Americans All

Race and Ethnic Relations in Historical, Structural, and Comparative Perspectives

AMERICANS ALL

Race and Ethnic Relations in Historical, Structural, and Comparative Perspectives

PETER KIVISTO
Augustana College

Wadsworth Publishing Company
Belmont, California
A Division of Wadsworth, Inc.

Editor: Serina Beauparlant
Editorial Assistant: Jason Moore
Production: Forbes Mill Press
Designer: Robin Gold
Print Buyer: Barbara Britton
Permissions Editor: Jeanne Bosschart
Copy Editor: Robin Gold
Illustrator: Patty Arnold
Cover: Patty Arnold and Robin Gold
Signing Representative: Elizabeth Covello
Compositor: Forbes Mill Press
Printer: Malloy Lithographing, Inc.

 *This book is printed on
acid-free recycled paper*

International Thomson Publishing
The trademark ITP is used under license

Printed in the United States of America

1 2 3 4 5 6 7 8 9 10—99 98 97 96 95

Library of Congress Cataloging-in-Publication Data

Kivisto, Peter, 1948–
    Americans all : race and ethnic relations in historical,
structural, and comparative perspectives / Peter Kivisto.
        p.   cm.
    Includes bibliographical references (p.) and index.
    ISBN 0-534-24366-5 (acid-free paper)
    1. United States—Ethnic relations.   2. United States —
Race relations.   I. Title.
E184.A1K48   1995
305.8'00973—dc20   94-12581

For my children, Sarah and Aaron

Contents

Preface xvii

PART I THINKING ABOUT RACE AND ETHNICITY 1

Chapter 1 Ethnic and Racial Dimensions 2
History and Social Structure 3
Ethnic Identities and Experiences 6
Five Lives 6
Generalizing from the Specific Case 11
Making Visible the Invisible 12
Why Can't They Be Like Us? 14
Nobody Knows the Trouble That I've Seen 15
Ethnic Groups 16
Group Definitions and Boundaries 17
Choosing Names 18
Intergroup Relations 18
The Big Picture: What is Ethnic America? 21
The Melting Pot 22
Cultural Pluralism 26
Alternative Images of Ethnic America 27
Summary 28

Chapter 2 Toward a Conceptual Map of Ethnic Relations 30
The Emergence of Ethnic Studies 30
Clarifying Concepts 32
Nations, Nationality, and Nationalism 33
Minority Groups 35
Race 38

Ethnicity and Ethnic Groups 42
   Religio-Ethnic Groups 44
   Racial Groups 45

Ethnic Relations 46
   Assimilation 48
   Pluralism 50

Toward a New Model 52
   Marxism and Social Classes 53
   Rational Choice Theory 54

The Social Construction of Ethnicity 56
   Ethnogenesis 57
   Ethnicization 57
   Emergent Ethnicity 58
   The Invention of Ethnicity 58

In Groups, Out Groups, and Group Position 62
   The Psychology of Prejudice 63
   The Sociology of Prejudice and Discrimination 64

Explaining Ethnic Differences 66
Summary 70

Chapter 3   **Demographic Profile of America's Main Ethnic Groups** 72

The Politics of Counting Heads 72

American Indians 74
   Population Decline and Recovery 74
   Rural and Urban Dwellers 77

European Americans 80
   The Old Immigration 82
   The New Immigration 84
   The Contemporary Situation 87

African Americans 89
   The Slave Trade and Population Growth 89
   The Great Migration 92

Hispanic Americans 98
   Mexican Americans 98
   Puerto Ricans 100
   Cuban Americans 100
   The Other Hispanics 101

Asian Americans   102
    Chinese Americans   103
    Japanese Americans   104
    Filipino Americans   106
    Korean Americans   107
    Other Asian Groups   108
Summary   109

PART II   **SOCIOLOGY MEETS HISTORY**   111

Chapter 4   **European Migration from Colonial America to the Civil War**   112
Social Change and Key Actors   112
    Economic Forces   112
    Political Forces   115
    Cultural Forces   116
Albion's Seed   117
    The Puritans   118
    The Cavaliers   118
    The Quakers   118
    The Scotch-Irish   119
    Transplanting the Old World to the New   119
    Nineteenth Century English Migration   120
    Scots in the Nineteenth Century   122
    The Core Society: Anglo-Saxon Protestant   124
Erin's Children in America   124
    The Colonization of Ireland   125
    Emigration and Exile   126
    Immigrant Destinations   128
    Finding Work   128
    Communal Activities and Organizations   130
    The Catholic Church in America   132
    Nativism   133
Germans in America   136
    Settlement Patterns   136
    The Early Ethnic Community   138
    Economic Immigrants   139

	Intraethnic Conflict	140
	Interethnic Encounters	143
	Summary	143
Chapter 5	**Coercive Pluralism and the Politics of Exclusion, 1492–1865**	145
	Coercive Pluralism	145
	The First of This Land	147
	The Market Period (1600–1775)	149
	The Conflict Period (1775–1850)	151
	Relocation Policies	153
	Beyond the Middle Passage	155
	The Ideology of Racism	157
	Slavery and the Plantation	159
	The Origins of an African American Culture	161
	The Community of Slaves	163
	Slave Revolts	165
	Free Persons of Color	167
	External Challenges to the Peculiar Institution	168
	The Politics of Conquest	170
	Travelers to Gold Mountain	173
	Summary	176
Chapter 6	**From Immigrants to Ethnic Americans, 1865–1940**	177
	Becoming Ethnic Americans	179
	Peasants No More: The Italians	180
	Finding Work	182
	The Ethnic Community	183
	Ethnic Stereotypes and the Mafia	188
	Politics	189
	Generational Change	190
	The Birth and Maturation of Polonia in America	192
	The Homeland	194
	Emigration	195
	The Immigrant Community Takes Shape	196
	Labor and Politics	198

Cultural Values	200
Interethnic Relations	201
Generational Change	202
The Jewish Diaspora	203
Early Immigration	203
Mass Immigration	204
The Early Community Presence	205
The Ethnic Community Evolves	207
Anti-Semitism	211
Upward Mobility	212
The Irish and Germans Revisited	213
The World of Work	213
Politics	215
The Erosion of Ethnic Communities	217
Intermarriage	218
Summary	219

Chapter 7   **The Color Line: From the Civil War to the Civil Rights Era**   **222**

From Emancipation to Jim Crow: African Americans	223
Reconstruction	223
Reasserting White Domination	226
Leadership in the African American Community	228
Southern Race Relations	231
The Promised Land	234
The Development of the Black Community	236
Black Culture	237
The Hispanic Presence in the United States	238
Mexicans in the Southwest	239
Mexican Immigration in the Early Twentieth Century	240
The Depression and Repatriation	243
Prejudice and Discrimination	244
The Bracero Program	246
The Ethnic Community	246
Cubans and Puerto Ricans	248

The Chinese and Japanese: A Comparison   249
   The Chinese and Immigration Restriction   249
   The Bachelor Society   251
   Chinatown as an Ethnic Island   252
   Anti-Chinese Activity   253
   Chinatown and the Outside World   255
   The Transformation of Japan   256
   *Emigration and the Role of the Japanese
     Government*   257
   Getting a Foothold in America   258
   Prejudice and Discrimination   259
   *The Ethnic Community and Generational
     Differences*   260
   World War II and Internment   262

Native Americans During the Reservation Era   263
   Reservations as Total Institutions   264
   The Dawes Act and Acculturation Policies   265
   Responding to Defeat   267
   Stereotypes   269
   The Indian New Deal   269

Summary   271

PART III   YESTERDAY, TODAY, AND TOMORROW   273

Chapter 8   **European Americans: The Twilight
of Ethnicity?**   274

Suburbanization and White Ethnics   276

Does Ethnicity Matter?: The Case for
Cultural Transmission   278
   The Polish Americans   281
   Italians   281

The Debate Over an Ethnic Revival   283
   The Hansen Thesis   283
   Political Ethnicity   284

Symbolic Ethnicity   286
   Evidence from Census Findings   287
   Ethnic Options   288
   The Privatization of Ethnicity   289

The Invention of Ethnicity 290
   Regional Identities 291
   A European American Identity? 292

Jewish Exceptionalism? 294
   The Core Jewish Population 295
   Continuity and Change 295
   Intermarriage 298

The Specter of Race 300
   White Attitudes About Governmental Actions 302
   The Politics of Hate and Racial Divisiveness 304

Summary 306

Chapter 9 African Americans: The Enduring American Dilemma 308

The Civil Rights Movement: 1940–1970 311
   Phase I: Nonviolent Confrontation and
     Legislative Lobbying 312
   Phase II: Militancy and Black Nationalism 318

Two Lingering Controversies: Busing and Affirmative Action 321
   Busing and School Desegregation 321
   Affirmative Action 326

Housing and Residential Segregation 336
   Public Housing 336
   Alternatives to Public Housing 339
   Equal Housing Opportunity 340

The Declining Significance of Race? 343
   The Black Middle Class 345
   Poor Blacks 349

Into the Future 353

Summary 353

Chapter 10 American Indians: The Continuing Plight of the First of This Land 355

Termination 356

Searching for Alternatives to Termination 358

Urbanization   359
> *Adjusting to Urban Life*   360
> *Intermarriage*   362
> *The Ethnic Community in the City*   363

Political Activism   364
> *The Red Power Movement*   365
> *Competing Political Goals*   367

Ongoing Conflict with White America   368
> *The Chippewa Spearfishing Dispute*   369
> *The Blackfeet and Oil Exploration: Limiting Development*   371
> *Land Disputes: The Legacy of Treaty Violations*   372

Development Plans on Native American Reservations   374
> *Exploiting Natural Resources*   374
> *Tourism and Gaming*   375

Quality of Life on Reservations   376
> *Housing*   377
> *Health Issues*   378

Native Americans in the White Mind   379

Uncertain Futures   382

Summary   383

Chapter 11 Hispanic Americans: Into the Mainstream or on the Margins?   385

Pan-Hispanic Unity or Ethnic Distinctiveness?   386

The Bilingual Issue   387

Cuban Americans   390
> *Settlement Patterns*   394
> *The Enclave Economy*   396
> *Political Participation*   397
> *Are Cubans Assimilating?*   398

Puerto Ricans   399
> *Settlement Patterns*   402
> *Economic Status*   403
> *The Ethnic Community*   407
> *Integration or Isolation?*   409

Mexican Americans 410
   Chicano Politics 413
   Socioeconomic Status 418
   Current Economic Problems 420
   The Problem of Marginalized Youth 422
Summary 422

Chapter 12   **Asian Americans: The Myth of the Model Minority** 424

The Model Minority: Myth and Reality 425
The Resurgence of Anti-Asian Views 427
Japanese Americans 429
   The Third Generation and Beyond 431
   Changes in the Ethnic Community 432
   The End of the Japanese American Community? 434
Chinese Americans 435
   Pre-1965 Developments 436
   Post-1965 Developments 439
Korean Americans 444
   Immigrant Entrepreneurs 445
   Conflict Between Koreans and African Americans 447
   Korean Ethnic Churches 448
   Adhesive Adaptation 449
   Scenarios for the Future 451
Filipino Americans 452
   Immigration Since 1945 453
   The Ethnic Community 455
Summary 457

Epilogue 460

References 463

Index 505

PREFACE

Race and ethnicity have played and continue to play crucial roles in shaping the nation's social, cultural, and political character. The sheer complexity of race and ethnic relations over time, the passions that they evoke, and the problems they have produced make it vitally important for students to expand their understanding of the multicultural world they inhabit. Sociology can perform a vital role in facilitating greater understanding. These assumptions are the basis of this book, which will introduce students to the central importance of race and ethnic relations in America's past and present.

During the past three decades, a veritable flood of work has been published on this subject, which indicates the dramatic escalation of interest in racial and ethnic differences within the academic community as a whole. Not surprisingly, this interest coincides with profound changes in the nature of race and ethnic relations, brought about most dramatically by the civil rights movement and the resumption of mass immigration since 1965. We will attempt to make sense of these changes by using the new body of scholarship in an interdisciplinary manner.

In particular, we will review recent trends in social history and historical sociology, especially the emphasis among practitioners in these fields to write history "from the bottom up," which is to say, to write about ordinary people who with limited resources and power were nonetheless agents in shaping their own lives. I have employed an interpretive theoretical approach to the topic, treating racial and ethnic identities, cultures, communities, and relations as socially constructed and variable. This general approach is used in addressing the long-standing debates between assimilationists and pluralists, as well as in exploring the more recent scholarly debates over such topics as the "ethnic revival," "symbolic ethnicity," and the presumed "declining significance of race."

This book differs from other texts in the field because it is far more historically grounded. In some texts history is simply ignored; in others history functions as essentially a backdrop to the present. This book shows how the past continues to impinge on the present by using in-depth case studies of major racial and ethnic groups. Moreover, the book is structured in terms of historical periods, which allows you to revisit various groups in different sections of the book and trace their particular historical trajectories. Specifically, the book examines three periods, which roughly run from: (1) the founding of the republic to the Civil War; (2) the end of the Civil War to the immediate period around World War II; and (3) mid-century to the present.

A second difference from other texts is that this book has a genuinely comparative perspective. Not only are specific similarities and differences between and among groups highlighted, but also the attention given to distinct differences in terms of time, place, and circumstance will help you comprehend the reasons for differing contemporary situations. For example, this is important in understanding the reality of the current Asian experience that makes possible the "myth of the model minority."

This book is also unique because of the attention given to the inner workings of racial and ethnic communities, which includes extended discussions of aspects of particular group's cultures, institutions, leaders, resources, and internal divisions. This connects to the concept of seeing members of groups as makers of their own lives and histories. The book pays considerable attention to the impact of prejudice, discrimination, and exploitation. But unlike some texts, it resists the reductionist temptation to view racial and ethnic minorities as mere victims. Ample evidence of legacies of oppression is complemented by extensive inquires into the various ways that individuals responded and groups mobilized to improve their situations.

One aspect of internal differences within groups revolves around other important social divisions, particularly class and gender differences. This book is distinctive in its attempt to reveal the

This World War I poster by Howard Chandler Christy promoted citizenship as a force that transcended ethnic differences. Courtesy of the Library of Congress.

interconnections and the tensions that exist between race and ethnicity and both class and gender. Thus, rather than viewing women as a distinct minority group, accorded a chapter in a manner parallel to chapters on African Americans and Jewish Americans, this book seeks to understand, for example, how the experiences of Irish women differ from that of both Irish men and of women from other groups. Another division — that of age or generation — is also discussed in greater detail here than in other texts.

I believe that W.E.B Du Bois was in fundamental ways right when he wrote, in 1903, "the problem of the twentieth century is the problem of the color-line." This book, unlike most textbooks, has a thematic core, one that seeks to indicate the continuing validity of Du Bois's claim as we approach the twenty-first century. Understanding is a prerequisite for any attempts to create a more equitable and just social order. Without preaching or indoctrinating, this book is an attempt to help you better understand our highly diverse society. This book is a sustained attempt to illustrate the continuing significance of sociology in identifying and assessing both the dynamics of racial conflicts and the forces that might serve to create a more harmonious society.

Acknowledgments

Writing can be a lonely undertaking. I spent literally hundreds of hours in from of my computer screen in very quiet surroundings. Similarly, over the past several years, I have spent a great deal of my professional life in equally quiet circumstances, reading the books and articles that informed what I was writing. Writing and reading are, indeed, two very solitary endeavors. It is only possible, however, to produce a book such as this one if a person is afforded ongoing support in many forms from a wide array of colleagues, friends, and relatives. In this respect, I consider myself to be remarkably fortunate.

I would like to single out two people who were, in their own ways, especially helpful. Werner Sollors, from Harvard University, has not only commented on various parts of this work, but also has been generous in the extreme in responding to both versions of my previous work and to numerous queries. He is chiefly responsible for providing me with the title of the book. Second, Stanford M. Lyman, at Florida Atlantic University, has been shaping my thinking and encouraging me since 1974, when I first took a graduate school course from him at the New School for Social Research. For twenty years, I have benefited from his critical insights and his unflagging support.

A number of other scholars have helped to clarify my overall understanding of the issues pursued in this book. Some have done so by engaging in ongoing dialogues and debates with me over the years. Others have provided useful comments on various sections of the book or work that led up to the book. Given my interest in the work of those seeking to bring sociology and history into a fruitful dialogue, it's not surprising that this list includes both sociologists and historians. Among those I would like to single out for thanks are Richard Alba, Thomas Archdeacon, Harry Bash, Dag Blanck, Raymond Breton, Rose Brewer, John Bodnar, Martin Bulmer, Kathleen Conzen, Eike Durin, Herbert Gans, Philip Gleason, Stephen J. Gold, Richard Helmes-Hays, Gary Heath, Melvin Holli, Tracy X. Karner, Mike Karni, Olavi Koivukangas, Auvo Kostiainen, James McKee, Rick Maddox, Fred Matthews, Ewa Morawska, Janusz Mucha, Joane Nagel, Robert Nakamaru, John Pollitz, Peter Rachleff, Moses Rischin, Harald Runblom, Alice Scourby, M. Mark Stolarik, Bill Swatos, Rudy Vecoli, Arthur Vidich, and R. Stephen Warner.

Margaret Abraham, Hofstra University; Peter Adler, University of Denver; Donna Barnes, University of Wyoming; James Button, University of Florida, Gainsville; Joseph Carroll, Colby-Sawyer College; Valerie Carter, University of Maine; Grant Farr, Portland State University; Clarence Lo, University of Missouri, Columbia; David Musick, University of Northern Colorado; and C. Gray Swicegood, University of Illinois, Urbana provided perceptive and extremely helpful reviews to Wadsworth, and I would like to thank them for the assistance they provided in making this a better book than it otherwise would have been. I would like to single out for thanks Anne Hastings, University of North Carolina, Chapel Hill. From a very early stage in the evolution of this project she consistently supplied especially sage advice.

I have been very fortunate to have had the opportunity to work with a fine group of people at Wadsworth, including Jason Moore, Jeanne Bosschart, Hal Humphrey, Liz Covello, and most especially the publisher's Sociology Editor, Serina Beauparlant. In addition, it has been a most rewarding experience to work with Robin Gold, my copy and design editor at Forbes Mill Press. At my home institution, Elizabeth Walsh has, with ample measure of patience and good humor, reformatted, edited, and in other ways improved the manuscript. I have benefited from the company of Dave Hill, Mike Kirn, Sonja Knudsen, Bradley Levinson, and Steve Zdatny.

Finally, my family has been in my corner all along, including my mother and my two sisters, Kay and Kathy. My father had taken a keen interest in progress on the book, but sadly died before it was completed. My wife, Susan, and my children, Sarah and Aaron, have been involved in the everyday routines of writing for more than two years and have been consistent sources of both inspiration and diversion. Although they may not always realize it, they have made it all worth while.

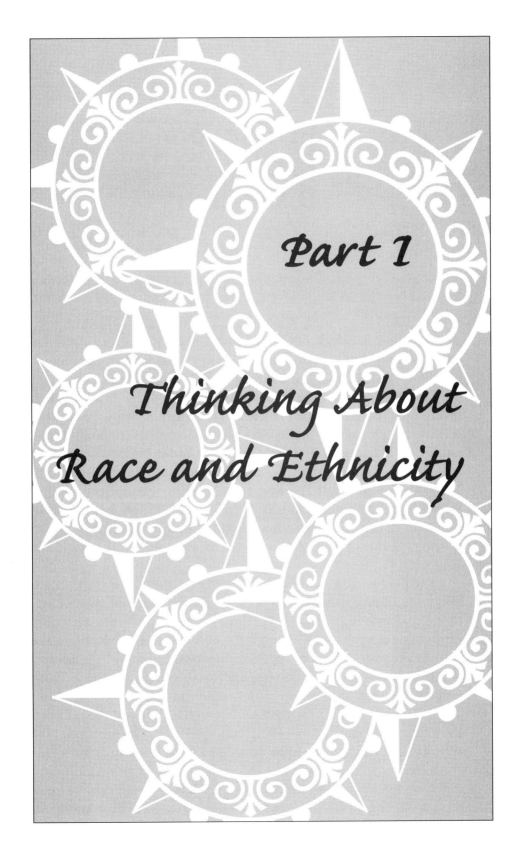

Part 1

Thinking About Race and Ethnicity

ETHNIC AND RACIAL DIMENSIONS

Diversity is a hallmark of the American experience. And America has always been a nation of nations—a society composed of numerous ethnic, racial, and religious subcommunities.

The United States has been and continues to be an immigrant receiving nation. Long before the birth of the nation the continent served as a magnet for settlers from Europe and as the final destination for African victims of the slave trade. For 500 years the indigenous peoples of North America confronted wave after wave of sojourners and settlers, first from a select number of western European countries and later from the rest of Europe, from various points in Asia, from Africa, from Latin America, and from virtually every other place on the face of the globe (Hughes and Hughes, 1952).

The new nation, born a little over two centuries ago, adopted relatively liberal immigration policies during much of its history, thereby ensuring not only an expanding, but also an ever-changing populace. Though the ebb and flow of immigration has varied over time, immigration has never completely ceased, and the result is a composite population that is perhaps more heterogeneous than that of any other nation in the world (Handlin, 1959). One recent upbeat commentator characterized America as the "first universal nation" (Wattenberg, 1991). The ethnic diversity of America accounts in no small part for the uniqueness of the American experiment. But the ability of the many groups inhabiting America to live in relative harmony has always been precarious, requiring individuals and groups to engage in a constant renegotiation of their rights and obligations. Americans have had to define and redefine what it means to be a citizen in a pluralist society (Williams, 1977).

For example, what did citizenship mean for a black American denied the right to vote in many southern states prior to the 1960s? What does it mean now that the right to vote has been extended to them and is in fact backed up by federal law? What do white southerners think about this change? Similarly, why were Native Americans denied citizenship rights until 1924, even though their ancestors had inhabited the land long before the arrival of Europeans? What does it mean for them today to be simultaneously citizens of the United States and of various tribal nations? What do non-Indians think about such "dual allegiances"? Asking these kinds of questions is essential if we are to understand the powerful impact race and ethnicity have had throughout the history of the United States.

History and Social Structure

This book provides you with the tools needed to arrive at a better understanding of the ethnic dimension to our collective social life. These tools include a variety of concepts and a theoretical perspective that can serve to make sense of what would otherwise be a mind-boggling mountain of facts. The conceptual map in Chapter 2 provides a way to look at both history and social structure.

Unlike many sociological studies of ethnicity, this book pays considerable attention to history because, as we shall see, the past continues to exert its influence on the present in many ways that we often fail to appreciate. Social historians and historical sociologists have attempted to bring sociology and history into fruitful contact in an effort to better understand the past. We will extensively review the works of many scholars operating in this interdisciplinary arena, especially in Part II.

Social structure refers to the institutional arrangements of a society, including the distribution of power and various resources possessed by individual and groups. Social structure entails constraints, and those constraints are more burdensome for those with the least power and the fewest resources. For example, if discrimination prevents some categories of people from obtaining jobs that

Figure 1.1   *Two Croatian children celebrating the day their parents became American citizens, circa 1922.*

Source: Courtesy of the Swenson Center.

pay well, those people will be forced, due to economic circumstances, to live in inadequate housing in ghetto neighborhoods. There, among other things, they will find schools are inferior to those elsewhere. Their children are thereby prevented from obtaining an education that would allow them to work their way out of poverty. Clearly, social structure can and does perpetuate social inequalities over time. But social structure also enables people to act: It makes possible certain kinds of activity that would otherwise be impossible. For example, in a country with democratic values and the rule of law, disenfranchised groups can challenge existing social arrangements. Legal challenges to job discrimination can be mounted, and political campaigns can be mobilized to elect officials committed to social change.

Social structure has a profound impact on the lives of members of a society, and it is a central focus throughout this book. But social structure should not be seen as simply determining the outcomes of individual opportunities, meaning people are mere puppets, pulled by the strings of powerful social forces. We are the products of our social world, but we also have a say in what that world will look like. Thus, it is not enough to look only at social structure. We must examine how people—as individuals and also as members of collectivities—go about the business of shaping, changing, preserving, and otherwise responding to their social environment.

This chapter highlights a number of problems that confront anyone trying to comprehend the role played by ethnicity and ethnic relations in our national life. Problems arise when we try to: (1) understand ethnicity as a lived phenomenon that is experienced differently by different people; (2) define the nature of the ethnic group; (3) identify the characteristic patterns of inter-ethnic relations in the nation; and (4) depict ethnic America as a whole. Each of these will be explored in the remainder of this chapter.

We see at the outset an extraordinarily complex picture. To make sense of that picture requires that we pay attention to several levels of analysis. It is essential to study both individuals and the circumstances in which they find themselves. One level focuses on individual social actors in the process of creating and defining their own lives. Here we are interested in their beliefs, their desires, and the motives behind their actions. The second level locates individuals in concrete historical and geographical circumstances. Here we are interested in how changing circumstances serve to either constrain or enable individuals in their social interactions. The focus shifts to the group and to both inter- and intragroup relations.

In sociology, both individual and group analyses are seen as operating at the micro-level. In contrast, the third, or macro, level is primarily concerned with the whole rather than with the parts, with American society in general rather than with the discrete ethnic pieces that constitute it. The macro-level entails examining the impact of the state, economic conditions, and cultural factors on ethnics and ethnic groups, as well as the impact that the ethnic factor has on the society as a totality. As we will see in Chapter 2, these levels interpenetrate each other, and such analytic distinctions should not be equated with a view that sees them as empirically discrete or autonomous.

Ethnic Identities and Experiences

People's ethnic and racial backgrounds can be a benefit or a burden and are relatively more or less important to different individuals. People attempt to embrace their ethnic ancestries or repudiate them. Ethnic and racial identities are a source of pride or shame. People accept their identities as givens that cannot be changed, or they attempt to modify them in some respects. In short, people experience race and ethnicity in a multiplicity of ways.

Five Lives

Consider the following examples, which are not meant to be representative, but, on the contrary, are intended to suggest something of the wide range of possible encounters with the ethnic factor in America.

An Italian American

Jerre Mangione was born in 1909 and grew up in Rochester, New York. His parents were Italian immigrants who, with relatives and other acquaintances from their native Sicilian village, emigrated to America in search of economic opportunities that did not exist at home. In his memoirs, Mangione relates what it was like to grow up in a world that was at once a southern Italian village transplanted in urban, industrial America and at the same time a bustling metropolis inhabited by an incredibly diverse array of people.

For some, the old world remained a source of solace and comfort because traditional values and modes of conduct were preserved. For Mangione, and others like him, his parents' world was increasingly too parochial, and the lure of America created a gulf between him and his parents. He recalls, for example, that he "became increasingly resentful of my parents for being more foreign than anyone else. It irked me that I had not been born of English-speaking parents . . . " (Mangione, 1978: 14). For their part, his parents wanted their children to remain close to them and their culture while being successful.

These dual goals caused a complicated bind for his parents, but also provided them with a way of reconciling their differences with their children. In school, Mangione found himself identifying with Jews more than fellow Italians because in his view the former were more interested in intellectual pursuits and the latter were too boisterous. His route out of the transplanted village was accomplished not by open rebellion, however, but by entering Syracuse University. Though his parents and relatives felt a sense of loss when he departed for the university, they also felt a sense of pride and expectation regarding their son's future. Thus, coming of age for Mangione entailed maintaining a relationship with his family while distancing himself from his inherited immigrant culture.

A Mexican American

In a different place, a generation later, echoes of this narrative are heard again. Richard Rodriguez grew up in Sacramento, California, the son of Mexican immigrants. Sent to Roman Catholic parochial school by his parents, he began his education knowing very little English. The nuns at the school told his parents that to be successful he would have to learn English. His parents and the school successfully encouraged Rodriguez to break with his native tongue, and he became a scholarship student. As a beneficiary of affirmative action programs, he went to Stanford University and then on to graduate school at Columbia University and the University of California at Berkeley.

Like Mangione before him, education was a vehicle for Rodriguez's upward mobility and for entry into a cosmopolitan American society. In his autobiography, poignantly titled *Hunger of Memory* (1981), Rodriguez reflected on the painful side of this move. A major consequence of his educational success was his growing distance from the Spanish language, and with it the ability to communicate freely and easily with his parents. This led to a "bewildering silence" that served to separate parent from child, which was never overcome: later Rodriguez's mother referred to him as "Mr. Secrets" (Rodriguez, 1981: 5, 173–195). There is, in short, a tragic dimension to this account that is lacking in the preceding one.

This autobiography introduces another dimension: race. Although many things contributed to childhood insecurity, perhaps none was more significant than skin coloration. Rodriguez's dark skin was a source of shame and inferiority, partly the result of racial slurs directed at him, but also the result of his reaction to the way Mexican Americans viewed complexion. He knew about home remedies designed to lighten skin color (a mixture of egg white and lemon juice concentrate) and he understood the aesthetic implications of such efforts: beauty was associated with fair or light skin. He also realized that his mother saw dark skin as "the most important symbol of a life of oppressive labor and poverty" (Rodriguez, 1981: 119).

Rodriguez became alienated from his body: the scholarship boy would develop his mind to compensate for the inadequacies of his body. In adulthood, as with language, Rodriguez continued to wrestle with the social implications attached to such physical attributes as skin color (Rodriguez, 1981: 111–139).

An African American

For Maya Angelou, a black woman growing up in the American South, race loomed large as a force shaping her life. Like Rodriguez, she was a victim of the aesthetic view that valued whiteness and she sometimes fantasized about waking from her "black ugly dream," in which her "kinky mass" of hair was replaced by long blond locks (Angelou, 1969: 2). Unlike Rodriguez, however, she also confronted a virulent form of racism. Far from the heterogeneous ethnic milieu of Mangione's Rochester, the segregated South was defined by a much simpler divide: the "color line" separated black from white.

Furthermore, it was understood that white supremacy was challenged only at great risk. Angelou relates an incident in which the grandmother who helped raise her was informed that "[a] crazy nigger messed with a white lady today" and therefore night riders would be combing the countryside in search of a black male who would likely be the victim of a lynching. Angelou was forced to participate in the indignity of hiding her crippled uncle Willie to protect him from such vigilante "justice" by covering him with potatoes and onions in a storage bin. The precariousness of black life was an everyday reality, though she learned to hold in check any public expression of contempt for many whites, whom she saw as "cement faces [with] eyes of hate" that exhibited a perverse desire to perpetuate the "ugliness and rottenness" of racial oppression (Angelou, 1969: 14–15).

In many ways, Angelou's early life paralleled that of Richard Wright, who, in his powerful chronicle of his formative years, *Black Boy* (1937), concluded that active resistance to oppression was futile and that the options available to him were inadequate: being the "genial slave," internalizing anger and directing it toward other blacks, or seeking escape in sex and alcohol. Rejecting each of these, he decided that his only chance to succeed on his own terms entailed migrating to the North (Wright, 1937: 276–285). The important difference between Angelou's and Wright's respective experiences was gender. At age eight, Angelou was raped. In reflecting on this and subsequent events she concluded that "[t]he Black female is assaulted in her tender years by all those common forces of nature at the same time that she is caught in the tripartite crossfire of masculine prejudice, white illogical hate and Black lack of power" (Angelou, 1969: 231).

A Chinese American

Jade Snow Wong was born in San Francisco's Chinatown. Her father was a businessman in the Chinese enclave, who, as a Christian convert, was not as traditional as some of his contemporaries. Nonetheless, his wife had had her feet bound in childhood, and he considered both her and their six daughters inferior to men. After fifteen years of anxious waiting by the father, the first male child in the family was born, named Forgiveness from Heaven. Then Wong clearly understood the subservient role of women in the Chinese family (Wong, 1945: 28–29). Despite this and the rather rigid demands for filial obedience and respect for elders, her early years were far less traumatic than those of Maya Angelou.

Jade Snow Wong's family sought to preserve much of Chinese culture, including language, while collectively partaking of such aspects of American mass culture as the newspaper comic sections and movies, where "they shared the excitement of six-shooters, posses, runaway stagecoaches, striking cobras, the unconquerable Tarzan, and organized apes" (Wong, 1945: 71). Only as she got older did Wong begin to feel the tension between the world of Chinatown and that of the larger host society.

While attending college (a decision she made that was viewed ambivalently by her parents), she began to distance herself from Chinatown. Upon learning in a sociology class that in America children are considered individuals with rights and an ability to make their own decisions, she came to the stark realization that her parents "had not left the Chinese world of thirty years ago." This provoked her into an act of rebellion when she decided to accept an offer to go to the movies with a young man without first asking for her father's permission. This seemingly inconsequential challenge to authority was of major significance for Wong insofar as it provided her with what she would describe as "a measure of freedom" (Wong, 1945: 125–129).

Subsequently, Wong learned that gender discrimination, though manifested differently, existed in American society. For her, it was overlaid with racial discrimination. Ultimately Wong established her independence by becoming a potter, but she set up a shop in Chinatown, preserving her ties to the ethnic community in contradistinction, for example, to Mangione.

A Native American

N. Scott Momaday is an American Indian, or Amerindian — a member of the Kiowa tribe. His memoir, *The Names* (1976), is both an autobiographical account of his childhood and adolescence and an act of recovery and imagination. It is a lyrical portrait of the author's sense of connectedness with his ancestors and with the lands they inhabited. In stark contrast to Angelou and Wong, there is no discussion of prejudice and discrimination. He describes matter-of-factly the world of his grandfather: "the Kiowas had been routed in the Indian wars, the great herds of buffalo had been destroyed, and the sun dance prohibited by law." He describes his grandfather's understanding that in the wake of this tribal catastrophe, he "had his own life to live" and he sustained himself as a farmer (Momaday, 1976: 28–29).

Actually, Momaday's mother was not a full-blooded Native American, and she only gradually came to see herself as an American Indian, a journey undertaken later by her son. Momaday grew up in a middle-class home. Both of his parents were college educated and, like their son, were artists and teachers. Because

Momaday's mother had a tense relationship with her parents, the family decided to move from Oklahoma to the Southwest, and so Momaday grew up among Navajo and Jemez peoples rather than the Kiowa. Momaday's embrace of his heritage was thus not restricted to a particular tribe, but was decidedly pan-Indian.

Momaday's description of his relationship with his parents suggests an idyllic childhood in which many of the anxieties and generational conflicts noted in the previous vignettes appear to have been absent. Similarly, his relationships with other Native Americans, as well as with non-Indians, are depicted as being re-markably unproblematic. Perhaps because his parents had already, by entering the middle class, established a bridge between the two cultures, Momaday conveys in the memoir a sense of his ability to live comfortably in both Indian and non-Indian worlds. Momaday planned for his college education with parental help, not resis-tance, as Mangione and Wong faced. Thus, Momaday described a scene in which he poured over college catalogues with his father and mother.

Generalizing from the Specific Case

What can these brief synopses of five lives reveal about the ethnic experience? First and foremost they provide insights into the sub-jective character of ethnicity, illustrating differing influences on the creation and maintenance of personal identities. Second, these vivid and poignant writings permit us access to the inner world of these writers, providing us with an opportunity to understand the pain, joy, anger, ambiguity, and sustenance that ethnic identity and affiliation can provoke. These stories help us appreciate the variegated and complicated nature of this phenomenon. For this reason, autobiographies are an invaluable resource. So are other documentary resources, such as letters and oral histories. Add lit-erary sources, for the fiction and poetry of ethnics can be read not simply for their artistic merit, but also as social-historical docu-ments (Skardal, 1974; Early, 1993; Ferraro, 1993). Finally, the ethnographic tradition in sociology and anthropology has made considerable contributions, such as *Street Corner Society* (1943), William Foote Whyte's classic study of an Italian slum, and *Tally's Corner* (1967), Elliot Liebow's highly acclaimed study of black ghetto men.

These sources reveal much, but they also raise questions that are not easily answered. The initial question covers the representativeness of these five examples: How typical are they? For example, to what extent can Mangione be seen as typical of the Italian immigrant? Did most second generation Italians seek liberation from the confines of America's Little Italies the way he did, or were most intent on preserving their ties to the ethnic community? As a Sicilian, and thus the offspring of parents from Italy's most economically underdeveloped region, was Mangione's experience similar to or profoundly different from the experiences of northern Italians, who migrated from a region that had witnessed greater industrialization?

Similar questions can be directed at the other four examples. Can we speak about Rodriguez's case as an instance of the Hispanic experience (thereby including Mexicans, Puerto Ricans, Cubans, and other Latin Americans), or should we limit the scope of generalization only to the Mexican American experience? How is Wong's account of life in Chinatown similar to or different from the experiences of Japanese, Korean, and Filipino Americans? Does the pan-Indian sensibility conveyed in Momaday's memoir capture the world view of the far less cosmopolitan, poor American Indians who have spent their lives on isolated reservations? Does Angelou's life in the rural South dovetail with or significantly diverge from the lives of African Americans residing in inner city ghettos in northern cities? How typical is her portrait of the role of the extended family for African Americans? The questions about ethnic identity go on and on.

We must note that each of the five people presented is a skilled writer, and all except Wong make a living writing. All five are considered professionally accomplished. This suggests that in some fundamental way these individuals are decidedly atypical.

Making Visible the Invisible

Many ordinary people also provide documentation of their lives, sometimes at the behest of interested journalists or scholars. One autobiographical collection of particular note exists because of the initiative of social reformer and journalist Hamilton Holt, who commissioned a diverse array of individuals to write or to narrate for transcription brief autobiographical sketches, or what he called

Figure 1.2   *An African American soldier shortly after World War I.*

Source: Courtesy of the Swenson Center.

"lifelets." First published in 1906, *The Life Stories of Undistinguished Americans, as Told by Themselves* (Holt, 1991) is a collection that includes, in the language of the time, the life stories of a Polish sweatshop girl, an Italian bootblack, a Negro peon, a Chinese man, an Irish cook, and a Syrian clerk. This vivid and often blunt work illustrates the ability of ordinary people to provide articulate and compelling accounts of their lives. Nonetheless, even here the same questions must be raised, though these individuals are probably more representative of their peers than our five cases.

Some suggest that for this reason such documents should not be considered valuable resources for social scientific or historical inquiry. But just like any other type of data, this kind of material can only be used beneficially if its limitations are appreciated and if interpretations are made with great care. The best way to ensure autobiographical material is used appropriately is to juxtapose it with other data. Assessments of any first person document require determining whether the person in question is particularly unique or even idiosyncratic or is in some important ways typical of many other members of an ethnic group. The person must be placed into context, by considering the historical time frame, the particular place, and the circumstances and events in which (and often in response to) a document was created.

Most ordinary people, however, have not left documentary traces that could help elucidate the character of their lives and the distinctive role of ethnicity in shaping those lives. The limited quantity of evidence available to scholars has produced, at least in part, what historian Anne Firor Scott (1984) has referred to as the "historical invisibility" of such people. Because ordinary people are often viewed as objects of history rather than as subjects who have a role in shaping their social world, ethnicity was for a long time a relatively neglected dimension in history and the social sciences (Vecoli, 1970).

The considerable body of scholarship produced during the past quarter century by sociologists and historians, and particularly by those operating at the boundary between the disciplines — historical sociologists and social historians — has done much to remedy this neglect (Kivisto, 1990; Morawska, 1990; Archdeacon, 1985; Vecoli, 1979). Furthermore, by treating ordinary people as subjects of history, as authors of their own lives, such work has sought to make visible that which was heretofore invisible.

Why Can't They Be Like Us?

Two pitfalls in the study of ethnicity must to be identified. The first pitfall — borrowing from a title of one of sociologist Andrew Greeley's (1971) books — is reflected in the question, "why can't they be like us?"

Although generalizations about the constituent members of different groups and comparisons between and among groups are essential, they become distorted when ethnocentrism intrudes. The term ethnocentrism was coined by the early American sociologist William Graham Sumner (1940 [1906]: 13–15) to refer to the tendency to use one's own group as a standard or norm by which to assess other groups. This practice yields invidious comparisons.

Insofar as the individual's membership group is viewed as a positive ideal, all other groups are judged by how far they deviate from this ideal — groups relatively similar to the membership group are evaluated more favorably and groups manifesting greater differences are judged in a negative manner. Although ethnocentrism can affect any study of ethnicity, it is more likely to be a problem when members of privileged or dominant groups in a society seek to describe and assess less privileged and relatively powerless groups.

Nobody Knows the Trouble That I've Seen

Conversely, the second pitfall emanates from members of groups who are less privileged and relatively powerless, from groups falling victim to ostracism and oppression. Some members of such groups argue that the essence of what it means to be a member of that particular group can only be lived and experienced; it cannot be comprehended from the outside. Ethnic identity is therefore fundamentally ineffable, its meaning and significance being accessible only to insiders. This pitfall, which stems from what sociologist Robert Merton (1972) has called the "insider-outsider debate," denies the social scientist or historian the ability to provide valid interpretive accounts of ethnic group life and the beliefs and actions of members therein — unless that scholar also happened to be a member of that particular group.

Accepting this position means denying the possibility that the human condition is sufficiently universal to transcend ethnic differences. This position, which Merton dubbed "extreme insiderism," also implicitly denies that the tools used by social scientists and historians can actually add to our ability to know or to understand. This suggests that the questions posed after the five brief autobiographical glimpses presented earlier are unanswerable.

Peter Rose (1978: 25) has responded to the "extreme insider" position by suggesting that scholars can overcome the difficulties of being an outsider insofar as they are able to "experience things vicariously." Scholars cannot provide first-person accounts, and they should not be apologists for their subjects. Scholars contribute distinctive modes of inquiry that emphasize comparative studies that constantly move back and forth between the particularities of distinct groups or subgroups and more general patterns of social action and interaction. As Rose (1978: 27) notes, all groups institutionalize their behavior patterns, set criteria for the conferring or denying of status, indicate the tolerance limits of accepted and expected behavior, and maintain social systems of great intricacy even when they, themselves, have great difficulty articulating their character.

Social scientists and historians can employ their methods and theories to assist all of us — insiders as well as outsiders — in comprehending how these processes occur for different groups at various times and places.

Ethnic Groups

Rose's discussion shifts the focus of analysis from the individual to the ethnic group. Individuals as members of varying ethnic groups are shaped by the distinctive character of those groups. Therefore we must understand the dynamics of ethnic group formation, maintenance, transformation, erosion, revival, and the like. Indeed, in the chapters that follow, inter- and intragroup relations will receive more attention than the individual's experience of ethnicity. Underlying each level of analysis, however, is an appreciation that all groups are the creations of social actors acting in complex ways with others.

What groups are we interested in examining? Because ethnic groups are socially constructed and defined, what is and what is not an ethnic group can change over time and in different places. Definitions will be contested, with some opting for one definition and others for an alternative definition. Two examples can help explain this. First, consider a man who emigrates to America directly from Spain (that is, not via Latin America). He might consider himself to be a Spaniard or a Spanish American. This might be reinforced by those around him in America and by officially sanctioned definitions. If, however, he came from the Basque region in Spain not only might he prefer to be seen as a Basque, but if he supports the claims of Basque nationalism, he might vehemently deny that he is a Spaniard (Douglass and Bilbao, 1975).

Second, consider a woman departing in the nineteenth century from Sicily. Her understanding of who she is may well revolve around the village or region she came from. Thus, she sees herself as Sicilian, not Italian. Once in America she may slowly come to redefine her self image — aided and abetted by the definitions imposed on her by those she encounters in America. Her sense of being a Sicilian may give way or merge first with a sense of being an Italian, and still later transformed into being an Italian American (Foerster, 1919).

Group Definitions and Boundaries

Although the boundary parameters of a particular group may not be disputed, there may be a question about whether it is an *ethnic* group. The *Harvard Encyclopedia of American Ethnic Groups* (hereafter the *HEAEG*, Thernstrom, et al. 1980) includes in the list of groups represented the following: Amish, Copts, Hutterites, and Mormons. The advisory editors of this volume concluded that these groups met the criteria for inclusion in the encyclopedia as bona fide ethnic groups, though some might protest that these are religious groups and not ethnic groups. Appalachians, however, are not accorded an entry, though some have contended that out of this region of the United States is an emerging ethnic group (Marger and Obermiller, 1983).

The matter of who gets included within the boundaries of a group and who gets excluded introduces further complications. Who in America is black? What if one quarter of an individual's ancestry is white? Is that person black? What about the person whose ancestry is half black and half white? What about the person whose ancestry is $^{1}/_{32}$ black and $^{31}/_{32}$ white (Davis, 1991)? Where do we locate in America's racial definitions those people described in the *HEAEG* as "tri-racial isolates," peoples with ancestries derived from white, black, and American Indian origins (Berry, 1963)? Why, in contrast to most of the rest of the world, does this country not recognize any mixed racial categories between black and white — such as the designation "mulatto" (Starr, 1992: 274)?

The related issue of the relationship between race and ethnicity poses further problems. Who are today referred to as African Americans are also referred to as blacks (and have been designated at other times as Negroes and Afro-Americans). Two of these definitions — Negroes and blacks — emphasize race, and the other two find their parallel with other ethnic groups: Irish Americans, Chinese Americans, Mexican Americans, and so forth. Is a person with ancestry derived from Africa necessarily an African American? For instance, what about such a person who happens to have been born and raised in the Dominican Republic? Is that person black? Is that person an African American?

Choosing Names

Finally, what we call various ethnic groups has changed over time, and there is often a lively debate over which name is preferred, as the example just cited illustrates. For people of African descent, Negro was the most commonly used label up to the 1960s, when the term black came to replace it. In the late 1960s, a majority of African Americans preferred Negro over black, but that changed. Now if one sees the word "Negro" in print, it is a good indication that the publication was written prior to 1970. The term Afro American also has received some popularity, though it gave way by the 1980s to African American. Today both African American and black are widely used both inside and outside of the group.

Similar shifts can be seen for Hispanics, partly because some ethnics prefer to use a particular national identity, such as Cuban or Mexican, rather than the more pan-ethnic label Hispanic. The term "Latino" vies at present for general acceptance with Hispanic. The indigenous peoples of the North American continent have also carried different labels. Through much of the past, the term "Indian" was imposed on them by Europeans. During the 1960s this term was held in disrepute and the term "Native American" gained in popularity and general usage. More recently the term Indian has gained a comeback in usage, along with the related designations American Indian and Amerindian.

These examples show the fluid, imprecise, ambiguous, and sometimes contradictory character of group definitions. We are studying social constructs that human beings are continually renegotiating and articulating.

Intergroup Relations

Groups undergo this continual process of redefinition and its members seek to advance their individual and the group's interests by interacting with other groups. Thus, the next dimension we'll consider is that of intergroup relations.

Though not the whole story, submerged tensions and overt conflicts have characterized much of the history of ethnic relations. From Benjamin Franklin's condemnation of the use of the German language in America during the nation's founding period to the current acrimonious debates concerning bilingual education in the public schools, the future of transplanted cultures in general, and language maintenance in particular, has been an open question. From the first concerted attempt to curtail open immigration — the passage of the Chinese Exclusion Act of 1882 — to the incarceration of the Mariel boat people, refugees from Communist Cuba, ethnic factors have been at the core of the discourse about who should and who should not be accepted into American society. From the first treaties enacted between American Indians and the United States government to the present court cases brought by various tribes demanding the enforcement of nineteenth century treaties permitting tribal governments to claim sizeable areas across the country, North American native peoples have sought to deal with the consequences of conquest. From the many slave revolts and conspiracies that occurred prior to the Civil War to the numerous urban riots of the 1960s, African Americans have challenged the persistent legacy of racial oppression and injustice.

Competition for jobs has historically been an important source of friction among groups. This can be seen in the rise of the labor movement in the last century, when non-whites were frequently denied union membership (racial animosity thereby serving as a barrier to class solidarity) and in the current battle over affirmative action programs to redress past discrimination.

Paralleling competition in the economic arena is the recurring quest for political power. For example, at the local level, the political machines that became a crucial force in many American cities during the late nineteenth and early twentieth centuries pitted various ethnic groups against both the native-born and other ethnic groups, while ensuring that others were effectively denied the political franchise. Today, in the process of ethnic succession (wherein ethnic groups that had obtained sufficient rewards exited declining cities for the suburbs), the groups have changed, but the struggle for what is perceived to be an equitable piece of the pie continues.

In the cultural realm, newcomers, outsiders, and marginalized peoples have always wrestled with the implications to their own

Figure 1.3   *Greek Americans celebrating the Fourth of July,*
symbolically linking their Greek past to their
new homeland.

Source: Courtesy of the Swenson Center.

culture of various modes of adaptation to and acceptance of the
dominant culture. Whether they opted to embrace incorporation
into the larger culture (and thereby forsake their inherited cultural
tradition), resist such incorporation, or blend ancestral and American cultures is and has been an ongoing decision members of
ethnic groups have had to make. This means responding to the
demands imposed by elites intent on Americanizing the diverse
peoples of the nation in an image solely defined by these elites.

Although much has changed over time, these examples suggest
that the potential for conflict remains and imply that understanding the present requires understanding the past. The problems
generated by ethnic differences have not been resolved. Some
groups have improved their lot in America with each succeeding
generation, while for others the picture is not so clear. Some groups
have a vested interest in preserving the status quo while others are
intent on effecting various kinds of social change. In the continuing drama of social reality, the ethnic dimension of that drama
continues to be a powerful divisive force.

Mutual hostility and conflict, however, do not tell the whole story. Ethnic history amply illustrates the myriad ways in which many people from differing ancestral backgrounds have managed to forge cooperative and harmonious relationships with many outside of their own ethnic group. In towns and cities where ethnic groups lived and continue to live side by side with other groups, what historian Rudolph Vecoli (1991) refers to as a "spirit of neighborliness" became a common characteristic of everyday social life: people cared for their neighbors' sick children, helped neighbors through tough economic times, and so on regardless of ethnic identities. Similarly, in the workplace and in schools various modes of mutual accommodation and working together have been established. Ethnic differences have not prevented friendships from developing, and the willingness to marry across group boundaries is a powerful testament to people's abilities to transcend ethnic divisions.

On the other hand, another way that group members have related to others is simply to avoid contact. Many new immigrants report confronting neither overt hostility nor cooperation, but mostly a sense of isolation from people outside of their own group.

The Big Picture: What is Ethnic America?

Earlier we asked what it meant to be an ethnic in America. An equally crucial question is this: What does it mean to be an American? Can we speak about a typical American as, for example, the principal characters do in Gish Jen's (1991: 67) recent novel about an extended Chinese family in post-World War II America? In the novel, the immigrant protagonists find themselves talking about the "typical American" when they want to criticize people and their behaviors. When irritated, they complain about a "typical American no-morals" or a "typical American just-dumb." What is interesting in this fictional illustration is that the characters find it increasingly difficult to decide what is and what is not "typical" the longer they are in America. They have learned to appreciate the complexity and the diversity contained within what can be called the American character.

Perceptive observers who have traveled throughout the country—from the famous observations recorded by Alexis de

Toqueville in *Democracy in America* (1981 [1835]) after his visit to America a century and a half ago to the more recent accounts provided by his fellow countryman, Jean Baudrillard (1988: 82)—have commented on this phenomenon.

Discussions about ethnicity in America often rely on metaphors and evocative images designed to capture the social relationships created by an extraordinarily heterogeneous population. Anselm Strauss (1991:287) explained this tendency: "The early decision to throw the country open to virtually all peoples of the world was fateful for the nation, and consequential for the development of American imageries, including those pertaining to mobility, rurality, cities, frontier, and industrialization." The United States has been described in numerous ways, including as a melting pot, a mosaic, a symphonic orchestra, a salad bowl, and a kaleidoscope. The first new nation, a nation of nations, and the first universal nation are only a few of the images used at various times. Why do we so frequently use these and similar characterizations of America's ethnic character? Two primary reasons account for this. First, the sheer complexity of America encourages, and perhaps even demands, attempts to generalize and to provide an overarching picture of the American scene. Second, these metaphors and images have built into them not only descriptions about what America looks like, but also evaluations about how it ought to look.

The Melting Pot

Without doubt the melting pot has been the most powerful and enduring metaphor, but as historian Philip Gleason (1964) suggested, this symbol of fusion has also been a source of considerable confusion. To greater or lesser extent our thinking about ethnicity has been shaped by this particular metaphor; we should examine it to better understand its impact on our thought.

The notion of America as a place where diverse peoples are melded, blended, or fused has a long history. Perhaps the first person to use this imagery in print was the French immigrant farmer J. Hector St. John de Crèvecoeur, who has been described as the first spokesperson of our national consciousness (Rischin, 1990: 64). In his *Letters from an American Farmer* (1904 [1782]: 39), composed shortly after the nation achieved independence from Britain, de Crèvecoeur saw America losing its non-American past as "individuals of all nations are melded into a new race of men" (we can assume that he included women in this process as well). Out of this would come a new culture (including a new religion) and a new society. De Crèvecoeur believed that all of the people residing in the new nation—Europeans, Africans, and what he referred to as Polynesians—would intermix in what he called a "smelting pot," yielding something novel and precious. The metaphor, thus, refers to metallic compounds like brass that are the unique creations of combining unlike metals.

Although this imagery did not gain general acceptance in the nineteenth century, others, such as Ralph Waldo Emerson, the American frontier historian Frederick Jackson Turner, and Theodore Roosevelt, used this metaphor. The person most responsible for popularizing the melting pot metaphor, however, was Israel Zangwill, a Jewish playwright residing in England. On October 5, 1908, his play, *The Melting Pot*, opened in Washington, D.C., in the midst of the most wide-scale immigration that the country had ever witnessed. This immigration brought large numbers of eastern and southern European immigrants, groups whose religion and culture differed significantly from the older American stock. Many earlier immigrants made invidious comparisons between established Americans and the newcomers. They questioned whether the new arrivals were competent to become citizens and whether it was appropriate to include them in the social fabric. Others, especially from the ranks of social reformers and political progressives, were quick to defend the immigrants.

In short, Zangwill's play entered into, and became a centerpiece of, an intense national debate on immigration and American citizenship. One of the audience on opening night was President Roosevelt, who proclaimed it a great play (Mann, 1979: 98–106). Roosevelt saw the play as an endorsement of his faith in the ability of the nation to absorb the new arrivals and as support for his call to abandon immigrant cultures. Opposed to the "hyphenated American," he promoted a process of rapid and complete Americanization. Those more sympathetic to and supportive of immigrant heritages—such as Jane Addams, the social worker chiefly responsible for the establishment of Hull House in Chicago—also responded favorably to the play.

The critics noted that *The Melting Pot* was not an artistic success. It was, however, popular with audiences, chiefly because of its optimistic view of America's capacity to incorporate diverse peoples. Something of a melodrama, the play is a love story whose protagonists are David Quixano, a Russian Jew, and Vera Revendal, a Christian also from Russia. David emigrated after an anti-Semitic campaign resulted in the massacre of Jews from his home community. He met and fell in love with Vera, who worked at a settlement house that David went to for help in getting established in his new surroundings. Convinced that their love could overcome their cultural differences in America, though it would have been doomed in Russia, David's beliefs were tested when he learned that Vera's father was the military officer responsible for the massacre.

After breaking off the relationship, he ultimately concluded that a fresh break with a painful past is possible, and in the climax of the play the two are reunited on a tenement rooftop in the immigrant enclave in lower Manhattan, with, according to Zangwill's stage directions, the Statue of Liberty's torch twinkling in the background. David's concluding speech is described by the playwright as prophetic:

> There she lies, the great Melting-Pot—listen! Can't you hear the roaring and the bubbling? There gapes her mouth [he points east]—the harbour where a thousand mammoth feeders come from the ends of the world to pour in their human freight. Ah, what a stirring and a seething! Celt and Latin, Slav and Teuton, Greek and Syrian,—black and yellow—["Jew and Gentile—Vera interjects] Yes, East and West, and North and South, the palm and the pine, the crescent and the cross—how the great Alchemist melts and fuses them with his purging flame! Here shall they all unite to build the Republic of Man and the Kingdom of God. Ah, Vera, what is the glory of Rome and Jerusalem where all nations and races come to worship and look back, compared with the glory of America, where all races and nations come to labour and look forward! (Zangwill, 1909: 198–200)

For at least the first half of the twentieth century, this emotionally-charged symbol became the dominant way in which Americans thought about the relationships of the many ethnic groups in the country to one another and their bearing on national unity. The symbol is, as Philip Gleason (1964: 34–35) has indicated, ambiguous and confusing. First, it is not clear whether the melting pot should be seen as descriptive or prescriptive. Second, does it refer only to cultural fusion or to biological fusion (that is,

Figure 1.4   *Ford Motor Company's first graduating class from their English school posing in the Melting Pot.*

Source: *Outlook*, CXIV, 1916: 197.

intermarriage) as well? Third, is it only the immigrant who is changed, or does the host society change, too? Because people can answer these questions in various ways, many could claim to support the symbol while disagreeing with other supporters about the actual concrete implications of the melting pot.

Clearly, many cultural, economic, and political elites during the two decades after Zangwill's play reacted in one of two ways to the idea of the melting pot. On the one hand, those who manifested a nativist hostility to the European newcomers (usually combined with an equally or greater hostility to racial minorities) feared that American culture — seen as a product of western European, and particularly British, influence — would be irreparably damaged by unbridled immigration (Solomon, 1956). In a particularly influential book, *The Passing of the Great Race* (1916), Madison Grant sought to prove scientifically that southern and eastern European immigrants were intellectually, morally, and physically inferior to native-born stock (see also Stoddard, 1920; Fairchild, 1926). The newcomers were seen as contributing to increases in social problems such as poverty, illiteracy, and crime, and they were blamed for undermining the standard of living of the working class by accepting lower wages than Americans (Billington, 1938: 322).

On the other hand, those with a more optimistic view about the transformative capacity of American society urged on the immigrants' Americanization campaigns. These campaigns were intended to eradicate all vestiges of the new arrivals' cultural heritages (language, folkways and mores, and so forth) while instilling in them what were deemed to be genuinely American attitudes and behaviors. Perhaps nowhere was this position more vigorously pursued than by the automobile industrialist Henry Ford. Ford established language and citizenship training schools for workers in his plants, and in graduation ceremonies, as shown in the photograph in Figure 1.4, workers entered a large pot dressed in native garb, only to emerge in American attire, holding their naturalization papers and American flags and singing the national anthem. Central to this viewpoint is the element of loss, specifically the loss of one's past. American culture would be forged at the expense of old world cultures.

Cultural Pluralism

The melting pot was not universally accepted. Those who embraced diversity and the preservation of ethnic allegiances and heritages were opposed to the creation of a homogeneous American culture and society. Culture critics welcomed the infusion of new cultural influences on America. For example, in 1916 Randolph Bourne (1977) called for the establishment of a "trans-national America." What Bourne envisioned by this is not entirely clear, but he certainly intended to preserve and integrate foreign cultures into American culture, thereby transforming and rejuvenating the latter (Blake, 1990).

The most sustained and influential early critique of the melting pot thesis came from philosopher Horace Kallen. In an article published first in 1915, titled "Democracy *Versus* the Melting Pot," Kallen (1924: 122–123) contended that the demands for "100 percent Americanization" were antithetical to democratic ideals. Moreover, they were contrary to an important sense of self-identity, which he saw as based on an appreciation of and identification with one's ancestral background. He provided an alternative to the melting pot metaphor by suggesting that America could be seen as an orchestra. He wrote that, "As in an orchestra every type of instrument has its specific *timbre* and *tonality*, . . . so in society, each ethnic group may be the natural instrument, its temper and culture may be its theme and melody and the harmony and dissonances and discords of them all may make the symphony of civilization" (Kallen, 1924: 125).

The melting pot came under increasing attack after 1960. Nathan Glazer and Daniel P. Moynihan voiced their conviction in *Beyond the Melting Pot* (1963) that the metaphor was wrong. At the outset of their study, which focused on five major groups in New York City (Irish, Italians, Puerto Ricans, Jews, and African Americans), they boldly proclaimed, "The point about the melting pot . . . is that it did not happen" (Glazer and Moynihan, 1963: v). Michael Novak, a polemicist and self-proclaimed advocate of ethnics of eastern and southern European origin, issued a more provocative attack in *The Rise of the Unmeltable Ethnics* (1972). Arguing for a deeply-rooted psychic need to maintain ethnic attachments, Novak argued that the forced efforts to destroy ethnic attachments had been a decided failure. He concluded that white ethnics would be a important political force in the foreseeable future.

Alternative Images of Ethnic America

In short, the melting pot, as description and as prescription, was under attack. Any number of alternatives were offered in its place. Some, such as a cultural rainbow or a kaleidoscope, suggest an aesthetic perspective that values diversity. Another example is the image of a mosaic, in which the individual pieces of colored tiles are placed in various relationships to other tiles to produce an integrated whole based on maintaining distinctiveness. This image has served Canada, also a heterogeneous, immigrant-receiving nation (and thus like America in many respects) as its most powerful symbol of identity. It has been used less frequently in America, though when David Dinkins was elected New York City's first African American mayor, he proclaimed the city to be a "gorgeous mosaic" (New York Times, 1990: 20). The imagery of a tapestry conjures up a similar perspective.

Although these images have gained increased currency in recent years, images from the kitchen appear to be the most popular, perhaps because food remains one of the most important artifacts of ethnic and racial groups. America has been characterized as a soup, stew, or salad bowl. No one has analyzed the relative popularity of each of these alternatives, but I suspect that the salad bowl has become the most frequently used metaphor. What is implied by this, and related alternatives to the melting pot? Quite simply, they portray America as a nation in which different groups maintain their distinctive identities: a tomato is always a tomato; it does not become part of the lettuce. The salad dressing is the part of the civic culture that holds these diverse elements in a palatable harmony.

The salad bowl is, however, as confusing a metaphor as is the melting pot for several reasons. First, some foods simply do not go well in a salad. Does this mean that some foods should be excluded from the salad bowl? Second, some parts of a salad are clearly dominant while others offer little more than a subtle garnish. Should this be taken to suggest that for a proper harmony of tastes, careful limits need to be established, with some items in the salad being introduced only in small doses? Third, as with the melting pot thesis, it is not clear whether those who prefer the salad bowl view it as descriptive or prescriptive.

Clearly, this image offers a rather static view of how groups interact with one another. If the melting pot overlooks continuity and resistance to change, treating every group as being fused in the great cauldron, the salad bowl suggests the opposite. Artichokes and tomatoes will not blend or fuse to create something new. In the world of ethnic groups, this metaphor glaringly fails to address the reality and the consequences of intermarriage, which is an extremely important contemporary phenomenon.

These metaphors are all problematic because they each fail to capture the complexity of America's heterogeneous population. We consider these metaphors because they are frequently used in everyday characterizations of ethnicity and are related to major theories concerning the dynamics of ethnic relations.

Summary

In the simplest circumstances, ethnicity is an extremely complicated factor in social life. Given the ethnic diversity that characterizes the United States, the complications become even more daunting.

Indeed, the task of understanding the significance of ethnicity over the course of the nation's history can be formidable. This chapter introduced readers to the many dimensions of ethnicity that must be considered. These dimensions range from the micro-level to the macro-level. On the micro-level, we introduced the impact that ethnic identities have on different individuals and how individuals respond to those identities. From the macro-level, we looked at the overarching impact of ethnicity on American society at large and the reciprocal impact of American society on ethnics and ethnic groups. The significance of the ethnic group was explored, with emphasis given to its role as a mediator between the micro- and macro-levels.

The dilemmas of studying ethnicity as an outsider were reviewed, including the problems brought about by ethnocentrism. The insider-outsider debate revealed another facet of the problem by raising the issue of whether outsiders are capable of understanding what it means to be an insider. We also discussed the tendency in much research to ignore the lives of certain categories of relatively powerless people. Throughout the chapter the importance of examining ethnicity in historical and structural terms was stressed. The next chapter builds on this discussion by providing a conceptual map that is intended to assist in the quest to more fully comprehend ethnic America.

TOWARD A
CONCEPTUAL MAP
OF ETHNIC
RELATIONS

2

Ethnic groups exist because a sufficient number of individuals with similar ancestral backgrounds identify with like others and exhibit a willingness to engage in collective behaviors that create the group. Ethnic relations are not possible in culturally homogeneous societies (for example, Iceland), because ethnic relations depend on the interactions of two or more ethnic groups. The study of ethnic relations covers three related topics: interethnic relations, intraethnic relations, and ethnic identity.

When we speak about ethnic relations, we also are speaking about race relations. The latter is a subset of the former. The relationship between ethnicity and race is often a matter of considerable confusion, so in this chapter we will clarify how these — and other related — terms are used in the social sciences in general, and sociology in particular. To place this discussion into historical context, we shall first look briefly at the way in which ethnic studies developed in America during the first half of the twentieth century.

The Emergence of Ethnic Studies

Sociology's contribution to the study of ethnicity derives from two key features of its approach: First, the careful examination of behavioral, cultural, and organizational differences among groups, and second, the search for sociocultural factors that contribute to these differences and that furthermore contribute to shaping the character of interethnic relations. By searching for sociocultural factors — such as economic competition for scarce resources, political conflict, or cultural differences — sociology directs us away from explanations that rely on biology. By turning to the social world to explain group differences and relations, sociology repudiates efforts to use instincts, genes, or other biological notions to study ethnicity.

A thumbnail sketch of the history behind the sociocultural approach introduces it as well as some of the central figures associated with its advance. A major reaction to biological racism began to be evident early in the century, and though it derived from several sources, historian Carl Degler (1991: 59–104) considers the anthropologist Franz Boas as the most important scholar in this reorientation of the social sciences.

Clearly, Boas had a profound impact on the development of cultural anthropology, including the training of such well-known scholars as Alfred L. Kroeber, Ruth Benedict, Robert Lowie, and Margaret Mead. But Boas's thought extended beyond anthropology to other disciplines. In sociology, important scholars of African Americans who came under Boas's influence, such as Howard Odum and Edward B. Reuter, revised their earlier views which were based on biological racism and embraced sociocultural interpretations on matters related to race. Psychologists were slower to make the shift — because the discipline was so attached to the notion of instincts — but by the 1920s change was apparent here as well (Cravens, 1978: 191–193; Gossett, 1965; Wiley, 1986; Barkan, 1992).

In sociology this shift was most visible among the members of the sociology department at the University of Chicago, or what became known as the Chicago School (Matthews, 1978, 1987; Wacker, 1983; Persons, 1987). The two major figures behind this shift were W.I. Thomas and Robert E. Park. Thomas was the major force at Chicago prior to his departure due to an unfortunate scandal. His monumental study (written in collaboration with the Polish émigré sociologist Florian Znaniecki) on *The Polish Peasant in Europe and America* (1918) was a landmark work that set the stage and served as a model for subsequent empirical research (Wiley, 1986; Creelan and Granfield, 1986). This study replaced the concept of instinct with that of attitude, and employed Thomas's social psychology which was based on what he referred to as the "four wishes" — for experience, security, response, and recognition. In interpreting the

Polish immigrants' responses to their new environment, he used such concepts as personal disorganization, social disorganization, and reorganization.

Robert E. Park employed and adapted these concepts in his work and was perhaps the first sociologist to state that the study of the European immigrant and the study of racial groups should proceed in the same manner (Wacker, 1983: 9). Although Park's work was not always consistent and he made no particular attempt to be systematic, he was perhaps the principal force in severing the sociology of ethnic studies from explanations based on presumed innate hereditary dispositions. The generation of graduate students he trained reflected this perspective, as evidenced in works of his students that became classics in the field. A short list of contributions includes: St. Clair Drake and Horace Cayton's *Black Metropolis* (1945); Louis Wirth's *The Ghetto* (1956 [1928]); Everett Hughes's *French Canada in Transition* (1943); and E. Franklin Frazier's *The Negro Family in the United States* (1939) and *The Negro in the United States* (1949). What these studies had in common was an appreciation of "the complexity and fluidity of ongoing group life" and a refusal to employ theories that imposed overly rigid or oversimplified interpretations (Lal, 1986: 281; Lal, 1990; Kivisto, 1990).

Race, racial groups, and race relations were thus to be construed as ethnicity, ethnic groups, and ethnic relations. But what did Park and the Chicago School mean by these terms? What do we mean by them? Our purpose here is not to provide a detailed history of these concepts. Instead, we seek to clarify them to provide working definitions. Before addressing these particular questions, we will turn first to two related terms: nationality groups and minority groups.

Clarifying Concepts

Ethnicity has received considerable attention in recent years from scholars in the social sciences and history. This is a virtue insofar as contemporary discussions of a perplexing topic can build on a substantial body of research and of theory development. For a variety of reasons, however, including imbalances regarding which groups do or do not get studied (Lavender and Forsyth, 1976), scholars have taken widely divergent approaches. Not only do the

Figure 2.1   A Swedish American club, with members dressed in
traditional provincial garb, circa 1910.

Source: Courtesy of the Swenson Center.

ways we look at this subject vary considerably, but also the precise
parameters of what it is we are studying are unclear (Petersen,
1982).

Some scholars define the subject matter somewhat differently
than others: many prefer to speak about ethnic groups and others
have defined their subject matter as the study of nationalities, minorities, or racial groups. Sometimes the term ethnic group is used
as a virtual synonym for these terms. Although they are related,
there are important differences.

Nations, Nationality, and Nationalism

Nationalities are groups with a sense of peoplehood and with a political agenda that calls for creating or preserving a nation state.
Nationalism provides the ideological justification for, among other
things, the territorial claims of the group and the implications such
claims have relative to other groups (Gellner, 1983; Horowitz,
1985; Kedourie, 1985; Smith, 1986; Hobsbawm, 1991). Nationalism
is a potent force in the modern world, especially in areas where

political, cultural, and social boundaries have been subject to dramatic changes in complex histories over long periods of time (Kristeva, 1993).

Thus, the conflict in the Balkans that pits most centrally Serbs against Croatians, but also includes Slovenes, Macedonians, Albanians, and Montenegrins, developed from nationalist aspirations. The fragmentation of the Soviet Union into the Baltic areas of Lithuania, Latvia, and Estonia and the Asian republics that include Azerbaijan, Tadzhikistan, Kirgizistan, Turkmenistan, and Uzbekistan provides another vivid indication of nationalism's central significance. In western Europe as well, nationalist movements have risen to prominence in numerous places in this century. Examples include the Welsh and Scottish in Britain, the Basque and Catalonian in Spain, and the Occitan in France. Throughout much of the Third World nationalism has been a very divisive force. Recent examples include the ongoing strife in Lebanon, the civil war in Sri Lanka that involves the Sinhalese and Tamils, and the numerous conflicts in Africa that are based, at least in part, on tribal differences. In North America, the Quebecois separatists have recurrently during the past quarter century demanded that the province of Quebec remove itself from the Canadian confederation and declare itself an independent nation.

In the United States, nationalism is a relatively insignificant force—especially when viewed in comparative perspective. This is not surprising because the United States is largely a nation of voluntary immigrants, and immigrants are usually not in a position to make the territorial claims that underpins nationalism. Nonetheless, this particular designation has been applied to the United States, though more commonly several decades ago, as seen in the titles of such books as Louis Adamic's *A Nation of Nations* (1944), Oscar Handlin's *Race and Nationality in American Life* (1948), and Brown and Roucek's *Our Racial and National Minorities* (1937). Nationalist ideas can be seen among relatively small segments of the African American population and among American Indians (that is, two groups not composed of voluntary immigrants), though not as especially significant features of intragroup relations and ideologies.

Fundamentally, this country is unique because nationalist ideologies have generally not been advanced by societal subgroups. Somehow America differs from the rest of the world—or at least most of the world—in patterns of interaction across and among the diverse groups that make up the nation's citizenry. The term nationality groups is too restrictive: In global terms, nationality groups should be seen as a subset of ethnic groups, the former being seen in some multi-ethnic nations but not in others (Connor, 1978; O'Brien 1991).

Minority Groups

Although *nationality group* is too restrictive to capture the character of American situation, the more commonly used designation *minority group* is too expansive. As the Brown and Roucek title cited earlier illustrates, this term can be linked to that of nationalities. Indeed, as Philip Gleason (1991) has indicated, the earliest use of the term minority, in the nineteenth century, linked it with nationalities. In the United States, however, the term acquired a new definition that severed this connection: The term minority gained popularity as an alternative to the term race. *Race* tended to be used in a biological sense, and the term minority was intended to emphasize the centrality of social and cultural factors. Gleason saw the publication of sociologist Donald Young's textbook *American Minority Peoples* (1932) as the beginning of the widespread utilization of the term "minority." Indeed, at present, the authors of some textbooks on this topic continue to define their subject matter in terms of minority groups (for example, Vander Zanden, 1973; Newman, 1973; Farley, 1982; Schaefer, 1988).

Although attempts to delineate what constitutes a minority group vary somewhat, most definitions share the view that minority groups occupy a subordinate position in a society in allocation of wealth, prestige, and power (Schermerhorn, 1978: 13–17; Francis, 1951; Rose and Rose, 1948; Wirth, 1945). Differential markers identify minority groups, and on this basis they are denied full participation in the institutions of the society. Minority groups are thereby perceived to be victims—the objects of prejudicial attitudes and discriminatory actions by the majority group. Parenthetically, note that discussions of minority groups imply the existence of a majority group, which is the dominant group in a society usually depicted as benefitting from its ability to force other groups into the role of subordinates.

Figure 2.2   *A Mexican American family, circa 1921.*

Source: Courtesy of the Swenson Center.

Several problematic features are inherent in the concept of the minority group. The first point is that the term conjures up the numerical representation of the group in a society. When the concept was first applied to the United States, two groups in particular were singled out for designation as minority groups: African Americans and Jewish Americans. Both were, in fact, numerical minorities. If we look at South Africa, however, we discover that apartheid entailed a relatively small minority oppressing a sizeable numerical majority of the population. Since Wirth's (1945) discussion of this issue, most of those employing this term have contended that majority and minority do not refer to absolute numbers and can be seen as synonyms for dominant and subordinate (Blalock, 1967).

The second, and more serious point, is a lack of attention paid to defining what constitutes the majority group and who should and who should not be included. To take one example, in contemporary discussions of the current dilemmas of African Americans, there is often a lack of clarity concerning the dominant group they confront. At one extreme, a restrictive definition suggests that the majority is limited to White Anglo Saxon Protestants (WASPS). At the other extreme, the majority is white America. But in this instance, should Hispanics be included under the rubric of the white majority? What about American Jews, who have a long history of confronting anti-Semitic exclusion?

The third point is related to the second: majority-minority terminology encourages examining a society in an essentially dichotomous fashion. In a highly complex and heterogeneous society such as the United States, attempting to depict its social character by utilizing these terms encourages an oversimplification that can obscure some important issues while distorting others. That is to say, as we focus attention on the relationship that exists between a subordinate group and a dominant group, we fail to pay sufficient attention to the relationships between and among subordinate groups. For example, the dominant-subordinate relationship diverts attention from the often strained relations between African Americans and Jews as well as the tensions that exist between African Americans and Hispanic Americans. Further, we tend to overlook the very significant differences that persist among various European-origin groups (Greeley, 1974).

The fourth point addresses the matter of what counts as a minority group. The examples cited above could suggest that the term is roughly equivalent to ethnic group. However, minority group is used by most practitioners to include a variety of other groups as well, including women, religious sects, homosexuals, and both the physically and mentally disabled. Although broad generalizations can include these and perhaps other groups, they can only be made by ignoring that which is distinctive about each of the groups. This is a mistake in the study of ethnic relations, for which a considerable amount of theoretical work has been produced that is based on features of ethnicity that make it a relatively unique phenomenon.

Parallel to this, an ever-expanding literature on feminist theory proceeds with a similar desire to recognize and comprehend features that are unique to gender issues (Harding, 1987; Smith, 1990).

Race

Thus, in my view nationality is too restrictive for our use and minority group is too expansive or general. But what about race? Throughout its history, American society has been permeated by race relations issues and by the consequences of racism. Thus, we must examine the varied ways in which race and racial groups have been defined and acted upon by different social actors in differing times, places, and circumstances. Does this mean that race is a useful analytic tool for exploring these issues, and if so, how should we conceptualize the connection between race and ethnicity?

The general consensus among sociologists is that race fails as a useful theoretical concept. The reason for this failure can be seen by a brief look at the history of the use of racial theory. The classificatory list of races by the Swedish taxonomist Linnaeus in the eighteenth century was the first of numerous attempts to identify the varieties of Homo sapiens and determine what should and what should not be considered truly human. Linnaeus divided humankind into four major varieties: white, red, yellow, and black. He argued that these physical differences were correlated with personality differences (Rose, 1968: 33).

Nineteenth Century Racialist Thought

By the time Arthur de Gobineau published *The Inequality of Human Races* (1915 [1853–55]) in the middle of the nineteenth century, the pattern was set. Thereafter repeated efforts were made to not only classify, but also to illustrate the inferiority of various races and the superiority of others. Gobineau divided the races into the strong and the weak, with whites or Aryans constituting the former, while other groups were located in the latter category. He contended that the strong, due to their tendency to migrate, would inevitably conquer the weak, and in the process provide the weak with the benefits of civilization. He warned, however, of the dangers that racial mixing would bring about. In his view, racial differences were rooted in human nature and not in social conditions. Thus, the domination of some races by others was not only inevitable, but also in a perverse way was beneficial to superior and inferior races alike (Bolt, 1971; Banton, 1987: 1–64; Stone, 1985: 21–22). De Gobineau described the age of the European colonization of much of the rest of the world, and his quasi-scientific theory served well as an ideological justification for conquest.

As William Stanton (1960) indicated, similar thinking was used by Southern slaveholders in the United States to justify the institution of slavery. But such thinking extended beyond African and Asian origin groups. During the peak of mass immigration from eastern Europe in the early part of this century, race theory was employed to discredit the new arrivals. As Madison Grant's diatribe against these newcomers, *The Passing of the Great Race* (1916), illustrates, this mode of thinking was extremely pliable. Where predecessors might have viewed all Europeans as members of the same race, Grant provides a new classificatory schema that delineates the superior races (the Nordic peoples from western Europe) from the inferior, which he identifies as originating from the "Mediterranean basin and the Balkans." Here, racial theory was used in the interest of the immigration restriction movement. As Grant (1916: 92) argued, "Our jails, insane asylums, and almshouses are filled with this human flotsam and the whole tone of American life, social, moral, and political, has been lowered and vulgarized by them."

Darwinism and Eugenics

Several important figures in the early history of American sociology were deeply influenced by this kind of thought. Like Edward Alsworth Ross, they frequently sought to apply Darwin's theory of natural selection to human society. They were also influenced by the hereditary arguments of the eugenicist Sir Francis Galton. Perhaps aware of the scientific shortcomings of previous racial theories, such innovations were intended to redress the deficiencies of earlier expressions. The conclusions drawn, however, differed little from those less influenced by Darwin and Galton. Ross could have been parroting Grant when he concluded, in The Old World in the New (1914), that the fit were not surviving and as a result American society was experiencing a "certain decay of character." Franklin Henry Giddings, Ross's contemporary, thought that many new immigrants could not be incorporated into American society.

Like Ross, Giddings felt that their presence was detrimental to the well-being of American society, fearing the superior Anglo-Saxons would end up "sinking to the level of their more brutal competitors" (Giddings, 1893: 237). This conviction led Giddings to active participation in the Immigrantion Restriction League; he even served for a time as its vice-president.

Racialist Thought Challenged

By the 1920s race theories that were purported to be rooted in biology had come into disrepute (Benedict, 1959). Though they never entirely disappeared from the social sciences, racial theories ended up occupying an extremely marginal position. As the examples just presented illustrate, the reasons are twofold: they are based on bad science or pseudo-science and they carry racist political implications. These reasons were evident during the heyday of the Eugenicist movement around the turn of the century, and they can be seen in the more recent claims by figures such as Arthur Jensen and Richard Herrnstein that black IQs are lower than those of whites, and this difference can explain not only differences in academic achievement but in occupational status, too. As Troy Duster (1990: 9) has observed, "In this century, the empirical research on the genetics/IQ controversy and the attendant policy injunctions have had a remarkably varied history. However, one consistent pattern emerges: the more privileged strata have at each juncture raised the 'genetic' question about those at the lower end of the socioeconomic ladder."

In recent decades, scholars have been highly suspicious of the "received truth" about racial differences. Anthropologist Frank Livingstone (1962), for example, emphasized the lack of clear-cut divisions among human population groups, which led him to conclude that "if races have to be discrete entities, then there are no races." In other words, racial classifications have no scientific basis. This led to the call for a nonracial approach to the understanding of human diversity. Not all have agreed with this conclusion, but few dispute the assertion that the boundaries distinguishing groups are at best imprecise (Dunn and Dobzhansky, 1952; Coon, 1965; Banton and Harwood, 1975).

Geneticists have continued to study the differences in gene pools in humankind. The prevalence of illnesses such as sickle cell anemia among African Americans and Tay-Sachs among Jews can be viewed as indications of the validity of the biological approach. In contrast to these physical maladies, however, attempts to apply the findings of biology to explain social and cultural differences, particularly to explain inequality, have failed (Yinger, 1985: 158–159). As geneticist N.P. Dubinin (1956: 69) wrote in a book published by UNESCO that summarized the status of research on race at midcentury, "Theories of the alleged inequality of human races have no scientific basis."

Sociobiology

Before leaving this topic, we should note one recent effort to resuscitate a biological understanding of race (and ethnicity) because it comes from a prominent scholar in the field. Pierre van den Berghe, who in his early career used a historical approach quite at odds with the biological (1965; 1967; 1970), shifted his thinking as a result of the impact of sociobiology (1978; 1981; 1986; 1990; see also Lopreato, 1990). A self-fashioned iconoclast and anarchist, van den Berghe (1981: 2) became disenchanted with a perspective that, in his estimation, was too dismissive of biology's role in the sociocultural realm. He faulted this view for its severing of the link between the social and the cultural approaches on the one hand and the biological on the other; then he united them so that biology plays the central role in explaining group attachments and intergroup relations. He wrote, "My basic argument is quite simple: ethnic and racial sentiments are [an] extension of kinship sentiments" (van den Berghe, 1981: 18).

With this simple assertion he attempted to establish a model that assumes that human beings seek to maximize their fitness for survival by favoring, through nepotism, those sharing one's genes. Therefore, genetics influences the construction of in-group and out-group definitions, which means that there is something immutable about the problematic, conflict-ridden character of race and ethnic relations.

Van den Berghe does not argue, as the racial thinkers noted earlier do, that some races are inferior and others superior. He does not seek to justify racial oppression on the basis that the members of some racial groups will, because of their favorable genetic inheritances, inevitably obtain more power, wealth, and status than members of groups not so favorably endowed. Instead, he challenges those who assume that it is possible to create social environments conducive to racial harmony. He believes individual self-interest is bound up with the interest of the racial group, which leads to competition and conflict among groups for scarce resources. This rather fatalistic view limits the role of human consciousness in effecting social change and also limits (or denies) the relative autonomy of social and cultural factors.

In this respect, van den Berghe's work bears a remarkable similarity to that of William Graham Sumner, who in an earlier period of American sociology was convinced that efforts at societal reform and improvement were largely doomed to failure (Sumner, 1906; Kivisto, 1978). Sumner used the term "ethnocentrism" to account for what he saw as the universal tendency to advance the interests of one's own group at the expense of others. In effect, van den Berghe attempts to use what he sees as the contributions of sociobiology to explain the underlying cause of ethnocentrism.

Conceptual models, however, should not be judged by whether one agrees or disagrees with their political implications. Rather, they should be assessed on their usefulness or lack of usefulness in helping to make sense of aspects of our world. Van den Berghe is too reductionist. That is to say, biology is used to explain too much, at the expense of explanations that are rooted in social and cultural factors. Criticisms of sociobiology in general, such as Marshall Sahlins' (1976), have made the same point in considerable detail. Like any other grand theory, van den Berghe's overgeneralizes, and thus oversimplifies. He is not willing to consider history — which is muddled, complicated, and subject to varied and partial interpretations — seriously enough.

Because of this, the sociobiological approach does not help us understand ethnic phenomena. That no studies to date have fruitfully employed van den Berghe's model is perhaps the best indication of its limited utility. An approach rooted in the social and cultural sciences, which does not need to avail itself of biology, provides a far more promising basis for dealing with this subject.

*E*thnicity and Ethnic Groups

Most definitions of ethnicity have two central features: a shared culture (see, for example, Ware, 1940) and a real or putative common ancestry. The ethnic group should be seen as a distinctive type of group. E.K. Francis (1947) saw the ethnic group as a subtype of *Gemeinschaft* groups. *Gemeinschaft*, which can be roughly translated as community, implies a type of group characterized by its involuntary nature (that is, you are born into it) and by the member's familiarity with and emotional bonds to other group members. As such, Francis considers the ethnic group to be a secondary group with some of the features of primary groups.

Werner Sollors (1981: 259–260) noted that the term "ethnicity" is of relatively recent origin: the first use of it appeared only fifty years ago. Sollors locates its initial use by W. Lloyd Warner, an anthropologist at the University of Chicago. Warner used the term in his famous community studies particularly "Yankee City" (Newburyport, Massachusetts), to highlight cultural differences he observed in the city.

The adjective "ethnic" was used at least a century earlier, but not widely until the publication of William Graham Sumner's *Folkways* in 1906. Since then both ethnicity and ethnic have gained wide acceptance, but no consensus has been reached about precisely what they mean. In a study intended to discover the various ways that ethnicity has been defined in major social science journals, Wsevold Isajiw (1979: 1) found that a sizeable majority of writers on the subject simply avoided dealing with the matter of definition.

The editors of the *Harvard Encyclopedia of American Ethnic Groups* (Thernstrom, et al., 1980: vi) presented the following list of features that in varied combinations can be seen as defining ethnicity:

- common geographic origin
- migratory status
- race
- language or dialect
- religious faith or faiths
- ties that transcend kinship, neighborhood, and community boundaries
- shared traditions, values, and symbols
- literature, folklore, and music
- food preferences
- settlement and employment patterns

- special interests in regard to politics in the homeland and the United States
- institutions that specifically serve and maintain the group
- an internal sense of distinctiveness
- an external perception of distinctiveness

This is a loose and broad listing. The editors cast their net widely, which resulted in a selection of 106 groups for inclusion in their volume and a sense that this was to be seen as a minimum number of ethnic groups. Two features are actually consequences of ethnicity rather than attributes of the phenomenon: migratory status and settlement and employment patterns. Furthermore, some features seem to be more important than others. Since the editors do not provide criteria for the implementation of these features to concrete ethnic groups, an ambiguity (that they admittedly recognize) remains about what, in essence, ethnicity is.

Isajiw (1979: 25) offers a particularly parsimonious definition of the ethnic group when he describes it as "an involuntary group of people who share the same culture or the descendants of such people who identify themselves and/or are identified by others as belonging to the same involuntary group." This definition combines, as he notes, both a subjective and an objective component. With the provisos that follow, this definition will be used throughout this book.

Religio-Ethnic Groups

Isajiw finds fault with definitions that include religion as one of the attributes of the ethnic group (compare Gordon, 1964 and Schermerhorn, 1978). Although Isajiw is right to argue for preserving an analytic differentiation between religious groups and ethnic groups, religion is often a critical aspect of culture. Along with language, common folkways and mores, and a shared history, religion should be considered as one of the building blocks of culture. Thus, Baptists do not constitute an ethnic group, because it is a religion open to people regardless of their ethnic background. For some groups, such as Jews, the ethnic cannot be separated from the religious, and they might properly be viewed as religio-ethnic groups. The editors of the *HEAEG* included Mormons, but it is more appropriate to consider Mormons as a religious group like the

Baptists. The editors also included the Amish and Hutterites, and here the religio-ethnic designation is correct, for members of these groups trace their ancestry to Germanic sources as well as to particular dissident religious movements. Greeks, given their connection with Orthodox Christianity, might also be appropriately seen as a religio-ethnic group.

Racial Groups

As religio-ethnic groups are a subset of ethnic groups, so racial groups should be considered a subset of ethnic groups. Racial definitions are socially defined and use differentiating physical features such as those associated with skin color to serve as markers of identity. Racial markers are used to define relationships of dominance and subordination. Based on a person's particular racial markers, others may attribute favorable or unfavorable personality characteristics: the person will be seen as intelligent or unintelligent, industrious or lazy, rational or emotional, trustworthy or untrustworthy, and so forth. Based on a person's racial markers, others may be more or less willing to enter into social relationships with the person.

Racial definitions vary according to time and place. Some societies do not make sharp distinctions between racial groups, but see them in a fluid manner, taking into account the impact of interbreeding. By developing definitions of mixed-bloods (mulatto, sambo, and so forth), such societies portray racial definitions along a continuum. In contrast, other societies — and the United States falls into this category — make especially sharp distinctions between groups (Cross, 1991).

Robert Park (1950), in an insightful essay titled "Behind Our Masks," argued that in the latter case a great deal of importance is attached to racial differences. These societies are generally characterized by considerable racial hostility and conflict. The reason is that by forcing individuals to, in effect, wear their race like a mask, it becomes difficult for members of another group to see that person as an individual. Instead, the person is nothing more than a representative of the race. If people cannot view members of another race as individuals, with distinctive personalities, fears, desires, aspirations, and so forth, they cannot develop harmonious relationships with them. Race has been the most divisive force throughout the entire history of the United States.

Given this, does it make sense to make a sharp contrast between ethnic groups and racial groups? M.G. Smith (1982) thinks so, and he argues that it is a mistake to subsume race under the more general concept of ethnicity. His reason is that race is a reality in nature, or in other words that somehow biology actually counts.

This book proceeds with a different understanding. Racial groups are ethnic groups. When race is socially defined as important, those definitions carry with them real and profound consequences. We will employ the definitions used in the society, but will not mistakenly consider these as rooted in, and thus determined by, biology or nature.

We should not view these concepts in an overly rigid manner. This is because the definitions we employ are second hand, based on the logics-in-use of social actors who are constantly defining and redefining their world and the people who inhabit it. To use the phrase of sociologist Herbert Blumer (1954: 3–10)—a product of the Chicago School and the original spokesperson for a tradition of sociology that he referred to as "symbolic interactionism"—we need to use "sensitizing concepts" that assist us in comprehending how people interpret the social world. A summary of the relationship among the terms we have examined thus far is contained in Figure 2.1's Venn diagram.

Ethnic Relations

In one of the more systematic attempts to develop a general theory of ethnic relations, R.A. Schermerhorn (1970: 12) emphasized that the ethnic group must be seen as a "collectivity within a larger society." The ethnic groups must be considered in relation to other groups as well as to the society at large.

But what is the range of possible relations? At one extreme is an unwillingness on the part of a more powerful group to permit a less powerful group of people to exist. Genocide, the programmatic extermination of a people, has been an altogether too frequent occurrence in the modern world. In this century, two genocidal campaigns—the Turks against the Armenians in the second decade of the twentieth century (Dadrian, 1989) and the Nazi

Figure 2.3 *Clarifying Concepts.*

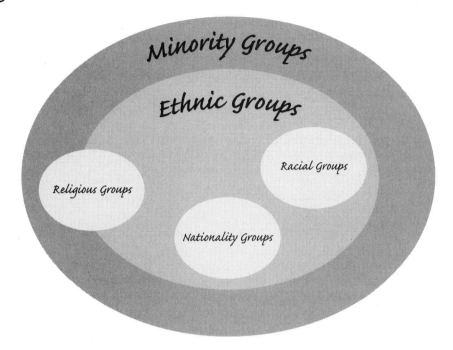

Germans against Jews and gypsies or Romanies—have left bitter memories for survivors and their children, many of whom now live in the United States. The only group in America, however, to have confronted what can be seen as genocidal campaigns is the American Indian. Though these campaigns may not have achieved sufficient political or public support to have become a coherent governmental policy, nonetheless the net result of the treatment of the Native American has appropriately been described by Russell Thornton (1987) as a holocaust.

Another possible response of a more powerful group to a less powerful one is to either deny entry or expel the less powerful from the territory controlled by the more powerful group. Many have advocated this option at various points in American history. Furthermore, it has been implemented on several occasions, beginning with the rise of anti-Chinese sentiment in the nineteenth century. Asian-origin groups have been the principal targets of such efforts, though Latin American, Middle Eastern, and selective European-origin groups have also been subject to such attempts. Although immigration laws have been used to deny entry to various groups, wide-scale, governmentally sponsored policies of ethnic expulsion have not been characteristic of American ethnic relations.

A third option, which has not shaped ethnic relations in this country in a significant way, is secession. Ethnic groups with territorial claims sometimes attempt to leave an existing nation state to establish a new one. Secessionist movements are nationalist movements. The Québecois separatists in Canada are a contemporary example. In other cases, what are called "irredentist" movements attempt to promote the voluntary exodus from one nation to another or to fuse a territory with a nation. The rationale used by movement adherents is that the territory is the natural homeland of the group. Such movements often elicit challenges from ethnic groups and political forces opposed to such an undertaking. This can be seen in eastern Europe among some Albanians in the Kosovo region of Serbia. These attempts cause much of the ethnic conflict in the world today. In the United States, because an overwhelming majority of Americans are voluntary immigrants or their offspring, this phenomenon has been limited to only two groups, African Americans and American Indians. Moreover, in both cases, such movements have attracted only limited support within the group.

This leads us to two types of ethnic relations that are applicable to the American setting: assimilation and pluralism (Abramson, 1980; Gleason, 1992). Assimilation is a theoretic articulation of the melting pot metaphor; pluralism is a parallel conceptualization of the salad bowl. Both have been used as key explanatory concepts in discussions of American ethnicity and have been the objects of extensive theoretical discussions and elaborations.

Assimilation

Assimilation can be defined as the incorporation of an ethnic group's members into the larger society. This definition, however, raises a number of questions, because the term incorporation is unclear. Milton Gordon (1964: 71) cites, in his seminal study on the topic, seven types of assimilation. Three do not actually refer to assimilation, but rather to preconditions for assimilation. These have to do with the absence of various impediments to harmonious or cooperative social relations: "attitude receptional assimilation" refers to the absence of prejudice; "behavioral receptional assimilation" signifies the related absence of discrimination; and "civic assimilation" is based on a situation free of institutional conflict in the political and cultural arenas.

The four remaining types do signify aspects of incorporation. One, "identificational assimilation," addresses the subjective or social psychological dimension of assimilation, and the other three deal with objective, external aspects of inclusion: "cultural assimilation" concerns modeling behavioral patterns after those of the dominant society; "structural assimilation" refers to the entry of ethnic group members into the institutions, neighborhoods, and primary groups of the dominant society; and "marital assimilation" refers, quite simply, to intermarriage.

Gordon did not claim that these types of assimilation were necessarily connected in a series of stages. He avoided depicting assimilation as an inevitable course of events. This set him apart from a perspective held by many of his predecessors, such as Robert Park, who at one point in his career spoke about a four-staged "race relations cycle" which was portrayed as moving inevitably from contact through conflict and accommodation to assimilation, (Park, 1950; Lyman, 1972; Matthews, 1978; Lal, 1983, 1990). Gordon's main objective was to construct a topology for comparative purposes, but he did suggest that if these modes of assimilation were to occur in sequential order, marital assimilation would be the last to occur.

In discussions about assimilation, two somewhat different versions of assimilation are frequently depicted. William Newman (1973: 53–67) summarized the two possibilities diagrammatically. A + B + C = D describes a situation in which cultural, structural, and marital assimilation take place. This is the purist expression of the melting pot, for the groups that enter the cauldron are transformed into something new — into a heretofore nonexistent entity. This subset of assimilation might properly be called, as Gordon does, "amalgamation."

A + B + C = A (where A is the dominant group) describes a situation in which all groups are transformed except the dominant one, which becomes the template used to reshape the identities of the other groups. This has been referred to as Anglo-conformity and as Americanization. In this model, the dominant model and the host society in general are not changed by the process of ethnic group interaction. This has a peculiarly one-sided character: change for subordinate groups, and stasis for the dominant group.

Pluralism

Similarly, two variations of the pluralist model can be distinguished. Again, Newman (1973: 67–87) provides a useful schematic portrait. A + B + C = A + B + C portrays a situation in which ethnic groups maintain their distinctiveness and their separateness. In contrast to the changes that occur in both the amalgamation and the Anglo-conformity models, ethnic persistence over time and in spite of interaction is the central defining feature of this version of pluralism. This is the most pristine expression of the salad bowl: distinctive identities and boundaries are preserved just as is the lettuce even after its interaction with the tomatoes, peppers, olives, and artichoke hearts.

A second, somewhat modified form of pluralism sees group identities preserved, but simultaneously changed via interaction with other groups and the dominant society: A + B + C = A1 + B1 + C1. Borrowing from the title of the book by Nathan Glazer and Daniel P. Moynihan (1963), Newman refers to this scenario as "beyond the melting pot." In this version of pluralism, African Americans remain different from Italian Americans, but African Americans are also different from Africans and Italian Americans are different from Italians. The difference is the product of the shared civic experience both groups — and, of course, all others — have had due to their ongoing contact with society at large and the complex patterns of interaction with other groups.

Just as the public arguments of proponents and opponents of the melting pot have been heated, so frequently have been the scholarly debates between assimilationists and pluralists. In the midst of these exchanges, however, a substantial body of empirical research has been produced, particularly in sociology and history, that helps clarify and put into perspective these theoretical discussions. Neither extreme position — amalgamation or radical cultural diversity — can provide compelling overarching descriptions of America yesterday, today, or in the foreseeable future. Evidence can and has been amassed to support and to critique both of the modified alternatives. Moreover, recently efforts have been undertaken to assess both the conceptual strengths and weaknesses of these positions.

The modified assimilationist position is, in effect, a model of change. The dynamic factors that produce the predicted change have not been sufficiently developed by assimilationist theorists, however. Modernization theorists, including Marxists, have seen industrialization as a destroyer of ethnic attachments, and, indeed, of all attachments rooted in tradition. From this perspective, ethnicity's demise leads to the emergence of powerful class-based allegiances. But, as we shall see, the empirical evidence provides compelling proof that a simple analysis of a progressive shift from ethnicity to class does not adequately capture the relationship between the two.

Force can only account in part for a decision to abandon ethnic attachments. Indeed, the demand to renounce one's ethnicity can lead to an intensified commitment to ethnic identity. Ethnic commitment can be a form of resistance to enforced compliance with the dictates of a dominant group or societal elites. Surprisingly little attention has been paid both to factors that stimulate a desire to leave the confines of the ethnic group and the lures of the host society in attracting people to it. Furthermore, assimilationists often underplay the persistence of ethnic antagonism and the power of forces intent on ensuring that assimilation does not occur.

The research agenda pursued by assimilationists tends, not surprisingly, to focus attention on measuring the perceived degree of assimilation. They use a variety of indicators dealing with rates of socioeconomic mobility, civic participation, social integration, cultural accommodation, and intermarriage rates, and they have paid scant attention to indicators of ethnic persistence.

By contrast, pluralists address precisely those issues that assimilationists ignore. The persistence of markers of cultural identity (language, values, behavior, and so forth) and the continuing impact of ethnicity on political orientation, educational achievement, and socioeconomic status have been explored extensively by pluralists (Greeley, 1974; Parenti, 1967).

The Primordialist Perspective

An important question that divides pluralists concerns the reasons for ethnic persistence. Some theorists such as Clifford Geertz (1973), Edward Shils (1975), Harold Isaacs (1975), and Pierre van den Berghe (1981), adhere to what has been described as a primordialist perspective, which sees ethnicity as a deeply rooted, and immutable, universal given. Most primordialists do not agree with van den Berghe's biologically based version of primordialism.

Instead, they treat ethnic persistence as a mysterious given. Shils (1975: 122) states, simply, that ethnicity is predicated on "a certain ineffable significance [that] is attributed to the tie of blood." In a similar vein, Geertz (1973: 259) writes that ethnic allegiance manifests a powerful coercive force due to "some unaccountable absolute import attributed to the very tie itself." Primordialists do not quite put it in these terms, but they seem to see ethnicity as the result of a not fully understood, but nonetheless extraordinarily powerful psychological attachment to the group.

This view is problematic because it devalues the role of historical and social structural conditions that act to either reinforce or to undermine ethnic loyalties. Ethnic identity may meet certain psychological needs, but it is not an immutable given, a basic part of the human condition (Glazer and Moynihan 1975; McKay, 1982; Scott, 1990). Furthermore, primordialists cannot account for why ethnic identities wane and even disappear.

The Circumstantialist Perspective

Circumstantialists, a term that gained currency when used by Glazer and Moynihan (1975: 19–20), or "optionalists" (Gleason, 1983: 919), provide a more compelling sociological basis for understanding ethnicity. They contend, quite simply, that societal, cultural, and environmental factors combine to create conditions that either sustain or undermine ethnic attachments for particular groups at different times. Ethnicity can wax or wane, depending on the circumstances. This particular perspective will be the basis of our discussion of ethnic identity and ethnic group formation and maintenance.

Toward a New Model

Until recently theoretical discourse about ethnicity has been limited chiefly to polemics that pitted assimilationists and pluralists against each other. The sterility of these debates has become increasingly apparent, and efforts are underway to develop alternative theoretical models that can account for both persistence, which is the focus of pluralists, and change, the central concern of assimilationists (Kivisto, 1989: 11–23; see also Higham, 1982). As the long-time student of ethnicity, J. Milton Yinger (1986: 39) commented, "neither the assimilationist thesis nor the persistence-of-ethnic-difference antithesis is adequate."

Thus, we have arrived at a situation aptly described by Ewa Morawska (1990: 218) in the following way: "The assimilation paradigm in its classical version has been abandoned on account of its excessive simplicity, and the 'ethnicity-forever' approach that replaced it is also passing away." If both of these theoretical perspectives can be faulted for seeing only part of the larger picture, one might think that a successful alternative model would incorporate both approaches into its overarching theoretical model. This has been attempted by a variety of reductionist theorists intent on identifying a single analytical factor in the study of ethnicity and ethnic relations.

Marxism and Social Classes

Some Marxists, particularly those who see themselves as the most orthodox, have made a persistent attempt to use class as the pivotal concept in defining various types of social relations, thereby reducing ethnic differences to class differences (Cox, 1948; Parkin, 1979; Bonacich, 1980; Steinberg, 1981). A related danger is "to subsume ethnicity, not to class but to power" (Zunz, 1985: 61). In both instances, ethnicity is epiphenomenal: it is a mystified version of class relations (Anthias, 1990). In other words, this thinking holds that ethnic divisions are actually superficial and do not reflect the most important kinds of social divisions. Moreover, to the extent that people view ethnic divisions as central, they do not see that the real underlying social divisions are class-based or are a matter of who has and who does not have power. Marxists are not alone in advancing this position. Around the turn of the century, the German sociologists Ludwig Gumplowicz and Gustav Ratzenhofer suggested that in the modern industrial age ethnic conflict (actually, they used the term "race conflict") would progressively give way to class conflict. This view was embraced by many American sociologists, including Robert Park during the earlier phase of his career (Matthews, 1978; Lal, 1990; Lyman, 1992).

The problem with this view is that the empirical evidence does not bear it out. Although class divisions are certainly a major form of societal differentiation and the consequences of social class location are profound, other divisions are also important in their own right. Attempts to minimize their importance illustrates a failure to appreciate the actual character of self-identity in the modern world. Sociologist Georg Simmel (1955) contended that the individual in the contemporary world is enmeshed in what he referred to as a "web of group affiliations," each making various demands of allegiance.

Among the most important affiliations are those based on ethnicity, social class, gender, and religious affiliation. Others include place of residence (urban, rural, or suburban), regional location, occupational status, and marital and family status. Ethnicity, thus, should be seen as one potential mode or aspect of individual identity (Dashefsky, 1976). Ethnicity can be a more or less significant aspect of identity, depending on the combined role of several variables. Table 2.1 provides a summary of some of the more significant variables.

Anya Peterson Royce (1982: 1) wrote, "It is developed, displayed, manipulated, or ignored in accordance with the demands of particular situations." Ethnicity can interact in complex ways with other aspects of identity, at times in a mutually reinforcing manner, but at other times it competes with these other modes of identity in terms of the relative importance or saliency attached to them. For example, middle-class blacks might highlight features of their class identity when they are at work, since that environment would bring them into contact with many middle class whites. Their shared class identities would serve as a basis for commonality. On the other hand, if middle-class blacks live in a predominantly black neighborhood, with many working class and poor blacks, they may accentuate their racial identity and downplay their class identity, again to accentuate that which these middle class residents share with the people around them at the moment.

Rational Choice Theory

Another recent attempt at a general theory to account for ethnic identity and behavior is rational choice theory (Hechter, et al., 1982; Hechter, 1986; Banton, 1983). Derived from economics, rational choice theory assumes that people act to maximize their economic and social positions. They weigh their actions in terms of the costs involved and the potential benefits that might accrue. This

Table 2.1   VARIABLES AFFECTING THE IMPORTANCE OF
ETHNIC GROUP AFFILIATION

Tend to Increase Importance	Tend to Decrease Importance
1. Large group (relative to total population)	Small group
2. Residentially concentrated by region and community	Residentially scattered
3. Short-term residents (high proportion of newcomers)	Long-term residents (low proportion of newcomers)
4. Return to homeland easy and frequent	Return to the homeland difficult and infrequent
5. Different language	Dominant language
6. Different religion from dominant group(s)	Share religion of dominant group(s)
7. Different race	Same race
8. Involuntary immigrants	Voluntary immigrants
9. Culturally different society	Culturally similar society
10. Attracted to political and economic developments in land of origin	Repelled by those developments
11. Homogeneous in class and occupation	Diverse in class and occupation
12. Low average level of education	High average level of education
13. Victim of a great deal of discrimination	Little discrimination
14. Resident in a society with little social mobility	Resident in open-class society

Adapted from Yinger, 1984.

theory has considerable appeal insofar as it can help us to understand that ethnic affiliation and ethnic competition (as opposed to individual competition) can be based on rational calculation. In other words, when individuals perceive ethnic bonding as personally advantageous, collective ethnic action is likely to result, and when other groups are viewed as impediments to goals, interethnic competition and conflict will occur.

This perspective has considerable merit, but does not provide an overarching explanation of ethnicity. Instead, it must be combined with a view that considers the nonrational character of ethnic phenomena. This is not to suggest that the "blood-and-guts" perspective of the primordialists (including the sociobiologists) should somehow be grafted onto this paradigm. Rather, we need to recognize that the historically embedded character of ethnicity produces nonreflective, habitual forms of identification and action that cannot be construed as rational (Thomas, 1909; Lyman, 1990a).

Ethnicity can produce powerful attachments that do not elevate the economic or social status of the individuals, but instead connect people to a past. This can, when ethnicity is not a particularly important aspect of identity, manifest itself as a form of nostalgia for a past that had largely disappeared. To the extent that factors such as nostalgia can reinforce ethnic identity, we can appreciate the limitations of rational choice.

Ethnic identity, thus, can be influenced by rational considerations, but not necessarily so. Ethnic identity can also be shaped by traditional modes of conduct, whose habitual character is not rational. Ethnic studies must consider both possibilities and attempt to sort out their respective roles in particular instances. This approach demands that careful attention be paid to how people shape their own lives. Careful attention must also be given to the muddle of historical contingency and the complexities of concrete historical events. Grand theories cannot be sustained. As Herbert Gans (1985: 303) has suggested, paradigms that can profitably guide ethnic research must be "more situationally sensitive" than most of those employed in the past.

The Social Construction of Ethnicity

In this book, we use a new approach that builds on some of the most compelling insights of earlier theories. We begin with the rather simple sociological assumption that ethnicity is a social construction, and we will incorporate strands from a variety of theories into this general orientation. The social construction of ethnicity has been referred to by a number of terms, which I'll discuss in the following sections.

Ethnogenesis

Anthropologist Eugene Roosens (1989) has defined the social construction of ethnicity as ethnogenesis. His position is essentially an instrumentalist one that is indebted to a perspective similar to that of rational choice, and with its inherent limitations. In his view, ethnicity emerges and is sustained over time when leaders make rational choices—based on self interest—that require efforts to mobilize ethnic identity and collective action. Although not the whole picture, Roosens is instructive insofar as he indicates that the role of ethnic leadership must be considered, and thus we must carefully examine the inner workings of ethnic communities.

Ethnicization

Jonathan Sarna (1978) describes a process that he calls ethnicization. Referring specifically to immigrant groups in America, he argues that at their time of arrival these groups were highly fragmented with little communal unity. This changed over time as a result of two factors: ascription and adversity. Ascription refers to the definition of group identities and the assigning of individuals to particular groups by outside agents, particularly by political and economic elites in the larger, host society. The connection between ascription and adversity is a reciprocal one insofar as those chiefly responsible for defining the ethnics also confront ethnics from a position of power and are frequently a source of hostility and exploitation.

Hostility and exploitation cause the creation of ethnic communities that are designed to meet the immediate social, political, and cultural needs of the ethnics. Sarna's characterization of this process may place too much power in forces outside the ethnic group, thus overstating the powerlessness of the ethnics in defining who they are and in confronting the dominant society. In other words, the ethnic is viewed too simply as a victim, thereby downplaying the active role ethnics had in shaping their own lives. Nonetheless, the virtue of Sarna's perspective rests with its call to locate or contextualize the ethnic group in relation to the larger society.

Emergent Ethnicity

This perspective is echoed in William Yancey, Eugene Ericksen, and Richard Juliani's (1976: 391) emergent ethnicity thesis. The authors downplay the impact of cultural heritage and argue that rather than being an ascribed attribute, ethnicity is structurally conditional. Of central importance are the intersecting influences of occupational location, residential patterns, and institutional affiliations. The result is that, "As society changes, old forms of ethnic culture may die out but new forms may be generated." Douglass and Lyman (1976) concur with this position, but concentrate on individual actors, rather than the ethnic group, in exploring the strategies actors employ in accepting or rejecting aspects of ethnicity while creating a self-identity.

The Invention of Ethnicity

A social constructionist term that has been developed recently originates with Werner Sollors (1989): the invention of ethnicity. His choice of words derives from a similar notion put forward by historian E.J. Hobsbawm, who has written about the "invention of tradition." Hobsbawm (1983: 1) defines invented tradition as: "a set of practices, normally governed by overtly or tacitly accepted rules and of a ritual or symbolic nature, which seeks to inculcate certain values and norms of behavior by repetition, which automatically implies continuity with the past."

Speaking about invention is a problem for some scholars because of connotations that they see in the word. Herbert Gans (1992) believes that the term can lead one to think that the act of ethnic invention has no connection with the past, but is simply conjured up in the present. Moreover, he thinks the word places too great an emphasis on agency, which is to say on individual actors creating their world, and not enough on the role of social structure. In any case, those who have used invention built upon earlier social constructionist theories while remedying some of the earlier versions' shortcomings.

Sollors uses this particular term to challenge the primordialist belief that ethnicity is at bedrock an irrational or preconscious form of cultural attachment, rooted in either blood or a past lost in the fog of time. Ethnic identity necessarily appeals to tradition, and tradition is something created, sustained, and refashioned by people. However, Sollors also wants to avoid those who see ethnicity as merely a rational construct of those intent on manipulating it for political or economic ends (compare Glazer and Moynihan, 1975). Although he does not dismiss this instrumentalist position completely, he does not want to reduce all of what counts as ethnic to such means-ends calculations.

An interdisciplinary group of historians and social scientists has further developed this concept by suggesting

> ethnicity itself is to be understood as a cultural construction accomplished over historical time. Ethnic groups in modern settings are constantly recreating themselves, and ethnicity is constantly being reinvented in response to changing realities both within the group and the host society. Ethnic group boundaries, for example, must be renegotiated, while the expressive symbols of ethnicity (ethnic traditions) must be repeatedly reinterpreted. By historizicing the phenomenon, the concept of invention allows for the appearance, metamorphosis, disappearance, and reappearance of ethnicities (Conzen, et al., 1990: 38).

This process of invention must be seen in a dialectical or reciprocal way, for not only do immigrants and indigenous peoples shape ethnic definitions and boundaries, but so does the dominant group in the society and so do the other groups that make up the societal totality. Differences in political, economic, and cultural power must be considered in analyzing this ongoing process of constituting and reconstituting ethnicity. Some groups have found themselves in an advantageous position by having greater resources that can be employed to construct a favorable and pragmatically useful identity. Other groups have had fewer resources and less power and, as a result, have had far less say in this process. Their identities have, to a comparatively greater extent, been imposed from the outside.

Furthermore, within and outside of different groups, two or more versions of ethnic identity and group definition usually compete. The invention of ethnicity perspective calls attention to this situation and to the intragroup struggles for dominance that generally result. Furthermore, given the assumption that this process of group definition is never completely accomplished, the invention of ethnicity perspective demands that we pay careful attention to changing circumstances.

Figure 2.4 *Jewish workers in the needle trades, circa 1920.*

Source: Courtesy of the Swenson Center.

Finally, the invention of ethnicity model questions the extent to which we can speak about a clear and singular American cultural and societal core or center. The process of ethnicity is a two-way street. Ethnics adapt to American culture. At the same time, ethnics influence and transform that core culture. Almost three quarters of a century ago the historian Arthur Schlesinger, Sr., made a case for a research agenda that studied not only the impact of America on the ethnics, but also the impact of these diverse groups on America. To date, historians and social scientists have too frequently ignored the latter part of this equation. Those arguing for a new theory of ethnicity, however, have echoed Schlesinger by contending "that what is distinctively American has been itself a product of this synergistic encounter of multiple peoples and cultures" (Conzen, et al., 1990: 54).

The invention of ethnicity approach is not an example of grand theory. It does not seek to be predictive or to develop propositions from which law-like patterns of behavior can be derived. Instead, the model is conceived in a manner that fully accords with Blumer's (1954), "sensitizing concept" in that it orients us to an appreciation of the place of human agency in creating social worlds. Given this character, it is appropriate to complement this perspective with other conceptual tools.

Ethnic Boundaries

One concept particularly relevant to the invention of ethnicity is that of ethnic boundaries. Fredrik Barth (1969) is generally credited with establishing the singular importance of boundaries in the definition of ethnic groups. He rather bluntly contends "[t]he critical focus of investigation from this point of view becomes the ethnic *boundary* that defines the group, not the cultural stuff that it encloses" (Barth, 1969: 15). He is referring to social, rather than territorial boundaries. Boundaries can be rigid or flexible, expansive or constrictive, permeable or impenetrable. They are subject to change. For example, Hasidic Jews and the Amish have rather rigid, constrictive, and impenetrable boundaries. Outsiders cannot easily enter, and insiders leave only with difficulty and often at the expense of ending all relationships with groups members. On the other hand, in situations where intermarriage rates are high, boundaries are flexible, expansive, and permeable. Through intermarriage, a person may be one-eighth Irish, and on this basis may chose to identify with and participate in Irish American organizations for either limited or extended periods of time.

The ethnic boundary "canalizes social life — it entails a frequently quite complex organization of behavior and social relations" (Barth, 1969: 15). The boundary is seen as both enabling certain kinds of relationships to exist and constraining or limiting others. The ethnic boundary is the principal device that distinguishes the respective character of intragroup and intergroup relations (Carling, 1991: 302–305).

I disagree with Barth's dismissal of the "cultural stuff" (behaviors, attitudes, traditions, and so forth) because this "stuff" is the source of the rationale for defining boundaries in one way or another. Rather than posing this in an either/or manner, as Barth does, the relationship between ethnic boundaries and cultures can be viewed as interconnected and mutually reinforcing.

Institutional Completeness

Similarly, Raymond Breton's (1964) concept of institutional completeness is valuable because it calls attention to the fact that an institutional presence is an essential ingredient for the creation and maintenance of *collective* ethnic identity (which, in turn, is a pre-requisite for the preservation of individual ethnic identities). Ethnic institutions perform a number of valuable services for members of ethnic communities, including functions related to employment, the acquisition of political rewards, welfare, ethnic cultural expression, recreation, the adjudication of conflict within and outside of the ethnic enclave, and so on.

Some groups have had the ability to create institutional networks that perform a wide range of tasks on behalf of constituents, thereby binding them to the community. These are institutionally complete ethnic communities. Two good examples are the Chinese throughout their history in America and the Italians during the periods of mass immigration. Other groups have, for various reasons, been less successful in achieving institutional completeness. The English and and the Danish are two examples.

Breton (1964: 204) speaks about "social entrepreneurs" who attempt to fulfill what they see as the needs of an ethnic "clientele." Another way of posing this is in terms of ethnic leaders and the mass of the ethnic community. Recently, attention has been paid to the role of ethnic leaders (Higham, 1978; Bodnar, 1985; Greene, 1987). Their backgrounds, especially their social class backgrounds, their bases of support, the resources at their disposal for mobilizing ethnic-based action, and the nature of the coalitions they form are topics that help answer questions related to the particular character of an ethnic community.

Connected to analyses of leaders must be an examination of the ordinary members of the ethnic group. How internally unified or divided are they? To what extent do they act as either supporters or detractors of potential candidates for leadership? What reasons underlie differing exhibitions of loyalty to leaders? What are the bases of loyalty or, in other words, what kind of appeals to legitimation are made — on traditional, charismatic, or legal-rational grounds?

In Groups, Out Groups, and Group Position

The invention of ethnicity, ethnic boundaries, and institutional completeness are concepts that assist in comprehending the internal dynamics of ethnic groups. Ethnic groups, however, never exist in a vacuum and are possible only insofar as the definition of "we" is linked to definitions of "they." This section focuses on prejudice and discrimination—the process by which some groups are accepted by the larger society (in-groups) while others are excluded (out-groups). We'll also look at negative attitudes toward out-group members and actions taken that are designed to prevent their full and equal inclusion into the larger society.

The Psychology of Prejudice

As See and Wilson (1988: 226) have contended, in an earlier period in ethnic studies much attention was devoted to the psychological dimension of intergroup boundaries, with most of the focus on prejudice. Prejudice refers to individually held negative attitudes about a group of people that are often accompanied by a strong emotional aversion to members of that group.

Arnold Rose (1951: 11) sees prejudice as "nearly always accompanied by incorrect or ill-informed opinions." This view was shared by psychologist Gordon Allport, who in his book, *The Nature of Prejudice* (1958: 7), treats prejudice as "thinking ill of others without sufficient warrant." This suggests that prejudice is the product of a lack of knowledge, and therefore education can be a valuable tool in eradicating such attitudes.

Allport, however, along with many other psychologists of his generation, viewed prejudice as more problematic than this lack of knowledge perspective would suggest. Allport attempted, in his notion of the "prejudiced personality" (1958: 371–384; see also Rokeach, 1960), to incorporate psychoanalytic theory into research on ethnic prejudice. This also is seen in T.W. Adorno and his colleagues' (1950) thesis of the "authoritarian personality" and in related versions of "frustration-aggression" theory (for example, Dollard, 1937). Despite differences, these approaches owe a shared debt to Freud. In the first place, they placed great emphasis on early childhood socialization. In the second, they viewed prejudice as the product of pathology.

This view holds that the prejudiced person manifests a personality disorder that involves intense insecurity and anxiety, a feeling of powerlessness, and internalized rage against parental authority. The result is an outlook that considers the external world to be threatening and evil and that reacts to this generalized perception in an often rigid and superstitious manner. Central to these psychoanalytically inspired theories is the concept of projection: the process by which an individual externalizes aggressive attitudes onto a group that functions as a scapegoat. The scapegoat becomes the object of prejudicial beliefs (Kovel, 1970; LeVine and Campbell, 1972: 117–135).

Beyond the specific shortcomings that some psychologists have found with psychoanalytic theories of prejudice, more far-reaching limitations have been noted. First, the theories fail to account for the societal contexts in which prejudice appears. Second, by defining prejudice as pathological, these theories fail to consider the possibility that prejudice might also be the result of normal socialization into a world characterized by intense ethnic rivalries and animosities (compare, Sherif and Sherif, 1953; Pettigrew, 1958).

The Sociology of Prejudice and Discrimination

Concerns with the limitations inherent in the psychology of prejudice have been voiced frequently (Park, 1950: 213–232; Schermerhorn, 1978: 6; Francis, 1976: 263–268). Recent work by social psychologists has tended to abandon this earlier psychoanalytic approach in favor of cognitive and learning theories (Tajfel, 1969, 1978, 1981), which consider the impact of larger societal forces on individual prejudice.

To the extent that these theorists treat individual prejudice as essentially derivative, they agree with Herbert Blumer's (1958) definition of prejudice as a "sense of group position." In this deceptively simple formulation, Blumer shifts the focus of attention from individual attitudes to history and politics. As Stanford Lyman (1984: 110) said in commenting on this move: "Attitudes in turn were merely the lowest form of expression of these historically established positions, and were not irremediably correlative with conduct." Without referring explicitly to Blumer (Killian, 1970), most scholars in ethnic studies today work with a similar understanding of the psychology of prejudice.

The significance of Blumer's definition can be seen in the analysis of derogatory expressions, stereotypes, and humor. Different groups have been variously characterized as lazy, miserly, drunken, morose, happy-go-lucky, cunning, inscrutable, hot tempered, or stupid (Allen, 1990). These stereotypes are not interchangeable. Why is it that African Americans are stereotyped as lazy and Japanese Americans are not? Why is it that Jewish Americans are depicted as miserly and Italian Americans are not? As an illustration of a derogatory expression directed at Irish Americans, why did the vehicle used by the police to transport arrestees to jail become known as the "paddy wagon"? In the realm of ethnic jokes, why does one ask how many Polish Americans it takes to change a light bulb and not how many German Americans? The answer rests, not in the psychological proclivities of the individual employing such negative expressions, but in the location of these groups in relation to each other and the society at large.

Stereotypes, derogatory expressions, and jokes are invidious distortions of a sociocultural truth. Those groups least successful socioeconomically are often deemed to be lazy if they are more highly represented in the ranks of the unemployed than the general population. Those who are employed in unskilled, low-paying, dead-end jobs may be deemed stupid. The stereotype addresses a truth: these groups are not as successful as other groups. The stereotype is invidious because the members of the group are blamed for this state of affairs. This kind of stereotyping is prevalent in America because of the high premium placed on individual achievement.

In a parallel way, the view of people as cunning or miserly is applied to groups that have been more, rather than less, successful than the general population. The invidious distortion here questions the means by which such groups got ahead, viewing their advancement as being based on less than scrupulous means. This, too, serves to justify a person's own place in the social hierarchy, for the implicit message is that the person is more morally upright than those who are more successful.

Discriminatory actions reinforce existing ethnic relationships by denying out-group members equal access to jobs, homes, neighborhoods, education, income, political power, influence, and status. Such actions can be crude or subtle, overt or covert. A person, for example, may be denied a job interview because her address identifies her as a resident of a black ghetto. A realtor may tell a middle class black couple that a suburban home they want to see has already been sold, only to show the house to a white couple a few hours later.

Sometimes discrimination is the intentional result of prejudicial attitudes. At other times it may be unintentional. A person who does not harbor prejudicial attitudes may be pressured into acts of discrimination. The connection between prejudice and discrimination is not a simple matter of cause and effect. Robert Merton (1976) illustrated this by identifying four different types of individuals. Unprejudiced nondiscriminators, or "all-weather liberals," are willing to act on their beliefs even in the face of pressure to do otherwise. At the other extreme, the prejudiced discriminator, or "all-weather bigot," is equally consistent and will continue to discriminate even when confronted by societal demands to end discrimination. In contrast, the other two types reveal an inconsistency between attitudes and actions. In both cases, the individual gives in to social pressure. Unprejudiced discriminators, or "reluctant liberals," give in to social pressure to discriminate, and prejudiced nondiscriminators, or "timid bigots," yield to opposite pressures.

Beyond individual manifestations of discrimination is the issue of institutional discrimination. This refers to patterns of discrimination at the societal rather than individual level, and includes widespread practices, laws, and customs that perpetuate existing inequalities. The most powerful expression of institutional discrimination in this nation's history was the institution of slavery.

Explaining Ethnic Differences

What, then, are the causes of the differences in group position in America? What contributes to ethnic stratification (Shibutani and Kwan, 1965)? Some, like the neoconservative social theorist Thomas Sowell (1981), believe that the differences are due to differing cultural characteristics. Simply put, some groups are seen as having cultural values that synchronize with the dominant cultural values of America, permitting them to achieve success. Other groups harbor values at odds with the dominant culture's values, and consequently are unable to be upwardly mobile.

Focusing on the role of culture in explaining perceived differences across ethnic groups has considerable merit. Ethnic cultures must be investigated as potential sources for inequalities. For example, early in this century Jews—for a variety of reasons rooted, at least in part, in cultural differences — used education as a vehicle for upward mobility, while Italians were suspicious of education's virtues. Jews were also more successful economically than their Italian counterparts.

When, however, cultural explanations are not linked to social structural explanations — Sowell's unfortunate tendency — the result is something like blaming the victim. The analysis resembles a morality play in which those presumed to be possessing the proper virtues (hard working, emotional control, family oriented, and so forth) are justly rewarded, while the morally deficient have only themselves to blame.

The equally short-sighted reverse perspective, common among many sociologists, is to ignore culture and attempt to use social structural factors alone as causal variables. In an influential work, Stephen Steinberg (1981) provides what amounts to an antithetical explanation to that of Sowell. Steinberg looks at Jewish success and attempts to disparage the cultural elements central to that success by focusing instead on such factors as the level of urbanism and occupational skills derived from the pre-migration milieu.

The point is obvious: Both culture and social structure must be considered. Moreover, they need to be viewed in a reciprocal manner: culture shapes social structure, which in turn shapes culture. Moreover, both social structure and culture must be linked to the role of individuals as active agents engaged in creating their social worlds (Pedraza-Bailey, 1990: 61–62). Individuals confront their cultures and social structures as both constraining their ability to act and as enabling them to act (Giddens, 1984).

That being said, what must be considered in determining the precise ways in which both culture and social structure manage to constrain or enable certain courses of action? What, in short, would be contained on a conceptual map that plotted the different life courses of individuals who happen to be members of different ethnic groups?

Though by no means a complete map, I would include the following crucial considerations:

1 How groups became a part of American society relates to the amount of power and resources (financial and human capital) they have to influence their position in the social hierarchy (Kinlock, 1974; Kuper, 1975). Voluntary migration, involuntary migration,

Table 2.2   TYPES OF ETHNIC GROUPS BASED ON MODE OF
               INCORPORATION INTO THE UNITED STATES

I.   Voluntary Immigrants
A.   Economic immigrants
1.   Skilled immigrants (including "brain-drain" immigrants)
2.   "Middlemen minority" or trader immigrants
3.   Poor immigrants
B.   Political refugees
II.   Imported Slaves
III. Victims of Colonial Conquest

and colonial domination constitute the three ways in which ethnic groups have been incorporated into America. The differences have had pronounced differential impacts (see Table 2.2), and therefore consideration of these differences is an essential starting point. The ability of each group to preserve its inherited culture and social institutions is important, for they provide an important mechanism for individuals to adapt to and become part of America.

Most Americans live in this country because they or their ancestors voluntarily migrated. This includes the Swedish peasant who left home in the nineteenth century to acquire farmland in the Midwest, the Jew who fled religious persecution in czarist Russia, the Cuban who fled to Miami after Castro's victory, and the Dominican who left last year to find employment in New York City. We must consider the forces that pushed voluntary immigrants out of their homeland, as well as timing and migration patterns, including chain migration, individual versus family migration, and so on (Thistlethwaite, 1960; Tilly, 1990). We must ask, who left: the poorest of the poor or a middle stratum? Did they leave for economic, political, or religious reasons? Did they view their migration as permanent or temporary? The reverse side of this equation involves determining the pull factors that brought immigrants not simply to America, but to particular places in America. Settlement location (that is, urban or rural, established communities or frontier settlements, and so forth) plays a key role (Conzen, 1991), as do the skills and educational levels that immigrants bring to America.

Although some similar considerations pertain to involuntary immigrants and colonized peoples, these immigrants had far less freedom of initiative than the voluntary immigrants. Involuntary immigrants describes Africans who were the victims of the international slave trade; colonized peoples refers to Native Americans. African slaves were unfree and powerless. They were stripped of much of their cultural heritage and denied the resources or opportunities to create a new communal institutional presence in America. Native Americans found their worlds undermined by the desire of the more powerful European colonizers to acquire their lands. Both involuntary migrants and colonized peoples had less power than voluntary immigrants, and the implications of this must be taken into account. Without ignoring how such groups sought to shape their own lives, we must determine the nature of and the reasons for the constraints imposed by more powerful groups (Rex, 1983; Williams, 1990).

2 The nation's economy has changed from an agrarian one to an industrial one to what some call a post-industrial or advanced industrial society. Concurrently, these changes transformed the class structure. Different kinds of employment possibilities exist depending on the particular historical period. The working class, for example, has often been divided between skilled and unskilled workers, sometimes leading to what Edna Bonacich (1972) has referred to as the "split labor market." These split labor markets have often been defined in terms of racial differences, with blacks, Asians, and Hispanics disproportionately located among the ranks of the unskilled. Here class and ethnicity or race turn out to be mutually reinforcing. In addition, some industries exhibit what can be termed ethnic succession. The meatpacking industry, for example, was once an important source of employment for Europeans, especially Poles, Lithuanians, Germans, Irish. Although such groups are still represented, the work forces at packinghouses today include large numbers of Mexicans and Southeast Asians. Earlier generations left for other jobs because the work is hard and very dangerous and pay levels have declined in recent years, whereas these are perhaps the first jobs the newly arrived can find (Lamphere, 1992).

Economic changes also contribute to different entrepreneurial possibilities. Economic niches in various industries or businesses have characterized many groups (Light, 1972; Bonacich, 1973). For example, prior to the 1960s, Jews were prominent merchants in black ghettos, whereas today they have been replaced in many major cities by Koreans. Jews have been historically prominent in the garment industry; today in Miami the same industry is an important source of ownership and employment opportunities for Cubans. The relationship between class and ethnicity is important—sometimes mutually reinforcing. Employment discrimination, which has proven to be especially burdensome to some groups, while not to others, is related to class and ethnicity.

3 The political realm, particularly citizenship is linked to the ways in which the economy shapes ethnic relations (Shklar, 1991). Some groups whose members were permitted to become citizens easily did so quickly while others did not. Some groups involved themselves in the political process while others distanced themselves from it. For others, especially Native Americans, Africans and Asians, citizenship was long denied, and even when granted, the remnants of institutional discrimination remained. Understanding why these observed differences occurred is essential.

4 The culture of America has evolved from its primarily Anglo-American roots to reflect the multicultural character of the nation. Ethnic cultures have also transformed over time. Some have all but disappeared, and others remain alive. Some have had a significant impact on American culture; others have had little or no effect. Some ethnic cultures made the transition into American society relatively painlessly; for others a profound culture conflict ensued. This conflict was sometimes generational, as first-generation immigrants hung on to their old-world cultures, while their children, who grew up in America, rejected much of the ancestral heritage, identifying instead with American culture (Hansen, 1938; Kivisto and Blanck, 1990; Ueda, 1992).

Summary

We began this chapter with an overview of sociology's repudiation of biological explanations and sociology's development of a sociocultural approach. This chapter included discussions of the limited utility of two concepts: nationality groups and minority groups.

We have defined ethnicity and ethnic groups and have indicated their relationship to race and racial groups. After discussing central forms of intergroup relations, the two most important types for the United States were analyzed: assimilation and pluralism. A review of their respective strengths and weaknesses lead to a discussion of various alternatives to both positions, culminating in a discussion of variations in the social constructionist approach. We then explored the issues of prejudice and discrimination. With all of these pieces in place, we presented a brief conceptual map that included a number of things that must be examined in attempting to understand the big picture.

What all of this indicates is that a wide range of variables must be considered if one is to begin to comprehend the continuing role of ethnicity in America. Furthermore, to understand the present, we must consider the past. To this end, chapters four through seven provide a historical survey that will inform the remainder of the book, which focuses on the present and possible futures of America's main ethnic groups. Before moving to history, however, a demographic and geographic profile of those main groups will help locate their respective places within American society.

DEMOGRAPHIC PROFILE OF AMERICA'S MAIN ETHNIC GROUPS

In the chapters that follow, we will examine the ethnic character of America by dividing the population into five very broad headings. The five lives presented earlier, in the first chapter, were chosen to reflect these major ethnic divisions: Native Americans or American Indians; European Americans; African Americans; Hispanic Americans; and Asian Americans. This chapter will provide a brief overview of the sizes of each of these groups over time, compared with one another and the overall American population. We will also discuss geographical concentration and dispersal. Each of these five major divisions is composed of many distinct groups, and we must recognize that the differences among groups within each division are frequently profound. Nevertheless, a rather cursory examination of the shifts in size and location of these five groups will illustrate the accuracy of Portes and Rumbaut's (1990: xvii) characterization of America as a "permanently unfinished" society.

The Politics of Counting Heads

Before providing an overview of each group, a few points about the data are appropriate. In the first place, the manner in which the U.S. Census is conducted is often controversial. The 1990 census was marked by complaints that some groups, especially African Americans and Hispanic Americans residing in inner cities, were undercounted. The Bureau of the Census has conceded that these charges have considerable merit and has offered revised estimates intended to rectify the undercount. This is nothing new: The first census ever conducted by the federal government was a crude endeavor to count people chiefly for revenue-collecting purposes. Various practical decisions were made at the time to ease the job of census enumerators in what was clearly an arduous task in a largely rural nation. Native Americans in the hinterlands were excluded from consideration on the grounds that they were not sources of revenue, while the "New Jersey Compromise" declared that each slave would be counted as three-fifths of a person (Kaplan and Van Valey, 1980: 9).

The Bureau of the Census decided not to classify people on the basis of religion, but rather on the basis of national-origin. Thus, Jews were not counted as Jews, but as Russians, Poles, Romanians, and so forth. Finally, though other examples of problems with the data could be cited, I will simply note that official statistics capture only legal residents and not illegal immigrants. For this latter category, we are forced to rely on extremely limited and problematic information.

One final point: These data are for the United States of America, a nation whose boundaries have expanded considerably during the two centuries under consideration. The American Indian population extended from the Atlantic to the Pacific, but the numbers offered here attempt to count only those residing in what was at any particular point in time the United States. Similarly, Hispanic-origin peoples lived in various places in the American Southwest that were incorporated into the nation in the nineteenth and early twentieth centuries (for example, Arizona and New Mexico became states in 1912). When those territories were outside of the United States, these people were excluded from consideration.

Despite these and many other shortcomings, the portrait provided is a generally accurate account of the sizes of the major ethnic categories. The first obvious fact to be aware of is that European-origin residents have constituted and continue to constitute not only the largest ethnic grouping, but an absolute majority of the population.

In the two-hundred-year period between the first official United States census — in 1790 — and the most recent, the population of the country as a whole grew over sixty fold from 3,929,000 to 248,700,000. During this time span the population grew steadily. At the beginning of the twentieth century the population had risen to 76,094,000. Not until two decades later would the decennial census first exceed 100 million. A half century later, in 1970, the figure exceeded 200 million for the first time. A variety of demographic factors account for this dramatic increase, chiefly changing fertility rates and health care improvements which reduced the infant mortality rate and expanded the average life expectancy of the population. Immigration, however, is a major factor contributing to the current population, which we will see as we examine each of the following groups.

American Indians

We do not know the size of the indigenous population of North America prior to the arrival of European colonists half a millennium ago. The population estimates for the peoples living in North America above the Rio Grande at the beginning of the sixteenth century range from less than one million to about 18 million. C. Matthew Snipp (1989: 9) concluded that it is reasonable to assume "a range for the pre-Columbian North American population size of 2 million to 5 million."

Population Decline and Recovery

Defined by tribal units, the population encountered by Europeans was highly diverse. Columbus, reflecting his confusion about where he had landed, dubbed the indigenous peoples he met "Indios," and this externally imposed name, or variations thereof, became the collective name for the panoply of tribes across the continent, which ranged between 150 and 200. In the northeast, the politically powerful Iroquois were an important force, while the southeast included such significant tribes as the Creek, Cherokee, and Shawnee. The plains states and the northwestern United States were home to the Cheyenne, Shoshone, and Blackfeet, and the Comanche, Apache, and Navajo tribes played an important role in the southwest's history.

The consequences of contact with Europeans (and perhaps Africans as well) proved devastating for the American Indian population, which declined precipitously between 1492 and 1890. By 1890, the population had plummeted to only slightly more than a quarter of a million (Thornton, 1987). William Denevan (1976: 7) described the magnitude of this tragic depopulation by writing, "the discovery of America was followed by possibly the greatest demographic disaster in the history of the world." Although a variety of factors contributed to this situation, including deaths due to military campaigns and to policies that were intended to be genocidal, two stand out as most significant. The first was famine. Famine occurred frequently when conflict over land between Native Americans and European settlers resulted in the forced relocation of tribes to other territories, thereby upsetting the ecological relationship a tribe had with the land of its ancestors and jeopardizing a particular way of life. The second, which Snipp (1989: 15) considers to be the most important, was communicable diseases, for which the American Indians had far less resistance than Europeans because they had not previously been exposed to these illnesses. Various diseases—headed by smallpox, but also including cholera, diphtheria, influenza, typhoid, measles, and scarlet fever—had a far more devastating impact on Native Americans than on Europeans.

By the end of the nineteenth century, Vermont lawyer Thomas Farnham's prediction—made a half century earlier—was being realized: "A melancholy fact, the Indians' bones must enrich the soil before the plow of civilized man can open it. " (Pearce, 1967: 65). As the continent was opened up for settlement by immigrants, Farnham—ethnocentrism aside—rightly suggested that this was achieved at the expense of the continent's first inhabitants.

Native Americans were pushed off of their ancestral lands, as European settlers moved westward. Once widespread throughout the eastern United States, as well as the west, the Indian population steadily shifted westward during the nineteenth century. The current population distribution reflects these forced migrations and official governmental policies that were designed to relocate Indians west of the Mississippi and thereby out of the mainstream of the newly emerging American society.

During this century the Native American population has rebounded and has steadily grown. As Figure 3.1 illustrates, between 1900 and the present the population has grown each decade with the exception of the decade between 1910 and 1920, when the influenza epidemic that swept the nation in 1918 was the probable cause for a slight decline. During the first half of the century the population increased by about 46 percent. After 1950 the growth

Figure 3.1   *American Indian Population Growth, 1890–1990.*

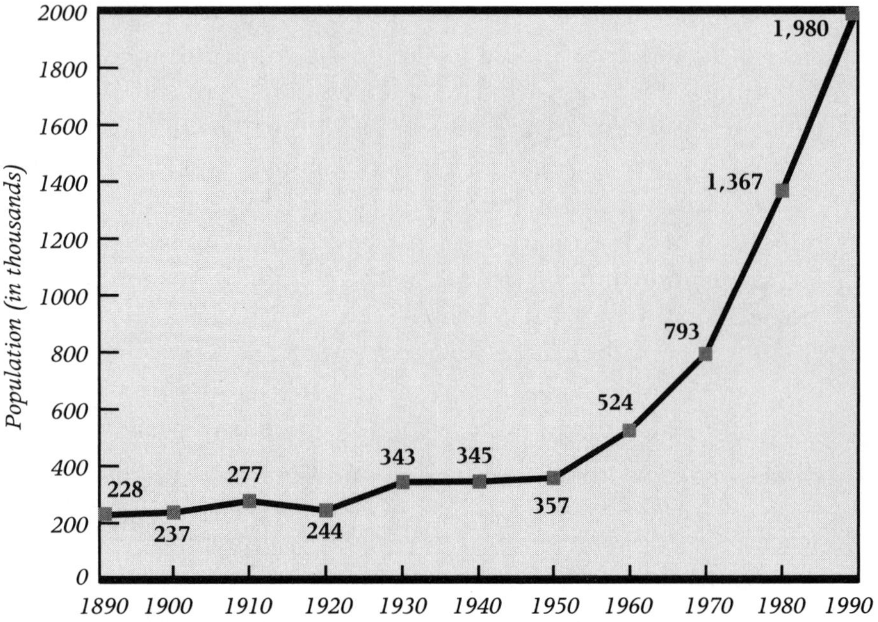

Source: U.S. Bureau of the Census, 1975, 1984, 1991b.

was far more dramatic, increasing by 282 percent. In 1980 the American Indian population, reported by the U.S. Bureau of the Census at 1,367,000, exceeded one million for the first time in nearly 300 years (Snipp, 1989: 64–66). This figure rose to 1,980,000 in the 1990 census. The increase in terms of tribal size is seen in Table 3.1, which reports the twenty largest tribes that account for almost two-thirds of the total Native American population.

Despite this growth, American Indians constitute only 0.8% of the American population. Furthermore, this growth may level off as fertility rates decline. Since 1965, there has been a decline in fertility among all Native American women under age 45. Their fertility rate, however, has been greater than that of European-origin women. In 1980, American Indian women had an average of 2.4 children, while European-origin women had only 1.8 children per woman. Although the trend may be toward a convergence, these present differences serve to explain why the Indian population has grown as rapidly as it has.

Table 3.1 TWENTY LARGEST AMERICAN INDIAN TRIBES (1980 CENSUS)

Tribe	Population Size	% of American Indian Population
Cherokee	232,080	17.0
Navajo	158,633	11.6
Sioux	78,608	5.8
Chippewa	69,064	5.1
Choctaw	50,220	3.7
Pueblo	42,552	3.1
Iroquois	38,218	2.8
Apache	35,861	2.6
Lumbee	28,631	2.1
Creek	28,278	2.1
Blackfeet	21,964	1.6
Papago	13,297	1.0
Pima	11,722	0.9
Seminole	10,363	0.8
Chickasaw	10,317	0.8
Alaskan Athabaskan	10,136	0.7
Cheyenne	9,918	0.7
Shoshone	9,830	0.7
Potawatomi	9,715	0.7
Tlingit	9,509	0.7
Total of 20 Tribes	878,916	64.5

Source: Adapted from Snipp, 1989: 324–332.

Rural and Urban Dwellers

An important feature of the Native American population is its rural character. The establishment of the reservation system helps explain the persistently rural location of American Indians in a larger

Table 3.2 POPULATION SIZES OF THE 16 LARGEST AMERICAN INDIAN RESERVATIONS (1980 CENSUS)

Reservation	1980 Population
Navajo (AZ, NM, UT)	104,968
Pine Ridge (SD)	11,882
Gila River (AZ)	7,067
Papago (AZ)	6,959
Fort Apache (AZ)	6,880
Hopi (AZ)	6,601
Zuni Pueblo (NM)	5,988
San Carlos (AZ)	5,872
Rosebud (SD)	5,688
Blackfeet (MT)	5,080
Yakima (WA)	4,938
Eastern Cherokee (NC)	4,844
Standing Rock (ND, SD)	4,800
Osage (OK)	4,749
Fort Peck (MT)	4,273
Wind River (WY)	4,150
Total of 16 Reservations	194,739
Percentage of U.S. Indian Population	14.3%

Source: U.S. Bureau of the Census, 1980.

society that became increasingly urban and industrial after the Civil War. There are at present 279 federal and state reservations. Although some, such as the Navajo nation, are quite expansive and contain relatively large populations, most exist as smaller units. Table 3.2 reports the populations of the sixteen largest reservations, and Figure 3.2 identifies their geographical locations. About two-thirds of the Native Americans living on reservations reside in communities with fewer than 4,000 inhabitants. Approximately 53 percent of the population lives on or near Indian lands. Almost half

Figure 3.2   Indian Lands and Communities.

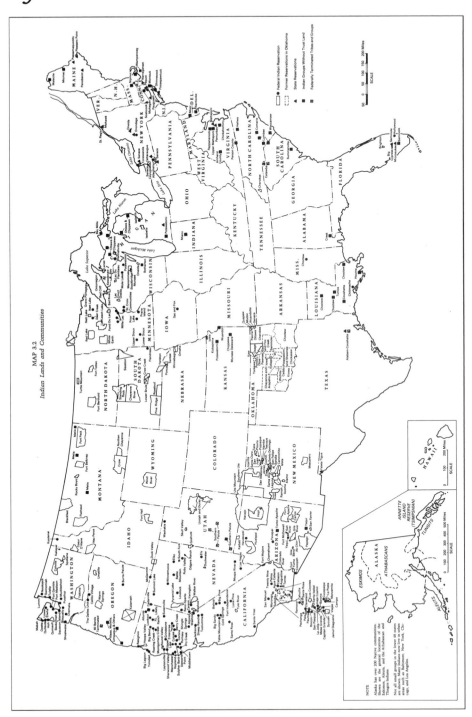

Source: Bureau of Indian Affairs, 1986.

of these (or 25 percent of the total American Indian population) reside on reservations (Snipp, 1989: 84–88).

Many Native Americans moved to cities in search of jobs as early as the nineteenth century, but during the 1930s, the reservation population expanded as the Depression produced widespread unemployment among these urban dwellers, prompting many to return to their rural origins. Most remained on reservations or in the surrounding communities until after World War II. The war itself contributed to the exodus from the reservations, as 25,000 Native Americans volunteered for or were drafted into the military, while an additional 40,000 moved to cities to work in war industries.

Nonetheless, by 1960 only 30 percent lived in cities. That figure rose to 45 percent a decade later, climbing to 49 percent in 1980. The slower increase during the 1970s is partially attributed to the emergence of economic opportunities on some reservations. Over half of all Americans resided in cities by 1920, but a majority of American Indians continued to reside in rural areas over a half century later. Thus, they continue to be much more rural than any other ethnic group.

Out-migration from rural areas often takes place in stages, with the first move being to towns and cities near reservations, such as Gallup, New Mexico; Rapid City, South Dakota; Ponca City, Oklahoma; and Scottsbluff, Nebraska. From these bases many American Indians move to larger metropolitan areas. Although sizeable Native American enclaves are found in New York, Detroit, and Chicago, the ten largest urban populations exist in cities west of the Mississippi (see Table 3.3).

One further point: Four centuries of interbreeding with Africans and Europeans (including Spaniards) has made the "pure-blood" American Indian rare (Snipp, 1989: 27). In the 1980 census 6,754,800 individuals indicated some Indian ancestry. Only 18 percent of those indicating some Indian ancestry identified their race as American Indian.

European Americans

In stark contrast to Native Americans, Americans of European origin constitute the largest segment of the American populace. In fact, they are a sizeable majority. This is because until relatively

Table 3.3   U.S. METROPOLITAN AREAS WITH 10 LARGEST
INDIAN POPULATIONS (1980 CENSUS)

Metropolitan Area	1980 Population
Los Angeles–Long Beach, CA	47,234
Tulsa, OK	38,463
Phoenix, AZ	27,788
Oklahoma City, OK	24,695
Albuquerque, NM	20,721
San Francisco–Oakland, CA	17,546
Riverside–San Bernadino–Ontario, CA	17,107
Minneapolis–St. Paul, MN	15,831
Seattle–Everett, WA	15,162
Tucson, AZ	14,880

Source: U.S. Bureau of the Census, 1980.

recently a majority of immigrants came from various European nations, partly because of immigration laws that favored them over
immigrants from elsewhere in the world. Although claiming, as
historian Oscar Handlin (1973) does, that American history is the
history of voluntary immigration overlooks both the history of
those who were here before the immigrants and those forced here
by the slave trade, a vast majority of people in America today
are here because their ancestors emigrated from their homelands
in Europe.

The cumulative total of immigrants arriving between 1630 and
1790 was well under one million. The first half of the seventeenth
century saw high rates of immigration, but by the eighteenth
century the numbers had fallen. While many immigrants came for
economic reasons, America also appealed to those seeking either
religious or political freedom. Indeed, the Puritans and other
religious dissidents who sought refuge and freedom of religious expression were among the earliest arrivals in New England.

The Old Immigration

From the colonial period through the immediate aftermath of the American Revolution, European immigrants came from northern and western Europe. In fact, they came from a rather small number of countries, and of these one is of singular importance: England. In the 1790 census, 82.1 percent of the white population originated from England. All other countries contributed relatively small percentages, with the 7.0 percent from Scotland and the 5.6 percent from Germany ranking as the second and third largest groups respectively. Small numbers of Irish, Dutch, French, Jews, and Scandinavians made up virtually all of the remainder of the European-origin population. The sheer difference in size between the English and the other groups accounts in no small part for the distinctive role the English heritage had in shaping the political, cultural, and social fabric of the emerging nation.

The 1790 census did not include American Indians who lived in territories far from population centers, so we cannot accurately compare the sizes of the European-origin and indigenous populations (Kaplan and Van Valey, 1980: 9). People of African origin, however, were counted, albeit in accord with Article I, section 2 of the United States Constitution, which counted them for revenue purposes as three-fifths of a person. In this earliest census people of European ancestry accounted for 3,172,444 individuals, or 80.73 percent of the total population, while African Americans numbered 757,208 individuals, or 19.27 percent of the total (U.S. Bureau of the Census, 1909).

The U.S. government did not begin to compile systematic statistics on immigration until 1820, but an estimated 250,000 immigrants arrived between 1776 and 1820, when the stream of immigrants from Europe started to expand dramatically. The increase that began around 1830 lasted until 1924 when legislation was passed restricting unbridled immigration.

This increase during the nineteenth century has been primarily attributed to two developments. The first was the industrialization process in America which created larger demands for labor. The second was the rapid population growth in Europe during the same period, which resulted in fewer economic opportunities for many people on the continent (Easterlin, 1980: 476–479). Industrialization in Europe could not keep pace with demographic changes.

Furthermore, industrial development occurred more rapidly in some regions than in others. When economic opportunities existed at home, people were not likely to make the uncertain trip across the sea; when prospects were slim, however, or the opportunities appeared to be far more restricted than reportedly was the case in the United States, "America fever" often swept a region.

Between 1820 and 1830, 106,508 immigrants arrived, as did nearly a half million in the following decade, and between 1841 and 1850, the United States gained more than one million immigrants for the first time. In each subsequent decade from 1850 to 1930, the number of legal immigrants from Europe exceeded two million, ranging from a low of 2,065,270 during the Civil War decade to a peak of 8,136,016 during the first decade of the twentieth century.

Immigration was encouraged by liberal immigration laws. Not until 1875 did the new nation, which was resource rich but population poor, enact any legislation to restrict unbridled immigration. The Immigration Act of 1875 barred prostitutes and convicts from the country, and the Alien Labor Contract Law of 1885 banned importing contract laborers. These legislative initiatives did not reduce in any appreciable way the growing wave of immigration (Hutchinson, 1981).

Until after the Civil War the vast majority of European immigrants were from northern and western Europe, which includes the following countries: Belgium, Denmark, France, Great Britain (including England, Scotland, and Wales), Germany, Ireland, Luxembourg, Netherlands, Norway, Sweden, and Switzerland. Overall, the religious orientation of these people was predominantly Protestant, so the characterization of America during this formative period as being fundamentally White Anglo-Saxon Protestant — or, to use what is now often seen as a pejorative term, WASP — is quite accurate.

America during the pre-Civil War period was fundamentally agrarian, so it is not surprising that most immigrants resided in rural areas. The frontier with large tracts of land available for cultivation addressed the "land hunger" of many arrivals. There were differences among the groups arriving prior to the Civil War. The Irish, for example, tended to be more urbanized than other groups, while Scandinavians — Swedes, Danes, and Norwegians — settled in the frontier of the upper Midwest, where they purchased land

Table 3.4   EUROPEAN IMMIGRATION, 1820–1930

Years	Northern and Western[a]	Southern and Eastern[b]
1820-30	103,119	3,389
1831-40	489,739	5,949
1841-50	1,592,062	5,439
1851-60	2,431,336	21,324
1861-70	2,031,642	33,628
1871-80	2,070,373	201,889
1881-90	3,778,633	958,413
1891-1900	1,643,492	1,915,486
1901-10	1,910,035	6,225,981
1911-20	997,438	3,379,126
1921-30	1,284,023	1,193,830
Total	18,331,892	13,944,454

[a]Comprising Belgium, Denmark, France, Germany, Luxemburg (1925–1930), Netherlands, Norway, Sweden, Switzerland, and the United Kingdom.
[b]Southern and eastern Europe comprises all countries on that continent not listed above.

Source: *Annual Report of the Commissioner General of Immigration for 1930.*

and helped create a rural culture in that region of the country (Miller, 1985; Norman and Runblom, 1988).

The New Immigration

As Table 3.4 reveals, however, after 1880 the number of immigrants from eastern and southern Europe rose rapidly. From 1890 to 1930 immigrants from these areas exceeded those who had predominated earlier. In the nation's peak decade of immigration, 1901–1910, 6,225,981 individuals came from eastern or southern Europe. The largest groups were Italians, Jews (from various countries in Europe, but particularly from Poland and Russia), and Poles, but every European country contributed to this mass movement of peoples, including Albanians, Byelorussians, Bulgarians, Croatians, Czechs, Estonians, Finns, Greeks, Hungarians, Macedonians, Montenegrins, Portuguese, Romanians, Russians, Serbians, Slovaks, Slovenes, Spaniards, and Ukrainians.

Collectively, these groups differed considerably from the earlier arrivals. Only a minority were Protestant Christians; Christians were more likely to be Roman Catholic (Dolan, 1975) or Orthodox (Saluotos, 1964). The vast majority of non-Christian arrivals were Jews (Rischin, 1962), though small numbers of adherents of Islam (Naff, 1985) were also present. Religious differences were compounded by cultural and linguistic differences and by the impoverished state of most of these immigrants. Hostility toward these new arrivals prompted a move to limit the nation's open door policy, based on the view that those groups least like those from northern and western Europe should not be admitted (Higham, 1970).

In 1891, 1903, 1907, and 1917 the definition of inadmissibles was expanded, and in 1906 the Basic Naturalization Act mandated knowledge of English as a requisite for becoming a citizen. These efforts to limit immigration culminated in an initial quota law in 1921 and a more stringent one in 1924, the National Origins Act, which limited immigration to 2 percent of the national origin of the foreign born of 1890. As Table 3.5 indicates, though immigration did not cease, this law marked the end of migratory movements from Europe on the grand scale of the 1880 to 1924 period (Hutchinson, 1981).

Throughout this entire period, however, not everyone stayed. Some did not find economic success in America, and others simply could not adjust to the new social environment. Unfortunately, accurate data on the levels of return migration do not exist. Many people, especially during the period when steamship travel was quite cheap, moved back and forth several times, which distorts the statistical portrait we have. Perhaps 30 percent of all immigrants returned home. Some groups, however, had higher return migration rates than others.

The rate of return for Italians, for example, was quite high. A survey conducted by the magazine *Survey* in 1912 reported that 74 percent of northern Italians returned home, while 41 percent of southern Italians did. The difference is presumed to be due to the job opportunities at home: northern Italy was the nation's industrial heartland, and as employment became possible in the homeland,

Table 3.5   IMMIGRATION TO THE UNITED STATES, 1820–1970

Year	All Countries	European Countries	Percent European
1820	8,385	7,691	92
1821–1830	143,439	106,508	74
1831–1840	599,125	495,688	83
1841–1850	1,713,251	1,597,501	93
1851–1860	2,598,214	2,452,660	94
1861–1870	2,314,824	2,065,270	89
1871–1880	2,812,191	2,272,262	81
1881–1890	5,246,613	4,737,046	90
1891–1900	3,687,564	3,558,978	97
1901–1910	8,795,386	8,136,016	93
1911–1920	5,735,811	4,379,564	76
1921–1930	4,107,209	2,477,853	60
1931–1940	528,431	348,289	66
1941–1950	1,035,039	621,704	60
1951–1960	2,515,479	1,328,293	53
1961–1970	3,321,677	1,129,670	34
	45,162,638	35,714,993	79

Source: U.S. Bureau of the Census, 1975.

many émigrés returned. Southern Italy, by contrast, was an industrial backwater, so such opportunities did not materialize for Sicilians, Calabrians, Neapolitans, and others from the Mezzogiornio — the region of Italy south of Rome.

Between 1880 and 1930, many economic immigrants—Italians and others — were what is referred to as "birds of passage," that is individuals intent on making money in America so they could return home and improve their economic lot there (Piore, 1979). In contrast, some groups, such as Jews, showed low rates of return migration. Jews came with more marketable skills than many of their counterparts and therefore were able to find a niche in the economy, principally in the garment industry (Steinberg, 1981). For them it was economically advantageous to remain in the United States. Moreover, many were also religious and political refugees fleeing anti-Semitic persecution. There was, quite simply, no home to return to, so they were willing to view themselves as permanent residents of America earlier than others were.

Since 1930, more than six million Europeans immigrated to the United States. Most migrated for economic reasons. Among those arriving, however, were individuals fleeing Nazi Germany, displaced persons (DPs) seeking a new home after the ravages of World War II, and anti-Communists who sought political exile after much of Eastern Europe was incorporated into the political orbit of the Soviet Union. Tragically, only 21,000 Jews were admitted into the country during Hitler's years in power (Wyman, 1984).

The Contemporary Situation

European Americans are distributed throughout the country in such a way that they constitute a majority of each region, though differences remain in the distribution of particular groups. The English are spread rather evenly throughout the country. The Irish remain more concentrated in New England and the Mid-Atlantic states, while a German concentration persists in the Midwest. Swedes, Norwegians, and Danes are still regionally significant in the upper Midwest and the Pacific Northwest. Many smaller groups can still be found in significant numbers in specific locales: a large Finnish population resides in the Upper Peninsula of Michigan and northern Minnesota; Belgian enclaves are found in western Illinois and the area around Green Bay, Wisconsin; Croatians are concentrated in northern Iowa and Minnesota's Twin cities; Slovenes are in coal mining communities in western Pennsylvania; and Swiss colonies are in Wisconsin (Allen and Turner, 1988; Ward, 1980).

Although differences in fertility rates varied greatly among the various European groups and compared to the other groups under review, the sheer volume of European immigration made this group the largest in the nation. In 1980, when most European Americans were members of the third or later generations and were far removed from the immigrant experience, the U.S. Census asked a question about ethnic ancestry for the first time in sixty years. About four-fifths of the American population traced its ancestry to one or more European countries in 1980. Although precise figures are not available, these figures are lower than they were prior to 1965, when the immigration law paved the way for larger numbers of immigrants from other parts of the world to enter the United States.

Because intermarriage is and has been a common feature among European origin groups, many people could and did claim multiple ancestries. The results indicate that 49,598,035 people reported that they are at least in part of English origin, while an only slightly smaller number — 49,224,146 — indicated all or some German ancestry. The other largest European ancestry groups, in rounded figures, were as follows: Irish, 40 million; French, 13 million; Italian, 12 million; Scottish, 10 million; Polish, 8 million; and Dutch, 6 million. This compares with 21 million African Americans, 8 million Mexican Americans, and 7 million American Indians (U.S. Bureau of the Census, 1983). The problems associated with self-reporting were evident in 1990, when a similar question was posed. Germans ranked first with 57,947,374 individuals reporting all or some German ancestry. Meanwhile, the figure for the English group declined to 32,651,788, placing the group third in the rank order (U.S. Bureau of the Census, 1992: 1).

As a religio-ethnic group, Jews provide additional complications in determining population size. As noted earlier, Jews are not included in census data as a distinct group because the Bureau of the Census viewed Jews as a religious group, and this information was gathered on the basis of national origin, not religious affiliation. Thus, Jews are counted among various national groups, especially Russians and Poles. The Council of Jewish Federations (Kosmin, et al., 1991) conducted a national survey of the Jewish population in 1990 and found a "core Jewish population"— which includes Jews by birth, converts, and secular Jews (those reporting no religion or defining themselves as "atheists" or "agnostics")— of 5,515,000 individuals. This is slightly larger than the 5.4 million figure reported in 1970, when a similar survey was conducted. In addition, another 1,325,000 people, such as those who have either converted to another religion or have been raised in a household with another current religion (that is, the children of intermarriage), could be considered part of the total. Thus, Jews are one of the larger European-origin ethnic groups, about the same size as the Swedes and the Dutch.

One of the most significant features of European-origin ethnic groups in America today is the high level of intermarriage among these groups. The single and multiple ancestry listings contained in Table 3.6 provide some indication of the level of intermarriage, since we can assume that multiple ancestry listings reflect inter-marriage. Actually, these data underemphasize the actual level of intermarriage because people with multiple ancestries had the op-tion of listing only one ancestry. We'll discuss this phenomenon and its implications for the redefining of group boundaries further in Chapter 8.

African Americans

African Americans are the only group of involuntary migrants to America, the victims of the demand for cheap labor in the Western Hemisphere. Their history in America is as old as that of European Americans. It is generally assumed that the first contingent of Af-ricans in America, numbering about 20, landed in Virginia in 1619 (Craven, 1971). Three decades later this number had reached 1,600. The legal status of these African Americans was ambiguous. Initial-ly they were indentured servants, as was the case with many other migrants, such as many early Irish arrivals. As servants, Africans could work a period of servitude and then obtain their freedom. Clear evidence exists of free Africans in the seventeenth century. Gradually, however, indentured servitude was extended in length until it became a lifetime status — in short, a perverse extension of the concept of private property.

The Slave Trade and Population Growth

The triangle of the slave trade linked Africa, Europe, and America, with the Dutch, British, French, and Portuguese playing particu-larly active roles. Although most Africans brought to the Western Hemisphere came from a relatively concentrated area in Western Africa, recent evidence suggests that because some African tribes were involved in the slave trade, members of other tribes were cap-tured from further into the interior of the continent than was

Table 3.6   ANCESTRY OF EUROPEAN AMERICANS IN 1980

Ancestry Group	Number of People	% of Total	% Reporting Single Ancestry	% Reporting Multiple Ancestry
English	49,598,035	26.34	47.88	52.12
German	49,224,146	26.14	36.45	63.55
Irish	40,165,702	21.33	25.74	74.26
French	13,672,734	6.85	25.63	74.37
Italian	12,183,692	6.47	56.50	43.50
Scottish	10,048,816	5.34	11.67	88.33
Polish	8,228,037	4.37	46.25	53.75
Dutch	6,304,499	3.35	22.28	77.72
Swedish	4,345,392	2.31	29.65	70.35
Norwegian	3,453,839	1.83	36.51	63.49
Russian	2,781,432	1.48	49.60	50.40
Czech	1,892,456	1.01	41.68	58.32
Hungarian	1,776,902	.94	40.93	59.07
Welsh	1,664,616	.88	18.52	81.48
Danish	1,518,273	.81	28.23	71.77
Portuguese	1,024351	.54	60.17	39.83
Swiss	981,543	.52	23.98	76.02
Greek	959,856	.51	64.16	35.84
Austrian	948,558	.50	35.82	64.18
Slovak	776,806	.41	46.52	53.48
Lithuanian	742,776	.39	45.70	54.30
Ukrainian	730,056	.39	52.20	47.80
Finnish	615,872	.33	43.50	56.50
Belgian	360,277	.19	34.09	65.91
Romanian	315,258	.17	44.94	55.06
Croatian	252,970	.13	42.64	57.36
Slovene	126,463	.07	50.28	49.72
Serbian	100,941	.05	49.16	50.84
Latvian	92,141	.05	60.30	39.70
Basque	43,140	.02	53.81	46.19
Bulgarian	42,504	.02	50.60	49.40
Albanian	38,658	.02	56.10	43.90
Icelander	32,586	.02	40.30	59.70
Estonian	25,994	.01	64.30	35.70

Source: U.S. Bureau of the Census, 1983.

previously realized. Most slaves, however, came from agrarian tribes located in West Africa (Herskovits, 1941). John Blassingame (1972: 2) declared a "majority of them belonged to the Ibo, Ewe, Biafada, Bakongo, Wolof, Bambara, Ibibio, Serer, and Arada tribes." These tribes lacked the centralized governments and armies that characterized some tribal states such as the Yoruba, Ashanti, Dahomey, and Mandingo. These latter groups were generally powerful enough to prevent enslavement, while the former lacked an ability to protect themselves. The diversity of those Africans ensnared in this trade created a highly fragmented collectivity: very different cultures and languages were represented. This heterogeneity, combined with their forced uprooting had, as we shall see later, a bearing on African Americans' ability to maintain elements of their African heritage.

We do not have precise figures concerning the number of Africans brought to this hemisphere, but it is estimated that between 8 and 10 million people were forcibly removed to the Americas between 1502 and 1860 (Tannenbaum, 1946; Woodward, 1971). The vast majority ended up in the West Indies and South America. Philip Curtain (1969: 87–93) believed that the overall number was about 9.6 million and that of this only 5 percent ended up in North America. Using his estimates, the number of Africans imported into this country was approximately 480,000. Although the slave trade was viewed ambivalently by many of the founding figures of the country (many of whom owned slaves), and although this ambivalence allowed legislation to be enacted in 1808 that prohibited the slave trade, slaves were brought into the country illegally until the eve of the Civil War (Nash, 1989).

Though relatively small numbers of Africans have emigrated to the United States since the Civil War, and though their numbers have increased during the past three decades, the period of mass migration for African Americans was effectively over by 1860. In contrast to European Americans, the population growth of African Americans has not been due to the infusion of new people for more than a century.

During the eighteenth century, the African American population grew from 27,000 to 1,002,000. Between 1619 and 1770, the eve of the American Revolution, the percentage of the total population of the United States that was of African origin rose from 1 percent to 21.4 percent. Blacks were highly concentrated in the

South, with about 40 percent living in Virginia (Low and Cliff, 1981: 685). This regional concentration persisted into the twentieth century.

Because of the slowing and eventual stoppage of the migration from Africa by the Civil War, the African American population grew chiefly as a result of increased birth rates and declining death rates. Birth and death rates affected European Americans as well, but they also experienced immigration on a grand scale into the twentieth century. As Table 3.7 illustrates, the African American population declined as a percentage of the overall population from 1810 on. Since 1900 the number has ranged between about 9 and 12 percent of the population, with 29,986,060 reported in the 1990 census constituting 12.1 percent (U.S. Bureau of the Census, 1971: 11; 1992).

The Great Migration

African Americans did not enter the industrial work force in northern states during the period of peak European immigration, and many have questioned why the migration northward, which increased after World War I, was so long delayed. Farley and Allen (1987: 110–112) cite three major reasons for this. First, agricultural employers in the South demanded a large work force of sharecroppers, and freed slaves and their offspring provided a readily exploitable supply of cheap labor. Thus, southern business and political interests combined to make it difficult for labor recruiters to seek African Americans who would move to northern cities. The Freedmen's Bureau pushed workers into long-term contracts with plantation owners, thereby tying them to the land. These contractual arrangements often plunged workers into debt, which made efforts to migrate all the more difficult.

Second, most African Americans were illiterate and socially isolated so were limited in their ability to ascertain employment prospects in the industrial sector of the national economy. It was some time before African American voices such as that of the influential newspaper, the *Chicago Defender*, were heard in the American South.

And third, racist animosity made it difficult for those who did venture to northern cities to find employment. Not only were employers frequently opposed to hiring blacks, but also organized

Table 3.7   AFRICAN AMERICAN POPULATION SIZE AND AS PERCENT OF THE TOTAL, 1790–1990

Year	Number	Percent of Total Population
1790	757,208	19.3
1800	1,002,037	18.9
1810	1,377,808	19.0
1820	1,771,656	18.4
1830	2,328,642	18.1
1840	2,873,648	16.8
1850	3,638,808	15.7
1860	4,441,830	14.1
1870	5,392,172	13.5
1880	6,580,973	13.1
1890	7,488,676	11.9
1900	8,833,994	11.6
1910	9,797,763	10.7
1920	10,463,131	9.9
1930	11,891,143	9.7
1940	12,865,518	9.8
1950	15,042,286	10.0
1960	18,871,831	10.5
1970	22,580,000	11.0
1980	26,945,025	11.7
1990	29,986,060	12.1

Source: U.S. Bureau of the Census, 1975, 1992.

labor was equally hostile. Unions were generally not receptive to opening up their unions to these new arrivals (Franklin, 1967; Rachleff, 1984). This situation was exacerbated because African Americans were used by employers as strikebreakers in numerous instances. Furthermore, the prospects for land acquisition in the

Midwest and Great Plains were extremely limited because the policies of the Federal government favored European immigrants.

The Great Migration began during the period of World War I, when the demand for labor in basic industries could no longer be met by European immigration, and when U.S. entry into the war meant that many workers left their industrial jobs as they entered the armed forces. Aggressive labor recruitment brought waves of rural African Americans to northern cities, and once initial settlements were established, chain migrations developed in a manner parallel to the overseas migrations of America's immigrants. Streams of migrants from such southeastern states as Georgia and the Carolinas headed for Boston, New York, Philadelphia, Pittsburgh, and other major urban centers in the Northeast, while those from states closer to the Mississippi headed for Chicago, Detroit, Cleveland, and other large and moderate-size urban centers in the Midwest, as well as to key cities in border states, such as Nashville and Memphis.

Despite racial conflict, prompted partly by employment competition after the war, migration northward continued. Prices of the three main export crops in the South — cotton, sugar, and tobacco — fell during the 1920s and 1930s, which reduced production and caused rural unemployment. Mechanization occurred far more slowly in the South than in other regions of the country, so agriculture was far more labor intensive than elsewhere. Nonetheless, mechanization and various technological innovations in southern agriculture came about during the 1930s, assisted in part by New Deal programs (Farley and Allen, 1987: 112–117). This reduced the need for as large a labor force as in the past and created economic incentives to leave rural areas. Black agricultural labor became increasingly obsolescent, as the title of Sidney Wilhelm's book, *Who Needs the Negro?* (1970), suggested. Some former agricultural workers headed for southern cities such as Birmingham and Atlanta, but most job opportunities were above the Mason-Dixon line because the South lagged behind the North in industrial development.

The exodus of African Americans from the South continued unabated until 1970. Despite race riots after World War I in such cities as Chicago, Philadelphia, Washington, D.C., Omaha, and East St. Louis, World War II again stimulated migration as the demand for laborers grew in war-related industries. The movement continued in the Cold War era. Not only did the migration to the Northeast and Midwest persist, but, also, the West Coast, particularly California, became an important destination. In 1910 more than 90 percent of African Americans resided in the South, but by 1970 only a slight majority — 52 percent — did.

Since 1970 this trend has reversed: the South has attracted more African Americans from the Northeast and Midwest than have gone to these two areas. This can be attributed chiefly to expanded employment opportunities in the South, while opportunities were drying up in the northern "rust belt." Although movement to the West has continued, the rate of migration decreased from previous decades. Roughly half of African Americans now reside in the South and the other half elsewhere in the country.

Coinciding with the movement out of the South was a move from a rural to an urban world (McAdam, 1982). The urban ghetto had been home to earlier migrants, but as they gained a foothold in the American economy, they progressively moved out of central cities, first to neighborhoods that afforded home ownership possibilities — neighborhoods of row houses, duplexes, and relatively modest detached homes — and then to the crabgrass frontier, the suburbs that sprang up after World War II.

African Americans became the main inhabitants of urban ghettos, and in many cities, they came to constitute a sizeable percentage of the total population, as the white middle class moved to the suburban fringe. In some cities blacks are an absolute majority of the population, and in others they account for large pluralities. On the other hand, as Table 3.8 reveals, they are decided numerical minorities of at most around a quarter of the population of Standard Metropolitan Statistical Areas (SMSAs), which includes urban and suburban populations. Farley and his colleagues (1978) characterized metropolitan America in the second half of the twentieth century as "chocolate city, vanilla suburbs."

Furthermore, blacks are far more likely than other ethnic groups to reside in residentially segregated neighborhoods. This tends to be more pronounced in northern cities, with Chicago and Cleveland being the most racially segregated in the entire country. This residential pattern is characteristic of the South and West, as well. The index of dissimilarity is a measure of residential segregation used by demographers to permit comparative analyses. Table

Table 3.8 BLACK AND HISPANIC POPULATIONS OF THE
TWENTY LARGEST METROPOLITAN AREAS

Standard Metropolitan Statistical Area	Black Population		Hispanic Origin Population	
	Number (1,000)	% of Total Metro.	Number (1,000)	% of Total Metro.
New York	3,279.3	18.1	2,499.2	13.8
Los Angeles	1,291.7	9.3	4,072.78	29.3
Chicago	1,698.1	20.7	811.1	9.9
San Francisco	543.4	8.9	893.5	14.7
Philadelphia	1,133.2	19.1	176.6	3.0
Detroit	954.1	20.4	87.1	1.9
Boston	206.5	5.5	103.6	2.8
Dallas-Fort Worth	552.8	14.7	400.2	10.7
Washington, D.C.	995.1	26.7	122.1	3.3
Houston	689.1	19.1	667.5	18.5
Miami	536.1	17.5	858.5	28.0
Cleveland	444.3	16.0	44.9	1.6
Atlanta	653.4	23.6	33.7	1.2
St. Louis	431.1	17.4	26.1	1.1
Seattle-Tacoma	105.1	4.4	54.5	2.3
Minneapolis–St. Paul	60.0	2.5	26.0	1.1
Baltimore	606.8	25.6	24.5	1.0
Pittsburgh	187.0	8.1	13.2	.6
San Diego	138.9	5.8	425.7	17.9
Tampa–St. Petersburg – Clearwater	200.0	9.8	116.4	5.7

Source: U.S. Bureau of the Census. 1991b.

Table 3.9　INDEXES OF THE RESIDENTIAL SEGREGATION OF BLACKS, HISPANICS, AND ASIANS FROM NON-HISPANIC WHITES FOR METROPOLITAN AREAS, 1980

Cities	Blacks	Hispanics	Asians
Atlanta	77	31	39
Baltimore	74	38	44
Chicago	88	64	46
Cleveland	88	55	42
Dallas	79	49	43
Detroit	88	45	48
Houston	75	49	45
Los Angeles	81	57	47
Miami	78	53	34
New Orleans	71	25	54
New York	81	65	49
Newark	82	65	35
Philadelphia	79	63	47
St. Louis	82	32	44
San Francisco	74	41	47
Washington	70	32	31
Average	79	48	43

Note: These are indexes of dissimilarity which were calculated from census tract data. Data are shown for all metropolitan areas with 250,000 or more black residents in 1980, except Memphis.

Source: U.S. Bureau of the Census, Census of Population and Housing: 1980, Public Use Samples, Summary Tape File 3.

3.9 reports the indexes of dissimilarity for blacks, Hispanics, and Asians in sixteen cities throughout the country. In all instances, African Americans are more segregated from whites than either Hispanics or Asians, and in several cases, their level of segregation is more than double that of the other two groups. We'll discuss the political, economic, and cultural implications of these demographic patterns in subsequent chapters.

Hispanic Americans

The demographic history of Hispanic Americans is complicated because it includes people incorporated into the American polity as a result of the colonial expansion westward in the nineteenth century—people who, like American Indians, preceded European settlers—and it includes the illegal immigrants who crossed the Rio Grande in search of work in America's farms and factories. It includes voluntary migrants who came to this country in very similar ways and for similar reasons as many Europeans, as well as people who came here for unique programs of contract labor. It includes a group of people whose land of origin was acquired by the United States in the Spanish American War and who have citizenship status because they reside in a U.S. territory. And it includes political refugees, people fleeing Communism or, more recently, right-wing death squads.

Hispanic, or Spanish-language peoples, now total more than 15 million people and slightly more than 7 percent of the total U.S. population. They are the second largest minority group after African Americans. As Table 3.10 reveals, Hispanics are heavily concentrated in a select number of states. They originate from various points in the Western Hemisphere south of the United States, including Central and South America, as well as the Spanish-speaking islands of the Caribbean (Bean and Tienda, 1987).

Mexican Americans

The largest group of American Hispanics is the Mexican. According to a 1985 census report, Mexicans accounted for 60.6 percent of the Hispanic population, numbering 10,269,000 (U.S. Bureau of the Census, 1987). Five years later the number had risen to 11,586,903 (U.S. Bureau of the Census, 1991a). The earliest Mexican Americans became a part of this nation as a result of conquest, particularly as a result of the 1846 war with Mexico and the subsequent Treaty of Guadalupe Hidalgo, which ceded Mexican lands along the border to the United States in 1848. What became Texas, for example, had approximately 5,000 Mexican residents when

Table 3.10 TEN STATES WITH THE LARGEST HISPANIC
POPULATIONS

Rank	State	Population	Percent of Total State Population
1	California	4,544,000	19.2
2	Texas	2,986,000	21.0
3	New York	1,659,000	9.5
4	Florida	858,000	8.8
5	Illinois	636,000	5.6
6	New Jersey	492,000	6.7
7	New Mexico	476,000	36.6
8	Arizona	441,000	16.2
9	Colorado	339,000	11.7
10	Michigan	162,000	1.8

Source: U.S. Bureau of the Census, 1980.

Anglos arrived, while New Mexico had in excess of 60,000. When the Mexicans in Arizona, California, and Colorado are added to this, these citizens by conquest numbered more than 100,000.

During the nineteenth century the number of legal immigrants was relatively small, with only 28,000 entering the country between 1820 and 1900 (U.S. Immigration and Naturalization Service, 1985: 2–4). Immigration became a significant factor during the first three decades of the twentieth century: the approximately 50,000 Mexicans who entered the United States between 1900 and 1910 were followed by more than 675,000 during the next two decades. This immigration was the result of the protracted and bloody Mexican Revolution (1909–1922) and of the need for labor in the aftermath of the restrictive immigration laws passed in the 1920s.

The easy access to Mexican labor made Mexicans attractive to employers in agriculture and industry, at first only in the Southwest, but later in northern cities such as Chicago and Milwaukee. The flow of immigrants was curtailed in periods of economic downturn, as during the Great Depression when many Mexicans were forced to repatriate. Since 1920, more than two million Mexicans have migrated to the United States. Furthermore, official statistics are always problematic, partly because illegal immigrants are not counted. This is particularly significant for Mexicans, because the border between the two countries is exceptionally permeable and permits relatively easy access to the United States.

Puerto Ricans

The second largest Hispanic group is the Puerto Rican. The 2,562,000 immigrants reported in 1985 account for 15.1 percent of the Hispanic population—considerably smaller than the Mexican (U.S. Bureau of the Census, 1987). By 1990, the number had declined to 1,955,323 (U.S. Bureau of the Census, 1992). Residents of Puerto Rico also have easy access to the U.S. mainland, but the reason is different. The United States acquired Puerto Rico in 1899 in the treaty that concluded the Spanish-American War. The island's colonial rulers were changed, with the residents failing since then to become an independent nation or to achieve statehood. Residents were granted citizenship rights in 1917 under the terms of the Jones Act. This allows Puerto Ricans to move freely between the island and the mainland.

Emigration from the island was not widespread during the first several decades of the current century. Although statistics are problematic because as citizens Puerto Ricans were not counted in official immigration statistics, it is estimated that in 1920 only 12,000 had left for the mainland. They settled chiefly in New York City and later in various other cities in the Northeast. The number rose to 53,000 a decade later and reached about 90,000 during World War II (Moore and Pachon, 1985: 33).

With the advent of low-cost airfares in the 1950s, the population grew dramatically, reaching nearly 900,000 by 1960, and this trend continued into the 1970s, when recessions in the United States prompted an out-migration back to the island. Though the movement to the mainland persisted, more Puerto Ricans returned to the island during this time than moved the other way (Feagin, 1984: 302).

Cuban Americans

Cubans are the third largest Hispanic group, with a population of 1,036,000 that accounts for 6.2 percent of the total (U.S. Bureau of the Census, 1987). Cuba also became a colony of the United States after the Spanish-American War, but unlike Puerto Rico, this island became an independent republic in 1902. Cuba was, however, economically and politically dependent upon its much more powerful neighbor. Relatively small numbers of Cubans settled in Florida between 1900 and 1950, frequently finding employment in cigar manufacturing (Pozzetta and Mormino, 1986). The number of Cubans rose to 79,000 by 1960, heavily concentrated in the Miami area.

After the revolution that brought Fidel Castro to power in 1959, the number of émigrés seeking political exile increased, so that by 1973, 273,000 additional immigrants had entered the United States. Most of these were either wealthy business people or white collar professionals, former government officials, and other members of the middle class who were hostile to Castro and communism. Since 1980 slightly less than 130,000 additional Cubans have arrived in Florida, including approximately 10,000 of them after taking refuge in the Peruvian embassy in Havana in 1980 and many who departed from the Cuban port of Mariel—thus becoming known as the *Marielitos*. These later arrivals were poorer and less educated than those who preceded them, which added a class dimension to the Cuban community (Moore and Pachon, 1985: 36).

The Other Hispanics

An additional 3,072,000 Hispanics, or 18.2 percent of the total, round out the overall population. The three countries from Central America and the Caribbean that have, as of 1990, contributed the most immigrants are, in descending order, the Dominican Republic, El Salvador, and Guatemala, but also included are sizeable enclaves from Nicaragua, Panama, Honduras, and Costa Rica. Costa Rica has the most stable democracy in the region and the healthiest economy and, not surprisingly, also sends the smallest number of emigrants.

The four leading sources of immigrants from South America are, in descending order, Columbia, Ecuador, Peru, and Argentina. Immigrants have also come from Chile, Venezuela, Bolivia, Uruguay, Paraguay, and elsewhere in the region. Paraguay has sent the smallest contingent of emigrants, though for reasons quite different than Costa Rica. Paraguay was ruled until recently by an authoritarian regime headed by General Stroessner, whose repressive rule not only stultified the politics of the country but kept the land-locked nation economically underdeveloped. Although this might have been a trigger for emigration, his opposition to the voluntary exit of citizens made it extremely difficult for people who wanted to leave to do so.

The size of these national-origin groups taken singly makes them less significant than the Mexican, Puerto Rican, and Cuban populations. In some instances — notably the Dominicans, Columbians, and Ecuadorians — because of clustering in certain cities, viable ethnic communities have emerged. This tends not to happen with other groups that are both quite small and geographically rather dispersed.

Although the Hispanic population now constitutes the second largest minority group, continuing immigration and the high fertility rate among these groups (the Cubans being an exception) compared with non-Hispanic whites and African Americans, make it the largest growing segment of the American population (Bean and Tienda, 1987: 205–232). The U.S. Census Bureau (1986) has projected these trends into the next century, and on the basis of current patterns of growth, Hispanics will outnumber African Americans and become the largest minority group in the country by the year 2080. This projection, it should be noted, is highly speculative. This growth will only occur if immigration rates remain at current levels, return migration does not become an important variable, and fertility rates continue to remain higher than those observed among the rest of the population. Obviously, one or more of these is subject to change in the future.

Asian Americans

Asian Americans do not have as lengthy a history in America as do Hispanics, but given the different groups involved, this history is nonetheless complex. The four largest groups are the Chinese, Japanese, Filipino, and Korean. The dramatic growth of these four since 1960 is summarized in Table 3.11. Added to this are immigrants from the Indian subcontinent and recent arrivals from Southeast Asia, including Vietnamese, Laotians, Cambodians, and Thais.

Table 3.11   GROWTH OF THE FOUR LARGEST ASIAN AMERICAN
GROUPS SINCE 1960

Year	Groups			
	Chinese	Japanese	Filipino	Korean
1960	237,292	463,514	181,614	32,000[1]
1970	436,062	591,020	336,731	69,130
1980	812,178	716,331	781,894	357,393
1985	1,079,400	766,000	1,051,600	542,000
1990	1,505,203	1,004,645	1,450,512	836,987

[1]This is an approximation. Koreans were not counted as a separate ethnic group until 1970.

Source: U.S. Bureau of the Census, 1975, 1984, 1987, 1991b.

Chinese Americans

The first group to arrive were the Chinese. Coastal Chinese have historically exhibited a willingness to leave China during periods of crisis and upheaval. Two early waves of emigration had occurred during the seventh century and during the Ming Era (1368–1644), with most of the Chinese settling in various locales in Southeast Asia. Only in the nineteenth century, when developments in travel by sea made trans-Pacific mass migration possible, did Chinese arrive in North America. Very few Chinese had arrived in the United States until 1850. Push factors that prompted a desire to exit China included economic disasters, caused in part by floods and resulting in widespread famine, and the political turmoil that occurred during the Taiping Rebellion (1850–1864). The primary pull factor was the discovery of gold in California, an event of world historical significance. A great number of Chinese, generally young men, many of whom were unmarried, came as sojourners intent on making money in the gold fields and then returning to China (Lyman, 1974).

The U.S. Census for 1860 reported 34,933 Chinese. That number rose to 105,465 by 1880 and peaked at 107,488 in 1890 (U.S. Bureau of the Census, 1975). In 1882, however, the Chinese Exclusion Act was passed, the nation's first restrictive immigration legislation directed at particular nationality or ethnic groups. Provisions called for barring additional Chinese from entering the country for ten years and forbade the naturalization of those already in the country (Hutchinson, 1981; Lyman, 1974). This prohibition was subsequently extended every ten years until 1904, when an unlimited extension was instituted. This situation did not change until World War II. Considering that the Chinese in America were overwhelmingly male, it is not surprising that the number of Chinese declined during the first half of the twentieth century. The Chinese population reached a nadir of 61,639 in 1920.

The prohibition on Chinese immigration was lifted during World War II because China was an ally of the United States in the war against Japan. Beginning in the 1940s, small numbers of Chinese again began to emigrate to America. Not until the 1960s, when low-cost airfares combined with a new more liberal immigration law — the Immigration Act of 1965 — did a new wave of immigrants begin to arrive. These newcomers were from either Hong Kong or Taiwan, because emigration from the People's Republic of China was prohibited. Though sociologist Robert E. Park had noted the decline of the Chinese in America and had predicted the death of Chinatowns in the 1920s, by the 1960s, these new arrivals had resuscitated the ethnic community — and Chinatowns in America's major cities have grown during the past quarter century. The population rose from 435,000 in 1970 to 1,079,000 by 1985 and reached 1,505,245 in 1990 (U.S. Bureau of the Census, 1987, 1992), mean-ing that the Chinese are the largest group of Asian Americans at present.

Japanese Americans

The Japanese arrived later than the Chinese and under rather unique circumstances. The intense opposition of Japan's government to emigration had taken the form of legal prohibitions against emigration beginning as early as 1639. This was part of Japan's plan to remain isolated from Western influence. Though the legal prohibition continued after Commodore Matthew Perry entered Japan in 1853, it became more difficult to restrain those intent on emigrating. Only a small number emigrated prior to 1880, most of these going to Hawaii (which was an independent kingdom when the first Japanese arrived, but later became part of the United States) as contract laborers (Takaki, 1989: 43).

Since the Exclusion Act of 1882 only applied to Chinese, the Japanese were not restricted in their immigration to the United States until the Immigration Act of 1907 granted the Executive Branch the right to exclude certain categories of persons if they were deemed to be harmful to labor interests. Though the Japanese were not singled out in the legislation, a general antipathy toward all Asian immigration had grown and the increased demand for immigration restriction could be met partly by the discretionary character of the law.

For its part, the Japanese government played an activist role in migration policy and in determining who would be granted passports. According to Ronald Takaki (1989: 46), Japan was intent on accomplishing two things: sending only those who would prove to be good representatives of Japan in the West, and ensuring that Japanese immigrants would be well treated. The Chinese example — in which Chinatown was portrayed as a vice district full of social problems, and anti-Chinese hostility was all too evident — apparently affected their actions. As a consequence, the Japanese were a much more select group of immigrants, not only in comparison to the Chinese, but also to most European immigrants.

As part of what was known as a "Gentleman's Agreement" entered into by Japan and the United States in 1907, Japan agreed to curtail emigration considerably. Japan succeeded in getting the United States to permit the immigration of parents, wives, and children of Japanese residents of the United States. This meant the ethnic community developed with a far more advantageous sex ratio than did the Chinese. The consequences can be seen by comparing the sizes of these two groups over a half century. While the Chinese population declined from 105,465 in 1880 to 74,954 by 1930, the Japanese rose from a mere 148 to 138,834 during the same time period.

Japanese were barred from any additional immigration after 1924. Furthermore, the devastating consequences of World War II for Japanese Americans, which will be discussed in detail later, resulted in a stagnation of what was a rapidly growing group. Since the 1950 figure of 141,768, however, the population has grown steadily, reaching 700,747 by 1980 (the growth appears even more dramatic because Hawaii became a state in 1959 and its sizeable

Japanese community was added to the total after that date). Immigration during the past four decades has averaged about 45,000 per decade (U.S. Immigration and Naturalization Service, 1985). At present, the Japanese are the third largest Asian group with 1,004,645 (U.S. Bureau of the Census, 1991b).

Filipino Americans

The Filipinos' immigration history parallels that of Puerto Ricans in some important respects. Both were Spanish colonies for several hundred years, and Spanish culture, including Roman Catholicism, was deeply embedded in the culture. Both the Philippines and Puerto Rico became colonies of the United States after the Spanish-American War in 1898. In both instances residents were accorded the right to travel to the United States because they were not defined as aliens. Although the Filipinos were more Westernized than their other Asian counterparts, they nonetheless confronted America's generalized hostility to Asians, or, to employ the term more commonly used at the turn of the century, "Orientals." In contrast to Puerto Ricans, the Filipinos fell under the dictates of the anti-Oriental legislation that denied them the ability to become naturalized citizens. They were considered nationals ineligible for citizenship (Kitano, 1985: 236). Despite this racist hostility, Filipinos took advantage of job opportunities in the West and by 1930 approximately 110,000 were living in Hawaii and 40,000 on the mainland. This wave of immigration was composed chiefly of single young men, many of whom found employment as agricultural laborers (Takaki, 1989; 58).

In 1934 the similarity with Puerto Rico ended as the Philippines became an independent nation under the terms of the Tydings-McDuffie Act. The Filipinos were defined as aliens and granted a minuscule quota of fifty entrees per year, thereby ending immigration on a large scale for three decades. Actually, a relatively small second wave of immigration took place after World War II, when many of the immigrants were veterans of the war. Given the fact that the United States has maintained a military presence in the Philippines since World War II, it is not surprising that a small but continuous stream of Filipinas has immigrated as the wives of U.S. servicemen (Chan, 1991: 40).

The Immigration and Naturalization Act of 1965 again opened the doors for a substantial wave of immigration. This legislation, which went into effect in 1968, eliminated the national quotas that were in place since 1924 with hemispheric quotas. Although preference was given to resident aliens and dependents of American citizens, the bill also gave preferential treatment to individuals (and their families) possessing job skills deemed valuable by authorities. This stimulated increased migration from the Philippines of educated white collar professionals, particularly health professionals (doctors and nurses), teachers, and engineers (Muñoz, 1971: 29). This is an example of what has been referred to as the "brain drain" from the Third World.

The Filipino population expansion since 1968 has been dramatic. The 343,000 Filipinos reported in 1970 grew to 775,000 a decade later, and by 1990 they numbered 1,450,512 (U.S. Bureau of the Census, 1991b). At present the Filipino population is the second largest Asian group, a close second to the Chinese.

Korean Americans

The fourth Asian group is the Korean. Though the Shufeldt Treaty of 1882 provided a legal basis for Korean immigration, very few Koreans actually came to the United States during the nineteenth century. The first wave, numbering little more than 7,000, entered the country between 1903 and 1905 prompted by economic disasters at home brought about by drought, a locust plague, a cholera epidemic, and famine (Kitano, 1985: 230). As with the Japanese, this group went to Hawaii, where its members found employment as plantation laborers. This migratory wave was short lived because the Japanese began to dominate Korea, finally making it a colony in 1910. After 1905 the Japanese demanded a cessation of emigration, except for a limited number of wives, including "picture brides," to help redress the sex ratio of the Korean émigré community. Although some Koreans returned home and about 2,000 relocated to the West Coast of the United States, most remained in Hawaii.

Thus, prior to World War II Koreans were a decidedly small component of the Asian American population. Though, as with the Filipinos, a small stream of immigrants continued to enter the country after World War II—wives of American servicemen, war orphans, and students — the numbers amounted to less than 20,000 between 1945 and 1968. The 1965 immigration law again was the impetus for an explosion in growth of the Korean population. This third wave was substantially larger that the previous two and can be characterized as largely derived from the middle class, including both professionals and entrepreneurs. This group is also, due to a long history of missionary activity in Korea, composed primarily of Protestant Christians (Hurh and Kim, 1984).

The 69,130 Koreans in the United States in 1970 increased to 357,393 a decade later, and by 1990 the number had reached 836,987, making Koreans the fourth largest Asian group (U.S. Bureau of the Census, 1991b).

Other Asian Groups

A number of other groups complete the portrait of Asian Americans. One group, Asians from the Indian subcontinent, have a history in America similar to that of Koreans and Filipinos. Included in this group were Hindus and Muslims, though a majority were Sikhs (Takaki, 1989: 295). Other groups are more recent — post-1965 — arrivals. These include relatively small numbers of Pacific Islanders from a variety of islands in the Polynesian, Micronesian, and Melanesian island chains. However, most significant are immigrants from Southeast Asia (also referred to as Indochina). Many of these immigrants are political refugees, victims of the Vietnam War and its devastating consequences on the entire region. The largest of these groups is the Vietnamese, with a current population of more than a quarter of a million. The Vietnamese are followed, in descending order of size, by Laotians (particularly a group of heretofore isolated peoples called the Hmong), Cambodians, and then all other groups combined.

By 1990 Asians accounted for about 2.4 percent of the U.S. population. Some projections suggest this may rise to 4 percent by the year 2000. For this increase to occur, immigration levels will have to remain high because the overall fertility rate for all Asian groups is lower than for the U.S. as a whole.

Despite constituting a small minority of the population, regional concentration increases the Asians' influence in the western states, especially California and Hawaii. While 56.4 percent of Asians reside in the western part of the country, only 19.1 percent

Table 3.12   REGIONAL DISTRIBUTION OF THE FOUR LARGEST
ASIAN GROUPS, 1990

	Northeast	Midwest	South	West
Japanese	8.9	8.5	10.7	71.9
Chinese	24.9	7.9	12.3	54.9
Filipino	10.3	8.8	12.5	68.4
Korean	21.5	14.3	20.2	44.0

Source: U.S. Bureau of the Census, 1991b.

of the U.S. population does. Table 3.12 depicts the regional distributions of the four largest Asian groups. Note that the Japanese are the most regionally concentrated, while the Koreans are the least.

Summary

This chapter reviewed the complex ways in which the heterogeneous population of the United States grew from the period of colonial expansion to the present. We examined the reasons for the precipitous decline of the Native American population and factors that have contributed to its growth since 1890. We surveyed the dramatic expansion of European immigration, then reviewed the shift in place of origin from western Europe during the earliest phase to southern and eastern Europe during the mass immigration period that extended from 1880 to 1924. The victims of the slave trade contributed substantial numbers to the American populace, and even after the termination of the slave trade African Americans constituted a significant minority community in the United States. We reviewed the long history of an Hispanic presence, focusing on the oldest and largest Hispanic group, Mexicans. We also reviewed the immigration history of the two next largest groups: Puerto Ricans and Cubans. Similarly, we surveyed the growth of the Asian population in the United States since the nineteenth century by looking at the four largest Asian groups: Chinese, Japanese, Filipino, and Korean. We looked at the impact of changes in immigration laws since 1965 on the dramatic expansion of both the Hispanic and Asian American populations.

This demographic and geographic profile of ethnic America provides a context by which to understand the changing character of inter- and intra-ethnic relations over time. To obtain a clearer understanding of the different ways in which America impinged upon and shaped the destinies of the various ethnic groups and subgroups, and in turn how these groups responded both to other groups and to America at-large, we must pay attention to the historical dimension. The next four chapters will survey, in necessarily broad brush strokes, two historical periods: the period from the colonial era to the Civil War; and the period of industrialization, extending from the end of the Civil War to a general period around World War II. The five chapters after that will take up the immediate past and the present for each of the major groups.

The historical sections are not merely a backdrop to the present. Rather, the past continues to exert its influence on the present, in ways frequently not discernible to people engaged in the routines of their everyday lives.

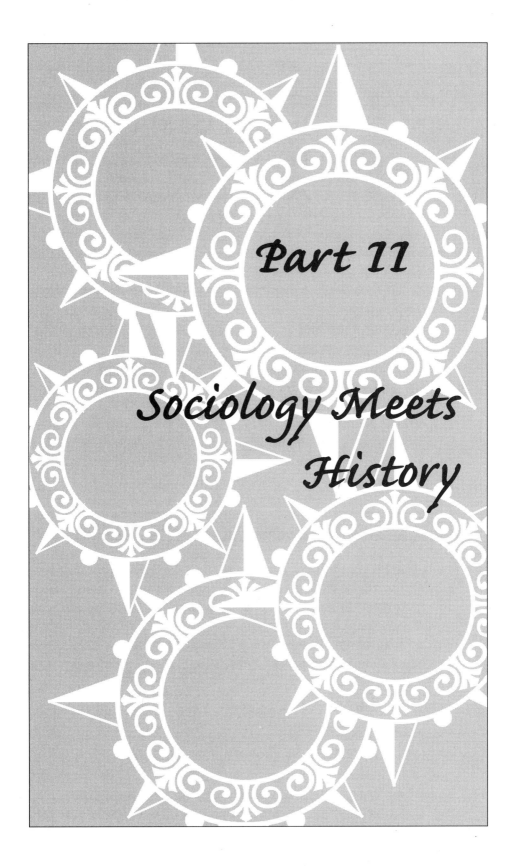

Part 11

Sociology Meets History

EUROPEAN MIGRATION FROM COLONIAL AMERICA TO THE CIVIL WAR

4

In this chapter we will examine the major social processes that formed the nation between the colonial period and the Civil War, and their relevance for the peopling of America by Europeans during this time. First, we will review key features of the economic, political, and cultural forces that channelled social change in certain directions. We will then discuss the three major European immigrant groups of this period: the British, Irish, and Germans. We shall look both at the ways that these social forces affected each group and how the groups responded to those forces.

Social Change and Key Actors

The period from 1760 — just prior to the American war of independence — to the Civil War was critically important to immigration and its impact on American society. Economic, political, and cultural forces shaped the experiences of those already in America as well as those of new immigrants. The impact of these societal forces continued long after the Civil War ended.

Economic Forces

The first of these processes was economic. Given the obvious economic success of the United States in the nineteenth and twentieth centuries, it is ironic, Rowland Berthoff (1971: 3) observed, that "American society began in a long series of business failures." During the seventeenth century, mercantilist policies encouraged state-chartered business ventures in the Americas. Major European powers sponsored a variety of undertakings prior to American independence. Some short-lived ventures had little impact on subsequent developments, such as the colony established by Sweden, and populated by Swedes and Finns in the Delaware River Valley in 1638 (Weslager, 1988; Koivukangas, 1988). New Sweden directly competed with both Dutch and English ventures in the fur and tobacco trade. The Dutch took over the colony in 1655, but ultimately lost it to the English (Wittke, 1939: 35). As a consequence, there was no continuity between this initial Swedish settlement in North America and the later migration of approximately 1.3 million Swedes (and 350,000 Finns). Although Swedes became an important group because of their sheer size and their regional concentration in the upper Midwest, they were relatively inconsequential to the formative history of the United States.

Dutch businesses in New York state had a more lasting impact. After 1620, the Dutch West India Company became a dominant economic force along the Hudson River, and the Dutch were heavily concentrated in this area. By 1790, 80 percent of the 100,000 Dutch in the United States resided within a 50-mile radius of New York City (Swierenga, 1985: 1). However, the Dutch lost to the British in the struggle for dominance so that by the beginning of the nineteenth century the Dutch had ceased to be a major economic force. Unlike the Swedes, the Dutch did not become invisible. They continued to have a regional impact, and the 250,000 Dutch immigrants found an ethnic subculture already in place. Although Dutch settlements in western Michigan and Iowa had a profound impact on those particular geographic areas, the relatively small size of the group limited its ability to have a larger impact on the nation.

The subsequent history of the Dutch in America is replete with internal conflicts brought about by linguistic and cultural differences, but particularly by religious conflicts. The Reformed Church in America was established in 1628, one of the earliest denominations in America. In the nineteenth century, the Reformed church confronted schisms and competing church bodies (Swierenga, 1985; Taylor, 1983).

The British met the Dutch and all other challengers and became the dominant economic force in North America. (As Table 4.1 illustrates, in the 1790 census, 82.1 percent of the white population

Table 4.1   EUROPEAN ORIGIN POPULATION IN 1790 BY NATIONALITY

Nationality	Number	Percent
English	2,605,699	82.1
Scotch	221,562	7.0
Irish	61,534	1.9
Dutch	78,959	2.5
French	17,619	0.6
German	176,407	5.6
Jewish	1,243	0.1
All Other	9,421	0.3
Total	3,172,444	100.0

Source: U.S. Bureau of the Census, 1909.

originated from England.) The British colonial empire actually extended from Newfoundland to Barbados and Tobago (Wells, 1975). Franklin Scott (1963: 9) aptly described the British in North America as "the shock troops and the pace setters of European occupation." In the settlements along the Atlantic seaboard the British dominated major businesses such as shipping and steel production and were the major group in banking and finance. Furthermore, on the frontier they had more influence than any other European group.

Economic development proceeded in two directions that affected immigration. First, the emergence of a capitalist industrial order, gradual at first, but accelerating dramatically in the nineteenth century, brought a demand for cheap labor. This demand was met by voluntary immigration and by the slave trade. The second development involved land. The vast frontier of the North American continent fueled land speculation, and large landowners bought vast tracts of land with the intention of selling them at a profit to the millions of land hungry farmers and peasants throughout Europe. These developments began to have an impact prior to the war of independence. Indeed, between 1760 and 1776 the level of migration reached the highest ever seen in Europe's and Africa's relationship with the Western hemisphere (Bailyn, 1986a: 24).

Political Forces

The economic domination of the British coalesced with political domination. British laws, institutions, and political sensibilities were transplanted to North America. In a more philosophical sense, the political ideals of those who shaped the American Revolution derived from Enlightenment thought in its various forms and was, therefore, not simply British. Nonetheless, the concrete political form of the new republic was most indebted to the way in which these ideas developed in a British setting (Commager, 1977; Bailyn, 1986b).

But the United States' political self-definition was based on its anti-colonialism and, therefore, on its ability to distance itself from its origins. Unlike Canada, which has continued to maintain its ties to Britain, the United States became, in Seymour Martin Lipset's (1963) phrase, "the first new nation." He meant that the United States was the first large colony to successfully free itself from the domination of a colonial power via revolution. The revolution's challenge to monarchial government meant that the new nation had to wrestle with competing definitions about what representative government meant and what form it should take.

Particularly important to ethnic and racial groups was how notions about democracy emerged. As historian Bernard Bailyn (1967: 60; 230–319) has indicated, for colonists hostile to British rule, a "contagion of liberty" swept the new republic, but at the same time many influential revolutionary leaders expressed their fears about the dangers that would result if political power was granted to "weak or ignorant" people. Thus, although the nation was conceived as a democracy, who was and who was not eligible for citizenship became an important question. Citizenship, and how it was granted and denied, became a major means of incorporating some groups into not only the American polity, but also social life in general, while excluding others. Although the history of incorporation and exclusion is a complicated one, as we shall see in this and subsequent chapters, race became the most powerful determinant of inclusion and exclusion.

Cultural Forces

Cultural development was related to the economic and political forces. Two aspects of culture concern us here. The first relates to the identification of certain core values that are deeply embedded in American culture. Although a number of values could be noted, none have had the enduring impact on national identity as the following trio: freedom, equality, and individualism. When the French traveler Alexis de Toqueville visited the United States during the 1830s and subsequently presented his impressions in his now classic *Democracy in America* (1981 [1835]), he identified these three as central to what differentiated America from Europe. In his opinion, America represented an entirely new kind of society, seen, for instance, by de Toqueville's need to coin a new word—"individualism"—to describe one of the nation's core values.

None of these values was perceived in an entirely and unambiguously positive way. De Toqueville appears to have understood the virtues of each, but he also saw their darker sides. Freedom, for instance, could lead to behavior devoid of any sense of civic responsibility or obligation to others. Equality could demand—and in fact de Toqueville thought that it did so—a general leveling in America in which people of genuine talent were not rewarded and where a comfortable mediocrity was pervasive. Individualism could result in pure selfishness.

In the more than 150 years since de Toqueville's analysis, commentators on the American character have repeatedly returned to the major impact of these values. Thus, Lipset (1963) has written about the tension that he thinks exists between freedom and equality. Freedom, in a competitive market economy, results in the generation of inequality, and attempts to redress gross inequalities frequently do so by constraining freedom. Robert Bellah and his colleagues (1985: viii) suggested that individualism in the late twentieth century has "grown cancerous," resulting in a society in which we no longer even have a language, and therefore an ability, to speak about collective responsibilities. Despite the ambiguous legacies of these central values, they were nonetheless an integral part of the core culture.

The second important issue related to culture is the extent to which culture is dynamic and open to outside influences or is static and closed. Obviously, this affects the extent to which a culture chiefly shaped by its British origins in the seventeenth and eighteenth centuries was either preserved or transformed by the waves of immigrants — voluntary and involuntary — as well as by the indigenous people. Put bluntly, would America always be a white Anglo-Saxon Protestant culture, or would it continue to refashion itself into what the early twentieth-century social critic Randolph Bourne (1977) referred to as an ever changing "trans-national America"?

Albion's Seed

To assess the extent to which America is stamped by the British imprint, we must first answer the following question: Who are the British? In one sense, the answer appears simple: they are people who originated from the British Isles. Yet, as with all national, ethnic, and racial definitions, what appears self-evident actually has a historical dimension that makes it far more complicated (Furer, 1972). The British were not always British. In fact, as David Hackett Fischer (1989: 6) has observed, the earliest recorded name of Britain was Albion. This name was used by Greeks as early as the sixth century B.C.E. (Before the Common Era). Though this name was used for another thousand years, it gave way to Britain. Those we refer to as the British are, however, a remarkably heterogeneous people whose sense of collective identity has changed extensively over time.

Fischer (1989: 7–11) has argued that America's folkways — the values, customs, and meanings that make up a normative structure — bear the heavy imprint of the nation's British founders. These can be seen in a wide range of human activities and attitudes, including our language; religion; education; cuisine; work and leisure habits; attitudes regarding wealth and inequality; views about marriage, the family, and sexuality; architectural preferences; and general political orientations (including views of power, freedom, and social order). Fisher doesn't see a unified culture derived from British roots, however. Instead, he sees in pre-revolutionary America four distinct folkways based on the different socio-economic, political, and religious orientations of four large waves of emigration from Britain that occurred between 1607 and 1775.

The Puritans

The first wave involved the Puritans, who originated in eastern England and arrived in America between 1629 and 1640. Central to Puritan theology was its understanding of a covenant with God and the need for the commonwealth to be composed of members who had found redemption. They were therefore a part of the chosen or elect, and their leaders fused religion and politics into a theocratic mode of authority. The result was an insular community that was frequently at odds with outsiders. Although many historians accord the Puritans with a particularly large role in defining a national identity for the fledgling nation, Fischer believes the picture is not that simple. He contends that the other three groups have had a larger voice in the invention of a national identity than has frequently been appreciated.

The Cavaliers

The second group, arriving between 1640 and 1675, came from southern England to Virginia and consisted chiefly of cavaliers (a royalist elite) and their indentured servants. Far less democratic and far more elitist and traditionalist (they tended to remain faithful to the Anglican Church) than their counterparts in Massachusetts, these cavaliers became a central force among the slave-holding class and offered an ideological defense of slavery based on their distinctive world view and folkways.

The Quakers

The third group came from the North Midlands of England and Wales and entered the Delaware Valley (especially Pennsylvania) between 1665 and 1725. These were largely members of the dissident pacifist sect known as the Society of Friends or the Quakers. Their egalitarian ideals starkly contrasted with the Virginia royalists. The Quakers' religious and political toleration distinguished them from the Puritans (Baltzell, 1979). The religious convictions of the Quakers put them at odds with slavery, and from their ranks developed, in the 1770s, the first antislavery society in the western world (Bailyn 1967: 245).

The Scotch-Irish

The final group to arrive from Britain (1717 to 1775) did not originate in England, but rather came from Scotland and Northern Ireland. The latter group, sometimes referred to as the Ulster Irish, was actually the product of a dual migration, first from Scotland to Northern Ireland and then to America. Thus, these people collectively are often referred to as the Scotch-Irish, though this migration also included Scots who migrated directly from both the Scottish Lowlands and Highlands. These people lived on the borderland of Britain and were frequently ambivalent about their incorporation into Britain. Some endorsed British — tantamount to English — rule while others fiercely resisted it.

Immigrants settled on the colonial frontier, in the backcountry, which meant in the western parts of states from Pennsylvania to Georgia, pushing into the new outposts of Kentucky and Tennessee. In short, the Scotch-Irish clustered in a region known today as Appalachia. They had a pronounced influence on frontier politics, particularly in their promotion of aggressive campaigns of forced relocations of American Indians.

Transplanting the Old World to the New

The obvious differences among these four groups make it difficult to speak about British America as a singular, coherent culture. Bonds such as language and a shared (if contested) history allow us to speak at another level about British culture in America. From the seeds of this culture we can find the tensions — the ambiguities and the contradictions — that have existed and continue to shape our national culture: a belief in equality versus a justification of the unbridled accumulation of wealth by individuals; a premium placed on liberty versus a systematic denial of liberty to people because of their skin color; theocracy versus religious freedom; and the belief in democratic participation versus the demand that decisions be made by elites.

Berthoff (1971: 21) has noted the British immigrants' desire to recreate that which was familiar to them in America, to transplant as much of their old social order as possible. He observes, however, that the lack of a strong central authority in America made this difficult. Although he is partially correct, many also sought to break with the past. This desire can be seen most explicitly in the revolutionary era, when settlers were divided over the issue of whether to remain loyalists or endorse the anti-monarchial, anti-colonial position. Some British loyalists found conditions in the newly established nation sufficiently unappealing that they migrated to Canada, where they could remain under British tutelage (Hansen and Brebner, 1940).

The multifaceted British culture rather quickly and rather decisively became dominant, and all immigrant groups that followed had to respond to this cultural imprint (Hansen, 1940b). For example, the English language became the language of the nation in both politics and commerce, an achievement reached without legislation mandating English as the country's official language. Some groups responded by attempting to identify with this culture and sought incorporation into the larger society. A small contingent of French Huguenots, Protestants who fled France after Louis XIV's revocation of the Edict of Nantes (which had granted religious freedom to non-Catholics), adapted to the new culture so completely and were so readily accepted that they experienced "rapid social and religious disintegration" (Butler 1983: 5). By 1750 they had all but disappeared as a distinct religio-ethnic group.

All other groups were judged by the British Americans in terms of how similar or how different their cultures were from the dominant culture. Though what being British American meant was not always clear, people often seemed to know which groups were most like the British and which were most unlike. The latter frequently became the objects of prejudice and discrimination.

Nineteenth Century English Migration

After the revolution British settlers continued to come to America. Though there was relatively little migration between the American Revolution and the War of 1812, when the two nations entered into a more cooperative political relationship, the increase in immigration was unprecedented. Charlotte Erickson (1980: 325) estimates that the figure was around 410,000. The main motive for emigration was economic. One of the most persistent rationales for migrating was economic independence.

Indentured servants were no longer part of this flood, so immigration became a self-financed move, and the poorest members of British society were not represented in the ranks of nineteenth-century immigrants. Farmers, who found greater opportunities in America, came instead of farm laborers. Fewer migrants came from the agricultural sector, however, and more from the industrial sector. Particularly noteworthy was an increase in workers from the more advanced industries, such as textiles, metal working, and engineering. The arrival of these immigrants also signaled the introduction of technological innovations in basic industries, such as textiles and iron, brought about by the Industrial Revolution (Erickson 1980: 329). After 1850, however, many immigrants were unskilled laborers, such as workers in building trades and mining.

These immigrants entered a country whose language and culture was far more familiar than any other immigrant group. This did not mean, however, that the world they entered was a mirror image of the old country. Wilbur Shepperson (1965) has studied English immigrants who became disenchanted with America and chose to repatriate and argues that assimilation into the new world for these settlers was not as easy as is popularly assumed. Some returned home because they harbored such a romanticized portrait of America that they could not bear the harsher realities. Others returned because they were unwilling to accept features of American life that were different from British life.

Nonetheless, most of the British adapted to the new environment with far greater ease than any other settlers. Although they founded ethnic societies similar to other immigrant groups, these organizations were relatively short-lived as the British soon opted to join American voluntary organizations. This was easier because no language barrier existed. Thus, a distinctive ethnic community did not emerge and maintain itself over time as was typical for most other groups. To be sure, elite organizations such as the St. George's Society served as a mark of identity for Anglophiles, and numerous self-help associations—fraternal societies, trade unions, and cooperatives (based on the Rochdale model)—were founded, but many did not survive past the first generation. By blending into the host society as rapidly as they did, the British became, in Charlotte Erickson's (1972) words, "invisible immigrants."

Scots in the Nineteenth Century

The Scots, including those from Ulster, the Lowlands, and the Highlands, could also be called invisible immigrants. The transition, however, occurred more slowly due to the outsider status of this group in relation to the English. Scots counted for approximately half a million people by the end of the colonial period, constituting almost 15 percent of the population (Anderson, 1970: 34). In occupational status, they were second only to the English and Welsh, being well-represented among the merchant class as well as among artisans, clerks, politicians, and officers in the military (Graham, 1956: 11).

The Scotch-Irish and the Lowlanders brought Presbyterianism to the United States. The Calvinist theology of the denomination stressed the centrality of the Bible, and as a result, the literacy rate was quite high. Officially established in this country in 1684, the Presbyterian church sought to establish congregations wherever substantial settlements of Scots and Scotch-Irish existed. Relatively few clergy emigrated, however, so many parishes could not readily find ministers. The Presbyterians became involved in experiments in higher education at an early date to remedy this problem. The church established numerous small colleges and seminaries throughout the country, as well as several elite institutions — Princeton University being the most important.

Presbyterianism was theologically at odds with Anglicanism, so the denomination had a strained relationship with the Episcopal Church (the Anglican Church in America shorn of its allegiance to the King or Queen as the head of the church after the American Revolution). Religious friction did not, however, result in a serious wedge between the Scotch-Irish and Scots on the one hand and the English on the other because by the nineteenth century the English were split between the Episcopal Church adherents and those aligned with a variety of dissenting church bodies, such as the Methodists, Baptists, and Quakers. Religious distinctiveness did not prevent the Scots and Scotch-Irish from identifying with British America.

The Scotch-Irish played a central role in the westward expansion of the nation; their prominence on the frontier distinguished them. Here they came into contact and conflict with other groups. They had a conflictual relationship with English Quakers and

Germans, but these conflicts were far less consequential than were their relationships with both American Indians and the Irish.

The Scotch-Irish forged a sense of self-identity based on their close proximity in cultural, political, and economic terms to the English. The name Scotch-Irish is actually an Americanism that the Scotch-Irish embraced in the 1840s as a way of differentiating themselves from the Irish when the mass exodus of Irish Catholics began (Jones, 1980: 895). The Scotch-Irish actively participated in anti-Catholic campaigns during the 1840s. They joined such nativist organizations as the American Protestant Association, which believed the nation had been founded as a Protestant republic and was now under assault by the hordes of Catholics arriving in the country. The Scotch-Irish also participated in mob actions against Irish Catholics, including a vicious attack in 1844 on Irish Catholic churches and homes in Philadelphia (Jones, 1980: 906). What transpired here was a continuation of old, unresolved hostilities because animosity toward Roman Catholicism had been imported from the British Isles, where its focus had also been the Irish.

Scottish Highlanders were Catholic and spoke Gaelic, so they were culturally similar to the Irish. Although Scottish Highlanders tended to remain aloof from anti-Irish actions, they also were fortunate because anti-Catholic sentiments were not often directed at them. Their Scottish national identity buffered such actions. The lack of hostility directed at the Highlanders can be seen by the rather rapid demise of Gaelic and the equally rapid assimilation into the larger body of British America—aided by high levels of intermarriage in the nineteenth century.

Like the English, the Scots and Scotch-Irish continued to arrive in America throughout the nineteenth century. Although Canada was the principle destination for these groups after the American Revolution, America continued to receive members of both groups in large numbers. In both Scotland and Ireland, changes in agriculture forced people off the land, and in Ireland the dislocations that this caused were compounded by population pressures. Industry was not sufficiently expansive to serve as an alternative to displaced farmers and farm laborers, so powerful migration push forces existed since the second decade of the nineteenth century. This pressure was greatly exacerbated by the famine during the 1840s that inflicted untold hardship and suffering on the residents of both Ireland and Scotland. When these new arrivals entered the United States, they discovered a core culture that was decidedly British; although adjustments to the new milieu were inevitable, they assimilated quickly and identified with other Americans of British origin (Donaldson, 1980: 915).

The Core Society: Anglo-Saxon Protestant

Although there was considerable diversity among the various components of British America, these immigrants were melded into what Charles Anderson (1970: 41) described as "the larger Anglo-Saxon Protestant core society." Furthermore, British Americans, due to this cultural hegemony and their dominant location in the American economy and polity, were in a position to attempt to dictate the terms of entrance for other ethnic groups. Other groups were forced to react to this in a reciprocal process of adaptation to British American folkways while seeking to preserve aspects of their own cultural heritages. As Thomas Archdeacon (1983: 94) suggested, "The pattern of combining cultural accommodation with resistance was common to all non-British European immigrant groups."

This pattern can be seen in the two largest non-British groups in America during the first half of the nineteenth century, the Irish and the Germans.

Erin's Children in America

Ireland is located on the periphery of Europe. Its geographic marginality had isolated it long enough to create a distinctive culture that served as a powerful vehicle for creating a national identity (O'Grady, 1973: 1–8). This Gaelic culture became fused with Catholicism as early as the eighth century. Religion was adapted to the unique features of the culture, and the affinities between Gaelic culture and Catholicism made the fusion of culture and religion relatively easy. Both stressed collectivism over individualism. The hierarchial authority of the church, in effect, closely resembled that of the paternalistic Irish family. Both religion and culture placed a premium on obedience to dogma and to authority figures. Those virtues most closely associated with the "Protestant ethic," such as initiative, enterprise, and innovative action, were viewed unfavorably by the Irish Catholics, who stressed instead the importance of tradition, community, and conformity (Miller, 1985: 116). The culture was both conservative and capable of effecting powerful resistance to challenges to its legitimacy.

The Colonization of Ireland

The English involvement with Ireland began as early as 1169, when Dermot MacMurrough, the Irish king deposed in a civil war, invited troops from King Henry II of England into Ireland to help MacMurrough regain his throne. Thus began Ireland's long and troubled relationship with British imperialism. Between the twelfth and thirteenth centuries, the English acquired more and more land in Ireland, especially in the eastern part of the island, in the regions of Leinster and Munster. By end of this period the English controlled two-thirds of the country. Though Gaelic Ireland has a cultural unity, which served as a basis for resistance to British domination, it did not have the political structures necessary for nationhood. So the English were able to expand their control without serious resistance. In this colonization activity the English attempted to replicate the English feudal order in Ireland. In the process, they introduced new agricultural technologies and prompted a more market-oriented agriculture (Miller, 1985: 11–25; McCaffrey, 1976: 11–29).

Between 1600 and 1800 an even more far reaching transformation of Ireland occurred. First, Catholics lost control of most of the land they once held, thereby putting Protestants in a position of economic supremacy. Second, Scottish Presbyterians entered Ireland, which changed the social character of Ulster. Third, revolt against British control broke out at the same time as the English civil war. Although the conflict raged for a decade, the final outcome occurred when Oliver Cromwell's Puritan army crushed the revolt. The devastation of war and the famine and plague that followed reduced the Irish Catholic population by as much as one-third. Many clerics and soldiers fled to the European continent, while many hundred poor Irish were forcibly deported to Virginia or the West Indies (Miller, 1985: 21).

The assault on the Irish Catholics intensified in the waning years of the seventeenth century. The Church of Ireland, which was a wing of the Anglican Church, successfully sought the passage of draconian laws designed to punish Catholic communicants for their rebellion against the crown. In the 1690s, both the British and Irish Parliaments passed the so-called "Penal Laws," which had a pronounced impact on all aspects of social life. Economically, Catholics were deprived of the right to purchase land from Protestants or to pass on their land to their children, although primogeniture was practiced among Protestants. Politically, Catholics were deprived of the right to vote, serve on commissions, and sit in Parliament. They could not own weapons or be members of the armed forces.

Religious persecution accompanied these measures, as bishops were exiled, religious orders and Catholic schools were banned, and importation of new priests was forbidden. In short, during this period, known as the "Protestant Ascendancy," the 25 percent of the citizenry who were Protestant had succeeded in erecting a "wall of suspicion and antagonism" between themselves and the majority Catholic populace (Blessing 1980: 525; see also Miller, 1985: 21–25 and McCaffrey, 1976: 21–22). Ireland was incorporated into the British realm in 1801, when it officially became part of the United Kingdom of Great Britain and Ireland. This status remained in effect until the Irish revolutionary upheaval in the early twentieth century resulted in the Irish Free State in 1920 — with the six counties of Ulster (that is, Northern Ireland) remaining a part of the United Kingdom. As events up to the present in that troubled region attest, the wall has not yet been dismantled in Ireland.

Emigration and Exile

The Irish had a powerful presence in the United States during the nineteenth century. In stark contrast to the Scotch-Irish, Irish Catholics did not migrate in significant numbers until after 1815. Migration prior to that time was quite common, but the destination was primarily England, with some Irish moving to the continent. Those who arrived in America during the colonial period were often either indentured servants or criminals who had first been sent to the West Indies (Lockhart, 1976). Some settled in Maryland because of its reputation for greater religious tolerance than the other colonies only to find that this tolerance had limits — a law was passed that limited the number of Irish Catholic servants admitted into the colony (Blessing, 1980: 525).

From their first encounter with America, the Irish confronted anti-Catholic and anti-Irish prejudice and discrimination. Most of the Irish in America were poor, though they brought various skills that helped them obtain work. A small contingent of wealthy Irish Catholics also resided in some colonial cities, particularly New York and Philadelphia. The poor Irish settled in residential concentrations in some cities, the beginning of the Irish ethnic enclave or ghetto. Thus, what would later be characterized as the "shanty Irish" and the "lace curtain Irish" were in evidence at an early date.

An ever-expanding stream entered this embryonic ethnic community between 1815 and 1845; after 1845 the stream became a major river. The increase was partially due to Irish population growth. In a century's time the population expanded from three million to more than eight million. Although demographers have indicated that population growth occurred throughout all of Europe during the eighteenth and early nineteenth centuries, the growth was higher in Ireland (Connell, 1950). Ireland accommodated this population increase until the early nineteenth century.

War in Europe between 1793 and 1815 resulted in heightened demand for Irish agricultural products, particularly potatoes and wheat. The inflated prices at which these goods were sold, principally to Britain, made this period relatively prosperous. When the Napoleonic wars ended with the peace defined at the Congress of Vienna, however, the price of Ireland's agricultural goods dropped considerably, leading to a period of economic depression. To protect their own economic interests, landlords attempted to force tenant farmers off the land. The combined effect of the depression and the enclosure movement served as a powerful push factor, and the exodus out of Ireland began in earnest in the 1820s. A series of blights and several seasons of inclement weather that produced bad harvests compounded the problem within the agricultural sector.

As late as 1845, the number of Scotch-Irish continued to outnumber the number of Irish Catholics in America (Miller, 1985: 193–279). But this changed as a consequence of the extremely destructive potato blight that struck in 1845 — the Great Famine began. In the wake of successive crop failures, widespread starvation and disease took a terrible toll. Between 1845 and 1851 an estimated million people died as a result of starvation or disease. An equal number emigrated, and most went to the United States. Within half a decade the population of Ireland was reduced by a quarter. Many believed that the British government had failed to respond adequately to the crisis, which further fueled anti-British sentiments (Wittke, 1956: 8).

Immigrant Destinations

The exodus had a major impact on the receiving country, as well: Between 1841 and 1860, the Irish supplied more immigrants to the United States than any other country. In the first of these two decades Irish immigration accounted for fully 45.6 percent of all immigrants entering the United States. In the following decade that number dropped somewhat to 35.2 percent. In contrast with those who had arrived prior to 1845, this cohort was decidedly poorer and, lacking economic resources or marketable skills, they found themselves in impoverished conditions that were rife with crime, disease, various social pathologies, and human misery. They became, in effect, America's first truly impoverished ghetto dwellers.

Though Irish immigrants settled virtually everywhere throughout the country, including the rural agricultural communities of the Midwest as well as the Pacific coast states, they were heavily concentrated in the northeastern states. They settled principally in urban rather than rural areas. Large concentrations of Irish could be found in New York, Philadelphia, and Boston, as well as in smaller cities throughout the region. They were also well represented in the mining centers of Pennsylvania.

Finding Work

Some of the immigrants, especially those originating in sections of Ulster and Leinster — centers of the textile industry that were more industrialized than the rest of Ireland — had some exposure to urban industrial life. For others, however, the trans-Atlantic crossing meant moving from an agrarian to an urban world, and the transition was often very difficult. Unskilled Irish males found employment in factories, mines, railroads, and similar occupations that placed a premium on hard physical labor. The Irish were especially well represented among the ranks of laborers who dug the canals that opened transportation and commerce between the East and the Midwest. Skilled laborers entered an economy that could use their skills, so they did not experience a loss of job status as a consequence of migration. Entrepreneurs operated a variety of business establishments in the ethnic community, most prominently saloons and boarding houses. Some of the Irish acquired middle class professional jobs, especially as clerks and teachers (Blessing, 1980: 531).

Irish immigration was distinguished from many other groups by the relative parity in the sex ratio of immigrants. While other groups were overwhelmingly male — a ratio of 9:1 was not unusual — more females than males entered the United States from Ireland between 1880 and 1910. No other large European-origin group counted so many women among its ranks (Daniels, 1990: 141). This was not because the Irish emigrated as family units. Instead, unmarried females, like their male counterparts, exhibited a willingness to make the journey alone. As Hasia Diner (1983: 50) points out, "it indicates that economic motives for migration remained paramount. Irish women did not migrate primarily to find the husbands they could not find at home." As in Ireland, many men and women remained celibate, and others entered matrimony only late in life.

Though women found employment in a variety of places, two types of work stood out (the women exhibited less occupational diversity than their male counterparts): in factory work, especially textiles and clothing manufacturing (some had prior experience), and in domestic service as maids. The latter was especially important and, according to Diner (1983: 74), the "Irish female immigrant's preferred job." This is noteworthy because domestic work — which generally required living in the home of one's employer, and thereby foregoing a considerable degree of freedom and privacy — was avoided by women from many other groups.

For Irish women, who were less intent than their counterparts from other groups on getting married and establishing a family, domestic service afforded a security they could not get from factory work, which fluctuated with marketplace cycles (Horgan, 1988). Being a maid could isolate a person from other Irish people because ongoing interaction with the employer could cause an abandonment of the ethnic community. This, however, was not true with Irish domestics. Instead, they maintained a remarkably high degree of identification with and participation in Irish America. Diner (1983: 153) concluded that ethnicity proved to be more powerful than gender, and, in the final analysis, "Their economic assertiveness and strong sense of self did not jar with those cultural traditions but proved instead to be the mechanism for blending old-world ideals with American needs."

One striking feature of the economic status of the Irish as a whole was the lack of upward social mobility they experienced during the nineteenth century. This was evident during the period up to the Civil War and persisted throughout the century. Blessing (1980: 531) observed that, unlike any other immigrant group arriving during this period, their "occupational mobility during the late 19th century appeared almost as small as that of American blacks." As a result, the Irish poor were confined to inner city ghettos, where levels of crime, violence, alcoholism, poverty, and social disorganization helped create a growing perception among other Americans that the Irish were a social problem. The perceived threat of what was known at the time as the "dangerous class" within the ethnic community concerned both nativists who were hostile to the Irish and more sympathetic social reformers (Wittke, 1956: 40–51).

Communal Activities and Organizations

The Irish became involved in politics soon after they arrived in the United States. Many have argued that the Irish had a unique penchant for politics (Levine, 1966; Erie, 1988). Clearly, the Irish had certain advantages compared with other immigrant groups, such as facility with the English language and familiarity with Anglo American laws and customs (Shannon, 1963: 60). They also had a keen interest in homeland politics: The surge of Irish nationalism had an impact not only in Ireland, but also among the immigrant population (Brown 1966). Given the residential clustering of this sizeable ethnic group in key American cities, the heads of local Democratic political machines saw the Irish as potential political support.

The Irish leaned toward the Democratic Party because they felt the Republicans harbored deep-rooted anti-Catholic attitudes. The result of this conviction was that from the 1840s the Irish began to be incorporated into big city political machines, though the Irish did not control those machines until after the Civil War. According to sociologist Steven Erie (1988: 31), the Irish attraction to machine politics stemmed from their "intense group solidarity, and the high value they placed on the economic rewards of politics." Municipal patronage was particularly important. This, however, did not substantially materialize during the antebellum era, as the Irish had first to gain a foothold in existing political machines. Thus, although the beneficial consequences of involvement in machine politics was not realized until later, between 1840 and the Civil War the stage was set for Irish ascendance in urban politics.

Irish voluntary organizations began during the colonial period when the first, known as the Charitable Irish Society of Boston, was founded in 1737. Like a number of subsequent early organizations, these were largely dominated by Protestants and by "lace curtain" Catholics. Similar organizations with more inclusive, working-class memberships emerged after 1840. These mutual aid or fraternal organizations were frequently local efforts, but later efforts were directed at national institutions. Though the membership differed between early and later organizations, they shared similar mission statements. First, most organizations proclaimed charitable goals, providing assistance to orphans, widows, the aged, the destitute, and so forth. Second, the organizations sought to enhance the status of the Irish in America. This objective was usually accomplished by a variety of historic celebrations (for example, the promotion of St. Patrick, the patron saint of Ireland) and by efforts to redress prejudice and discrimination.

Early leaders of these organizations — some of whom were local political functionaries, newspaper publishers, clerics, or business owners — played an important mediating role between the ethnic community and the host society. They sought to reduce the level of animosity directed against Irish Catholics. At the same time they served as mentors for the rank-and-file immigrants, helping them see themselves not as Irish exiles in America, but as Irish Americans (Greene, 1987: 17–36).

One further type of voluntary organization that appeared in the 1840s had a somewhat different purpose: the workers' association. The American union movement was still in its formative stages, but the Irish involvement was pronounced. Although some of the early voluntary organizations were distinctly ethnic in character, the Irish also became involved in transethnic organizations. For example, they were prominently represented in the leadership of unions formed by tailors, iron mill workers, shoemakers, masons, waiters, stonecutters, dockworkers, and coal miners (Wittke, 1956: 216–218). This activity brought them into contact with native-born Americans and with other ethnic groups and served as a location for both cooperative ventures and for conflict.

The Catholic Church in America

The Irish immigrant entered a world that was overwhelmingly Protestant, but the Irish had a greater impact on American society in the area of religion than on any other area. The Irish dominated the development of Roman Catholicism in nineteenth-century America, and they were chief contributors to the leadership of the church. The first American bishop, John Carroll, was Irish. Native-born Americans and French Catholics also played a key role in the church hierarchy, but their relatively small numbers and their identification with Anglo American culture caused them to seek acceptance by the host society (Fallows, 1979: 129–131).

The character of American Catholicism changed after the famine years. The immigrants arriving after 1845 were poorer and more attached to a Catholicism that had a political character. Nationalism and religion had been linked to provide the immigrants with an ideological source of resistance to British rule. Catholicism was seen as a bulwark against absorption into the Anglo American mainstream. Although most immigrants understood the need to adapt to new circumstances — they had, after all, embarked upon a voluntary emigration, and the return rate for the Irish was, comparatively speaking, quite small — they sought to find ways to preserve elements of their religion and culture.

The number of Catholics rose fourfold in the decades between 1830 and 1860, exceeding three million by 1860. Although other groups counted for some of this growth, a majority of the church at this time was Irish. In the city of Philadelphia alone 23 new parishes were founded, almost all under Irish American sponsorship (Clark, 1977: 55–56). Furthermore, priests and nuns emigrated from Ireland to establish and maintain parishes and related religious institutions.

Though contemporaries from other groups also played a role in the expansion of a Catholic institutional presence, most notably the German Catholics, none was as powerful as the Irish. Theirs was a grassroots movement. They came to dominate the church from the bottom up. Although their control of the hierarchy didn't come until later in the nineteenth century, when non-Irish officials had either died or retired, by 1860 they were clearly going to dominate the church. This meant that Catholics arriving in large numbers from southern and eastern Europe, particularly Italians and Poles, confronted an Irish-dominated institution. The ultimate impact of Irish control was felt around the turn of the century.

While the Irish Catholic church leaders created a position for themselves in which they could be the arbiters of competing efforts to shape American Catholicism, they also saw themselves struggling against the forces of Protestantism's "righteous empire." To prevent their offspring from losing their attachment to their heritage the Irish Catholics established parochial schools at great financial cost, as alternatives to public schools. Public schools were seen as powerful forces promoting Americanization. The Irish were not opposed to Americanization per se. Rather, they sought to have a role in defining what was entailed in becoming an American. They believed that public schools were controlled by Protestant elites who were generally hostile to Catholicism and desirous of eradicating all traces of old world cultures, except the British. Thus, the Irish feared that the future of their religion and culture was at stake, and parochial schools could provide them with the ability to dictate the terms of Americanization for Irish immigrants.

Nativism

This defensiveness partly reflects the conservatism and traditional character of the immigrant heritage, but it also reflected the attitudes of the larger society. The Irish were the first among the voluntary mass immigrant groups to confront intense antipathy. Hostility occurred not only as individual prejudice and acts of discrimination, but also acquired an organizational presence through such anti-Irish groups as the Native American Party, the Order of United Americans, the Order of the Star-Spangled Banner, and the Know-Nothing or American Party.

Since the revolutionary era Americans had harbored ambivalent feelings about foreigners. Part of the national self-image that citizens embraced involved viewing their new republic as a safe refuge for those escaping from oppressive conditions in the old world. They were concerned, however, that recent arrivals were so different that they could not fit into the fabric of American society or, worse, that the new immigrants would degrade the quality of life. Nativism recurred in American life in somewhat cyclic fashion, seemingly prompted by changes in national confidence: optimism promoted toleration and acceptance, while a loss of confidence tended to generate xenophobia. Various kinds of internal stress could unleash actions predicated on fear and hatred (Jones, 1960: 147–148; Higham, 1970).

Given the impact of the Irish mass immigration in the 1840s, it was not entirely surprising that, as Philip Taylor (1971: 239) observed, "Opponents of immigration became vociferous in the second quarter of the nineteenth century." The Irish were not the only target, although they were recipients of the most intense and sustained nativist animosity. Anti-Irish agitation had three components. First, the Irish were viewed as a social problem. They were accused of being prone to alcoholism, brawling, and crime, and they were condemned for placing a heavy burden on charitable institutions due to their poverty. However overstated, there was obvious truth to these charges. The problem with such nativist complaints was that they failed to adequately analyze the social roots that had spawned such problems. Instead, the nativist engaged in a campaign of blaming the victim.

The second component was political. The swelling numbers of Irish in major cities combined with their tendency to engage readily in political activities fueled anxiety about their potential impact. The Irish were seen as ignorant people susceptible to manipulation by scheming political operatives. Their attachment to machine politics, with its fraud and violence, suggested to nativists that the Irish were not capable of becoming responsible citizens. The clearest indication of the pervasiveness of these attitudes can be seen in the success of the secretive Know-Nothing party, which managed to elect 6 governors and 64 members of Congress in the early 1850s, while controlling a number of state legislatures (Jones, 1960: 157; Dinnerstein, et al., 1990: 122). Part of the party's platform called for limiting political offices to the native born and extending to 21 years the period required for naturalization. Another aspect of political hostility could be seen among social reformers who viewed the Irish as an impediment to such causes as abolitionism, the women's movement, and temperance (Wittke, 1956: 116). These opinions were not without foundation because the Irish exhibited little sympathy for these political movements.

The third component was religious. Anti-Catholicism was directed at other groups as well, but as the Irish position in the church solidified, the Irish and Catholicism were closely identified. Hostility to Catholicism was partly political: The Catholic church was viewed as authoritarian and antidemocratic, and the Vatican's support of various oppressive regimes in Europe suggested to some that it posed a threat to political freedom (Jones, 1960: 148–149). Furthermore, charges were often made that the papacy was intent on extending its political influence in the United States.

Conspiratorial accusations were frequent and often voiced by prominent citizens. Samuel Morse, the inventor of the telegraph, published a polemical pamphlet, titled *A Foreign Conspiracy Against the Liberties of the United States*, directed at a Catholic mission society. The influential Protestant clergyman Lyman Beecher contended, in *A Plea for the West*, that Catholics were plotting to take control of the western United States by encouraging huge numbers of Catholic immigrants to settle on the frontier. Perhaps the most infamous of these inflammatory writings was Maria Monk's *Awful Disclosures of the Hotel Dieu Nunnery of Montreal*. Though subsequently discredited, Monk's sensationalist claims that the nunnery was rife with illicit sex between priests and nuns, and that the babies born from these encounters were murdered, were widely read and believed (McCaffrey, 1976: 93).

The combination of these components of anti-Irish animosity created a heightened potential for conflict. Interpersonal contact with Irish Catholics was avoided, so when they began to enter a neighborhood in significant numbers, established residents exited — an early instance of neighborhood succession in American cities. Attacks on Irish homes and Irish Catholic institutions occurred with regularity throughout the country, but perhaps the two most dramatic events were the 1834 burning of the Ursuline convent outside of Boston and the 1844 riot in Philadelphia.

Two final points must be made about anti-Irish prejudice and discrimination during this period. First, a common source of ethnic strife was absent: Hostility was not motivated by fear that the Irish posed a competitive threat to jobs. The economy in the country demanded a large-scale infusion of workers, so the Irish were not seen as displacing others from positions. Nor were the Irish accused of lowering the living standard of the American worker, perhaps because organized labor was too weak during this time to make such a claim.

Second, the Irish had a conflictual relationship not only with native Americans, but with many other immigrant groups, too. For example, the Germans and the Irish were often at odds with one another in spite of opportunities for a variety of cooperative activities. Though this became more troubled after the Civil War, the Irish encounter with African Americans already offered evidence of strain. Emanating from some groups, such as the Swedes, were echoes of nativist complaints. In endorsing nativism the Swedes made a status claim for themselves as a group that identified with the English-speaking Protestant establishment and was therefore worthy of acceptance by it (Ander, 1931).

Germans in America

The Germans arrived in the Americas during the colonial period, but under somewhat different circumstances than most other European sojourners. Germany did not become a unified nation state until 1871, so what we refer to as Germany was actually several autonomous principalities. As a result of this situation, there was no colonizing nation state encouraging settlement in the New World. The German immigrants, therefore, established themselves in colonies founded by the European colonial powers and, as a consequence, were an ethnic minority.

Settlement Patterns

Although Germans were found in the Dutch colony of New Amsterdam, the first distinctly German settlement in North America was Germantown, Pennsylvania, founded by Mennonites in 1683. Germans were attracted to Pennsylvania because of the religious tolerance that its founder, William Penn, made the hallmark of the colony. These early arrivals were followed later by other religious dissenters, Pietists, and various nonconformist groups including the Schwarzenau Brethren (commonly referred to as the Dunkers) and the United Brethren, or Moravians. The latter group, led by Count Nikolaus Ludwig von Zinzendorf, engaged in missionary work among the American Indians. Numerically, these groups were outnumbered by Lutherans, under the leadership of Heinrich Melchior Mühlenberg, and Reformed church members, who began arriving in the eighteenth century (Faust, vol. 1, 1909).

This early emigration took place chiefly among groups, rather than only individuals or families because so much emigration was prompted by a quest for religious freedom (Rippley, 1984: 29). Economic motives also played a part in pushing people out of Germany and into the American colonies. For example, in 1709 a sizeable migration occurred as people left the Palatinate, an area in southwestern Germany, to escape economic devastation brought about by overpopulation, the affects of the Thirty Years War, heavy taxation, and bad weather (Conzen, 1980: 407).

These immigrants were quite diverse economically. Few were very poor and most possessed at least limited skills. Some were actually rather well off economically, reflective of their flight to America being prompted primarily by religious and not economic concerns. These arrivals included various kinds of artisans and entrepreneurs. Most Germans, however, were farmers intent on acquiring land in America so they could continue as farmers.

German immigration continued unabated until the revolution, dropping after that to a near standstill due to warfare in both Europe and America. Though heavy German immigration did not revive for several decades, the Germans had established themselves as the largest non-British European group in colonial America. Although population estimates during this period were often imprecise, the first U.S. Census, in 1790, indicates that nearly 9 percent of the new nation's citizens had German background. Germans tended to locate on the borders of the frontier rather than along the coast, and in these less-populated regions their impact was pronounced. Pennsylvania's population was one-third German and was clearly the center of German settlement (U.S. Bureau of the Census, 1975).

The Germans developed a reputation as successful farmers, often capable of success where others had failed; they often bought land from English and Scotch-Irish farmers. The German's land was usually passed on to eldest sons, and younger sons were assisted in acquiring land on the western frontier. Thus, the Germans became an important force in the settlement of the Midwest, moving from Ohio to Nebraska in an effort to remain in farming. Early observers, such as Benjamin Rush, Benjamin Franklin, and J. Hector St. John de Crèvecoeur depicted them as practical, hard working, and thrifty. This assessment appears to have been widely held. The Germans not only proved to be efficient farmers but they also were innovators in the crops they planted and the methods they used. The Germans, in turn, developed somewhat negative images of British American farmers, who were, for instance, seen as careless in their farming methods (Billigmeier, 1974: 29–31).

The Early Ethnic Community

Germans generally lived in ethnic enclaves. Although some religious sectarians preferred to limit contact with outsiders, most immigrants were not opposed to living in close proximity to non-Germans. Germans were nevertheless criticized for their presumed tendency to be clannish and for their intense desire to preserve their culture. Franklin was not alone in voicing a fear that not only would German culture persist in areas of high concentration, but would also absorb British American culture (Billigmeier, 1974: 35). Nonetheless, because of their advantageous socioeconomic position and because they were willing to mingle with British Americans, the members of this first stage of German immigration assimilated quickly. Kathleen Conzen (1980: 409) reports that even in the heart of German America (the so-called Pennsylvania Dutch country) there was abundant evidence of the erosion of German culture. Names were Anglicized, the English language began to replace German in the economic realm and even in the churches, and intermarriage increased over time.

A distinctly German presence did not disappear, however, partly due to some Germans' efforts to maintain aspects of their traditional culture. The proliferation of German language newspapers (a reflection of the immigrants' high rate of literacy), the creation of organizations intent on raising ethnic consciousness, and the establishment of a system of parochial schools checked the assimilative trend.

Economic Immigrants

When new immigrants began to arrive after 1820, they found a German institutional presence already in place. These immigrants were less likely either to have been part of a group migration or to have emigrated for religious reasons. Religiously motivated emigration didn't cease: Orthodox Lutherans fled Prussia when the state mandated the merger of the Lutheran and Reformed churches. Pietists left in small numbers and founded utopian communities such as Harmony in Indiana and the Amana Society in Iowa. The motives of the vast majority, however, were chiefly economic, similar to those of other immigrants arriving at the same time.

Mass immigration began relatively slowly in the decade of the 1820s, when fewer than 6,000 Germans arrived. The number swelled to nearly 125,000 during the following decade. The decadal numbers continued to grow until the peak decade of the 1850s, when 976,072 immigrants arrived. Between 1820 and 1859, nearly 1.5 million German immigrants arrived in the United States. Moreover, during the three decades beginning with 1830, German immigration was 31.1 percent of total immigration (U.S. Bureau of the Census, 1975: 105).

Some of these new arrivals originated from the southwestern provinces that had contributed heavily to the colonial immigration (the Palatinate, Württemberg, and Baden). Other areas also became points of origin, with increased numbers from the north and east. After the 1850s, emigration levels from east of the Elbe increased dramatically. Although emigrants from the southwest continued to be primarily farmers, those from northcentral Germany were more likely to be urban artisans. The Germans from the east were predominantly day laborers and servants. As these occupational differences suggest, the later-arriving easterners were poorer than the earlier cohort.

A portion of the post-1820 population settled in the regions favored by those who preceded them. The vast majority, however, settled in the frontier communities in the midwestern United States. German communities emerged in the major cities of this region, and sizeable concentrations developed in Cincinnati, Detroit, Chicago, Milwaukee, and St. Louis (Conzen, 1976). Large German enclaves also sprang up in smaller cities in border states, such as Louisville and Memphis, as well as cities west of the Mississippi such as Davenport and Dubuque in Iowa and Omaha, Nebraska. Surrounding each of these urban settlements were Germans engaged in farming (Hawgood, 1940: 54–90). The only ethnic groups with a larger percentage of the immigrant population residing in a rural milieu were the Scandinavians.

Outside the Midwest, German communities developed in New Orleans, San Francisco, and various places in Texas, most prominently San Antonio and Austin. By choosing parts of the country that lacked the clearly defined and established elites of cities along the Atlantic coast, the Germans were able to play an active role in creating a regional identity. They achieved power and influence more rapidly than might otherwise have been the case.

Some immigrants left Germany for political reasons. Known as the "Forty-eighters," these were victims of the abortive revolutions that convulsed Europe in 1848. In German-speaking Europe, these revolts resulted in considerable bloodshed, especially in major cities such as Berlin and Vienna. Initiated by a loosely held together coalition of liberals and radicals of various strains and ranging from communists to anarchists, the uprisings were somewhat spontaneous attempts to overthrow reactionary and oppressive regimes. The battle cry echoed both the ideals of the American and French Revolutions, with core values centering on notions of liberty, equality, and fraternity. When the revolts were crushed, many Germans were forced into exile, among them several thousand Germans who fled to America. Though they were a very small part of the pre-Civil War mass migration, their impact was felt both within the German American community and, to a lesser extent, in the larger society as well (Wittke, 1952).

Intraethnic Conflict

The "Forty-eighters" were an intellectual stratum that was not only more politically radical, but also more politically outspoken than most of their fellow countrymen and countrywomen. These political émigrés' anticlericalism and secularism compounded tensions. Religious Germans, regardless of their form of religious expression, took offense at this Enlightenment-inspired challenge to the Christian faith.

Germany contained a complex array of political, religious, regional, and class differences. Given the immense size of the immigrant population, it is not surprising that virtually the full spectrum of differences could be observed in the United States. This ethnic community's deep internal divisions made it impossible to forge institutions that included members from every quarter. Instead, institutions reflected various ideological orientations and competed with other institutions for the allegiance of the immigrants (Conzen, 1980; 416).

The "Germantowns" or "little Germanies" provided immigrants with a transplanted version of the old world in the new. Mutual aid societies, dramatic associations, singing clubs, athletic associations, lodges and fraternal orders, and a variety of other organizations catered to this clientele. Restaurants, saloons, and cafes became vital places for socializing, and German-owned businesses provided the immigrants with goods and services that reminded customers of the homeland. The German language press offered a wide selection of newspapers, and each paper often catered to particular religious or political segments of the ethnic community. Attending to the cultural and social needs of its residents, the ethnic enclave was, to use Raymond Breton's (1964) term, "institutionally complete."

Religious divisions played perhaps the greatest role in preventing a unified community from arising. Within Protestantism, Lutherans had pronounced differences with Reformed churches and with the Pietist sects. The arrival of German Catholics further complicated the religious picture. The relationship between German Protestants and Catholics can be characterized as one of mutual antagonism. Catholics were forced to confront a nation in which anti-Catholicism was rising. Furthermore, they had to stake out a place in the American Catholic Church, and address the challenge posed by growing Irish domination.

Even within Lutheranism there were divisions, as the earliest arriving Lutherans had accommodated themselves to the American denominational scene and had come to identify in many ways with Episcopalians. Members of this branch of Lutheranism expressed a willingness to interact in an ecumenical fashion with other denominations from the nineteenth century into the twentieth. In contrast, many of those who arrived after the late 1830s were traditionalist Lutherans who had become disgruntled with ecumenical undertakings in Germany.

One of these groups settled in Missouri and, under the leadership of C.F.W. Walther, founded what became known as the Lutheran Church, Missouri Synod. The Missouri Synod Lutherans sought to protect themselves from theological positions at odds with their beliefs. They built their own churches, seminaries, colleges, and parochial schools rather than joining established Lutheran institutions. Although the overt rationale for this isolationism was religious, an unintended consequence was the maintenance of the German language and culture (Billigmeier, 1974: 57–60).

Besides religious differences, political divisions precluded German American unity and harmony. The Germans willingly engaged in the political controversies of the day, and they were especially vocal over the issue of slavery. Except for small pockets of German America in the southern slave-owning states, the German American community was overwhelmingly opposed to slavery. This did not, however, establish a basis for unity. Germans who had arrived prior to the Forty-eighters were often aligned with the Democratic Party because, in their opinion, it best advanced the Jeffersonian ideals of freedom and equality. They were not attracted to the Republican Party which they associated with nativism and with temperance advocates.

Unfortunately, the Democratic Party was also associated with pro-slavery forces, and this presence in the party caused an increasing amount of ambivalence, but not enough to cause the Germans to bolt to the Republicans. This part of German America became known as the "Grays." Challenging their position were the "Greens," primarily Forty-eighters, who joined ranks with the Republican party when it was founded in 1854. The Greens viewed the Grays as too hesitant and too moderate in their opposition to slavery, and the Greens urged more active involvement in the abolition movement (Rippley, 1984: 52–53).

These religious and political differences resulted in a system of parallel ethnic institutions, as "church" and "club" Germans competed with each other to forge a German American identity (Conzen, 1980: 416). Both were able to play off of the comparatively favorable stereotypes of Germans: industrious, efficient, innovative, and the like. The former, however, sought to meld such positive images with notions of Christian devotion and obedience, while the latter wanted to incorporate views related to rationalism and free-thinking.

In a country that was, as historian Jon Butler (1990) described, "awash in a sea of faith," religiously-inclined Germans were in a strategic position to advance their particular construction of German America and be assured it would be well received by the larger society. Indeed, some of the negative stereotypes that arose about the Germans centered on agnostic and atheistic tendencies. Linked to this was a condemnation of their political radicalism. In short, precisely those features of the Greens that served to distinguish them from their contemporaries helped to ensure that their version of German America would be less attractive to the host society.

Interethnic Encounters

German workers began to be involved in the embryonic trade union movement in the United States and in political activities. Those arriving in the wake of 1848 and later often brought with them a familiarity with, if not an explicit endorsement of, socialism and also practical experience in political activism. Because many were skilled workers, they proved to be a source of leadership in both leftist political organizations and the more militant trade unions. In this regard, the Germans were quite different from their Irish contemporaries, who as peasants and unskilled workers were far less likely to embrace socialism or the more radical versions of trade unionism.

On the eve of the Civil War the Germans were well positioned in the hierarchy of ethnic groups in America. Since the Scandinavians were all Protestant and were less inclined to be active in free-thinking, radical, or labor activities, their general image in the larger society was perhaps a bit more positive than that of the Germans. The Germans had a decided edge over the Irish, however, and their active involvement on the Union side in the war enhanced their position. Thus, during the immigration hiatus brought about by the war and attendant economic conditions, the Germans were poised to enhance their social status in America when mass migration resumed.

Summary

In this chapter we have seen that the quest for economic opportunity was a prime cause of the Atlantic migration of western

European immigrants between the colonial era and the Civil War. Many immigrants were also attracted to America by the promise of religious and political freedom. The British were by far the more numerous and the most powerful. In all areas of social life, they established themselves as the principal architects of the new nation—shaping its political institutions, developing and expanding its economy, and defining a national culture.

The two largest non-British groups to arrive during this period were the Irish and the Germans. The Irish had a long history of conflict with the British, and this spilled over into the New World. The Irish had relatively fewer resources than other immigrants and had a difficult time achieving economic security. They managed, however, to create a solid ethnic community to promote their interests in America, though in a setting of intense prejudice and discrimination. The Irish were the primary victims of anti-Catholic sentiments, and religious conflict continued well beyond the Civil War.

In contrast, the Germans advanced economically rather quickly because of the skills and economic resources that they brought with them. Germans had opportunities to assimilate into Anglo America, and many chose to do so. Others sought to preserve their heritages, and they used the ethnic community to achieve this. The Germans were more fortunate than the Irish because the British were more favorably disposed toward them. The Germans did not have to spend as much time and energy seeking acceptance and combating discrimination. They did have to deal with far more internal divisions in the ethnic community than did the Irish. Indeed, a variety of political, religious, regional, and economic differences characterized the German American community, and these differences often led to intraethnic tensions and conflicts.

Both of these groups shared one important thing with the British. They were white, and as the next chapter will amply indicate, they were all beneficiaries of their racial identity. Race proved to be the major factor contributing to differing levels of acceptance and success in America.

COERCIVE PLURALISM AND THE POLITICS OF EXCLUSION, 1492–1865

Race was increasingly used to differentiate those deemed qualified for inclusion into the fabric of the larger society from those considered unqualified. Thus, the indigenous population of the Americas, the involuntary migrants from Africa, and the voluntary immigrants from Asia and Latin America confronted far greater social barriers than did European immigrants.

In different ways these groups were either excluded from participation in the national economy or were prevented from occupying positions in preferred occupations. They were likewise stymied in their attempts to become involved in the political process. Sometimes citizenship was denied to them, and sometimes they found it difficult or impossible to vote and otherwise engage in political life. Historian Eric Foner (1990: 68) has argued that, "In effect, during the first half of the nineteenth century, race supplanted class as the line of division between men (women were denied the right to vote until the following century) who could vote and those who could not." Assessments of who would be accepted in other arenas of social and cultural life were similarly based on race.

Coercive Pluralism

Lawrence Fuchs (1990: 80–86) has referred to the nation's collective response to these groups as one that entailed various forms of "coercive pluralism." For American Indians, he described the form of pluralism as "predatory," by which he meant that the original occupants of the continent were defined as outsiders who, insofar as they stood in the way of European settlement, were to be pushed aside. The integrity of the American Indians' traditional ways of life was thoroughly disregarded.

In contrast, Africans confronted a system of "caste pluralism." Africans were forcibly brought into the country and consigned to a particularly oppressive place in the economic system (Fuchs, 1990: 87–109). In an otherwise class-based economy, which permitted individual mobility, Africans were relegated to a subordinate position based on race-specific ascriptive criteria. This meant that not only would Africans not experience individual upward mobility or intergenerational mobility, but also that they were severely circumscribed in every aspect of their lives by the white majority. Slavery was only one form of caste pluralism. Although caste pluralism defined the period up to the Civil War, the elimination of slavery did not spell the end of caste pluralism.

The third type of coercive pluralism Fuchs (1990: 110–127) defined was "sojourner pluralism," which characterized the situation of two particular groups in the antebellum period, Mexicans and Chinese, and later was applicable to other Hispanic and Asian groups. As the term suggests, these groups were perceived as temporary residents in the country, composed of individuals who wanted to come to America for a limited period of time to take advantage of economic opportunities. The expectation was that they would eventually return to their respective homelands. Whites were frequently ambivalent about the presence of these groups in America (Saxton, 1990). As a result these sojourners were not as oppressed and constricted as were the blacks. Mexicans and Chinese, however, were often seen as competitive threats to European-origin workers in the labor market, and thus were early victims of white working class racism (Roediger, 1991). Not surprisingly, early campaigns urging immigration restriction riveted on precisely these groups.

The historical experiences of these groups differed appreciably based on the differential consequences of these three types of pluralism. In this chapter we will discuss the early implications of these differences. When compared to the histories of the groups treated in the preceding chapter, we can appreciate the gulf that separated those inhabiting a world of "voluntary pluralism" (Fuchs, 1990: 69–75) from those forced into any of the three coercive pluralisms.

The First of This Land

The 500th anniversary of Christopher Columbus's voyage prompted renewed reflection on how we should interpret the encounter between European and American civilizations. Although some prefer to refer to the expedition's landing as a "discovery," others have suggested that more appropriate characterizations might be "invasion" or "conquest" (Sale, 1990; Heller, 1991). Clearly, each of these terms carries political and moral connotations. Some scholars have offered "encounter" as a less evaluatively charged term, but its very attempt to be neutral is an effort to underestimate the devastating impact that the arrival and settlement of Europeans had on Native American civilization.

We must be careful about generalizing about American Indian social organization because of limitations in anthropological knowledge and because of the diversity among tribes across the continent. For example, some tribes — including the Iroquois and the Pueblo — permitted only monogamous marriages, while others allowed men to have more than one wife. Nonetheless, some broad general statements can be made. Extended families were common, and especially with the death of a spouse, it was usually assumed that the dead person's family would care for the surviving spouse and children. Clans were organizations that linked kin members in even larger extended kinship networks. Associations performed many of the mutual aid activities characteristic of clans, but were not based on kinship. Moieties were tribe subdivisions similar in their social utility to clans or associations (Leacock and Oestreich, 1988).

Tribes refer to what might be seen as governmental units. They were often composed of a number of bands, the smallest such unit generally consisting of 25 to 250 members living in close proximity and operating as an economically interdependent unit. Individual membership in a band was often based on birth, a form of ascribed identity, but, for example, the Comanche tribal members could move from band to band "as their own best interest and personal obligations dictated" (Foster, 1991: 69). Bands chose their leaders from male elders who were considered to possess wisdom. These leaders served as members of tribal councils, and from their ranks an overall leader of a tribe — the chief — would be selected. In some instances, groups of tribes formed even larger units, referred to as federations — the most powerful of which was the Iroquois, composed of five northeastern tribes: the Mohawk, Onondaga, Oneida, Seneca, and Cayuga.

Contact with Europeans exhibited considerable variation, ranging from tranquillity and cooperation (some whites even opted to assimilate into tribal cultures) to duplicity, violence, exploitation, and extermination. In part, these variations were based on the proclivities of differing Native American tribes: some were warlike and others essentially peaceful; some had the power to resist outsiders while others were forced by necessity to accommodate to newcomers (McNickle, 1962).

Hernando De Soto's journey of 1539–1543 through what is now the southeastern United States resulted in some of the first encounters between the two civilizations, and in its course each of the varied kinds of contact previously noted could be witnessed. The Creek, for example, greeted De Soto's band peacefully, but the Spaniard's response was to take captives. His troops engaged in a fierce battle with the Choctaws. Some tribes, such as the Quapaws, sought to evade contact. Others, such as the Chickasaws, were hospitable, even permitting De Soto to spend a winter with them. When he demanded women and carriers to accompany him as the expedition resumed in the spring, however, the tribe reacted by killing several of his group and a number of his horses (Debo, 1970: 30–33).

Europeans differed in their general orientations toward the indigenous peoples they encountered. The French were perhaps the group that was, comparatively speaking, freest from racist attitudes and the least hostile. The Spanish were the most hostile and exhibited the most intense expressions of racism. The British and the Dutch manifested more varied and ambiguous responses.

Finally, the nature of Native American-European interaction was dictated by differing historically conditioned circumstances. Several periods of political and economic relationships linking American Indians and Europeans can be identified between the initial European contact with the Americans and the time by which competing European nations established permanent settlements in the new world. We will use the classificatory scheme of Stephan Cornell (1988: 12), who has identified six stages, two of which concern the period under discussion in this chapter. They are: (1) the market period, which persisted into the latter part of the eighteenth century; and (2) the conflict period, which ran from the end of the eighteenth century to the middle of the nineteenth or shortly past that time.

The Market Period (1600–1775)

During the earliest part of this period, European interests in the Americas were chiefly motivated by economic considerations, and political interests associated with permanent settlement overlaid the economic. The first period brought European mercantile interests into contact with new goods and raw materials. Native Americans were allowed to enter into relationships with European commercial interests. The fur trade, which was prompted by prosperity and fashion in Europe, was the glue that held American Indians and Europeans together (Bolt, 1987: 20–26).

In exchange for furs, Native Americans received European goods, including such practical items as blankets, woolen goods, cooking utensils, knives, axes, and firearms. They also obtained glass beads, alcohol, and tobacco. These items increasingly entered tribal life, where they replaced many more traditional goods and caused considerable change in the material culture (Jennings, 1976: 98–99). Goods such as firearms, metal implements, and woolens, made obsolete many items from the existing material culture, which was mainly based on stone, clay, wood, fiber, hides, and bone. When American Indians concluded that the Europeans had superior goods to trade, they quickly developed a demand for those goods and exhibited a willingness to substitute them for traditional items. Similarly, American Indians expanded their desires for non-utilitarian goods. Cornell (1988: 23–24) observed that although it is a mistake to view Native American cultures prior to European contact as static, the arrival of these settlers set off an unprecedented process of economic change. Thus, the American Indian population began to be incorporated into a European-centered world economic system (Wallerstein, 1974). Furthermore, since the economy was integrally linked to the rest of tribal society, the effects filtered throughout all facets of the society (Sahlins, 1972).

According to Cornell (1988: 12) this was a period of "willful Indian participation in the fur trade and [of] extensive Indian diplomatic efforts to exploit unusual political opportunities and maintain their own autonomy." European nations fiercely competed with their rivals, and they sought to elicit the support of different tribes. Similarly, many tribes played one European nation against another and frequently perceived other tribes as competitors. This became a complex and extremely fluid drama. For example, in the middle of the seventeenth century, the Dutch supplied the Mohawks with weapons that the Mohawks used against the Susquehannocks. The Dutch were motivated by a desire to wrest control of the Delaware River Valley from the small Swedish colony that had been established there in 1638 (Jennings, 1976: 23–25). For an extended period of rivalry, the French and English simultaneously sought to create alliances with the Iroquois Confederacy, and in the southeastern United States, three European nations — Britain, Spain, and France — did the same with the Choctaws, Chickasaws, and other tribes (Champagne, 1992).

During this period, warfare between Indians and Europeans broke out at some junctures, but the desire on both sides to establish trade links promoted diplomacy. The potential for conflict should not be underestimated. For example, in the Pequot War of 1637, the Pequots, located in the Connecticut River Valley, suffered a debilitating loss, which included 600 to 700 Indians being burned alive and countless others sold into slavery in the West Indies (Hauptman and Wherry, 1990). Overall, however, this period was characterized by something of a symbiotic relationship between Native Americans and Europeans.

The consequences of this encounter were profound. Traditional patterns of authority and social relations, including gender relations, often eroded and were transformed (Driver, 1969; John, 1988). The potential for increased tribal wealth set off increased tension with other tribes, who were seen as competitors. Inter-tribal warfare over control of the fur trade, for example, led to the near extermination of the Huron by the Iroquois in the middle of the seventeenth century. In addition, tribes increasingly neglected agriculture for hunting, thereby transforming a self-sufficient subsistence economy into one based on the dictates of the market. Ecological damage resulted as the exploitation of fur-bearing animals (the killing was expanded for trade rather than for consumption) over time jeopardized the basis for trade relations with Europeans (Cornell, 1988: 23).

In spite of this, political developments brought this period to an end. Specifically, the British triumph over their European counterparts undid the ability of American Indians to negotiate with various competing interests. The Treaty of Paris, signed in 1763, was a watershed event because it provided for British domination of all lands heretofore held by the French. If this was not sufficiently problematic, the fur trade served as a basis for permanent European settlements in which the Native Americans increasingly became superfluous, their hunting roles taken over by the offspring of immigrants. By the time the colonies freed themselves from British rule, a new era of relations between Indians and Americans was dawning.

The Conflict Period (1775–1850)

This period was defined by conflict over land. The primary factor generating this conflict was the increased demand for land by the citizens of the new republic. The Revolutionary War had placed a heavy strain on the new nation's treasury, and political leaders saw westward expansion as a way of alleviating these financial woes. The desire to push the U.S. boundaries toward the Pacific was shared by a wide range of the American citizenry, including farmers, land speculators, and entrepreneurs interested in exploiting new areas for their valuable raw materials. Furthermore, immigration began to grow and many of the newcomers believed that their chances for success were better if they settled somewhere other than the Atlantic seaboard. Increasingly, Native Americans were seen as being in the way, and a process of displacement began.

Europeans found an ideological justification for their policy of Indian removal from ancestral lands in the Manifest Destiny doctrine. In part, this term reflected the belief that the United States was destined to control the continent from the Atlantic to the Pacific. To some this meant incorporating Canada and Mexico into its ultimate boundaries. The concept was also based on the religious belief held since the Puritan period that the United States had a providential mission to tame the continent and Christianize it (Dinnerstein, et al., 1990: 87–89).

Roy Harvey Pearce argued in his study of white images of the American Indian, *Savagism and Civilization* (1967), that the American Indian was seen as religiously and morally incomplete and as an impediment to civilization. Although some Europeans — Catholics earlier than Protestants — saw it as their Christian duty to convert these nonbelievers, others were less sanguine about the prospects of "civilizing" them and sought merely to remove or eliminate the American Indians. For example, troops sent by George Washington to pacify the Iroquois uttered the following toast: "Civilization or death to all American savages." (Wax, 1971: 15 and 47–50).

The nineteenth-century writer Herman Melville captured what he referred to as "the metaphysics of Indian hating" in his novel *The Confidence Man* (1964 [1857]). In essence, the Indian hater infused hatred with morality; one could hate with a clear conscience. The reason for this rested with the notion of historical inevitability. The American Indian was doomed by the advance of civilization.

Ronald Takaki (1979: 80–107) observed that this "metaphysics" shaped the thought of many involved with what was the frontier of the United States in the early nineteenth century. It could be seen, for example, in the case of Lewis Cass. He was the governor of Michigan Territory for nearly two decades, after which he served as the Secretary of War. In an article published in the *North American Review* in 1827, Cass wrote on what he saw as the character and the fate of the American Indian: "He never attempts to imitate the arts of his civilized neighbors. His life passes away in a succession of listless indolence, and of vigorous exertion to provide for his animal wants, or to gratify his baleful passions . . . [H]e is perhaps destined to disappear with the forests . . . " (quoted in Takaki, 1979: 83).

This thinking was prominently displayed by Andrew Jackson, whose actions were especially important in expropriating Indian land. Jackson became U.S. President as the champion of common folk, an egalitarian democrat. Yet his political rise was based in no small part on his vicious campaigns against Native Americans. Jackson first came into national prominence as the commander of troops in the Creek War of 1813–1814, during which time he characterized the American Indians as "savage bloodhounds," "blood-thirsty barbarians," and "cannibals" (Takaki, 1979: 95–96).

During the decades leading up to his presidency, open conflict and warfare escalated. Although some tribes accommodated defeat in a manner that permitted remaining on traditional lands, a series of Indian wars ensued. Until recently scholars have studied these conflicts from the perspective of Europeans and Americans. Even when sympathetic to the Native Americans, scholars have not explored what wars with colonialists and Americans meant to these people, how they understood their situation, and what they hoped to accomplish.

Scholars are now beginning to redress this lack of attention. Joel Martin (1991) examined the events leading up to the 1814 Battle of Horseshoe Bend, in which Muskogees engaged in what he refers to as a "sacred revolt." Similarly, Gregory Evans Dowd (1991) explored the role of militant Indians and prophets in prompting a "spirited resistance" by four major Indian nations, Delaware, Shawnee, Cherokee, and Creek. In both accounts, religion proves crucial to providing a rationale for resisting the threat that outsiders posed to the American Indian's way of life.

The most violent wars pitted Americans against two formidable tribal confederations: the Iroquois in the Northeast and the Creek in the Southeast. The campaign against the American Indians was intended to remove any who were perceived to be in the way of westward expansion.

Relocation Policies

During Jackson's presidency, this process led to the forced relocation of a number of tribes in the eastern United States, including Cherokees, Seminoles, Ottawas, Potawatomis, Shawnees, Kickapoo, Delaware, Peorias, Miamis, and the Sauk and Fox. As early as the Louisiana Purchase in 1803, the possibility of exchanging Indian lands in the eastern part of the country for land west of the Mississippi had been contemplated.

In continuity with British law, the Americans proceeded with a view that recognized the right of Native American ownership. For the Cherokee, a series of 13 treaties extending from 1721 to 1798 resulted in the loss of about 82,000 square miles of tribal lands (Thornton, 1990: 41). Although in practice treaty rights were often not considered, such violations were in defiance of the law. Thus, governmental policy had to consider the law in establishing policies that effectively removed Indians from their lands. What cannot be underestimated was the inordinate amount of pressure placed on Native Indians, combined with interference in the internal affairs of tribes, that was designed to encourage relocation.

This was especially evident when the Five Civilized Tribes — Cherokees, Choctaws, Chickasaws, Creeks, and Seminoles — resisted removal efforts. In defiance of the treaties these tribes signed with the federal government, the states of Georgia, Alabama, and

Mississippi asserted their legal right to incorporate these tribes into their legal jurisdictions. When the tribes appealed to President Jackson, he turned a deaf ear and sided with the states. Even when these actions were voided by two Supreme Court rulings — *Cherokee Nation v. Georgia* in 1831 and *Worcester v. Georgia* in 1832 — the pressure did not end (Cornell, 1988: 45–50). The ultimate outcome is vividly illustrated by the Cherokee, who finally moved to what is now Oklahoma in a wrenching migration of misery, starvation, and death that became known as the "Trail of Tears."

During this time the status of the American Indians was uncertain. They were neither citizens or aliens. They were neither persons or slaves. Murray Wax (1971: 47) made the interesting observation that since the late eighteenth century American Indian affairs had been under the purview of the War Department. He noted that had their affairs been located in the Commerce Department, Native Americans would have been seen as a purely domestic issue. On the other hand, had they been located in the State Department, Indian tribes would have been defined as sovereign foreign nations. The choice of the War Department reflected the ambivalence of the situation: it "implied that, in the last analysis, the relations were those of control and subjugation of peoples [within the boundaries of the United States but] outside of the frame of the Union" (Wax, 1971: 47).

This situation did not mean that the United States government refused to enter into treaties with tribes. The government did so without explicitly recognizing the tribes as independent nations, although treaties by definition are transacted between autonomous nations. Congress ended this activity in 1871, but it was common practice during the late eighteenth and first half of the nineteenth centuries, reflecting the considerable uncertainty about the Indian's place in American society.

In one of the first sympathetic accounts of Native Americans written by a white person, Helen Hunt Jackson (1881) aptly characterized this period as "a century of dishonor." Cornell (1988: 45 and 50) described the period as the Indian's "descent into powerlessness," and claimed that by the end of the Civil War "the Indians were rapidly disappearing as major actors on the intergroup stage." This set the stage for the reservation system — an institution in which Native Americans were defined as wards of the nation — already in evidence since mid-century.

Beyond the Middle Passage

The institution of slavery decisively shaped the lives of all Africans in the United States, free persons as well as slaves (Berlin, 1974; Williams, 1990). Slavery was by no means unique to the United States, or to western civilization. Indeed, it has been practiced in virtually every part of the world, including Africa. Wherever slavery has taken institutional form, it has operated in similar ways. Slavery has been succinctly and accurately defined by sociologist Orlando Patterson (1982: 334–342) as "human parasitism." The motivation behind slavery is to subjugate another person or persons. The reasons behind such practices vary, but usually entail an economic impetus to get others to do burdensome work at minimal cost, status considerations, and sometimes political factors. Slavery operates through a process of systematic degradation of the slave, who by being reduced to property owned by another, experiences what Patterson (1982) refers to as "social death."

African slaves were imported into the Americas from the seventeenth century on, where, as Figure 5.1 reveals, most ended up in the Caribbean and South America. All of the principal European colonizing nations engaged in the slave trade, and in British North America slaves were found along the entire Atlantic coastal area, in urban centers as well as in rural sections. In colonial America, as with the rest of the western hemisphere, slavery was practiced for decidedly economic reasons: slavery provided an abundant source of cheap labor.

Africans, by being violently uprooted from their homelands, were controlled by slaveholders far more readily than other groups would have been. Thus, Native Americans were not enslaved in large numbers because their familiarity with the environment meant that escape and return to their tribe was a distinct possibility. Africans had nowhere to go in America (Stampp, 1956: 23; Fredrickson, 1981: 58).

The irony of the existence of slavery is most evident with Thomas Jefferson. As David Brion Davis (1966: 3) wrote, "Americans have often been embarrassed when reminded that the Declaration of Independence was written by a slaveholder" and that slavery was practiced in all thirteen colonies prior to the American Revolution. Although powerful ideological justifications for slavery existed, many slaveholders felt guilty or morally

Figure 5.1 *Destination of the Atlantic slave trade, 1701–1810.*

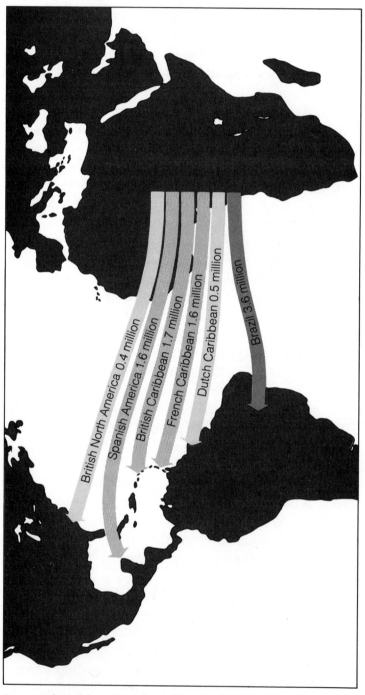

Source: Adapted from *The Atlantic Slave Trade*, Philip D. Curtin, The University of Wisconsin Press, 1969: 215. Reprinted by permission.

ambivalent about owning slaves while espousing republican ideals of government.

Why were Africans singled out for slavery? A number of rationalizations have been offered by apologists for the practice of slavery, including the argument that the southern climate demanded Africans since Europeans could not survive as laborers in that environment. George Fredrickson (1981: 79) contends that racial prejudice is not the primary cause of slavery; rather economic considerations are the primary causal agents. The planter class in the southern states determined that it was economically advantageous to use slave labor rather than indentured servants or wage laborers. Race prejudice justified slavery, but did not produce it.

The Ideology of Racism

Two intertwined features of the ideology of racism involved the claim that Africans were intellectually inferior and were barbarians incapable of becoming civilized on their own. This latter aspect derives from deeply rooted images that link blackness to evil in Judeo-Christian thought (Jordon, 1968; Wood, 1990). Thus, the ideology of race characterized the African as the eternal "other," standing outside of and being fundamentally hostile to civilization. A modified version of this thesis viewed African cultures as simple and primitive, incapable of contributing to the construction of major historical civilizations (see Bernal, 1987, for a powerful critique of this view).

This expression of race ideology linked the notion of savage to that of child and served as a basis for claiming that blacks were forever in need of parental guidance and discipline. The image of the savage implied unbridled sexuality. The image of the child conveyed a powerful anti-black stereotype that involved such negative traits as immaturity, laziness, irresponsibility, and moral underdevelopment. This last mentioned trait was often associated with the belief in the criminal tendencies of blacks (Takaki, 1979: 109–128).

This stereotype justified a caste system in a society otherwise defined in class terms. For individuals of African descent, unlike other migrants who found niches in the American economy, there was no possibility for upward mobility or individual advancement. Instead, the entire race was consigned to a subservient place in not only the economy, but the society at large. The ideology advanced the belief that not only were blacks incapable of success at anything other than menial labor, but also that they were unfit for citizenship.

Politicians and civic leaders in the South offered powerful ideological rationales to protect the slave system from the challenges posed by those opposed to it as well as by those ambivalent about its existence. Perhaps the most sophisticated were those articulated by two southern slavocrats, Henry Hughes and George Fitzhugh, who invoked the newly-emerging discipline of sociology for their respective theses. In 1854 Hughes published his *Treatise on Sociology*, while Fitzhugh's work was titled "Sociology for the South." Both works were designed to establish an intellectual justification for slavery. In other words, these writers viewed slavery as both morally and politically good; they saw it as essential for the preservation of morality and social order.

Hughes, influenced by the writings of Auguste Comte and the utopian writer Charles Fourier, defined his understanding of slavery as "warranteeism." The subordination of Africans was necessary, in his view, for two reasons. First, he feared the mixing of the races that he believed would result if blacks were released from the confines of the plantation. Second, he thought that treating them as equals would undermine the stability of southern society and wreak havoc on the region, to the detriment of all — whites and blacks, alike.

This particular assertion made his claims distinctive from many other slavocrats. He saw warranteeism as beneficial to slaves. This rather startling conclusion was based on the conviction that freedom was a poor basis for organizing society. In Hughes's assessment, the wage laborers in the northern states, especially the poor and oppressed recent immigrants who were subject to market fluctuations and the political power of industrial capitalists, inhabited a far more precarious world than did the slave. Although wage laborers confronted unemployment due to economic conditions or illnesses and injuries, anxiety regarding affordable housing, the fear of an impoverished old-age, and related uncertainties, the slaves lived with the certainty that their physical needs were taken care of from cradle to grave.

With this conviction, Hughes (1854: 292) concluded his *Treatise* in glowing fashion:

Then, in the plump flush of full-feeding health, the happy warrantees [that is, the slaves] shall banquet in PLANTATION-REFECTORIES; worship in PLANTATION-CHAPELS; learn in PLANTATION-SCHOOLS; or in PLANTATION-SALOONS, in the cool of the evening chant old songs, tell tales, . . . and after slumbers in PLANTATION-DORMITORIES, over whose gates Health and Rest sit smiling at the feet of Wealth and Labor, . . . [here] shall be the fulfillment of Warranteeism.

Of course, the reality of slavery was far different from this ideological portrait. Nonetheless, this portrait of a *Gemeinschaft* world in which owners and slaves engaged in a system of reciprocity where owners not only had rights but obligations, and slaves could find contentment on the plantation, had a profound impact on racial thought well into this century. We see a version of this world-view articulated in Margaret Mitchell's best selling novel, *Gone With the Wind*. This genre of literature, written after the Civil War, has been dubbed the "moonlight and magnolia" school, a romanticized portrait of the antebellum South produced by apologists for the "lost cause."

Slavery and the Plantation

Slavery has been described by historian Kenneth Stampp (1956) as "the peculiar institution"— despotism in a country that defined itself as democratic. Though slavery was practiced in northern states, and though urban slavery existed in both the North and the South, slavery is most intimately associated with the plantations of the South. Whites in the antebellum South can be divided into four major categories: the planter class, the independent yeoman farmer, the middle class (business people, professionals, artisans, and so on), and poor whites who worked as wage laborers or tenant farmers. The yeoman farmers constituted more than half of the white southern population. The vast majority of white southerners, including the typical yeoman farmer, did not own slaves. Who, then, were the slaveowners? Almost three-quarters of slaveowners were relatively small farmers who owned less than 10 slaves. Only three thousand families throughout the South owned more than one hundred slaves (Stampp, 1956: 30–31).

Slaves were concentrated in relatively large agricultural units. The majority lived on plantations containing more than 20 slaves.

As Stampp (1956: 31) wrote, "That the majority of slaves belonged to members of the planter class, and not to those who operated small farms with a single slave family, is a fact of crucial importance concerning the nature of bondage in the ante-bellum [sic] South." In short, slavery and the plantation were integrally connected.

The plantation can be seen as an instance of Erving Goffman's (1961) "total institution." Goffman used the term in *Asylums* to describe a mental hospital he had studied, but saw it as an apt characterization of a variety of similar institutions ranging from prisons to monasteries. Such institutions circumscribe the entire life of individuals who are part of them: they work, play, eat, and sleep in the institutions. Furthermore, the subordinate members of such institutions are forced to undergo rituals of incorporation into the institution that are intended to sever their connections with their pasts — rituals appropriately characterized as "degradation ceremonies." Individuals in these institutions are the recipients of discipline and authority designed to ensure that they do not challenge their subordinate status (Goffman, 1961; Foucault, 1979). For historian Stanley Elkins (1959), the Nazi concentration camp served as an analogy to the plantation.

The peculiarity of the plantation was that it operated internally as a "total institution" while being part of an international economic system. The Industrial Revolution in England, for example, would not have been possible without the availability of cotton (Hobsbawm, 1969) so the emergence of modern capitalism was connected to a noncapitalist form of labor exploitation — slavery. "In this essential respect, the Old South emerged as a bastard child of merchant capital and developed as a noncapitalist society increasingly antagonistic to, but inseparable from, the bourgeois world that sired it" (Fox-Genovese and Genovese, 1983: 5).

The planter class occupied an ambiguous place between two worlds, feudal and capitalist. The cultural trappings of the planters (recall the discussion in Chapter 4 on the cavaliers) were more reminiscent of the feudal world than that of modern capitalism and were based on a social order that increasingly pitted the bourgeoisie against wage-labor. Slavery's goal was to generate profit in the world market, so the planters had to conduct themselves as rational, calculating business persons (Genovese, 1969).

Although the state functioned as a prop to defend slavery, southern slavery was distinctively a private institution. Public democracy served as a bulwark to protect private despotism. The color line dividing blacks and whites differentiated the realms of democracy and despotism. As William Freehling (1986: 26) described it:

> Two colors, two abilities, two regimes, with nothing in between. Alas, the in-between condition intruded. Mulattoes were sometimes born. Blacks were sometimes freed. Whites were sometimes stupid. Slaves were sometimes brilliant. Democratic and despotic suppositions were sometimes inseparable. Schizophrenic confusion often returned.

The Origins of an African American Culture

Within these oppressive conditions Africans constructed a community. As did other migratory peoples, they used aspects of their ancestral cultures. The problem for Africans was that the involuntary character of their migration, combined with slaveholders's efforts to repress expressions of African culture, resulted in a greater degree of uprooting than was the case for voluntary migrants. Furthermore, unlike most other groups, Africans were not able to maintain communication links to the homeland.

Some scholars have concluded that African Americans had their pasts thoroughly eradicated, thereby making them simply and totally the products of their American experience. This was Robert E. Park's opinion. His student, the African American sociologist E. Franklin Frazier (1963: 23), summarized this position when he argued "because of the manner in which Negroes were captured in Africa and enslaved, they were practically stripped of their social heritage."

This conclusion was challenged by anthropologist Melville J. Herskovits in his trailblazing study, *The Myth of the Negro Past* (1941). He argued that he had discovered remnants of African culture in the Americas and specifically in the United States in a number of relatively isolated enclaves in coastal regions of South Carolina, Georgia, and Florida. The most well-known is the Gullah community on coastal islands off the South Carolina mainland, where linguistic, religious, and artistic evidence of Africanisms is apparent (Creel, 1988).

Although Herskovits rebuts the view that all vestiges of African culture disappeared in America, subsequent research indicates that Africans lost far more of their ancestral culture than did voluntary immigrants. The extent to which Africanisms survived is testimony to the ability of those cultures to address the hardship confronted by the slave community as well as the tenacity of slaves in their attempt to hang on to aspects of their past despite intense repression and acute social disruption and deprivation (Holloway, 1990).

Lawrence W. Levine (1977) has gone beyond the Frazier-Herskovits debate to argue that what should be explored are not African survivals, but rather how African culture was transformed by its interaction with the culture of white southerners. Particularly important to him are the many and complex ways in which slaves sought to subvert or to resist oppression and exploitation. For example, Levine found that the trickster in African myths was also a common feature of slave tales. Depicted in stories in divine, human, or animal guise, the trickster succeeded in a contest of wills against those more powerful by using deceit and cunning. Slaves became tricksters as they sought to practice the frequently-repeated aphorism, "White folks do as they pleases, and the darkies do as they can." Reports from the era indicate the prevalence of slaves who "lied, cheated, stole, feigned illness, loafed, pretended to misunderstand the orders they were given," and did damage to the masters' property, crops, and livestock (Levine, 1977: 122).

These expressions of discontent reinforced the slaveowner's view of Africans as "a troublesome property" and served as an inducement "to make them stand in fear" (Stampp, 1956: 86–191). Indeed, the Sambo stereotype cast the slave as fundamentally infantile and therefore in need of stern "parental" control (Elkins, 1959: 81–89).

Moreover, such modes of resistance did not challenge the status quo by articulating an ideology of liberation. Many scholars have recently acknowledged that the quest for freedom — individual and collective — was powerfully expressed by slaves and was fueled chiefly by religion. The Africans' desire for liberation en masse had begun early as members of different African tribes quickly came to see their fates intricately intertwined. The horror encountered on the slave ships was so profound that these vessels are appropriately seen as the first "incubators of slave unity across cultural lines" (Stuckey, 1987: 3).

Though slaveowners sought to inculcate a Christianity designed to convince the slaves that they should accept their fate on earth and concentrate on heavenly reward — encouraging slaves to be docile, obedient, and respectful — slaves found a message of freedom in this religion. Actually, the slaves' religious expression was a mixture of African religious tradition and Christianity. Scholars continue to debate the relative importance of Protestant Christianity and African religions in this syncretistic religious expression (Blassingame, 1972; Genovese, 1972; Levine, 1977; Lincoln and Mamiya, 1990).

Out of this mutual influence of African folk religion and Christianity emerged a rhetoric of resistance to racial oppression. Christianity proclaimed a message of salvation that provided a rationale for activist involvement in political and social struggles for liberation. Perhaps the most important feature of African folk religion in shaping the religious character of the slave community was its emphasis on a communal rather than an individual orientation. African American religion was exceedingly complex and ambiguous, as various tensions persisted between what Lincoln and Mamiya (1990: 10–16) refer to as dialectical poles, including other-worldly versus this-worldly; communal versus privatistic; and resistance versus accommodation.

The Community of Slaves

Slaves were not able to construct an institutional community similar to those created by voluntary immigrant groups. Slaves could not establish mutual benefit societies, fraternal organizations, businesses, political associations, and the like. So it is not surprising that one central institution stood out as crucially significant in defining the slave community: the family. Unfortunately, our understanding of the slave family is limited and subject to considerable controversy because the African American has too often been reduced to what was referred to earlier as "historical invisibility."

Slaves were not free to enter into marriages in the manner of free whites; rather, such unions either required the consent of slaveowners or were actually arranged by them. Robert Staples (1988: 304) reports many instances in which young women, upon reaching puberty, were forced into marriage. The reason for this was economic, namely the slaveowners' desire to breed a new generation of plantation laborers.

Furthermore, since slaves could be sold at will, marriage unions could be dissolved by the owner. The extent to which this practice of separating family units at the slave trading block was actually employed is uncertain. Historians Eugene Genovese (1972) and Herbert Gutman (1976) saw this as a relatively infrequent occurrence, although they understood that its very possibility generated uncertainty and anxiety in slaves. John Blassingame (1972: 91), however, believes the practice to have been very common and estimates that perhaps as many as one-third of all marriage unions were terminated by the sale of one of the partners. Since no consensus has emerged among scholars about the respective merits of these two positions, it is difficult to know the extent to which the typical African family that emerged from slavery was or was not a stable, dual parent nuclear family (Fogel, 1989: 451).

A lack of clarity about gender roles and the respective impacts of African culture versus the conditions imposed by servitude also affected Africans' family lives. What was clear to early students of African America, such as W.E.B. Du Bois (1970 [1909]) and E. Franklin Frazier (1939), was that the illegitimacy rate for blacks in the post-Civil War period was much higher than the white rate. Both attributed this situation to the demoralization brought about by slavery. Frazier further talked about what he saw as a dual family structure in the African American community: male-headed families and female-headed households. In his view, this division was the consequence of "widespread illegitimacy" (Frazier, 1939: 483).

The prominent role of women as the heads of households in many African American families, and the difficulties in sustaining dual parent families has been duly noted by Blassingame (1972: 78), but he finds evidence that indicates that Africans placed a high value on family stability. Furthermore, the family "was in actuality one of the most important survival mechanisms for the slave."

However different in form from white families and from the families of free Africans, the slave family managed many of the usual functions, especially those associated with child-rearing. Blassingame (1972: 79) writes that because slave parents were chiefly responsible for raising their children, "they could cushion the shock of bondage for them, help them to understand their situation, teach them values different from those their masters tried to instill in them, and give them a referent for self-esteem other than their master."

One persistent challenge to the integrity of the family and to monogamous relationships was the sexual exploitation of African women by whites. The African man, whether he was a husband or not, was powerless to ward off the advances of the master or his sons or employees. Doing so would put the slave's life at risk, which instilled in him a profound sense of powerlessness (Blassingame, 1972: 88). The slaveowner's power was not confined to the sexual realm, but also shaped all facets of slave life. Both kind and cruel masters sought to perpetuate the subordination of their slaves. The former did so by attempting to elicit consent and compliance, while the latter did so by instilling fear and by punishment.

Slaves did not simply accept this fate as inevitable or as deserved—in other words, they did not resemble Elkin's (1959) characterization of them as reduced to "infantile dependence." This can be seen in several ways. First, the tricksterism previously noted suggests a form of resistance. Second, many slaves ran away. Although most did so without plans or a desire to leave friends and families forever, those who "decided to follow the North Star to freedom faced almost insurmountable obstacles" (Blassingame, 1972: 110). Though most runaways were ultimately caught and punished, some managed to get either to northern states that had abolished slavery or found refuge in various backwater regions. Third, slaves revolted or engaged in conspiracies designed to overthrow the oppressors.

Slave Revolts

Herbert Aptheker (1943) provided the first attempt to assess the prevalence of slave revolts, and in this benchmark work he contended that more than two hundred revolts occurred during the era of legal slavery. Subsequent scholarship has questioned that number, but clearly slaves were willing to revolt and a number of major rebellions or conspiracies occurred (Genovese, 1972; Genovese, 1979). Slaves in the United States did not manage to mount the large-sized challenges to slavocracies that occurred in various places in the Caribbean and Latin America, but the failure had less to do with the slaves's inclinations to revolt than with their lack of ability to gather the resources that made insurrections possible. The largest revolt in the United States occurred in Louisiana in 1811, and it involved between 300 and 500 slaves — a relatively modest figure compared with the numbers involved elsewhere in the Americas (Genovese, 1972: 588).

Three of the most well-known challenges to slavery were those led by Gabriel Prosser in 1800, Denmark Vesey in 1822, and Nat Turner in 1831. In addition, there was the attack on the Harpers Ferry arsenal by John Brown, a white man with apocalyptic visions. The first two were aborted conspiracies; the second was led by a former slave who had managed to obtain his freedom. Nat Turner's rebellion was a bloody affair involving about 70 slaves. One feature of these revolts was that religion was linked to a keen sense of the meaning of freedom as it emanated from Enlightenment political thought. Slaves took seriously the goals expressed in the Declaration of Independence (Patterson, 1991). As Genovese (1979: 45) writes, "Each [of the major revolt leaders] projected an interpretation of Christianity that stressed the God-given right to freedom as a fundamental doctrine of obligation underlying a political vision that itself reflected the new ideologies of the Age of Revolution."

Although all revolts failed, they reflected the desire of slaves to be free and revealed the fear of revolt felt by slaveowners. Every aborted or failed insurrection was met with renewed repression. Religion's role in challenges to the legitimacy of slavery was sufficiently pronounced that after Turner's revolt, free Africans were either forbidden by law to preach to slaves or were forced to register and preach under the surveillance of whites (Genovese, 1972: 257). As the early historian of the American South, and an apologist for slavery, Ulrich B. Phillips (1918) concluded, white southerners had considerable anxiety about the potential for violent slave uprisings. Nonetheless, slavery did not cease to exist because of the slaves' efforts alone.

These three insurrectionary leaders reflect the African American community's diversity in the antebellum era and describe their position in the society at large. In the first place, as Prosser, a blacksmith, and Turner, a jack-of-all-trades and an "exhorter," indicate, there was considerable internal differentiation in the slave community. One major division on the plantation was between house slaves and field hands — the former had far more contact with whites and often developed a social distance from laborers. Many slaves were artisans or skilled tradespersons and often functioned as leaders (not unlike their class counterparts in the urban white working class). Furthermore, there was a substantial number of urban slaves, most of whom were domestic servants.

Free Persons of Color

Moreover, not all Africans were slaves. At the onset of the Civil War, a half million "free persons of color" lived in the United States (Berlin, 1974). Some were descendants of the earliest African arrivals in America, who had been defined as indentured servants rather than slaves and had worked through their indentured period and become free. Others, like Vesey, managed to become free in their own lifetimes. In most instances this was due to the abolishment of slavery in northern states or to the manumission of slaves by individuals who could no longer live with the incongruity of democratic ideals and despotic practices. For example, the Quakers made a collective decision after the American Revolution to uphold the ideals of the new nation by freeing their slaves (Sowell, 1981a: 195). Many slaveowners, torn by what they perceived to be economic necessity and morality, chose to manumit their slaves on their deathbeds.

Free Africans found employment in cities; many possessed craft and artisanal skills, but others worked chiefly as unskilled laborers. They differed from slaves in many ways. For instance, although no more than two percent of slaves could read, most free persons of color were literate (Woodson, 1968: 227–228). Free Africans were often racially mixed. They were not accepted by white society, but they often sought to distance themselves from the mass of Africans. They lived, as Adele Logan Alexander (1991) has written of the free women of color who were her ancestors, "ambiguous lives." They sought to emulate the mores of white society and to distance themselves from the world of the slaves. This did not prevent some mulattoes from owning slaves, however.

One parallel with other immigrant groups was the creation of voluntary ethnic institutions "as a means of coping with the difficulties that plagued their lives" (Greenbaum, 1991: 95). One of the earliest examples of a mutual aid society was the Free African Society, established in 1778 in Philadelphia. Soon thereafter the

Prince Hall Masonic Lodge was founded in Boston, as was the African Union Society in Newport, Rhode Island. Similar undertakings were seen in the South during the early part of the nineteenth century.

Under financed and in some instances (especially in the South) operating in secret, most of these organizations were relatively short-lived. Nonetheless, some managed to survive throughout the antebellum era, and where failures occurred, there were repeated efforts to forge new organizations. Because their resources were more limited than their white counterparts, African voluntary organizations were primarily local in nature. Though there were few successful efforts to establish regional or national umbrella organizations (Johnson, 1934; Babchuk and Thompson, 1962), some of these organizations became the basis for later commercial ventures, such as the Atlanta Life Insurance Company (Greenbaum, 1991: 105).

External Challenges to the Peculiar Institution

Slavery cast a powerful shadow over free Africans' lives, even if they resided in antislavery northern states (Pinkney, 1987: 13–15). There were forces in the larger society urging the abolition of slavery, however. Opponents of slavery in European America were heard prior to the American Revolution, but the ideology of the revolution itself served as a powerful stimulus to abolitionism. As Gary Nash (1990: 25) suggested, "the revolutionary generation drank deeply from the wells of antislavery ideology," but their abolitionist efforts in the years just after the revolution failed to put an end to the "peculiar institution."

During the nineteenth century the abolitionist movement continued to challenge the slavocracy. Throughout the northern states slavery was progressively abolished. In 1807, further slave importation was prohibited by federal law (Du Bois, 1969 [1896]) — a fact that did not in actuality stop the illicit slave importation until the very eve of the Civil War. As new states became part of the union, a political conflict ensued over whether they should be free or slave states.

In this context, the Underground Railroad was a sophisticated and well-financed operation that defied the Fugitive Slave Law (which granted slaveowners the right to repossess slaves who had fled to freedom in the North) and may have assisted as many as 100,000 Africans escape from involuntary servitude (Franklin, 1967; 253–260). The Abolitionist Movement gained in militancy with the ascendance of such powerful leaders as William Lloyd Garrison and the important black abolitionist, David Walker (Stuckey, 1987: 98–137).

The leading spokesperson for African Americans in the nineteenth century was Frederick Douglass. Born into slavery, Douglass fled to the North, where he became prominent in abolitionist circles. He was active on the lecture circuit, published the antislavery newspaper *North Star*, and wrote his autobiography which provided a compelling account of the degradation inherent in involuntary servitude. Douglass keenly understood that eliminating slavery would not end the problems Africans confronted. He spoke out against discrimination in the North: the preferential treatment given to immigrants in the job market at the expense of black workers, segregated institutions, and the petty injustices that free people of color confronted daily (Huggins, 1980). Nonetheless, he believed that none of these problems could be adequately addressed until slavery had been outlawed.

Historians continue to debate the factors that finally resulted in the end of slavery. Particularly important to the debate is the question of whether or not slavery was profitable. Eugene Genovese (1972) viewed slavery as inefficient and thought that plantation owners tended to exhaust the soil, compelling a perpetual quest for new land. In addition, he saw slaveowners as essentially precapitalist, antibourgeois aristocrats willing to subjugate profit to honor, luxury, and leisure.

Economic historians Robert W. Fogel and Stanley L. Engerman (1974), employing the sophisticated quantitative methods of cliometricians, presented a powerful argument that suggests slavery was highly profitable, and not moribund, prior to the Civil War. Indeed, they considered the plantation economies, due to economies of scale and the intensive utilization of cheap labor, to have been more profitable than northern agriculture. Their findings imply that the institution of slavery did not end because of economic shortcomings. Rather, the reasons must be sought in the political and social realms (compare, Smith, 1987; Lyman, 1991). This will be seen more clearly in Chapter 6, when the history of emancipation is addressed.

The Politics of Conquest

Mexicans were incorporated into the United States as the nation pushed its borders westward, so the initial population was not composed of voluntary immigrants. Actually, the indigenous peoples of what became Mexico confronted two different conquests. The first was the Spanish invasion in the sixteenth century, which resulted in the destruction of the Aztec empire between 1519–1521 by Hernando Cortés's forces. The Spanish conquistadors were primarily motivated by the riches they thought could be provided by the mineral wealth of the Americas. They established permanent settlements, and with the missionaries, sought to introduce Spanish culture into the region (Stoddard, 1973: 177–179).

In the process they confronted the matter of whether their policies toward the indigenous peoples would entail incorporation, pluralism, or some form of exclusion. Certainly, there was tension among Spaniards about this issue, as reflected in the famous debate between Bartolomé de las Casas and Juan Ginés de Sepúlveda in the middle of the sixteenth century. The latter, using Aristotle's understanding of the "natural slave," argued that domination of Indians was just because of their sins (especially the sin of idolatry) and what he referred to as their "rude nature." Subjugation was considered necessary to spread the Christian faith. It was essential that the weak among the natives were protected from the stronger. In short, Sepúlveda provided a philosophical and theological justification for colonial domination and for the enslavement of the natives.

Las Casas argued that the Indians were fully human and therefore equals of the Spaniards. Although he did not disagree with the proselytizing efforts of Catholic missionaries, he forcefully challenged the arrogance of those who, in his view, failed to realize that nobody is born enlightened. Las Casas argued that all must be guided and taught—in short, he urged the colonizers to have a sense of humility and compassion.

This debate occurred in Spain, and though some suggest that las Casas was the more persuasive of the two, a ruthless campaign of subjugation continued to characterize the Spanish relationship to the Indians. The indigenous population declined precipitously, and over time interbreeding resulted in mixed bloods, or mestizos, making up a substantial majority of the Mexican population.

Spanish control of territory north of the present Mexican-United States border included all or part of Texas, New Mexico, Arizona, California, Nevada, Utah, Colorado, and Wyoming. Hispanic settlement in these regions was sparse. At the end of the seventeenth century, the Pueblo revolt in what is now Arizona and New Mexico provided temporary relief from an oppressive system of forced labor and cultural suppression. Though resistance did not entirely disappear, and pockets of autonomy persisted, the Spaniards were successful over time in tightening their control of the Indians.

John Chavez (1984: 20) contended, "Once the Spanish authorities realized that the riches of the north would take great effort to develop, their enthusiasm for the region waned." Political authorities viewed this region as essentially a defensive buffer against other European powers: the French in Louisiana and the English and Russians on the Northwest coast. Catholic missionaries saw it as rich ground for conversion activities.

In the early nineteenth century an independence movement arose in Mexico, headed by Miguel Hidalgo y Costilla. In 1821 Mexico freed itself from Spanish rule and established the nation as a republic three years later. During this period, the newly-formed Mexican nation sought to economically develop its far northern regions and to increase the region's population. The central government failed, however, to successfully integrate that territory into the new polity (Weber, 1982), hindered in part by conflictual relationships with some Native American tribes, such as the Apache.

Even before independence, Mexicans were confronted with the escalating incursion of Anglo Americans into their northern territory, especially in Texas and California. As early as the Louisiana Purchase of 1803 it became increasingly clear to government officials that the United States, and not the European powers, posed the greatest threat to the region. Nonetheless, little was done early on to stop Anglos, who took advantage of commercial opportunities. As a consequence, by 1828 Anglos were the majority of the population in Texas, and their numbers continued to rise there and elsewhere (Chavez, 1984: 29).

Actually, both demographic and political factors created differences in Anglo American–Mexican relations in each of the border states (Hraba, 1979: 237–238). For example, Texas had only about 5,000 Mexican inhabitants, who were overwhelmed by the Anglo presence. During these years the economy revolved around large cattle ranches and livestock ownership.

New Mexico had about 60,000 inhabitants, which included a powerful landowning elite and a complex social hierarchy from a history of interbreeding with Indians. A stratified social order defined in terms of the Spanish Society of Castes defined social distance between pure-blooded Spaniards and the Indians (Stoddard, 1973: 75). Hispanos took these caste gradations seriously, which was reflected in the intensity of their anti-Indian sentiments. The Spanish population was isolated from the central government because of the presence of the Apaches between major settlements in New Mexico and the central government's base in Mexico City. During most of the nineteenth century overt conflict between Anglos and Hispanos did not materialize, and alliances were formed between elites from both communities. Potential conflict over land lurked in the background, however.

In contrast, Arizona was only sparsely populated, with perhaps 1,000 inhabitants. Development occurred more slowly, and the relationship between Anglos and Hispanos was less strained than elsewhere. The economy developed more fully after 1880, with the beginning of copper mining.

California was dominated by a handful of powerful ranchers who had a particularly strained relationship with Mexico. These landowners were not entirely adverse to severing ties with the central government. The problems for Mexico's central government were compounded during the 1840s when the influx of substantial numbers of Anglo settlers got underway.

Tensions between the United States and Mexico intensified over time. Texans revolted against Mexican rule and established the Republic of Texas in 1836. A decade later, American rebels in California, under the "Bear Flag" banner, attempted to found the California Republic. Also in 1846, the Mexican War began. It concluded two years later with the signing of the Treaty of Guadalupe Hidalgo, which ceded Mexico's northern frontier to the United States. As a consequence, the United States expanded by more than 525,000 square miles. When the Gadsden Purchase was signed in 1853, additional land was acquired from Mexico, establishing what are today the boundaries between the two nations.

Shortly thereafter gold was discovered in California, which set off a gold rush that brought thousands of Anglo settlers into the frontier. The decade of the 1850s saw increasing conflicts over the control and ownership of land, resulting in the progressive displacement — through legal and extralegal means — of Hispanos. Chavez (1984: 43) captured the significance of the war and its immediate aftermath when he wrote, "We can date to 1848 the modern Chicano image of the Southwest as a lost land."

Travelers to Gold Mountain

The mass immigration of Chinese to America did not begin until 1849, the year gold was discovered in California. In the ensuing decade, 34,000 Chinese immigrated to the United States, settling almost entirely in California (Kitano and Daniels, 1988: 19).

Most of the immigrants came from two southeastern provinces, Guangdong and Fujian (Chan, 1991: 5). These coastal Chinese have historically been a diaspora people, evident in two earlier waves of emigration: during the seventh century and during the Ming era (1368–1644). In these instances sojourners settled in various parts of southeast Asia, such as the Philippines, and some traveled as far as Africa. An Imperial Edict of 1712, which threatened a death penalty for émigrés who returned to China, served to slow the migratory flow, but it picked up again in the nineteenth century. At that time, trans-Pacific travel improvements allowed the mass emigration to the Americas. During this century Chinese settled in Hawaii and in coastal areas from Canada to Peru (Lyman, 1974: 6–7).

The push factors propelling Chinese out of China included such natural disasters as floods and crop failures, which resulted in famine conditions. The devastation caused by the Taiping Rebellion (1850–1864), which resulted in perhaps as many as 10 million deaths, was an additional stimulus.

The initial pull factor was remarkably singular: the quest for gold. For this reason, the typical Chinese immigrant was an adult male traveling alone. Indeed, more than 90 percent of those seeking the "Gold Mountain," as they referred to California, were male. Whether they were unmarried or married with a family left behind in China, their general goal was to get rich quickly and return to China, where they could live as wealthy individuals. Thus, the Chinese have been described as "sojourners" or "birds of passage" (Daniels, 1988: 16).

Figure 5.2 *Portrait of an early Chinese immigrant to California.*

Source: Chinese in California Photographs courtesy of the Balch
Institute Library.

During the 1850s most Chinese were involved in mining; by
1860, although surface deposits for gold had been depleted and
most white prospectors had given up and moved on to other work,
85 percent of the Chinese remained in the gold fields. Not until the
beginning of the transcontinental railroad construction would the
Chinese find an alternative employment for a significant number
of workers. Most Chinese (and, indeed, most white miners) did
not get rich prospecting for gold; many, perhaps as many as half,
of these failed miners returned to China. Those who remained, either by choice or because they did not have the money to return,
began to find alternative modes of employment. They began to
settle in cities, the most important being San Francisco. In these
urban settings, they moved into ethnic enclaves that became
known as Chinatowns.

Soon after the first wave of immigrants, a merchant strata developed. Settling both in mining locales and in cities, the merchants opened stores and restaurants that provided both provisions imported from China as well as American-made products. In addition, merchants played an important role in meeting the social needs of immigrants, assisting with health care and death benefits, leisure time, and so forth. Sucheng Chan (1991: 30) wrote, "Merchants played such a crucial role that they became the wealthiest members and the most important leaders of the community," while constituting perhaps 3 percent of the community in rural areas and maybe as much as 10 percent in cities.

During the decade beginning in 1850, the foundation of the Chinese ethnic community was in place, albeit often in embryonic form. Several features defined it. The community was dominated by the business elite, which over time created powerful coordinated organizations that enhanced their position in the community. The Chinese also transplanted an institutional structure from the homeland, in which three types of organization were most prominent. Two performed similar functions: clan associations and speech or territorial associations (*hui kuan*) were involved in mutual aid, employment, recreation, and commerce. The third type was secret societies, criminal bands, or what E. J. Hobsbawm (1959) has called "primitive rebels," nonideological and opportunistic outsiders who were willing to work for the highest bidder. They, too, provided goods and services to the immigrants, the three most important involving gambling, drugs, and prostitution (Lyman, 1974). In this overwhelmingly male community—a "bachelor society"—many of the women were prostitutes, often living, according to Roger Daniels (1988: 16), "in a condition of semislavery."

The Chinese were subjected to intense prejudice. Indeed, anti-Chinese attitudes had preceded the Chinese themselves, as the United States had been inundated with unfavorable reports from sailors, missionaries, traders, and other travelers to China. The Chinese were described in these accounts as being superstitious, dishonest, cruel, lacking in courage, intellectually inferior, lecherous, and xenophobic. One clergyman went so far as to characterize them as "marginal members of the human race" (Lyman, 1974: 55–58). This hostility resulted in concrete actions to stem the flow of immigration almost as soon as the Chinese arrived. Within this context of isolation and simmering hostility the Chinese community in America grew and developed.

Summary

In this chapter we have seen the barriers that race posed to the fulfillment of the democratic ideals of the American republic. We have seen how race has determined who would and who would not be caught up in coercive forms of pluralism: predatory, caste, or sojourner. Native Americans suffered from the perception that they stood in the way of the nation's westward expansion. Government policies, economic decisions, and the actions of thousands of white settlers suggested that the indigenous peoples of the continent were in the way and had to be forced aside.

Blacks, in contrast, were economically vital for the growth of the nation's economy. The institution of slavery defined a long legacy of the oppression of blacks by whites. The involuntary migration of Africans and their subjugation was motivated by a simple economic need: the need for labor. Slavery provided a readily available supply of inexpensive workers who were relatively powerless to challenge those who exploited them. Racism served as an ideological justification for slavery, and though not all whites embraced racialist thought, the vast majority did. Even many abolitionists thought that blacks were intellectually and morally inferior to whites. The outlawing of slavery did not end such ideas. Equal justice and the equality of opportunity did not materialize after emancipation. It took whites more than a century after the Civil War to begin to consider seriously the possibility that biological notions of inherent inferiority are mistaken.

The black-white division cast a shadow over white relationships with other people of color. This was true for the first Asian group to arrive in America: the Chinese. Such racist ideas were also evident with the Mexicans, although not quite as pronounced because Mexicans could to some extent claim European origins and were not perceived to be quite as "foreign" as the Chinese. The imposition of racial definitions on all Asian and Hispanic groups took a heavy toll on group members and made their ability to gain a foothold in America more difficult to accomplish than the whites' ability. We'll discuss this further in the following chapters.

From Immigrants to Ethnic Americans, 1865–1940

In the eight decades between the end of the Civil War and the end of World War II the United States emerged as the most powerful nation in the world. This produced monumental changes in virtually every facet of American life. Central to this was industrialization, which transformed the nation's economic basis and introduced the machine technology that challenged the pastoral ideal of America as well as its rural character. Midway through this period—in 1920—the majority of the American population resided for the first time in urban rather than rural settings.

Economic change was linked to political change. America's relative isolation from international conflict eroded as the country became a major world power. The Spanish-American War of 1898 was an initial indication of this change; for the first time since the Mexican-American War a half century earlier, the United States acquired territory via conquest. Entry into World War I—a late entry due in no small part to the rather widespread influence of isolationist sentiments—signaled the nation's inability to separate, as it had once attempted to do, the conflicts of the old world from the new world. By the end of World War II, the nation had become the leader of the western bloc in an emerging world order that entailed a perpetual state of military preparedness: the Cold War.

Although in conjunction these economic and political changes account for much of what redefined America, other consequential developments also had an impact on ethnic relations. Changes in the mass media and in communications provided new ways of shaping images of America's identity and conveying its values and

Figure 6.1   A Greek American couple arriving at their wedding reception, circa 1911.

Source: Courtesy of the Swenson Center.

ideals to ever-larger audiences. The advent of the motion picture, the phonograph record, and the radio were particularly important. The expansion of railroads and the development of the automobile brought people into closer proximity with others and challenged regional and rural and urban divisions. These set the stage for what social scientists and cultural commentators at the middle of the twentieth century called "mass society."

Among the cultural changes were challenges to established religions from several quarters. First, secularization began to be felt, especially after the disillusion that followed World War I and the challenge posed by science (seen most vividly in the famous Scopes trial). Second, Protestantism had to deal with a rapidly expanding Catholic minority as well as with other smaller religions, especially Judaism. Third, within Protestantism battles emerged between progressive forces intent on accommodating modernity rather than resisting it (such as the Social Gospel movement) and traditionalists who fought a cultural battle against change.

Within this general socio-cultural context, ethnicity exerted its pervasive influence on American society, and was, in turn, influenced by that society. New groups entered America, adding to its heterogeneity. Some older groups virtually disappeared as distinctive ethnic entities. Others sought to redefine their place in America, reacting to new circumstances and challenges.

Becoming Ethnic Americans

The largest wave of immigration in the country's history occurred between 1880 and 1930, during which time 27,788,140 immigrants entered the United States. The vast majority came from Europe (U.S. Bureau of the Census, 1975: 119). This immigration brought millions of eastern and southern Europeans who differed in many respects from the western European immigrants who had preceded them. These new immigrants entered an unfamiliar world in search of employment opportunities that eluded them at home. They frequently confronted not only economic exploitation but nativist hostility.

Sympathetic scholars reflecting on this generation of immigration characterized these immigrants as alienated. Oscar Handlin's Pulitzer-prize winning history of these new arrivals, *The Uprooted* (1973) contains a classic portrait of alienation. The book attempts to provide an ideal typical portrait of the southern and eastern European immigrants, whom Handlin views (mistakenly, as we shall see) as primarily peasants.

Handlin viewed these new immigrants as politically and culturally conservative, religiously devout, and attached to the intimate and familiar world of the village and to an agricultural way of life. He considered their world-view to be defined by a hierarchical conception that not only placed them near the bottom of the pyramid but required them to defer to those at the top who were in positions of authority. Handlin argued that migration would only occur under conditions of extreme duress, such as dire economic crises in the homeland.

The immigrants entered an urban industrial world diametrically different from the world they had previously inhabited. The dislocations proved disorienting. The immigrants' old values and ways of life no longer worked in America. Communal attachments were destroyed by an all-pervasive and previously unknown individualism. The uprooted metaphor reflected this, for these immigrants had lost their old world, but were not yet established in the new. They confronted an existential crisis that Handlin (1973: 97) described in the following manner:

> Loneliness, separation from the community of the village, and despair at the insignificance of their own human abilities, these were the elements that, in America, colored the peasants' view of the world. From the depths of a dark pessimism, they looked up at a frustrating universe ruled by haphazard, capricious forces.

Although Handlin captured much of the anxiety and the misery of the immigration experience, subsequent scholarship has challenged his portrait. Three major problems mar his ideal type: (1) it is too general; (2) it depicts the immigrants solely as victims and not as actors involved in constructing their own lives; and (3) it fails to appreciate the powerful impact of the ethnic communities that sustained and nourished their respective members.

Recently, John Bodnar's *The Transplanted* (1985) has challenged the general thrust of Handlin's work. As the choice of metaphors in titles suggests, Bodnar downplayed the alienating consequences of migration and offered, instead, a perspective that stresses the role of the family, ethnic institutions, the church, labor unions, and political organizations in promoting the interests of immigrants. This perspective looks carefully at the role played by leaders, who frequently developed from the ethnic community's middle class. Bodnar did not simply dismiss Handlin's work. Rather, he provided a corrective to Handlin's overemphasis on alienation. Bodnar urged appreciating the extent to which immigrants were able to effect a transplantation that brought elements of the old world into the new while adapting aspects of the new world into their everyday lives.

This general perspective has been used by recent scholars of ethnicity and is reflected in the summaries of the new arrivals—Italians, Poles, Jews—and for those who arrived earlier—the Irish and Germans. Other than the English, these were the five largest immigrant groups after the Civil War.

Peasants No More: The Italians

Although Italians were present in colonial America, and a growing stream of immigrants arrived during much of the nineteenth century, large numbers of Italians did not immigrate until after 1880. Between 1820 and 1830, for example, only 439 Italians entered the United States; between 1881 and 1890, the number rose to 307,309. The subsequent three decades brought even more immigrants, with 2,045,877 Italians arriving in the peak decade of 1901–1910 (U.S. Bureau of the Census, 1975: 105–106).

Italy was not unified as a nation state until 1861, so it is not surprising that Italians were defined in a far more localized manner than were some other ethnic groups. People tended to see themselves in terms of the most immediate geographical identity: the village. They also were likely to define themselves on the basis of different regional identities: Neapolitan, Abruzzian, Calabrian, Sicilian, and so forth (Lopreato, 1970).

Particularly significant is the division between immigrants from the northern regions, such as the Piedmont, Lombardy, Tuscany, and Veneto, and those from the Mezzogiorno, which is the designation for those regions south of Rome. Although northern Italy experienced extensive industrialization during the late nineteenth and early twentieth centuries, the south remained economically underdeveloped (Cinel, 1981). Handlin's characterization does not describe northern Italian immigrants, many of whom were artisans or part of the industrial proletariat. But the image of the peasant existing in a semi-feudal condition is in some respects an accurate portrayal of those who chose to depart from southern Italy. The two components of the Italian immigrant population differed in available resources and preparedness for an urban industrial setting (Lopreato, 1970: 33–35; Ramella, 1991).

Italians migrating prior to the Civil War tended to originate from northern Italy. Though some of these arrivals settled in rural areas, most Italians opted for cities. By 1860 the largest concentration of Italians was in California, and San Francisco was a particularly important destination (Cinel, 1982a). Second and third in size, respectively, were New York and Louisiana, with New York City and New Orleans attracting most of these immigrants (Nelli, 1983: 40). Immigrants to San Francisco and New Orleans after 1860 continued to be mostly from northern Italy. This explains why, in terms of economic location, home ownership, and the development of community organizations, residents of San Francisco and New Orleans appear to have adjusted faster and more thoroughly than their counterparts in New York (Baily, 1983).

During the mass Italian migration period, an overwhelming majority came from the Mezzogiorno and settled primarily in the northeastern United States, with the heaviest concentrations in New York, New Jersey, and the industrial cities of New England. Many also settled in the Midwest in cities such as Chicago, St. Louis, Kansas City, and Cleveland (Barton, 1975). These individuals moved from an agrarian world to an industrial one. As early as 1919 Robert Foerster observed that the Italians in America tended to avoid farming. Along with Hungarians, the Italians were the least likely European group to move into American agricultural occupations (Hutchinson, 1956: 178).

Finding Work

Italians found work in a wide range of industries and provided the burgeoning economy with a large supply of unskilled labor. They worked in such industries as construction (where they obtained so-called "pick and shovel" jobs); various manufacturing concerns, including cotton, woolen, and silk mills; stonecutting, and coal and iron ore mining. They found employment with railroads and as longshoremen. Women were well represented in the garment industry (Caroli and Kessner, 1978). In short, Italians worked throughout American industry. Their jobs demanded long hours for low wages and were frequently dangerous. Work-related accidents were common occurrences, and tragedies such as the one related in Gabriel Iamurri's (1951: 49) autobiography were part of everyday life for the "greenhorns":

> [soon after three other deaths on the job] a friend of mine carrying a case of dynamite and caps together on his shoulders, as he was told, fell down and the case of dynamite with the caps exploded and my poor friend Jimmie, poor Jimmie, was torn to pieces — died. No one of the concern ever shed a tear over him.

One distinctive feature of Italians in the labor market was the role played by the labor boss or the padrone. This was an adaptation of practices common in southern Italy, where the padrone served as a labor broker in what has been described as a form of indentured servitude. The padrone in America functioned as a mediating link between employers and new immigrants unfamiliar with the American environment (LaSorte, 1985: 95–99). As with some other groups where the padrone system operated, such as Greeks and Mexicans, the padrone often exploited the newcomers.

He demanded kickbacks and overcharged workers for such things as transportation fees to work sites and for provisions at those sites. Since the immigrant paid a fee for a job, padrones had an incentive to discharge workers routinely to ensure additional fees from new workers (Alba, 1985: 52).

The padrone system, not surprisingly, fell into disrepute by 1900, and though it persisted into the twentieth century, the new arrivals coming during the decades of peak immigration knew far more about the United States than did those who came a few decades earlier; the new arrivals frequently had friends, family members, or former villagers who could show them the ropes.

Other notable occupations were in the service sector. Italians found jobs in restaurants and in the retail fruit and candy trade. They worked as barbers, and young males worked as shoeshine boys. Italians were rag pickers. They ran shops that produced macaroni, religious artifacts, and artificial flowers. Italian women were well-represented in these trades. Some Italians found employment as musicians and entertainers (Hutchinson, 1956: 178).

Not all immigrants chose to remain in America. These were commonly seen as birds of passage — primarily single young men who planned to work in America just long enough to earn capital that could improve their economic status back home. More than 4.5 million Italians arrived in the United States between 1880 and 1930, and some estimates place the return migration at about 50 percent (Caroli, 1973; Nelli, 1980: 547). Though some migrants returned home and stayed, others made more than one voyage to America. Cinel (1982b) observed that some Italians were seasonal migrants, coming to America to escape springtime poverty in Italy only to return home in the winter. Because official statistics do not make it easy to determine if and when this was occurring, we cannot easily differentiate those who left America for good from those who went to Italy for visits. Clearly women and children became a more prominent feature of the latter phase of the great migratory wave, which began the ethnic community shift from a male-dominated one to one with an increasing number of families.

The Ethnic Community

Italians were heavily concentrated in large cities, but they also settled in smaller towns and cities. They formed an integral part of the iron mining communities in Michigan and Minnesota, for example (Vecoli, 1987). Ethnic enclaves emerged in both large and small cities. In the larger cities, such as New York, Chicago, Philadelphia, Baltimore, Boston, and St. Louis, these enclaves often were dubbed "Little Italies" (Nelli, 1970; Harney and Scarpaci, 1981). Within these "foreign colonies" much of the first and second generation resided. The smells, sounds, and sights of these enclaves indicated the Italians' ability to transplant elements of the homeland to America.

In some cities residential patterns were determined by the region, or even the village, of origin. Harvey Zorbaugh (1929: 164) described village affiliations of the Sicilians in Chicago's Little Italy by the streets in which they lived. Those from Altavilla resided on Larrabee Street, those on Townsend came from Bagheria, those on Milton came from Sambuca-Zabut, and so on. Thus, the immigrants and their offspring remained connected with their cultural origins. Thomas Kessner (1977: 16) discovered a similar pattern in New York City. As Robert Harney (1976: 11) put it, Little Italies provided the immigrant generation with a "cultural breathing space" between peasant society and urban-industrial America.

Two additional points are necessary to avoid a tendency to romanticize these communities. First, Little Italies were slums. The tenements provided substandard housing units for residents, and conditions were unsafe, unhygienic, and overcrowded. In general, this was the only kind of housing available to poor immigrants. As early social reformers such as Jacob Riis, Hamilton Holt, and Jane Addams suggested, the newcomers suffered considerably because of their poverty and the problems of social disorganization, such as crime and domestic upheaval (compare Riis, 1971 [1890]; Woods, 1903; Tomasi, 1978). The poverty that characterized the lives of many Italian immigrants was graphically described by American social reformer Charles Loring Brace (1872: 194), based on his visits to New York's Little Italy:

> In the same room I would find monkeys, children, men, and women, with organs and plaster casts, all huddled together; but the women continuing still, in the crowded rooms, to roll their dirty macaroni, and all talking excitedly; a bedlam of sounds and a combination of odors from garlic, monkeys, and dirty human persons. They were, without exception, the dirtiest population I had ever met.

Brace's comments did two things at once: they provided a description of poor immigrants struggling to survive by being street musicians and by begging, and they illustrated the negative attitudes that even social reformers tended to hold.

Second, many non-Italians resided within these communities. In some quarters Italians lived next to Irish families, and in other cities Jews and Italians experienced considerable residential mixing. The ethnic community allowed the continuation of old world cultural patterns while providing opportunities for social interaction with members of other ethnic groups (Yancey, et al., 1985).

Within the institutional matrix of Little Italy an ethnic community was forged. Families developed as women followed men and as the migrations of entire families became more common. The family proved to be a resilient institution, and in a new environment it enabled immigrants to negotiate cultural differences and economic obstacles (Yans-McLaughlin, 1977).

Mutual aid societies, churches, Italian-language newspapers, and banks contributed to various facets of group welfare. Rudolph Vecoli (1964) argued that the family in Mezzogiorno culture was a selfish institution that demanded such devotion that nonfamilial institutions were necessarily rather weak; he also contended that he could see the imprint of this cultural trait on the contadini (peasants) in Chicago. Although this may be an accurate depiction of the traditional family, forms of mutual aid emerged even before migration, and once in America they developed quickly. These efforts were designed, as Humbert Nelli (1983: 115) wrote, to "deal with sickness, loneliness, and death" in a setting where the family could not undertake such welfare functions alone.

The centrality of work led to the close connection between mutual aid societies and incipient labor unions. The development of working class consciousness melded with traditional notions of cooperation to encourage collective solutions to economic problems rather than notions of individual mobility. Labor union involvement was one way in which immigrants interacted with non-Italians. The meaning that unionists imputed to their labor organizations varied considerably, depending chiefly on the differing political orientations of those involved. Moderates tended to believe unions functioned to improve workers' lives as they pertained to wages, benefits, length of the work day, safety, job security, and the like. Militants—including democratic socialists, communists, and anarchists—viewed unions as vehicles for revolutionary change. Although most radicals came from the industrial north, where they had often been introduced to radicalism prior to migration, some areas of southern Italy also contributed to immigrant radicalism (Gabaccia, 1988). Most Italians did not embrace political radicalism, so their attitudes regarding labor unions tended to have a moderate, reformist orientation.

Roman Catholicism

The church's role in the immigrant community is debated, but the general consensus is that comparatively speaking the church was weak. The pietism that characterized the Irish was uncharacteristic of the Italians. Italy had a long history of hostility to the Roman Catholic church; some of this was due to secular ideals, some to the continuing impact of magic in place of religion, and some to anti-clerical sentiments. This does not mean that the church was irrelevant, for Italians used it to mark the major events of life (baptism, marriage, and funerals) and as the focus of religious festivals, which were communal celebrations (Lopreato, 1970: 87–93; Tomasi, 1975). Over time, these rituals were transformed and modified by new social patterns that arose in America, but they also served as a powerful source of connectedness with the old world (Cowell, 1985).

Two facts conspired to further weaken the role of the church in the immigrant community. First, Italian priests and nuns did not migrate in large numbers, which deprived the first generation of a sufficient number of Italian-speaking priests. Second, by the time of mass Italian immigration, the Irish had ascended into positions of control of Catholicism in this country. The church became an institution that fueled hostility between the two groups (Femminella, 1985). As a result, the Italians did not send their children to parochial schools in great numbers. Although the Irish did so to avoid the impact of Anglicization in the public schools, the Italian aversion to parochial education was partly due to a desire to protect their children from "Irishization."

Education and Upward Mobility

A more general aversion to public education was also evident, part of a legacy from the homeland. In southern Italy peasants were suspicious of education and most children spent very little time in school. A compulsory education law passed in 1877 met stiff resistance, widespread noncompliance, and even riots and the burning of schoolhouses. Alba (1985: 59) characterized the tension between peasant culture and mandatory state-sponsored education by the contrasting value accorded to being *buon educato*, or knowledgeable about society's mores and folkways, and being *ben instruito*, the result of book-learning. The former, based on the preservation of tradition, was considered unreservedly good, while the latter was viewed with considerable suspicion.

As a result of this general dislike of educational institutions, Italians in America did not use education as a vehicle for upward mobility until the emergence of the third generation after World War II. Instead, truancy and dropping out were common through the first four decades of the twentieth century, and characteristic of both the first and second generations (Oliver, 1987). Although many immigrants and their children from all ethnic groups left school early, the Italians appear to have done so to a far greater extent. Richard Gambino (1974: 256) reported that in 1931, while the graduation rate for all students in New York City had risen to 42 percent, only 11 percent of Italians graduated high school. In a study of a mining community in the upper Midwest, a similar pattern emerged. Throughout the 1930s, the Italians (and French-Canadians) had lower rates of high school completion than the three other large ethnic groups in the community: English, Swedes, and Finns (Kivisto, 1991; see also Smith, 1969).

This orientation toward education affected upward mobility. Some Italians were economically successful, especially those who operated their own businesses. Northern Italians were overrepresented in the ranks of this sector of the ethnic community. Many Italians saw their or their children's living standards improve as a result of participation in various successful campaigns of organized labor. Although Thomas Kessner (1977) contends that both Italians and Jews in New York City advanced quite quickly, the patterns were different. In particular, because the newly emerging white-collar class was based on educational credentials, Italians — in contrast with Jews — did not enter this new middle class in large numbers during this period. This did not change until the 1950s.

Although not all employers preferred Italian workers over other ethnics (compare Bodnar, et al., 1982: 85; Korman, 1967: 45),

Italians provided ample evidence that they were willing to work hard. Italians tended to view work as a means of survival and not in terms of individual career mobility paths. They worked to establish a foothold in the American economy; despite often meager wages, Italians saved considerable sums of money (Nelli, 1983: 63–64). The prevalence of banks such as the Bank of Italy (which later became one of the nation's largest banks, the Bank of America) indicated their penchant for saving. One chief goal was home ownership, and with opportunities to purchase homes, Italians exhibited considerable residential mobility.

Ethnic Stereotypes and the Mafia

Italians confronted considerable negative imagery in their attempt to become a part of the larger society. In a study of ethnic stereotypes conducted by Daniel Katz and Kenneth Braly (1933), Princeton University students saw Italians as artistic, impulsive, passionate, quick tempered, musical, and imaginative. In short, Italians were seen as being guided by their emotions and not their intellects. As such, they were seen as fit for manual but not mental labor. Some of this imagery is not inherently negative, so it is not surprising that when Emory Bogardus (1933) conducted his first study of social distance in the 1920s, Italians fell somewhere in the middle of the thirty groups studied: not as readily accepted as groups such as the English, Germans, and Swedes, but far more accepted than blacks, Chinese, Turks, and various racial minorities.

One part of the negative stereotype not mentioned in the Katz and Braly study involves crime. Overall, Italians had a lower crime rate than many other ethnic groups, and were not as readily identified with many other social problems (for example, the alcoholism rate was comparatively low). Nonetheless, the existence of the Mafia colored perceptions of the association of ethnicity and criminal activity. During this era organized crime grew in power and influence, in no small part due to Prohibition, and many prominent gangsters came from various ethnic groups, including Irish, Jews, and Germans. The public, however, believed there was a powerful link between Italians and organized crime, which was seen in the Mafia.

The Mafia functioned mainly in Sicily, but it operated throughout southern Italy in a fashion quite similar to the Chinese secret societies noted in the preceding chapter, and like them they can rightly be seen as examples of "primitive rebels" (Hobsbawm, 1959). The institution was transplanted to the United States, including the familial features of the organization that were exaggerated in the "Godfather" movies. One explanation for the Mafia's existence in this country was provided by Daniel Bell (1965), who suggested that it functioned as a mechanism for upward mobility for a segment of the population whose legitimate channels of mobility were cut off. Whatever the reasons, the role of Italians in criminal syndicates proved to be, well beyond this period, a particularly troublesome phenomenon for Italians seeking acceptance by the host society.

Politics

Italians were slower to enter the political arena than were the Irish. Though most Italians were, especially by the New Deal era, Democrats, a segment of the more prosperous, especially northern Italians, had identified with the Republican party and had, at least for a time, brought some southern Italians into the fold. Democratic allegiance was affected by the class location of the majority of Italians — the working class ravaged by the Depression endorsed Roosevelt's policies.

A small but important segment of Italians continued to support various radical political positions. Carlo Tresca was the most important radical outside the ethnic community. He was a prominent organizer in two of the era's most famous strikes, the 1912 textile workers strike in Lawrence, Massachusetts, and the 1916 Patterson, New Jersey, silk workers strike. The celebrated case of Nicola Sacco and Bartolomeo Vanzetti — two anarchists tried, convicted, and, in 1927, executed for murder — highlighted the efforts the government was willing to make to get rid of immigrant radicals (Pernicone, 1979). On the fiftieth anniversary of their execution, the state of Massachusetts officially declared that justice had not been served by the trial that led to their conviction (Nelli, 1983: 154–155).

Both interethnic and intraethnic conflict were produced by Benito Mussolini's rise to power in Italy and the ascendance of fascism (Salvemini, 1977; Bayor, 1978). During the 1920s support for Italian fascism among Italian Americans was widespread, as it was in many other quarters. Many Italians thought that Mussolini would solve the social and economic problems besetting Italy while gaining respect for Italians from Americans. This latter aspect of support suggests that events in the homeland were perceived to have a direct bearing on acceptance in America. During the 1930s, when the character of fascism became clearer, support waned considerably. Conflict intensified between anti-fascists and sympathizers. At the eve of World War II, despite the continual erosion of fascist support, some questioned the "divided loyalties" of Italian Americans.

Generational Change

While these political events were transpiring, larger changes occurred. In the interwar years the second generation came of age and tensions arose between children and parents. Marcus Lee Hansen's (1938) essay on "The Problem of the Third Generation Immigrant" suggested that though the first generation is forced to live with an inherited, foreign culture, the second, anxious about its place in America, opts quickly to abandon it and seeks to Americanize. In his view, only when the third generation appears is an appreciation of the heritage of the immigrant generation possible. Although subsequent research has cast considerable doubt on the universality of Hansen's thesis (see, for example, several essays in Kivisto and Blanck, 1990), generational changes were underway.

For example, in Caroline Ware's (1935: 193) study of Italians in New York's Greenwich Village, she discovered pronounced generational differences regarding values and beliefs about the family. Although 88 percent of older Italians thought that divorce was not permissible in any circumstances, only 39 percent of younger Italians agreed. Similarly, the younger were more willing to question the authority of fathers, large families, and traditional strictures about young women being in the company of men. In some instances, it seems that the immigrant generation had already abandoned some elements of traditional mores, and the second generation merely took that trend further. For example, fully 70 percent of older Italians disagreed with the practice of arranged marriages, while the figure soared to 99 percent for their younger counterparts.

Figure 6.2 *An Italian American family, circa 1925.*

Source: Courtesy of the Swenson Center.

Throughout this entire period American mass culture began to have an impact, simultaneously shaping the perceptions of Italians and the larger society. The dance and musical tastes of the new ethnics and those who had been in America for generations served as a basis of commonality. Movies were a primary vehicle for creating what Elizabeth Ewen (1980: 46) has referred to as "a new visual landscape of possibility." The silent film, Ewen points out, transcended language barriers.

During the first two decades of the century numerous movies were made about Italian immigrants. Films played upon stereotypes, such as the 1911 film *Italian Blood*, in which passion drives a jealous Italian immigrant husband into a rage that nearly results in the death of his children. Many films, such as *The Black Hand* (1906), focused on the Mafia, but rather than simply displaying a disdain for the presumed criminal proclivities of Italians, they often provided sympathetic — if generally melodramatic — portraits of the immigrant victims of such activities. Two films, *The Italian* (1915) and *One More American* (1918) captured the flavor of the ethnic community and gave audiences moving accounts of the difficulties that the immigrants confronted. Ironically, the star in both of these features was George Beban, an Irish American (Brownlaw, 1990: 316–320). Such films disappeared in the interwar years, in the period of immigration restriction. The movies, as well as other forms of entertainment, became more "American" and less "foreign."

This change reflects a transformation, which is not to suggest that the ethnic community had outlived its usefulness. William Foote Whyte's (1943) classic ethnographic study of "Cornerville" (Boston's North End) indicated that as the second generation came of age in the 1930s, other Italians continued to be the individual's primary reference group and the ethnic world defined such central norms as respectability, honor, and duty. But youth increasingly desired to move out of the ghetto and into the mainstream. Commenting on the youth that were Whyte's focus, Arthur Vidich (1992: 20) wrote that they were not rebels hostile to American society, but rather "sought a way to get into it." The opportunities to do so considerably improved after mid-century.

The Birth and Maturation of Polonia in America

The first sustained sociological study of the immigrant in America that sought to interpret the lived experiences of the immigrants was William I. Thomas and Florian Znaniecki's *The Polish Peasant in Europe and America* (1918). Their analysis of the immigrant world is not unlike that of Oscar Handlin's "uprooted thesis"— not surprising since Handlin was influenced by their work. Thomas and Znaniecki spoke about the "disorganization," both personal and social that migration brought about. The authors devoted sections of their multivolume work to such topics as marital breakdowns, unemployment and welfare dependency, youth delinquency, murder, "sexual immorality," and "demoralization." In short, considerable attention was paid to immigrants as a social problem and as victims of circumstances.

This study differs from Handlin's essentially monochromatic analysis in two important ways, however. First, Thomas and Znaniecki (despite the title of the book) understood that the Polish immigrants were a diverse group; though primarily of peasant origin, they were also artisans and other skilled workers, unskilled proletarians, disgruntled intellectuals, and a variety of other types (see also Keil, 1979). Differing social class backgrounds contributed to the internal diversity of the ethnic community as it emerged in America.

This leads to the second point. Thomas was, along with Robert E. Park, a central figure in the Chicago School of Sociology, and both social scientists were convinced that ethnic communities and the organizations they created assisted the immigrants in overcoming disorganization and adjusting to their new homeland. Active participation in the ethnic community's institutional network dispelled the loneliness and anomie that Handlin so vividly and poignantly emphasized. Moreover, Thomas and Park were convinced that involvement in the ethnic community did not keep the immigrant from entering the mainstream. To the contrary, the ethnic community actually aided in the process of Americanization (Wiley, 1986; Kivisto, 1990). Since the publication of Thomas and Znaniecki's classic work, a substantial body of research has been conducted on Poles in America, much of which supports the general thrust of its major arguments.

There are some similarities between Polish and Italian immigrants. For both groups mass migration to America did not begin until the latter part of the nineteenth century. Among the few Poles who went to America earlier were two who served notably in the American Revolution, Count Casimir Pulaski and Thaddeus Kosciuszko. Both became important symbols for the Poles who arrived over a century later: Poles could claim to be among those involved in the founding of the republic and sharing its ideals and aspirations. Most of those who arrived during the early nineteenth century were political refugees, including liberal reformers and intellectuals who took part in aborted uprisings in the Russian controlled section of Poland in 1830–1831 and 1863 (Greene, 1980: 791).

The Homeland

A second commonality between Italians and Poles is that national unification occurred late for both. The Poles' nation was partitioned three times between 1772 and 1795, and an independent nation did not materialize until 1918. During this time, the eastern part of Poland was controlled by Russia; the south fell first into Austria's orbit and was incorporated into the Austro-Hungarian empire after 1867; and the western region was part of Prussia and, after German unification in 1871, part of Germany (Morawska, 1989: 238). The fact that three different powerful neighbors ruled sections of the would-be nation intensified already existing regional differences.

Although the territory of Poland was economically fairly self-sufficient in the eighteenth century, this changed as industrialization advanced in western Europe. Industrialization prompted a growing need for food products, raw materials, and a source of labor from the more underdeveloped territories of eastern Europe. Western European economies began to penetrate this periphery and produced far-reaching economic changes. In addition, the abolition of serfdom (begun in 1807 in Prussia, undertaken in Austria in 1848, and completed in the Russian sector by 1864) increased the percentage of land owned by peasants, and propelled even more peasants into the ranks of day or seasonal laborers. Combined with a rapidly growing population — the rate exceeded the growth of Europe as a whole — these push factors contributed to a heightened migratory pressure and intensified over time (Morawska, 1989: 241–243).

At the same time, industrial enterprises began to penetrate Poland and increasing numbers of Poles found employment in mining and manufacturing. This meant that the migrants to America were not only the peasants noted in the title of Thomas and Znaniecki's book, but also the industrial working class, many of whom had some experience in, or at least exposure to, organized labor.

Emigration

As Poles left for various destinations, Germany, due to its proximity, was one important country to receive them. For many Poles this was a step in a series of migrations that culminated in a final move to America. Others made the Atlantic migration directly, especially after the first arrivals had settled and began sending those back home information about opportunities in the United States. Letters — written by a third party if the immigrant was illiterate — were commonplace. They both kept the new arrivals in touch with events back home and provided a vital link with others contemplating emigration. In addition, many Poles reported traveling back and forth at least once, thereby providing first-hand accounts of America (Balch, 1910, 460–461; Thomas and Znaniecki, 1918). Steamship lines and labor recruiters also encouraged Poles to emigrate because of the increased demand for labor in industrializing America.

Beginning in the 1850s Poles from Prussian-controlled territory began to arrive in a steady stream that continued to grow until 1890. Then the numbers of immigrants from western Poland declined and were replaced by the migration from Russian and Austro-Hungarian Poland. In all, between 1850 and the end of World War I, approximately 2.5 million Polish immigrants came to America, 2 million of whom arrived after 1870 (Greene, 1980: 790–791).

These overwhelmingly economic immigrants frequently saw themselves as temporary sojourners ultimately intending to return to Poland. They were described at home as *za chlebem* (for bread) emigrants. Although this suggests that they were motivated by abject poverty, and thus had extremely low expectations, Ewa Morawska's (1985) community study of Poles in Johnstown, Pennsylvania, suggested that they had a higher, though realistic, sense of what they could obtain. She titled her book *For Bread with Butter* to convey an appreciation of their vision of a better life.

Immigrant destinations depended on the pull factors associated with job availability combined with the forces of chain migration networks (Golab, 1977). Approximately 95 percent of Poles worked in industry as unskilled laborers and were heavily concentrated in coal mining, steel production, and slaughtering and meat-packing (Morawska, 1989: 253). The inhuman working conditions in these industries stimulated labor activism, and reform-minded progressives sought to alleviate the human degradation by legislation to make working conditions at least safe for workers. Upton Sinclair's *The Jungle* (1906), which focused on the slaughterhouses in Chicago, was one of many exposés of the industrial misery that Polish workers (and, of course, others) encountered.

The Immigrant Community Takes Shape

The geographic concentration of Poles was rather pronounced. They settled in the middle Atlantic and midwestern states, especially around the Great Lakes. Thus, Pennsylvania, Ohio, Indiana, Illinois, Michigan, Wisconsin, and Minnesota had Polish colonies in their major industrial cities. Chicago became the undisputed center of Polonia in America, as 400,000 Poles had settled in the city by 1920. Along with Chicago, six other cities became major Polish destinations: New York, Pittsburgh, Buffalo, Milwaukee, Detroit, and Cleveland. Early in the twentieth century half of the nation's Poles lived in one of these seven cities, with another 20 percent in mining communities in Pennsylvania (Balch, 1910: 263–264; Morawska, 1989: 253; Daniels, 1990: 220).

In these burgeoning urban industrial cities, Polonia was born. One central institution in these ethnic communities was the Roman Catholic church. Like the Italians, Poles had to contend with a church already dominated by the Irish, but unlike the Italians, the Poles made demands for Polish-speaking priests and for representation in the ranks of the hierarchy. The majority of Poles were particularly religious, partly because religion and nationalism were intertwined in Poland, and religion was a key ideological source of resistance to external domination. This connection had an impact in America, where a poor immigrant group invested heavily to create a powerful religious presence in their midst. Ethnic parishes grew from less than 20 in 1870 to about 800 by the middle of the 1930s (Greene, 1975; Wrobel, 1979; Parot, 1981).

Within parishes, considerable conflict often pitted priests against church councils. In addition, conflict with the Irish-dominated American church was endemic. One of the most obvious examples was the Reverend Francis Hodur, who led a group of dissidents out of the local diocese, was subsequently excommunicated, and in response established an independent church body, the Polish National Church in 1904 (Greene, 1975: 112–113; Orzell, 1982). Though only a minority of Poles ultimately joined this break-away church, it did reflect the attitudes of a substantial number of Poles. The church hierarchy realized this and sought to accommodate Poles by supplying them with Polish-speaking priests and by elevating Poles into leadership positions.

Besides churches, Poles built numerous ethnic institutions, including two large national organizations, the Polish National Alliance and the Polish Roman Catholic Union. Both actively engaged in homeland issues, with the former seeking a secular Poland and the latter one in which the church played a central political role. In addition, countless local mutual aid societies, social clubs, and culture centers arose. Many were affiliated with churches, bearing names such as the Holy Name of Jesus Society. In Chicago, the Union of Small Polish Clubs was an umbrella organization for individual clubs that were based on the village of origin, so new arrivals could meet and renew ties with acquaintances and friends from home.

Still another institution was the tavern, a preserve of workingmen often located in the shadow of the factory. In the early period of the colonies, the tavern was the most important place for single men, who frequently resided in boarding houses, to socialize. Even after other institutions developed and the community was transformed by the presence of women and children, the tavern remained important. The tavern owners, like other small businessmen in Polonia — primarily the owners of butchershops, markets, restaurants, small merchandise stores, and the like — were community leaders. According to John Bukowczyk (1987: 37–38), immigrant entrepreneurs:

> became pillars of the fragile Polish immigrant enclaves because they commanded sufficient resources to help poor, jobless, lonely, and sometimes desolate peasant immigrants hang on, settle in, and perhaps even prosper. The successful business owners translated immigrants' letters, held their money, found them jobs, kept them out of jail, and generally showed them how to get by in what must have been, for men and women who spoke little or no English, extremely bewildering surroundings.

Labor and Politics

Polish support for organized labor was a critical prerequisite in many unionization attempts. The small socialist element in Polonia was not especially successful in attracting a mass following. In large part this is because the Catholic church was hostile to socialism, which it identified with the forces of secularism. This did not mean, however, that Poles were uninterested in labor unions, nor did it imply that they lacked militancy. Indeed, as Victor Greene (1968) illustrated in his study of striking miners in Pennsylvania, Poles were often an especially militant group among the workers.

This has also been pointed out more recently in James Pula and Eugene Dziedzic's (1990) study of the role of Poles in the 1912 and 1916 textile strikes in New York Mills, New York. Poles were chiefly responsible for forming an affiliate of the United Textile Workers of America and they managed to forge an intraethnic alliance that united a disparate ethnic workforce composed of—in addition to Poles—English, Welsh, Scottish, French-Canadian, Italian, and Syrian workers. Such labor activity reflected a sense of solidarity that, though often fragile, was based on mutually reinforcing ethnic and class identities.

Poles were also actively engaged in intraethnic political involvements. Although slow to develop their own municipal leaders, Poles were a force to be reckoned with in urban machine politics, if for no other reason than the sheer force of numbers. Polish involvement in Chicago's political life illustrates a similar process elsewhere (Kantowicz, 1975). In the early twentieth century both Republicans and Democrats vied for the votes of immigrant groups who were being incorporated into the body politic. But after the watershed election of Anton Cermak, the Democratic party dominated because of its ability to capture the loyalty of large ethnic constituencies, among them the Poles.

The Democratic machine, which survived longer than other machines throughout the country, extended through the "glory days" of Richard Daley's long tenure as mayor and functioned, according to Dianne Pinderhughes (1987), as a "static hierarchy" of ethnic and racial groups. In this hierarchy blacks were consistently located at the bottom, the Irish generally at the top, and eastern and southern European groups in the middle. A group was accorded differentially distributed selective rewards depending on its location in the hierarchy. In this way, the Polish community in

Figure 6.3   *Working class taverns, such as this one owned by a Belgian American (circa 1910), were a common feature of ethnic enclaves.*

Source: Courtesy of the Swenson Center.

Chicago found a niche in the political arena, one that placed them solidly in the Democratic camp.

At the national level, this meant that Polish Americans became a part of the New Deal coalition. They were supporters of programs that laid the basis for the nation's welfare state, and they supported an enhanced governmental role in the economy, particularly in terms of labor-management relations.

In connection with this, they were an active force in the formation of the Congress of Industrial Organizations (CIO), which achieved considerable success in organizing low-skilled industrial workers during the 1930s. More militant than the American Federation of Labor (AFL), which primarily attracted skilled workers, the CIO sought to avoid the mistakes of the Industrial Workers of the World which identified too closely with socialism. This was important for non-socialist Poles who had a history of labor activism but were opposed to radical political ideologies. Bukowczyk (1987: 79–80) stated that Poles "played a central role in sparking the wave of union-organizing activity that virtually remade industrial America between the early 1930s and the early 1940s." Indeed, during the critical years of 1935–1937 about one quarter of the CIO membership was composed of Slavs, and Poles were by far the largest Slavic group. By the next decade approximately 600,000 Poles were members of the CIO.

These labor and political activities resulted in Poles interacting with other groups, but this did not erode Polonia. Rather, such activities preserved ethnic attachments. Poles realized that the political power they possessed was based on their voting as a bloc. Furthermore, Poles were intent on seeing an independent Poland. They continued to involve themselves in homeland politics, thereby ensuring the salience of ethnic allegiances.

Most Poles were members of the industrial working class, operating at its lower tiers, which resulted in a situation in which class identities and ethnic identities proved to be mutually reinforcing. As Lizabeth Cohen (1990) has argued, workers' organizing activities were based on a desire for economic security; neither conservative or radical anticapitalists, they sought a form of "moral capitalism" that provided due compensation for their labor and protection during economically troubled times.

Cultural Values

The immigrant world-view transplanted into Polonia affected attitudes regarding work. Poles tended to believe that humankind had to endure ceaseless hard work (Lopata, 1994) — work was to be endured rather than being a means toward upward mobility. They were also suspicious of secular education in public schools as a means for individual advancement. Instead, they understood education to be, according to John Bodnar (1976: 1) "for the purpose of retaining the cultural, linguistic, and religious values of the group." For this reason Poles created their own educational institutions, such as Alliance College in Pennsylvania, and they pressured local school boards to provide Polish language classes. They were concerned about what they perceived to be the rampant materialism of American society — a concern that was strongest among religious Poles. But this concern was also evident among secularists and radicals, who worried about the impact of an aggressively acquisitive society on egalitarian aspirations.

More than anything else, Poles were motivated by what John Bodnar (1982; 1985) terms "pragmatism." They were not overly motivated by political ideologies, but rather by which potential course of action would achieve steady employment and economic well-being. One particularly important manifestation of this pragmatic orientation was homeownership. Commentators frequently observed that Poles saved money, even if this created hardships, so they could purchase homes. Poles exceeded all other ethnic groups in homeownership rates in the interwar years (Bodnar, et al., 1982: 258). Helena Lopata (1994) sees property ownership as a culturally-transplanted "status competition," it is probably primarily related to a quest for security and a stake in urban neighborhoods. Home purchases were like union efforts: both promoted security and stability (Slayton, 1986).

Interethnic Relations

Perceived challenges to jobs or neighborhoods often caused conflict. Particularly important to American race relations was conflict that pitted Poles against blacks—a battle fought in what Ira Katznelson (1981) has aptly referred to as "urban trenches." Thaddeus Radzialowski documented the conflict that emerged between the two groups in Chicago over job competition (1976) and in Detroit over housing (1982; see also Zunz, 1982). He summarized the underlying reason for this conflictual relationship in the following way:

> The origin and much of the fear or dislike of blacks felt by Polish Americans (and vice versa) is not to be found in a mysterious, deep-seated sexual fear or a retardation at one of the Freudian stages of development, or even of a profound guilt at the past treatment of blacks; rather it is to be found to a significant degree in the brutal, violent, and desperate conflict between them for poorly paid jobs [and for a limited supply of adequate and affordable housing]—a conflict often deliberately fostered in the name of greater profits (Radzialowski, 1976: 18).

The migration of African Americans from the rural South to America's northern cities began in earnest about the time of World War I, precisely when Poles were attempting to gain a foothold in many of the same cities. This suggests the reason for the anti-black animus that grew over time. Poles could also have perceived other recently arrived immigrant groups as rivals, and though there was obvious evidence of conflict among such groups, it paled by comparison to the animosity that characterized the black-Polish relationship. The two European groups with which conflict was evident were the Germans and Jews—the product of hostilities transplanted from the homeland. Although these tensions did not disappear, they were not as consequential as black-Polish conflict. In Chicago, for example, African Americans had relatively more harmonious relations with Italians and Jews. The Poles were most like the Irish insofar as both had tense and frequently overtly hostile relationships with blacks (Drake and Cayton, 1962 [1945]: 180–181).

Generational Change

Although continuity with cultural traditions characterized the Polish American community through the decade of the 1930s, changes were seen that, after World War II, emerged more powerfully to transform Polonia and Polish American ethnic identity. Poles had confronted their share of nativism, and during the 1920s community leaders fought to enhance the status of Poles in America. By the 1930s, the more vehement anti-Polish sentiments had begun to subside. The stereotype that persisted was that of the "dumb Pollack," an invidious distortion of a social reality: Poles were overwhelmingly located in the ranks of unskilled workers, and as a group they were relatively slow to climb the socioeconomic ladder into the middle class. Their treatment by the mass media reflected this: Unlike Italians and Jews, Poles were largely missing as both major and minor characters in the American cinema. When they were included, it was usually as stolid members of the working class—precisely the class that received the least attention from Hollywood (Woll and Miller, 1987: 210).

By the 1930s, the second generation came of age, and as with other groups, generational conflict intensified. Though most of the second generation still participated in the institutional life of Polonia and many continued to speak Polish at home, they were different from their parents. John Bukowczyk (1987: 71) wrote of the second generation, "The majority did not object to the idea of ethnic intermarriage; and most, while retaining Polish customs, had absorbed a great deal of American culture." Parents and ethnic leaders alike shared a growing concern that they were losing their offspring to America and they increasingly voiced the fear aptly characterized by the title of Bukowczyk's book: *And My Children Did Not Know Me.*

The Jewish Diaspora

In *The Transformation of the Jews* (1984), Calvin Goldscheider and Alan S. Zuckerman observe that in less a century, the center of world Jewry shifted from Europe to America. Indeed, at present there are more Jews in the United States than there are not only in Europe but also in Israel, the Jewish state founded in 1948 after the Holocaust. How and why did this movement take place?

Jews have been a diaspora people for centuries, living in exile from their homeland in the Near East. Scattered throughout the world (there was, for instance, a Jewish community in China at least until the communist revolution in the 1940s), they were principally located throughout Europe and northern Africa. Wherever Jews settled they were a minority group, and thus they were forced in various ways to adapt to the cultures of the dominant society. The result was considerable diversity, as seen in language differences. Jews located in the Iberian Peninsula spoke Spanish or Portuguese. Those residing in central and eastern Europe spoke various regionally-distinct dialects of Yiddish, a language produced by the interplay of Middle High German, Hebrew, Aramaic, and the language of the host culture, which included, for example, Hungarian and Polish (Lavander, 1977; Goren, 1980: 571). Different social environments also contributed to differences in economic standing and in the ability to be, to a greater or lesser extent, incorporated into the dominant society.

Early Immigration

Prior to the period between 1880 and 1924, during which mass immigration brought nearly 2.5 million Jews into the United States from eastern Europe, two distinct settlements had already occurred involving the Sephardim and the Ashkenazim. Sephardic Jews, who originated in Spain or Portugal, arrived first. They had been expelled from both countries after 1492 as a result of the Inquisition, and they moved in large numbers to Holland and England.

The first Jewish community in North America involved 23 Sephardic Jews who settled in New Amsterdam in 1654 (Marcus, 1970). Settlements of Sephardic Jews developed in South America even earlier, and a number of prominent trader and merchant families—with names that reflected their Iberian origins, such as Gomez, Lopez, and Rivera—played a role in both North and South America (Goren, 1980: 574). The earliest enclaves in the United States developed in such cities as New York, Newport, Philadelphia, Savannah, Charlestown, and Richmond. In these enclaves, synagogues were constructed as the focal point of Jewish communal life.

Although their numbers never exceeded more than a few hundred, Sephardic Jews exerted considerable influence over the Ashkenazic Jews emigrating from Germany in the eighteenth century. By the second decade of the eighteenth century this latter group outnumbered the Sephardim (Sklare, 1971: 6). Nonetheless, the total Jewish population prior to the nineteenth century was quite small. It is estimated that soon after the American revolution the Jewish population in the new nation was about 2,000.

Mass Immigration

During the first half of the nineteenth century German Jews continued to enter the country, however. Their numbers grew to about 15,000 by 1840, increased to 50,000 a decade later, and then expanded to 150,000 in 1860. By 1880 the numbers had reached approximately a quarter million (Glazer, 1957: 23). At that they were, it should be noted, a distinct minority in the country, constituting only about 0.5 percent of the population as a whole.

The ethnic community that they established confronted the new arrivals during the peak immigration era. German Jews were economically far better off than their eastern European counterparts. The Ashkenazim were typically artisans, traders, and merchants who left Germany because of tax burdens and other restrictions—some directed solely at Jews—that stifled their ability to be as successful as they otherwise might have been. So they came to the United States not out of dire poverty, but with capital and human resources that could work to their advantage.

They settled in both established cities on the Atlantic seaboard, in the emerging commercial cities in the Midwest, and in hundreds of small towns (Sharfman, 1977). Many began modestly as peddlers, expanding when successful to shop ownership, and from there, for the most successful, to owning a chain of stores or a major department store. They also played a key role in merchant banking (Sklare, 1971: 7).

German Jews were more cosmopolitan than both Sephardic and eastern European Jews. They had been influenced by Enlightenment ideas and many had abandoned their religion. In addition, because they had greater opportunities to assimilate, many did so, though often with difficulty. Karl Marx's father, for example, was a successful middle class lawyer who converted to Lutheranism not out of religious conviction, but because it enhanced his economic prospects. For a young intellectual named Rahel Varnhagen, however, the process proved psychologically costly as she learned that the ability to simply will the abandonment of one's religio-ethnic origin had limits. Tempted by the desire to assimilate, for example by converting to Christianity and marrying a Gentile, Varnhagen painfully concluded that she could not escape her Jewishness. She came to define herself as a "conscious pariah" (Arendt, 1974).

The Early Community Presence

In the United States, German Jews attempted a balancing act, seeking acceptance and even incorporation into the larger society while maintaining a sense of Jewish identity. The Reform movement was a reflection of this effort. Orthodox Jews were traditionalists and therefore hostile to rationalism, liberalism, and the various currents of modernist thought. Many of the more educated Jews who were not prepared to abandon religious belief sought to incorporate these ideas into Judaism rather than using their religion as a bulwark against them.

Though Reform Judaism had its origins in Germany, among higher status Jews, it proved to be far more successful in America, where it did not have to confront a powerfully entrenched traditional community. Less than twenty years after the founding of Temple Emanuel in Davenport, Iowa, the members voted to abandon Orthodoxy in favor of Reform Judaism. In addition, various fraternal and mutual aid societies, or what were called *Landsmannschaften*, were established. One notable organization, B'nai

B'rith, was founded in 1843 to enhance the social status of Jews and to challenge anti-Semitism.

The Jewish community changed appreciably after 1880 as a result of the mass immigration of Jews from throughout eastern Europe, especially from Poland, Russia, Lithuania, Hungary, and Romania (Perlman, 1991). These Jews lived in far more difficult circumstances than did their western European counterparts. They were poorer and they resided in the part of Europe that was least changed by industrialization (Kahn, 1978). Furthermore, anti-Semitism was a greater problem for them during the nineteenth and early twentieth centuries. Religious hatred was a key to prejudicial attitudes, as Jews were depicted by Christians as "Christ-killers." A small segment of the Jewish community functioned as a "middleman minority" (Bonacich, 1973). These Jews worked as tax collectors, rent collectors, and traders and were held in contempt both by those who held the reins of power and by those below them in the class structure, who confronted them as economic adversaries.

As a whole, eastern European Jews were outsiders, forced to live in far more isolated circumstances than other Jews in Europe. They were, to use sociologist Georg Simmel's (1955) term, "strangers": people who stayed, though they were seen as potential wanderers. They resided in ghettos, which had first been self-imposed and later were made compulsory due to the rise of anti-Semitism. Even after legal barriers were relaxed, Jews continued to exist in self-isolation—in but not fully a part of the larger society (Wirth, 1928).

Immigration was prompted by a combination of factors. Economic changes had undermined the economic livelihood of small merchants, artisans, and similar members of the group. Furthermore, political conflict intensified the always-latent anti-Semitism and a number of pogroms occurred, particularly in Russia: in Odessa as early as 1871, followed by attacks elsewhere in 1881, 1889, and over an extended period from 1903 to 1907. As a result, Jews were political as well as economic migrants and moved to the United States with the intention of remaining. In contrast with many groups, the return migration rate for Jews was very low.

Jews provide the starkest contrast to the ideal typical immigrant presented in Handlin's *The Uprooted* (1973). They were primarily urbanites rather than rural dwellers. They did not come from the peasantry, rather many were part of the industrial proletariat. Unlike other working class arrivals, Jews brought with them skills that helped them find an economic niche in America. Particularly important was work in the needle trades, for they became the most important immigrant group in the garment industry. Between 1900 and 1925, more than 60 percent of the Jewish working class worked in this industry.

The Ethnic Community Evolves

Many new arrivals were influenced by socialism either prior to migration or afterwards. Jews contributed greatly to the political left in America, and by World War I they were one of the two most radical ethnic groups, the other being the Finns (Liebman, 1979; Kivisto, 1984). Although both of these groups contributed rank-and-file members in large numbers to various socialist organizations during the era, Jews, unlike the Finns, also provided these organizations with many national leaders. Jews also figured prominently in the labor movement.

Many other Jews were intent on preserving Orthodox Judaism in their adopted country, and they were frequently in conflict with the radicals. These Orthodox Jews also found themselves in disagreement with Reform Jews, whom they believed had watered down Judaism and thereby failed to appreciate that being a chosen people necessarily set Jews apart from Gentiles. The assimilative orientation of earlier arriving Jews was resisted (Liebman, 1973).

Eastern European Jews settled in a more concentrated manner than had earlier Jews. They opted for large cities on the East coast and the Midwest, where they resided in ethnic enclaves such as New York's Lower East Side, South Philadelphia, Chicago's West Side, and Boston's North End. These slums were rife with disease and danger, but an ethnic community quickly evolved. In New York the proximity of the neighborhood to the center of the garment industry linked residency and work (Wirth, 1928: 195–240).

The Family

Central to the ethnic community were four institutions: the family; fraternal and mutual aid societies; religious institutions; and labor organizations. The family in eastern Europe was an integral part of the *shtetl* (the Jewish village in eastern Europe), and the *shtetl* was seen as a kind of extended family. The tension between the family and the larger ethnic community that characterized Italians did not exist here. The nuclear family was embedded in a larger network of socially prescribed kin obligations. Gender roles were rigidly defined, with men's worlds involving both economic pursuits and religiously defined scholarly learning. Women were confined to the domestic realm, where they often assumed a dominant role. Mothers' expressions of love for their children embodied the "notions of suffering and sacrifice for the sake of the children" (Farber, et al., 1988: 407–408). Marriages were typically arranged, and the matchmaker (*shadchen*) had considerable power, but with the sometimes daunting responsibility of ensuring that marriages remained intact over time.

Change took place in America. For instance, nonreligious Jews rebelled against the idea of arranged marriages, opting for the romantic love that they saw in the Gentile world. Arthur Hertzberg (1989: 198) also contends that because fathers had such a difficult time in the workplace their authority eroded at home. The mother became the central figure in the family unit, the "source of family loyalty for her children because she was their protector." She thereby defined the terms of appropriate conduct, based not on the Talmudic tradition to which she had been excluded in Europe, but in terms of a kind of "folk religion."

Contrary to the commonly held image of the Jewish family as one of great durability, Hertzberg (1989: 198–200) stresses the frequency of desertion by fathers. He offers an antidote to those who romanticize the immigrant Jews' penchant for marital stability. A sizeable majority of families did have two parents present, however, and although comparative data is not conclusive on this point, it appears that compared to other ethnic groups at the time, the Jewish family was quite strong. Many women entered the work force, especially in the garment industry. Women reoriented and renegotiated their roles in the domestic realm and sought new opportunities and possibilities outside of the home (Glenn, 1990; Weinberg, 1988).

Fraternal and Mutual Aid Societies

New fraternal organizations and mutual aid societies emerged. Because of the divisions within the community, this often entailed a dual system of halls and enterprises because neither religious nor radical Jews were willing to participate in social activities with those from the other camp. Actually, there were several cross-cutting currents of intragroup conflict: between political radicals and conservatives; between the religiously devout and the secular; between German and non-German Jews; between the economically well-off and the poor (in New York they were described respectively as uptown and downtown Jews); and between the greenhorns and those who had been in America for some time.

The tensions could be acutely felt, as seen in the following example derived from a letter to the editor of a Jewish newspaper (in a personal column referred to as a "bintel brief"). An anonymous young man wrote:

> Permit me to ask you how to act in the following situation. I have been here but a short time, and fell in love with a girl, who is American born. She, like all American girls, loves to dance, to attend balls, and above all to have a good time, and I am a socialist, who having just come from such a revolutionary country, do not care for that. When it comes to love, I love her with my innocent heart. If I should ask her whether she loves me too, she would no doubt be unable to refuse me and would say that she loves me. But I know in my own heart that if I too attended dances, balls, she would certainly love me. I cannot influence her with my socialist ideas. Can you perhaps explain to me how one can get those follies out of her head? (quoted in Metzger, 1971: 240)

Despite these cleavages and the problems—personal and social—that resulted, a vibrant ethnic community based on Yiddish culture arose. Credit-lending institutions, *Landsmannschaften*, neighborhood organizations, educational enterprises, and the like grew rapidly. Yiddish language newspapers proliferated (Jaret, 1979). In New York City alone, 20 daily Yiddish papers were published between 1885 and 1924; at this latter date, as the more Americanized second generation came of age, 7 still remained in circulation. Various newspapers served different audiences: *Yiddishes Tageblatt* (Jewish Daily News) was read by religious and Zionist Jews (that is, Jewish nationalists); *Vorwaerts* (Jewish Daily Forward), under the editorship of the influential Abraham Cahan, was a socialist paper; and communists read *Freiheit* (Waxman, 1983: 47–48).

A thriving Yiddish theater sought to entertain and sometimes to edify. As Irving Howe (1976: 460) wrote, "It was a theater

superbly alive and full of claptrap, close to the nerve of folk sentiment and outrageous in its pretensions to serious culture." Drama,
music, and comedy were an integral part of this milieu, and it later
became a training ground for entertainers who ultimately found
national popularity: Al Jolson, Eddie Cantor, George Jessel, Sophie
Tucker, Jack Benny, Fanny Brice, and many others.

Religious Divisions

Religious Jews were divided into three major expressions, and they
created an institutional presence that reflected these theological
differences. The religiously devout from eastern Europe did not
embrace the German-dominated Reform movement, and after 1880
Orthodox Judaism gained momentum and became the main vehicle
for an anti-accommodationist stance toward the dominant culture.
This served as the institutional home of traditionalists, that part of
the Jewish community intent on not developing social relationships with Gentiles, while demanding the strict observance of Jewish law (halacha). The Orthodox founded yeshiva to educate their
children, avoiding public schools for the same reason as those Catholics who sent their children to parochial schools. Orthodox Jews
also established a few institutions of higher education, the most important being Yeshiva University in New York City. Within Orthodoxy the many differences spread individuals and groups on a
continuum from the ultratraditionalist to the moderately traditionalist (Glazer, 1957: 60–78; Heilman and Cohen, 1989).

Reform Judaism, though representing a minority of the
Jewish religious, was particularly influential because of the higher socioeconomic status of its adherents. Modeling themselves after Protestant Christians, Reform Jews established a system of
Sunday schools for religious instruction, and they founded a seminary for rabbinical training. They were inclined, however, to send
their children to public schools and to universities. They sought
accommodation with the outside world rather than segregation
from it. They were instrumental in the development of the
free-thinking Ethnical Culture Society, which began in 1876.

The Conservative movement established a middle ground,
which became an attractive alternative for many post-1880 immigrants. Unlike Reform Judaism, which had its origins in Germany,
Conservative Judaism was a distinctly American phenomenon. The
Jewish Theological Seminary, founded in 1887, became a center of

theological life for Conservative Jews. This was the religious choice of middle class or lower middle class non-German Jews, and because eastern Europeans far outnumbered German-Jews by the end of mass migration, this was the fastest growing branch in the twentieth century (Sklare, 1972 [1955]; Woocher, 1986).

Political and Labor Organizations

The final institutional component of the Jewish community involved radical political organizations and labor organizations. Though not all Jews attached to the union movement were radicals, socialists, communists, anarchists, and labor-Zionists played a crucial role in forming and leading many organizations. Gerald Sorin (1985: 70–71) argued that the proletarianization of the majority of immigrants was a necessary, but not sufficient cause to explain the significance of radicalism for a sizeable segment of the Jewish community. He argues that radicalism was a secular substitute for the Jewish religion that preserved a religiously-rooted sense of social justice. Jewish radicalism was deeply connected to the Jewish past, while having a tense relationship with central elements of the traditional culture (Liebman, 1979). In terms of Breton's (1964) institutional completeness thesis, radical political organizations and militant trade unions served the part of the ethnic community that was disaffected from the religious side.

Anti-Semitism

From these key institutions, a vibrant Jewish community arose. From the outset it confronted nativist hostility. Although there was a rising general antipathy toward essentially all of the new immigrant groups, according to John Higham (1970) no other group was subjected to as much hatred as the Jews. For example, the Ku Klux Klan was not only hostile to blacks; it was also intensely anti-Semitic. The link between anti-black and anti-Semitic attitudes was poignantly seen in the 1915 lynching of Leo Frank. Frank was a Jewish businessman in Atlanta who was unjustly accused of the murder of Mary Phagan, a 14-year-old girl who worked in his pencil factory (Lindemann, 1991: 194–272).

In addition to the hostility of violence-prone hate groups, a pervasive genteel animus toward Jews could be seen in the thinking of political, business, and religious leaders, as well as among academics and intellectuals. The old stereotypes of Jews originally involved the portrait of Christ-killers. This persisted, but was not the most prominent facet of stereotypes during this era. Instead two contradictory images arose. The first expanded upon the long-held characterization of Jews as Shylocks seeking power through money. This translated into a fear of Jews controlling government and the banks. Prominent in this perspective was the notion of the "International Jew." Henry Ford, for instance, embraced as the truth an infamous tract titled "The Protocols of the Learned Elders of Zion," which had presumably been written by Jews in Russia, but was actually a fabrication of Russian monarchists. The tract purports to outline a conspiratorial plan for establishing a worldwide Jewish dictatorship (Ribuffo, 1986).

The second image singled out the Jews as being particularly prone to radicalism. Although this was true, anti-Semitism fused with anti-radicalism in the United States, especially after the Russian Revolution and the Red Scare era in America (Higham, 1970). Not bound by logical consistency, anti-Semites both condemned the Jew for presumably controlling Wall Street and for fomenting communism. The irrationality of this can be seen in Ford's writings in his newspaper, *The Dearborn Independent*, in which he accused Jews not only for capitalist and communist conspiracies, but also for short skirts, bootleg liquor, and the corruption of baseball (Wirth, 1928: 271).

Upward Mobility

Despite this hostility, during the interwar years upward mobility was evident as Jews moved out of the working class and into the middle class. Some did so via business success. Others used higher education and joined the emerging white-collar work force. Many entered teaching and government service. The trend from business to the professions began at this time, though it became far more pronounced after World War II. As Jews applied to professional schools — law, medicine, and so on — they confronted discrimination based on the fear that if merit were the sole criteria for admission into these institutions, Jewish enrollment would overwhelm that of Gentiles. Thus, major universities, such as Harvard, Yale, Chicago, and Columbia, implemented quota systems whereby Jewish admissions were limited to a certain percentage of class size.

Other changes that signaled the beginning of a new relationship with the non-Jewish world were linked to this occupational shift. Jews began to move out of the ethnic enclave during this period for dwellings in better neighborhoods of cities, and later this became a mass migration to the suburbs (Sklare and Greenblum, 1967).

In both the workplace and in neighborhoods, interaction between Jews and non-Jews increased and afforded the possibility of new relationships. This period also witnessed an exodus from Orthodoxy, and Conservative Judaism was the major beneficiary. Linked to this was a trend toward overcoming the cultural differences between German and East European Jews (Swatez, 1990).

Although poised for more dramatic changes, Jewish America remained more insular than other European origin groups because of anti-Semitism and the desire among Jews to preserve a distinctive ethnic identity. Jews, for example, had a considerably lower rate of intermarriage than other new immigrants.

The Irish and Germans Revisited

During the period of mass immigration of eastern and southern Europeans into America, those often thought of as the older immigrants also continued to come. For example, more than 1.5 million English immigrants entered the United States between 1880 and 1930. The peak decade of German immigration occurred between 1880 and 1890, during which time slightly less than 1.5 million people entered the United States. During the 50-year period beginning in 1880 the total number was just under 3 million. During the same period, slightly less than 1.75 million Irish left their homeland for America (Bureau of the Census, 1975: 105). Despite these numbers, these groups constituted less of the overall immigrant population that they had prior to 1880.

The World of Work

As a consequence, although older arrivals were increasingly at home in America, these new arrivals provided a renewed need for the German and Irish institutional networks forged earlier (Handlin, 1970; Kamphoefner, 1987). Many of the newer immigrants were members of the industrial working class. Germans arrived possessing fewer marketable skills than the earlier cohort, which had a solid middle class, many artisans and crafts workers (bakers, brewers, shoemakers, and so forth), and a large number of farmers. Thus, there was a class division between the old and new immigrants (Luebke, 1990: 166–167). This distinction was not as pronounced among the Irish since much of the earlier generation had found employment as unskilled workers in an urban industrial environment, so their experience paralleled that of the new arrivals. Nonetheless, a modest Irish middle class had grown by the latter part of the nineteenth century and the "lace curtain" Irish often looked with either disdain or embarrassment at their poorer countrymen and countrywomen (Fallows, 1979: 45–59).

These two groups provide rather different portraits of the extent to which generational upward mobility was occurring. The Germans had a relatively high rate of upward mobility, both among farmers in the Midwest (Curti, 1959; Conzen, 1985) and among their urban counterparts (Bergquist, 1984). The lack of similar resources stymied a parallel pattern of mobility among the Irish, who had, according to Patrick Blessing (1980: 531) a "dismal record of movement up the occupational ladder." The Irish lack of mobility differentiated them from all of the other major European immigrant groups and placed them closest to blacks in their job mobility performance. Furthermore, the Irish who rose into the middle classes generally did so via politics or the priesthood and not the business world (Thernstrom, 1973; Sowell, 1981: 35–36).

Both German and Irish workers contributed to the labor movement around the turn of the century. The Germans were involved in craft unionism best represented by the American Federation of Labor, but for the more radicalized workers this also meant involvement in socialist-inspired labor and political involvements (Keil and Jentz, 1983).

Although the Irish had been used as strikebreakers earlier, this role went at this time to blacks, Italians, and other newcomers. Instead, the Irish were an increasingly important constituency of the American labor movement and were seen across the labor spectrum. Denis Kearney, who headed the anti-Chinese organization the California Workingman's Party, was one of many Irish who played prominent leadership roles in organized labor. Before the new unions emerged, the Irish achieved notoriety from activities in the

Pennsylvania coalfields of the secret organization known as the Molly Maguires, which combined labor agitation with nationalist hostility to the British (many of whom owned and ran the mines). The Knights of Labor was the most militant union of the nineteenth century, and its leader was the Irish American, Terence V. Powderly. In the twentieth century the successor union, the Industrial Workers of the World, was headed by another Irishman, "Big Bill" Haywood, whose militancy ultimately took him to the Soviet Union, where he died and was buried in the Kremlin (Dubofsky, 1969).

Politics

The Germans voted and otherwise used the political process to advance their perceived interests. They were, nonetheless, relatively slow to provide politicians to the national political arena, mainly because of the internal conflicts that had persisted in German America. For example, middle class business interests founded the National German-American Alliance, but it was rejected by labor activists and socialists and generally dismissed by church organizations, as well. The goals of the Alliance included fighting the growing threat of prohibition and promoting German language instruction in public schools (Luebke, 1990: 172).

On the political left, democratic socialists went to the polls to support presidential candidate Eugene V. Debs. In Milwaukee, which had a heavy concentration of Germans, the socialist journalist Victor L. Berger was elected to the U.S. House of Representatives. Given the group's size, the Germans remained underrepresented as political office holders.

In contrast, the Irish, as Edward Levine (1966: 138) has written, were "given to politics." Notably, the Irish controlled Democratic political machines in various big cities, after having helped create them earlier in the nineteenth century. Tammany Hall was a force in New York City for more than a half century, and there were comparable powerful organizations in Chicago, San Francisco, Pittsburgh, Jersey City, and Albany, with weaker versions existing in many other cities. These machines became entrenched because of their appeal to the ethnic loyalty of coethnics and their ability to deliver various rewards such as patronage jobs. When challenged, as by socialists and progressive trade unionists, the machines resorted to political repression, fraud, and other illegal means to preserve their control (Erie, 1988).

In relation to other ethnic groups, the Irish succeeded in establishing a rigid ethnic hierarchy that placed them at the top and accordingly permitted them to define the precise allocation of rewards (Clark, 1975; Pinderhughes, 1987). The New Deal and the subsequent reorientation of power from the local to the national level undermined these machines from the 1930s on; the reign of Richard Daley was the end of an era in urban politics.

Homeland politics were important for both groups. Woodrow Wilson's refusal to endorse the cause of Irish independence tested the Irish allegiance to the Democratic party. But finally, the Irish Free State was established and Irish Americans continued to ally themselves with the Democratic party. At the same time, they continued to push for uniting Ulster with the new Irish state — a cause that continues to elicit support from many Irish Americans, as seen in support for the Irish Republican Army.

Homeland politics fostered and reinforced ethnic identity. For the Germans, however, homeland issues profoundly affected the ethnic community and led to the rapid erosion of its institutional framework. When the United States entered World War I on the British side, a wave of anti-German hostility swept the country. The German language was banned in several states, and boycotts of German business, vandalism of property, harassment, and physical attacks occurred in the heat of patriotic fervor. This proved to be a devastating blow to German America, as many Germans opted to indicate their loyalty to America by abandoning their ethnic community. Thus, many chose to speak only English at home as well as in public, and it was common to Anglicize last names (Holli, 1981).

Their support for ethnic institutions declined. The number of German language newspapers after the war was reduced to one-fourth of the number published in 1910 (Conzen, 1980; 423). Even in the bastion of religio-ethnic identity, the Lutheran Church, Missouri Synod, congregations began to replace the German language with English in services and business meetings. Ethnic institutions experienced a precipitous decline in memberships and many closed their doors permanently.

In the interwar years various episodes of intraethnic conflict occurred. German American support for Hitler triggered intraethnic conflict (Bayor, 1978), though due to the bitter memories of

World War I, American Germans were far less inclined to exhibit support for Hitler than the Italians were for Mussolini. The Ku Klux Klan included among its enemies not only blacks and Jews, but also Catholics, with the Irish being perhaps the most hated group. On the other hand, some Irish lent their support to the anti-Semitic campaign of Father Charles Coughlin's Christian Front. Coughlin was known as the "radio priest" and for his anti-Semitism, anti-Communism, and pro-Fascist political positions (Blessing, 1980: 542).

The Erosion of Ethnic Communities

Despite these manifestations of conflict, and the persistent salience of ethnicity in fostering them, the interwar era was characterized by social processes that undermined ethnic communities and forced a redefinition of ethnic identity — changes that had their most visible impact after mid-century. Public schools proved to be a powerful Americanizing force, providing students with a multi-ethnic environment (Weiss, 1982; Fass, 1989). New patterns of friendship and dating that transcended ethnic boundaries began to be seen. Catholic parochial schools were more successful in preserving ethnic affiliations, but even here Catholics from different ethnic backgrounds were exposed to one another (the Missouri Synod schools were more successful in maintaining religio-ethnic boundaries). Similar changes were observed in multi-ethnic workplaces.

Although ethnic enclaves survived throughout this period, they became chiefly the residence of the working class. People who made their way into the middle class, a phenomenon that typified the Germans more than the Irish, often moved out of ethnic neighborhoods. Similarly, white-collar workers were forced to be more geographically mobile, thus detaching themselves from traditional institutional and personal affiliations.

Instead of ethnic lodges and social clubs, individuals were increasingly likely to join parallel nonethnic organizations such as the Elks or Kiwanis. Labor unions, especially the Congress of Industrial Organizations (CIO) founded in the 1930s, tended over time to replace earlier ethnically based workers' organizations. A similar pattern can be detected in other arenas of social life, as complex webs of group affiliation made ethnicity one of several competing claims for an individual's allegiance (Simmel, 1955).

Throughout the twentieth century mass culture progressively replaced ethnic culture. This can be seen, for example, in changing musical preferences. Although both Germans and Irish sought to some extent to cling to traditional music, they — and especially youth — were more attracted to all-inclusively American music, whether big band music, jazz, country, or other types of popular music. The radio and the recording industry played a key role in redefining musical tastes (Greene, 1990). The film industry stopped producing films directed to particular ethnic audiences and instead sought a common denominator in producing mass appeal movies.

Intermarriage

Many factors both within and without the German American and Irish American communities eroded the salience of ethnicity for members of these groups. Though far from irrelevant, ethnicity was less powerful and consequential than it had been at any point in their respective histories. As assimilationists have argued, perhaps intermarriage should be treated as the most crucial variable in assessing whether or not group boundaries will be preserved over time. If so, intermarriage trends prior to World War II suggest that for both the Irish and the Germans the viability of the ethnic community was being undermined.

Two major barriers existed to intermarriage: race and religion. The racial barrier has been powerful for most groups, but especially black and white marriages. Somewhat more controversial is the argument that religion began to replace ethnicity as a barrier to intermarriage. In other words, people began to marry out of the ethnic group, but within the religious group of their parents. This thesis, referred to as the "triple melting pot" was first presented by sociologist Ruby Jo Reeves Kennedy (1944). In a study of intermarriage trends in New Haven, Connecticut, from 1870 to 1940, she contends that ethnic intermarriages increased for all groups except Jews, but they did not occur randomly. British, German, and Scandinavians intermarried mutually, based on the common link of Protestantism. A similar pattern occurred for the Catholic groups in the city: Irish, Italians, and Poles. Although Will Herberg's (1955) *Protestant-Catholic-Jew* popularized this notion during the 1950s, recent scholar Cheri Peach (1980) has questioned the claim that religion replaced ethnicity as a determinative factor in mate selection.

Kennedy's (1944: 333) data clearly shows that outmarriages for all of the Christian groups discussed in this chapter increased over time. Although 93.05 percent of the Irish chose an Irish mate in 1870, the figure declined to 45.06 percent by 1940. The percentage for Germans during the same time fell from 86.67 to 27.19. This might not have been expected for the newer arrivals as well, but Kennedy found that although the decline for Italians was not great—from 97.71 percent in 1900 to 81.89 percent in 1940—the Polish went from 100.00 percent to 52.78 percent in the same four decade period.

In this the Italians most resembled Jews, who in 1940 had an in-marriage rate of 93.70 percent. Can religion account for these two exceptions? Probably religion accounts for high in-marriage rates for the Jews, but the Italians were less religious than the Irish and Poles, so religion probably wasn't the determining factor. New Haven had one of the highest concentrations of Italians anywhere in the country, and the ready availability of potential Italian mates can likely account for this difference. Italians in other locales had higher rates of intermarriage than in New Haven. As this suggests, we must consider the unique characteristics of any locale in making sense of intermarriage rates.

Lowrey Nelson's (1943) study of Minnesota's rural Wright County found that during the 1930s endogamy remained powerful among the three main groups in the region: Germans, Swedes, and Finns. Although the Germans were not the most endogamous, 80 percent of Germans married Germans. Rural areas with high concentrations of particular groups allowed the preservation of "ethnic islands." This provided a slower rate of change than was evident in urban settings.

Summary

We have examined the different experiences of three major groups that were part of the mass immigration that occurred during the fifty years after 1880: the Italians, Poles, and Jews. They brought with them different languages and cultures. They possessed

Figure 6.4   *A Swedish American amateur baseball team, circa 1935.*

Source: Courtesy of the Swenson Center.

different resources and occupational skills. They confronted different adjustment problems in America and different levels of prejudice and discrimination. They interacted in differing ways with other ethnic groups. These differences account for the observable differences in how each group responded to their new home and, in turn, how they were received by the host country.

During this same time, Germans and Irish immigrants also arrived, but they were able to identify with and participate in already established ethnic communities. By this time, the Germans and Irish who arrived earlier had adjusted and improved their situations. The Germans had proven to be rather successful economically. In contrast, the Irish were slow to exhibit economic upward mobility. Their main areas of success occurred in politics and religion, where the Irish gained footholds in urban machine politics and the hierarchy of the Roman Catholic Church.

Despite differences, the evidence suggests that for these and all other European-origin ethnics, the first half of the twentieth century was a watershed era. The movement out of the ethnic community and into the larger society began, sometimes fitfully, and sometimes with tensions, conflicts, and regrets about the disappearance of old bonds and allegiances. The prevalence of intermarriage provided new understandings of what it meant to be a pluralist or multi-ethnic country. Except for the Jews, whose intermarriage rates remained low until the late 1960s, the question would increasingly be posed: what does ethnic identity mean to a child whose parents come from different groups? The most far-reaching implications of this trend would not be evident until the second half of the century.

THE COLOR LINE: FROM THE CIVIL WAR TO THE CIVIL RIGHTS ERA

7

In an oft-quoted passage, W.E.B. Du Bois (1961 [1903]: 23) contended, "The problem of the twentieth century is the problem of the color-line — the relation of the darker to the lighter races of men in Asia and Africa, in America and the islands of the sea." In other writings he suggested that white workers were "compensated in part by a public and psychological wage" that was based on the racist belief in the inferiority of people of color (Du Bois, 1973 [1935]). Thus, white workers refused to join with Africans, Asians, and Hispanics in establishing a class consciousness that transcended racial boundaries because they derived a benefit from their racial identity. Similarly, white citizens frequently sought to deny the rights and benefits of citizenship to nonwhites. Whites excluded nonwhites from their neighborhoods, social organizations, unions, athletic clubs, churches, schools, and other institutions. Transracial friendships were infrequent, and when they occurred, often involved risks and a price for both parties. Interracial marriages were even less likely and were, in fact, banned by antimiscegenation laws in many states.

The color line operates along two axes: first, that of dominance and subordination; and second, that of inclusion and exclusion (Blumer, 1965: 323; Lyman, 1994). We will illustrate this by providing an overview of how the color line was drawn during the first four decades of the present century. In doing so, we will see the implications of this line for people of color in America.

From Emancipation to Jim Crow: African Americans

On January 1, 1863, President Lincoln signed the Emancipation Proclamation, which declared that slaves in all areas under the control of the confederacy were free. The proclamation did not include slaves in the border states or in southern states under total or partial Union control. Most important, it did not succeed in freeing one slave. The proclamation was designed to become a rallying cry for the Union forces when the North was not doing very well in the war. Furthermore, the proclamation ensured that France and England, despite their desire for southern cotton, would not join the Confederate cause due to opposition in those nations to slavery (McPherson, 1982).

Reconstruction

The Reconstruction Acts provided for further governmental actions in the immediate aftermath of the Civil War, during what became known as the Reconstruction era. After the Confederacy's defeat, several critical matters related to reintegrating the South into the Union had to be addressed. These included the terms under which Confederate states would be readmitted, who among Confederate supporters should be punished, whether rebels should be barred from seeking public office, and a host of related matters. Another facet of Reconstruction dealt with the rebuilding of the southern economy. The central issue of freed slaves revolved around redefining the role and status of Africans in American society (Frazier, 1949: 123–146; Franklin, 1967: 297–323; Litwack, 1979; McPherson, 1982).

The first action, in January 1865, was the proposal for the Thirteenth Amendment to the Constitution, which would abolish slavery throughout the nation. Two months later Congress passed legislation establishing the Freedmen's Bureau, which was intended to protect the interests of former slaves. By the time the Amendment was ratified, at the end of 1865, Lincoln had been assassinated and Andrew Johnson, a southerner, undertook a policy of Reconstruction that was designed to enhance the interests of the white small holder farmers. He did not press for citizenship for blacks and was not opposed to the passage of "black codes" in

Figure 7.1 *African American women working in a northern factory during World War I.*

Source: Courtesy of the Swenson Center.

several southern states that were intended to both revive the southern economy and reassert the role of the white landowning class. These laws required former slaves to sign labor contracts, permitted whipping, and allowed jail sentences for unemployed blacks (Foner, 1988: 199–201).

Johnson's efforts to avoid policies aimed at integrating blacks into the political system and into a new position in society were challenged by Radical Republicans in Congress. Not only was he nearly impeached, but Congress also passed the Civil Rights Act of 1866 over Johnson's veto. This act both granted various rights to African Americans and provided a role for the federal government in protecting these rights. Congress also succeeded in passing both the Fourteenth and Fifteenth Amendments to the Constitution. The Fourteenth granted citizenship to all African Americans and provided for equal treatment under both federal and state laws. The Fifteenth made it unconstitutional to deny citizens the right to vote on the basis of race.

African Americans attempted to assert their autonomy and to stake out a new place in American society (Du Bois, 1973 [1935]). Although some free persons of color had owned land in the ante-bellum era (in fact, some had also owned slaves), the number of property owners rose dramatically between 1860 and 1870. For example, black rural land ownership in the upper South rose over fourfold during that decade (Schweninger, 1990: 154). Those who had acquired artisanal skills on the plantation sought to use them as independent laborers.

One important legacy of the Freedmen's Bureau was the creation of schools to educate former slaves. From these developed what became some of the most important institutions of higher education for several generations of African Americans: Atlanta University, Fisk University, Hampton Institute, and Howard University. Taking advantage of these opportunities, a cadre of educated blacks emerged and formed the basis of both a middle class and a leadership stratum.

During a period that extended only to 1877, at which time the last federal troops were removed from the South, blacks entered the political process at the state and local level. At the national level, blacks were elected to the Senate and the House of Representatives. Several served as lieutenant governors, secretaries of state, state treasurers, and related high-ranking positions at the state level, as well as being represented in state legislatures. Thomas Nast's political cartoons and D.W. Griffith's 1915 film, *The Birth of a Nation* both portrayed blacks as unfit for involvement in a democracy and as making a travesty of legislative decorum, but historian Eric Foner (1988: 410) concluded that:

> Biracial democratic government, a thing unknown in American history, was functioning effectively in many parts of the South. Men only recently released from bondage cast ballots and sat on juries, and, in the Deep South, enjoyed an increasing share of authority at the state level, while the conservative oligarchy that had dominated Southern government from colonial times to 1867 found itself largely excluded from power.

Not only were attempts to recreate a labor system based on caste temporarily curtailed, but also many reform policies, such as those related to education and taxation, benefited poorer whites and blacks. This, however, did not last, and when Reconstruction came to an end, a new system of racial oppression replaced the former (Scott, 1994).

Before this happened, African Americans asserted themselves in ways that established the foundation for a distinctive black community. One important underlying feature of this gestation period of the free black community is its social distance from the white world. Two interrelated phenomena accounted for this situation: white resistance to racial equality and the black "quest for self-determination" (Foner, 1988: 89). This relative autonomy was seen in family life, churches, schools, and farms (Williamson, 1986: 48; Foner, 1988: 612).

Fifty years after the end of the Civil War and 50 years before the major triumphs of the civil rights movement, Griffith's *A Birth of a Nation* (based on Thomas Dixon's 1904 novel, *The Clansman*) provided a white supremacist reinterpretation of the antebellum South and the Reconstruction era. The slave period was depicted in a glowingly romanticized fashion that resembled the earlier-cited antebellum writings of Henry Hughes (1854). Moreover, freed Africans are depicted as intellectually and morally inferior to whites. Employing white actors in blackface, Griffith is not subtle in his contempt for former slaves. His polemic was designed to show that though they attempted to act like whites, blacks were incapable of genuinely patterning their lives after whites. In one caption of this silent film epic, Griffith wrote, "Meanwhile the former slaves ape the manners of their former masters." Blacks whip whites, place a former master in chains, sexually assault innocent white women, and are depicted as corrupt, vulgar, superstitious, and incapable of self-rule.

Reasserting White Domination

The film was greeted with hostility by many blacks and by some whites, but was highly regarded by large movie-going audiences. It reflected the firmly entrenched belief in the inherent inferiority of blacks, a belief that was shared by most whites, North and South (Pieterse, 1992). Such thinking gained currency in the decade following emancipation, during which white Southerners reasserted their claim to race supremacy through the political system and by extralegal terroristic tactics.

The first challenge to blacks occurred in the political arena, as efforts were made to disenfranchise them. Blacks were, beginning in the 1890s, excluded from both running for elective office and voting. Because the Fifteenth Amendment prohibited denying citizens the right to vote on the basis of race, other criteria were employed to circumvent this prohibition. The two most widely used devices were literacy tests and the poll tax.

Reducing African Americans to political powerlessness was just the first step in efforts to institute a new form of caste society predicated on race. Next came laws that mandated racial segregation. Although de facto segregation was actually more characteristic of the North than the South, what became known as the era of Jim Crow in the South redefined race relations far differently than advocates of Reconstruction had in mind. In a somewhat piecemeal fashion, a series of laws were enacted in southern states that required the segregation of blacks and whites in public accommodations, schools, residences, streetcars, and the like. Thus, around the turn of the century, began what historian C. Vann Woodward (1974) has termed the "strange career of Jim Crow." "Jim Crow" referred to a series of laws passed in the South that were designed to repress blacks. The origin of the term is uncertain.

African Americans found that, in spite of white supporters in both the North and South, such as advocates of the Social Gospel (White, 1990), there was not enough support to prevent the institutionalization of Jim Crow. In fact, such laws were found to be constitutional in the 1896 Supreme Court case, *Plessy v. Ferguson*. The plaintiff, Homer Adolphus Plessy, argued that because he was only one-eighth black, the state of Louisiana's laws pertaining to railroad segregation should not apply to him. The court did not rule in his favor. Rather, it declared that racial segregation was constitutionally permissible if segregated facilities were equally provided to both races. This doctrine of "separate but equal" remained the law of the land for more than a half century.

Plessy also permitted states to determine who was and who was not to be defined as a "Negro." Thus, a school reserved for whites could deny admission to a young girl who was one-sixteenth black. In short, a color line divided the races into two discrete camps (Baker, 1964 [1908]; Lyman, 1991). The problem with this, as the two examples in the preceding paragraph attest, is that there was a long history of racial interbreeding (Williamson, 1980). In some cosmopolitan parts of the South, such as Charlestown and New Orleans, the antebellum period witnessed racial definitions expressed in very subtle distinctions. Categories in use included mulatto (one-half black), quadroon (one-quarter black), octoroon (one-eighth black), sambo (three-fourths black), and mango (seven-eighths black). This changed in the age of Jim Crow.

Leadership in the African American Community

This hardening of the color line meant that the black community developed in isolation from other groups. As African Americans were progressively excluded from participation in the larger society, they withdrew into a world of their own. Historian Joel Williamson (1986: 54) has described how this shaped the leadership within the community:

> Out of this fragmentation emerged what amounted to a new black "nobility." The new noble was, perhaps, a minister or a bishop, the principal of a school, the president of an insurance company, or a political boss. Like the feudal lord, he offered his followers protection and maintenance, and he demanded loyalty and labor in return. He was invariably the self-conscious strong man who brooked no opposition within his domain.

In Zora Neale Hurston's novel, *Their Eyes Were Watching God*, (1978 [1937]), the reader is provided with a vivid portrait of such a leader in the character Joe Starks, a successful businessman who is the unofficial "mayor" of the black enclave in a Florida town. He exhibits a mixture of hard work, shrewdness, manipulation, and petty tyranny. At the national level, leaders in this mold, operating with considerable personal charisma, included such religious figures as Daddy Grace and Father Divine, as well as the nationalist Marcus Garvey (Williamson, 1986: 55).

Garvey was one of three black leaders to rise to national prominence during the early part of the twentieth century. The other two were Booker T. Washington and William Edward Burghardt (W.E.B.) Du Bois. They presented three different leadership styles and different, if sometimes overlapping, programs for responding to the new racial order in America. Washington was by far the most powerful and influential of the three. Born in slavery, Washington

Figure 7.2   *The family of an African American born into slavery, but working at the time for the U.S. Government, circa 1900.*

Source: Courtesy of the Swenson Center.

later founded Tuskegee Institute, a vocational training school in Tuskegee, Alabama, (Washington, 1963 [1901]) that was financially supported by northern progressives and had on its board several ranking Protestant reformers who were part of the Social Gospel movement (White, 1990: 66). From this base, Washington became an advisor to Presidents Theodore Roosevelt and William Howard Taft, members of Congress, and governors (Harlan, 1983).

Washington's success came because he did not directly challenge the system of institutionalized racial inequality. In his famous "Atlanta Compromise" speech of 1895 he set the terms for a racial peace that resonated well with many whites. It called for a situation of "mutual progress" in which blacks could expect increased opportunities for economic advancement. In turn, African Americans would neither demand racial equality nor integration. He sought to accommodate to what he viewed as the realistic limitations that existed in the nation. This explained the emphasis of

Tuskegee on vocational training in such areas as carpentry, farming, and teaching. Recent evidence has indicated that this portrait of Washington as the consummate "Uncle Tom" who capitulated to the whites rather than challenge their moral authority was not entirely accurate. Behind the scenes, Washington funneled money to support legal challenges to segregation and political disenfranchisement (Harlan, 1983).

The moderate accommodationist position articulated by Washington was challenged most forcefully by W.E.B. Du Bois, who many saw as the heir of Frederick Douglass. Du Bois was born and raised in Massachusetts and his life was quite different from that of the southerner Washington. Du Bois, for example, became the first African American to receive a doctorate from Harvard University. Like Washington, he wanted to bring African Americans into the mainstream, but he refused to limit their socioeconomic positions to the working class and lower middle class. To do so, he believed, would result in the consignment of blacks to permanent servility. Instead, he urged the promotion of what he termed the "Talented Tenth," a stratum that he wanted to be provided with the best education possible (Du Bois, 1961 [1903]: 85). From their midst would come intellectuals, educators, clergymen, lawyers, doctors, and other professionals who collectively functioned as a vital leadership for the African American masses (Broderick, 1959: 74).

Through the organization of the Niagara Falls Conference of 1905, out of which sprang the National Association for the Advancement of Colored People (NAACP), Du Bois posed a direct challenge to Washington's leadership and to his racial policies. The NAACP was a liberal assimilationist organization that advocated, according to Joel Williamson (1986: 68) the "immediate assimilation of black people as equal citizens in the Republic." Its economic stance basically supported laissez faire capitalism. Although Du Bois moved from this position over the course of his career, embracing first socialism and later Pan-Africanism (he died in Ghana in 1963 shortly after becoming a citizen of that country), the NAACP maintained its liberal reformist orientation.

A third approach to remedying the subservient position of African Americans was found in the program advanced by Marcus Garvey. Born in Jamaica, Marcus Garvey offered a version of black nationalism that encouraged the belief that blacks could not develop within the confines of a white-dominated society. Indeed,

Garvey advocated an exodus to Africa, and was seen by followers as a "black Moses" (Cronon, 1955; Redkey, 1969). He founded the Universal Negro Improvement Association (U.N.I.A), which was based on the quest for self-respect and dignity; in this, his approach was indebted to Washington, under whom he studied, and Du Bois would not have disagreed.

Garvey differed, however, from the other two major black leaders by opposing integration, instead endorsing a nationalism that mandated racial separatism. Garvey's quest for "racial purity" elicited support from such white supremacist groups as the Ku Klux Klan and Anglo-Saxon Clubs. Sometimes leaders from these white supremacist groups were invited as speakers at U.N.I.A. meetings; they found common ground in their advocacy of racial separatism (Cronon, 1955: 188).

Another aspect of Garvey's nationalism was its hostility to socialism. His economic policies called for the development and expansion of black capitalism. He did not believe that African Americans had a future in America, so he urged their return to Africa, calling first upon pioneers with skills to build new societies on the African continent. He created a shipping company, the Black Star Line, which was intended to facilitate the anticipated migration out of America. Garvey's organization was inherently unstable, and built on personal charisma and on slippery financial footing, so it is not surprising that it failed. He was convicted of fraud and was ultimately deported to Jamaica. As with the approaches of Washington and Du Bois, however, Garvey's nationalist ideals were revived again in subsequent decades.

Southern Race Relations

Throughout the period between the Civil War and World War I, African Americans remained heavily concentrated in the South. In 1910, 89 percent lived in that region of the country. They remained in southern agriculture. By 1910 about one-quarter of African American farmers owned their own farms, in contrast to about three-fifths of white farmers. The remainder of both blacks and whites in agriculture worked as tenant farmers or sharecroppers (Geschwender, 1978: 162–164).

Black and white farmers confronted similar economic difficulties, including high interest rates, mortgage debt, and the cost of shipping their crops by rail. Populism in the Midwest and the South was a political response to economic distress caused, populists argued, by financiers and industrialists. The populists' political objectives included a more egalitarian society that challenged the capitalists' economic power (Goodwyn, 1978). In the southern states, this populist vision took form in the Southern Farmers' Alliance. Race became a barrier to a unified alliance of tenant farmers because the Alliance excluded blacks from membership. Although there were fraternal relations between the Alliance and the Colored Alliance, based on a clear understanding of a shared position in the southern class system, racism undermined the formation of an integrated movement (Schwartz, 1988: 101; Geschwender, 1978: 164–168).

The failure to develop a biracial populist movement served the interests of the economically powerful. They were in a position to play race against race, and their domination of the region not only kept African Americans in a position of caste subordination, but also helped "to maintain a captive force of tenant labor, [and] to control agricultural labor costs" (Schwartz, 1988: 286). The racial division also mitigated the efforts of some in organized labor to mobilize the southern workforce. Historian Peter Rachleff's (1984) richly documented case study of the unsuccessful efforts to overcome racial divisions in Richmond, Virginia, serves as a microcosmic assessment of the South in general.

Underpinning this new social system in the South was the perpetual threat of violence and terror. The actions of groups such as the Ku Klux Klan and the Knights of the White Camellia were clearly intended as an extralegal reinforcement of a social order stratified along racial lines. The burning of property, beatings, and lynchings became an integral part of the social order. The result was the reestablishment of an interracial "etiquette" code in which blacks were expected to conduct themselves in a manner of servile politeness in the presence of whites. As Bertram Doyle (1936: 205) commented, this race specific etiquette was "a form of social control." Indeed, violations of the code could result in serious consequences, up to and including lynching — which became an endemic feature of Southern life (Raper, 1933; Shapiro, 1988).

Two classic community studies of southern cities were conducted during the 1930s, John Dollard's (1937) study of "Southerntown" and the monograph of Allison Davis, Burleigh Gardner, and

Figure 7.3   Caste and Class in the Deep South.

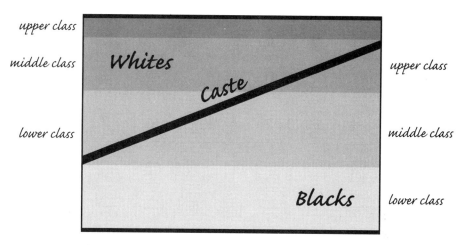

Source: Adapted from Davis, et al., 1941: 10 and 455.

Mary Gardner (1941) on "Old City." Both provide compelling documentation that the communities were divided along both class and caste lines, with a white class structure and a black class structure each further divided along caste lines. In Figure 7.3, derived from Davis and her colleagues (1941), it is clear that the upper class in the black community — professionals and business people serving the black community — are higher than the lower echelon of the white caste in socioeconomic position.

Nonetheless, the caste barrier was erected to ensure that there were advantages to being white, regardless of location in the class hierarchy. Dollard (1937) singles out three ways in which whites benefited at the expense of blacks: whites gained in economic, social status, and sexual ways. The last actually applied only to white men, who were described as having sexual access to both black and white women. Because a central tenet of the caste system revolved around the prohibition of black men engaging in sexual relations with white women, this obviously meant that white women also were restricted in their access to potential sexual partners (Dollard, 1937: 134–172; see also Davis, et al., 1941: 25).

Within the black community, an emerging class structure was based on occupation. The small upper class and the middle class were composed of owners of businesses that serviced a black clientele, professionals such as doctors and lawyers, and members of the clergy. Overlaying and reinforcing these internal economic divisions was the prestige attached to light skin by African Americans. Those in the upper and middle classes were disproportionately light-skinned, while poor blacks were more often dark-skinned. Dollard (1937: 69) observed, "Consciousness of color and accurate discrimination between shades is a well-developed Negro caste mark; whites, of course are not nearly so skillful in distinguishing and naming various shades." Color consciousness in the black community played a significant role in upward mobility, choice of marital partners, and the like.

The economy of the South continued to be dominated by the importance of three major crops: cotton, tobacco, and rice. Changes in Southern agriculture, especially felt in the cultivation of cotton, progressively undercut blacks' ability to remain on the land. Until 1910, cotton production expanded chiefly because of westward movement and led to the migration of blacks within the South. After 1910, however, expansion ceased. Several factors produced severe economic hardship for blacks engaged in cotton production. The boll weevil infestation destroyed crops and reduced the amount of acreage under tillage. A worldwide depression in cotton prices during the 1920s added to the problems, followed by the advent of increased mechanization and the payment of government subsidies to farmers. The combined impact of these changes served as a powerful migratory push force (Wilhelm, 1970; Fligstein, 1981: 8–19; Daniel, 1985).

The Promised Land

But economic factors alone do not entirely explain the move out of the South. Intertwined was a desire to escape the subordination of the caste system and the ever-present reality of violence perpetuated by whites. In a sense, African Americans exiting the South were "refugees," and not simply workers moving to improve their economic condition (Tolnay and Beck, 1992: 105). Many African Americans looked to the North as a "promised land" (Grossman, 1989; Marks, 1989; Lemann, 1991). An excerpt from a letter written by a would-be migrant to the offices of the *Chicago Defender* newspaper poignantly illustrates this combination of economic and political motives:

> Sir: I am writing you to let you know that there is 15 or 20 fam-
> ilys wants to come up there at once but cant come on account
> of money to come with and we cant phone you here we will be
> killed they dont want us to leave here & say if we dont go to war
> and fight for our country they are going to kill us and wants to
> get away if we can if you send 20 passes there is no doubt that
> evey one of us will com at once [sic] (quoted in Fishel and
> Quarles, 1970: 250).

Nonetheless, blacks were slower to enter urban industrial
America than other groups. Robert Park (1950: 167)) once said
that people in the modern world could be divided into two categories: "those who reached the city and those who have not yet
arrived." Though an overstatement, it contains an important sociological insight. African Americans were late arrivals, and this
had far-reaching ramifications because they had to contend and
compete with groups that had some prior experience in an urban
industrial setting.

A northern migration began to occur about the time of World
War I, produced partly by the demand for labor in war industries.
This migration expanded during the 1920s, as the immigration restriction law that was passed in 1924 dried up the supply of immigrant labor. The depression reduced, but did not entirely stop, this
flow northward, and World War II fueled the movement of even
greater numbers into northern cities (Fligstein, 1981: 76). In many
respects, the African American migration was akin to the transoce-
anic migrations of many other ethnic groups. Blacks migrated not
by steamship, but by rail. The Rock Island Line, for example,
served as the link between rural farmers in Mississippi and Louisiana and jobs in such urban centers as St. Louis and Chicago. Railroads on the East Coast, such as the Baltimore and Ohio, brought
blacks up the Atlantic seaboard to various northern cities.

Whatever economic opportunities the "Great Migration" afforded, it did not result in entering anything that remotely resembled the "promised land." Indeed, African Americans quickly
learned that much of the racial exclusion and discrimination they
had experienced in the South would be replicated in the North.
The movement north sparked racial hostilities. Around the time of
World War I, for example, there were serious race riots in numerous cities, including Chicago, Philadelphia, Washington, D.C.,
Omaha, and East St. Louis. Similar events occurred during World

War II; riots in New York's Harlem and Detroit were among the most severe and destructive.

African Americans were forced to reside in separate worlds in northern cities. In their famous investigation of Muncie, Indiana, both in the 1920s and the 1930s, Robert Lynd and Helen Lynd (1929; 1937) portrayed a northern city not unlike those encountered by Dollard and Davis and her colleagues. The Lynds (1937: 463) concluded that the "cleft between the white and the Negro population of Middletown [their pseudonym for Muncie] is the deepest and most blindly followed line of division in the community." This meant that the less than 6 percent of the city's population that was black had to attend a segregated YMCA, YWCA, American Legion post, and similar clubs and social organizations. Churches were de facto segregated, and black children were relegated to a separate corner of the city's main park. Moreover, the Ku Klux Klan had a powerful presence in Muncie, and during this period elicited rather widespread support from the mainstream of the white community. African Americans were systematically excluded from skilled trades. Most were relegated to the most menial occupations. In all of this, Muncie was a microcosm of larger patterns of prejudice and discrimination that blacks who migrated North confronted.

The Development of the Black Community

The most systematic and richly detailed study of black life in the North between the world wars is found in St. Clair Drake and Horace R. Cayton's *Black Metropolis* (1962 [1945]), a community study of a major destination for southern blacks: Chicago. Between 1900 and 1940, the African American population of Chicago increased more than tenfold. Referring to the black enclave as "Bronzeville, the authors depict it as a "world within a world." Bronzeville developed a rich institutional complex, including churches, businesses, voluntary associations, and newspapers (including the influential *Defender*). This community was connected to African Americans nationwide.

Furthermore, there were countless ties to the outside world of whites. For one thing, social reformers set up operations in Bronzeville to address a variety of social problems. Schools were another connection. In addition, the local political machine brought blacks into its fold, albeit in a subordinate position (Pinderhughes, 1987). During the 1930s both the organizing efforts of the Congress of Industrial Organizations (CIO) and of the political left, especially the Communist party, sought class alliances that transcended racial boundaries, with limited success (compare Naison, 1983, for a look at communist influence in New York's Harlem).

Bronzeville was, according to Drake and Cayton (1962 [1945]: 396) removed from the outside world, while being:

> organically bound up with American life. Negroes attend the same movies, read the same daily newspapers, study the same textbooks, and participate in the same political and industrial activity as other Americans. They know white America far better than white America knows them. Negroes live in two worlds and they must adjust to both.

In this milieu a distinctively black musical idiom emerged — the blues — that played a major role in shaping a distinctively American popular music (see, Jones, 1963). Rooted in the rural South, this secular music (as compared with spirituals) took instrumental form in southern cities, especially New Orleans, as jazz was born. In northern cities this music was central to the rise of rock-and-roll. But the cross-over from the black to the white world took time.

Black Culture

In this general context a cultural movement arose within African America, centered not in Chicago, but rather in the nation's intellectual capital, New York City. The Harlem Renaissance was the first great blooming of a distinctly African American culture, a literary movement that had both cultural and political implications. Principal figures such as Alain Locke, Langston Hughes, Countee Cullen, Zora Neale Hurston, Jean Toomer, and Claude McKay reflected the heterogeneous character of this largest of the African American communities. Its inhabitants included African Americans from both the North and South and also the West Indies (Huggins, 1971; Lewis, 1981).

The writers associated with the Harlem Renaissance tried to articulate a common consciousness of what it meant to be black in

America. Deprived of ongoing connections with their African roots, blacks who migrated to the North also felt the lack of a regional heritage, which prior to this time been centered in the South. Furthermore, just as the economic and political positions of African Americans had been largely determined by whites, the images of blacks in American culture were determined by the white-controlled media and cultural outlets. The American cinema, for example, was thoroughly Eurocentric and reinforced negative stereotypes of African Americans, exhibited a morbid fear of interracial sex, and provided only one positive role for blacks, that of "loyal servant"—evident in films ranging from *The Birth of a Nation* to *Gone with the Wind* (Lyman, 1990b).

The central ideological figure of the literary movement, Alain Locke, argued in reaction that racial unity should be fostered by an awareness of a common cultural tradition. He saw such an effort as a first opportunity for self-determination (Huggins, 1971: 58). Calling for the birth of the "New Negro," the Harlem Renaissance writers attempted to change racist notions of subservience and inferiority. They sought to redefine the African American image in the larger culture as a prelude to redefining the social, economic, and political position of blacks.

This cultural movement was short lived, but it did succeed in educating future generations of African Americans, who, after World War II participated in the modern civil rights movement.

The Hispanic Presence in the United States

Hispanic immigration was chiefly a Mexican phenomenon until after 1940, with relatively small numbers of Puerto Ricans and Cubans also entering the country during this time (Burma, 1954). After the Mexican-American War about 80,000 Mexicans resided in the United States, chiefly in border regions. Although a few thousand Mexicans opted to repatriate to Mexico after the conquest, most remained and were joined by a small, but steady stream of immigrants. Mexican migration from the middle to the end of the nineteenth century was quite small; slightly more than 13,000 immigrants were reported for the entire half century by the Commissioner General of Immigration (U.S. Bureau of the Census, 1975).

Mexicans in the Southwest

Although Mexicans in the United States were accorded citizenship rights, the rapid settlement of Anglos on the western frontier jeopardized their socioeconomic and cultural positions. Demographic change reduced the Mexican population to a minority in regions of the Southwest, though New Mexico was an exception. The completion of railroad connections between California and the eastern United States allowed 120,000 Anglos to enter that state in 1887 alone which reduced California's 12,000 Mexicans to a numerical minority (Moore, 1970: 19). In Los Angeles, for example, the Mexican-American population declined from 75.4 percent of the city's total population in 1850 to only 19.3 percent by 1880 (Griswold del Castillo, 1979: 35).

Political conquest was followed by economic domination and a challenge to Hispanic culture. The Anglo exploitation of the Southwest's natural resources in mining, lumbering, and agriculture combined with the growth of business ventures and industrial development. These developments intensified during the 1880s.

Viewing the Hispanic and Anglo frontiers as increasingly "interlocked," Sarah Deutsch (1987: 13) argued, "This renewed Anglo assault posed an even greater challenge to the territory's Hispanics." It resulted in the loss of substantial amounts of land, sometimes through legal means and other times through outright fraud. Some land went to private interests and the federal government also appropriated substantial holdings into the national forest system. Although wealthier Hispanos often managed to hold onto their land, the poorer and less educated did not. For example, the infamous Santa Fe Ring, dominated by Anglos, but also involving wealthier Mexicans, acquired vast tracts of land formerly held communally by residents of small Hispanic towns. Over several decades the 2 million acres of community land was reduced to 300,000 acres (Cortés, 1980: 707).

This challenge did not occur without resistance to the Anglo incursion. Some secretive societies, such as the Mano Negro (Black Hand) and Gorras Blancas (White Caps), engaged in guerrilla tactics, destroying telegraph lines and railroad ties, but they were also willing to use the courts and public opinion in their struggle to protect their interests (Cortés, 1980: 708). In the famous Lincoln

County War, which began in 1876, New Mexican sheep ranchers, who were largely Mexican, fought Anglo cattlemen as the latter began to enclose fields with barbed wire, thereby denying access to open lands used for sheep grazing (Moore, 1970, 14).

Despite this struggle, the Mexican position in the Southwest eroded considerably. Loss of land was accompanied by loss of jobs. Anglo control of the economy meant that Mexicans were essentially excluded from the middle class and were consigned to the lowest tier of unskilled laborers within the working class. The downward social mobility landed them in unskilled positions as agricultural day or seasonal laborers, on railroads, and in mines and manufacturing.

Anglo domination entailed a progressive marginalization of Mexicans into what some scholars have referred to as a colonized status that produced the "barriozation" of the Mexican populace (Camarillo, 1979; Berrera, 1979; Romo, 1983). Thus, Mexican Americans can be viewed in terms of Robert Blauner's (1969) "internal colonialism" thesis. Blauner argued that when a group is subjugated by a more powerful and numerically larger group, the colonized group ends up economically and politically weakened and its indigenous culture is threatened. Confined to a residential ghetto, Mexican Americans became isolated politically and religiously as control of the Roman Catholic church slipped from them (Griswold del Castillo, 1979: 139–170).

The loss of economic and political power did not occur in New Mexico to the extent that it did elsewhere — an Hispanic elite managed to maintain its position, although this required accommodating to Anglo settlers. Anglos were slower to settle in New Mexico so their numbers did not overwhelm the Mexican population. New Mexico was not admitted to statehood until 1912, partly due to the belief in Washington that the territory had not been sufficiently "Americanized" (Weber, 1973; Daniels, 1990: 308).

Mexican Immigration in the Early Twentieth Century

In the twentieth century immigration increased dramatically. The border's permeability allowed Mexicans, especially those living near the border, to respond rapidly to job opportunities in the United States. Seasonal and temporary work was attractive to workers because it did not require permanent migration.

Figure 7.4   *The harsh realities of immigrant life are revealed in this Mexican American funeral, circa 1920.*

Source: Courtesy of the Swenson Center.

Employers increasingly came to appreciate the benefits of a "reserve army of the unemployed." These workers' labor power could be exploited during labor shortages, while they could just as easily be dismissed during economic downturns (McWilliam, 1948).

Although the Mexican experience has been characterized as an instance of coercive pluralism, there are also similarities with the European experience (Deutsch, 1987: 213). Mexicans departed their homeland for chiefly economic reasons, but like some Europeans, economic factors were overlaid with political ones, especially as a result of the Revolution of 1910 in which Porfirio Díaz's dictatorship was overthrown. Díaz pushed industrial development in Mexico, but the dislocations it caused divided the nation into the beneficiaries and the losers. Liberals were disenchanted with him, and under the leadership of Francisco I. Madero, they managed to drive Díaz from power.

In the ensuing chaos, Mexicans poured into the United States. Some estimates suggest that as much as 10 percent of the population emigrated during this period. Government statistics regarding Mexican immigration are problematic because they cannot account for illegal entries, but they do reveal something of the extent to which migration increased after 1900. During the first decade of the twentieth century nearly 50,000 Mexicans legally entered the Unites States, almost four times the total for the preceding half century. In the second decade 219,004 Mexicans immigrated and were followed by 459,259 during the 1920s (U.S. Bureau of the Census, 1975: 107).

Responding to opportunities in the American labor market, Mexicans began to move into urban industrial settings. The largest populations were located in the following southwestern states (ranked in descending order of size): Texas, California, Arizona, New Mexico, and Colorado. In addition, Mexicans moved into the burgeoning industrial cities of the Midwest, particularly Chicago and Detroit (Bogardus, 1934: 16). Their sojourner status is symbolically reflected in their early living arrangements in the Mississippi river town of Silvis, Illinois. Newly arriving Mexicans found work with the community's major employer, the Rock Island Line and were housed in boxcars in the railroad yards! These housing conditions were repeated elsewhere (Moore, 1970: 21).

Mexicans industrial workers were received ambivalently by Anglo workers. Mexicans were sometimes imported by industrialists as strikebreakers, which produced anti-Mexican hostility from organized labor. This employer strategy of divide and conquer tended to be a rather effective way of stymieing labor organizing. International Harvester, for example, brought many Mexicans into the Midwest. This impeded unionization by establishing a racially segmented labor force in which Mexicans occupied the bottom of the occupational hierarchy (Berrera, 1979). The Mexican American situation supports Edna Bonacich's (1972) "split labor market" theory, which sees recent immigrants and racially-marginalized groups excluded from higher-paid jobs and as a source of cheap labor.

Like blacks and Asians, Mexicans were often not welcomed into the union movement. But when Mexicans were involved, they were often actively involved. For example, Mexicans played a major role in the struggle to obtain union recognition in Arizona's copper mines. They participated in two of American labor's major battles, the 1913 Wheatland Strike in California, and in Ludlow, Colorado. They were involved in organizing efforts of the United Mine Workers, the Western Federation of Miners, and the Industrial Workers of the World (Deutsch, 1987: 94–95, 110)

The border communities from Brownsville, Texas, to San Diego acquired distinctive features because the border between the two nations allowed considerable movement back and forth (Garcia, 1981; Heyman, 1991). Illegal immigration was common and attempts to control it resulted in an adversarial relationship between Mexicans and the Immigration and Naturalization Service's Border Patrol, along with local authorities such as the Texas Rangers. Illegal immigrants were vulnerable to abuses from these agencies. Many illegal immigrants were dependent on the padrone system for employment because of their legal status and their unfamiliarity with the language and culture. In this, they were like Italians and Greeks: victims of the system's exploitive character.

The Depression and Repatriation

Despite the problems, Mexicans continued to come to the United States in response to job opportunities. Communication networks between Mexican Americans and those in the homeland provided would-be migrants with information and advice. World War I and the end of the European mass migration meant that opportunities for Mexicans existed over an extended period of time. The depression finally stopped large-scale migration. With the rise in unemployment, many Mexicans voluntarily returned to Mexico. That country was also hard hit by the depression, however, and there were still would-be immigrants. Few were admitted, with the number of Mexicans obtaining visas in the hundreds rather than thousands for most years of the 1930s. It became routine practice to deny visa requests by identifying Mexicans under the bureaucratic designation LPC (that is, "liable to become a public charge" or in other words, a recipient of welfare or unemployment relief). Scapegoating was common as Mexicans were blamed for filling up relief rolls (Stoddard, 1973: 23–24).

As one means of dealing with the crisis of unemployment during the 1930s, Secretary of Labor William Doak advocated ousting aliens from the country. Many counties and municipalities agreed.

Abraham Hoffman (1974) documented the forced repatriation policies of the County of Los Angeles. Concluding that it was cheaper to pay transportation costs rather than maintaining Mexicans on relief rolls, the county chartered trains and paid for one-way tickets, generally shipping individuals to Mexico City — far from the border where re-entry would be possible. Ricardo Romo (1983: 162) described the impact of this campaign on the East Los Angeles barrio:

> Panic gripped the Los Angeles *colonia*, which by 1930 had become the unofficial Mexican capital of the United States. Mexicanos, poorly organized politically, highly visible in segregated communities, and misunderstood socially and culturally, became the target for immigration raids that touched the lives of at least one of every three Mexican families.

The result of the combined effects of voluntary and forced repatriation was that the Mexican-born population in the United States declined from 639,000 in 1930 to 377,000 a decade later (Moore, 1970: 42). One unanticipated result of this policy was that many Mexicans, even after a relatively short stay in the United States, found themselves alienated from their homeland. They were often seen as having become too Anglo or "gringo."

Prejudice and Discrimination

Economically troubled times generally intensify prejudice and discrimination. For Mexican Americans this meant that the repertoire of negative stereotypes that already existed, though declining over time, were still acutely felt during the 1930s. These included persistent images of Mexican laziness and corruption. There was a generalized perception that they were present-oriented, complacent, subjugated to nature, seekers of immediate gratification, non-intellectual, emotional, superstitious, and traditional (note that many of these resemble stereotypes of Italians). In addition, the notion of machismo was applied to males. Linked to machismo was the representation of Mexicans as violent-prone.

Early movie portrayals, in what were pejoratively known as "greaser" films, such as *Tony the Greaser* (1911) and *The Greaser's Revenge* (1914), were the stock-in-trade of films about Mexicans during the first two decades of the twentieth century. In them, according to Allen Woll and Randall Miller (1987: 243), "the 'greaser'

Figure 7.5   *A Mexican American bride, circa 1930.*

Source: Courtesy of the Swenson Center.

robbed, murdered, pillaged, raped, cheated, gambled, lied, and displayed virtually every vice that could be shown on the screen." Although this negative imagery softened over time, the difficulty with speaking proper English proved to be a source of jokes with the advent of talking films (Woll and Miller, 1987: 245; Miller,

1978). In addition, as Chon Noriega (1991) observed, films depicting Mexican Americans were often of the social-problem genre, as seen in the 1935 film *Bordertown* in which the lead character (played by Paul Muni) is a violence-prone manager of a prohibition-era casino.

Not surprisingly, in Bogardus's (1959) social distance studies, Mexicans were located in the bottom third of the 30 groups he studied in both 1926 and 1946. Their social distance score was only slightly better than those of African Americans, Asians, and Turks.

The Bracero Program

Nonetheless, the value of Mexican labor became increasingly obvious, especially to employers in the Southwest, both in agriculture and manufacturing. With the outbreak of World War II, the demand for workers grew and it was hoped that Mexicans would temporarily meet that demand, as they had done during World War I. Unlike the earlier wartime period, however, the Mexican economy in the 1940s was doing well, so migratory push forces were not strong. This situation led to the implementation of a program of contract labor known as the "bracero program."

Begun in 1942, this program enticed Mexicans with the offer of higher wages than could be obtained at home if they would temporarily migrate. It carried the explicit expectation that when their services were no longer needed, Mexicans would return to their homeland (Moore and Pachon, 1985: 137). Suspended after the war, as soldiers returned home and again entered the workforce, the bracero program was later resumed because it gave employers considerable flexibility in meeting labor needs. Although this program was a boon to these temporary workers, it was not viewed favorably by Mexican Americans, many of whom thought that they were being passed over for jobs because the immigrants, it was believed, worked for less than American workers.

The Ethnic Community

In this context, characterized by considerable fluidity of the Mexican American population, an ethnic community emerged. For a variety of reasons the community was less developed than those among European immigrants. Mutual aid societies were relatively slow to develop into formal organizations, as Mexicans were in-clined to rely more on informal kin networks. The Roman Catholic church was quite weak. Since the nineteenth century, conservative traditionalists and liberal reformers had sought to control Mexican politics. In this struggle the church hierarchy sided with the con-servatives. This resulted in a disaffection with Roman Catholicism by those who disagreed with its generally accommodationist and conservative orientation. This split within Mexico was replicated in the Mexican American community and was further exacerbated by the lack of an adequate supply of Mexican or Spanish-speaking priests. Parishes were often assigned priests with little familiarity with Mexican Americans or their culture. The pervasive poverty combined with the relative ease by which Mexicans could return home also contributed to the underdeveloped state of the ethnic community.

In his study of the "Back of the Yards" neighborhood of Chica-go, Robert Slayton (1986: 183) noted that the Mexicans "never de-veloped the same institutions [as European-origin groups], or when they did, established them over a much longer period of time." They, thus, relied much more heavily on the settlement house founded by the University of Chicago than did other ethnic groups in the area. The informality of their self-help network was seen by the fact that the central mutual aid institution was a pool hall, which was "a combination information center, hiring agency, job and housing referral service, and bank" (Slayton, 1986: 181).

During the interwar years, however, a middle class arose and developed a sense of self-identity and an organizational presence. Its leaders sought to develop a mentality within the entire Mexican American community that stressed a dual consciousness — Mexi-can in culture, but politically American. They invested in various local community institutions, especially the Roman Catholic church, and they got involved in political affairs at the local level, concerned about such issues as educational opportunities for their children and prospects for economic advancement.

These concerns were most visibly pursued in a national orga-nization that represented the middle class interests, the League of United Latin American Citizens (LULAC). Essentially a civil rights organization, LULAC's objectives and tactics resembled those of the NAACP and B'nai B'rith. LULAC waged an ongoing campaign against Anglo prejudice and discrimination (Garcia, 1991). For example, in the aftermath of what became known as the "zoot-suit riots" in Los Angeles during 1943 (Mazón, 1984) that pitted U.S. servicemen against young Mexican Americans, LULAC was instrumental in combating the resultant intensification of Anglo hostility.

Although middle class leaders played a major role in shaping Mexican American consciousness, Mario T. Garcia (1989: 145) argues "they did not monopolize it." El Congresso del Pueblo de Habla Espanola (the Spanish-Speaking Congress) was a working class counterpart to LULAC that had ties to left-wing political organizations, including the Communist Party. It was concerned with discrimination, jobs, housing, education, and the problem of youth crime and delinquency in the barrio. In addition, Mexican American workers joined with other border proletariats in the CIO's International Union of Mine, Mill, and Smelter campaign to unionize the lead, gold, silver, zinc, and copper mines and refineries in Arizona, New Mexico, and Texas (Garcia, 1989: 175–198).

Cubans and Puerto Ricans

As the Mexican American community evolved, the two other Hispanic groups under consideration, Cubans and Puerto Ricans, remained relatively small. Cuban immigration remained very low until the 1960s, despite the island's close proximity to the mainland and the U.S. role in Cuban history since the Spanish-American War. The impetus for immigration was the revolutionary overthrow of the corrupt dictator Fulgencio Batista. The small contingent of Cubans arriving in the late nineteenth and early twentieth centuries settled in a few small enclaves in southern Florida, and many found employment in cigar factories owned by fellow Cubans. The heaviest concentration was in the Ybor City section of Tampa (Pozzetta and Mormino, 1986). Given their small numbers, they did not have a pronounced impact on the ethnic composition of southern Florida until after mid-century.

Puerto Rico became a commonwealth of the United States, and after 1917, Puerto Ricans were granted U.S. citizenship. This meant that they could legally move to and from the mainland freely. Nonetheless, until 1930 the numbers were low. Only 1,513 Puerto Ricans were living in the United States in 1910. The early immigrants were largely political exiles. Labor migrants began to arrive in the 1920s and continued during the depression years, due to a long-term drop in world prices for the island's two main export crops, sugar and tobacco. Migratory pressures were heightened by the destructiveness of two powerful hurricanes that hit Puerto Rico in 1928 and 1932.

By 1940 there were nearly 70,000 Puerto Ricans on the mainland. Unlike Cubans, they did not opt for Florida, but instead settled in New York City and its immediate environs. In 1940, 87.8 percent of all Puerto Ricans in the continental United States lived in New York City (Fitzpatrick, 1980: 860). Only the beginnings of an institutional presence were evident during the interwar years. This changed after 1945, as cheap airfares provided easy access to the mainland and resulted in a dramatic increase in immigration.

The Chinese and Japanese: A Comparison

As Figure 7.6 indicates, the Chinese population in America nearly doubled between 1860 and 1870, and it continued to grow until 1890, when it reached a peak of 107,488. Thereafter, the population declined, its nadir being 1920, when U.S. Census data report a total of 61,639. From this low point, the population again began to grow slowly (U.S. Bureau of the Census, 1975).

The Chinese and Immigration Restriction

This demographic overview reflects a unique feature of the Chinese experience: the Chinese were the first group to be singled out by immigration restriction forces. Efforts aimed at stopping the further migration of Chinese began in California, but as they moved into other parts of the country, Chinese exclusion became a national cause (Barth, 1964). Organized labor played a particularly important role in restriction efforts. White workers in the labor movement viewed the Chinese in racial rather than class terms: whites saw Chinese workers as a competitive threat rather than as allies in the struggle against capitalist exploitation. Samuel Gompers, the head of the American Federation of Labor, was a vocal spokesperson for the demand: "The Chinese must go" (Saxton, 1971). But organized labor was not alone in this call. When President Rutherford Hayes called for a stop to "the

Figure 7.6   Chinese and Japanese Residents in the United States, 1880–1930.

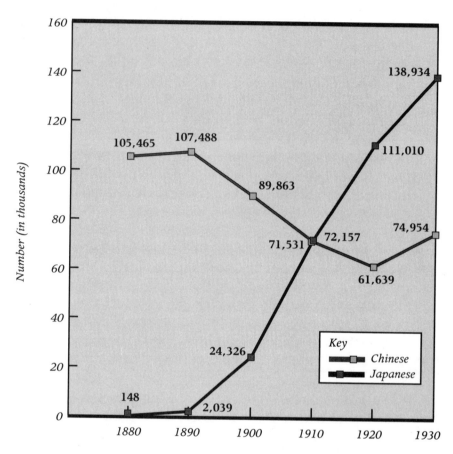

Source: U.S. Census Data, 1975.

present Chinese invasion," he reflected a widely held public sentiment for restrictive legislation (Takaki, 1989: 103).

Immigration restriction laws passed in California proved to be both constitutionally suspect and ineffectual. In 1882, however, a national Chinese exclusion act became law. It prohibited further Chinese immigration of laborers for a period of ten years. Certain exceptions, such as those for merchants and students, made the law cumbersome and provided the Chinese ways of circumventing its impact. Despite protests by the Chinese government and spokespersons in the United States, the prohibitions were not merely extended a decade later, but the Geary Act imposed even harsher burdens on the Chinese. The merchant category was redefined in a more restrictive way, and all Chinese were required to carry certificates of residence (Lyman, 1974: 66–67). A decade later immigration restriction was again continued, and this persisted until the national legislation of 1924 that halted mass migration across the board.

Actually, migration did not cease altogether. By getting themselves classified as merchants or students, some would-be immigrants were admitted under false pretenses. In addition, though precise figures are hard to come by, illegal immigrants found their way into the country. The 1906 earthquake in San Francisco destroyed records on Chinese immigration and citizenship, so authorities could not dispute Chinese claims that they had been born in America. Because it was permitted to bring relatives to the United States, it was possible to claim that a child had been born in China who should be permitted entry papers. This led to a practice known as the "slot racket" or "paper son" migration (Wong, 1988: 238).

The Bachelor Society

The Chinese community in America continued to be heavily male dominated. In 1860 there were 1,858 males for every 100 females. That ratio worsened in ensuing decades, reaching 2,678 males per 100 females in 1890. By 1920 the ratio had improved substantially, but still remained at the skewed figure of 696 men per 100 women. By the outbreak of World War II the most balanced sex ratio of Chinese America to that date was reached: 285 men per 100 women (Lyman, 1977: 147). As a consequence of the imbalance, throughout this period the family had difficulty developing as an integral part of the ethnic community. Most Chinese women in America were either the wives of merchants or prostitutes (Hirata, 1975; Nee and Wong, 1985). Most men were either single or married with families in China, forced to live in a "bachelor society" (Siu, 1952; Nee and Nee, 1973; Lyman, 1977). Those who were married and forced to live apart from their wives and children were members of what Betty Lee Sung (1967) has called "mutilated" families.

The consequence of this was the strengthening of the other institutions of the Chinese American community. In China religion tended to be family-centered, partly because of the central role of devotion to ancestors. In America, however, religion was frequently linked to non-familial institutions. In many instances temples and shrines were erected by clans and *hui kuan*. Secret societies were also known to have been the sponsors. According to Stanford Lyman (1974: 48), these religious centers "operated much like a sacred but theatrical enterprise, providing services in the form of festival celebrations, dragon parades, deity propitiation, and individual prayer in return for contributions."

Chinatown as an Ethnic Island

Ordinary Chinese were heavily dependent upon clans and *hui kuan* for other facets of everyday life: jobs, housing, socializing, adjudicating conflict, relationships with the host society, and welfare. In turn, these institutions (and more indirectly, this was true for the secret societies, as well) were controlled by the merchant class, which over time solidified its position as the ruling elite in the community.

Though conflict was common within the community, it was not permitted to threaten the power of the merchant class (Lyman, 1977: 103–118). To ensure against this, clans often divided the turf to work cooperatively rather than competitively. Sometimes this meant that certain clans controlled certain business enterprises. The Dear clan became associated with fruit and candy stores, while the Yee and Lee were associated with better restaurants. In other instances, the division was geographic. Thus, the Lee clan was dominant in Philadelphia, the Toms in New York City, the Loys in Cleveland, and the Moys and Chins in Chicago. Overarching merchant associations were established to help ensure cooperation, with San Francisco's Chinese Consolidated Benevolent Association, or Six Companies, serving as the model for similar ventures.

The immigrants' dependence on the ruling elite and the community institutions meant that it was in the interest of that elite to preserve the Chinese ghettos as something approximating what Ronald Takaki (1989: 230) termed "ethnic islands." The elites' position was based on an ability to control a highly dependent group. They were aided and abetted by intense racism on the part of the host society. Even if the Chinese had sought to assimilate, they would have discovered powerful barriers to admission into the larger society.

Anti-Chinese Activity

The Chinese were heavily concentrated in the western part of the United States. Although San Francisco quickly became the undisputed center of Chinese America, many Chinese found employment in rural areas and small towns on the frontier. Economic survival was precarious because of the intense discrimination they confronted. Chinese were driven from agricultural work in California in the 1890s as a consequence of a series of racially-motivated labor actions. Chinese were denied work in the canneries and on the fishing vessels in Astoria, Oregon — a demand put forth by the local white labor union. Chinese were the victims of punitive or harassing laws such as a tax assessed on foreign miners. In San Francisco's cigar industry, the creation of Chinese owned companies led white businesses and workers to use, for the first time in American history, the "union label." In this case, a white band was placed on cigars and smokers were urged to buy these cigars because they had been made by white workers (Lyman, 1974).

In this inhospitable climate, Chinese carved out an economic niche in two business enterprises: restaurants and laundries. Ronald Takaki (1989: 92) noted that laundries did not exist in China, so this can not be seen as an instance of transplantation. These two areas provided opportunities because of the gender imbalance on the frontier. Both occupations were construed as being "women's work." The shortage of women in this region permitted the Chinese to assume these roles, thereby establishing a form of structured ethnic subordination circumscribed by an understanding of a gender division of labor.

Even here, however, if the Chinese were perceived as a threat to white businesses they could confront harassing laws. Thus, in response to the pleas of white-owned laundries, the San Francisco city council passed an ordinance that mandated the use of a horse-and-buggy for the delivery of laundry. This meant that it was a misdemeanor to carry baskets suspended on a pole over the shoulder for the same purpose. This was an explicit assault on the Chinese laundry business.

These were not the only expressions of anti-Chinese attitudes. The Chinese were the victims of mob violence in numerous places. In several cases they were forcibly driven from localities. For example, in California they were expelled from Humboldt County and from Eureka. In Washington, they were similarly cast out of Seattle and Tacoma (Lyman, 1974: 60–61). In 1871 somewhere between 18 and 21 Chinese immigrants were killed by hanging or burning in Los Angeles. In 1885, 31 gold miners were murdered on the Idaho-Oregon border. Two years later in Rock Springs, Wyoming, at least 28 coal miners were killed (Kitano and Daniels, 1988: 22; Storti, 1991).

The animosity directed at the Chinese was evident after the San Francisco earthquake of 1906. Although the city was the recipient of an unprecedented outpouring of aid from around the country, city leaders thought it an opportune time to rid themselves of the Chinese. Thus, they refused to direct any aid to the rebuilding of Chinatown. The Chinese managed to rebuild on their own.

During the first few decades of the twentieth century not only did the Chinese population decline, but it also became more concentrated in a select number of cities. Smaller ethnic communities in places such as Butte, Salt Lake City, and Denver saw their Chinese enclaves shrink (Lee, 1949). At the same time, a move from rural areas to cities made the Chinese an even-more urban-based group. San Francisco continued to have the largest Chinese population, but sizeable communities also existed in Oakland, Los Angeles, Portland, and Seattle (after the earlier expulsion some decades before). These cities reflect the heavy concentration of Chinese on the Pacific coast. In 1900, 66.5 percent of Chinese resided in the Pacific region; that figure dropped to 56.6 percent by 1940 (Lyman, 1977: 135). Outside of the West coast, cities with large Chinese enclaves included New York City, Chicago, and Boston (Chan, 1991).

Given that the African American population in the West was quite small, that part of the country developed a racial sensibility that pitted Asians against white Europeans. It was a bifurcated understanding in which the Chinese were readily lumped together with other Asians. In numerous states marriages between whites and Orientals were prohibited. Due to prohibitions against immigrants becoming citizens, by 1920 over two-thirds of Chinese remained aliens, disenfranchised from participation in the American political system.

On the other hand, their location in a racial hierarchy defined in terms of black and white—the larger racial division in America—suggests a rather ambiguous location. James Loewen (1988) and Robert Seto Quan (1982) studied two small Chinese communities in Mississippi, where Chinese made a livelihood by operating stores that served African Americans. Both sociologists indicate the dilemma this small contingent of a middlemen minority confronted. While they sought to carve out a space for themselves that elevated their status vis-à-vis blacks, white Southerners tended to confine them to the segregated world of blacks.

Chinatown and the Outside World

Despite their social isolation, the economic pursuits of the Chinese brought them into contact with members of other ethnic groups and with the larger economy. In addition, Chinatown itself was not economically isolated because Chinatown relied on the tourist trade. It played off of the outsiders image of Chinatown as a world inhabited by the "exotic other." This imagery continued to be tinged with a negative cast, replete with notions of lurid tong wars, opium dens, and prostitution. Nonetheless, the merchant class managed quite successfully to sanitize these images to make the gilded ghetto attractive to tourists.

Within Chinatown, business enterprises often got their start from a system of rotating-credit, whereby individuals received necessary capital to begin a business from a collectively funded supply of capital. This provided the ethnic community both with a measure of autonomy from external economic interference and with a sense of internal mutual interdependence (Light, 1972). Over time this system served the merchants of Chinatown well, and by the third and fourth decades of the twentieth century, this enabled the socioeconomic elevation of a sector of the Chinese American community.

Very few individuals, however, left the ethnic island for the larger society. A few Chinese had acquired college educations; some of this group had actually entered the United States from China as students and for one reason or another had not returned. Part of the student group has been referred to as the "stranded" educated. They chose educational training for entry into fields such as medicine, pharmacy, dentistry, chemistry, and engineering (Kwoh,

1947; Lyman, 1974: 133). Because of their educational credentials, they were poised to exit Chinatown — and the control of its ruling elite. Prejudice and discrimination, however, made it difficult to sever these ties — as was seen in the case of Jade Snow Wong.

World War II proved to be a watershed event for Chinese America. When Pearl Harbor was attacked and war was subsequently declared against Japan, the United States' war propaganda machinery redefined the Chinese. Because China was under siege by Japan, the Chinese became our de facto allies. Thus, Americans had to learn how to distinguish, as a headline from *Time* magazine (December 22, 1941) put it, "your friends from the Japs." Although such repugnant distinctions actually do little to define ethnic differences, the net result of this event was that it reduced the level of prejudice directed at the Chinese in America. This provided breathing space that, in the immediate post-war years, allowed the emergence of a middle class that was no longer intimately tied to the ethnic community.

Of course, this event had profound, devastating consequences for the Japanese in America. Although in many ways Americans were unwilling to distinguish among the various Asian groups in the country, the differences are pronounced. From the outset the Chinese and Japanese migrations exhibited considerable differences. The Japanese did not begin to arrive until late in the nineteenth century, some four decades after the arrival of the first wave of Chinese.

The Transformation of Japan

Japan emerged from a self-imposed isolation that had extended over two centuries to become an increasingly powerful nation state, and in this regard it was different from China. Commodore Matthew Perry's entry into Japan in 1854, and his refusal to depart until the nation ended its seclusion marked the end of a long period in Japanese history and the fitful beginning of a new relationship with the outside world (Petersen, 1971: 152–153; Takaki, 1989: 43). Perry's intrusion revealed the weakness of the central state and the limits to Japan's military strength. It marked the beginning of the end of the rule of the Tokugawa clan. Japanese society at this time could be divided into the following classes: a small stratum composed of the emperor, *shogun*, and nobility; the *samurai*, a warrior class; peasants; artisans; and merchants. The peasantry composed more than three-quarters of the nation's total population. They had been economically squeezed by Japan's rulers, which led to a series of peasant riots (Petersen, 1971: 153–156).

The Tokugawa emperor was overthrown in 1868 in what became known as the Meiji Restoration. Although Japanese society exhibited a division between traditionalists and modernists, the new head of state plunged the country headlong into modernization and industrialization. The Japanese were absorbed by the Occident and by western ideas, which generated a feeling of inferiority and fueled a reaction on the part of ultranationalists, traditionalists, and militarists. This could be seen, for instance, in the growth of emperor worship, which was particularly evident among the *samurai*, since they had been displaced by modernization (Petersen, 1971: 156; Takaki, 1989: 46).

Within two decades Japan made considerable strides in expanding the economy, accomplishing this chiefly by developing agriculture and the rural-based silk and textile industries (Lockwood, 1954; Dore, 1959). The government played a central role in developing communication and transportation systems, in introducing new technologies into the country, in establishing a new comprehensive educational system, and in founding new industries. The government also strengthened the military and, in the 1890s, initiated a policy of imperialist expansion that led to war with China in 1894 and with Russia in 1905. The latter elevated Japan to major world power status.

Emigration and the Role of the Japanese Government

Within this context emigration to the West started. Economic dislocations for many peasants, combined with demographic pressure brought about by rapid population growth fueled the desire to emigrate. Japan's inheritance system was based on primogeniture, which meant that the oldest son acquired the land of the parents, and younger sons had to look elsewhere for an economic livelihood. Given Japan's land scarcity, agriculture could not support most of these sons, and Japan's industrial development was not sufficiently advanced to absorb them either (Takaki, 1989: 49). Thus, they became prime candidates for emigration. Unlike most countries, the Japanese government played an active role in shaping and controlling emigration. This often took, especially in the early phase, the form of governmentally-arranged forms of contract labor (Daniels, 1988).

The first group of contract laborers went to Hawaii, before it became a part of the United States. These sojourners were employed on plantations. After 1885, due to an exacerbation of economic problems, the number of emigrants increased, with Hawaii and California being the two major destinations. Two features of the Japanese government's role in emigration were significant. First, due to concerns about outsiders' perceptions of the Japanese, the Japanese government did not send the poorest peasants, but instead those from the middle strata, often with agricultural skills that would serve them well in the future. Second, the Japanese took an active interest in the well-being of their expatriate community, intervening when they thought it necessary.

Between 1885 and 1924, approximately 480,000 Japanese immigrated to either Hawaii or the U.S. mainland (Takaki, 1989: 45). Many, however, returned to Japan after a short period of employment. Thus, U.S. Bureau of the Census (1975) data indicate that in 1920 there were 111,010 Japanese in the country (this figure excludes Hawaii, where that number was exceeded). As with the Chinese, the immigrant community was heavily male-dominated.

Getting a Foothold in America

Japanese found work in a wide range of occupations, including mining, mill work, lumbering, cannery work, and as railroad laborers. More than 40 percent were employed in agriculture. As a consequence, the Japanese were more rurally based than the Chinese. Furthermore, those who did reside in cities tended to be more residentially dispersed than the Chinese. Cities did not experience the proliferation of Japantowns or Little Tokyos in the same way that Chinatowns emerged, though in the center of Japanese America — Los Angeles — such an enclave grew (Lyman, 1986). In 1920, the three cities with the largest Japanese communities were Los Angeles, San Francisco, and Seattle, with smaller but sizeable settlements in Oakland, Tacoma, and Portland. The only city not on the Pacific coast with a comparably sized Japanese community was New York City.

Immigration was possible because the restrictive acts of 1882 and 1892 did not apply to the Japanese. In fact, they would not confront similar restrictive legislation until 1907. They did, however, face racism similar to that experienced by the Chinese, although they were spared from some of the negative imagery. In this regard, the Japanese government, acutely aware of anti-Chinese sentiments, sought to ensure that this would not be repeated for the Japanese.

When Theodore Roosevelt was president, one issue that Japan raised with the United States was the admission of women to redress the unbalanced sex ratio. This addressed both the issue of prostitution and the ability of the Japanese in America to create a viable ethnic presence. The so-called "Gentleman's Agreement" was entered into in 1907. Among its terms, Japan voluntarily limited the number of immigrants to stem the tide of restrictionist demands (Kitano, 1969: 28). This agreement permitted the admission of relatives of immigrants. Arranged marriages were common in Japan, and this practice was used to join women in Japan with men in America, with "picture brides" arriving in the United States to see their husbands for the first time. This practice was condemned by the anti-Oriental lobby, but it proved the basis for a second, American-born generation (Wakatsuki, 1979).

As Evelyn Nakano Glenn (1986: 109–111) has shown, a substantial number of women entered the labor force as domestics. They worked for a variety of reasons: to build up a nest-egg in case they wanted to return to Japan; to add to the family's finances, especially after the arrival of children; or as the sole wage earner if a spouse died or for whatever reason became unemployed. Domestic service provided opportunities for women with family responsibilities and with limited English-language and marketable job skills.

Because of the skills Japanese American males brought to agriculture and the ability to use a rotating-credit system, some Japanese acquired prime agricultural land, and many others found success as tenant farmers. Ivan Light (1972) suggests that their success in this area was due to their familiarity with Japanese methods of intensive cultivation and because they were responsible for introducing some crops to the regions where they resided.

Prejudice and Discrimination

Whatever the reasons, conflict with white landowners was quickly apparent. California passed an Alien Land Act in 1913 that prohibited the Japanese from owning land. Because Japanese agricultural workers were needed during World War I, little was done to stop the Japanese from circumventing the law. When competition between Japanese and whites renewed after the war, however, a new act was passed in 1920 that prohibited "aliens ineligible for citizenship" from both owning and leasing agricultural land. There is an ongoing debate among historians about whether or not the law was effective (Higgs, 1978). What is clear is that the Japanese were the victims of considerable discrimination during this period.

The Japanese not only found ways to minimize the impact of discriminatory legislation, but also they were willing to challenge it in court. Race became the focal point of a 1922 Supreme Court decision, *Ozawa v. U.S.* Takao Ozawa was a legal immigrant who had resided in the United States for two decades, graduated from high school, attended college, was employed, spoke English even at home, and went to church. He was also, according to the government, ineligible to be naturalized. Ozawa's challenge was a novel one, for rather than disputing the racially exclusionary intentions of the law, he argued that he should be exempt because in his view Japanese were actually Caucasians. The Supreme Court was unpersuaded (Lyman, 1991: 207–208). Sojourner pluralism continued to describe the Japanese situation.

In the 1930s working-class Japanese frequently sought to participate in the push for unionization, though they discovered that they were often not welcomed into the labor movement, or when permitted to join, were pushed into racially segregated union locals. In some instances, they created their own unions, as did fruit stand peddlers in Los Angeles. This evoked the ire of organized labor, which viewed it as an expression of ethnic solidarity and a challenge to class solidarity. Hypocrisy aside, this reflected the double bind that confronted Japanese workers.

The Ethnic Community and Generational Differences

In spite of prejudice and discrimination, Japanese were remarkably successful in various entrepreneurial ventures. Two fields, related to agriculture, stand out as especially important: produce markets and gardening. By 1929 there were more than 700 Japanese-owned markets in Los Angeles (Light, 1972: 17). The Japanese gardener was so common that gardening was to the Japanese what restaurants and laundries were to the Chinese. A willingness to undertake business risks and using an ethnic-based credit system were common. Moreover, Japanese got into businesses that required little initial capital investment and were portable and easily liquidated. All these features made the Japanese quite successful. They did not limit themselves to a few areas, but ran hotels, restaurants, dry cleaning establishments, and numerous other businesses (Sowell, 1981: 167).

The Japanese were culturally and socially distinct, but were economically interdependent with the larger society. When the second generation came of age between 1920 and 1940, a considerable amount of intergenerational tension resulted. The use of terminology to distinguish the generations — *Issei* for the first and *Nisei* for the second — highlighted the differences. Although, as we have seen, tension was characteristic of most groups, it was perhaps more pronounced in the Japanese case. Exacerbating the typical differences in generational experiences was the fact that the immigrant generation was consigned to alien status while their children were citizens. Furthermore, while Buddhism was the dominant religion among the *Issei*, Christianity became more attractive to the second generation, especially to those intent on assimilating. This caused considerable conflict. The *Nisei* acquired English language skills, and over time it became clear that many had not retained a working knowledge of Japanese.

At the institutional level, two nationwide organizations were created, each devoted to addressing the major concerns of these two generations. The immigrants were represented by the Japanese Association of America, which Kitano and Daniels (1988: 57) described as "semiofficial organs of the Japanese government." The *Nisei* found a voice in the Japanese American Citizen's League. As the name suggests, the second generation stressed the fact that, unlike their parents, they were citizens.

A dramatic change in Japanese America occurred over a two decade period beginning in 1920. At that time, only 26.7 percent of the Japanese in America were native born. By 1940, fully 62.7 percent were (U.S. Bureau of the Census, 1975). In other words, those born in the United States — primarily second generation, but also some third — were a sizeable majority. The *Nisei* were inclined to define themselves as neither "too Japanesy" or "too American" (Lyman, 1977: 155), and they were intent on preserving aspects of their ancestral past. At the same time they chose those elements of

American culture that they found most appealing and conducive to maintaining a distinctive Japanese American identity.

World War II and Internment

World events conspired against an easy or gradual melding of two cultures. Prior to the attack on Pearl Harbor, many young Japanese American males had already enlisted. In various ways the community sought to dispel the suspicion that they harbored "dual loyalties." They feared the worst, and after Franklin Delano Roosevelt signed Executive Order 9066, these fears were realized. The order granted to the Secretary of War the right to declare any region of the country a military region. If deemed necessary, the Secretary had the authority to remove any or all persons from the area. There was no explicit mention of the Japanese, but they, and not the Germans or Italians, were singled out for wholesale removal from their homes on the West Coast. General DeWitt, the military official in charge of the removal, believed that the Japanese continued to harbor allegiances to the Japanese government. He crassly declared, "A Jap is a Jap, and it makes no difference whether he's a citizen or not" (Daniels, 1972: 46).

Not surprisingly, the decision to remove Japanese Americans to internment camps in remote regions of the plains and Rocky Mountain states was greeted with delight by the political right and by those who had earlier supported immigration restriction. The jingoistic newspaper magnate William Randolph Hearst endorsed the policy editorially. Japanese Americans discovered that they could find no solid sources of support anywhere across the political spectrum. Liberals, including Earl Warren and Walter Lippmann, joined conservatives in approving the relocation. Likewise, Roger Baldwin and the American Civil Liberties Union did not defend the constitutional rights of Japanese Americans, nor did Carey McWilliams, an otherwise sensitive spokesperson for oppressed ethnic groups. Even on the far left, with the Communist Party, the policy was not criticized (Daniels, 1972: 68–81). Devoid of outside support, some resisted, some challenged the decision in court, and some opted to go to Japan, but most relocated with no overt resistance.

The camps, ten in all, were constructed like military barracks and were located in desolate and isolated areas: Manzanar and

Tule Lake in California, Poston and Gila River in Arizona, Amache in Colorado, Topaz in Utah, Minidoka in Idaho, Heart Mountain in Wyoming, and Jerome and Rohwer in Arkansas. Over time, increasing numbers of Japanese were permitted to leave the camps, either because they were needed in the labor force or to fight in the European theater. About 22 percent of *Nisei* males refused to affirmatively answer loyalty questions and were not considered for military service. These "no-no boys" did so as a protest against internment. Seeking to prove their loyalty to America, despite its act of injustice, many others served with valor. One of the most highly decorated units in American military history was the Nisei-composed 442nd Regimental Combat Team (Takaki, 1989: 397–402).

This internment caused the loss of jobs, savings, homes, and status. Tetsuden Kashima (1980) argued that the evacuation legacy also resulted in a deep sense of personal inferiority, a proclivity to noncommunication and inarticulateness, and a shying away from any discussion of this hurtful topic. The aversion to talking about this devastating event resulted in a kind of social amnesia in Japanese America. Many *Sansei* (third generation) only learned about the camps when they went to college in the 1960s. From this nadir in Japanese American history, the victims of internment were forced to rebuild their lives in the postwar era.

Native Americans During the Reservation Era

Cornell (1988: 12) refers to the third period (the earlier periods were the market and conflict periods) of Indian relations with Euro-Americans as the reservation era. Though reservations had been set up before the middle of the nineteenth century, and they continue to exist up to the present time, Cornell believed they were central to the Indian experience after 1850, extending to the 1930s.

During this period, the subjugation of the Indians was completed (Spicer, 1962). The process moved westward: To establish military control over the frontier regions, a series of forts was constructed to quell resistance. Though no one event spelled the final defeat of the Indians, the surrender speech of Chief Joseph of the Nez Perce tribe, after being caught trying to flee to freedom in Canada, spoke to the situation of other tribes as well. He said:

I am tired of fighting. Our chiefs are killed . . . The old men are all dead . . . It is cold and we have no blankets. The little children are freezing to death. My people, some of them, have run away to the hills, and have no blankets, no food; no one knows where they are — perhaps freezing to death. I want to have time to look for my children and see how many I can find. Maybe I shall find them among the dead. Hear me, my chiefs. I am tired; my heart is sick and sad. From where the sun now stands I will fight no more forever (quoted in Nabokov, 1991: 180–181).

Reservations as Total Institutions

The conquered were relocated to reservations, which, like plantations, can be viewed as "total institutions" (Goffman, 1961). The differences, however, were pronounced. Plantations were founded for economic reasons and were connected to an international market place; such was not the case with reservations. Generally established on the most arid and inhospitable land, Native Americans had little success with their agricultural endeavors. They were isolated and cut off from larger markets. They were frequently unable to even make the reservations into subsistence economies, thereby furthering the notion that American Indians had to be treated as wards of the state.

If land was known to have minerals that could be potentially exploited, it was not included within the reservation boundaries. Furthermore, if tribes did manage to derive a living from the lands via agricultural production, as did the Apaches on the San Carlos Reservation, they could find their livelihoods jeopardized by white encroachment. In this particular case, Mormon settlers upstream diverted the water supply that the Apache farmers depended upon, thereby ruining the Apaches economically (Spicer, 1962: 543–549). By the last quarter of the nineteenth century, it was clear that the Native American would not be an impediment to white economic interests.

Reservations were constructed as a means of political containment and not to allow American Indians to acquire economic self-sufficiency (McNickle, 1962; Vogel, 1972). Tribes found themselves in a dependency relationship with agents of the federal government. These agents constituted the real power on reservations. Not all Native Americans lived on reservations, but the tentacles of the federal government held in place even those who did not. For example, the Oklahoma Cherokee did not reside on a reservation, but the Principal Chief of the Cherokee Nation was appointed by the President of the United States, not by the Cherokee themselves.

Denied the right to become citizens, regulated in their movements off of the reservations, stifled from engaging in many traditional religious practices, and victimized by unscrupulous Indian agents, the indigenous peoples of the Americas and their social world reached their nadir (Lurie, 1968: 69–70; Josephy, 1969). The American Indian's lack of power and inability to engage in self-determination combined with the fact that their population reached its low point in 1890. At this time governmental policy changed by directing attention to the issue of what Cornell (1988: 56) refers to as the "cultural transformation" of the Indian. The Bureau of Indian Affairs (BIA) was the primary governmental agency responsible for this task, and it did so by implementing policies that were underpinned by a combination of coercion and coaptation. The goal was the acculturation of Indians into the dominant culture.

The Dawes Act and Acculturation Policies

Policy makers saw tribal organizations as the major impediment to acculturation and pressed for legislation that would end collectively held land by making the American Indians into individual property owners. A severalty law, formally the Indian Allotment Act, but generally known as the Dawes Act, was passed in 1887, despite the objections and apprehensions of many Indians. Although a complicated law that did not apply to all reservations, in general terms it was designed to allot to Native American families title to 160 acres of reservation land, with smaller parcels granted to single individuals. The land was to be held in trust by the federal government for 25 years, during which time it could not be sold or leased. Reformers believed that by replacing tribal identities with the centrality of the autonomous individual, Native Americans were being prepared for full incorporation into the body politic. Thus, allotment was considered to be a prerequisite to citizenship (Bolt, 1987: 99–100; Cornell, 1988: 56–58; Foster, 1991; 82).

The Bureau of Indian Affairs initiated various actions that undermined traditional tribal practices. For example, it used its authority to force school children to attend boarding schools on

Figure 7.7   *A Native American family from the Sac and Fox tribe, circa 1900.*

Source: Courtesy of the Swenson Center.

reservations, thereby separating them from their families. The bureau established courts, set up new forms of social organization, and suppressed practices the bureau found offensive, such as polygamy. Certain Indians willing to work with the BIA were rewarded and elevated to leadership positions. In conjunction with missionaries who moved onto reservation lands to convert Native Americans to Christianity, the BIA attempted to instill white culture.

Some American Indians did become farmers and did incorporate much of the outside culture. Recall that this happened with N. Scott Momaday's grandfather, and that his offspring obtained college educations and entered the middle class. The Dawes Act did not succeed in abolishing reservations or tribes; however Native Americans who did obtain individual land allotments found it difficult to be successful farmers, chiefly because the land they were given was of such poor quality. Momaday's grandfather was the exception rather than the rule.

One other feature of the Act compounded the American Indian's plight. A provision built into the law allowed a land grab on Indian territory. The provision in question allowed any "surplus" land after allotment to be held by the government and allowed the government the right to sell it to anyone. As a result, between 1887 and 1934, 86 million acres of land, more than 60 percent of the total, was purchased by non-Indians (Wax, 1971: 54; Cornell, 1988: 44).

Outright fraud and deception, combined with debt payments that Indians could not meet also contributed to the loss of land. Thus, by the 1930s Native Americans were more impoverished and were considerably more land poor than before the Civil War. Furthermore, acculturation reformers concluded that their efforts had been largely a failure, and like the abolition movement after the end of slavery, the energies of this reform movement dissipated (Bolt, 1987: 100–101).

Responding to Defeat

The Native American response to this situation reflected their plight. Several religious movements emerged that, albeit different in appearance, shared many of the characteristics of other religions of the oppressed. One of the most significant was the Ghost Dance movement. Beginning sometime in the 1870s and extending into the twentieth century, perhaps even beyond the 1930s, the Ghost Dance movement proved to be a recurring if sporadic feature of many Indian tribes. It was particularly prevalent among Plains Indians. In defeat, many Indians held views similar to that of a Blackfeet named Flint Knife, who banefully commented, "I wish that white people had never come into my country" (quoted in Nabokov, 1991: 184).

This wish took the form of a chiliastic cult after a Paiute Indian named Wovoka had a revelation and began to expound a millennial prophecy based on what he claimed he had seen in the world of the dead. He contended that dead ancestors were alive and would be reunited with the living if Indians participated in a mystical ghost dance. In addition, prosperity would return (the bison that had been killed off were with the dead) and whites would disappear. The movement was generally pacifistic, because advocates believed that the end was near and active struggle against whites was not necessary (Wax, 1971: 138–141).

Under the emotional influence of the cultic ritual dance, some American Indians felt that they had acquired mystical powers that led them to believe that they were immune from the destructiveness of U.S. Cavalry bullets. In the tragic case of the Oglala Sioux in South Dakota, a confrontation between Native Americans empowered by the ghost dance and frightened, inexperienced soldiers led to the massacre at Wounded Knee, in which 300 defenseless Indians — men, women, the aged, and children — were gunned down (Niehardt, 1961; Wax, 1971: 140; Brown, 1970).

Related religious practices developed elsewhere, including the Dreamer Movement and the Drum Cult (Josephy, 1971; Spindler and Spindler, 1984). Another religious response was the peyote cult (La Barre, 1975). This particular cult took institutional form in the Native American Church, which was incorporated in 1918. The Church was congregationally decentralized and had relatively little in the way of a formal creed or organizational structure. It was a syncretistic religion that used Christian imagery as well as traditional tribal religions. Centered primarily in the Southwest, it appealed to a population that was impoverished and semi-nomadic (Wax, 1971: 141–144).

These religious expressions have been depicted by some as essentially apolitical, and thus as a form of passive acquiescence to circumstances. Like the Christianity of the slave quarters, however, they provided the basis for active resistance that occurred later. In addition to providing a semblance of an alternative to their present condition, millennial religions were a vital stage in the emergence of a pan-Indian consciousness. This consciousness did not deny the distinctiveness of various tribal identities, but fused that identity with a larger identity. An overtly political response to oppression was not felt until after World War II.

Stereotypes

Throughout this time period, American Indians confronted numerous problems related to employment, housing, health care, education, and other issues. The most enduring social problems within the Native American community were connected to the persistence of poverty, chronic unemployment, and alcoholism. They shaped the two most powerful negative stereotypes of the Indian: lazy and drunken.

Hollywood's outpouring of western movies generally portrayed the American Indian as the savage enemy of white settlers on the frontier. In fact, most films from D.W. Griffith's *America* (1924) to John Ford's *Stagecoach* (1939) and *Drums Along the Mohawk* (1939) were fixated on the frontier period. Although this image generally did not extend to views regarding contemporary Indians, it made it difficult to appreciate the incredible destructiveness that the conquest of the Indians entailed. Furthermore, little room was left to explore more positive relationships between Indians and whites. The one exception to this general tendency was *The Vanishing American*, which depicted corrupt whites and a virtuous Indian protagonist. Broaching the topic of interracial love, a relationship between the Indian and a white teacher on the reservation could not be consummated — death was used as a formulaic cinematic device for avoiding this possibility (Woll and Miller, 1987: 328–329).

The Indian New Deal

All American Indians became citizens in 1924, thereby permitting them the right to vote and otherwise be involved in the political process. This reversed the Supreme Court decision of four decades earlier in the case of *Elk v. Wilkins*, in which John Elk was denied the right to revoke his tribal membership to become a citizen of the United States. The Indians's response to this Act of Congress was decidedly ambiguous. Although some welcomed it, others saw it as a threat to the future of tribal organizations. This ambivalence was obvious in the differing reactions to military service during World War II. On the one hand, both individuals and tribes were willing to challenge the legitimacy of efforts to draft Native Americans. On the other hand, many Indians volunteered to serve in the military

(Bolt 1987: 107; Lyman, 1991: 226–229). The tragic death of Ira Hayes, brought about by alcoholism, is recounted in a song by Bob Dylan. Hayes was a soldier decorated for valor at Iwo Jima but condemned to second class citizenship after the war. This poignantly illustrates that even if Native Americans were expected to serve the nation at war, they would have to, in Stanford Lyman's (1991: 229) words, "wait for a long time before being granted the full measure of their citizenship and civil rights."

The most deleterious effects of the Dawes Act were amended during the first term of Franklin Roosevelt's administration. John Collier, the Commissioner of Indian Affairs, had a long history of involvement in progressive activities as executive director of the American Indian Defense Association. Collier proposed legislation that would have ended the land grab allowed under Dawes, promoted tribal home rule, and validated the desire to preserve American Indian culture by encouraging such activities as school courses in native history (Collier, 1945).

Although the Indian Reorganization Act of 1934 (IRA) proved to be a watered-down version of Collier's proposal, it nonetheless set the stage for a renewed orientation toward a central role for tribes in political and economic affairs. Not all Indians embraced the plan, including those who were assimilationists and those who simply distrusted any policy initiated by the federal government. Some Indians and non-Indians accused the policy of being a form of socialism (Collier, 1945: 91–93). This charge was echoed a half century later by Ronald Reagan's extreme right-wing Secretary of the Interior, James Watt. Although many were ultimately disappointed with the results of the IRA, Christine Bolt (1987: 127) indicated its singular importance when she wrote that, "For the first time in its history, the bureau [that is, Bureau of Indian Affairs] was not concerned with parting the Indians from their 'surplus' land or obliterating their culture."

The shifting policies of the federal government, combined with the varied responses of Native Americans, led to considerable ambiguity. This is reflected in the decision whether to remain on the reservation or move into the larger society. Although a sizeable majority of American Indians resided on or near Indian lands, a growing number began to leave, generally in the quest for work. This movement ebbed and flowed based on employment opportunities. In the long run, substantial Indian settlements developed in a number of major cities. Despite this movement, the urbanization rate of Indians lagged far behind that of the general population (Steiner, 1968).

Those who entered cities confronted prejudice and discrimination, and tended to be unable to find a viable economic niche. The Caughnawagas (or "Christian Mohawks") proved to be the exception rather than the rule. Hired to build a bridge across the St. Lawrence River in the late nineteenth century, they proved themselves capable of working in high steel, a dangerous vocation that Murray Wax (1971: 164) said meshed with their "warrior ethos." Since the construction of skyscrapers afforded job opportunities in cities, urban enclaves of the tribe emerged in Brooklyn, Buffalo, and Detroit. During construction boom periods these urban communities thrived; during economic downturns, many Indians returned to the reservation. Generally, they managed to create a coherent functional ethnic community in an urban setting—successfully transplanting a rural-based culture into the heart of the metropolis. Unfortunately, for the vast majority of Indians who moved to cities after World War II, this success was not replicated.

Summary

This chapter showed that what W.E.B. Du Bois referred to as the "color line" has served as the major obstacle to social harmony and to the possibility of extending freedom and equality to all people. After the Civil War a new form of racial oppression was established that ensured the domination of white Americans and the subordination of all peoples of color. The color line was used to determine who would and who would not be incorporated into the American political process and into the civic culture. Race was the principle criterion for determining who would be insiders and who would remain outsiders. Its rigid application allowed all white ethnics to develop bonds across ethnic boundaries with other whites. Quite simply, the differences between white ethnics became less consequential as the differences across the racial divide became more pronounced.

The stark division between blacks and whites—implicitly denying the reality of extensive racial mixing—was used by whites after emancipation to reassert a caste system. How white

Americans thought about blacks shaped the nature of racial definitions for the other racial minority groups considered in this chapter: Hispanics, Asians, and Native Americans. Each group experienced racially motivated actions from whites that were designed to ensure their subordination and exclusion.

All of the groups considered in this chapter responded to the challenges posed by racism. All attempted to improve their position in America. They had fewer financial and human capital resources than white ethnics had. Nonetheless, like European-origin groups, each created an ethnic community, established a leadership, created alliances with other groups, and in other ways responded to its particular circumstances. In each case an educated middle class defied the odds and emerged. Because of the prevalence of racism, the middle class among these groups could not leave their communities of origin. Instead, they served as a leadership stratum and supplied their respective communities with professionals and entrepreneurs. The role of this elite—what Du Bois referred to as the "talented tenth"—was crucial in the civil rights struggle that emerged after mid-century.

Part III

Yesterday, Today, and Tomorrow

EUROPEAN AMERICANS: THE TWILIGHT OF ETHNICITY?

In the second half of the twentieth century, America underwent changes as far-reaching and all-encompassing as those during the earlier transformation from a rural-agrarian to an urban-industrial nation. The new epoch is reflected in some of the terminology used to describe contemporary society, such as advanced industrial or a postindustrial society (Bell, 1973; Giddens, 1973). Although scholars disagree about the extent to which a distinct break with the earlier phase of industrialization occurred, nonetheless, there is general agreement about some of the implications of these changes.

Beginning in the late 1940s the American economy grew, and heightened productivity levels resulted in a two-decade period of unprecedented prosperity. The growth of large-scale national (and, later, international) corporations and the simultaneous decline of smaller local and regional industries were connected to this prosperity. These new corporations were huge bureaucratic enterprises requiring a large cadre of educated workers in white-collar positions — legal, accounting, advertising, design, administrative, and so on. At the same time, due chiefly to automation, relatively fewer blue-collar workers were needed. In addition, because of government's new role in the Keynesian welfare state created during the New Deal and because of the military's expanded role in American society during the Cold War, huge government bureaucracies also provided job opportunities for the new middle class.

C. Wright Mills (1951) was one of the first sociologists to systematically explore this reshaping of the class structure. His book

Table 8.1 CHANGE IN ETHNIC SOCIAL STANDING OVER THE PAST 25 YEARS

Ethnic Group	1964	1989	Change
British	6.37	6.46	0.09
French	5.73	6.07	0.34
Irish	5.94	6.05	0.11
Swiss	5.50	6.03	0.53
Swedes	5.41	5.99	0.58
Austrians	5.06	5.94	0.88
Dutch	5.60	5.90	0.30
Norwegians	5.48	5.87	0.39
Scotch	5.73	5.85	0.12
Germans	5.63	5.78	0.15
Italians	5.03	5.69	0.66
Danes	5.20	5.63	0.43
French Canadians	5.08	5.62	0.54
Japanese	3.95	5.56	1.61
Jews	4.71	5.55	0.84
Finns	5.08	5.34	0.26
Greeks	4.31	5.09	0.78
Lithuanians	4.42	4.96	0.54
Spanish Americans	4.81	4.79	−0.02
Chinese	3.44	4.76	1.32
Hungarians	4.57	4.70	0.13
Czechs	4.40	4.64	0.24
Poles	4.54	4.63	0.09
Russians	3.88	4.58	0.70
Latin Americans	4.27	4.42	0.15
American Indians	4.04	4.27	0.23
Blacks	2.75	4.17	1.42
Mexicans	3.00	3.52	0.52
Puerto Ricans	2.91	3.32	0.41
Gypsies	2.29	2.65	0.36

Source: National Opinion Research Center, 1991. These surveys asked people to rank the "social standing" of various groups using a scale in which 1 was the lowest standing and 9 was the highest. The numbers shown are averages.

was an indictment of the middle class's conformity in its quest for financial security and status. He, like other social critics of the immediate postwar era (for example, David Riesman, et al., in *The Lonely Crowd* [1950]), stressed the shift to an increasingly homogenized mass society. According to these critics, one consequence was a decline in the significance of both class and ethnic identities. Rather than being class consciousness, the new middle class was portrayed as opportunity consciousness. If an individual thought his or her ethnic background was an impediment to upward mobility aspirations or to chances for social inclusion, ethnicity would be downplayed or repressed as much as possible.

The ranks of the new white-collar class swelled as the children of the working class acquired college educations, the credentials that permitted their ascent in the social hierarchy. Many college students had served in the armed forces, which proved to be a training ground in improved intergroup relations, at least among white ethnics (blacks and Asians were forced to serve in segregated units). Veterans were able to take advantage of the GI Bill, which provided them with student assistance payments. College became a means to leave urban ethnic ghettoes and, in the process, helped those with a desire to forget their ethnic past to do so (Bensman and Vidich, 1971).

Suburbanization and White Ethnics

The sons and daughters of working class ethnics departed the ethnic enclave in droves for the suburbs. Policies of the federal government, particularly those relating to housing and transportation, encouraged the rapid expansion of American suburbs. The American housing stock in cities had declined because of a lack of investment during the depression and war. Furthermore, the urban infrastructure needed large-scale upgrading, particularly in older cities in the East and Midwest. The Federal Home Administration (FHA) and Veteran's Administration (VA) guaranteed home mortgage programs and, combined with the Department of Transportation's expressway system construction financing, propelled white-collar workers into the suburbs, where they built new homes rather than encouraging them to remain in cities. The result was a gulf between those ethnics who went to college, entered the middle class, and moved out of the city, and those who did not go to college, but remained in both the blue-collar work force and the city.

The connection between ethnicity and class suggests that for blue-collar workers, ethnicity and class identities had been mutually reinforcing, while for the middle class, the connection between class and ethnicity was less clear. The importance of ethnic identity did not disappear, but changes were clearly underway in both cities and suburbs, with somewhat different results. Some differences can be seen by comparing two ethnographic studies conducted during the 1950s and early 1960s by the same sociologist, Herbert Gans (1962; 1967) — one in an Italian neighborhood in Boston, and the other in the suburban New Jersey tract development known as Levittown.

In Levittown, ethnicity continued to shape interactional patterns. Ethnic subcommunities were one basis for friendship, which meant that for the small number of Chinese, Japanese, and Greek families who did not have a developed subcommunity, Levittown could be a lonely place to live. Anti-Semitism, though not seen as especially problematic, nonetheless was evident and did limit interaction between Jews and Gentiles. In many ways ethnicity, however, was increasingly a less consequential factor in defining attitudes and everyday behaviors. Gans pointed to areas in which ethnicity continued to play a role, while identifying areas where it did not. While German names were in evidence in the local Lutheran Church and Irish names in the Catholic parish, indicating the persistence of an ethnic character related to religious affiliation, ethnic divisions did not determine patterns of interaction in many other realms of social life. The spirit of neighborliness often served as a catalyst for friendships based on shared professional or leisure time interests (Gans, 1967: 85, 162).

Gans's study of the Italians in Boston's West End suggests a more pervasive persistence of ethnicity in the lives of these "urban villagers," when compared to their suburban counterparts. Noting the retention of the Italian language by the second generation, the continuation of the immigrant generation's relationship with Roman Catholicism, and the survival of food and drinking habits, Gans (1962: 35) observed that:

> Social relationships are almost entirely limited to other Italians, because much sociability is based on kinship, and because most friendships are made in childhood, and are thus influenced by

residential propinquity. Intermarriage with non-Italians is unusual among the second generation, and is not favored for the third.

An aversion to politics at the local level and a lack of interest in state and local politics further reinforced the relative isolation of the West End from the outside world.

But change took place, here, too. The second generation did not pass the Italian language on to the third. Neither generation expressed an interest in Italy. Italian names were Anglicized. Outside institutions intruded into the everyday lives of West Enders. Of particular importance was the public school system, which introduced youth to a world outside of the ethnic enclave. Gans (1962: 181–196) saw the impact of consumerism and the mass media, especially television, in drawing West End residents into the larger society, though he saw a "selective acceptance" of consumer goods and the media (for further discussion of this general pattern of change during the 1950s, see Vidich and Bensman, 1958, and Berger, 1960).

In his rich ethnographic accounts Gans provided an awareness that both ethnic persistence and change can be detected. He indicated that ethnic identity and ethnic affiliation were destined to not remain the same as they had been at an earlier historical period. But it is not clear whether this meant that ethnicity was fading into oblivion or merely adapting to new circumstances. Gans's snapshot of a specific point in time cannot by itself reveal future trends. Furthermore, as with all ethnographic accounts, we must question how much we can generalize from this particular case.

Does Ethnicity Matter?: The Case for Cultural Transmission

Sociologists have engaged in a sustained debate over whether or not a process of straight-line assimilation is underway among European ethnics, or, to use the phrase of Richard Alba (1981), whether these groups were experiencing the "twilight of ethnicity." In a long series of books and articles, Andrew Greeley (for example, 1974; 1975; 1988; Greeley and McCready, 1975; Greeley, et al., 1980) challenged this conclusion, arguing that ethnicity continues to shape people's values and behaviors.

Greeley's work was meant to challenge those who, like Gans, saw a fading role for ethnicity among the third and subsequent generational offspring of European immigrants. Unlike Gans, Greeley's work does not rely on ethnographic research, but uses National Opinion Research Center surveys of relatively large national samples, many of which were conducted during the 1960s and 1970s. Thus, his work has a scope that is lacking in community studies.

A wide range of attitudinal and behavioral topics were explored in Greeley's research. These included such personality attributes as conformism, anxiety, authoritarianism, moralism, and trust. Attitudes regarding such diverse topics as families and children, politics, race relations, and religion were also explored. Similarly, behaviors investigated included those associated with topics ranging from such diverse matters as political participation to drinking patterns. In addition, he looked at ethnic differences in educational attainment and socioeconomic mobility. Throughout this ongoing research, one recurring question was constantly posed: Does ethnicity matter?

The results of Greeley's investigations do not provide a simple response to the question. For example, in a comparison of individuals with Irish, Italian, and British ancestry, several hypotheses based on an assumption of differences in cultural heritages (for example, Irish would be more "trusting" than Italians because the former were more religious than the latter) on various personality traits were not supported. Other hypotheses were supported. At some level, as Greeley (1974: 100) observed, the Italians are more like the British than like the Irish, perhaps suggesting that they were assimilating while the Irish were not. Despite the mixed findings that emerged from his research, Greeley (1974: 319) argued that ethnicity does matter, though he qualified his answer: "to some extent some dimensions of the ethnic culture do indeed survive and enable us to predict some aspects of the behavior of the children, grandchildren, and great grandchildren of immigrants." He suggested, though with little empirical support, that people tend to look to the ethnic community in establishing a variety of interpersonal attachments, including marital partners, close friends, recreational partners, and informal associates (Greeley, 1974: 306–307).

If Greeley is right, why is this the case? He attributed this to differential socialization processes brought about by differing ethnic family structures (Greeley, 1974: 320). He did not assign a role to nonfamilial institutions of the ethnic community and paid scant attention to changes within ethnic communities. This is a product of the research strategy he pursued. These data did not address the issue of change versus continuity within ethnic institutions. He paid virtually no attention to the particular historical experiences of specific groups. In short, he did not attempt to locate ethnic identity in either social structural or historical contexts.

During the second half of the twentieth century the institutional network of most European American ethnic communities eroded considerably. This process was underway earlier, but it accelerated. Mutual aid societies, athletic clubs, cultural organizations, and the like all declined in membership. The immigrant generation died off and their children and grandchildren did not need these institutions to assist them in their quest for economic security, a political voice, or enhanced status. Foreign language newspapers ceased publishing as native-born ethnics no longer maintained what Joshua Fishman (1966) termed "language loyalty." In an ecumenical era, many Christian churches lost their distinctively ethnic character and consciously downplayed their ethnic origins. Thus, what was once the Swedish Evangelical Lutheran Church might be renamed the First Evangelical Lutheran Church.

It is not surprising that the pace of change varied both across and within groups. Among the particularly relevant factors cited in Table 2.1 are group size, degree of residential concentration, length of time in the country, religious affiliation, homeland concerns, and the degree of educational and occupational mobility. Looking just at the Scandinavian groups in America, differences in the pace of ethnic erosion occurred. The Danish presence faded rather quickly and, although somewhat slower, the Swedish presence did too. At the other extreme, Finns, and to a lesser extent, Norwegians, preserved an institutional presence and a stronger sense of ethnic identity for a longer period of time. Even so, the movement for all four groups was in the same direction. Relatively little empirical research has been conducted on particular groups, especially earlier-arriving groups and Protestant groups. Large European American groups such as the English, Germans, Irish,

French, Swedes, and Norwegians have not been the objects of sustained sociological inquiry.

The Polish Americans

Poles have not been widely studied, but Neil Sandberg (1974) studied the Polish Americans in Los Angeles (not a representative community because of the continuing clustering of Poles in the Great Lakes region), and his findings challenged Greeley's persistence of ethnicity theory. Rather, Sandberg saw a progressive decline in the intensity and significance of ethnic identity from the immigrant generation to the third and fourth generations. He also saw a connection between a decline of ethnic identity and affiliation and the Poles' move out of the working class and into the middle class. Sandberg traced the decline in ethnic institutional affiliations, which was even seen in the area of religion. Recalling that, in comparative terms, Polish immigrants had exhibited a higher level of religiosity than a number of other immigrant groups, this is an especially significant change. Sandberg saw decline in ethnic church attachment as well as religious attendance. Linked to this is a decline in parochial education support. This is not to say that ethnicity has disappeared because it can be detected even in the fourth generation.

We can look at certain cities, most notably Chicago, and still find evidence of a functioning Polish American community, so Polish American ethnicity might be more salient than is the situation for most European Americans. In part, this can be attributed to events in their homeland. Actually, since Sandberg conducted his study, the rise of the Solidarity Movement in Poland and the eventual demise of communist rule were potent issues that mobilized the Polish American community, and in this regard it may exhibit some similarities to both that of the Irish (for whom Northern Ireland is an ongoing concern) and Jews, for whom the fate of Israel is an important concern.

Italians

James A. Crispino (1980), in his research on the Italians of Bridgeport, Connecticut, and its suburban environs (a representative site for Italians), came to conclusions similar to those of Sandberg.

Figure 8.1   *Italian Americans attend a wartime rally in New York City, 1944.*

Source: The Leonard Covello Photographs courtesy of the Balch Institute for Ethnic Studies Library.

Crispino chronicled the demise of mutual aid societies, neighborhood bars, athletic clubs, and the like in the city and noted that there was no evidence of recreating the ethnic enclave in the suburban ring of the city. Acculturation was evident. For instance, in areas related to the traditionalism investigated by Greeley, such as the prevalence of distrust of others and fatalism, Crispino's research indicated generational decline in traditional attitudes. His subjects overwhelmingly supported legalized abortions under certain circumstances and so disagreed with the official teaching of the Roman Catholic church. In addition, he discovered a decline in ethnic identification.

Perhaps most problematic for Greeley's cultural transmission thesis is the fact that structural assimilation is also apparent. Crispino (1980: 94) reported a "decline in strong attachments to kin, especially those at some distance, and ethnic friends, and their replacement by considerations of class and presumably common interests in the selection of close associates." A linked issue is intermarriage. Although neither Sandberg nor Crispino directly addressed intermarriage, a study conducted by B.R. Bugelski (1961) of Poles and Italians between 1930 and 1960 in Buffalo, New York, found that both groups had a precipitous drop in in-group marriages during these three decades. For Italians, the in-group marriage rate fell from 71 percent in 1930 to 27 percent in 1960; the corresponding figures for the Poles are 79 percent in 1930, which dropped to 33 percent in 1960. These finding led Bugelski to suggest that by 1975 in-group marriages would be rare.

The Debate Over an Ethnic Revival

The ethnicity perspective, which derived from the work of sociologists like Greeley, gained popular expression during the early 1970s in the writing of Michael Novak (1971), who described "unmeltable ethnics." In contrast, a different argument reflected a contemporary resurgence of interest in ethnic identity that presumably involved a return to various modes of ethnic affiliation.

The Hansen Thesis

Actually, there are two different, though not necessarily mutually exclusive, versions of the ethnic revival theory. One focuses on the dynamics of generational change and is essentially psychological, and the other is political. The generational theory was initially formulated by historian Marcus Lee Hansen (1938: 195) and summarized by the pithy claim that "what the son wishes to forget the grandson wishes to remember." Hansen's "principle of third generation interest" was based on his understanding of the social psychology of second and third generation ethnics. Whereas the former were seen as insecure about their place in America and therefore sought to abandon their ethnic past to fit into the society outside of the ethnic world, the third generation was at home in

America. Their secure status permitted a curiosity about and a pride in their ancestry.

If Hansen is read literally, the evidence overwhelmingly suggests that his hypothesis is incorrect (Appel, 1961; Nahirny and Fishman, 1965; Lazerwitz and Rowitz, 1964; Abramson, 1975; Greene, 1990). If freed from its generational formulation, however, Hansen's thesis suggests that ethnicity must be treated as a flexible and variable phenomenon. This general perspective could account for the growth of ethnic celebrations, genealogical interests, travel to the ancestral homeland, an interest in ethnic artifacts, ethnic cuisine, ethnic language and literature, and the dramatic expansion of interest in ethnicity by scholars from a variety of disciplines (TeSelle, 1973; Tricarico, 1984, 1989; Archdeacon, 1985; Fishman, et al. 1985). Although these manifestations of ethnicity must be acknowledged, it is difficult to determine the extent to which this "voluntary" interest in one's ethnic background has permeated large sectors of European America. Actually, it appears that this voluntary ethnicity is limited to a rather small sector, generally composed of the more highly educated members of the middle class.

Political Ethnicity

Numerous ethnically based nationalist social movements exist elsewhere in the industrial world, including the Welsh and Scottish in Britain, the Occitan in France, the Flemish in Belgium, the Basques in Spain, and the Québecois in Canada. According to Anthony Smith (1981: 156), what is distinctive about the United States that makes this ethnic revival weak and politically ineffectual is the "lack of an autonomist, let alone separatist, nationalist component of the ideology of 'neo-ethnicity'." Simply put, this revival in the United States was not linked to land—it entailed no territorial claims. Given the steady erosion of ethnic communities, ethnic solidarity did not prove to be an especially viable source of collective action (Rothschild, 1981; Nagel and Olzak, 1982; Nielsen, 1985).

A more political, interest-based form of resurgent ethnicity did occur at approximately the same time as this more apolitical, nostalgic form of ethnic return, however. Nathan Glazer and Daniel P. Moynihan, in their seminal work *Beyond the Melting Pot* (1963), considered the five major groups in New York City that they scrutinized, including three European-origin groups — Jews, Italians, and Irish — as constituting in effect political interest groups that vied competitively in the political arena. Although Glazer and Moynihan did not highlight this in their work, emergent ethnicity was closely connected to racial politics, especially in major American cities with large black populations (Weed, 1971; Yancey, et al., 1976; Polenberg, 1980).

In a study of Italians and Irish in Providence, Rhode Island, during the height of the civil rights movement, John Goering (1971) discerned a reemergence of ethnic identification as a crucial form of self-identification. He observed that this identification had little effect in terms of concrete actions aimed at political mobilization. Instead, it was largely associated with a questioning of the American dream brought about by the belief that the civil rights movement had granted blacks government-sponsored benefits at the expense of white working-class ethnics. Although the first form of ethnic interest derived from the educated middle class and often suburban offspring of European immigrants, this conservative defense against perceived challenges to their neighborhoods and jobs came from working-class and lower-middle-class urban ethnics, that is, those who have not gotten out of the ethnic enclave.

Jonathan Rieder's (1985) ethnography of the Jews and Italians in the Canarsie section of Brooklyn provided a vivid account of how these two ethnic groups, different in history and politics, managed to find common ground in their collective quest to protect their neighborhood. They are united by a fear that their neighborhood is vulnerable to the pathologies of the ghetto (crime, drugs, teen pregnancies, and a general decline in civic responsibility) brought about by the incursion of blacks and Hispanics into a predominantly white section of the borough. Both ethnic groups, although they expressed it in different ways, viewed affluent liberals as being unconcerned or outright hostile to them. Though these white ethnics were an important component of the liberal coalition that made up the Democratic party since the New Deal, they have shifted to embrace conservatism. Although Rieder provides ample evidence of the racist thinking of many of these white ethnics, including some violent and other unpleasant acts by a very small minority, he also indicates that the obvious discontent and anxiety they feel about their future is not entirely unfounded.

However romanticized their collective descriptions of the neighborhood a generation ago might be, it was once a haven and it might not be so in the future (see also Sleeper, 1990).

What is at stake here is not Italians and Jews returning to their ethnic roots, but European ethnics finding a common cause against changes in the city that they believe have occurred because of the increased proximity of non-European ethnics. If, earlier in the century, Italians entered into conflictual relations with Jews, Irish, or other European ethnics, today those things that generated such conflicts have either disappeared or have become inconsequential compared with forces that have produced or reinforced racial tensions and hostilities.

Symbolic Ethnicity

The notion of an ethnic revival in America is problematic, even though there are clear cultural and political manifestations of ethnic interests (Stein and Hill, 1977). Ethnicity has not disappeared for many if not most European Americans, as the earlier assimilationists predicted. But neither has it exhibited an ability to resist change. Most evidence suggests that the salience of ethnicity for these groups has declined in recent years. There is little to suggest that this trend will be reversed.

The theory of "symbolic ethnicity" accounts for both the indicators of the persistence of various manifestations of ethnicity and its simultaneous more pervasive gradual decline. This concept was formulated by Herbert Gans (1979) and is applicable to ethnics from the third generation and beyond. Gans saw ethnicity for most European Americans as having a low level of intensity, thus occupying an individual's attention only sporadically. The decline in ethnic organizations and cultures does not permit more substantive manifestations of ethnic identity or affiliation. Rather than relying on community or culture, the third generation and beyond uses symbols, primarily out of a sense of nostalgia for the traditions of the immigrant generation. According to Gans (1979: 203–204):

> most people look for easy and intermittent ways of expressing
> their identity, for ways that do not conflict with other ways of
> life. As a result, they refrain from ethnic behavior that requires
> an arduous or time-consuming commitment, either to a culture
> that must be practiced constantly, or to organizations that

demand active membership. Second, because people's concern is with identity, rather than with cultural practices or group relationships, they are free to look for ways of expressing that identity which suit them best, thus opening up the possibility of voluntary, diverse, or individualistic ethnicity.

Until 1980 government census takers did not question members of the third and later generations about ethnic background, categorizing them as "native white of native parentage." The 1980 census, however, did incorporate questions that permitted an inquiry into the relevance of ethnic background for such variables as residential location, cultural differences, economic attainment, and intermarriage (Hout and Goldstein, 1994).

Evidence from Census Findings

Stanley Lieberson and Mary C. Waters (1988) believe these data show a progressive decline of the ethnic factor in shaping European Americans' lives. For example, though differences persist regarding the spatial distribution of groups, in part based on length of time in the country, the trend for all groups is to spread out across regions of the United States over time. Conceding that census data are not the most useful for considering cultural issues, nonetheless they found that in terms of three culturally-shaped issues—fertility, marriage rates, and educational attainment—a clear convergence has occurred or is underway. Although some differences remain in the propensity to marry, these differences are fading. No statistically significant differences were observed across groups for both fertility patterns and educational attainment. Similarly, "for the most part socioeconomic inequalities among white ethnic groups are both relatively minor and unrelated to patterns of ethnic inequality found earlier in the century" (Lieberson and Waters, 1988: 155).

Lieberson and Waters (1985, 1988) concluded that there is a trend toward increased intermarriage with other European Americans, seen especially among younger cohorts, and involving both ethnic groups from northwestern Europe as well as those from south central Europe. This conclusion supports Richard Alba's work (1985), which also utilized data from the 1980 census. Alba found intermarriage among native-born non-Hispanic whites to be widespread. It is more widespread among those individuals of mixed rather than single ancestry, but since more and more people are of mixed ancestry, this suggests increased intermarriage rates in the future. Alba (1985: 17) noted one irony in this trend: as people acquire ever-more complicated mixed ancestries, multiple ancestry actually "increases the probability of sharing some common ancestry with a spouse."

So what does this mean for ethnic identity trends? There is evidence of a considerable amount of flux in terms of ethnic identification (Lieberson and Waters, 1986). For the 13.3 million respondents who identified their ancestry as "American" or "United States" in the 1980 census, national origins are either unknown, unimportant, or both. One's ethnic ancestry has no apparent relevance for current sociopolitical matters. These "unhyphenated whites" may constitute a new ethnic group that "is in the process of forming" (Lieberson, 1985: 179).

Ethnic Options

Most respondents, however, did opt to identify with, by claiming ancestry in, one or more European ethnic groups. The census data do not reveal what this meant to these individuals. Was it merely a fact of birth that a person was, say, Irish and German, or did these identities mean something to the individual? Mary C. Waters (1990) explored this through a series of in-depth interviews with third and fourth generation ethnics in suburban Philadelphia and San Jose, California.

Her general conclusion was that ethnicity does mean something for her subjects. She discerns in their attachment to ethnic identity a desire for a sense of community, while they are also intent on preserving a sense of individualism. Thus, their ethnicity takes on a voluntaristic cast. Taking part in a St. Patrick's Day parade or preparing ethnic dishes for holiday meals are examples of ways of connecting intermittently with an ethnic past without great outlays of time and energy. They pick and choose features of the ethnic tradition to valorize, while ignoring or abandoning others, such as a tradition that is sexist. Likewise, although the immigrant culture might have demanded that a woman's role is in the home, a dual-career household composed of third or fourth generation ethnics will not perpetuate the values that endorse that particular gender division of labor (Waters, 1990: 168).

Waters (1990: 155) concurs with Gans that this can be seen as symbolic ethnicity, which, she believes, "is not something that will easily or quickly disappear, while at the same time it does not need very much to sustain it. The choice itself — a community without cost and a specialness that comes to you just by virtue of being born — is a potent combination."

Furthermore, Waters (1990: 112–113) provides evidence of what she refers to as "cultural syncretism." By this she means the tendency by ethnics to consider various interethnic marriage combinations as decidedly positive because such unions are seen as establishing a healthy and beneficial balance between the differing imputed emotional traits of various ethnic groups (for example, the "emotional" Italian and the "reserved" Irish). Although her subjects made frequent use of such ethnic distinctions, she noted that when asked to describe how the traditional values of their own ethnic group differed from others, respondents routinely argued, regardless of which group they were from, that their particular group placed a high premium on family, education, hard work, religiosity, and patriotism (Waters, 1990; 134).

The Privatization of Ethnicity

The symbolic ethnicity thesis was further confirmed in a survey research project undertaken by Richard Alba (1990: 65–69) in New York state's capitol region, which includes Albany, Schenectady, and Troy. In his sample, two-thirds of respondents identified ethnically, and of this group only one-quarter said that ethnicity was very important to them, about two-fifths said it was somewhat important, and one-third attached no importance to it. The older immigrant groups (English, German, Dutch, and French) attached less importance to ethnicity than the newer immigrant groups, such as Italians and Poles. Alba found that women tended to attach greater importance to ethnicity than did men (compare di Leonardo, 1984).

Moreover, those who attach some importance to their ethnic identity, the largest category, believe that ethnicity must be consciously nurtured if it is to survive. In other words, they think that ethnicity is at risk of fading away into insignificance.

Alba (1990) documented the progressive unlinking of ethnic identity from ethnic social structure. The erosion of ethnic institutions and neighborhoods, the declining role of ethnic culture, the expansion of intermarriage, the prevalence of nonethnic bases for friendships and other modes of social interaction, and the lack of discrimination based on one's ethnic background all contribute to this. Like Gans, Lieberson, and Waters, Alba did not conclude that this means that ethnic identity will entirely disappear for these white ethnics in the foreseeable future. Rather, he contended that as ethnic identity is severed from ethnic social structure, it increasingly becomes privatized, and (echoing Waters) as such resonates with American notions of individualism. This suggested to him the possibility that what Thomas Archdeacon (1990) referred to as an "ethnic hum" might persist for many generations.

The Invention of Ethnicity

Ethnicity for European Americans has not disappeared, but it is undergoing various reformulations, taking at least three different forms. We have only focused on one: symbolic ethnicity, which entails an attempt to remain at least nominally connected to a particular European-origin group. Some manifestations of symbolic ethnicity illustrate the profound erosion of ethnic tradition. Two related examples will suffice to illustrate this point. In the center of Helsinki, Finland, a drinking establishment, "St. Uhro's Pub," is named after the patron saint of Finland who, according to legend, saved farmers by casting the grasshoppers out of the country. No one in Finland celebrates St. Uhro's day, however, and not surprisingly since he dates only to the 1950s—the invention of a small band of Finnish Americans in northern Minnesota. They decided to create a counterpart to St. Patrick as a source of pride in things Finnish (Kaups, 1986). Clearly, the original signs of Finnish ethnicity no longer served as meaningful markers of ethnic identity. However contrived this attempt was, it also indicated the presence of a conviction about the need for preserving ethnic allegiance and for enhancing the status of the group vis-á-vis other groups.

St. Patrick was a real historical figure, and although a considerable body of legend surrounds him, he was the patron saint of Ireland, the person primarily responsible for Christianizing the nation. The Irish in America have celebrated St. Patrick's day since 1737, but over time the celebration has been transformed. Once a religious event, it is now secular. Some use it as a political event to show support for the Irish Republican Army. But for most people of Irish descent, it is merely an occasion to engage in a nostalgic tribute to one's ancestors. Furthermore, in recent decades it has increasingly taken on the character of a panethnic celebration: organizers of parades and related festivities frequently refer to March 17 as a day during which everyone can be Irish.

Moreover, as events in recent years in New York City (the site of the nation's largest St. Patrick's Day parade) indicate, precisely what it means to be Irish is a matter of controversy. The Irish Lesbian and Gay Organization was banned from participating in the 1992 parade by the sponsoring organization, the Ancient Order of Hibernians. Although members of the homosexual group argued that one can be both gay or lesbian and Irish, the Hibernians countered by arguing that homosexuality was an affront to Irish Catholic tradition (*New York Times*, 1992b: A16). In short, one group wanted to change and the other preserve an inherited cultural orientation.

Regional Identities

A second type of invention involves the emergence of new ethnic groups based chiefly on geographic region. This can be seen most clearly in Appalachia and among people from Appalachia who have moved to cities, such as Cincinnati, Pittsburgh, and Chicago, to find work. Though one can identify various European ethnic groups that make up this population—the most predominant one being Scotch-Irish—their relative isolation fused ethnic groups into a new regionally based identity. Elements of the traditions of several different ethnic groups compose part of the Appalachian identity. But the identity is also shaped by shared features of life in the hollows—the remote and self-contained valleys—of this region, which have been characterized by being both economically disadvantaged and isolated from the outside. This self-construction of Appalachian identity is reinforced by outsiders, who often refer to the residents of Appalachia with the pejorative term, "hillybillys." Marger and Obermiller (1983) argued that what is occurring here is an instance of "emergent ethnicity."

One can see a similar process developing in the Upper Peninsula of Michigan, another geographically remote region whose people are composed of a variety of ethnic groups, including Finns,

Swedes, Norwegians, Poles, Irish, Italians, and Cornish. The regional identity there is a product of the composite impact of the various ethnic groups. A sense of distinctiveness and alienation from the more urban Lower Peninsula has fueled regional consciousness. A distinctive speech dialect serves as a marker of identity when residents travel "downstate." When the state's tourist bureau began a campaign to promote the state a few years ago, it distributed red bumper stickers with the slogan: "Say yes to Michigan!" Almost immediately, green bumper stickers began to appear on cars in the Upper Peninsula with their response: "Say ya to da U.P., eh!" During the past two decades there has been increased usage of the self-identification term "Yupper." Its use is embraced by some residents of the region while decried by others. This is yet another example of this second type of reformulation of ethnicity, although of more limited applicability than the first.

A European American Identity?

The third trend is based on the assumption that among European-origin groups we may be witnessing not merely the lingering vestiges of past inherited ethnic identities, but the construction of a new one. Alba (1990) pointed to the emergence of a new ethnic group that he refers to as the European Americans. Although he does not use the language of the "invention of ethnicity" perspective, this process is clearly what is involved when he (1990: 292–293) wrote:

> Ethnic distinctions based on European ancestry, once quite important in the texture of American social life, are receding into the background. Yet this development does not imply that ethnicity is any less embedded in the social fabric, but rather that the ethnic distinctions which matter are undergoing a radical shift. The transformation of ethnicity among whites does not portend the elimination of ethnicity but instead the formation of a new ethnic group: one based on ancestry from anywhere on the European continent. The emergence of this new group, which I call the "European Americans," with its own myths about its place in American history and the American identity, lies behind the ethnic identities of many Americans of European background.

Though Alba did not stress this, the manner in which many European Americans forge this panethnic identity is based on their

Figure 8.2   *A Greek American float in a parade, circa 1968.*

Source: Courtesy of the Swenson Center.

conceptualization of other non-European groups — on their understanding of "we" versus "them." Micaela di Leonardo (1984: 234)
made this connection when she wrote of a symbolic ethnicity that
uses "rhetorical nostalgia" in celebrating one's own past, while
criticizing or denigrating other ethnic groups. Such nostalgia
becomes a substitute for an appreciation of the differences in historical experiences of various groups. For example, to argue, as so
many European ethnics do, that their culture placed a high premium on close-knit families is to implicitly criticize groups such as
African Americans because of the prevalence of single-parent
households in that group. Similarly, the belief that one's ancestors
imbued subsequent generations with a willingness to engage in
hard work can be used as a way of blaming those groups who suffer
from persistently high levels of unemployment and underemployment for their economic circumstances.

   This approach fails to recognize, among other things, the historical impact of exclusionary hiring practices and organized
labor's opposition to inviting some groups into its ranks. Mary
Waters (1990: 147) detected a similar underside to symbolic

ethnicity and bluntly concluded that one of the reasons that "symbolic ethnicity persists [is] because of its ideological 'fit' with racist beliefs." We shall return to this issue of race relations later, but before doing so, we will look at one ethnic group that does not fit these general trends: Jews.

Jewish Exceptionalism?

Because the U.S. Census posed its ethnic ancestry questions in terms of national identity and not religious identity, Jews are not identified by their religio-ethnic identity in the 1980 census. Instead, they are lumped into such national groups as Poles and Russians. In addition, Alba's Capital Region study contained relatively few Jews, while Waters did not include Jews in her project. Thus, the question arises: might the trends described in the preceding section be inapplicable to Jews? Substantial research that attempts to answer this question has been devoted to Jewish Americans.

What might contribute to the persistence of differences between Jews and non-Jews? First, the lingering power of anti-Semitism has made discrimination and exclusion more problematic for Jews than, for instance, have anti-Italian or anti-Polish sentiments for Italians or Poles. At the same time, Jews have been, as a group, remarkably successful in socioeconomic terms. This provided them with the resources to both combat anti-Semitism while undertaking actions to preserve the strength of the ethnic community. The fusion of religion and ethnicity for Jews differentiates them from other European-origin groups (the Greek Orthodox community may be an exception). The memory of the holocaust and the ongoing concern with the future security of Israel have bolstered a sense of group allegiance, and have overcome many of the divisions within the ethnic community. In combination, these factors raise the possibility that the future of the Jewish community and of a distinctive ethnic identity might be different from that of other European Americans.

Sections of Jewish America that show continued vitality are intent on remaining in fundamental ways aloof from the larger society. This can be seen in the Hasidic community, which has its center in Brooklyn (Mayer, 1979). In addition, there has been a modest return to religious Orthodoxy (Danzger, 1989; Kaufman

1991). Furthermore, during the Carter presidency and again after the collapse of the Soviet Union, Jews have emigrated from that region. An enclave located near Coney Island in Brooklyn is referred to by local residents as "Odessa by the Sea," while emigrants from Israel have taken up residence in the borough of Queens (Shokeid, 1988). The presence of new arrivals can inject renewed vitality into an ethnic community. Taken together, however, all of these Jews compose a very small percentage of the total Jewish American population.

The Core Jewish Population

According to the 1990 national Jewish population survey, 6,840,000 Jews were identified by ethnic background or by religious preference. Of this number, 1,325,000 had either converted to another religion or were children currently being raised with another religion. Of the 5,515,000 that constitute what the survey authors refer to as the "core Jewish population," 77 percent were born Jewish and identify with the Jewish religion, 3 percent were non-Jews who converted to Judaism, and 20 percent were secular Jews, born Jewish but claiming no religious identity (Kosmin, et al., 1991: 6).

The difference in size between the core Jewish population and the total ethnic background and religious preference figure illustrates that changes have occurred within American Judaism. These changes have been brought about mainly by expanded opportunities for inclusion into the larger society in recent decades. Since the 1950s, as Jews were incorporated into the fabric of America's civil religion, which was seen as rooted in a shared Judeo-Christian heritage, their place in America seemed more assured. Since that time, the level of anti-Semitism has markedly declined. This has permitted structural and cultural assimilation and raised questions about the possibility of integrating into the larger society while preserving a unique group identity (Waxman, 1983; Cohen and Fein, 1985; Glazer, 1985; Silberman, 1985; Hertzberg, 1989).

Continuity and Change

During the past two decades, there is growing evidence of changing patterns of institutional affiliation and religious observance, heightened levels of geographic mobility and residential dispersal, shifts in attitudes on political and social issues, a lessening of support for Israeli policies toward the Palestinians and their Arab neighbors, changes in interpersonal relations, and rising rates of intermarriage.

Some scholars argue that these changes point to assimilative patterns not unlike those experienced by other European American groups (Glazer, 1985; Hertzberg, 1989). Gans thinks that symbolic ethnicity is increasingly an apt term to characterize Jewish America, and, before he wrote about symbolic ethnicity in general terms, he had argued that what was occurring as early as the 1950s in the suburbs was the development of "symbolic Judaism" (Gans, 1956; 1979). At the other extreme are those who, like Calvin Goldscheider (1986: 9–10) contended that, "the American Jewish community is a powerful and cohesive community. It has strong anchors of social, religious, and family life; it is neither diminishing demographically nor weakening Jewishly." This position sees American Judaism changing but not eroding, transforming itself to meet the particular circumstances and demands of the present. This transformation is depicted as being resistant to the corrosive impact of the assimilative process.

A major survey research project directed by Steven M. Cohen (1988) contains a careful and systematic attempt to assess the merits of these two positions. The study, conducted in 1981, entailed a survey by mail and phone of 4,505 Jewish households in the greater New York area, which, as Table 8.2 indicates, has a considerably larger Jewish population than any other city. Cohen examined a variety of attitudinal and behavioral topics, dividing them into three major categories: religious ritual observance, Jewish communal affiliation, and interpersonal relations (friendships and marriage). The conclusions distilled from these data provide a somewhat mixed picture. In terms of ritual observance, Cohen noted that across generations there are patterns of both declining and increasing practices, indicating a considerable amount of what he terms "intergenerational flux."

This fluidity is seen in other aspects of Jewish social life as well. The role played by intermarriage in prompting assimilation has, in Cohen's view, been overstated. He contended that although intermarriage rates continue to grow, the rate of growth has tapered off since the 1960s. According to Cohen, the effect of intermarriage on

Table 8.2   TWENTY LARGEST U.S. JEWISH COMMUNITIES

Community	Jewish Population
New York, NY	1,742,500
Los Angeles, CA	500,870
Chicago, IL	248,000
Miami (Dade County), FL	241,000
Philadelphia, PA	240,000
Boston, MA	170,000
Washington, DC	157,335
Metro West, NJ	111,000
Baltimore, MD	92,000
San Francisco, CA	80,000
Cleveland, OH	70,000
Detroit, MI	70,000
Bergen County, NJ	69,300
Ft. Lauderdale, FL	60,000
Orange County, CA	60,000
South Broward, FL	60,000
Atlanta, GA	50,000
Phoenix, AZ	50,000
Palm Beach County, FL	45,000
Pittsburgh, PA	45,000

Source: Singer, 1988: 233

involvement in Jewish life has been minimal. Furthermore, he saw conversion by a non-Jewish spouse as a remedy to the problem that intermarriage poses to Jewish identity and group affiliation.

Cohen (1988: 96–109) constructed what he calls a "typology of Jewish commitment," which derives from combining the findings from his three indices. He defined five categories and cited their respective sizes in the population: observant (10 percent), activists (17 percent), affiliated (49 percent), holiday (15 percent), and inactives (10 percent). On the basis of this overall portrait, Cohen concluded that a modified, "moderate transformative" view most adequately captured the character of Jewish life in greater New York (where 30 percent of the nation's Jews resided). He further suggested that these conclusions can be extrapolated to the country at large. This tends to overlook the role of Jewish population density and propinquity in shaping attitudes and behaviors. What about Jews in other parts of the country, where they are a smaller minority of the overall population?

A study of a midwestern city with a considerably smaller Jewish population was modeled after Cohen's New York study to see if such extrapolation was warranted (Nefzger and Kivisto, 1990). The findings also provided somewhat mixed results. For example, in the area of ritual observance, although this community did not have an Orthodox institutional presence, and therefore did not contain those Cohen identified as highly observant, there were still clear parallels between the two communities. In the other two indexes, however, there were important differences. In the area of communal affiliation (which includes involvement in both religious and secular Jewish organizations) the midwestern Jews ranked significantly higher than those in greater New York. The situation is reversed for the interpersonal index, where New York Jews ranked higher. The midwestern community shows a voluntaristic affiliation with Jewish religious organizations and a growing tendency to choose friends and marital partners without regard to ethnic background.

In terms of friends, 63 percent of respondents reported that at least two of their three closest friends were Jewish, a figure considerably lower than that obtained in Cohen's study, but similar to that found in numerous other community studies (Fishman, 1987; Cohen, 1988). Particularly notewothy is that the figure for 25- to 34-year-olds is lower in every city studied, and outside of the New York area, it drops appreciably. As the proximity to other Jews diminishes by geographic region, so does the likelihood of having mainly Jewish friends.

Intermarriage

Similar patterns are evident for intermarriage. Cohen's dismissal of the implications of intermarriage for Judaism are not reflected in other regions of the United States. According to Marshall Sklare

Figure 8.3   *Present identity of spouse for Jews by birth by year of marriage.*

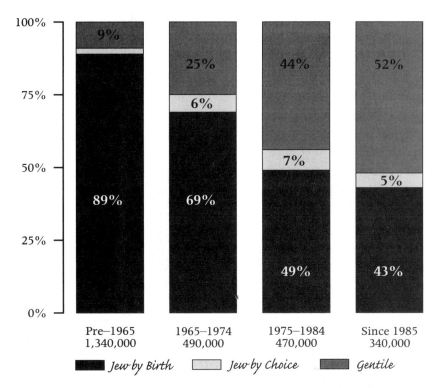

Total = 2,640,000 currently married persons (excluding institutional population

Source: From *Highlights of the CJF 1990 National Jewish Population Survey*, Barry A. Kosmin, et al., 1991:14. Reprinted by permission.

(1971: 191), intermarriage did not become a particular topic of concern for Jews until the 1960s. Between the 1950s and 1970s, the intermarriage rate of Jews increased from 3.7 percent to 11.8 percent (Glenn, 1982: 557). This was quite low in comparison with the rates for other European Americans. Evidence from a number of community studies shows that the intermarriage rate has increased since the 1970s, and one study argued that a "sharply rising incidence of intermarriage among Jews" is seen in the Midwest and West (Sandberg, 1986: 557). The 1990 national Jewish population survey found that 68 percent of Jews are married to Jews-by-birth, 28 percent are married to Gentiles, and 4 percent are married to spouses who converted to Judaism. As Figure 8.3 indicates, however, if we look at the identity of the spouse by year of marriage, the differences over the past three decades are profound. Only 9 percent of pre-1965 marriages involved Gentile spouses, but the number soared to 52 percent for marriages after 1985 (Kosmin, et al., 1991: 13–14).

The overall figure remains lower than that for other European Americans (Spikard, 1989: 229–230). Religion appears to play a role in keeping the rate of outmarriage lower than that of other groups. Jewish parents have historically been more opposed to their children dating or marrying Gentiles than Gentile parents have been opposed to their children dating or marrying Jews. Egon Mayer (1980: 516) has argued that this opposition by Jewish parents has waned considerably, however, and he attributed the rise in intermarriage, in part, to what he refers to as "Jewish default."

Although marital indicators imply increased assimilation, there are other indications that Jews still retain a distinctive identity. Jews have traditionally been more liberal than many other white ethnics, and they remain so. Similarly, they remain closely identified with the Democratic party, at a time when many other white ethnics from the former New Deal coalition have bolted to the conservatism offered by the Republican party. In addition, the question of the Jewish homeland, Israel, still remains a potent stimulus to ethnic identity. Anti-Semitism has not disappeared, and in the late 1980s and early 1990s various white supremacist groups ranging from the KKK to the Aryan Nation, replete with their skinhead youth contingents, have justifiably revived concerns among Jews. This intensified ethnic identities and boundaries.

In short, at present it appears that Jews *might* follow the pattern of other European ethnics, but it is by no means clear that they *will* do so. There is also evidence of vitality, and the intertwining of religion and ethnicity may maintain a distinct Jewish American presence.

The Specter of Race

Public opinion polls capture something of the changes that have transpired during the past half century. What has happened to the color line while boundaries dividing different white ethnic groups have eroded considerably? Changes in white racial attitudes since the 1940s are difficult to summarize both because the trends are ambiguous and because different analysts can and do interpret changes in various ways.

There is rather clear evidence that a substantial majority of whites have come to endorse equality and integration in principle (Taylor, et al., 1978). For example, in 1942, 54 percent of whites believed that blacks should be required to occupy separate sections on streetcars and buses, but by 1970, 88 percent of whites disagreed with this stance. Subsequent public opinion polls have dropped this question, reflecting the fact that the number of whites accepting integrated transportation systems was approaching 100 percent. The percentage agreeing that whites and blacks should attend the same schools rose from 32 percent in 1942 to 90 percent by 1982 (Schuman, et al., 1985: 72–79).

Questions about residential segregation suggest a more favorable attitude about open housing than in the 1940s, but the change is not as pronounced as in other areas. This is partly because this issue was often posed in terms of rights, including the rights of whites to sell their homes to whomever they want. Given the importance attached to individual rights in America, it is not surprising that the rights of whites and the rights of blacks could conflict. Nevertheless, in a 1982 National Opinion Research Center (NORC) survey, 71 percent of whites either disagreed or disagreed strongly with the statement that whites have a right to keep blacks out of their neighborhoods if they want to (Schuman, et al., 1985: 79–81).

These principles are not as overwhelmingly supported in areas of intimacy in social relations. For example, during the past decade 34 percent of white Americans agreed that there should be laws prohibiting racial intermarriage (see Figure 8.4). A majority of whites—60 percent—disapprove of marriages between whites and nonwhites (Schuman, et al., 1985: 75). Thus, what Robert E. Park long ago saw as the last major barrier to assimilation still remains in place.

Looking at the preferred kind of social contact with blacks, it is clear that in matters related to residential and school integration, whites are far more comfortable in situations with small numbers of blacks. This suggests that whites prefer to interact with blacks in a context in which whites are in the majority, and black interactants

Figure 8.4   *Attitudes toward laws against intermarriage.*
Laws against intermarriage (NORC): "Do you think there
should be laws against marriages between blacks and
whites?"   1. Yes   2. No.

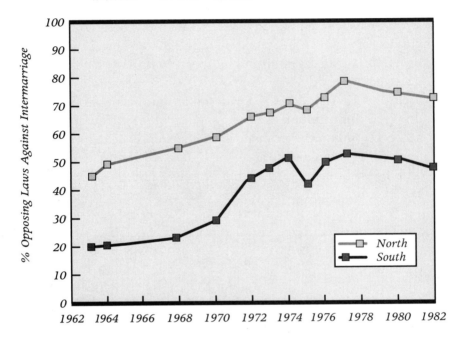

Source: Reprinted by permission of the publishers from *Racial Attitudes in America* by
Howard Schuman, Charlotte Steeh, and Lawrence Bobo, Cambridge, MA: Harvard
University Press. Copyright © 1985 by the President and Fellows of Harvard College.

find themselves in a situation where they must conform to white
expectations and work at fitting in. Although some analysts have
concluded that this is an indication of persistent racism, it is a gross
oversimplification to reduce this solely to racism. Issues related to
social class also have an effect, as whites manifest a greater willingness to interact with blacks from the same class background than
with blacks from a lower class background than their own.

White Attitudes About Governmental Actions

When turning from principles to ways of effecting change, or in
other words, to questions related to implementation, whites are far
more divided. In general, the majority of whites do not support the
federal government having a major role in initiating policies to

remedy problems such as school and residential segregation, inequitable treatment in the labor market, and related issues (Schuman, et al., 1985: 86–104). As we shall see in greater detail in the next chapter, in two areas—busing to achieve school integration and affirmative action policies—the pronounced split in white opinions has made these implementation practices highly charged political issues.

Although public opinion surveys provide valuable data, there are limits to their utility. They fail to reveal some of the complicated reasons that affect people's attitudes. Furthermore, attitudes do not necessarily translate into behaviors. For example, although 86 percent of whites in 1982 said they would vote for a black presidential candidate if he or she were qualified, in local and state races, whites have been far less willing than this suggests to cast their votes for black candidates. The reason for this reluctance is not easy to unravel. Is it because of latent racism or because the voters genuinely believe the candidate is not as qualified as the opponent? Is it due to disagreement over the candidate's platform and general political orientation?

Whites are a large majority of the nation's population, and as such are characterized by a great number of divisions. They cannot be seen in monolithic terms. The opinion polls reviewed above indicate, for example, the differences that persist between southern whites and whites elsewhere in the nation—the former remain more conservative in their racial attitudes than the latter. Similarly, more highly educated people have more liberal racial attitudes than those with less education.

Michael Omi and Howard Winant (1986) pointed to a shift in the configuration of race relations since the 1960s. A conservative reaction not only to the civil rights movement but also to the loss of the Vietnam War, the transformations brought about by the 1960s counterculture, and the growing stagnation of the American economy led to electoral victories first by Richard Nixon, and then, in 1980, by the most ideologically-motivated president of the century, Ronald Reagan. The backlash that was part of this shift to conservatism was frequently motivated by what can be seen as the politics of resentment. White ethnics, especially poor and working class whites, felt that they had been left behind by liberal politicians. The Reagan administration contended that the federal government did not have a legitimate role in promoting social change and sought to roll back the government's role in matters related to racial and class inequality. Omi and Winant (1986: 113) wrote, however:

> There were clear limits to any attempt to undo the effects of the "great transformation." In the aftermath of the 1960s, any effective challenge to the egalitarian ideals framed by the [civil rights movement] could no longer rely on the racism of the past. Racial equality had to be acknowledged as a desirable goal. But the *meaning* of equality, and the proper means for achieving it, remained matters of considerable debate.

The Politics of Hate and Racial Divisiveness

A resurgence of white supremacy marks the far right-wing response to black advancement and takes a number of organizational forms. All of these groups combine a virulent racism with an equally virulent anti-Semitism. The Ku Klux Klan has experienced something of a revival since the early 1970s, especially in the South and along the entire Atlantic coast, under the leadership of David Duke. West of the Mississippi has the greatest concentration of various neo-Nazi groups, including Tom Metzger's White Armed Resistance (WAR) and many loosely organized skinhead youth gangs with names such as Youth of Hitler and Confederate Hammerskins. Several groups see themselves as "Christian patriots," including Posse Comitatus, the Golden Mean Society, the Order, and Identity Christians. They are alike in their hostility to what they refer to as ZOG (that is, Zionist Occupied Government). They are convinced that they are a "chosen people" engaged in a righteous war against blacks, whom they refer to as "mud people" (Omi and Winant, 1986: 113–118; Aho, 1990; Langer, 1990). These groups are small in number but nevertheless dangerous. They are responsible for terrorist acts throughout the country, including shootings, lynchings, and beatings (Marable, 1983: 231–253). They have also attempted to use the mass media to attract a larger audience, as Metzger's efforts to use public access television shows.

These extremists are largely outside of the conventional political process, though David Duke has made an effort to enter electoral politics. After being elected to the state legislature in Louisiana, he ran unsuccessfully for the governorship of the state. He lost the election, but garnered the majority of the state's white vote — despite his connection with the Klan and the American

Figure 8.5   *The adherents of neo-Nazi groups such as this one have increased in numbers in recent years.*

Source: Larry Fisher/Quad City Times.

Nazi movement. He proved to be an embarrassment to the Republican party, which sought to disassociate itself from him.

The Reagan and Bush administrations, as the major exemplars of mainstream conservatism, publicly repudiated the racism that characterized, for example, southern politics well into the 1960s. They espoused ideals of racial equality and harmony, and they appointed conservative blacks to highly visible governmental posts. But they achieved victory by driving a wedge into the New Deal coalition, one that split the party chiefly along racial lines.

The Democrats were increasingly seen as the party of racial minorities and the poor, but no longer as the voice of the white working class. Conservatives played on white resentment and a sense that governmental intervention on behalf of blacks had been at their expense. As with the 1988 Bush election campaign's Willie Horton advertisements, conservatives fueled the public's growing fear of crime and reinforced the association of violent crime with black males. Frequently, conservatives relied on subtle codes that aroused racial animosity without resorting to overt racist appeals. Although the electoral victories of conservatives since 1980 were the result of a combination of factors, with racial issues being only one of them, the repudiation of many liberal policies of the 1960s by a significant portion of the white voting population should temper the generally optimistic findings of the opinion polls reported above (Edsall and Edsall, 1991; Franklin, 1991: 1–21).

Summary

This chapter has surveyed the profound changes that have occurred within European-origin ethnic communities during the past half century. As earlier chapters have illustrated, these communities have often been at odds with one another. Conflict based on job competition, over political control, or because of cultural, religious, and linguistic differences have frequently pitted one group against another. Throughout American history, however, these groups have also constructed bridges to overcome differences. In short, from an early date one could point to various indicators that suggested assimilation was occurring.

The pace of change accelerated dramatically after 1950. Interethnic conflict declined precipitously. Ethnic communities and cultures eroded, ethnic allegiances declined in strength, and intermarriages increased among white ethnic groups. Although how change occurred varied for each group, with some assimilating more quickly than others, nonetheless, for all Gentile groups abundant evidence suggests the validity of Richard Alba's characterization of them entering the "twilight of ethnicity." For a number of reasons, Jewish assimilation remains distinctive. There is evidence of assimilation, especially during the past quarter of a century, but it is difficult to speculate about what the future holds for the Jewish American community.

Ethnicity has not disappeared for most European-origin Americans. Rather, several new forms of ethnicity may be emerging. The invention of ethnicity perspective calls attention to how ethnicity is currently being reshaped, whether in the form of symbolic ethnicity, the creation of new regional and ethnic identities, or the emergence of the European American.

The chapter also examined how race plays a role in this redefinition of ethnicity for European Americans. Although racial attitudes have improved, racism is a continuing problem. The majority of whites are opposed to governmental actions designed to overcome the legacy of racial oppression. There is a tendency to think that blacks are to blame for their problems. Most whites live in worlds apart from blacks, especially in the intimate worlds of friendships and marriages.

Nonetheless, this does not mean that all whites are, in effect, closet racists. Many, perhaps most, are not. Their orientations toward race relations are highly varied and often ambiguous. Some simply want to avoid the issue as much as possible. Its seeming intractability leads them to a fatalistic view of race relations or to mere indifference. Others overestimate the extent to which inequality has been overcome and the amount of opportunity actually available to blacks. For many well-intentioned people, one can point to countless acts, small and large, that are intended to do something to improve race relations. For all, race continues to cast its shadow over their definition of the American situation as we approach century's end (Franklin, 1991).

AFRICAN AMERICANS:
THE ENDURING
AMERICAN DILEMMA

In 1944 the Swedish economist Gunnar Myrdal published a monumental study on African Americans. Encyclopedic in its effort to cover all aspects of black life, *An American Dilemma* included analyses of major political, economic, and cultural forces that shaped the black experience in America. Furthermore, it provided extended discussions of social inequality and the persistent role of prejudice and discrimination. After presenting a vast body of data regarding the past and present circumstances of blacks in America, Myrdal provided tempered but, nonetheless, generally optimistic conclusions about the future.

The study was commissioned by the Carnegie Corporation, a philanthropic organization established by the estate of industrialist Andrew Carnegie, which wanted to derive implications for social policy from the study. Although it is not entirely clear why the corporation hired a foreigner who had conducted no prior research on race relations in America, a primary reason was the desire to get a fresh, outsider's perspective on the topic of race relations. Myrdal had ample monetary support and involved many prominent American scholars, including several black activists and intellectuals (Southern, 1987: 20–21).

The overarching thesis advanced in the study was noteworthy in several ways. Despite the range and complexity of the topics treated, Myrdal's conclusions about the future of race relations derived from a remarkably simple claim: the dilemma produced by the conflict between the American ideals of freedom and equality and the reality of black oppression would be resolved in favor of the realization of American values. Myrdal was an assimilationist who based his assessment of the future of race relations on the assumption that America had a unified cultural system with commonly shared core values. The race problem was located in the white mind which, as long as it harbored prejudicial attitudes that were translated into discriminatory actions, would ensure that the dilemma persisted. Thus, the solution to the race problem would occur when whites rooted out their own racism and treated blacks in a manner congruent with the core cultural values.

But Myrdal did not think that a mass therapy session was all that was necessary to cure the nation of white racism. On the contrary, he understood that the historical legacy of racial oppression had to be remedied. He called for the government to play a central role in improving the social condition of African Americans. As a central figure in the creation of Sweden's welfare state, Myrdal was an exponent of social engineering. This position had not been a particularly prominent feature of earlier American social science, but it was congruent with the expanded role of the state being advanced by advocates of the New Deal (Lyman, 1972: 99–120; Wacker, 1983: 80). This position contrasted with the laissez-faire views of one of the founders of American sociology, William Graham Sumner. Sumner contended that mores cannot be legislated or, in other words, laws do not change the way people think and feel. Myrdal's position starkly refuted this claim. In his opinion, government could and should involve itself in improving the living conditions and life chances of blacks, through expanded educational opportunities, job training, and the like.

Moreover, Myrdal called for racial integration. He abandoned Booker T. Washington's approach, which opted for developing blacks within the confines of a caste society. Prior to Myrdal commencing his research, Roy Wilkins of the NAACP expressed his concern that Myrdal might promote a renewed commitment to the Washingtonian position of development within the framework of a segregated world (Southern, 1987: 10). Instead, Myrdal endorsed the quest most closely associated with the views of W.E.B. Du Bois for the dual objectives of advancement and integration.

Myrdal placed relatively little emphasis on black activism as a means for changing their subordinate place in American society (Smith and Killian, 1990). When he discussed the presence of protest organizations within the black community, especially the

Figure 9.1   *This poor family, like millions of southern blacks, took part in the Great Migration to the North.*

Source: Library of Congress.

NAACP and the Urban League, he stressed the importance of their interracial character. He was sympathetic to such organizations and suggested that more organizations with somewhat different political orientations would be welcomed. Nonetheless, his general view was that due to their lack of power and experience, such organizations would ultimately play an essentially secondary role in the move to redefine the place of blacks in American society.

But an event that Myrdal mentions can be seen as signaling the beginning of a social movement that was far more consequential than he was able to imagine (Myrdal, 1944: 768–857). The event was a proposed march on Washington, D.C., orchestrated by the political and labor activist A. Philip Randolph. The planned march was motivated by Franklin D. Roosevelt's refusal to desegregate the armed forces, but was called off when Roosevelt signed Executive Order 8802, by which he established the Fair Employment Practices Commission. According to Doug McAdam (1982: 84), "That order marked the official termination of the earlier policy of executive inaction, and as such established an important, if largely symbolic, precedent."

The Civil Rights Movement: 1940–1970

Randolph was the most important black leader during the 1940s, an interstitial figure who bridged two generations of leadership. Although he was a unique leader in his own right, with a distinct operational base and political stance, he was in many respects the heir to the early Du Bois. Randolph was also a model for the new generation of protest organizers, most notably Martin Luther King, Jr. Randolph's success in pressuring the Roosevelt administration to take a more active role in the affairs of black America or risk a confrontation set in motion repeated attempts to stimulate change. Segregation continued as official policy of the military until after the conclusion of World War II. But in 1948 President Truman signed an executive order that was designed to end segregation — though integration did not occur immediately.

The civil rights movement intensified and grew during the 1950s, during a period of heightened international tensions brought about by the international struggle between the United States and the Soviet Union. Because both superpowers were intent on serving as a model for peoples throughout the world, racial oppression in the bastion of the "free world" proved increasingly to be an embarrassment and a political burden. Mass communications permitted the rapid dissemination of unsavory events such as the lynching of Emmett Till in 1955. Till was a teenage black from Chicago who, on a visit to relatives in the South, failed to understand the region's perverse "racial etiquette." After allegedly making a sexual remark to a white woman, he was attacked and killed by a vigilante mob. Because the Soviet Union made quick and effective use of this and similar events in their propaganda war, it became increasingly evident to some government officials and politicians that steps had to be taken to prevent racism from further tarnishing America's image abroad. In addition, given the centrality of racism to Nazi ideology, progressives were able to link the rationale for our participation in the war against fascism to the struggle for black rights at home.

This was also a period of unprecedented economic prosperity and one in which the middle class expanded. A growth economy demanded workers and resulted in low unemployment rates. This meant a reduction in the competition for jobs, which allowed a lowering of interracial tensions. There were decided limits to who were the beneficiaries of these new economic circumstances, however. Poverty did not disappear, as some thought it would. Instead, an affluent society was forced to confront the existence of those who stood outside — those whom Michael Harrington (1962) depicted as residents of the "other America." Blacks were disproportionately represented in the ranks of the other America, and their concentration in inner-city ghettos made them a highly visible feature of the urban landscape that highlighted both the gulf between comfort and want and the divide between blacks and whites.

Phase I: Nonviolent Confrontation and Legislative Lobbying

In this climate the modern civil rights movement developed during the 1950s and 1960s, built partly on already existing black organizations. The church played a key role, as did black colleges and the oldest civil rights organizations, particularly the NAACP and the National Urban League (Morris, 1984; Haines, 1988; Lincoln and Mamiya, 1990: 196–235).

In addition, several new organizations emerged. These included the Congress of Racial Equality (CORE), founded in 1942, which was an offshoot of the Fellowship of Reconciliation, a Christian pacifist group (Meier and Rudwick, 1973). Another key organization created in the midst of movement activism was the Southern Christian Leadership Conference (SCLC), founded in 1957. It began after discussions among some influential northern blacks such as A. Philip Randolph, Ella Baker, and Bayard Rustin, and southern clergy, the most prominent of whom would soon be seen as its leader, Martin Luther King, Jr. Aldon Morris (1984: 77) has described the SCLC as "the decentralized political arm of the black church." CORE and SCLC were alike in their advocacy of nonviolent protest, and in this they differed from the NAACP, which was more inclined to seek redress for injustice and racial inequality through the courts and the legislative system. The former groups were thus more militant than the NAACP, but not as militant as the Student Nonviolent Coordinating Committee (SNCC). A spin-off of SCLC, SNCC was construed at its inception in 1960 as a place for student activists to be connected to the larger movement while being able to act creatively and independently. Within a few years of its founding, this organization was transformed from having a reformist integrationist stance similar to these other groups into a radical, black nationalist one (Haines, 1988: 35–36).

This indigenous movement was, until the second half of the 1960s, quite unified in terms of its objectives. For example, considerable overlap in organizational support and membership existed. The major differences that generated conflict revolved around tactics, which ultimately involved conflicting assessments about the appropriate speed of change and the desirability of compromise with whites. Related to this were two relevant facts regarding the movement's relationship with whites. First, wealthy liberal whites and various foundations contributed financially to movement organizations. Parenthetically, J. Craig Jenkins and Craig Eckert (1986: 823) suggested that wealthy Jews, out of a longstanding concern about discrimination, may have been disproportionately represented among the contributors. Certainly this is true for one of the most important sources of foundation support: the Julius Rosenwald Fund. Movement organizations also derived support from prominent law firms, media executives, and from liberal politicians. Movement organizers found political backing from well-placed government officials in the central corridors of power especially after the election of John F. Kennedy.

Although much of the black leadership came from the middle class, it succeeded only insofar as it connected with the black working class and poor, which, as became increasingly clear, were far from docile. Blacks from all socioeconomic backgrounds pressed for dramatic social change. Although much of what transpired during two tumultuous decades involved considerable spontaneity and innovativeness (Killian, 1984), it was also encouraged by professional social movement organizers and paid staffs who utilized, through rational calculation, strategic resources (McCarthy and Zald, 1977; McAdam, 1982; Bloom, 1987).

Because of the middle class leadership base, the professional cast, and the role played by white elites, some have argued that the militancy of the civil rights movement was effectively contained by those who sought change, but only change within certain circumscribed limits. Some have argued that elite sponsorship amounted

Figure 9.2 *The sit-in at the Woolworth's lunch counter in Greensboro, North Carolina, was one of the pivotal dramatic events of the civil rights movement.*

Source: Jack Moebes/Greensboro News & Record Library.

to a form of social control (Piven and Coward, 1971). Recent historical studies of the movement have disputed this contention, reporting such support as essentially reactive rather than as controlling — playing, in other words, a secondary role (McAdam, 1982; Morris, 1984).

Challenging Jim Crow in the South

The first phase of collective action began in the South, where the Jim Crow system was challenged. Direct action took varied forms of peaceful confrontations with white rule. For example, in 1953 a boycott of city buses in Baton Rouge, Louisiana, challenged the "back of the bus" requirement. The local chapter of the NAACP was involved in this early, and partially successful, attempt to end segregation in public accommodations. Two years later a similar effort to end segregation on municipal buses began in Montgomery, Alabama. When Rosa Parks refused to take a seat in the back of the bus she was arrested. Out of this not entirely spontaneous action, an ad hoc committee was formed to boycott the bus line. Through his early involvement in the Montgomery Improvement Association, Dr. Martin Luther King, Jr., was catapulted into national prominence. The boycott was a year-long struggle that sought to make a moral argument while exhibiting the economic clout of black consumers. Since 75 percent of the public transit riders were black, the boycott put the bus company in financial jeopardy and had a direct impact on city tax revenues. The movement combined protest tactics with court challenges, which proved to be successful as the federal courts ruled against segregated busing (Blumberg, 1984; Haines, 1988).

In varied ways in different locales similar nonviolent actions were undertaken throughout the 1950s and into the early 1960s. These included sit-ins at segregated lunch counters, beginning with an initial demonstration at the Woolworth store in Greensboro, North Carolina. Several major episodes of this period occurred in a relatively short span of time. Among the most important was the CORE-initiated Freedom Rides. CORE sought the implementation of the federal ban on segregated interstate buses and organized an unsuccessful attempt in Albany, Georgia, to desegregate public facilities and a similar campaign in Birmingham, Alabama, which was a success.

Closely linked to these efforts was work designed to overcome barriers to political involvement, particularly impediments to voting. Thus, in 1958 a voter-registration drive in Tennessee's Fayette and Haywood counties was started. Similar drives were conducted in many places after 1960, especially in the Deep South. This activity culminated in 1964 with the implementation of Freedom Summer, a massive voter registration project in Mississippi that was made possible by an interracial coalition of civil rights volunteers, chiefly recruited from the North.

As Figure 9.3 indicates, the number of movement-initiated events grew slowly during the first half of the 1950s and increased thereafter; a dramatic escalation of activities occurred during the first half of the 1960s. In 1963 a massive March on Washington, D.C. took place, a little more than two decades after A. Philip Randolph had initially proposed such a protest. Two years later, with

Figure 9.3 *Number of Movement-Initiated Events, 1948–1976*

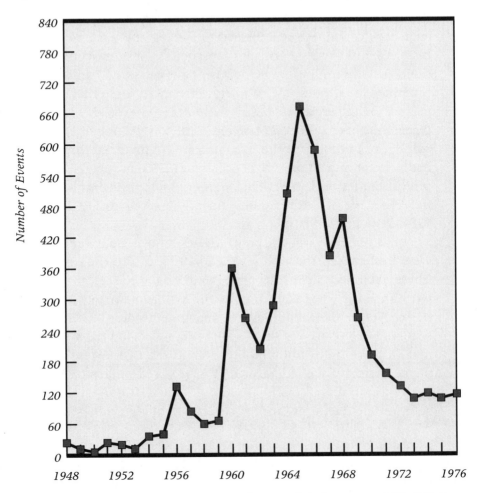

Source: From *Political Process and the Development of Black Insurgency 1930–1970,* Doug McAdam, The University of Chicago Press, 1982: 121. Reprinted by permission of the author and the publisher.

the voting rights struggle in Selma, Alabama, this phase of the civil rights movement, for all intents and purposes, came to an end (Garrow, 1978; Powledge, 1991: 620–628).

White Responses to the Civil Rights Movement

Throughout this phase the movement evoked varied responses from whites, but the challenge to the caste system began to under-mine the paternalism that permeated it. For instance, wealthy whites who traditionally made donations to buy gifts for poor black children stopped doing so (Bloom, 1987: 133). Their benevolence had been based on a sense of their own superiority and on the legitimacy of the "racial etiquette" of the South. The assertiveness of blacks was an indication to wealthy whites that these taken-for-granted assumptions were being seriously challenged.

On the one hand, black protest met stiff white resistance. This opposition to change entailed legislative challenges such as the gerrymandering law that was designed to prevent blacks from acquiring political power in Tuskegee, Alabama. It also involved defiance of court orders by southern politicians. The two most prominent challenges were Governor Orval Faubus's attempt to stop the integration of Little Rock's Central High School and George Wallace's similar stance against the introduction of black students to the University of Alabama. Citizens Councils were founded in many communities to provide an organizational base for white resistance. Moreover, the Ku Klux Klan underwent a revival. Along with other white supremacist organizations, the Klan was responsible for a wave of violence, taking form in the beatings of Freedom Riders; numerous murders, including those of three volunteers — James Chaney, Mickey Schwerner, and Andrew Goodman — working for Freedom Summer; and bombings of churches and homes (Blumberg, 1984; McAdam, 1988).

On the other hand, many whites, especially outside of the South, began to react to the incidents of violence perpetuated against unarmed, nonviolent protesters. The unleashing of police dogs on demonstrators, the wanton beatings, and similar events were documented and reached national (and international) audiences in daily newspapers, magazines, and television news. The leadership of the movement understood that if they were to be successful they had to vividly dramatize racial injustice to what was a "conscience constituency." In appealing to an otherwise passive public, leaders hoped that citizens would demand that their elected officials undertake policies that would advance equality. Indeed, part of this constituency was composed of elected officials, and, perhaps more indirectly, members of the judiciary.

Legislative and Judicial Decisions

The first major governmental decision came from the judiciary, and it occurred at the initial stage of protest activity. That decision was the 1954 *Brown v. Board of Education of Topeka, Kansas* case in which the segregation of public schools was declared to be unconstitutional. The courts argued — for the first time in its history basing a decision partly on the evidence amassed by social scientists — that segregated schools were inherently unequal. Therefore, the Court argued, the constitutional guarantee of equal treatment had been violated. Thus, the Supreme Court reversed *Plessy v. Ferguson* and with it the doctrine of separate but equal. A year later the court ruled that the implementation of this decision should occur "with all deliberate speed."

A decade later, the legislative centerpiece of the civil rights era became law: the 1964 Civil Rights Act, which contained a number of bans on discrimination, focused attention on employment discrimination (as well as discrimination by labor unions), and provided mechanisms to enforce educational integration. Although several other pieces of legislation and judicial decisions had a bearing on civil rights, two other acts combined with the Civil Rights Act to provide the most important bases for ending the Jim Crow era. These were the Voting Rights Act of 1965 and the Civil Rights Act of 1968. The former banned the discriminatory use of literacy tests in voter registration (the poll tax was prohibited by a 1966 Supreme Court decision) and provided for the use of federal marshals to enforce voting rights (Haines, 1988: 130–131). Title 8 of the latter act, or the Fair Housing Law, established provisions designed to promote open housing, although its enforcement mechanism was weak (Goering, 1986).

Phase II: Militancy and Black Nationalism

While these pieces of legislation were enacted into law, a second, far more militant phase of the movement commenced. The militancy of the second half of the 1960s is partially attributable to the mutual reinforcement of the civil rights struggle with other social movements. Together they represented a generalized legitimation crisis. Thus, the black struggle for racial justice influenced the emergence of parallel movements in the Hispanic and American Indian communities (and, to a lesser extent, the Asian). In addition, both the anti-Vietnam war movement and the youth counterculture attracted increased numbers of adherents and sympathizers. Not only were there important interconnections among these movements (for example, Martin Luther King, Jr., became increasingly vocal about his opposition to the Vietnam war during the last years of his life), but also their overarching impact on the nation presented a significant challenge to the status quo (Rollins, 1986). This is not to suggest, however, that there was a unified and coherent opposition. Serious and persistent tensions and conflicts existed among movements and within each movement.

Within the black community militancy was expressed in the form of Black Power, which was based ideologically, at least partially, on the position earlier espoused by Marcus Garvey. Some African American clergy were influenced by the powerful critique of American society offered by the black theology movement (Baer and Singer, 1992: 124–126). The Black Power idea was first expressed by Stokely Carmichael in 1966 when he was working within the integrationist framework of the earlier phase. The two organizations most closely associated with the idea—the Black Muslims (the Nation of Islam) and the Black Panthers—were opposed to integration. They opted, in somewhat different ways, for separatism and black nationalism (Carmichael and Hamilton, 1967; Blumberg, 1984). Rather than attempting to break the barriers that had been erected during the Jim Crow era, black nationalists sought to achieve power and economic development while preserving racial autonomy. The Black Muslims, led by Elijah Muhammad, had been in existence for some time, but they were revitalized when Malcolm X rose to prominence. To the dismay of many Muslims, he split from the movement, while rethinking his earlier positions and possibly moving to a new rapprochement with whites and with the mainstream of the civil rights movement. His assassination in 1965 ended this reevaluation and repositioning of his political views.

The Black Panthers were a product of the 1960s, formed by Huey Newton and Bobby Seale in Oakland, California, in 1966. The Panthers defined themselves as a self-defense organization, especially intent on protecting urban ghetto residents against police brutality (Blumberg, 1984: 126–127). Their ideological position changed rapidly, to embrace a third world perspective and, contrary to Garvey, condemn capitalism. Nonetheless, the actual program they advanced was reformist, replete with breakfast programs for school children and a presidential campaign by one of their chief figures, Eldridge Cleaver. In contrast, their style was that of the resistance fighter, and their leather jackets, berets, and weapons gave the public appearance of a militia. Their message was clear: they did not want into the American dream, which they considered to be a nightmare (Killian, 1975).

The Panthers became the focus of intense political repression. According to Doug McAdam (1982: 219), "In the late 1960s law enforcement officials at all levels of government responded to what they perceived to be the growing threat posed by insurgents by initiating a stepped-up campaign of repression designed to destroy the black-power wing of the movement." The Panthers were a major object of the FBI's Counter-Intelligence Program (COINTELPRO) and the victims of various police assaults. One notorious case was the 1969 killing of Mark Clark and Fred Hampton by the Chicago police, who fired between 800 and 1,000 rounds of ammunition into the victims' apartment (Blumberg, 1984: 127).

At the same time, a wave of urban riots swept the country, beginning as early as 1964 in Rochester, Harlem, and Philadelphia. Riots first acquired widespread national attention with the 1965 civil disorder in the Watts section of Los Angeles. During the next few years riots ultimately encompassed hundreds of cities, large and small (McPhail, 1971). These essentially spontaneous outbursts constituted a form of political theater acted out by relatively powerless people who had concluded that despite the changes that had occurred, their most basic grievances remained unmet. Hundreds of deaths and thousands of injuries resulted, and vast numbers of ghetto dwellers were arrested for violence and looting. Millions of dollars of property were destroyed or stolen during these uprisings, and in many places local and state police were joined by the National Guard, equipped with tanks and other military hardware reflecting an army occupation.

By the end of the decade the movement was winding down. Internal conflicts between various expressions of moderate support for integration and radical nationalism escalated and splintered the movement. Moderate organizations suffered from declines in outside financial support. The assassination of Martin Luther King, Jr., in 1968 robbed mainstream civil rights organizations of their most important national spokesperson. Repression and white backlash took a toll. The inability to achieve consensus about goals made cohesiveness impossible, mainly because the objective of ending Jim Crow had succeeded and a legislative apparatus was in place that provided mechanisms for addressing the legacy of the past (McAdam, 1982: 181–229).

Two Lingering Controversies: Busing and Affirmative Action

Although white attitudes toward the issue of justice and equality for blacks changed appreciably between the 1940s and 1980s, the principle of fair play did not necessarily translate into support for various policies to redress the legacy of segregation. This is evident in two highly controversial policies: busing and affirmative action.

Busing and School Desegregation

Busing was a mechanism for assisting in the desegregation of public schools. The initial phase of school desegregation entailed prohibiting legally mandated, or *de jure*, segregation. The focus was on the South. When the *Brown* ruling was made, less than one-tenth of one percent of black students in eleven southern states attended school with whites. Although many southern white elites determined that change would occur and began to develop desegregation plans, resistance to integration was intense in many places. The conflict was felt throughout the South, but racial politics in Little Rock, Arkansas, riveted the attention of the nation and reflected the dilemmas of change in the face of resistance. In Little Rock, local school administrators, with the support of some white business elites, began a plan to integrate the all-white Central High School. The plan was opposed by many whites. By 1956, however, some in the black community decided that the school system was not moving with "all deliberate speed." So they filed a lawsuit in federal court to bring the power of the federal courts into the dispute.

The school superintendent went forward with his plan, but as it was to be implemented in 1957, Governor Orval Faubus intervened to prevent the plan from being carried out. This resulted in a conflict between the state and federal governments, and culminated in President Eisenhower's decision to send National Guard troops to enforce the desegregation order. The citizens of the city responded the following year by voting to close the schools to terminate the integration policy. Ultimately, a coalition of influential and powerful white moderates intent on a peaceful transition from segregation waged a successful campaign, and the schools were reopened. Integration proceeded without widespread disruption. This leadership entered into a working relationship with the black community, and during the next few years, according to Irving Spitzberg, Jr. (1987: 9), the local economic elite, "on its own and apart from the public governmental system, desegregated many sectors of the economy as well as maintained modest desegregation in the schools."

This local initiative occurred in many other southern communities, but where it did not, involuntary, court-ordered integration plans were enacted. By the time the Civil Rights Act had passed in 1964, the percentage of blacks attending schools with whites stood at only 2 percent. Desegregation plans were enacted throughout the South by utilizing a provision of the act that granted to the Department of Health, Education, and Welfare the ability to impose financial sanctions on noncompliant school systems by cutting federal funding. By 1973, 46 percent of blacks in the South attended integrated schools.

Judicial Decisions

The trend toward integration was further enhanced by several Supreme Court decisions. In *Green v. New Kent Co.* (1968) the court ruled that freedom-of-choice plans were an unacceptable remedy to segregation, and in *Alexander v. Holmes* (1969) the court moved beyond the "with all deliberate speed" framework to order the immediate desegregation of all southern schools (Jaynes and Williams, 1989: 75). Finally, the *Swann v. Charlotte-Mecklenberg* (1971) case addressed the link between residential and school segregation, arguing that desegregation plans could not be limited to schools a student could walk to. Therefore, busing was an appropriate tool for achieving integration. This decision also raised the possibility that busing could go beyond established school district lines if residential segregation was so pronounced that the goal of integration could not be achieved within a district. Specifically, this introduced the possibility of incorporating suburbs into the desegregation plans of cities.

This particular court case had implications that went beyond the South. Included in the mandate to promote racial integration in

American schools was the elimination of not only *de jure* segregation, but also *de facto* segregation. In many northern cities, residential segregation was more pronounced than in the South, and where neighborhood schools existed this meant that segregated schools were the inevitable result. *De facto* segregation was specifically declared to be unconstitutional in the *Keyes v. Denver School District No. 1* (1973) case.

White Opposition

Nowhere was the conflict between the opponents and supporters of busing more acrimonious than in Boston, where Federal District Court Judge W. Arthur Garrity developed a plan that met with stiff resistance. Many lower-middle class and working-class white ethnics, especially Italians and Irish, felt that they were being treated unfairly because the impact of busing would be felt at their local schools and on their children. They argued that it would not have an impact on the children of affluent middle class citizens who either sent their children to private schools or lived in suburbs that would be untouched by the plan. For their part, white supporters of the plan often viewed the opponents as uneducated bigots.

Certainly, racism was a major factor in the busing controversy. Thomas Cottle (1976: 2) reported the reaction of one white student, who argued, "Nobody's busing me just so some niggers can get a better deal." As Ronald P. Formisano's (1991) case study of Boston indicated, however, the reality was more complicated, and the conflict cannot be reduced solely to racism. A core of anti-busing activists caught the attention of the media, and they had a constituency in white ethnic enclaves such as South Boston. According to Formisano, however, many whites were willing to give busing a chance. In addition, reasons other than simple racism accounted for a position against busing. For residents of working-class neighborhoods, the local school was seen as an integral part of the local community, a community which residents did not want to leave or see their children leave. Busing was seen as an assault on the neighborhood.

For white parents, the prospect of their children being shipped into lower-class black neighborhoods evoked fears of crime and drugs. Formisano (1991) observed that black-on-white crime was a troublesome reality and not simply a rationalization for racist hostility. Moreover, many blacks were at best ambivalent about busing. In one black neighborhood, there was dismay over the fact that an excellent school would have introduced whites, while many blacks in the area would have been bused elsewhere in the city. Some blacks argued that what they wanted was local neighborhood control of schools, and not integration.

Social Contact or White Flight

Although the conflict in Boston was more intense than in many places — where, in fact, integration plans were implemented without controversy — Boston nonetheless served as a microcosm of national patterns. It reflected the dilemmas caused by the unintended consequences of busing. The purpose of busing was to facilitate racial harmony by overcoming social distance between the races. Research had tested the hypothesis that increased social contact yielded more positive race relations over time (Zeul and Humphrey, 1971). This assumption underpinned school integration plans. In addition, research initially conducted by James Coleman and his associates (1966), and confirmed by subsequent studies, concluded that students from lower socioeconomic backgrounds benefited from the presence in schools of students from higher socioeconomic backgrounds. Meanwhile, the latter group did not perform less well due to the presence of the former. Together, these seemed to confirm the beneficial nature of policies designed to promote integration.

What policymakers had not foreseen, however, was the exodus of whites from urban public schools. In Boston, for example, 60 percent of students were white in 1973. By 1988 that figure had plummeted to 26 percent, and a disproportionate number of those whites attended a few prestigious schools in the system rather than being dispersed throughout the city. This phenomenon became known as white flight, and it took two main forms: a move from urban to suburban school districts and enrolling students in parochial schools or, especially in the South, in newly created "Christian academies." James Coleman, Sara Kelly, and John Moore (1975) concluded that white flight was so pervasive that it rendered busing a failed remedy.

Although the relationship between white flight and busing is complicated and somewhat uncertain, by 1980 in many urban public schools whites made up a very small minority of the student population (Pettigrew and Green, 1976; Rossell, 1976, 1988; Farley, et al., 1980). For instance, the white student population in the nation's capitol was only 4 percent, while only 8 percent in Atlanta, 9 percent in Newark, and 12 percent in Detroit (Orfield, 1983; Jaynes and Williams, 1989: 76). Even within schools a form of "resegregation within desegregated schools" often occurred as special academic programs effectively created what amounted to two schools within one, and each was racially quite distinct (Jaynes and Williams, 1989: 81–83).

The reason for white opposition to busing has been the object of scholarly debate. David Sears and Donald Kinder (1985: 1141) contended that opposition is an expression of what they refer to as "symbolic racism." They saw symbolic racism as having "its roots both in early-learned racial fears and stereotypes," and therefore having "little to do with the direct, tangible threats blacks might pose." In short, opposition is the consequence of early childhood socialization and does not derive from a perception of real intergroup conflict.

This position has been challenged by others. Lawrence Bobo (1983) did not deny the lingering impact of prejudicial attitudes derived early in life, but he argued that this is not a sufficient explanation. Rather, he concluded that when whites perceive black demands and potential gains as detrimental to white self-interest, they resist change. In effect, if whites think that their lifestyle and well-being are being jeopardized in a zero-sum game — one in which black gains necessarily are made at the expense of whites — they will be opposed to the demands put forth by the civil rights movement. Bobo (1983: 1208) argued that group conflict can best explain opposition, for whites opposed to such policies as busing "need not hold blatantly stereotypical beliefs or hostile orientations toward blacks."

Bobo's claims were supported by two carefully documented case studies of the school districts in Los Angeles and Baton Rouge conducted by Christine Rossell (1988). She found that real costs are attached to school desegregation for some whites. When the costs are weighed, a decision is made to either comply with the requirements of a busing plan or exit the school system. For example, white parents are less willing to permit their child to be bused to another school if that school has (or is perceived to have) lower average achievement scores or if such a move locates them with a student population from a lower social class than that of their previous school.

Because of the controversy generated by busing, black support declined from 78 percent in 1964 to 55 percent in 1978. Nonetheless, by that latter date, much of the tension had appreciably subsided. Many blacks have argued that they would prefer to see greater attention paid to improving the quality of public school education than to integration. Jaynes and Williams (1989: 76) noted that the major strides toward school integration took place between 1966 and 1973, during which time conflict was at its highest. On a more optimistic note, however, Rossell (1976; 1988) found that white opposition to busing was at its highest during the first year of desegregation. More recently, both black and white parents of children currently being bused find busing to be generally satisfactory, while a majority of students nationwide believe that busing does help to improve race relations and black academic achievement (Hochschild, 1985; Jaynes and Williams, 1989).

Affirmative Action

The busing issue has become less controversial over time, but affirmative action continues to spark intense debate. Those supporting the policy view affirmative action as a means for redressing past inequities. This position was aptly reflected in President Lyndon Johnson's 1965 speech at Howard University, where he said, "You do not take a person who for years has been hobbled by chains, and liberate him, bring him up to the starting line, and then say, 'You are free to compete with all the others.'" On the other hand, opponents perceive it as a form of reverse discrimination. They think that affirmative action permits unwarranted compensation to less qualified individuals, while adversely impacting individuals who have not practiced discrimination (Glazer, 1975; Pinkney, 1984; Sowell, 1989).

Affirmative action is not concerned with racial integration per se, but rather with improving the socioeconomic status of blacks (and other minorities). The rationale behind affirmative action plans is that merely terminating discriminatory laws and policies does not provide racial equity. This is because over time such historical practices have enhanced whites in their socioeconomic location at the expense of blacks. Indeed in many instances after the Civil War blacks were forced out of skilled jobs that they held. They thereby became victims of downward social mobility caused by racism and not by merit. The argument by supporters of affirmative action is that if parity is ever to be achieved, it will have to directly confront and remedy this historical legacy. Affirmative action reflects a shift in concern from equal rights to genuinely equal opportunity (Ezorsky, 1991).

The focus of affirmative action plans has been on employment and education. The constitutional basis of affirmative action constitutes part of the current debate. In the opinion of Stanford Lyman (1991: 200), the abolishment of slavery by the Thirteenth Amendment to the Constitution carries a mandate to

> remove the badges of slavery from all those to whom they are still affixed. The forms of race discrimination that derive their authority from the more than two centuries of involuntary servitude are the evil manifestation of such badges, and are, hence, the proper objects of legislative attention with respect to effecting the public interest.

Although this can serve as a persuasive constitutional rationale for general plans of affirmative action, the legal basis for the specific shape of current affirmative action policies is exceedingly complex. Efforts at enforcing nondiscrimination were evident as early as the presidency of Franklin D. Roosevelt, who during World War II, issued an Executive Order that opened defense-plant jobs to blacks. His successor, Harry S. Truman, proposed an expanded federal policy requiring equal employment opportunities. President Kennedy, through Executive Order 10925, prohibited racial discrimination by contractors doing business with the federal government and set up guidelines that were designed to encourage the hiring of blacks. During this administration the phrase "affirmative action" first came into use.

Implementation

The most important legal basis for affirmative action, however, derived from Title VII of the 1964 Civil Rights Act. The act was not limited to the government or to businesses that have government contracts. Rather, it banned discrimination in all aspects of employment and established the Equal Employment Opportunity Commission (EEOC) to investigate complaints and to refer violators to the U.S. Department of Justice, which was charged with prosecuting violators of antidiscrimination laws. This was soon linked to President Johnson's Executive Order 11246, which mandated the creation of affirmative actions plans that were to indicate the steps an employer was going to take to correct existing deficiencies (Jaynes and Williams, 1989: 315–316). Not only did affirmative action apply to employers, but also to labor unions and to colleges and universities.

One way of designing affirmative action plans was to establish concrete goals and timetables for achieving those goals. This approach was first advanced during Richard Nixon's administration. The administration's "Philadelphia Plan," required contractors doing business with the federal government to set numerical goals in the hiring of minority workers. In 1972 legislation was enacted, amending the 1964 Civil Rights Act, that granted to courts the power to enforce affirmative actions measures. Implementation of this enforcement provision occurred during the same year, as the state of Alabama was required by federal court order to hire one black state trooper for each white hired. This policy was to continue until blacks held one-fourth of the positions on the force (Hacker, 1992: 119–120). This particular shift in policy raised the politically controversial debate over quotas (Glazer, 1975; Fullinwider, 1980; Sowell, 1989).

The Charge of Reverse Discrimination

Not long after the implementation of affirmative action plans throughout the nation, opponents filed a series of court challenges. They argued that these plans, especially those with numerical quotas, constituted a form of reverse discrimination in which whites who themselves had not discriminated were being unfairly made to pay the price for the policies of the past. What such arguments tended to avoid addressing was that whites as a group had been the beneficiaries of historical practice. Though not always explicitly stated, underlying the charge of reverse discrimination was the belief that blacks were being given unjust preferential treatment insofar as less qualified blacks obtained positions at the expense of higher qualified whites.

A series of important early court challenges to affirmative action occurred during the 1970s. These included *Anderson v. S.F.*

Unified School District (1971), which questioned San Francisco's plan for increasing the number of minority school administrators, and *DeFunis v. Odegaard*, a case that challenged the University of Washington's law school minority recruitment plan. The most significant case was decided in 1978, however, in *Allan Bakke v. Regents of the University of California*. Bakke had been denied entrance to the medical school at the University of California, Davis. The basis for his complaint that he had been unfairly denied admission derived from the fact that sixteen of the one hundred slots available at the school were targeted for "economically and/or educationally disadvantaged persons," which could have included whites, but in practice had meant racial minorities (Sindler, 1978: 52). Bakke contended that such preferential treatment amounted to illegal discrimination. The university countered with the claim that their admissions plan increased the number of heretofore underrepresented groups in the student body.

Implicit in Bakke's position was the conviction that the sole criterion for admissions should be merit. This position raises two issues. The first involves what is and what is not an appropriate test of merit. Although some would argue that standardized tests, such as the Medical College Admissions Test (MCAT) are a valid measure of aptitude, others see such tests as biased in various ways. Critics see standardized tests as not only racially biased, but also biased in terms of people who have a facility for this particular form of testing, which places a premium on multiple choice rather than essay questions and on factual retention rather than reflective thinking (Hacker, 1992: 144). In any event, blacks as a group do not fare nearly as well as whites on standardized tests.

The second issue concerns the range of factors that institutions of higher education use in admission decisions. Colleges and universities have used and continue to use a variety of selection criteria that are not based on merit. To create a more cosmopolitan atmosphere, considerations are given to applicants based on their location in the country. Thus, a midwestern school might be particularly interested in students from either coast. College athletes are admitted partly by athletic ability, permitting their admission despite the fact that they are less academically qualified than others. Moreover, the children of privilege have often been granted special dispensations at elite institutions. As Andrew Hacker (1992: 129) wrote:

For years, so-called selective colleges have set less demanding standards for admitting children of alumni. (This by itself should show that affirmative action has a venerable history.) These privileged offspring know full well that other applicants with better records received rejection letters. Yet few of them are seen slouching around campus, their heads bowed in shame.

In the *Bakke* case, the Supreme Court ruled against the school's special admissions program and ordered Bakke admitted. In a second part of the ruling, however, the Court concluded that ethnic and racial background could be one factor among others in determining admissions. Seen by most observers as a compromise, the ruling did not deny the constitutionality of affirmative action. *Bakke* was followed by several other court decisions that addressed various other aspects of affirmative action plans. An important case in the area of employment was *Weber v. Kaiser Aluminum and Chemical Corporation* (1979). The company and the United Steel Workers Union had formulated a plan to increase the number of blacks in skilled labor positions. Brian Weber, a white worker, filed suit on the grounds that he had been denied admission to a skilled crafts on-the-job training program despite having more seniority with the company than many black candidates. The court did not rule in his favor, but instead concluded that voluntary goals and timetables such as those established jointly by the company and union were constitutionally permissible (Feinberg, 1985: 562; Pinkney, 1987: 215–216). Together, these two decisions were hailed by supporters of affirmative action and decried by opponents.

A conservative political agenda gained the upper hand in 1980, when Ronald Reagan was elected to the presidency, and continued into the Bush administration. One centerpiece of this agenda was a call for the elimination of affirmative action programs. Throughout the 1980s the executive branch urged the judicial branch to reverse earlier court decisions that legitimated this remedy to racial inequality. During this time a number of aging liberal members of the Supreme Court retired and were replaced by conservatives chosen by Presidents Reagan and Bush. The culmination of this process occurred when Justice Thurgood Marshall was replaced by Clarence Thomas. Marshall was an appointee of Lyndon Johnson. He had worked earlier as a lawyer for the Legal Defense Fund of the

NAACP and served as their counsel in the *Brown v. Board of Education* case. In contrast, Thomas, who as a graduate of Yale University's law school was a direct beneficiary of affirmative action, became an ardent neoconservative and quickly made his mark as one of the relatively few blacks appointed to important positions in the Reagan administration.

Although the Supreme Court now has a clear conservative majority, it did not during much of the 1980s. Instead, it was a deeply divided body, and this was reflected in the affirmative action cases. On the one hand, several decisions upheld the constitutionality of affirmative action. Included in such decisions was *United States v. Paradise*, a challenge to the previously-noted Alabama state police hiring plan. On the other hand, in the 1984 *Firefighters Local Union No. 1784 v. Stotts* case, the court ruled that the city of Memphis, Tennessee, was within its rights to maintain a seniority system that meant that blacks, as the last hired, would be the first fired. The mixed responses of the Supreme Court are an indication of the legal complexity of these issues. Despite this, to date affirmative action remains a constitutionally permissible means of redressing a legacy of racial inequity.

Changes in Public Opinion and Political Orientations

The American public is deeply split over whether or not policies that entail preferential treatment are acceptable. Prior to the civil rights movement, the majority of white Americans did not agree with the claim that blacks should have the same chance as whites to obtain any job. In 1944, for example, only 45 percent of whites agreed. In the ensuing several decades, that assessment changed dramatically, so that by 1972, 97 percent of whites agreed (Lipset and Schneider, 1978; Schuman, et al., 1985; Beer, 1987; Sigelman and Welch, 1991). Thus, there appears to be a consensus about the ideal of equal opportunity.

The conflict derives from disagreement over the appropriate mechanisms for ensuring equal opportunity. Sigelman and Welch (1991: 126–134) analyzed a variety of survey results on this issue. They concluded that it is difficult to provide a simple assessment of white or black attitudes regarding the appropriateness of affirmative action. Depending on the question and on what the respondent considers is and is not contained under this rubric, responses vary widely. They noted that some surveys suggest widespread support for affirmative action among both blacks and whites, citing respective levels of support as 96 percent for blacks and 76 percent for whites. Other surveys paint a very different picture, with low levels of support reported for both races: 23 percent for blacks and 9 percent for whites. For both races, the word "quota" conjures up negatives reactions. Blacks are far more likely to conclude that without affirmative action blacks would not have fared as well as they have in recent years; furthermore, they are only half as likely as whites to conclude that affirmative action inevitably leads to reverse discrimination.

The spectrum of quotas provided conservative politicians with a very effective racially-divisive weapon. When George Bush ran for the presidency, he persistently proclaimed his opposition to quotas. (Though he did not choose to broadcast this fact in 1988, in the 1960s he—like his predecessor, Ronald Reagan—had also opposed the 1964 Civil Rights Act). Part of the electoral success of Ronald Reagan and George Bush is due to the defection from the Democratic party by a bloc of working-class whites who believed that they, and not those higher on the socioeconomic ladder, were paying the price of black advancement.

The unraveling of the New Deal coalition, which had, among other things, brought blacks and blue-collar whites into the Democratic party, was a consequence of the perception that American society was addressing its racial problems by constructing what amounted to a zero-sum game: black gains were being achieved at the expense of whites. This attitude was exploited by the conservative Senator Jesse Helms, in his close electoral race in 1990 with Harvey Gantt, who was black. Helms ran a television advertisement that depicted a white who had been denied a job, and it asked the question: "You needed that job, and you were the best qualified. But they gave it to a minority because of a racial quota. Is that really fair?"

The Unintended Consequences of Affirmative Action

Some liberals who support affirmative action in principle have concluded that the unintended conflict it has generated can only work against black advancement in the long run. Therefore, they have called for efforts to pursue alternative policies that would unite rather than divide the potential coalitions in the American political arena (Wilson, 1978; Killian, 1991). William Julius Wilson

(1978) concluded that it would be better to place a premium on what he refers to as universal entitlement programs, rather than maintaining race-specific governmental social welfare policies. His assessment is based on the assumption that across-the-board entitlement programs—a good example being Social Security—are far more popular and more immune to attack by opponents of the welfare state than are programs targeted to particular audiences, such as racial minorities or the poor. It should be noted that Wilson is not opposed to affirmative action per se. Rather, he sees it producing a political impasse that, by generating a powerful white backlash, might result in stymieing reform. Policies aimed at full employment would, in Wilson's view, have more beneficial consequences than race-specific policies.

An important question is: who among blacks are the main beneficiaries of affirmative action? Andrew Hacker (1992: 131) argued that in the competitive quest for jobs, whites in highly trained and well-paid occupations face little threat to their economic livelihood from policies designed to grant preferences in job allocation to blacks. Rather, this threat is confronted by working class and lower-middle-class whites. He wrote, "One of the chief effects of affirmative action has been to pit whites with modest aspirations against blacks who want better lives for themselves." Wilson (1978) would not agree, though his position should not be seen as a total rejection of Hacker's. According to Wilson, blacks already in the middle class and those poised to enter it, as well as more highly skilled working-class blacks are those in a position to benefit from affirmative action. Poor blacks have not benefited. This position was supported by Feinberg (1985) who considered the economic growth of the 1950–1970 period (a tight labor supply forced employers to hire blacks) to have been the primary cause for economic gains experienced by poor blacks. The growth of the black middle class since 1970 is attributable, in part, to the role of affirmative action. We will consider the connection between class and race in more detail later.

The idea of "stigmatized achievement" is noted by opponents and allies of affirmative action alike (Carter, 1991; Steele, 1990; Sowell, 1981). This idea refers to the belief held by many that blacks have succeeded because of two standards, one based on achievement for whites and the other on racial criteria for blacks. The result is that the genuine achievements of blacks are not

Figure 9.4   *The irony is obvious in Margaret Bourke-White's Depression era photo of African Americans in a relief line.*

Source: Margaret Bourke-White, American, 1904–1971, World's Highest Standard of Living, gelatin silver print, 1937, 55.8 x 73.7 cm, Gift of Boardman/Edelston, 1992.560, photograph courtesy of The Art Institute of Chicago.

appreciated, and blacks are forced to confront suspicions that they are not really as qualified as their white peers. Although how whites perceive them is no doubt a real concern, in a recent study of 100 black men and women in professional and executive positions, Lois Benjamin (1991) did not see this concern translated into feelings of inferiority. On the contrary, her respondents viewed themselves as not only capable, but as having to overcome obstacles that whites did not have to confront in achieving success.

Improvement or Decline?

All of this leads to a simple question: have the conditions of blacks improved in terms of educational attainment, occupational location, and income? It is not surprising to learn that blacks have a less optimistic assessment than whites about the extent to which improvement in the black community has occurred since the civil rights era. For one thing, blacks believe that prejudice and discrimination remain a far more consequential force in their lives than whites assume to be the case. Furthermore, although blacks as a group indicate a positive assessment about change during the past two decades, not all blacks concur. Many believe the situation of black America has either remained unchanged or has gotten worse (Sigelman and Welch, 1991; Jaynes and Williams, 1989; Schuman, et al., 1985).

The reason for these differing perceptions is partly due to very different life experiences, but the course of change has also produced mixed results. Since 1940 there has been a sharp increase in the percentage of both blacks and whites completing high school, and during this period the gap in years of school completed by blacks and whites born since the late 1950s has nearly disappeared. Black rates of enrollment in college rose from the 1950s to the late 1970s, but since then have declined. The rate of college enrollment peaked in 1977 as slightly less than one out of two black high-school graduates .entered college. Furthermore, at that time, the figure for blacks was only a few percentage points lower than that for whites. Within half a decade, however, the gap had reappeared as white rates of enrollment rose to around 60 percent, while black rates dropped to about 40 percent (Farley and Allen, 1989: 188–208; Jaynes and Williams, 1989: 19–20; Farley, 1984: 194).

Blacks continue to be educationally disadvantaged. Early intervention to assist disadvantaged children, seen especially in the Head Start program, has been quite successful. Unfortunately, these programs are underfunded and cannot meet the need. Various standardized measures of educational achievement indicate blacks do not do as well as whites. Recent research by James Coleman, Thomas Hoffer, and Sally Kilgore (1981), which has indicated that students in private and parochial schools are more successful than public school students, suggested part of the problem. Black children are far more likely to attend public schools than whites, and in these institutions achievement is lowest. Conservatives have argued that a remedy to this is to force public schools to operate in a marketplace in which students would be treated as consumers who could pick and choose among the schools in the area. These are generally referred to as choice or voucher plans.

This view fails to consider one important fact. School integration was only partially successful, and this means that in many instances blacks and whites continue to attend racially segregated schools. Integration has occurred in many areas of the rural south and in the region's smaller and medium-sized cities, as well as in areas where school districts are county systems that link urban and suburban schools. Elsewhere, most blacks attend urban schools, while most whites in public schools reside and go to school in the suburbs (Farley, 1984: 193–199). Because public schools are funded primarily by local property taxes and because the class character of suburbs means that they have a far more solid tax base than cities, considerably more is spent per student on suburbanites than on their urban counterparts. Suburbanites have resisted attempts to bring urban blacks into their schools, and there is no reason to assume that various choice or voucher proposals would change that.

The economic status of blacks as a whole improved compared with whites between 1940 and 1970, but since then black incomes have leveled off or declined (Jaynes and Williams, 1989: 16–18). There is a bifurcation within black America between a now relatively sizeable middle class and a remaining core of poor blacks, who have a poverty rate more than twice the national average (Farley, 1990).

Housing and Residential Segregation

Housing policies have also been the sources of intense political conflict. An important connection exists between race and economic status when it comes to the provision of decent, safe, and affordable housing, which is a right of all Americans according to the Housing Act of 1949. Actually, the topic of housing must be sorted into two related but nonetheless distinct issues. The first involves the linkage between race and poverty and raises the topic of subsidized housing. This concerns the extent to which poor blacks are or are not able to obtain and pay for housing that meets certain minimum quality standards. The second issue deals with housing discrimination and pertains not only to poor blacks, but also to working-class and middle-class blacks seeking housing in white neighborhoods.

Public Housing

The United States was slow to establish laws aimed at improving the housing conditions of its citizens. Furthermore, to this date the

United States has resisted creating universal entitlement programs, despite the ideal set forth in the 1949 housing legislation. Throughout the nation's history powerful economic interests have resisted state intervention in housing markets. There was little support for the public ownership and management of housing (Fisher, 1959; Friedman, 1978). Only during the Depression did a coalition of labor, social reformers, religious leaders, and the construction industry push successfully for the passage of the United States Housing Act of 1937. This legislation provided only a limited role for governmentally run housing. Such housing was designed for the poor alone, and in this regard the public housing program differed from those in other industrial nations, such as Great Britain, where council estates were also intended to meet the housing needs of the middle class.

The reason for this limited government role was that the real estate industry convinced Congress that the government should not compete with private industry for tenants. Considering the poor to be incapable of generating profits for the industry, industry representatives were willing to concede that part of the market to the government. Public housing was built with federal monies, but the projects were managed by local housing authorities, who were required to charge rents high enough to cover operating costs. As a result, the poorest of the poor were excluded from the program because they could not afford the rents. Because blacks were overrepresented in the ranks of this lowest socioeconomic stratum, this policy had a negative impact on them.

The majority of public housing residents during the 1940s and 1950s was white. Moreover, segregated public housing projects were customary. New Haven, Connecticut, was one of the first cities to open public housing projects, and its approach was typical of cities throughout much of the country. At essentially the same time, three projects were built. Elm Haven in the black ghetto around Dixwell Avenue was solely occupied by blacks, while both Farnham Courts and Quinnipiac Terrace were located in white ethnic neighborhoods and were occupied entirely by white ethnics, predominately Italians and Irish.

By excluding the middle class from participation, public housing never gained the level of public support that council housing did in Great Britain (Bredemeier, 1955). A consequence of the limited scope of public housing was that during the post-World War II prosperity period, the program was vulnerable to attack by political critics. A submerged white working and middle class came out of the Depression and the war and, in this period of unprecedented affluence, found opportunities to purchase homes, largely by moving out of cities and into growing suburbs. Thus, throughout the 1950s and into the 1960s, the tenants of public housing were increasingly black and were poorer than before (Kivisto, 1986).

Hundreds of thousands of substandard housing units were demolished in slum clearance efforts. Urban renewal was an attempt to rejuvenate center cities, and linked to the plan was a call for constructing more public housing. Actually, Congress called for a 1:1 equation: for each unit of housing demolished, one should be built to replace it. Construction fell far short of this goal. Moreover, instead of the low-density, low-rise projects built in the first decade of the program, new units tended to be high-density, high-rise developments. This was seen as a cost-cutting mechanism—large projects suggested economies of scale. A second factor was that by building more low-density scattered sites, many public housing projects—now increasingly occupied by blacks—would have to be located in white neighborhoods. White resistance to residential integration stymied such efforts. Mayors and other local officials thought it would mean political suicide if they pushed such proposals. They found it expedient to build huge developments, such as Chicago's Robert Taylor Homes, in black ghettos.

These projects proved to be failures. Instead of being seen as part of the solution to the problem of poverty, public housing acquired the reputation of being part of the problem. By 1965 an absolute majority of public housing residents were black (Freedman, 1969: 140). Their poverty made it impossible for them to pay rents that would cover operating costs, and therefore maintenance suffered. This period saw a dramatic increase in the number of female-headed households, who were generally supported by Aid to Families with Dependent Children (AFDC) payments. Social problems including truancy and school dropouts, child abuse, alcohol and drug abuse, and crime escalated.

Public housing projects were increasingly described as "vertical ghettos," "federal slums," and "warehouses for the poor"

(Moore, 1969; Rainwater, 1970; Savas, 1979). Perhaps the most dramatic indication of this view was the fate of St. Louis's Pruitt-Igoe project. The high-rise development built in the 1950s was the recipient of a major architectural award. Within a decade, however, the project experienced such serious problems that the only solution the city had was to demolish it.

Alternatives to Public Housing

President Lyndon Johnson attempted to expand the welfare state legacy that first emerged during the New Deal in his call for a Great Society and in his War on Poverty. This period yielded the second major wave of welfare legislation. It took various forms that affected blacks because they were disproportionately poor (Patterson, 1981; Katz, 1989). The Great Society called for the expansion of older programs and the development of new ones. The Johnson administration, and later the Nixon administration, began efforts to find alternatives to conventional public housing rather than increase new construction for poor families

The alternatives relied in various ways on a greater role for the private sector. These included the Section 23 Leased Housing Program which used existing housing owned by private landlords. The program provided qualified applicants rent subsidies that made up the difference between the rent they could afford to pay (25 percent of the tenant's net income) and a market rent that provided the owner with a reasonable return on investment. This program became the model for its successor, which is still in place: the Section 8 program. Like Section 23, housing in the private sector is used, but unlike the earlier program, Section 8 provided incentives for new construction and housing rehabilitation. Finally, this led to a major experiment that was designed to further reduce government's role in housing provision. This took the form of the Experimental Housing Allowance Program (EHAP), which gave recipients direct cash outlays. Participants were provided greater flexibility compared with other programs (they could choose to move to better quality housing, invest in home improvements, or use the money for other needs). Additionally, many administrative responsibilities were removed from the purview of local housing agencies.

The effects of these programs on blacks are somewhat difficult to determine. Clearly, blacks have participated in Section 23, Section 8, and EHAP. But reliance on private sector landlords has meant that they have encountered housing discrimination, partly because, in contrast to public housing, blacks confront more competition from low-income whites for the limited number of available housing slots in these other programs.

Nonetheless, this trend set the stage for the aggressive privatization campaign undertaken during the Reagan administration. Thus, *The Report of the President's Commission on Housing* (1982) called for the "deprogramming" of a sizeable portion of the current public housing stock through sale, conversion, planned deterioration, or demolition. As critics argued, however, such efforts posed serious problems for poor blacks. First, the evidence pointed to the shortage of decent, safe, and affordable housing for such families that privatization schemes did not address. Second, there are at present no adequate mechanisms to handle cases of housing discrimination. Existing tools designed to do so are weak. The result is that alternatives to public housing fail to meet the shelter needs of poor blacks, especially for certain categories of families, such as female-headed large families. Coupled with cuts in benefits to poor people, the result of the conservative policies of the 1980s meant, according to researchers at the Urban Institute, that "beneficiaries will be increasingly impoverished" (Struyck, et al., 1983: 67).

Equal Housing Opportunity

A large majority of whites agree that blacks should have equal housing opportunities, while the majority also are opposed to any laws that prohibit discrimination (Levitan and Taggart, 1976). These contradictory responses can be explained by noting that whites are far less likely than blacks to believe that blacks are, in fact, the victims of housing discrimination. Thus, in 1989, 52 percent of blacks believed that blacks are generally discriminated against in attempting to obtain decent housing, while only 20 percent of whites agreed (Sigelman and Welch, 1991: 57).

An early challenge to housing discrimination came in the 1948 *Shelley v. Kramer* case, in which the Supreme Court banned restrictive covenants in the sale of property. Such covenants had been inserted into sale transactions in an effort to ensure that homes were not sold to certain ethnic groups, with blacks and Jews being singled out most frequently. Despite this ruling, the Federal Housing Administration (FHA) and the Veteran's Administration (VA) mortgage insurance activities willingly condoned such covenants, following the practice of the real-estate industry.

During the 1960s, several additional measures to combat discrimination were introduced. They included President Kennedy's Executive Order 11063, which banned discrimination in federally subsidized or financed housing. Title VI of the 1964 Civil Rights Act extended these provisions even further. The Civil Rights Act of 1968 provided the most sweeping changes for fair housing: Title VIII of the act prohibited discrimination in the sale, rental, and financing of all housing. In the same year, in *Jones v. Mayer*, the Supreme Court ruled that racial discrimination in housing had been outlawed more than a century earlier, in the Civil Rights Act of 1866. For 102 years after the passage of this post-Civil War legislation, the government had chosen to ignore it in practice. Thus, although the newer act appeared redundant, the 1968 act differed from the its predecessor because it added enforcement provisions that were heretofore missing.

But what has been the impact of this legislation on residential segregation since 1970? During that decade, residential segregation in 20 of the 25 cities with the largest black populations declined; some (including Houston and Los Angeles), substantially declined, but for most, it was very modest. Three cities remained unchanged, while Cleveland and Philadelphia ended up more segregated by 1980 (Taeuber, 1983). The cumulative change reflected a minor decline in residential segregation in cities.

During the same period, suburbs continued to grow. The black suburban population grew during the 1970s at an annual rate of 4 percent, in contrast to 1.5 percent for whites (Long and DiAre, 1981). In the 16 Standard Metropolitan Statistical Areas (SMSAs) with black populations of at least 250,000, an overall modest decline in segregation was observed. The reduction was equal to that seen in central cities. There is still a very high level of racial separation, however. In 1980, only 20 percent of blacks lived in suburbs compared with 42 percent of nonblacks (Farley and Allen, 1989: 142). The unanswered question at present is whether the suburbanization of blacks will lead to integration or whether we will continue to have, as Farley, Schumun, Biachi, Colasyto, and Hatchett (1978) have described the situation, "chocolate cities and vanilla suburbs."

However halting and limited, the black middle class has experienced enhanced housing opportunities, even though the obstacles to further integration have not disappeared (Farley and Frey, 1994). Blacks are moving to suburbs at a lower rate than Hispanics and Asians, and furthermore, within suburbs, blacks are more residentially isolated (Massey and Denton, 1988). Blacks have greater difficulties in achieving entry into desirable neighborhoods than other racial minorities, but the disadvantage of middle class blacks is not as pronounced as it was in the past (Massey and Fong, 1990).

For those not in the middle class, the situation is quite different. Within segregated neighborhoods in central cities, blacks confront a number of problems. Those seeking to purchase homes in predominantly black neighborhoods often encounter lending institutions that are engaged in the practice of red lining — which is a tacit practice of denying mortgages to would-be homeowners when the property is located in an area where such financial investment is deemed to be too risky. The National Committee Against Discrimination in Housing has concluded that neither the Department of Housing and Urban Development (HUD) nor the National Association of Realtors have established adequate strategies for combating red lining (Blackwell, 1985: 206).

An additional dilemma has resulted from the gentrification of some neighborhoods and from the conversion of rental apartment buildings to condominiums (Department of Housing and Urban Development, 1980; Sumka, 1978). In both instances, these trends have resulted in the displacement of low- and moderate-income families and have had a disproportionately negative impact on blacks. To date, neither the federal government nor local governments (who stand to benefit from these changes through increased revenues from property taxes) have taken substantial steps to control these processes or to address the problems of those most adversely impacted. Unfortunately, little empirical data exists on the fate of the displaced. Aside from impressionistic evidence, we know little about whether families have found alternative housing, and if so, what it is like in terms of quality, cost, overcrowding, and related indices.

$\mathcal{T}$he Declining Significance of Race?

To what extent is a black person's fate shaped by racial identity? To what extent by the individual's location in the American class structure? These are complex and controversial questions. Many social scientists of ethnicity have seen race as being a far more important determinant of a black's life chances than class location. Challenging this—some, especially orthodox Marxists, such as the black sociologist Oliver Cox (1948)—have placed a premium on class relations. For them, race is merely a subterfuge for what is at bedrock class exploitation. Clearly, class and ethnicity (including race) are intertwined. Milton Gordon (1964) understood the importance of wrestling with this interconnection when he called for the analysis of what he termed "ethclass" relations.

Although few would dispute the interconnectedness of race and class, explicit attempts to unravel the connections have elicited considerable debate. Nowhere was this more evident than in the thesis advanced by sociologist William Julius Wilson (1978) in his book, *The Declining Significance of Race*. Wilson attempted to historicize the connections by identifying three historical periods, each of which is defined in terms of differences in the respective salience of race and class. The periods he identifies are roughly the same as those used throughout this book.

During the first period—the antebellum era—racial oppression was paramount as blacks were consigned to a subordinate location in a caste system. The underlying rationale was economic: blacks provided a cheap and compliant supply of labor. Class differentiation among blacks was minimal and quite inconsequential. This gave way during the period from the end of the Civil War to the demise of Jim Crow to a new form of economic exploitation in which class acquired a significance that it did not previously have. Although race was still more important in determining the life chances of blacks than class, it was no longer the sole determinant. One of the changes that occurred during this period was the emergence of an internal class structure within black America, one that largely paralleled, while standing outside of, the class structure of white America.

Since 1965, the thesis continued, this second period has been superseded by a third in which race is no longer as powerful a force as class in determining blacks' life chances. First, as we have seen, white attitudes toward blacks have improved since the 1940s. Second, Wilson (1978: 150) stressed, the federal government played a new role in the drama of race relations. Previously it had served as a prop to the maintenance of economic subordination. Increasingly since World War II, however, the federal government has been a key force in the promotion of racial equality. Government action was instrumental in eliminating legal barriers to incorporation into the mainstream of the American economy and to active political involvement.

At the same time, changes in the American economy transformed the labor force. The white-collar, professional middle class expanded, which provided opportunities for upwardly mobile blacks. Simultaneously, due to a variety of factors that together can be referred to as processes of deindustrialization (for example, the expansion of automation and the export of factory jobs to plants in the Third World), structural unemployment grew, and poorer blacks were most adversely affected. In contrast to the economic expansion period from 1950 to 1970, these blacks, confronting a situation in which real purchasing power actually was declining, found limited opportunities for economic advancement. These included the working poor and a core of impoverished people at the bottom of the socioeconomic ladder that some have referred to as the "underclass." Wilson (1987) himself chose to call them the "truly disadvantaged." Wilson depicted a profound split within black America along class lines and described this bifurcation in the following manner:

> On the one hand, poorly trained and educationally limited blacks of the inner city, including that growing number of black teenagers and young adults, see their job prospects increasingly restricted to the low-wage sector, their unemployment rates soaring to record levels (which remain high despite swings in the business cycle), and their labor-force participation rates declining, their movement out of poverty slowing, and their welfare roles increasing. On the other hand, talented and educated blacks are experiencing unprecedented job opportunities in the growing government and corporate sectors, opportunities that are at least comparable to those of whites with equivalent qualifications (Wilson, 1978: 151).

This thesis has been criticized by those who thought that Wilson underplayed the continuing importance of racism in determining black opportunities. Thomas Pettigrew (1979), for example, argued that though change has occurred, the significance of race has not necessarily declined. Charles Vert Willie (1979) argued that we can speak about an "inclining significance of race" (actually undermining his counter thesis by relying on very limited data that is derived primarily from the pre-1965 period). Wilson did not claim that racism has been eradicated. He contended, however, that though racism was instrumental in the historical oppression of blacks, at present it is less consequential than class factors in shaping life chances. He made a case for looking carefully at the internal class stratification of black America, in particular the middle class and the poverty class.

The Black Middle Class

Two major and interconnected changes have occurred in recent decades: the black middle class has grown and it no longer finds itself confined to the black ghetto. Between emancipation and World War I the black middle class was very small — no more than 3 percent of the total black population, compared with 23.8 percent for whites. In 1910, 89.1 percent of blacks were either farm workers or unskilled industrial workers. The comparable figure for whites was 47.1 percent (Landry, 1987: 21). Most members of the black middle class were part of the old mulatto elite, and they owned businesses in service industries. They worked as barbers, caterers, tailors, and in other small business enterprises. Many served a white clientele (Katzman, 1973).

A half century later, with the expansion of urban ghettos brought about by migration from the rural South, the middle class grew. As Figure 9.5 indicates, it accounted for 13.4 percent of the black population. In addition, 25.7 percent of blacks were in the skilled working class. Although these figures lagged behind those recorded for whites, this nonetheless reflects a greater class differentiation within the black community than in the earlier period. Among the important professions in the middle class were doctors, lawyers, accountants, undertakers, and similar occupations. What made their professional lives different from the preceding era was that they were largely restricted to serving a black clientele. Black sociologist E. Franklin Frazier described this middle class in highly critical fashion in his controversial book, *Black Bourgeoisie* (1957).

Figure 9.5 *Black and white class structures in 1960.*

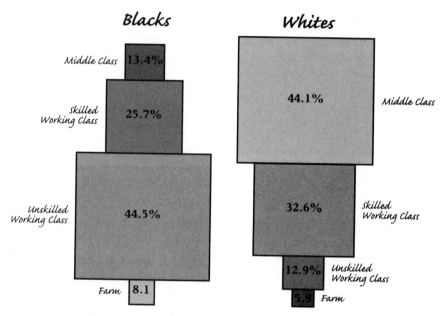

Sums do not equal 100.0 because of those for whom no occupation was reported.

Source: From *New Black Middle Class,* Bart Landry, University of California Press, 1987: 68. Copyright © 1987 The Regents of the University of California. Reprinted by permission of the publisher.

In a world of enforced or de facto segregation, middle class blacks lived in isolation from the white middle class. They generally obtained their educations from historically black colleges and universities. When they entered professional life, they both worked and lived in a largely all-black world. This, according to Frazier, had a profound impact on the world view of the black middle class. He criticized them for their tendencies toward conspicuous consumption and the pretentiousness of their "high society." He saw these behaviors, however, as manifestations of the inferiority imprinted on this stratum by racism. Theirs was a world of make-believe in which "the masks which they wear to play their sorry roles conceal the feelings of inferiority . . . that haunt their lives" (Frazier, 1957: 213; see also Drake and Cayton, 1962 [1945]; Landry, 1987: 78–85). This world has not entirely disappeared, as shown in Spike Lee's devastating critique of the mores of the children of these black bourgeoisie in "School Daze," his film about the social world of a black college.

Nonetheless, one consequence of the civil rights movement was the emergence of a new black middle class — one that was no longer tied to the black community, but instead was integrated into the fabric of the larger middle class (Wilson, 1978; Kilson, 1983; Landry, 1987; Banner-Haley, 1994). The educational attainment levels of blacks have increased since the 1960s, thereby offering the credentials that were a prerequisite for upward mobility (Zweigenhaft and Domhoff, 1991). According to Martin Kilson (1983: 86–87), the overall growth of the white-collar professional class permitted the rapid entry of blacks. They found employment "in national job markets — in national (white) banks, insurance companies, retail firms, industries, universities, and government agencies. The last employs the heads of 30 percent of white-collar black families, compared with 16 percent for whites."

Furthermore, from this middle class come the new black suburbanites, with the purchasing power to acquire homes in such communities and the desire to integrate into the mainstream. Like their white middle-class counterparts, many middle-class blacks have fled the problems associated with urban life for the relative security, better schools, and related amenities offered by the suburbs.

Wilson (1978) and Kilson (1983: 90) contended that the class location of the black middle class is sufficiently secure that their opportunities are now determined chiefly by economic and not by racial factors. That is, racism has not disappeared, but while "persistent racist practices by police, business firms, unions, and by hoodlums like the Ku Klux Klan continue to threaten all blacks, these practices are now a weaker constraint upon Afro-Americans than they were ever before" (Kilson, 1983: 90). This is what Wilson meant when he spoke of the "declining significance of race."

Others have questioned this conclusion. Bart Landry (1987: 193–233), for example, in the first comprehensive study of the black middle class since Frazier, cautioned against what he saw as an overly optimistic assessment of the black middle class. Although, as Figure 9.6 indicates, he believed that this class will continue to grow between now and the year 2000, there are many reasons to be concerned about this class in the future. The black middle class lags behind the white middle class in earnings, and some evidence indicates that blacks tend to get locked into middle-range managerial positions, so their chances of rising to the top of an organization are considerably more limited than

Figure 9.6 *The black and white class structure in 1981 and projected class structures for 1990 and 2000.*

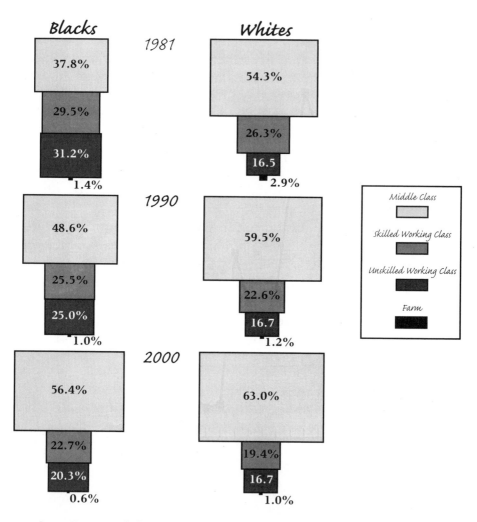

Source: From *New Black Middle Class*, Bart Landry, University of California Press, 1987: 219. Copyright © 1987 The Regents of the University of California. Reprinted by permission of the publisher.

those of whites. Furthermore, blacks are more adversely affected by economic recessions. Black entrepreneurs, aside from a small number of highly successful people, continue to earn less than whites and their businesses are often precarious; the failure rate is quite high. Thus, genuine parity with whites does not appear to be attainable in the near future (see also, Thomas, 1993).

Moreover, the impact of discrimination may have been understated in the declining significance of race thesis. Joe R. Feagin (1991), in a study of middle-class blacks in a number of cities, has documented the extent to which his respondents confront various discriminatory actions in their daily lives in public places — actions ranging from threats and harassment by strangers or the police to verbal epithets, rejection or poor service, and avoidance (for example, crossing the street to avoid passing a black male on a sidewalk). Such actions are far more common than many whites appreciate, and they take a heavy toll on blacks because, as Feagin (1991: 115) puts it, "you cannot accomplish as much as you could if you retained the energy wasted on discrimination."

Poor Blacks

One of Wilson's (1978) concerns was that the exodus of middle-class blacks from urban enclaves has further impoverished such communities, both financially and culturally. The middle class served as leaders of black ghettos prior to the 1960s and as role models for more disadvantaged blacks (Wilson, 1987: 3). Life in the inner city is shaped by poverty in the midst of an affluent society, an impoverishment that is characterized by high levels of unemployment and underemployment, a high percentage of female-headed households, high levels of crime and violence, low levels of educational attainment, substandard housing combined with relatively high rents, inadequate health care, and the like.

Although most inner city adults work, they do so at low-paying unskilled jobs, which offer few, if any, fringe benefits, little opportunity for advancement, and frequently little job security. There is also a stratum of nonworking poor. In the 1960s, two now-classic ethnographic studies, both conducted in Washington, D.C., explored the everyday lives of groups of men from this stratum: Elliot Liebow's *Tally's Corner* (1967) and Ulf Hannerz's *Soulside* (1969). Both capture features of the everyday lives of groups of "streetcorner men." Hannerz observed that those inner city residents with relatively stable lives are oriented toward the mainstream of society. The main reference of streetcorner men, however, is the immediate peer group. Hannerz (1969: 54–55) wrote that they "usually return day after day to the same hangout. There they talk and drink, play cards, and shoot crap, or just do nothing . . . There is continuous drinking . . . If they are not already alcoholics, they are well on their way . . . Many of the men have some kind of police record."

Liebow's (1967) account reinforced Hannerz's portrait. Liebow emphasized that though these men often father children, they tend to have little or no contact with them and are not inclined to provide financial support to them. These men often drift from job to job, exploit women financially and sexually, and often have tenuous and violent relationships with other streetcorner men. They are concerned primarily about the present, viewing their futures as too unpredictable for them to shape or influence. Liebow (1967: 70) contended that for these men, "the constant awareness of a future loaded with 'trouble' results in a constant readiness to leave, to 'make it,' to 'get out of town,' and discourages the man from sinking roots into the world he lives in."

The Moynihan Report

Women with children were increasingly forced to rely on various governmental support programs, the most notable being Aid to Families with Dependent Children (AFDC) and public housing. A rising percentage of women were forced to confront the dilemmas of raising children in poverty without a partner to share those responsibilities. This is what is meant by the "feminization of poverty." This increase in female-headed households prompted discussions about the "matrifocal black family," a line of inquiry that culminated in the 1960s in a highly controversial debate over what became known as the "Moynihan Report." This document was prepared in 1965 by sociologist Daniel Patrick Moynihan, then employed by the U.S. Department of Labor, and went by the title, "The Negro Family: The Case for National Action." Pointing to the dramatic increase in single-parent households in black America and the connection between such households and poverty status, Moynihan paid considerable attention to what he referred to as a "tangle of pathology," which included academic failure, crime and delinquency, unemployment, and out-of-wedlock births. Government policy, it was argued, needed to address family instability as part of the effort to combat poverty (Moynihan, 1965).

Critics countered the report's conclusions. Some argued that the report was based on a bias that saw the dual-parent nuclear family as superior to other family forms. For example, Carol Stack (1974) sought to illustrate the strengths of families that were headed by women. What others depicted as unstable family arrangements, she saw as flexible, exhibiting a creative reliance on extended kin networks. Others argued that by focusing on the family and on the behaviors of poor blacks, Moynihan's approach tended to blame the victims of poverty for their plight (Rainwater and Yancey, 1967; Valentine, 1968; Ryan, 1971). The role of culture and behaviors emanating from cultural values were seen as derived from the underlying structural conditions that were the true cause of poverty: racial oppression, economic exploitation, enforced segregation, and exclusion from meaningful participation in civic life.

Inner-City Poverty Today

Two decades later, inner-city poverty continues to be a serious unresolved problem. A recent ethnographic study in the tradition of Liebow and Hannerz documented the continuing significance of the problems that afflicted similar communities a generation earlier. Elijah Anderson's (1990) study of a Philadelphia neighborhood does not provide grounds for optimism concerning the future. Differences between earlier studies and his suggest an intensification of old problems such as teenage pregnancy and the arrival of new ones, particularly those associated with drugs — especially crack — and, related to this, violent crime. Furthermore, he saw a deterioration of stabilizing social networks due largely to the erosion of authority of what Anderson called the "old heads," mature men who traditionally served as role models for young men.

In a series of recent films directed by blacks, including *Boyz N the Hood, Straight out of Brooklyn*, and parts of Spike Lee's *Jungle Fever* concerned with the main character's crack-addicted brother, the ravages of crime and drugs and the sense of isolation from the larger society are poignantly and forcefully depicted.

Anderson's conclusions are reflected in national-level data. For example, though blacks compose no more than 13 percent of the general population, they account for 47 percent of prisoners in state and federal prisons and 40.1 percent of death-row inmates (Hacker, 1992: 180). The leading cause of death among black male youth is murder, usually committed by other black youth. Drug addiction is far more problematic among ghetto dwellers than outside such communities. Furthermore, AIDS has hit inner cities especially hard.

What accounts for the persistence of poverty and the exacerbation of the problems it produces? Why is it that an affluent society has in its midst an underclass that finds no significant place in the larger economy (Auletta, 1982)? The debate begun during the War on Poverty era continues unabated. Traditional liberals still argue that two factors are chiefly responsible: racism and a lack of governmental support for social programs. Conservatives have challenged this by arguing that it is precisely due to government programs that the cycle of poverty has not been broken. They contend that government programs have generated a dependency that has caused the inner city to actually be worse off at present than before the existence of significant government intervention (Murray, 1984). Although liberals focus on social structural factors, conservatives tend to pay greater attention to the cultural attributes and behaviors of the poor.

Wilson (1987; 1991) offered an alternative explanation from both the traditional liberal and the conservative approaches. He called it a social democratic account, one that stressed changes in the nation's occupational structure that limit upward mobility by the poorest poor. Like liberals, he stressed social structure, though unlike them he minimized the present impact of racial prejudice and discrimination. He gave conservatives their due, however, by also considering culture's role.

He viewed efforts to pit culture against social structure as a simplistic distortion of what is, in fact, a complex interplay between the two: "Poverty, like other aspects of class inequality, is a consequence not only of differential distribution of economic and political privileges, but of differential access to culture as well" (Wilson, 1991: 1). As a consequence, no simple solution is possible. Rather, what is needed includes increased job opportunities and increased access to political power as well as a renewed connection between the ghetto poor and the cultural beliefs and attitudes of the larger society. A sense of futility and fatalism reinforces a lack of success in the job market. Only when such views are replaced by a conviction that work is a means toward economic betterment will efforts to combat the problems of the truly disadvantaged succeed.

Into the Future

Although Wilson's analysis dealt with social policy, shaped largely by whites, blacks have acquired a political voice in the wake of the civil rights movement. Blacks have been elected to the United States Congress, and many cities, including the nation's five largest—New York, Los Angeles, Chicago, Philadelphia, and Detroit—currently have or have recently had blacks mayors. Though these electoral victories signaled empowerment, they did not necessarily indicate genuine integration of black candidates into the political process. Most black members of Congress represent predominantly black constituencies. In many major cities that have elected black mayors, a majority or large plurality of the citizenry is black.

The candidacy of Jesse Jackson highlighted the dilemmas of black involvement in the political process (Reed, 1986). A veteran of the civil rights movement, Jackson made a bid for the Democratic presidential nomination in 1988. He portrayed himself as not only a candidate of blacks, but of other racial minorities as well as blue-collar workers and the poor regardless of race. Dubbed the "Rainbow Coalition," his candidacy failed to get off the ground, due to its inability to attract sufficient numbers of white votes. But the Jackson presence was an indication of the effort to move from social protest to participation in the political mainstream without abandoning the objectives of the former.

Summary

The civil rights movement was one of the most important sources of social change in twentieth-century America. In this chapter we have reviewed its various stages, beginning with the work of A. Philip Randolph, turning to the early phase in the 1950s in the South, the subsequent move North, and its culmination in the militancy of the Black Power movement. We surveyed the central organizations and key leaders that played a role in this history, examining the types of resources that they had at their disposal, as well as the resistance that they confronted.

A number of legislative and judicial decisions came out of this period that were intended to overcome the legacy of racial oppression. After reviewing the most important of these, we turned to their net impact on the lives of black Americans. Going beyond general black-white differences on a number of quality of life measures, the increasingly different life chances of middle-class blacks and poor blacks were discussed. Although there is considerable debate about the levels of gains made by middle-class blacks, few would dispute that for poor blacks in the inner cities, life has gotten more difficult, not less so. Poor blacks are not misreading the situation when they conclude that social change has not improved their lives for the better.

Cornel West (1993) noted that a distressingly pervasive nihilism can be seen in these quarters of black America. Spike Lee's film, *Do the Right Thing*, depicted deep conflict-ridden fissures in contemporary race relations. Beneath any surface comity he sees the ever-present potential for venomous and destructive exchanges. The film implicitly indicts white America for a lack of will, while depicting the ambiguities and uncertainties in black responses to racial inequality: Malcolm X and Martin Luther King, Jr., advanced two very different responses to the condition of blacks, but in the end the viewer is left with both options, which is to say, with a lack of certainty about how to proceed. All of this was forcefully illustrated in the 1992 Los Angles riot. Black frustration was acted out in attacks on whites, Korean merchants, and others, while millions of dollars of property were destroyed. This is vivid testimony that a half century after Myrdal's monumental work, the American dilemma clearly continues to bedevil the nation.

AMERICAN INDIANS: THE CONTINUING PLIGHT OF THE FIRST OF THIS LAND

Native Americans occupy a unique place in America. Preceding chapters have chronicled the important role played by the federal government in defining their subordinate relationship to European Americans. Their relative lack of power meant that American Indians have had to learn to respond to shifting governmental goals and policies. This chapter traces the history of those shifts from the Indian Reorganization Act (IRA) of 1934 to the present. During the past several decades, Indians have mobilized resources that were not possible earlier. The result is that there have been gains for some Native Americans, but despite this, many remain both impoverished and political and social outsiders.

The Indian Reorganization Act discussed in Chapter 8 was hailed by advocates as the "Indian New Deal." It was intended by its supporters to preserve and strengthen Native American cultures. As such, it was designed to encourage resistance to assimilation. Proponents saw the IRA as a way to preserve tribal organizations and identities and to stop the loss of Indian lands that resulted from the allotment acts of the 1880s. In at least two ways this legislation and the underlying rationale advanced by John Collier has been subsequently called into question (Prucha, 1985; Cornell, 1988).

First, by the 1930s many Native Americans had only tenuous, if any, connections with tribal entities, and in many instances tribes had changed considerably due to acculturation. Thus, preserving traditional tribal organizations was frequently unrealistic. The second point is, ironically, a reflection of the government's willingness to impose on tribes non-traditional forms of government. Collier proposed a democratic process for electing tribal representatives and even drafted a constitution that many tribes adopted without revision. Francis Paul Prucha (1985: 66) observed that, "These tribal governments, with councils and tribal chairmen elected by majority vote, were Anglo-American inventions, which did not accord with traditional Indian ways."

As with other New Deal programs, the Indian Reorganization Act expanded the role of the federal government. This led critics both within Native American communities and outside of them to accuse the federal government of embarking on a new form of paternalism. Washington became more, rather than less, involved with the internal workings of Native American affairs. Indeed, the Bureau of Indian Affairs (BIA) and the Secretary of the Interior did play a determinative role in tribal decision making. Traditional tribal religious leaders, whose importance in tribal life was challenged as a result of these policies, frequently considered the elected leaders to be mere pawns of the federal government. They often refer to elected leaders disparagingly as "BIA Indians" (Prucha, 1985: 66; Deloria 1985). Nonetheless, the Indian Reorganization Act ended the allotment system, stimulated economic development on reservations, and promoted cultural preservation, including the centrality of tribal organizations to Native American identity.

Termination

The IRA was followed, during the Eisenhower administration, by a concerted effort to undo the Indian New Deal. The context for the policy shift included key economic and political features of the post-World War II landscape. The nation's economy grew dramatically, and the public generally believed in expanded opportunities for members of heretofore disadvantaged groups. Success was assumed to be an individual, not a collective, matter, however. In other words, individual Native Americans might be economically successful, but tribal units might not. This rather pervasive belief, stemming, in part, from the Cold War ideology of the 1950s, "placed particular value on national unity and conformity, and special groups, especially if they emphasized communal values, were considered out of line" (Prucha, 1985: 69). In fact, they were sometimes accused of embracing communistic ideals.

A new governmental approach to Native Americans was developed that became known as "termination." The head of the Bureau of Indian Affairs, Dillon S. Myer, argued that the relationship of Native Americans to the land, as reflected in the reservation system, had worked against their desire to achieve economic well-being. He contended that if the health, education, and economic situation of the Native American were to improve, it would have to occur outside of the tribal context. Termination entailed eliminating the reservations and severing the unique relationship that existed between the federal government and Native Americans (Burt, 1982; Fixico, 1986). In short, this new response by the federal government constituted an aggressive campaign of assimilation. Many liberals were sympathetic to this campaign because they considered reservations to be "rural ghettos" (Cornell, 1988: 121).

Most Native Americans were vehemently opposed to termination. In particular, the National Congress of American Indians (NCAI), a pan-tribal political organization formed in 1944, waged a battle against the policy. The NCAI was opposed to termination because of the threat to tribal entities posed by assimilation and because of the loss of land and federal protection that termination would bring about. The amount of opposition to termination is illustrated by the fact that only 3 percent of the total Native American population terminated its relationship with Washington. Furthermore, only 3 percent of Native American land was removed from the trust status accorded to reservations. Still, in two notable cases, those of the Menominee tribe in Wisconsin and the Klamath Indians in Oregon, Native Americans approved termination laws. Native American land in these instances was no longer held in trusteeship and all federally funded services, including health and educational ones, ceased. The economic and social consequences were disastrous. Menominee tribal members concluded it was in their best interest to return to the status quo ante: after a long legal battle their tribal status was finally restored in 1973 (Spicer, 1980: 114; Prucha, 1985: 70–85; Cornell, 1988: 123–125). The Klamath tribe has never been reinstated.

Searching for Alternatives to Termination

Termination was abandoned by the Kennedy administration, and since that time no administration, liberal or conservative, has attempted to revive the assimilationist strategy of the Eisenhower years. During the Great Society initiatives of the Johnson presidency, policymakers revived aspects of the IRA. They emphasized programs that were designed to strengthen communities and facilitate economic development. The new approach differed because Native Americans were accorded a far greater role in decision making. This was an attempt to avoid the charges of governmental paternalism and forced subservience of Indian communities. Community action programs were often funneled through the Office of Economic Opportunity (OEO) and other government agencies, such as the Administration for Native Americans, and not the highly-criticized BIA. These alternative sources of funding provided avenues for Native Americans to challenge tribal councils too dependent on the BIA. Not infrequently these programs served as training grounds for a leadership that used confrontational tactics to advance Native American issues (Prucha, 1985; Cornell, 1988).

The Nixon administration scuttled the activist element contained in OEO programs, though it urged enhanced possibilities for Native American involvement in community development. The slogan of this administration was "self-determination," and it took legislative form in the 1975 Indian Self-Determination Act. The argument was made by administration spokespersons that Native American independence should occur without ending tribal allegiances or withdrawing federal support (Spicer, 1980: 120). This was an attempt to steer a course between assimilation and total separatism. It was an ambivalent course.

This ambivalence has been evident in every subsequent administration. The Reagan administration made a concerted attempt to reduce the size of the federal government's involvement in domestic affairs, but Native Americans found a confusing situation. On the one hand, the administration contended that it was going to treat tribal governments with respect, relating to them on a "government-to-government" basis. This was viewed positively by most Native Americans. At the same time, however, draconian budget cuts were proposed, and Native Americans were understandably fearful of the negative consequences these cuts would have on already impoverished reservations (Cornell, 1988: 209–210).

An overall lack of interest in domestic affairs by the Bush administration meant that no new initiatives directed at Native Americans were undertaken. Thus, at present, self-sufficiency remains the goal for Native Americans. Concrete workable policies that can advance that goal have not yet been formulated, however. Later in this chapter we shall explore how Native Americans have responded to the various shifts in governmental policies from the IRA to the present.

Urbanization

Because of the centrality of the reservation system to the ongoing existence of tribes, Native Americans have lagged far behind the general population in their level of urbanization. Nonetheless, after 1945 the number of Native Americans seeking employment in cities increased. Partly a voluntary migration, this resembled the labor migrations of immigrant groups, but perhaps resembled more the migration of African Americans from the rural South to northern cities. Like the African Americans, Native Americans had other reasons to leave reservations, including serving in the armed forces and attending college. But there was something unique about the Native American experience: by the 1950s, urban migration was actively encouraged by the federal government. During the termination period, relocation to cities was seen as a way of breaking down tribal allegiances and promoting the incorporation of Native Americans into the national economy (Waddell and Watson, 1971). Furthermore, as Edward Spicer (1980: 113) has observed:

> The movement of Indians into cities has proceeded on a quite different basis from the urbanization of European or Asian immigrants. It is not characterized by the growth of extensive contiguous neighborhoods in which thousands of persons of similar cultural backgrounds live in subcultural enclaves. The urbanization of Indians in the United States has been a relatively small-scale movement of individuals and small family groups from quite different tribal cultural backgrounds.

Native Americans in cities were no longer under the direct jurisdiction of tribal governments or of the BIA, though the government established relocation centers designed to assist Native

Americans in acquiring jobs and adjusting to their new environment. During the early 1950s field relocation offices were set up in a number of cities that had become major destinations for Native Americans: Los Angeles, Chicago, Denver, Salt Lake City, Oakland, San Jose, Cleveland, and Dallas. Between 1950 and 1960, as the urban population of the whole country increased by almost 30 percent, the urban Native American population increased by 160 percent (Cornell, 1988: 130–131). Urban areas with the largest Native American populations are, in descending order of size, Los Angeles, San Francisco–Oakland, Tulsa, Minneapolis–St. Paul, Oklahoma City, Chicago, and Phoenix (Spicer, 1980: 111).

Native Americans find it difficult to maintain ties with other Native Americans because they are residentially dispersed in many cities. Churches often provide an important place for maintaining contact. Many Native Americans are Roman Catholic, though various Protestant denominations have also attracted members. Some religious groups have helped establish community centers for Native Americans. For example, in San Francisco the Society of Friends (Quakers) founded the Intertribal Friendship House. The center provided various social services to recent arrivals in the city and functioned as a gathering place. Although this particular center was run by whites, Native Americans also created their own organizations, such as the Bay Area American Indian Council, which offered similar services, but also promoted political involvement (Spicer, 1980: 112).

Adjusting to Urban Life

Native Americans had to overcome a number of obstacles to be successful in an urban setting. They confronted some discrimination in hiring, though the level of discrimination is not generally as high as that experienced by blacks (Mucha, 1984: 339). Their initial poverty meant that they tended to locate in ghetto neighborhoods, which had poor quality housing and lacked adequate community services and social amenities. Urban migrants also brought with them some social problems, the most troublesome of which was alcoholism. In the pre-1970 period, some Native Americans were either monolingual and had to learn English or they were bilingual, but their English-language skills were not well-developed. In either case, the acquisition of functional English-language skills was a prerequisite for occupational success.

Anthropologist Janusz Mucha (1984: 333), in an ethnographic study of Native Americans in Chicago, pointed to the cultural adaptations that had to take place for the Native Americans to succeed economically. He offered one particularly revealing case, that of a person who after many years in Chicago had become an electric plant designer. The individual had a difficult time during his early years in the city coming to terms with the competitiveness of the white employment world. He disliked what he referred to as the "dog-world" of whites, where everyone "barked and bit." He also had to learn to deal with a different conception of time (recall the similar reorientation many European immigrants from agrarian backgrounds also had to make at an earlier time in American history). Mucha (1984: 333) summarized the change that occurred in the following way:

> The "white" concept of time is a situation in which people are ruled by their watches, and it was very difficult to understand. Eventually, this person got used to the white concept of time and even came to the conclusion that it was the only correct concept when large groups of people who have to work together are involved. For about ten years, however, he was on the edge of being fired because of [persistent] lateness, and only his very good work record saved him.

Despite these various obstacles to economic betterment, because the job opportunities in cities far surpass those in rural areas, whether on or near reservations, urban Native Americans have a higher standard of living than rural Native Americans; furthermore, that difference will probably increase over time (Snipp, 1989: 320). Urban Native Americans can be found throughout the socio-economic hierarchy. They are located in the middle and upper middle class, the solid blue-collar working class, in the unskilled working class, and in tenuous circumstances of underemployment and chronic unemployment (Jarvenpa, 1985: 36).

This class diffusion has had an impact on various shifts in ethnic identity. Those at the top of the socioeconomic ladder often have limited contact with other Native Americans and with Native American institutions. Those at the bottom of the ladder are frequently recent arrivals from reservations, and their contact with the tribe often is intact. For the latter, frequent trips to the reservation are common. Indeed, many Native Americans show considerable movement to and from reservations.

Intermarriage

Connected to this internal class differentiation is the issue of intermarriage. Since intermarriage is seen as perhaps the key indicator of social acceptance, the contrast between blacks and Native Americans is instructive. Recall that Native Americans were located near the bottom of the ethnic social standing ranking (see Table 8.1). Their standing was only slightly higher than that of blacks (and Mexicans and Puerto Ricans). This being the case, the pronounced difference in intermarriage rates for Native Americans and blacks is remarkable. As we noted in the preceding chapter, the historically low rates of black-white intermarriage still persist. For Native Americans, however, the rate is very high (Sandefur and McKinnell, 1986).

Data from the 1980 census indicate that 53 percent of married Native Americans were married to non-Indians. To appreciate how unique this figure is, compare it with the rates for both blacks and whites. Only approximately 4 percent of blacks are married to non-blacks, and the figure for whites is only around 2 percent. This has prompted some in the Native American community to question whether this tendency to marry non-Indians means that Native Americans will, "in the not too distant future, marry themselves out of existence" (Snipp, 1989: 165; 157–158; see also Vogt, 1957).

The city has been a crucible for intermarriage. As Table 10.1 reveals, only one in five married Native Americans in metropolitan areas is married to a Native American, while for those residing on or near reservations the figure is closer to one out of two. Furthermore, Native Americans on or in close proximity to reservations have a variety of communal institutions that can assist intermarrieds maintain contact with the Native American community. In contrast, many intermarrieds in cities have few if any ties to Native American communities. This can be due to choice, as Native Americans seek to distance themselves from their Native American past — or perhaps merely from poor Native Americans in cities — as they assimilate into white society. But this can also be partially caused by the relative weakness of ethnic institutions in urban settings.

Table 10.1   MARITAL CHOICES OF AMERICAN INDIANS
(PERCENTAGES) BY PLACE OF RESIDENCE

Place of Residence	American Indian Husband and Wife	Indian Husband, Non-Indian Wife	Non-Indian Husband, Indian Wife	Total
Metropolitan	20.6	39.5	39.9	100.0
Nonmetropolitan	48.6	24.3	27.1	100.0
Off Reservation	20.6	39.5	39.9	100.0
On or Near Reservation	46.2	25.6	28.2	100.0

Reprinted from *American Indians: The First of This Land,* by C. Matthew Snipp, 1989: 160
© The Russell Sage Foundation. Used with the permission of the Russell Sage Foundation.

Whatever the precise reasons, clearly a segment of urbanized Native Americans are not part of the Native American community and do not choose to accentuate, or even claim, their Native American identity. Others are not part of the community, but choose, when they think it advantageous, to claim their Native American ancestry. For this segment of the population, Native Americanness becomes a form of symbolic ethnicity.

The Ethnic Community in the City

For those who remain attached to the Native American community—especially found in the ranks of working class and poor Native Americans—an institutional presence has developed. Such institutions have actually existed in cities since at least the 1920s, and their numbers have grown since the 1950s. But distinctive features have a bearing on ethnic identity. Most important, these institutions have tended to promote pan-Indian organizations and ethnic identity. Although pan-Indian ethnicity is not new, it is a more pervasive feature of the Native American population today, largely due to urbanization.

Although urban organizations have been established on a tribal basis, many community centers and organizations formed to advance the interests of urban Native Americans have been constructed across tribal boundaries. The connection between tribes and the federal government has been severed in cities, opening up the possibility of new forms of organization. This process has been further encouraged because white society has tended to be oblivious to tribal differences among urbanized Native Americans, defining native people by the supratribal designations "American Indian" or "Native American."

Robert Thomas (1968) considered pan-Indianism as an instance of the invention of a new ethnic group, one that replaces tribal identity with a more inclusive one. He believed that this is a way for Native Americans seeking inclusion in an urban-industrial society to preserve a sense of ethnic identity. For Thomas, the root motives for this invention are psychological and cultural. Cornell (1988: 146) disputed this by pointing to the political character of pan-Indianism: it provides Native Americans with the resources needed to mount effective campaigns to advance their political interests and improve their economic conditions.

In a study of the Native American community in Los Angeles, Joan Weibel-Orlando (1991) documented both the cultural preservation and the political activities of these institutions. Thus, this in-depth empirical study lent credence to both positions. It also pointed out something that both Thomas and Cornell tended to overlook: only a small minority of urban Indians actually involve themselves in these institutions. Only about 4 percent of the approximately 48,000 Native Americans in the Los Angeles area actually participate in the social world of the ethnic community.

Political Activism

The main vehicle for pan-Indian political activity until the 1960s was the National Congress of American Indians (NCAI). Its political stance was moderate and its tactics were nonconfrontational. The NCAI operated primarily by lobbying in Washington, and its chief objective was to fight termination. As such, the organization was committed to protecting the existing relationship between tribes and the federal government. Thus, supratribalism was designed to be a political means to protect the integrity of tribes and preserve the reservations. Of course, the NCAI also tried to find ways to foster economic development on or near reservations (Wax, 1971: 144–148).

Given this general orientation, it is not entirely surprising that the leadership of the NCAI was publicly hostile to the black civil rights movement and to the tactics of nonviolent civil disobedience. In part this was due to their belief in the appropriateness of conventional political activities. It can also be seen as a way of making invidious comparisons between blacks and Native Americans in an effort to display Native American activism in a more favorable light.

This stance was challenged during the 1960s. The National Indian Youth Council (NIYC), formed in 1961 by Native American college students, argued for more militant opposition to white society and to the detrimental effects of government policy. In contrast with the NCAI, the NIYC was inclined to be sympathetic to the black civil rights movement. In many ways the NIYC modeled its activities after the civil rights movement's more militant wing. The NIYC gave way to several other militant groups, the most influential being the American Indian Movement (AIM), which not only engaged in confrontational politics, but also endorsed the appropriateness of violence in some instances. Like the Black Panthers, AIM was founded in a city (Minneapolis in 1968) as a response to police mistreatment and harassment.

The Red Power Movement

Direct political confrontation dramatically escalated during the 1960s (Nagel, 1994), although there were actually activist stirrings in the late 1950s. These included the attack by Lumbee Indians of Robeson County, North Carolina, on a Ku Klux Klan rally in 1958, and a pan-Indian march on the Washington, D.C., headquarters of the BIA, in the following year. In the 1960s numerous local actions reflected a growing willingness to engage in civil disobedience and in political theater. For instance, the "fish-ins" and hunting in defiance of state laws were responses to what were seen as violations of treaties that had guaranteed special hunting and fishing privileges to Native Americans. Contestations over land ownership and the use of land by loggers and other developers was yet another early focus of conflict (Cornell, 1988: 189).

Such activism was a precursor to what became known as the "Red Power" movement. The three most dramatic events during this period that captured the attention of the national media were the occupation of Alcatraz in 1969, the 1972 Trail of Broken Treaties march, and the takeover of the community of Wounded Knee in 1973. The first action involved the occupation of the San Francisco Bay island that had formerly served as a federal prison. An ad hoc organization called "Indians of All Tribes" claimed that the island legitimately belonged to Native Americans. Its leaders proclaimed their intention of establishing a training school and a center for Native American culture and education. Several thousand Native American supporters and whites sympathetic to the movement visited the island during the 19-month occupation. But the government held its ground and finally in June 1971, without achieving their demands, the Native Americans withdrew from the island (Spicer, 1980: 121; Prucha, 1985: 81–82).

The other two events were initiated by AIM. The Trail of Broken Treaties march was in some respects a parallel to the 1963 black civil rights movement's march on Washington. By highlighting the long history of injustice suffered by Native Americans and the failure of whites to abide by treaties, protest organizers appealed to a moral constituency. AIM's goals and tactics were more militant, however. The demands, contained in the "Twenty Points" proposal, included abolishing the BIA and reinstituting the ability of tribes to enter into treaties with the federal government. Thus, AIM's objectives were far different from those of the NCAI and called for a complete reorganization of Native American relations with the U.S. government (Cornell, 1988: 195).

The Trail of Broken Treaties march culminated in the week-long occupation of the BIA headquarters, during which time demonstrators hung a sign from the building proclaiming it to be the American Indian Embassy. When threatened with expulsion, occupiers vandalized the building. The subsequent reaction to this dramatic event has been summarized by Prucha (1985: 82): "The BIA was dispersed and reorganized, and Congress investigated possible foreign influence in AIM. No one any longer doubted that Indian conditions were serious enough to lead to violence."

The site chosen for the third action was symbolic. On February 27, 1973, activists occupied the village of Wounded Knee — the site of the 1890 massacre of some 150 Native Americans participating in the Ghost Dance — located on the Oglala Sioux's Pine Ridge Reservation. The government surrounded the Native Americans with several hundred heavily armed FBI agents, U.S. Marshals, and BIA police. For 10 weeks the nation witnessed a violent siege that took two Native American lives and resulted in many injuries on both sides. The demands of the occupiers included the restoration of lands that, it was claimed, had been taken by whites in violation of treaties. AIM called for an end to government involvement in Native American affairs and condemned the purported corruption among tribal officials (Prucha, 1985: 82–83; Cornell, 1988: 3–4). When the occupation finally ended, none of these goals was met, but, like the actions that preceded it, AIM had captured the spotlight and drawn public attention to the situation of reservation life.

Competing Political Goals

The "Red Power" movement forced the government and the general public to ask, "What do Indians want?" The social movement elicited varied responses from white society, ranging from an intensified hostility toward Native Americans to growing support for their cause. Needless to say, within the Native American community, this movement also caused considerable debate and conflict. The Native American population is not a single, homogeneous group, but consists of peoples of great diversity, as we have seen in terms of geographic and social class locations, tribal identities, mixed versus full-blooded Native Americans, and so forth. Native Americans do not always agree on what they collectively want.

Cornell (1988: 151–156) makes two distinctions in classifying the variations in Native American goals. The first distinction deals with the structure of Native American–white relations. He distinguishes two different orientations: *reformative* and *transformative*. Reformative goals basically accept the existing structure of Native American-white relations, but seek to improve the welfare of Native Americans through a redistribution of resources, services, and rewards. Transformative goals seek not only a redistribution of rewards, but also a fundamental restructuring of Native American–white relations.

The second distinction lies in differences between *integrative* and *segregative* goals. Integrative goals essentially accept the presence and appropriateness of Euro-American institutions in Native American communities. The assimilation of Native Americans into the mainstream American culture and into the larger society's institutions is promoted. In contrast, segregative goals challenge the benefit of permitting the dominant group's economic and political institutions to take root within Native American communities. As such, segregative goals are "antiassimilationist and antiacculturational" (Cornell, 1988: 153).

In the aftermath of the militancy of the 1960s and 1970s, transformative goals gained adherents at the expense of reformative goals. Although advocates for reform are still a powerful presence in Native American communities, they are not nearly as powerful as they were prior to 1960. Thus, Native Americans are currently far more critical of the status quo then they were a few decades ago. Native Americans remain deeply divided, and quite ambivalent, about the appropriateness of primarily integrative goals versus essentially segregative ones.

Ongoing Conflict with White America

In recent years Native Americans have combined confrontational tactics with increased court challenges. Tribal and supratribal organizations have been created or strengthened (Legters and Lyden, 1994). These organizations rely on a cadre of educated Native Americans with leadership skills, supporters outside of Native American communities, and the media. They operate with better financial resources than in the past. Although a number of important transformative organizations exist, the Native American Rights Fund, founded in 1971, has been particularly instrumental in undertaking numerous court cases.

The 1975 Indian Educational Assistance and Self-Determination Act and related legislation and court rulings transformed the issue of tribal sovereignty. These permitted tribal control of mineral and other natural resources, and provided the legal basis for Indian gambling casinos. Many legal battles were based on claims of violations of treaty agreements between various tribes and the U.S. government. To capture the flavor of some of the areas of greatest conflict, a few illustrative examples will be reviewed briefly. These examples will look at the following three areas of dispute: over hunting and fishing rights, over control of natural resources, and over land claims.

The Chippewa Spearfishing Dispute

The Chippewas, located near Lake Superior, had ceded lands in what is now eastern Minnesota, northern Wisconsin, and northern Michigan to the United States government in a series of treaties entered into in 1836, 1837, 1842, and 1854. The Chippewas did not relinquish their rights to hunt, fish, and gather on these lands; they sold the land to the government but did not give up their right to the resources that had been essential to their economic survival. In Wisconsin, the Chippewas have historically harvested fish, deer, furbearing animals, waterfowl, and wild rice (Terry, 1991). During the ensuing century and a half the Chippewas have not consistently exercised these rights. It is important to note that this right to harvest is not held by individual Native Americans, but by the tribe.

Beginning in the 1970s, a controversy arose in northern Wisconsin over the right of the Chippewas to engage in spearfishing, a practice that is illegal for non-Native Americans. Opponents of the practice complained that Native Americans were given special rights not granted to others. Furthermore, opponents contended that old treaties could not possibly be applicable to present circumstances, and thus should no longer be legally binding. They also argued that when Native Americans became United States citizens in 1924, they gave up their tribal citizenships and thus such special privileges. Finally, they argued, treaties applied only to full-blooded Native Americans, and not to individuals who are only part Chippewa. Actually, these arguments are wrong on all counts. The Chippewas were not granted privileges: they never relinquished them in their treaties. The age of the treaties does not void them. Native Americans did not give up their tribal citizenships when they also became U.S. citizens. Instead, tribes are the arbiters of who is and who is not eligible for membership into the tribe. They use varying criteria for making such determinations, including the use of blood quantum or birthright.

Native Americans had confined their spearfishing to reservation land until 1974, when the Tribble brothers of the Lac Courte Oreilles Band of Chippewas crossed reservation boundaries to fish. They were subsequently arrested by Department of Natural Resources wardens. This act of defiance set the stage for a legal battle; it was a test case to challenge the legality of the state's right to enforce Wisconsin law against tribal members in areas under which treaty rights superseded state law. The Chippewas, in a report titled "A Guide to Understanding Chippewa Treaty Rights" (ndl., p. 2), indicated their conviction that by the 1970s they had acquired the necessary sophistication and skill to deal with the complicated legal system of the white world. The report stated that, "Time and familiarity with the system eventually provided the Chippewa with the ability to assert their rights within the legal forum of the dominant society." Indeed, after a nine-year legal battle, the Chippewas won their case in the U.S. Court of Appeals.

This set the stage for the intensification of conflict with whites, who argued that the decision was a direct threat to the economic livelihood of all non-Native Americans. The economy of the area was dominated by tourism and the timber industry. Whites feared that the ability of the Chippewas to exploit the region's natural resources would undermine their economic position. Spearfishing was only one example of how Native Americans were seen as having a potentially disruptive impact on the local economy.

Out of this economic conflict emerged an organized anti-Native American presence that included such local efforts in Wisconsin as Equal Rights for Everyone, Wisconsin Alliance for Rights and Resources, and Protect American Rights and Resources. These groups waged both a legal and media campaign to halt spearfishing. Their members picketed and used high-speed boats to disrupt the Chippewas when they sought to exercise their fishing rights. There were also scattered threats of violence, including shooting in the vicinity of spearfishers and the planting of pipe bombs. The threat of violence was associated with manifestations of racism, seen for example in bumper stickers that read "Save a Walleye, Spear an Indian" or "Spear a Pregnant Squaw, Save a Walleye." Native Americans were referred to as "Indian niggers" or "Red niggers" (Ivey, 1990; Terry, 1991).

On the other hand, not only were the Chippewas well organized, but they also received support from a variety of non-Native American organizations, ranging from the regional chapter of the environmentalist Green party to the human rights office of the Evangelical Lutheran Church in America. The end to this current dispute occurred in March 1991, when the Chippewas agreed to a court settlement that reaffirmed their traditional treaty rights. The Native Americans agreed to drop a $325 million law suit and to a limitation on the number of fish they could take from nonreservation waters. They also agreed to refrain from harvesting timber off of reservation land, thereby protecting the economic interests of whites in the timber industry. The agreement pleased some Native Americans and whites while it was received with either hostility or ambivalence by others.

The Blackfeet and Oil Exploration: Limiting Development

A conflict over oil development of a vast tract of land in Montana known as the Badger-Two Medicine region, part of the Lewis and Clark National Forest, pitted the Blackfeet Indians against the combined forces of the oil industry and the U.S. government's Forest Service. The Chevron Oil Corporation and Fina Oil and Chemical Company obtained the lease to this land and over several years worked to acquire the government's approval to conduct exploratory drilling. This created an ongoing conflict between those favoring exploration and those opposed to it (Cornell, 1988: 201). During the Persian Gulf crisis, an internal memo circulated within the Forest Service that urged the agency to take advantage of the public's fear of a loss of imported oil to push through approval. The memo's author pressed for relaxing existing procedures for environmental review and argued in favor of limiting public comment. Environmentalists were opposed to any attempt to drill in this land and argued that the area was home to the grizzly bear, which is an endangered species. They pointed to government studies that indicated drilling would disturb more than 7,000 acres of land and create air, water, and noise pollution (Baum, 1990).

The Blackfeet joined environmentalists in opposing oil exploration in the area. They shared the concern about the impact on the environment. But the Blackfeet were also concerned that it would upset their ability to practice their religion. Tribal leaders argued that the land was used as a place of spiritual renewal. Their sweat lodges were built along a creek for retreats as tribal members conducted traditional purification rites. There they make pilgrimages to the top of the mountains and fast in a practice known as "vision quests," conduct sun dances, and practice various other religious ceremonies. According to Tiny Man Heavy Runner, a chief of the Blackfeet, the idea of digging oil wells in this area is as much of a sacrilege as it would be to dig a well in St. Patrick's cathedral (Baum, 1990). The Forest Service contended that the Native Americans had not proved their case that the land is sacred. The Blackfeet failed to produce what government officials considered to be adequate documentation of their claims.

The Blackfeet battle with oil companies and their governmental supporters is an example of cultural conflict—the result of two competing and distinctive world views. Developers view the natural world as separate from humans, who, to survive and thrive, must exploit the resources provided by that world. Furthermore, individuals derive their definitions of personal identity from the social and cultural world they inhabit, not from the natural world. The natural world is not sacred, but profane.

In stark contrast, the Blackfeet identify with their natural environment, seeing themselves as a part of it, and thus finding their own identities in it. Any action that disrupts or profoundly alters the existing state of nature and the Blackfeet relation to it is condemned. From this perspective, such changes could destroy the distinct identity of the Blackfeet. Tribal elders attribute the contemporary ravages of alcoholism and drug abuse to a weakening of tribal identity. In their view, the exploitation of the region for oil and gas will exacerbate these problems and intensify the alienation experienced by many younger Blackfeet.

This particular conflict between proponents and opponents of economic development is an example of many similar battles between those who view land as a commercial resource and those who invest land with spiritual power. The Northern Cheyennes, for example, have waged a similar campaign against coal mining. Related concerns are fundamentally about the preservation of Native American identities. Some tribes, including the Crows and Navajos, have voiced their opposition to economic plans that would result in the influx of sizeable numbers of non-Native Americans. Native Americans fear that such an influx would produce assimilative pressures that many tribal members want to resist (Cornell, 1988: 201).

Land Disputes: The Legacy of Treaty Violations

The terms of many treaties that ceded lands occupied by Native Americans to whites have been followed. In other instances, violations have resulted in land disputes, many of which have persisted since the nineteenth century. As noted in the Chippewas case, the increased willingness of Native Americans to use the American legal system to redress injustices has resulted in several highly publicized court cases that had or continue to have far-reaching implications.

On the East coast, a number of challenges were made to Native American land cessations that had taken place during the colonial period. These involved Native Americans from tribes such as the Passamaquoddies, Penobscots, Wampanoag-Mashpee, and Narragansetts. For example, the Native Americans of Maine argued in federal court that they should be given title to millions of acres of land in the state. They based this claim on a 1790 federal law that required states to obtain the approval of the federal government prior to purchasing any Native American lands. According to the suit, Massachusetts (at the time the state controlled what is now Maine) failed to do this. If the court had ruled in the Native Americans' favor, the entire social and economic structure of Maine would have been placed in jeopardy. The apprehensions this caused among the white citizenry of Maine heightened tensions. Rather than continuing a long, protracted legal battle, Native Americans opted for a negotiated settlement that provided them with monetary compensation for lost lands (Prucha, 1985: 86).

A similar claim was made for much of Cape Cod, a major resort and tourist area. Like the Maine case, the basis for the claim rested on the legality of the state's original purchase of Native American land. The high property values of the Cape put the Native Americans in a position to make rather stiff demands for monetary compensation. In a parallel case, the Wampanoags unsuccessfully sought to reclaim land on Martha's Vineyard. Similar land claims have been made elsewhere along the Atlantic seaboard, in Rhode Island, New York, and South Carolina (Prucha, 1985: 86). And these claims have not been confined to this region of the country. The Puyallup in Washington state negotiated a settlement that netted the tribe $162 million, and the Sioux were awarded $106 million for the Black Hills in South Dakota. The Southern Pacific Transportation Company agreed to pay the Walker River Paiutes $1.2 million to settle a land dispute that began a century ago. (*New York Times*, 1990: 33; 1984: 17; 1989: 26).

In some instances, land rather than money was awarded. This occurred during the early 1970s in the Alaska Native Claims Settlement, which gave 40,000,000 acres of land in that state to the Native Americans, Aleuts, and Eskimos (Dinnerstein, et al., 1990: 326).

These land disputes are far from over. Numerous simmering controversies exist in various places throughout the nation. These include a dispute between the Chippewas in northwestern Minnesota and local white farmers over land ownership and the assertion of the Oneidas that they are the rightful owners of five million acres of land in central New York state.

Development Plans on Native American Reservations

Reservations were created in a way that made it difficult to incorporate them into the national economy. Not only were they located in areas generally remote from major transportation networks and manufacturing and commercial centers, but also they usually had few natural resources that could make them profitable. The preceding section focused on issues related to cultural conflict and the antidevelopmental logic that can be seen in some types of Native American-white conflict. This section explores some of the varied ways in which Native Americans have pursued economic development. Many reservation residents have not opposed development; rather, they have sought to find ways to control and channel it for the best interests of the tribe.

Exploiting Natural Resources

Several tribes, especially in the Midwest and the West, occupy land containing valuable oil, coal, and other mineral resources that have been mined by white-owned companies. Native Americans generally believe that there has been rampant exploitation by these companies, and that reservations have not been paid adequate royalties. In perhaps the most concerted attempt to rectify this, several dozen tribes founded the Council of Energy Resource Tribes (CERT) in 1975 to obtain better contracts with companies. Supplied with grant monies from the federal government, CERT employed skilled negotiators and rather quickly won a contract with Atlantic Richfield that provided the tribes $78 million in royalties for 20 years. Many subsequent contracts were also favorable to Native Americans. Government support for CERT waned after Ronald Reagan's election, however, and CERT proved to be far less successful than in the preceding decade (Dorris, 1981; Fixico, 1985; Ungeheuer, 1987).

Within tribal communities there was considerable dissension over the aggressive pro-developmental stance of CERT's leadership. Many questioned the impact of such a campaign on tribal cultures. AIM was as vigorous in its opposition to unbridled development as were various environmental groups, especially over the issue of uranium mining (Jorgensen, 1984; Feagin, 1984).

Efforts to find ways to end the endemic poverty of reservations continue. Five tribes — the Yakima Indian Nation in Washington, the Mescalero Apache tribe in New Mexico, Minnesota's Prairie Island Indian Community, and two tribes in Oklahoma, the Sac and Fox Nation and the Chickasaw Indian Nation — are among the seven applicants for Department of Energy grants given to sites willing to store thousands of tons of high-level nuclear waste on their land. Many consider this willingness as a sign of the economic desperation felt by tribal councils. As Keith Schneider (1992) has written, the request for grant proposals has "stirred political dissension and raised questions about whether the Government is taking advantage of hard economic times and rural poverty to gain a site for some of the nation's most dangerous industrial wastes."

Tourism and Gaming

Some tribes have promoted tourism to provide an economic base. This has been an important part of reservation economic life for some tribes for decades. Tourism can only work in some places and depends on the accessibility of the reservation, the scenic character of the landscape, and so forth. Furthermore, even where tourism is well-established, Native Americans are often disappointed with the economic returns it provides (Smith, 1982).

Tribes have attempted to find other ways out of a state of chronic poverty. Thus, the Moapa band of Paiute Native Americans in Nevada contemplated establishing a brothel on the reservation as a way of becoming economically self-sufficient (*New York Times,*

November 4, 1984). Taking advantage of the fact that state laws do not apply to reservations, many tribes have turned to organized gaming as a means of generating revenues for reservations. Initially, many tribes established bingo parlors, including the Mohawk Indians of Rooseveltown, New York, which built one of the nation's largest bingo parlors. Tribes throughout the country have constructed gambling casinos on tribal lands, including the Pequots and Seminoles in the East; the Chippewas, Oneidas and Sioux in the Midwest; and the Navajo in the West.

A National Indian Gaming Commission was established to oversee and coordinate gaming ventures. Supporters of gambling argue that it is a major industry and Native Americans are in a position to benefit financially from entry into such ventures. Critics counter such claims by arguing that many Native Americans will be victimized by gaming. Furthermore, they are concerned about the potential for corruption and about the possible influence of organized crime (*New York Times*, January 6, 1992).

Whatever the future of gambling on reservation lands, it shows that manufacturing has not been particularly successful. The Blackfeet have run a pen and pencil manufacturing plant, but in most instances, plans for industrial development have either not gotten started or have failed. In a review of three economic development plans formulated, respectively, by Navajo, Zuni, and Standing Rock Sioux, David Vinje (1985: 167) observed, "Manufacturing is not viewed as the key to economic development in the current plans." Instead, the focus is on social service activities (health care, provision for the elderly, and so on) in the public sector, and on improving the level of commercial businesses — stores, restaurants, gas stations, and the like — on reservations.

Quality of Life on Reservations

Reservations are sites of persistent poverty and high levels of chronic unemployment and underemployment. Overall, the income of Native Americans improved since the 1960s: Native Americans had a lower per capita income than blacks in 1969, but a higher income than blacks a decade later. Native Americans nonetheless lag far behind whites, especially on reservations. On 15 of the 16 most populated reservations, the proportion of families with incomes below the official poverty line ranged from a low of one-third to more than one-half (Snipp, 1989: 259). Since labor force participation is heavily tied to governmentally funded jobs, federal cutbacks in various programs during the 1980s have had a negative impact on reservation inhabitants.

Housing

The quality of reservation housing is considerably worse than that of the general population. Overcrowding is a major problem. Housing units are more likely to lack running water, indoor plumbing, and electricity than is the case for whites and blacks. This is partly because rural housing in general is characterized by deficiencies in these amenities to a greater extent than is urban housing.

An attempt to improve reservation housing in the 1960s and 1970s involved the BIA and the Department of Housing and Urban Development. Housing authorities modeled after the public housing program were created and controlled by tribes, the BIA, or by both. New construction undertaken by these authorities resulted in an expansion of housing stock, which somewhat reduced overcrowding. It also provided to poor Native Americans subsidized housing in which rents were assessed in terms of a family's ability to pay.

Appreciable improvements were made in the overall housing stock on reservations. For example, the percentage of Native American homes with complete bathrooms increased from 72 percent in 1970 to 90 percent in 1980. Nonetheless, this figure was still below that of whites (97.8 percent) and blacks (93.6 percent). Furthermore, some reservations are poorer than others, so general figures do not reveal the actual depth of poverty in some locales. In 1980, on the Hopi reservation, 55.5 percent of households did not have indoor plumbing, while the figure was 53.5 percent for the Papago. In addition, 15.9 percent of housing units on reservations did not have electricity, 16.6 percent did not have refrigerators, and 55.8 percent were without telephones. Clearly, parity in housing had not been achieved by 1980. Since that time, further improvements have been stymied because Native American housing assistance programs were abolished by the Reagan administration (Snipp, 1989: 96–126; Tippeconnic, 1990).

Table 10.2 MORTALITY RATES FOR SELECTED CAUSES
(PER 100,000)

Cause of Death	American Indians	All Races
Cardiovascular Disease	173.1	228.4
Malignant Neoplasms	88.4	133.5
Accidents	81.3	35.0
Auto	42.0	19.1
Other	39.3	15.9
Liver Disease and Cirrhosis	30.7	10.0
Diabetes	20.6	9.5
Pneumonia and Influenza	18.4	12.2
Homicide	14.5	8.4
Suicide	12.9	11.6
Tuberculosis	1.8	0.5

Source: Indian Health Service Chart Book Series, 1987.

Health Issues

American Indians may be the least healthy racial group in the
United States. The infant mortality rate is higher than average, and
the life expectancy of Native Americans is about 10 years shorter
than the national average. Death rates due to diseases including
pneumonia, diabetes, and tuberculosis are higher for them than for
other groups. The suicide rate slightly exceeded that of the general
population, and the death rate due to homicide is nearly two times
that of all racial groups. As Table 10.2 indicates, accidental deaths
are more than twice as common for Native Americans than for all
races (Indian Health Service, 1987).

Most staggering is the fact that deaths due to alcoholism are
five times greater for Native Americans than for all races. There is
a high incidence of liver disease and cirrhosis, and alcohol abuse is
also linked to accidental deaths, suicides, and homicides. Although, as Figure 10.1 indicates, during the 1970s there was a
noticeable decrease in alcohol-related deaths, alcoholism continues
to be an extremely serious problem. Not surprisingly, in a public

Figure 10.1 *Age-adjusted alcoholism-related death rates for American Indians and Alaska Natives and all races, 1970–1983 (per 100,000 population).*

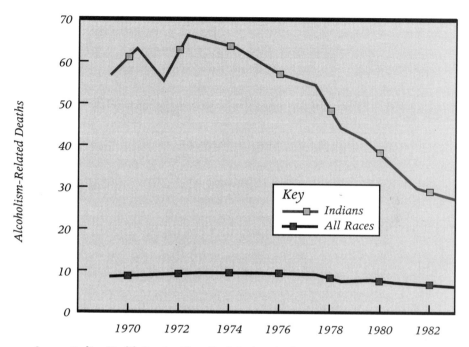

Source: Indian Health Service Chart Book Series, April, 1987.

opinion survey of Native Americans conducted by *The Arizona Republic* (1987), substance abuse was identified as the greatest problem facing Native Americans today. A troubling dimension to this problem has recently received media attention: the incidence of fetal alcohol syndrome. This refers to the mental and physical defects suffered by infants of alcoholic mothers. This serious problem has resulted in the jailing of a pregnant alcoholic woman to ensure that she refrained from drinking while carrying her child.

Native Americans in the White Mind

When whites think of race relations, they think of black and white relations. More recently, the impact of immigration has made whites more conscious of changes among both Hispanics and Asians. In contrast, among whites there is relatively little consciousness of developments within Native American communities except in communities located near reservations. This is partly because Native Americans are more rural than other racial groups and thus are more invisible to most whites and partly because of the relatively small size of the Native American population.

Whatever the reasons, white attitudes toward Native Americans differ from those directed at other racial groups. In the nineteenth century, Native Americans were perceived as museum pieces, as part of a premodern world that was destined to disappear entirely. This general attitude has not disappeared even today. For example, if one looks at how Native Americans are depicted in American movies, it is clear that they are generally portrayed as an "entertaining anachronism" (Bataille and Silet, 1980). Films about Native Americans are seldom about their current circumstances; rather, films are mainly portrayals of Indians on the American frontier (Woll and Miller, 1987: 328). Though about half of Native Americans now reside in cities, no film has been produced that explicitly examines the lives of urban American Indians.

Countless B-movies have been produced by Hollywood that depicted Native Americans as savage aggressors. These "cowboy-and-Indian" movies were the stock of matinees that shaped the attitudes of at least two generations of moviegoers. The frontier settlers were generally presented as the innocent victims of attacks in which women and children were routinely abducted, while men were the victims of brutal torture and death. These particular films rarely showed sensitivity to the fact that the western expansion of the nation entailed a form of colonial occupation, or that whites — soldiers and civilians — brutalized Native Americans and uprooted their lives in the process of conquest.

Beginning as early as the late 1940s, however, several movies either reflected a more ambiguous understanding of white and Native American relations or offered a sympathetic treatment of Native Americans. In the 1950 film *Broken Arrow*, the Apache chief Cochise (played by the non–Native American Jeff Chandler), is presented as an advocate of peaceful relations with whites, and Apache culture is treated in a favorable manner — although the perspective is somewhat romanticized and not entirely accurate historically. Indicating a very different attitude than that held by the public and reflected by Hollywood regarding black and white interracial love, the film also has a romantic relationship between a frontiersman (James Stewart) and a Native American woman played by Debra Paget (Woll and Miller, 1987: 330; Bataille and Silet, 1980: 49).

In the 1960s several Hollywood films were highly critical of American society in general, reflecting the growing hostility over the Vietnam War and the more militant phase of the civil rights movement. Members of the youth counterculture, known at the time as hippies, became interested in Native American cultures. They saw the Native American as a valuable model for alternative lifestyles that were more in tune with nature and that fostered harmony and cooperation rather than individual competitiveness. Although Hollywood films did not necessarily embrace this view, several movies did turn the tables, portraying Native Americans in a favorable light and whites as the aggressive victimizers. This could be seen, for example, in *Soldier Blue*, *A Man Called Horse*, *Tell Them Willie Boy Is Here*, and *Buffalo Bill and the Indians*. The film that perhaps best captured this sensibility was Arthur Penn's *Little Big Man*. Bataille and Silet (1980: 45) considered the film to be a powerful indictment of white-dominated culture in America and summarized its main message in the following way:

> The slaughter of Custer and his men was seen as a perfectly justifiable revenge for the atrocities committed by the cavalry on a peaceful people . . . Penn contrasts the organic culture of the Cheyenne with the confusing and destructive Anglo-Saxon society which is engulfing it. Civilization becomes disordered, hypocritical, self-seeking, and nihilistic with people living in constant fear and tension. The culture projects all of its hatred and insecurity onto its enemies.

Native Americans occupy an ambivalent place in the minds of whites. Images of the noble savage, the victim of conquest, and peaceful and harmonious communities living intimately connected to the natural world continue to coincide with negative images of drunken, violence-prone, and lazy Native Americans living in disorganized and impoverished tribal units. Non–Native Americans know little about people of mixed ancestry, especially those who, like Scott Momaday, have managed to remain connected to their Native American past while integrating into the outside society. Yet these people constitute a large and ever-growing component of the

Native American population. If intermarriage rates continue to remain high, as is likely, they will become even more typical.

Uncertain Futures

The futures of mixed-bloods will probably be quite different from full-bloods. Although those who are only part Native American have frequently embraced assimilation, many of this group, like European Americans, will express their sense of being Native American in various manifestations of symbolic ethnicity. They will choose to be Native American on some occasions and downplay or conceal this part of their ancestry at other times. As with similar members of other ethnic groups, these Native Americans do not rely to any great extent on ethnic institutions and their interpersonal relationships may be chiefly with non–Native Americans. They are assimilationists whose lives are shaped by the values of the dominant society. They are unwilling to let their Native American ancestry be an impediment to success, and not surprisingly they are better educated, and are far more upwardly mobile in socioeconomic terms than other Native Americans. They are urbanites with few if any ties to reservation residents.

Native Americans who have chosen to remain on or near reservations are more likely to be full-blooded. They differ from those involved in an assimilative symbolic ethnicity insofar as they are attempting to preserve not simply a sense of individual Native American identity, but a viable communal life as well. They are undertaking this while seeking to take advantage of those aspects of contemporary society that can help improve their lives. As C. Matthew Snipp (1989: 322) wrote, "That American Indians no longer wander the plains on horseback in search of wild game does not mean that there are no longer any 'real' Indians." Rather than treating what it means to be a Native American as unchanging, these native people have a more dynamic perspective that entails the construction of a Native American identity that preserves selective traditions while seeking ways to overcome economic isolation and deprivation.

This is not easily accomplished, as can be seen in recent developments in higher education. Beginning in 1968 on the Navajo's reservation in Tsaile, Arizona, tribes in 12 states have opened colleges on Native American land. At present there are 24 tribal colleges and 2 run by the federal government. Most are junior colleges and some are not fully accredited. Four are four-year institutions, with Sinte Gleska University in Rosebud, South Dakota, also offering a master's degree in education. What these institutions are attempting to do is twofold: first, to provide skills that can assist students in finding jobs, and second, to instill a sense of pride and appreciation of one's Native American identity. There are attempts to teach using values more in tune with Native American culture, such as downplaying individual competition and promoting ways in which students can learn by working together on common tasks.

The results so far are somewhat mixed. The dropout rate is quite high and students who go on to four-year colleges off of the reservation do not have a high rate of success. On the other hand, many graduates attribute their ability to acquire better jobs to the education they received at these institutions. Some outside observers have credited the colleges with impressive results in reaching native people who are not served by mainstream American educational institutions. The education offered has a practical character because administrators see their roles as that of training professionals needed on reservations, and students focus on certain areas where they see genuine local job opportunities. According to Michael Mariott (1992: A13), "Topping the list are usually studies in land and resource management and human welfare and health services."

Summary

On reservations, the lives of Native Americans are shaped by the community, which is beset with many serious social problems. Native Americans' lives are also frequently characterized by internal conflict and dissent; corruption by tribal leaders is a common complaint and source of strain. Nonetheless, this is home to many, and the familiarity of the reservation provides a sense of security not found elsewhere. Those who have left the reservation in search of employment in cities often return because of the loss of a sense of community. The problems they hoped to escape often follow them to cities, while the benefits of communal life do not. The fate of those who do not return has not been studied much so at present we know very little about their circumstances. What we do know about reservation Native Americans is that they have not succeeded in becoming self-sufficient, so they continue to depend on the federal government playing a prominent role (Prucha, 1985: 103).

HISPANIC AMERICANS: INTO THE MAINSTREAM OR ON THE MARGINS?

11

The Hispanic population in the United States has grown dramatically since 1965 due to the combined impact of increased immigration levels and high fertility rates for most Hispanic groups. If these trends continue into the twenty-first century, demographers project that the Hispanic population will increase by almost 238 percent by the year 2050. The same projections place the African American population growth at just under 94 percent, so the net result is that the Hispanic population would exceed that of the African American by 2050. The projections for population increase among non-Hispanic whites is less than 30 percent, that of Native Americans is just a little more than 109 percent, and the Asian at more than 412 percent. Thus one consequence is that the nation would be less white than it is now (U.S. Bureau of the Census, 1992). In this new ethnic mix, Hispanics would be a more significant component of the population.

Hispanics tend to be regionally concentrated so they can have an even greater impact than they would if they were evenly dispersed throughout the country. The culture as well as the political and economic character of some cities, particularly Miami and Los Angles, have been profoundly altered by the Hispanic presence. Miami has become a truly bilingual city in only three decades, due primarily to the presence of Cubans. One consequence of this increase is that the city's black population is now a smaller percentage of the city's overall population than it was prior to 1960. The same transition has occurred in Los Angeles. The Hispanic — largely Mexican — population of Los Angeles County is now 38 percent, only 3 percentage points lower than the white population. The black population has declined to 11 percent.

Both Los Angeles and Miami have experienced major urban riots in recent years: Miami in 1980 and Los Angeles in 1992. Each riot revealed that, unlike the essentially black and white character of the urban disorders of the 1960s, other groups were involved as well. The event that triggered the uprising in Miami's Liberty City was a jury's innocent verdict in a case in which police officers had been accused of beating to death a black motorcyclist. A larger underlying factor was that many blacks in Miami felt that the expanded Cuban American presence in the region had been detrimental to black interests. The Los Angeles riot has been described as the nation's first multiracial riot, involving blacks, whites, Asians, and Hispanics. The role of Mexicans is complicated, but as in Miami, clearly many blacks in Los Angeles believe that their place in the region has been undermined by the growing Hispanic population.

All of this illustrates that the Hispanic presence in the United States is becoming more pronounced over time. For Mexicans, this has international implications because Mexico is one of the most important trade partners of the United States. The debate over the North American Free Trade Agreement is an indication of the crucial economic ties between the nations. The strengths or weaknesses of the economies of the two nations at any particular time have had a direct bearing on the number of Mexicans who emigrated to the United States, legally or illegally. U.S. corporations, however, have found it beneficial to set up shop in Mexican border communities, as part of the Border Industrialization Program. These are referred to as *maquiladora* industries. Typically, U.S. manufactured parts are shipped to the Mexican plants, which have much lower labor costs, for assembly. The plants are either owned by U.S. firms or by Mexican firms under contract to the American companies. *Maquiladora* industries began in the mid-1960s and employed more than a quarter million persons by the late 1980s (Stoddard, 1987; Heyman 1991).

Pan-Hispanic Unity or Ethnic Distinctiveness?

Two terms are commonly used to describe Spanish-speaking people from the western hemisphere: Hispanic and Latino. The latter term has been embraced most recently, especially by younger people who consider the term "Hispanic" to refer too directly to their descent from a colonized people. Some do not agree with this negative assessment and use the terms interchangeably. Both collective terms describe a number of highly diverse nationality groups. This chapter will focus on the three largest groups, which in descending order are Mexicans, Puerto Ricans, and Cubans. But these three do not encompass all of Hispanic America. Other Hispanic or Latino groups that, according to the 1990 census, have at least 75,000 persons include Dominicans, Salvadorans, Colombians, Guatemalans, Ecuadoreans, Nicaraguans, Peruvians, Hondurans, and Panamanians.

The federal government employs the Hispanic label when dividing the nation into major racial and ethnic groups. Some within the various Hispanic communities have promoted a panethnic identity, seeing this as the basis for a powerful political alliance. According to a survey conducted in 1989 and 1990 by the Latino National Political Survey, however, the majority of people surveyed defined their identities in terms of national place of origin and not in panethnic terms. Figure 11.1 illustrates this tendency, which is more pronounced for the immigrant generation than for subsequent generations. Mexicans born in the United States are most likely to use the label, but most individuals from the second and subsequent generations of both Puerto Ricans and Cubans choose to call themselves "American." David Gonzalez (1992a) found that Cubans were especially reluctant to lose their distinctive ethnic identity by using a panethnic label. Thus, he reports bumper stickers in Miami that read "No soy Hispano, soy Cubano" ("I am not Hispanic, I am Cuban").

The Bilingual Issue

After English, more people in the United States speak Spanish as a first language than any other language. In regions where Hispanics are concentrated, Spanish is not only spoken in the home, but can also be heard on the streets, in schools, in businesses, and in public facilities. Although the wave of immigration since 1965 has brought many other people who do not speak English or do not speak it as a first language — especially various Asian groups — the

Figure 11.1 *Self expressions among Hispanic groups.*

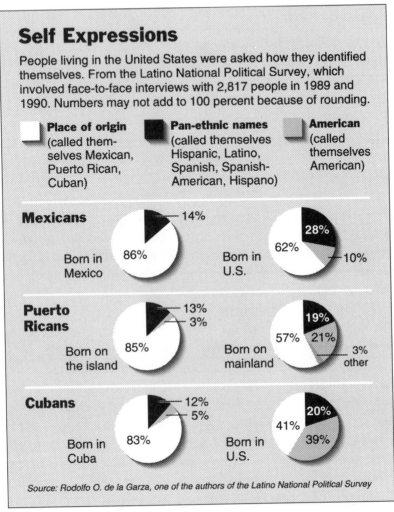

Self Expressions

People living in the United States were asked how they identified themselves. From the Latino National Political Survey, which involved face-to-face interviews with 2,817 people in 1989 and 1990. Numbers may not add to 100 percent because of rounding.

Place of origin (called themselves Mexican, Puerto Rican, Cuban)

Pan-ethnic names (called themselves Hispanic, Latino, Spanish, Spanish-American, Hispano)

American (called themselves American)

Mexicans

Born in Mexico — 86%, 14%

Born in U.S. — 62%, 28%, 10%

Puerto Ricans

Born on the island — 85%, 13%, 3%

Born on mainland — 57%, 19%, 21%, 3% other

Cubans

Born in Cuba — 83%, 12%, 5%

Born in U.S. — 41%, 20%, 39%

Source: Rodolfo O. de la Garza, one of the authors of the Latino National Political Survey

issue of bilingualism chiefly revolves around Spanish. In this context, it is worth noting that more people in the western hemisphere speak Spanish than speak English. This has led some nativists to raise fears that the privileged role of English in the United States is being placed in jeopardy by the "invasion" of new immigrants.

Since the 1960s, language rights have evolved, partly as a result of pressure from legislative and judicial changes. In 1968 Congress passed the Bilingual Education Act, which supported research into programs that would help school children with little or no English language proficiency. Two years later the Department of Health, Education, and Welfare issued a regulation related to Title VI of the Civil Rights Act of 1964. The regulation declared that if a student was not able to participate effectively in a school's educational programs because of English language deficiencies, the school district was required to implement actions designed to remedy the deficiency. In several judicial decisions, notably *Serna v. Portales Municipal Schools* (1974) and *Lau v. Nichols* (1974) the courts upheld these regulations, while failing to rule conclusively on whether there is a constitutional right to bilingual education (Piatt, 1990: 37–48).

Bilingual education programs have been in place for the past two decades. They have taken a variety of forms, ranging from intensive English immersion programs to academic courses taught in the native tongue while instruction to develop English language proficiency is provided. Whatever their form, the regulatory intent has been to help students make a transition to fluency in English. Although many proponents of bilingualism also sought to assist students in preserving their native tongue — thus becoming and remaining truly bilingual — this was not an explicit goal of such programs. Indeed, it was often assumed that in the long run, English would replace the native language. The implementation of bilingual programs has been extremely varied, and it is difficult to assess their effectiveness. Although much of the controversy over bilingualism has centered on education, language rights issues include the right to courtroom interpreters, the provision of multilingual voting ballots, the obligations of social service agencies to provide information in languages other than English, and broadcasting (Piatt, 1990).

A reaction to bilingualism began to mount by the late 1970s. A key demand of those opposed to bilingualism was for an amendment to the constitution that would declare English to be the official language of the United States. The organization chiefly responsible for spearheading this drive was U.S. English, founded by former U.S. Senator S.I. Hayakawa and Dr. John Tanton. The stated rationale was that the constitutional amendment would encourage assimilation. Spokespersons for U.S. English argued that proponents of bilingualism were hostile to assimilation and that this worked against the ability of non-English speaking immigrants to succeed economically in America. Such an amendment has been introduced into Congress in 1981, 1984, and 1988, and in each instance, it has been defeated. At the state level, however, "official English" legislation has been passed by 18 states.

Several prominent people served on the organization's board, including former television anchorperson Walter Cronkite, and it claimed a membership of 350,000. The group lost the endorsements of many earlier supporters, however, when it was revealed that Dr. Tanton had written in racist terms about the threat to the educated, English-speaking population from the rapid population growth of poor, uneducated non-English speaking people. To counter this perceived threat, he had advocated draconian measures to stop immigration and had proposed forced sterilization as a method of population control (Piatt, 1990: 20–23). Although earlier supporters then questioned the motives of U.S. English, many still continued to oppose bilingualism. Among them are some prominent individuals within the Hispanic community, including former Reagan aid Linda Chavez and writer Richard Rodriguez. Chavez (1991) considered the acquisition of English-language to be a prerequisite for poor Hispanics to move "out of the barrio."

This argument implies that it is necessary to learn English to succeed economically in America, and once you do speak the language, upward mobility will follow. Cubans are the most successful group, yet more than 46 percent of Cubans claim that they do not speak English well or at all. On the other hand, only 27 percent of Puerto Ricans, the poorest Hispanic group, claim that they don't speak English well (Bean and Tienda, 1987: 93). This suggests that much more than language determines the ability of ethnic groups to succeed in America. We shall explore some of the important factors that contribute to the differing experiences of the three largest Hispanic groups in the remainder of this chapter.

Cuban Americans

Cuba is only 90 miles from the U.S. coast, yet immigration levels remained relatively low until the 1950s. From the Spanish-American War in 1898 to 1959, Cuba was dependent on the United States, both politically and economically. The United States was responsible for ending Spanish control of Cuba, and subsequent Cuban governments relied heavily on American support. Although democratic government did not develop in Cuba, the economy developed throughout the first half of the twentieth century, which resulted in considerable foreign investment. It also permitted the growth of a class of wealthy entrepreneurs, many of whom created an essentially aristocratic lifestyle, and produced a middle class of small business people and educated professionals.

Although there was considerable poverty in Cuba because wealth was concentrated in a small segment of the population, Cuba was far from being the poorest of Caribbean nations. This is one major reason that immigration levels were so low until the late 1950s. Then, in little more than two decades—between the late 1950s and 1980—about 794,000 Cubans settled in the United States. The Cubans became the second largest Caribbean group to immigrate during this period, surpassed only by Puerto Ricans (Briquets and Perez, 1981: 26).

During the dictatorship of Fulgencio Batista, Cuba was perceived as a tourist mecca, especially for those interested in gambling. Organized crime elements from the United States developed a warm relationship with the Batista regime, which allowed the creation of casinos owned by crime syndicates. The regime was characterized by its corruption. Not surprising, this situation stimulated organized dissent to the dictatorship. During this time a revolutionary movement headed by Fidel Castro waged a guerrilla campaign against the dictatorship. Prior to the overthrow of the regime in 1959, the number of immigrants to the United States began to rise as conflict escalated. Among the arrivals during the 1950s were people seeking employment, as well as those who had run afoul of the dictatorship, and who were political exiles.

The number of people emigrating from Cuba rose dramatically after 1960, when the revolutionaries attempted to recast Cuban society into a Marxist one. They sought to pattern themselves after the Soviet Union, which became Cuba's main financial patron. In so doing, the revolutionary government found considerable support among the nation's working classes and poor and intense opposition from the upper and the middle classes. When it became clear that the regime would not create a liberal democracy, anticommunists sought political refuge, overwhelmingly in the United States. This is interesting because Cuban emigrants opted not to go to Spanish-speaking countries with similar cultures. In the three years between 1959 and 1962, 155,000 immigrants arrived in the

United States (Perez, 1980: 256; Daniels, 1990: 372–376). These immigrants came largely from the more privileged classes and included landed aristocrats, political elites, wealthy entrepreneurs, and many members of the professional middle classes. Not surprisingly, members of this phase of the Cuban migration were often referred to as the "Golden Exiles," although many immigrants were also from the lower-middle class or the working class.

This migration occurred during the height of the Cold War, and the presence of the Marxist government off the shore of Florida proved to be a powerful symbol of competing ideologies in the struggle between the United States and the Soviet Union. Thus, the U.S. government received these political exiles warmly. The relationship between the United States and Cuba soured quickly. On January 3, 1961, President Dwight Eisenhower severed diplomatic relations with the Castro regime, which did not stop the flow of out migration from Cuba. The Castro regime was ambivalent about emigration: The exodus of dissidents was a way of getting rid of potential troublemakers; however, the character of the migration resulted in a "brain drain" from the island nation (Boswell and Curtis, 1983: 47).

Many Cuban exiles thought that the Castro government could be toppled, and they hoped for a speedy return to their homeland. They viewed their stay in America as temporary so they can justifiably be seen as irredentists. Some in the exile community began conspiratorial plans to overthrow Castro, and in this they found support within the U.S. government, especially in the C.I.A. Clandestine groups mobilized with the ambition of retaking their island home. Such activities culminated in the early days of President Kennedy's administration with the ill-fated Bay of Pigs invasion of Cuba in April 1961. The failure of the Bay of Pigs attack led to the imprisonment of more than 1,000 of the invading force and proved to be a major foreign policy failure of the Kennedy administration (Boswell and Curtis, 1983: 7).

Tensions between Cuba and the United States escalated when intelligence sources discovered Soviet missiles on the island. When President Kennedy demanded that the Soviet Union remove the missiles, a major international confrontation occurred. Recently unclassified documents reveal that during the Cuban missile crisis, the world stood at the brink of a nuclear war between the superpowers. This tiny island loomed large in the history of the Cold

War, and, mainly for this reason, the Cuban immigrants in the United States were viewed far more positively than were their Hispanic counterparts from other countries.

One result of the missile crisis was the curtailment of air travel between Cuba and the United States and a suspension of legal emigration to the United States. This did not stop the exodus from Cuba, as more than 50,000 Cubans left between 1962 and 1965. Several thousand of them escaped to the mainland by boat or plane. The vast majority of those who left during these three years, however, did so by obtaining exit visas to third countries, the two most important of which were Mexico and Spain. This hiatus in legal migration ended in 1965 when Fidel Castro granted emigration rights to Cubans with relatives in the United States and flights between the two nations resumed. Flights continued until 1973, and during this time approximately 302,000 Cubans immigrated. They differed from those from the "Golden Exile" period: This group contained fewer middle-class professionals and considerably more lower-middle-class and working-class Cubans (Boswell and Curtis, 1983: 48–50). In contrast with the earlier arrivals, who were essentially political immigrants, economic considerations also played a role for these "Freedom Flight" immigrants.

From 1973 to 1979, the numbers of immigrants declined significantly — only 38,000 arrived during this entire period. Included were 3,600 political prisoners who were released from Cuban jails in 1978. The final phase of mass migration occurred in 1980 when approximately 125,000 Cubans departed from Cuba through the port of Mariel, and thus became known as the "Marielitos." Prior to this exodus the Cuban government had relaxed travel regulations by permitting visits of Cuban Americans to see family members. This was done to improve relations with the United States and to provide hard currency for the Cuban economy. An unintended consequence of this policy was that Cubans began to see first hand that those who had left the country were economically better off than those who remained. This fueled increased resentment toward the regime.

One response that had major international reverberations was that 11,000 Cubans sought refuge in the Peruvian embassy in Havana. This act triggered Castro's decision to allow emigration to the United States as a way of alleviating internal criticism. The large number of Cubans seeking to exit became an embarrassment for

Castro. He responded by including among the Marielitos a number of what he called "social undesirables," which included criminals, homosexuals, mental patients, and even some lepers (Boswell and Curtis, 1983: 51–57). One estimate of hard core criminals among this group was 5,000. The presence of these elements in this migration wave caused many Americans to respond unfavorably to their arrival, in stark contrast with the response to the arrival of the two earlier groups. Although the impact of social "undesirables" has often been overestimated, clearly the Marielitos differed from earlier arrivals in terms of social class, employment, and educational backgrounds. The Marielitos were poorer, with fewer occupational skills and lower educational attainment levels. The differences between early and later arrivals paralleled the changes that occurred among German immigrants in the last century.

Settlement Patterns

Cubans are a highly concentrated group geographically. Although Cubans can be found almost everywhere in the country, about 90 percent are found in only six states. Florida has about 60 percent of the total, and New Jersey ranks second with about 20 percent. Metropolitan Miami is the undisputed center of Cuban American life. Other cities that have received relatively large numbers of Cuban immigrants include New York City; Jersey City and Newark, New Jersey; Chicago; and Los Angeles. A substantial number of Cubans who first settled in other cities because of the refugee resettlement program eventually moved to Miami (Boswell and Curtis, 1983: 66–68).

More than 150,000 non-Cuban Hispanics reside in the Miami area; they come from Mexico, Puerto Rico, the Dominican Republic, and several countries in Central and South America. In addition, there may be as many as 50,000 French-speaking Caribbeans from Haiti. Cubans are by far the largest of the recent immigrant groups to the metropolitan area, however. At present, more than a half million Cubans live in the Miami area, and only Havana has more Cuban residents than Miami.

The result of this mass influx of newcomers is that Miami is now a genuinely multicultural and bilingual city. The 1990 census revealed that Hialeah (Florida) and Miami rank first and second in the nation in terms of the percentage of their populations that are

Figure 11.2 As the billboard attests, Miami is the undisputed capital of Cuban America.

Source: J. B. Diederich/Contact Press.

foreign born. For Hialeah the number is an astounding 70.4 percent, and for Miami it is 59.7 percent. In contrast, the figures for Los Angeles, New York, Chicago, and Detroit are, respectively, 38.4 percent, 28.4 percent, 16.9 percent, and 3.4 percent (U.S. Bureau of the Census, 1992: 11).

Prior to 1960, Miami was an aging tourist city, but the influx of immigrants from the Caribbean and Latin America has transformed not only Miami proper, but many surrounding communities in Dade County. Indeed, a mayor of Miami has described the city as a "boiling pot," and historian Raymond Mohl (1985: 52) considered the changes in this area to be a "twenty-year demographic revolution without precedent in American history."

Cubans are residentially concentrated in an area known as "Little Havana," a locality that extends outside of Miami proper to include other municipalities in Dade County. A once-declining section of the metropolitan area has been rejuvenated with the creation of the Cuban ethnic community. A rich and varied institutional structure created by the Cuban American community includes social halls, political organizations, mutual aid societies, newspapers, radio and television stations, and literally thousands of businesses. Most Cuban Americans are Roman Catholic, and the size of the local archdiocese has grown tremendously. Church-related organizations play a prominent role in the Cuban American community. Some Cubans, however, are practitioners of *santeria*, a syncretistic religious cult that links elements of African religions to Catholicism (Perez, 1980: 259). Evangelical Protestantism has also made some inroads into Cuban America.

The Enclave Economy

Many ethnic groups have established businesses that have proved to be highly profitable for the owners (Light, 1972; Waldinger, 1994). Edna Bonacich's (1973) "middleman minority" theory accounts for the success of these enterprises mostly because owners cooperate with other owners to limit competition and because the owners hire coworkers, to whom they pay low wages. Thus, in her view, ethnic economies can be avenues of success for ethnic entrepreneurs, but employees do not do as well as their counterparts in the larger or primary economy.

This argument was challenged by Kenneth Wilson and Alejandro Portes (1980), who, in a study of Cubans in Miami, argued that the "ethnic enclave economy" had not only proved to provide opportunities for entrepreneurial success, but also was beneficial to workers. They concluded that workers did as well working in the enclave economy as they would have done working outside. Although the argument has been questioned when applied to other groups, such as the Chinese, Mexicans, and blacks, it appears that for the Cubans, the ethnic enclave has been beneficial to both owners and workers (Wilson and Martin, 1982; Sanders and Nee, 1987; Portes and Jensen, 1989; Model, 1992). Portes and Stepick (1985) indicated that the existence of the ethnic enclave economy for Cubans in Miami and the lack of one for Haitians partially accounts for the fact that the former have fared better economically than the latter.

As early as 1972, Cubans owned more businesses than blacks in Miami, and the net worth of their enterprises was almost four times that of blacks. By the 1980s, the enclave economy consisted of more than 20,000 businesses. The vast majority were small businesses, including retail stores, gas stations, restaurants, cafes, pastry shops, pharmacies, and family-run grocery stores or *bodegas*. There are Cuban owned banks, construction companies, auto dealerships, and fishing fleets (Mohl, 1985: 57). As with Cubans in Tampa early in the century, Miami contains numerous cigar factories. The garment industry employs the largest number of people, however — approximately 25,000. Traditionalist family definitions historically kept women out of the work force, but more than half of Cuban American women work outside of the home. The garment industry attracts sizeable numbers of them (Sullivan, 1984). In addition, many import-export businesses have been established that have linked the enclave economy to Latin American markets. Finally, "Little Havana" contains thousands of white collar professionals, including doctors, pharmacists, lawyers, accountants, and the like.

The middle- and upper-class origins of the immigrants who arrived during the 1960s, combined with the impact of the enclave economy, make Cubans by far the most economically successful Hispanic group. In 1990, the average median household income for all Hispanics was $22,330, a figure well below the national median household income of $29,943. If we look at the median incomes of the largest Hispanic groups, the relative affluence of Cubans becomes apparent. Though lagging behind the national average, the Cuban figure of $25,900 is significantly higher than the Mexican, which is $22,439, and considerably higher than the Puerto Rican median, which is a low $16,169 (Current Population Reports, 1991c). Part of the reason for differences across Hispanic groups is the differing rates of female participation in the labor force. When compared with Mexicans, and especially Puerto Ricans, more Cuban households rely on two incomes than one. Some observers have concluded that at the individual level, Cuban American economic success has been somewhat exaggerated, but at the household level the success can be linked to what Perez (1986: 16) called the Cuban "family work ethic."

Political Participation

Cubans differ from other Hispanics both in levels of participation in politics and in their political orientations. Perhaps because Cubans view themselves as political refugees, and not economic migrants, they are considerably more active politically than other Hispanic groups. In contrast with Mexicans, Cubans have a high rate of naturalization, a prerequisite to involvement in American politics. In this regard, Cubans are more like recent Asian immigrants than other Hispanics (Puerto Rico is a special case because of the island's territorial status). Cubans also have a high rate of voter registration and turnout at elections (Portes and Mozo, 1985).

Cubans tend to be politically conservative. Their politics are shaped by their intense hostility to the Castro regime, so they have been fervently anticommunist. In contrast with Mexicans and Puerto Ricans, both of whom are overwhelmingly aligned with the Democratic party, Cuban Americans are chiefly identified with the Republican party. Although a relatively small immigrant group, the regional concentration of Cubans makes them a potent political force in southern Florida. It is estimated that Cuban Americans constitute 53 percent of all registered Republicans in the Miami area (Bouvier, 1992; 154). In Ronald Reagan's two presidential electoral victories, Cubans in Miami may have cast in excess of 90 percent of their votes for him. It is not surprising that the national Republican party has been quite active in its efforts to court this particular immigrant group.

At the local level, because Cubans have aligned themselves with conservative white business forces in the Miami area, tension exists between Cubans and blacks (Hero, 1992: 153–154). Many African Americans see the political ascendancy and economic advancement of Cubans to be at least in part at their expense. Thus, for example, as the city became bilingual, many jobs in the service sector, even low paying ones, often required Spanish language skills. The result was that employers often chose Hispanic applicants instead of blacks. The tension between blacks and Cubans took violent form in the 1980 Liberty City riot. In New York and New Jersey, where Cubans are a smaller part of the Hispanic population, they have tended not to enter into political alliances or coalitions with Puerto Ricans, Dominicans, or other Hispanic groups.

Are Cubans Assimilating?

As we have seen with other ethnic groups who have sizeable middle classes and have experienced upward mobility, the opportunities and temptations to assimilate increase over time. This may be the case with Cubans, but because they are only in the second generation, it is a bit early to discern with any precision what the future might hold.

Cubans in Miami have a vibrant ethnic community, so they are able to preserve much of their culture and to contain most of their social relations to the ethnic community. Thus, the ethnic community can serve as a buffer to prevent rapid assimilation. Cubans in other parts of the country, where the ethnic communities are not as large or institutionally complete, show greater indications of assimilationist tendencies. But even in Miami, considerable generational change can be seen. The second generation uses English with far greater ease than did their parents. The transition to English is being accomplished by the mixture of the two languages into something referred to as "Spanglish." Younger Cubans have greater opportunities to interact with Anglos, especially in school. For those who go to college, and this group is growing, interpersonal relations outside of the Cuban community increase.

Even within the ethnic community, cultural change is seen. As we have noted, the role of women in the workforce challenged traditional family definitions. In addition, courtship practices have been liberalized. Young Cubans are no longer required to have chaperones when they go on dates, though Cuban Americans still have lower levels of premarital sexual intimacy than do Anglos and other Hispanics. Cuban families have relatively low fertility rates compared with the rates that characterized pre-Castro Cuba. Finally, exogamous marriages have begun to increase. Thus, Cuban Americans appear to be between two worlds: poised in many respects to enter the mainstream, while seeking to preserve not only their individual ethnic identities, but their ethnic community as well.

Puerto Ricans

Despite the fact that Puerto Rico is close to the U.S. mainland and the island's residents have had citizenship rights since 1917, which permitted unrestricted migration, mass migration from the island did not occur until after World War II. Because of their legal status as citizens, Puerto Ricans are not, strictly speaking, immigrants. One consequence of their distinctive status is that a "circular migration," or movement back and forth between the mainland and the island has been very common (Kitano, 1991: 146). The relatively few Puerto Ricans in the country prior to World War II included a substantial percentage of political exiles, including socialists and nationalists. Mass migration was shaped largely by economic, and not political, factors, however. The economic stimulus to migrate was also influenced by demographic change. During the first four decades of the twentieth century, Puerto Rico's population doubled (Moore and Pachon, 1985: 32). This overwhelmed the job market, contributed to poverty and unemployment, and served as a powerful incentive to emigrate.

Puerto Rico's status as a colony of the United States meant that for several decades its rulers and laws were imposed by the federal government. The president appointed the governor of the island, and all laws were established by the U.S. Congress. During the first several decades of U.S. rule, peasants and small farmers (*jibaros*) lost much of the land they had held in the nineteenth century to large corporations that produced export crops, the most important being tobacco, coffee, and sugar. A professional class of *criollos* emerged that had ties to American corporations and was an important component of the island's population that supported the American presence. Ultimately, the island was primarily associated with one major export crop that was grown on large plantations owned by U.S. agricultural companies: sugar (Mintz, 1960). Poverty and debt were endemic features of life for the peasantry. The subsistence economy eroded as agricultural production became geared toward international markets. Thus, Puerto Rico lacked not only political autonomy, but economic independence, as well.

During the New Deal era, progressive reformer Rexford Tugwell was appointed governor of Puerto Rico by Franklin D. Roosevelt. Unlike his predecessors, Tugwell encouraged economic development. He saw a need for reforms of the agrarian economy and encouraged investment in industrial development. Tugwell's tenure as governor extended until 1946, when a Puerto Rican was chosen for the position. In 1947 Congress passed the Elective Governors Act, which granted to Puerto Ricans the right to choose their own governor. The following year Luis Muñoz Marin became the first elected governor. Congress permitted the island's residents to draft their own constitution and redefined Puerto Rico as a commonwealth (Daniels, 1990: 320–322). Although this newly defined relationship with the United States did result in greater political autonomy, it was not without critics. Some residents wanted statehood, while others sought to create an independent nation. In 1952, radical nationalists attempted to assassinate President Harry S Truman, and others fired shots in the U.S. House of Representatives.

Advocates of independence constitute a small minority of Puerto Ricans. For example, in a plebiscite held in 1967, less than 1 percent of voters supported the cause of nationhood. Statehood proponents have considerably more support, but in the same plebiscite, they mustered only 39 percent of the vote, while 60 percent of Puerto Ricans preferred to maintain their commonwealth status. One reason for this outcome is that their commonwealth status means individuals and businesses do not have to pay federal income taxes. This status does, however, set limits to political empowerment. So, for example, Puerto Ricans serve in the U.S. military (and when there was conscription, were subject to the draft), but they cannot vote for president. Although they elect a Resident Commissioner to the House of Representatives, that person does not have voting rights.

Tugwell's desire to bring industry to Puerto Rico was shared by Muñoz, who initiated "Operation Bootstrap" in an attempt to introduce industry to the island, especially to areas that suffered from chronic poverty. This program was in effect from 1948 to 1965 and promoted industrialization at the expense of reforms in the agricultural sector. The result was rapid social change, including the precipitous drop in the percentage of people employed in agriculture, from 50 percent in 1940 to only 10 percent by 1970. Lured by tax incentives and the prospect of a cheap labor force, multinational corporations flocked to Puerto Rico after World War II. Leading the way were U.S. corporations, which by 1970 owned 80 percent of all industrial enterprises (Bonilla and Campos, 1981). With industrialization came rapid urbanization. The middle class grew, as did a huge government bureaucracy that employed 30 percent of the workforce by the mid-1970s.

Despite these profound changes, unemployment grew. Industrial jobs did increase, but they only kept pace with the growth of the working age population. The decline in agricultural jobs meant that unemployment increased rather than decreased. One response to these social and economic dislocations was emigration to the mainland. That began in the late 1940s and became a mass exodus in the 1950s (Mills, et al., 1950; Senior, 1965). Bean and Tienda (1987: 24) observed, "So intense was the outflow of wage laborers that during the 1950s Puerto Rico provided the unusual spectacle of a booming economy with a shrinking labor force."

Settlement Patterns

During the 1940s, the annual number of Puerto Ricans who migrated was 18,700. In the following decade that number soared to 41,200 people per year—the peak of migration. By 1960 there were approximately 900,000 Puerto Ricans on the mainland. In the 1960s the annual rate of migration fell to 14,500. In 1970 there were 1,429,396 Puerto Ricans on the mainland, there were 2,013,945 in 1980, and the most recent census figures put the number at 1,955,323. This slight decline during the past decade indicates a return migration has been occurring in recent years (U.S. Bureau of the Census, 1992; Sánchez-Ayéndez, 1988: 176).

New York is to Puerto Ricans what Miami is to Cubans: the mainland location of choice. Although at least 75,000 Puerto Ricans are found as far west as California, and in Illinois, Florida, Pennsylvania, and Massachusetts, the heaviest concentration is in the greater New York area, which extends into New Jersey and Connecticut. Sizeable Puerto Rican communities have been created in a number of cities in this northeastern region, including Newark, Jersey City, and Patterson in New Jersey and Bridgeport and Hartford in Connecticut. By 1970, however, two-thirds of all Puerto Ricans resided in New York City. Since then New York Puerto Ricans have dispersed to other communities, but still approximately half of all Puerto Ricans on the mainland live in that city (U.S. Bureau of the Census, 1992; Sowell, 1981: 232).

The earliest arrivals concentrated in the section of Manhattan that became known as Spanish Harlem (Sexton, 1966; Glazer and Moynihan, 1963). Harlem had become the large black ghetto in that borough of New York City, so Puerto Ricans lived in close proximity to African Americans. Over time, Puerto Ricans also established enclaves in the South Bronx and Brooklyn. In contrast with Cubans, immigrants from Puerto Rico were quite poor. They were generally peasants or young urban dwellers without prior experience in urban industries, and thus without specialized skills that provided opportunities for economic advancement. In addition, the migration flow also lacked a significant middle class. As a result, unlike Cubans, Puerto Ricans did not develop an enclave economy.

Economic Status

Instead, Puerto Ricans found work outside of the barrio. They were highly concentrated in low-paying blue collar jobs and often found jobs working in service industries such as hotels, restaurants, and hospitals as bellboys, busboys, dishwashers, and orderlies. Many men found employment in industry as assembly-line operatives, while women early on found jobs in the garment industry. This changed over time as many textile firms left the Northeast in search of cheaper labor forces, either in the South or overseas. By the late 1970s, Puerto Rican women began to enter the clerical and sales workforces (Sowell, 1981: 236–237; Feagin, 1984: 305).

Puerto Ricans on the mainland have not fared well economically. Not only are they the poorest of the Hispanic groups, but they have lower median incomes than blacks living in close proximity to them. Only Native Americans have a lower median income than Puerto Ricans. Moreover, given that Puerto Ricans live in cities where the cost of living is high, they have persistently been over-represented in the ranks of the poor. The Puerto Rican unemployment rate has over time exceeded the national rate, even exceeding the 20 percent mark at times during the 1980s. There are several reasons for chronic unemployment, underemployment, and poverty. The immigrants' lack of human and financial capital put them at a disadvantage from the beginning. High school dropout rates and a lack of adequate occupational training compounded this problem.

The Role of Race

Another compounding factor is racial discrimination. Puerto Ricans frequently compete with African Americans for jobs, and it might have been assumed that the former would have fared better because the latter confronted racial discrimination in hiring practices. However, this has not been the case because many Puerto Ricans have been doubly stigmatized as black Hispanics. Like many other Caribbeans, Puerto Ricans have historically treated race in terms of color gradations and have not employed the stark black-white dichotomy that has characterized American race relations (Denton and Massey, 1989). They use various terms that recognize color gradations, such as *pardo*, *moreno*, *mulatto*, and *trigueño*. Clara Rodriguez (1989: 52) differentiated the Puerto Rican and the American perspectives by observing:

> In Puerto Rico, racial classification was subordinate to cultural identification, while in the United States, racial identification, to a large extent, determined cultural identification. Thus, Puerto Ricans were first Puerto Ricans, then blanco/a (white), moreno/a (black), and so on, while Americans were first White or Black, then Italian, Irish, West Indian, or whatever.

That American society did not take account of color gradations frequently came as a shock to Puerto Ricans. This is vividly illustrated in Piri Thomas's *Down These Mean Streets* (1967), an autobiographical account of growing up in a world of crime and drugs in East Harlem. He recalled the following scene from prison: Engaged in a conversation with a fellow Puerto Rican in the lunch line, Thomas failed to realize that there were two lines, one for whites and one for blacks. The shock of being defined as black occurred when a prison guard pushed him into the black line and the other Puerto Rican into the white line. Thomas recounts that this externally imposed racial definition resulted in considerable confusion about his sense of self-identity and left him with a simmering rage at the American racial order.

The precise extent to which racial discrimination in hiring has impeded Puerto Rican economic advancement is difficult to measure. Some evidence suggests that those with darker skin have not fared as well as those with lighter skin, and the *trigueños* in the middle find that they confront considerable ambiguity about their racial standing (Fitzpatrick, 1987: 104–116; Rodriguez, 1989). Moreover, at least one study suggested that darker-skinned Puerto Ricans, due to their greater marginality, are more likely to be involved in crime and various forms of deviant behavior (Berle, 1959).

Ethnic Competition for Jobs

Between 1970 and 1985 the economic position of Puerto Ricans deteriorated dramatically. At the same time, the economic well-being of Mexicans showed small improvements, while Cubans experienced considerable improvement (Tienda, 1989: 106; Ortiz, 1986).

Figure 11.3 *A Puerto Rican school organization in East Harlem (photograph by Leonard Covello).*

Source: Leonard Covello Photographs. The Balch Institute Research Library.

One contributing factor is variations in regional economic conditions. The heavy concentration of Puerto Ricans in the northeastern states placed them in declining cities in the Rust Belt. As the industrial bases of these cities have declined, hundreds of thousands of unskilled and skilled union jobs have disappeared.

Marta Tienda (1989: 108) pointed out that Puerto Ricans have never been singled out as preferred workers in particular jobs (in contrast, for example, with Mexicans in agriculture), and this puts them at a distinct disadvantage when job shortages occur. Comparatively lower levels of educational achievement and other aspects of human capital have translated into a competitive disadvantage in comparison with other groups. Thus, blacks and Cubans have fared better than Puerto Ricans in this region.

In New York City the character of the Hispanic population has changed in the past two decades. First, it has grown from 16.3 percent in 1970 to 24.4 percent in 1990. Although 20 years ago the overwhelming majority of Hispanics were Puerto Rican, they now compose only about half of the city's total Hispanic population. This is due to the rise in immigration—legal and illegal—of Central and South Americans. The Dominicans are by far the largest of the newer arrivals in New York. They rank second in size to Puerto Ricans—332,713 in contrast with the 1990 census figure of 896,763 for Puerto Ricans. Puerto Ricans often view the new arrivals as rivals for jobs and political influence. Part of the tension between Puerto Ricans and Dominicans is because the latter appear to be doing better economically, despite their relatively short stay in America. David Gonzalez (1992b: A–11) observed that though both groups "live on the struggling side of success, the Dominicans have made substantial economic progress in a single entrepreneurial generation, buying up bodegas, restaurants, and livery-cab fleets around the city."

The Impact of Return Migration

The inability to gain a solid foothold in the American economy has prompted increasing numbers of Puerto Ricans to return to the island. Since the 1970s, the earlier circular migration has been replaced by a growing return migration. Those who return tend to be from two sectors of the ethnic community: older Puerto Ricans who want to spend their remaining years in their birthplace and younger Puerto Ricans who confront the highest levels of unemployment. The young returnees are primarily men (Sánchez-Ayéndez, 1988: 176).

The decline in the number of young men relative to women can help explain the high proportion of female-headed households. The 53.3 percent figure of out-of-wedlock births is higher than for other Hispanic groups, second only to African Americans, and far exceeds the 14.9 percent for European Americans. In addition, Puerto Rican women have a lower level of participation in the labor force than other groups, so they are forced to rely solely on government assistance to a greater extent than other groups. The contrast between Puerto Ricans and blacks indicates that while 66 percent of Puerto Rican women are not in the labor force, only 49 percent of black women are not. Moreover, while only 28 percent of black female-headed households rely solely on public assistance, the number is 57 percent for Puerto Ricans (Falcon, Gurak, and Powers,

1990; Rodriguez, 1989: 32–34). This contributes significantly to the extremely low median income of Puerto Ricans noted earlier.

The Ethnic Community

Given the limited resources that immigrants brought with them and the relative lack of economic success of Puerto Ricans on the mainland, it is not surprising that the ethnic community is more fragile and less institutionally complete than that created by most other groups. The ability to return to Puerto Rico with ease also weakened the ethnic community; people ambivalent about whether to remain on the mainland or return to the island are less likely to commit resources to institution building. Despite these limitations, however, an ethnic community has emerged.

A central feature of the community has been the role played by the family. In Puerto Rico, prior to changes brought about by Operation Bootstrap, the extended family was of central importance. Today the nuclear family has become more important, especially in child rearing. The role played by "fictive kin," people who, though not related to a family, will informally adopt children during periods of family crisis (Sánchez-Ayéndez, 1988: 176–178) is significant. Further changes in family composition occurred on the mainland. Fitzpatrick (1987: 74) identified four types of household structures among Puerto Rican Americans. In addition to the modified extended family (where relatives such as grandparents may live in the household or in close proximity) and the nuclear family, he added two others: (1) blended families, where two parents are present, but some of the children are biologically related to only one of the parents; and (2) female-headed households. The family, regardless of type, was viewed by Sánchez-Ayéndez (1988: 186) as the "primary support system for first- and second-generation Puerto Ricans in the United States."

Like the Mexicans earlier, informal self-help organizations — ranging from social clubs and after-hour clubs to athletic clubs for youth — have played an important role in assisting immigrants to adjust to their new environment. In addition, a number of formal organizations have been created, many initiated by members of the relatively small middle class. Most are local rather than national in scope. Among the most established organizations in New York are the Puerto Rican Merchants' Association, the Puerto Rican Forum, Aspira (an agency promoting higher education), the Puerto Rican Community Development Fund, a social service agency staffed largely by Puerto Rican social workers called the Puerto Rican Family Institute, and the Puerto Rican Legal Defense and Education Fund. Some of these organizations, as well as the National Puerto Rican Coalition founded to lobby in Washington, operate at the national level (Fitzpatrick, 1987: 47–58; Padilla, 1987).

Puerto Ricans are nominally Roman Catholic, but their religious practice is that of a nontraditional folk religion, an amalgam of orthodox Catholicism and various forms of personalistic saint worship and spiritualism. Puerto Ricans have not been as committed to the institutional church as have some groups. On the mainland, they have tended to feel marginalized from American Catholicism due to its domination by Anglos. In the early years, most Puerto Rican parishes did not have Spanish-speaking priests, and though the church has changed this practice, this has not resulted in most Puerto Rican parishes being served by Puerto Rican priests. Many priests serving predominantly Puerto Rican congregations are Spanish-speaking Anglos. No prominent Puerto Rican clergy have risen to the rank of bishop (Daniels, 1990: 325). No more than one-third of Puerto Ricans on the mainland are estimated to be members of Catholic congregations, while perhaps an additional 6 percent have joined various Protestant denominations (Fitzpatrick, 1987: 136). In other words, a majority of Puerto Ricans are not involved with the institutional church. The church does have an important but somewhat limited role in the community.

Puerto Ricans have not created newspapers to the extent that most ethnic groups have. In fact, the main newspapers serving the Puerto Rican community in New York, including the influential *El Diario,* have not been owned or controlled by Puerto Ricans. Puerto Ricans have been involved in Spanish-language radio programming, and the availability of Spanish-language programming has been an important source for creating and sustaining group identity. More recently, two Cuban-owned television stations have provided Spanish-language programming. For both radio and television, the programming is intended for all Hispanics rather than specifically for Puerto Ricans (Fitzpatrick, 1987: 59–60).

Some of the community's institutions were created with outside funding, and they were dependent for their existence on the continuation of such funding. This was especially true during the War on Poverty in the 1960s, when neighborhood organizations were created with money from the federal government. This reliance on outside financial support is evident in a number of ways. For example, in a comparison of Polish and Puerto Rican participation in an ethnic parade in Philadelphia, Jo Anne Schneider (1990) noted that while the Polish parade committee was self-supporting, the Puerto Rican group relied on contributions from such corporate donors as Goya, Coca Cola, McDonald's, and American Airlines. In addition, indicating the Puerto Rican community's concerns about major social problems, their parade contingent included messages such as "Say No to Drugs" and "To Read Is Power." Schneider noted that while the sole focus of the Polish parade contingent was on ethnic pride, a major thrust of the Puerto Ricans revolved around issues related to impoverishment: unemployment, crime, drugs, the lack of day care, and so forth.

Integration or Isolation?

Some ethnic groups have used politics as a means to establish contacts with the larger society and improve the circumstances of group members. Political involvement has had a limited impact on Puerto Ricans so far, however. They have been somewhat slow to become actively involved in politics. In the past, the major political parties ignored this potential voting bloc. The 1960s marked a period of greater political involvement, and as a leadership stratum arose, sometimes emerging from the training ground of the period's antipoverty programs, Puerto Rican leaders have been courted by local political parties. Puerto Ricans are primarily affiliated with the Democratic party. Though they remain underrepresented in elective offices and political appointments in New York City, their numbers have increased in recent years. The future is unclear, especially because Puerto Ricans are now a smaller part of Hispanic New York than in the past. In cities where they constitute a smaller percentage of the overall urban population, they are even less politically influential, though, there is evidence of increased involvement in local and state politics, particularly in northeastern cities such as Hartford and Bridgeport, Connecticut, and Newark and Patterson, New Jersey (Hero, 1992; Moore and Pachon, 1985: 189–191).

Relations with other Hispanics and blacks have frequently been strained. Social interaction with Anglos is frequently limited, partly due to residential segregation. Thus, Puerto Ricans are far more marginalized and isolated from the rest of American society than Cubans. Nonetheless, those born on the mainland—the second generation—are beginning the process of creating an identity that reflects that their home is on the mainland and not back in Puerto Rico (Flores, 1985). In New York the second generation has been referred to as the "Nuyoricans," which shows the significance of New York City in the evolution of their definition of ethnic identity.

Unlike Cubans, Puerto Ricans are not poised to enter the mainstream. This is primarily because they have not been sufficiently successful economically to establish the preconditions for ending their marginality.

Mexican Americans

As the Mexican American community evolved and its middle class expanded, immigration also continued. The Mexican American population continued to be extremely fluid and highly diverse, complicated by the continuous arrival of newcomers. Mexican America is unique in this regard (Kerr, 1984; Burma, 1954). After World War II, Mexicans continued to enter the United States, attracted to higher wages than were available at home. The immigrants included both legal and undocumented individuals. An important component of this wave of immigration were those involved in the bracero program, which continued after the war. Although the need for workers in defense industries had ended, the bracero program continued to supply contract laborers to employers, especially in agriculture. For example, by the end of the 1950s, 75 percent of sugar beets and 90 percent of cucumbers were being harvested by braceros (Valdes, 1991: 142). Many Mexican Americans felt that they had been displaced by braceros in these jobs, and thus a demand to abolish the program gained support within the Mexican American community. The program was finally terminated in 1964, but by then the number of new braceros was quite small.

Immigrant workers were particularly vulnerable to changes in the economy. They were welcomed when there was a demand for labor, but when their labor was not needed, as during the Depression, pressures mounted to deport them. Migratory push forces mounted in Mexico during the late 1940s and early 1950s. The population of the nation grew rapidly. Many Mexicans migrated to cities along the U.S. border, and from there many were attracted to the higher wages north of the border.

The dramatic increase in migration during this period was met with demands to restrict immigration. In 1954 the government initiated Special Force Operation — more popularly known as "Operation Wetback" — to stop illegal entry into the country. Wetback was a slang term for Mexicans who had entered the country illegally by crossing the Rio Grande River. To curtail such activities, the federal government began rounding up and repatriating undocumented aliens. In addition to those who had recently arrived in the country, many long-term residents were also detected. Many legal aliens were also rounded up, thereby creating fear and anger in the Mexican American community. During the two-year period ending in 1956, the Immigration and Naturalization Service sought the deportation of 3.8 million Mexicans. Although only 63,000 were officially deported, more than one million returned voluntarily to avoid deportation proceedings (Stoddard, 1973: 26; Barrera, 1985).

By the end of the 1950s, the Mexican population in the United States had been reduced considerably; most who remained dated either their residency or that of their family to no later than the 1920s. In other words, the most recent arrivals had returned to Mexico. This situation did not continue, however, as the net flow of immigration increased in the 1970s and 1980s. For example, the number of resident aliens with permanent status who arrived during the 1970s was approximately 640,000, nearly triple that of two decades earlier (Daniels, 1990: 311).

The number of illegal aliens who entered the country during the past two decades is difficult to ascertain. Many enter for short periods of time before returning to Mexico. Some come and go frequently. Government estimates of illegal aliens have suggested that the numbers may be as high as 6 to 8 million, and one estimate even put the figure at 10 to 12 million. These are politically motivated estimates designed to mobilize public sentiment about the presumed problem of illegal immigration. More careful demographic estimates put the figure at between one and three million. A careful analysis of existing data by demographer David Heer (1990: 51) resulted in an estimate of about 1.8 million undocumented Mexicans. Although these aliens can be found throughout the United States, they are heavily concentrated in the border states from Texas to California.

Organized campaigns to control illegal immigration gained momentum during the 1970s and early 1980s. Legislation was proposed in Congress to reform current policies. Originally introduced by Republican Senator Alan Simpson and Democratic Representative Romano Mazzoli in 1982, a bill that was intended to give the federal government more power to control movement across the border was highly controversial. Mexican American groups, spearheaded by the League of United Latin American Citizens (LULAC) and the Mexican American Legal Defense Educational Fund (MALDEF), mobilized to defeat it. They contended that if enacted the law would increase discrimination against all Hispanics, not only undocumented immigrants. Moreover, they argued that illegals had rights that would likely be violated. The proposed bill had foreign policy implications after the Mexican Senate registered its concerns about the legislation (DeConde, 1992: 162–163; Gutierrez, 1991).

Nonetheless, prompted by President Reagan's claim that it was imperative that the United States regain control of its borders, a modified version of the bill, known as the Immigration Reform and Control Act, became law in 1986. It was the result of a delicate compromise that was designed to appease several interests and audiences simultaneously. The act did give the government greater power to control the Mexican border and also provided for a temporary-worker program, a key concern of the southwest's agribusinesses. One provision imposed sanctions on employers who employed illegal immigrants. To placate the opposition to the bill coming primarily from the Mexican American community, the act established an amnesty program. The program granted legal residency to all undocumented Mexicans who could prove that they had resided in the United States since January 1, 1982 (Hero, 1992: 170–171). To date, the precise impact of the law is difficult to determine.

It is also difficult to determine the impact of illegal immigration on the U.S. economy. Critics contended that illegal immigrants have a negative impact because they tend to drive down wages and they place additional financial burdens on public institutions such as schools. This has been challenged by economist George Borjas (1990), however, who argued that immigrants do not lower earnings or reduce employment opportunities. Lawrence Fuchs argued that undocumented workers actually create additional jobs. Douglas Massey noted that without illegal immigrants, some businesses, including the garment industry, would probably relocate to a third-world country (CQ Researcher, 1992; Bouvier, 1992; Thomsen, 1993).

Chicano Politics

From the 1940s to the 1960s, Mexican Americans became more politically assertive and, especially in the Southwest, began to demand an enhanced role in local and regional politics. Reformers pressed for the election of Mexican American officials to city councils, school boards, state legislatures, and so forth. Although the number of Mexican American elected officials did increase during the 1950s and 1960s, the numbers remained comparatively low. One reason was the persistence of discrimination. Another reason was that Mexicans were somewhat slow to become naturalized citizens and were thus ineligible to vote.

LULAC continued to play a key role in efforts to end discrimination and to achieve economic equal opportunity. LULAC grew from only 46 local councils in 1932 to more than 150 by 1960. Other older groups, such as the Congress of Spanish-Speaking People and the Alianza Hispano-Americano, declined in significance, but were replaced by new organizations. One of the most important civil rights organizations to emerge after World War II was the American G.I. Forum, which was founded in 1948 after a funeral home in Three Rivers, Texas, refused to provide burial services for Felix Longoria, a Mexican American veteran (Green, 1992). Mexican Americans who had served in the armed forces during the war expected past discrimination to end. When it was apparent that past inequities had not ended, Mexican American veterans used patriotic symbols in their efforts to combat discrimination against them (Hero, 1992: 76; Gomez-Quiñones, 1990: 60–63; Stoddard, 1973: 188–189).

At the same time, the Catholic church became more involved in the Mexican American community, promoting church-related activities that were designed to instill lessons in religion, ethics, and civic participation. Although the conservative sector of the Catholic church was especially concerned about the impact of atheistic communism on poor Mexicans, the more liberal elements in the church began to involve themselves in social reform. Liberals sought to alleviate the social problems besetting the Mexican American community (Gomez-Quiñones, 1990: 64).

Some new organizations focused their energies on explicitly political objectives. Among the most important were the Los Angeles–based Community Service Organization (CSO), the Mexican American Political Association (MAPA), the Political Association of Spanish-Speaking Organizations (PASSO), and the American Coordinating Council on Political Education (ACCPE). Voter registration drives, promoting Mexican American candidates for elective offices, and endorsing various Anglo politicians seen as sympathetic to Mexican Americans constituted the major activities of these organizations (Moore, 1970).

A campaign in Crystal City, Texas, served as a symbol of the new ethnic politics. In this relatively small city of 10,000, the 25 percent of the population that was Anglo controlled the city both politically and economically, excluding from effective political participation the 75 percent of the population that was Mexican. This changed in 1963, when a slate of working-class Mexicans, endorsed by MAPA, won a landslide victory. The tensions in the community prior to the election were high, and Texas Rangers were dispatched to the city at the request of Anglo politicians. Mexicans saw their presence as an attempt to intimidate Mexicans from going to the polls. The election received national attention, for it was the first time in the state's history that Mexican Americans had elected candidates from their community through the conventional political process (Stoddard, 1973: 190–194).

Mexicans were overwhelmingly identified with the Democratic party. In his presidential campaign, John F. Kennedy actively courted the Mexican American vote, seeing it as a potentially important voting bloc in some key electoral states, particularly Texas and California. Many middle-class Mexicans were actively involved in Viva Kennedy clubs. Nationally, Kennedy received approximately 85 percent of the Mexican vote (Gomez-Quiñones, 1990: 91).

These political developments were not without problems. Many organizations suffered from internal conflict and from a lack of effective leaders. For example, the Mexican slate in Crystal City was voted out of office in 1965, and many local chapters of political action organizations were relatively short-lived. Although Mexican Americans made gains during the 1950s and 1960s in education, employment, status, and political representation, they were far from reaching parity with Anglo Americans. Historian Juan Gomez-Quiñones (1990: 99) contended that because of the even greater gains in these areas experienced by Anglos, the gulf between the two may have increased. The optimistic expectations of the immediate postwar years gave way to bitterness and to a growing surge of militancy. Developments during the tumultuous decade of the 1960s have clear parallels with political activities in both the black and the Native American communities.

The movement that received the most widespread media attention nationally was the United Farm Workers (UFW), led by the CSO-trained Cesar Chavez. Like Martin Luther King, Chavez advocated nonviolence, but his organization was not strictly a civil rights organization like the Southern Christian Leadership Conference. Rather, it was a labor union that sought to unite Mexicans with other exploited laborers, including Filipinos, whites, and others.

Beginning in 1965, the UFW targeted selected large agribusiness concerns in California. It used strikes (*La Huelga*) and consumer boycotts — of lettuce and grapes — in an effort to obtain union recognition by growers and to end a century of "harvests of shame." Emerging at the height of the civil rights and the antiwar movements, the UFW presented itself as an organization of high moral purpose and was quite successful in its effort to convey a favorable image of its cause in the mass media. The UFW received the support of several prominent liberal politicians on the national level, including Robert F. Kennedy and George McGovern, and Jerry Brown at the state level. It was also endorsed by the AFL-CIO. Powerful opponents of the UFW included the Teamsters' Union and Ronald Reagan (who at one point referred to striking workers as "barbarians") when he was governor of California. The UFW succeeded in obtaining union recognition from several major growers and entered into contract negotiations with them (Majka and Majka, 1982). Similar drives were initiated in other parts of the country, often with the support of the AFL-CIO (Valdes, 1991).

During the same time period, more militant voices developed a new ethnic political expression that became known as *Chicanismo*. By identifying with the term Chicano, which up to the 1960s had been a derogatory expression applied to unskilled Mexican laborers, Mexicans fostered a positive collective self-image. This was intended to directly challenge the negative imagery harbored by many Anglos and was based on the conviction that Mexican Americans were the victims of conquest — not only economically exploited, but also suffering from political oppression and deculturation. The Chicano movement addressed all three of these problems. The cultural aspect entailed an effort to recover and preserve the ancestral culture. In promoting this project, movement adherents were hostile to assimilationists. Moreover, by stressing the importance of *la raza* ("the people"), they emphasized collective goals rather than individual upward mobility (Moore and Pachon, 1985: 182–183; Melville, 1983; Gutierrez and Hirsch, 1970; Steiner, 1970).

An urban expression of Chicano politics emerged in Denver under the leadership of Rodolfo ("Corky") Gonzales, who had gained familiarity with city politics through his work in Great Society antipoverty programs. Gonzales founded a civil rights organization called the Crusade for Justice, which sought to end discrimination in employment and housing. The Crusade for Justice organized a strike of high-school students to protest the lack of attention paid to the special needs of Spanish-language students and also focused attention on police brutality. Many of the activists were young, including college and high-school students as well as student dropouts. This was the case with other organizations, such as the United Mexican American Students (UMAS), the Mexican American Youth Organization (MAYO), and the Brown Berets, a militant organization that modeled itself after the Black Panthers (Gomez-Quiñones, 1990: 101–153; Moore and Pachon, 1985: 182).

Another manifestation of the decade of dissent was the short-lived career of the *Alianza Federal de Mercedes* (Federal Alliance of Land Grants), founded in 1963 by the former Pentecostal preacher Reies Lopez Tijerina. The *Alianza* sought to reclaim land for Mexicans that it believed had been taken from them illegally. Tijerina engaged in political theater when he and his supporters seized a section of New Mexico's Kit Carson National Park and used this dramatic event to call attention to the history of land expropriation by Anglos. Although this event resulted in a negotiated settlement that conceded some of the park's land to 75 Hispanic families, the *Alianza's* protests also resulted in violence, including a 1967 shootout between activists and the police at the Tierra Amarilla courthouse. Tijerina was convicted of destruction and assaulting law officers and was sent to prison for two years. Without his charismatic leadership, the *Alianza* began to crumble, and when Tijerina was released he no longer wanted to run the organization he had founded (Gomez-Quiñones, 1990: 115–118).

In numerous southwestern communities with large Mexican populations, separatists conducted third-party election campaigns under the banner of *La Raza Unida*, and, as in Crystal City, achieved some level of success. This prompted a number of Chicanos to attempt to establish a national, ethnically-based third party. *La Raza Unida's* political ideology was separatist, though its decision to be involved in conventional electoral politics moderated its militant tendencies. Like the more local efforts described earlier, the party declined in significance after the early 1970s, and by 1980 it was no longer a political force (Moore and Pachon, 1985: 183).

Actually, *Chicanismo* as a political ideology lost its appeal for many by the mid-1970s, and this led many Mexican Americans to either enter or return to the liberal wing of the Democratic party, where they embraced the liberal reformism characteristic of the period before the 1950s. This resulted in a reinvigoration of some of the older organizations, such as LULAC, in a shift that Mario Barerra (1985) referred to as "re-traditionalization." The difference was that by this time Mexican Americans were somewhat better positioned to demand a larger role in politics, at both the state and national levels. Between 1970 and 1988, the number of Hispanics elected to political offices increased from less than 800 to nearly 3,400. The vast majority of these officials were Mexican Americans (Fuchs, 1990: 263). One of the most successful younger Mexican American elected officials is Henry Cisneros. The former mayor of San Antonio, he has been mentioned as a potential vice-presidential candidate. In January 1993, he joined the Clinton administration as the Secretary of Housing and Urban Development.

Mexican Americans persist in favoring the Democratic party in state and national elections, usually by 70 to 75 percent of the Mexican American vote. Nonetheless, during the 1980s Mexican

Americans were actively courted by the Republicans. A sector of upper- and upper-middle-class conservative Mexican Americans has long supported the Republican party, though few were elected to public office. As a middle class has grown within the ethnic community, the question has been posed by political strategists: "Will Mexicans vote like Jews or like Italians?" In other words, as Mexicans become wealthier, will they become more politically conservative, and therefore inclined to the Republican party, as Italians have done, or will they maintain their historical allegiance to the Democratic party, as Jews have done? In addition to economic factors, some believe that the strong emphasis placed on traditional social values means that Mexicans can be attracted to political conservatism. Two things work against this, however. The first is the tradition of collective action rather than the individualism preached by the political right. The second is a deeply entrenched belief among Mexicans that the government should establish programs to assist the general welfare of the citizenry (*The Economist*, 1990).

Although political affiliation in the future remains an open question, current evidence does not suggest a shift to conservatism. In one test case, a former Reagan official, Linda Chavez, ran for a U.S. Senate seat in Maryland in 1986 and lost. She had campaigned on a platform that was opposed to affirmative action, bilingual education, and government welfare programs. Moreover, she was hostile to the politics of ethnic pride and preservation, urging instead actions designed to result in assimilation — including intermarriage (Chavez, 1991). Her political views remain a minority position within the Mexican American community.

Socioeconomic Status

The Mexican American poverty rate is similar to that of blacks. The unemployment level, though not as high as that of blacks or Puerto Ricans, is nonetheless higher than that of whites. Mexican Americans complete fewer years of school than non-Hispanic whites, blacks, and all other Hispanics (Bean and Tienda, 1987: 234, 304; Farley, 1990: 240; Aponte, 1991). Mexican Americans are more likely to attend predominantly minority schools than are blacks (San Miguel, 1987; Orfield and Monfort, 1988). Mexican Americans are proportionately underrepresented among college students, and they have a higher dropout rate than non-Hispanics.

Mexicans appear to be a distinctly disadvantaged group at the present, despite the efforts of Chicano politics to combat prejudice and discrimination.

This can be misleading, however. Many Mexicans are new arrivals, and as such have not had time to gain a foothold in the economy. Moreover, like Puerto Ricans, Mexicans are more youthful than the American public at large (Cubans, by contrast, are older than not only other Hispanics, but non-Hispanics as well). Since younger people tend to earn less than older people, it is not surprising that the median income of Mexicans is lower than the national average (Bean and Tienda, 1987: 65–71; Tienda and Lii, 1987; Sowell, 1981: 225–270).

Mexicans drop out of school to go to work. During periods of economic prosperity, Mexicans are more likely to remain in school, but during economically difficult times, when the principle wage earner may by unemployed, Mexican teenagers increasingly leave school to supplement the family income. Contrary to the view of the culture of poverty, which suggests that a fatalism about one's economic prospects undermines the work ethic, many observers see the Mexicans as having a powerful work ethnic. Work may not be seen as a means to upward mobility, but is it seen as an essential means for preserving the integrity of one's family. The centrality of the family among Mexicans contributes to their high rate of labor force participation (Becerra, 1988; Williams, 1990).

A recent study of Mexicans in the Los Angeles area revealed that 80.6 percent of Mexican men were currently in the labor force, compared to 66.7 percent for blacks and 76.2 percent for Anglos. Only 6 percent of Mexicans were receiving welfare payments, in contrast with 35 percent for blacks and 12 percent for non-Hispanic whites. Furthermore, 43 percent of Mexican American households with children were two-parent households. The comparable figures for blacks and whites were 14 percent and 16 percent respectively (Meyer, 1992; 32).

In addition, as with African Americans, the Mexican American middle class has expanded during the past two decades. The majority of these white-collar professionals work in service industries, though they are about evenly split between private sector and public sector employment. Most of those in the middle class are from the third or subsequent generations. Often they have moved out of the central-city barrio. Many reside in middle class neighborhoods that are predominantly Hispanic, however. This is partly due to the persistence of housing discrimination and partly due to choice (Hwang and Murdock, 1988). They are the most acculturated Mexicans, with the best English-language skills. But they also desire to maintain their ethnic background by continuing to shop in Mexican-owned shops and using the professional services of fellow ethnics — lawyers, accountants, doctors, and so forth. After 1982, when the problems of the Mexican economy intensified, middle-class professionals and skilled workers were among the newly arriving immigrants (Dinnerstein and Reimers, 1988: 115; Moore and Pachon, 1985: 93–94).

Current Economic Problems

The central-city barrios are home to the poorest Mexican Americans, and many new immigrants gravitate to these neighborhoods. Mexican American poverty is concentrated in these barrios. Workers are often exploited. For example, in Los Angeles Hispanics constitute a majority of the garment industry workforce. The sweatshops are often unsafe and unsanitary, and workers are expected to work long hours for very low wages. Edna Bonacich (1992: 173) reported that some workers in these enterprises were being paid only $50 a week, while working 11-hour days, five or six days a week. This situation is not confined to Los Angeles; indeed, similar conditions exist in the garment industry in other cities along the border, such as El Paso. In the Midwest, Mexicans are being hired in meatpacking plants that have restructured to eliminate labor unions. This industry has the highest rate of job related injuries. Thus, the industry is paying its workers considerably less than it did in the recent past and greatly reducing or eliminating fringe benefits, while doing relatively little to reduce the dangers on the job (Delgado, 1993).

But Mexican poverty is not only an urban phenomenon, for Mexicans continue to be an important source of agricultural labor. During the conservative political shift of the 1980s, many of the United Farm Workers' labor contracts were terminated, and California Governor Dukmejian worked with growers to reduce the influence of organized labor in the fields. Thus, Mexicans continue to confront annual "harvests of shame."

Figure 11.4 *American's new industrial belt is Northern Mexico.*

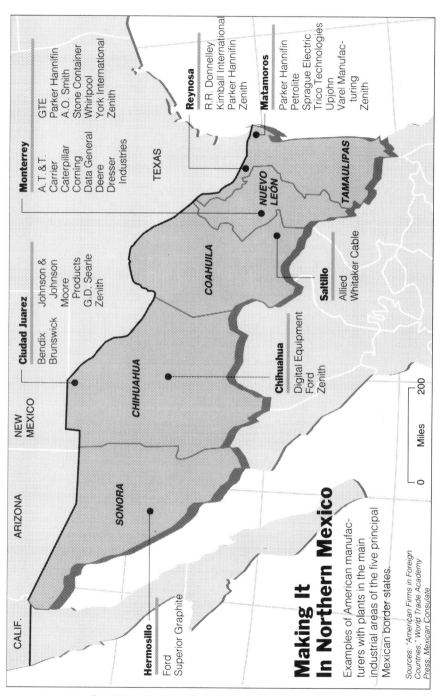

Making It In Northern Mexico

Examples of American manufacturers with plants in the main industrial areas of the five principal Mexican border states.

Sources: "American Firms in Foreign Countries," World Trade Academy Press; Mexican Consulate

Monterrey
GTE
Parker Hannifin
A.O. Smith
Stone Container
Whirlpool
York International
Zenith
A.T.&T.
Carrier
Caterpillar
Corning
Data General
Deere
Dresser
Industries

Reynosa
R.R. Donnelley
Kimball International
Parker Hannifin
Zenith

Matamoros
Parker Hannifin
Petrolite
Sprague Electric
Trico Technologies
Upjohn
Varel Manufac-
turing
Zenith

Ciudad Juarez
Bendix
Brunswick
Johnson &
Johnson
Moore
Products
G.D. Searle
Zenith

Saltillo
Allied
Whitaker Cable

Chihuahua
Digital Equipment
Ford
Zenith

Hermosillo
Ford
Superior Graphite

TEXAS
NUEVO LEÓN
TAMAULIPAS
COAHUILA
CHIHUAHUA
SONORA
NEW MEXICO
ARIZONA
CALIF.

0   200
Miles

The Problem of Marginalized Youth

Gang membership is an important source of identity and camaraderie for those barrio youth who feel particularly estranged from the larger society (Moore, 1978; Moore and Vigil, 1987). Gang membership becomes a source of self-esteem, or "honor" to the "homeboys." In her study of Chicano gang members in Chicago, Ruth Horowitz (1983: 81) wrote that honor "revolves around a person's ability to command deference in interpersonal relations." To command respect means that one cannot be perceived as weak. Any potential challenge or insult to the person's honor must be met directly, and often violently. The result is that gang membership entails a willingness to fight, and "gang banging" (that is, fighting rival gangs) becomes a frequent occurrence. In recent years the consequences of fighting have gotten more serious as guns—including automatic weapons—have become an increasingly important part of the gang's arsenal. Gang activities often revolve around the use and sale of drugs and involvement in criminal activities. The problems of the barrio—gangs, school dropouts and drugs—are, as Ray Hutchison (1992: 15) pointed out, "symptoms of declining economic opportunities."

Summary

Hispanics have become more prominent in American life in the recent past and, given current population growth projections, they will play an even greater role in shaping American society in the twenty-first century. The rapidity of recent developments make it difficult to predict what the future will be like.

Clearly the major Hispanic groups have had rather different historical experiences in America. Although there is considerable diversity within each group, we can make some comparative generalizations about the three groups discussed in this chapter. Cubans appear to be poised to enter the mainstream, while Puerto Ricans remain on the margins. The Mexican American community exhibits a more radical disjuncture between those who are upwardly mobile and those who remain caught in poor barrios. The middle class has expanded, but poverty characterizes a sizeable segment of the population, especially among the immigrant generation.

What does this mean for the future? Will Cubans preserve their ethnic enclave economy, or will younger Cubans move out of the ethnic community and into the larger society? Will intermarriage undermine Cuban American institutions? How will Cuban Americans respond to developments in the homeland? Will some, especially among the elderly, return to Cuba if Castro falls from power?

In a similar vein, will Puerto Ricans find an economic niche? Will they begin to exert greater political influence in the northeastern cities where they are concentrated? What are the prospects for continued return migration to the island? What is the likelihood that Puerto Ricans will develop alliances with other Hispanic groups?

Finally, to what extent will the largest immigrant group reshape not only the social and political character of the American southwest, but the culture as well? Will their political power expand? Will immigration increase or decrease? What will be the long-term impact of *maquiladora* industries? What will be the impact of the North Atlantic Free Trade Agreement?

These and countless other questions will only be answered after future examinations of these groups as they shape their place in this country and examinations of how the larger society responds to those actions.

ASIAN AMERICANS: THE MYTH OF THE MODEL MINORITY

During the 1970s and 1980s the Asian population in the United States grew rapidly. Asians, nonetheless, remain a small part of the total population, less than 3 percent in the 1990 census. Considerable diversity exists among the many groups originating from the Asian continent and the Pacific islands. In addition to the four largest groups that will be discussed in this chapter — Japanese, Chinese, Koreans, and Filipinos — about three dozen other groups are represented in the United States, including more than 500,000 people from both India and Vietnam. Hawaiians, who are Americans by conquest and annexation, have a current population of 256,081. Other groups with at least 75,000 residents include Pakistani, Cambodian, the Hmong, Laotian, and Thai (U.S. Bureau of the Census, 1992).

This chapter resumes the history of the Japanese and Chinese in America since the watershed World War II period. There are similarities in the subsequent histories of the two groups, but the differences are especially pronounced. In addition to these groups, the rapidly expanding Korean and Filipino communities will be examined. Although both groups can trace their histories to the early part of this century, they were very small groups until recently. They are, however, among the largest of the post-1965 immigrant groups. Again, though there are similarities between the two groups, important differences must be recognized, for these differences suggest rather divergent futures for these two groups.

The Model Minority: Myth and Reality

Some Asians have proved to be economically successful in a relatively short time. Many are educated middle class professionals who emigrated because of the perception of greater professional opportunities in America than could be reasonably expected at home. Many American-born Asians have experienced intergenerational upward mobility: though they have entered the professional white-collar workforce, their parents may have worked as agricultural workers or unskilled laborers. In addition, many Asian students — including relatively recent immigrants — have done very well academically. Asian students, for example, have higher average scores than white students on the Scholastic Aptitude Test (SAT). For example, for students whose family income exceeds $70,000, white students have an average composite SAT score of 998, while their Asian counterparts have an average of 1,066. The average score for Hispanics from the same income range is 932, and that for blacks is 854 (Hacker, 1992: 143).

Since World War II prejudice and discrimination directed at Asian Americans has gradually declined, and the images used to depict various Asian groups have shifted. Moon H. Jo and Daniel D. Mast (1993: 430) noted that as the most negative stereotypes were toned down during the 1950s, the image that began to emerge was initially neutral, rather than positive. Asians were collectively described as being "compliant, quiet, and docile." They were seen positively as polite, obedient, and hardworking, and they were portrayed as exhibiting high levels of family loyalty and responsibility. Beginning in the 1960s, but escalating to a peak by the 1980s, was a focus on the economic and educational achievements of Asians. This resulted in the rather widespread depiction in the American media and in scholarly publications of examples of the Asian "success story." Jo and Mast (1993: 431) wrote that, "The common theme of all these success stories is identified as Asian Americans' strong family and community ties, strong work ethic, academic excellence, self-sufficiency, low crime rate, and fewer requests for public assistance."

The characterization of Asian Americans as the "model minority" emerged out of this imagery. Without downplaying the genuine achievements of many Asian Americans, who have succeeded in spite of the legacy of racism and the difficulties associated with

Figure 12.1 *An engagement party for a Vietnamese American couple, circa 1986.*

Source: Courtesy of the Swenson Center.

acculturation, two features of the notion of a model minority are problematic and question the efficacy of the term. First, as this chapter will indicate, not all Asians have been successful. Not only have some groups been more successful than others, but also within each group significant sectors have not gained the foothold in the American economy that promises upward mobility. Some immigrant groups arrived with monetary and human capital that gave them a distinct advantage. Some groups settled in locales with expanding job opportunities, while others found themselves in places with fewer opportunities for economic advance. Some confronted intense competition from other groups, while others did not (Olzak, 1992). In short, many social structural and historical variables contribute to the likelihood of success, not simply the character of the members of any particular ethnic group.

Second, although some Asians have embraced the idea of the model minority — understandably preferring it to the negative images of the recent past — members of the dominant white society, and not Asians, created the image. In part, the model minority serves an ideological purpose. It makes an invidious comparison between the "successful Asians" and those racial and ethnic groups that have not achieved economic parity with whites and who continue to be viewed as second-class citizens — most notably, blacks. The term implicitly suggests that if blacks and less successful Hispanic groups such as Puerto Ricans and Mexicans would adapt the Asian work ethic and general lifestyle, they, too, would be successful. As such, the model minority concept contributes to the tendency to "blame the victim" (Takaki, 1989: 474–484).

The Resurgence of Anti-Asian Views

The perception of group success can have a darker side, and this has become increasingly evident since the early 1980s, during which time the Japanese economy outperformed the American. Nativism surfaced in tandem with increased concern that the Japanese economy was responsible for the decline in numerous U.S. industries, perhaps most important of which is the automotive. Moreover, as the Japanese began to invest in industries and real estate in the United States, a new version of the "yellow peril" hysteria grew that suggested the Japanese "invasion" posed a threat not only to American jobs, but also to America's culture and social fabric, as well.

The Japanese have been criticized for what are perceived to be unfair trade practices, which are seen as giving Japanese firms easy access to the U.S. market while limiting the ability of American businesses to penetrate the Japanese domestic economy. This has led to the reappearance of older stereotypes of the Japanese in particular, and the Asian in general, as sly, crafty, and unworthy of trust. The imagery of the Japanese is frequently tinged with envy or a sense of personal inferiority: this is evident in the widespread interest in Japanese approaches to management and organization.

Japanese are seen as being harder working than Americans. Recently this belief has taken on a novel turn insofar as it has been suggested that the Japanese work too hard. In fact, it has been argued that the Japanese—especially white-collar professionals and managers—literally work themselves to death. The implication of this perspective is that though Japanese perhaps work harder than Americans, it is not worth the price that they are forced to pay. This is an example of a compensatory myth, one that says that although they might be doing better than us economically, we really do not want to adapt their strategies for success.

These reactions are only the latest in a long series of shifting perceptions of various Asian groups produced by international relations. For example, during the Korean conflict and the war in Vietnam, animosity against the North Koreans, North Vietnamese, and the Chinese was intense. Wartime stereotypes focused on the presumed sadistic character of Asians. This racism is evident in such highly acclaimed films as the movie depicting the Korean War era, *The Manchurian Candidate* (1962) and in Michael Cimino's *The Deer Hunter* (1978), which appeared a few years after the peace accord that brought American troops home from Vietnam.

As America's future is increasingly being shaped by developments on the Pacific rim, international relations with the various nations of Asia may well intensify such stereotypes. The extent to which attitudes and beliefs about Asians spill over into characterizations of various Asian American groups is difficult to measure with any precision. In a number of well-publicized incidents, however, Asian Americans have been the victims of hate crimes. In one notorious case, Vincent Chen, a Chinese American engineer, was beaten to death outside of a Detroit bar by two unemployed auto workers who thought he was Japanese and thus somehow to blame for the plight of the American auto industry (Moore, 1988). Leaders of various Asian American organizations monitoring the level of prejudice and discriminatory actions have voiced concerns about the potential for a rather widespread revival of old negative stereotypes. At present the future is not clear (Jo and Mast, 1993: 434).

Japanese Americans

In the two decades after World War II, Japanese Americans managed a remarkable recovery from the devastating impact of the wartime internment. This did not occur without considerable difficulty, however. Thousands of *Issei* lost the businesses and farms that they had owned, and they were unable — due to age, educational background, acculturation problems, and discrimination — to find work in either skilled blue-collar jobs or in the expanding area of white-collar professional occupations. As a consequence, many turned to small business ownership and in particular to commercial gardening. For example, in Los Angeles, it is estimated that as late as 1960, as many as 75 percent of Japanese-owned businesses were contract-gardening related (Levine and Rhodes, 1981; Levine and Montero, 1973).

For the second generation, like the first, the internment was a nightmare. According to Harry H.L. Kitano (1988: 269):

> One of the unstated but constant concerns of the Nisei is that an event similar to the wartime evacuation should not happen again. However, for a long period after the event, many Nisei remained silent concerning the violation of their civil liberties; instead, they concentrated on reestablishing themselves in financially secure positions, with the hope that economic gain would somehow take care of most problems.

The *Nisei* did not generally follow in the footsteps of the immigrant generation. Rather than remaining in the ethnically based economic niche, the second generation instead entered the world of the white-collar middle class (Tsukashima, 1991). Even before World War II, they had used higher education — especially in technical fields such as engineering, pharmacy, and optometry — as a means of becoming upwardly mobile. William Petersen (1971: 114) noted that by 1940, Japanese Americans had higher levels of educational attainment than whites, and this differential has persisted over the past half century.

As the *Sansei*, or third generation, entered the workforce, these trends continued. The Japanese almost reached income parity with

Figure 12.2 *Manzanar Relocation Center, California, 1944 (photograph by Ansel Adams).*

Source: Marion Potts Photographs courtesy of the Balch Institute Research Libary.

whites by 1960, and a decade later their personal incomes were 11 percent above the national average, and their family income averages were 32 percent greater (Sowell, 1981: 175). In many respects, the Japanese American experience parallels that of Jewish Americans: both confronted considerable prejudice and discrimination, were set apart from the dominant culture (the Jews by religion and the Japanese by race and to some extent religion), used education as a vehicle for economic advancement, and have higher educational attainment levels and average incomes than the general white population.

Discrimination in the workforce has not been eliminated entirely. Another parallel with Jews is that both groups have tended to be excluded from top managerial or administrative positions in major corporate, financial, and educational institutions. There is evidence of a glass ceiling that upwardly mobile Japanese Americans bump into. Valued for their technical expertise, the Japanese are not similarly valued for their leadership capabilities. Thus, they are proportionately underrepresented in the ranks of high-level management (Kitano and Daniels, 1988: 170–171).

The Third Generation and Beyond

As the *Sansei* came of age they inhabited a world markedly different from that of their grandparents. Ethnic antagonism had declined, and most had not experienced the wartime incarceration. They were not encouraged to look at the painful past, but instead to the future. They have not been the victims of persistent prejudice in the way their ancestors were. Moreover, they are the beneficiaries of the relative economic success of their parents, which among other things provided them with the opportunity to pursue higher education (Lyman, 1977: 168).

Growing numbers from subsequent generations have grown up in racially integrated suburbs, where they are increasingly removed from the institutions of the ethnic community (Osako, 1984: 533; Lyman, 1986). Of the 28 percent of Japanese Americans who do not live in the American West, the suburbanites have not tended to create ethnic organizations, and their involvement in urban ethnic institutions is relatively infrequent. This is somewhat different in the West, especially California and Hawaii, where, due to the high concentration of Japanese, there is evidence of greater ongoing contact with and involvement in the ethnic community.

The third and subsequent generations were intent on fitting into America and willing to pattern their behaviors in ways that were designed to assist in that process. Their parents tended to lead quiet, conformist lives and got their children involved in what were seen as wholesome middle-class activities, such as YMCA programs, scouting, Little League baseball, and the like (Kitano, 1991:

221). On the job, in school, and in their neighborhoods, younger Japanese function in a world that is largely middle class and white. Their knowledge of contemporary Japan is often quite limited. Many *Nisei* believe this has resulted in a loss of the inherited Japanese culture as well as a devaluation of what they see as traditional character. In short, the *Sansei* are Americanized in a way that the *Issei* and *Nisei*, as well as most of their Asian counterparts, are not (Lyman, 1977: 168–169).

An indication of this change is that Japanese Americans tend to have few if any relationships with recent Japanese arrivals who are temporarily working in the United States for Japanese firms. This contingent of Japanese, known as *Kai-sha*, are in the United States for specified periods of time, after which the firms recall them to Japan. As they are well aware, if they or their families appear to be too Americanized upon their return to Japan, they not only have a difficult time adjusting to the homeland, but also their success with the company may be threatened. Thus, they tend to avoid activities that promote acculturative tendencies. A considerable cultural gulf separates these temporary sojourners from contemporary Japanese Americans.

Changes in the Ethnic Community

Generational changes have had an impact on ethnic institutions. The second generation initiated changes that posed a direct challenge to the traditional family. For example, many of them embraced the American family model by endorsing individuals' rights to chose their own marital partners on the basis of romantic love. Marital ties were considered more important than ties to blood relations (Yanagisako, 1985). Decision-making in the family was shared more equitably by spouses, and, as Stanford M. Lyman (1977; 169) wrote, child-rearing practices followed "the white middle-class ethos of love, equality, and companionship. The principles of *Bushido* gave way to those of Dr. Spock." This trend toward a decidedly American family model is even more characteristic of the *Sansei* (Kitano, 1988: 269).

A similar change characterizes religious institutions among Japanese Americans. Although many immigrants practiced Buddhism or Shintoism, a significant segment of the *Nisei* converted to Christianity, particularly to such Protestant denominations as the

Methodist and Presbyterian. This trend accelerated during World War II because the wartime hysteria resulted in equating allegiance to traditional Japanese religions with a loyalty to the Japanese government (Fukuda, 1990).

Since the 1960s, when members of the counterculture took a keen interest in Eastern religions, hostility to nonwestern religion declined considerably, and renewed interest in Buddhism can be among Japanese Americans. At present, the largest organization of Buddhists is the Jodo Shinshu Buddhist Churches of America. It currently has between 60 and 70 temples and a membership of approximately 150,000. Not all members are Japanese—many other Asian groups are also represented. Although there are several small Buddhist groups, most Japanese Americans are not affiliated with Buddhist or Shinto religious institutions. As with the family, changes set in motion by the second generation have been pushed further by the *Sansei* and the *Yonsei* (fourth generation).

Although changes in the family and religion provide evidence of acculturation, in areas of the country where there are high concentrations of Japanese Americans, a sense of ethnic identity is preserved by various kinds of ethnically based group activities—such as sporting activities and community service projects—that foster friendships and other in-group relationships. Even though there may be little traditional Japanese culture evident in the activities, they do preserve a sense of group identity.

Stephen S. Fugita and David J. O'Brien argued that for the California Japanese they studied in the late 1970s, while cultural assimilation was occurring, structural assimilation was not (Fugita and O'Brien, 1991; see also O'Brien and Fugita, 1991). It is uncertain whether this pattern will persist into the future. Moreover, the sites of their study—Gardena, Fresno, and Sacramento—are not typical of the communities where many Japanese Americans live insofar as they are communities with substantial Japanese American populations. As geographic dispersal in suburban America continues, this will likely have an impact on structural assimilation.

The *Nisei*-created Japanese American Citizens League (JACL) has continued to play a political role nationally. When the *Issei* were granted citizenship rights in 1952, the JACL conducted voter registration drives. The organization urged active involvement in mainstream American politics. This mostly meant working within the Democratic party. In Hawaii, and to a lesser extent California, Japanese candidates have been elected to national political offices since Daniel Inouye's election to Congress when Hawaii became a state in 1959.

The JACL has also functioned as a civil rights organization. Shortly after World War II, members began to demand compensation for the losses they had suffered as a result of the wartime evacuation. Minimal payments were made for business and property loses in 1948, but these inadequate payments were not accompanied by an admission that the government had violated the constitutional rights of Japanese Americans. This had to wait until the Carter administration created a Commission on Wartime Relocation and Internment of Civilians (Hosokawa, 1982). The Commission's final report, issued in 1983, recommended that each surviving internee be paid a tax-exempt amount of $20,000 and called for admitting that racial discrimination caused this violation of civil liberties. After much delay, President Reagan signed the Civil Liberties Act of 1988, which formally ratified the Commission's recommendations. Actual payments did not commence until 1990. Although the Act can be viewed as too little to late, it ended a long quest for justice.

As this mobilized activity indicates, the ethnic community has by no means disappeared. But considerable evidence suggests that it no longer plays the prominent role in the lives of Japanese Americans that it did earlier in the century.

The End of the Japanese American Community?

In *Come See the Paradise* (1990), a film set in the 1930s and 1940s, a young *Nisei* woman falls in love with an Irish American labor organizer. Not only is the couple forced to confront the enforced separation brought about by the war, but they also have to deal with her family's intense opposition to an interracial marriage. Until this point, the intermarriage rate for Japanese Americans had been very low, probably less than 2 percent. Since mid-century, however, the intermarriage rate of Japanese Americans began to rise dramatically (Spickard, 1989: 25–120; Kitano, et al., 1984).

Even during the earlier period, intermarriage rates were higher outside of the Western states, where Japanese were spread geographically and thus the likelihood of finding an in-group marital partner was considerably lower than in areas of high concentration. In some of these regions, more than 50 percent of Japanese Americans were intermarrying by 1960. The rise in intermarriage was not confined to regions of sparse Japanese American settlement, however. For example, by the mid-1970s, the out-group marriage rate in Los Angeles County exceeded 50 percent, and before the end of the decade it had risen to more than 60 percent (Kitano, 1988: 270). By 1985, more than half of all Japanese American marriages in Hawaii were exogamous (Barringer, et al., 1993: 144; Nakamaru, 1993).

No evidence suggests that this pattern will be reversed. Indeed, just as with Jews, there are few impediments from the ethnic community or from parents to discourage intermarriages. Even if parents might prefer that their child marry a Japanese American, they largely allow their children to choose. If they did not do so, they think, quite rightly, that their children would likely defy their wishes. Thus, here is another instance of intermarriage by default (Kitano, 1988: 271). The children of interracial marriages often felt a sense of marginality and ambiguity. Some have navigated this situation well, while others have not. Some have found themselves in environments that are supportive of their mixed identity, and thus they inhabit what Amy Iwaskai Mass (1992: 265) called "the best of both worlds." For others, however, their marginality has been a source of strain.

The prevalence of intermarriage raises the prospect of not only an erosion in the ethnic community, but also a decline in the salience of ethnic identity. Within and without the Japanese American community, the question has been posed: does intermarriage signal, as Mass (1992: 265) put it, "the end of the Japanese American community?" Although it is far too soon to see what the future portends, the possibility exists that, as Masako M. Osako (1984: 536) wrote, "Japanese-Americans may become the first nonwhites to merge biologically into the dominant American society."

Chinese Americans

The 1990 census reports 1,505,245 Chinese in America. This represents a nearly twentyfold increase from the 77,504 figure recorded in 1940 (U.S. Bureau of the Census, 1992; Wong, 1988: 235). One consequence of this dramatic population increase was that

Chinatowns grew. Thus, Robert Park's (1950: 151) prediction that Chinatown would disappear (made in the 1920s when the Chinese population reached its lowest level) did not happen. The increase was caused by a steady improvement in the sex ratio among Chinese Americans and by new immigration.

Pre-1965 Developments

Immigration took place in two stages. The first occurred during the two decades between 1945 and 1965, during which time growth was significant. Growth was far more modest, however, than the period after 1965. Because the Chinese were allies of the United States in World War II, the Chinese Exclusion Act of 1882 was repealed in 1943 and a token quota of 105 was established. After the war an act of Congress permitted 6,000 Chinese war brides of U.S. military personnel to enter the country, and this was subsequently expanded to include wives and children of U.S. citizens. As a result of the revolutionary upheaval in China that culminated in the victory of communist forces led by Mao Tse-tung and the forced withdrawal of nationalist forces led by Chiang Kai-shek, several thousand Chinese were granted permanent resident status under the provisions of the Displaced Persons Act. The passage of the McCarran-Walter Act in 1952 marked the end of racial criteria in determining eligibility for immigration (Kitano and Daniels, 1988: 37–40; Wong, 1988: 242; Chen, 1980).

The Chinese American population grew to 236,084 by 1960. Immigration during this period played a major role in redressing considerably the skewed sex ratio. Women accounted for 9 out of every 10 immigrants between 1940 and 1960 (Wong, 1988: 242); the sex ratio imbalance improved from 285.3 males per 100 females in 1940 to 134.5 males per 100 females in 1960.

The Growth of the Chinese Middle Class

Not all of the new immigrants gravitated to Chinatowns. Brides of servicemen, students, and others often lived outside of the ethnic enclave. At the same time, many residents also exited Chinatowns during the two decades after World War II. These were largely from the English-speaking second generation who were prepared to take advantage of new opportunities available because of postwar prosperity.

Many entered colleges and universities to pursue professional training. More than 80 percent of college-educated Chinese Americans went into professional occupations rather than business ownership. Stanford M. Lyman observed that the Chinese were highly selective in their choice of occupations. They opted for careers in engineering, medicine, pharmacy, dentistry, optometry, and chemistry, and tended to avoid positions in education and the law. They also exhibited a tendency to work for state and federal governmental organizations. This was, in Lyman's view, by design. The Chinese often had limited English-language skills, and they were concerned about prejudicial treatment from potential employers and clients. Thus, they selected careers that were seen as minimizing the problems associated with English proficiency and racism. Over time this trend has intensified as the Chinese middle class is largely based on people in technical fields and independent professions, while being underrepresented in managerial and proprietorial occupations (Lyman, 1974: 133–138).

Entry into the middle class stimulated a movement out of Chinatown and into the suburbs. This meant that the Chinese middle class came into contact with the white middle class in a way that was not possible a generation earlier. The movement to the suburbs frequently resulted in the clustering of Chinese in various suburban neighborhoods, however. Thus, many of New York's upwardly mobile Chinese located in Hempstead, Long Island, and those from Los Angeles moved to the San Gabriel Valley. Concerned that their children might loose much of their cultural heritage, the suburban middle class often established Chinese language schools and cultural centers to instill in their children an appreciation of their Chinese backgrounds (Zhou and Logan, 1991).

One consequence of upward mobility was that Chinatowns got smaller. For example, by the late 1960s, only one of six Chinese Americans in Chicago lived in Chinatown, while the figure was one in four in New York City (Schaefer, 1988: 359). As a result, the power of the ruling elite in Chinatowns eroded considerably. The middle class did not depend on this elite for their economic well-being, nor did they need to rely on them as mediators with the larger society.

Although Chinatowns remained tourist attractions, and thus continued to be economically viable, the community also continued to be beset with serious social problems. Poverty is endemic.

The Chinese American community is a divided one in which the successful tend to move out of Chinatown while those who have not made it remain. Housing problems include the prevalence of substandard units and a shortage of affordable units, resulting in overcrowding. Health care is inadequate — Chinatown residents suffer disproportionately from a number of serious illnesses and, in fact, are afflicted with one disease, tuberculosis, that is all but eradicated from the general population. Chinatowns have a serious suicide problem, as well as related mental health problems. Finally, crime, especially gang-related crime, has a negative impact on the community. Although often depicted in terms of juvenile delinquency, youth gangs are a perpetuation of the role historically played by the secret societies (Lyman, 1986: 142–149; Lyman, 1974: 151–168).

Homeland Politics

During the 1950s, most Chinese Americans supported the Chinese Nationalist cause and voiced their opposition to the communist takeover of the mainland. Since the People's Republic of China closed its doors to emigration, most Chinese arriving in the United States after 1949 were from either Hong Kong or Taiwan. These people were primarily hostile to the communist regime, which intensified anticommunist sentiment among Chinese in America. Given the political climate of the Cold War, and in particular the resurgence of "yellow peril" hysteria during the armed conflict in Korea, Chinese Americans became concerned that the reduction in anti-Chinese prejudice might be short-lived. Their worst fears were that they might suffer a similar fate to that of the Japanese during World War II. Not surprisingly, the ruling elite in Chinatown sought to reassure the American public that Maoist sentiment was minimal, and they worked actively to suppress the little support that existed (Lyman, 1974: 130–131).

Elements of the American political right-wing with an interest in Asia — such as the publisher Henry Luce, Representative Walter H. Judd, and Senator William F. Knowland — organized what became known as the "China lobby." Its main goal was to topple the communist regime on the mainland and return Chiang Kai-shek's government-in-exile on the island of Taiwan to power. When Senator Joseph McCarthy began his anticommunist witch-hunt, he and his sympathizers began a campaign of vilification against government officials and others accused of "losing" and "betraying" China.

Many Chinese Americans believed it was all the more imperative to do what they could to express loyalty to the United States and opposition to international communism. Thus, the Chinese American leadership cooperated with the China lobby. As Alexander DeConde (1992: 150) noted, they employed a variety of tactics "in the nation's Chinatowns to stimulate Chinese-American opposition to Mao Tse-tung's mainland regime."

Post-1965 Developments

The number of Chinese increased dramatically after 1965, as the Chinese represented the third largest immigrant group during recent decades, surpassed only by Mexicans and Filipinos. Between 1960 and 1980 the Chinese population expanded more than threefold because of these new immigrants, or *San Yi Man*. In 1990 the Chinese were the largest Asian group. Most immigrants came from urban areas and included both Mandarin and Cantonese speakers. Some came from the People's Republic of China by way of Hong Kong; they left because of the political turmoil and bloody violence brought about by the Cultural Revolution. Most, however, came from Hong Kong or Taiwan and they were motivated by primarily economic considerations (Takaki, 1989: 421–424).

As a result, Chinese Americans were once again composed primarily of immigrants, as the first generation rose from 39 percent of the total group in 1960 to 63 percent by 1980. A majority of the new arrivals settled in either California or New York, thereby revitalizing the Chinatowns in those states (Gold, 1992). The Chinatown in New York City, for example, grew from about 15,000 to more than 100,000 residents. Although many immigrants gravitated to traditional urban Chinatowns, others settled in suburban areas.

The choice of residential location was largely determined by the individual's economic status. Takaki (1989: 425) reported that the "different class backgrounds of the new immigrants has led to the formation of a bipolar Chinese-American community—one divided between a colonized working class and an entrepreneurial-professional middle class." The working-class immigrants are largely found in the traditional Chinatowns, while the more upwardly mobile and affluent have chosen suburbs. As one commentator put it, there is a major divide between the "Chinatown ghettos" and the "arriviste suburbs" (Awanohara, 1991). In New York City, reminiscent of the division between poor and affluent Jews at the turn of the century, the "Downtown Chinese" are employed in restaurants and the garment industry, while the "Uptown Chinese" are engaged in various professions and business enterprises (Kwong, 1987).

Many middle-class Chinese live in suburbs that are characterized by large numbers of Asians in general and Chinese in particular. Thus, in the New York metropolitan area, many middle-class Chinese live in multiethnic neighborhoods in Flushing and Elmhurst (Chen, 1992). In the Los Angeles area, Monterey Park has become known as the first suburban Chinatown (Fong, 1994). The majority of the community's citizens are of Chinese ancestry, and thus it has become known as "Little Taipei." Although the community elected its first Chinese American mayor during the 1980s, this ethnic transformation of Monterey Park produced a nativist backlash among some whites. Thus, Takaki (1989: 425) noted, "In 1986 a sign at a gas station near the city limits, for example, displayed two slant eyes with the declaration: 'Will the last American to leave Monterey Park please bring the flag.'"

Changing Chinatown: New York City

New York City's Chinatown, located in lower Manhattan, is the largest Chinese enclave, not only in the United States, but also in the western hemisphere. The population has grown so dramatically that it has spilled over into adjacent neighborhoods, including Little Italy. At present, approximately 150,000 Chinese inhabit Chinatown; perhaps as many as one of five are illegal aliens (Kinkead, 1992; Wong, 1982). As with other ethnic neighborhoods throughout the history of the United States, not all residents of Chinatown are Chinese; however, a sizeable majority of them are. Perhaps 80 percent are foreign born, and as many as half have resided in America for less than five years. As with Little Italies a century ago, many streets are defined in terms of the homeland region or the diaspora country of the immigrants. Thus, Peter Kwong (1987: 41) observed, "Groups with different dialects concentrate in separate sections of Chinatown: Fukienese on Division Street,

Burmese Chinese on Henry Street, Chinese from Taiwan on Centre Street, Vietnamese on East Broadway."

Residents find employment in a variety of occupations, but prominent among them are laundries, grocery stores, shops catering to tourists, and especially restaurants and the garment industry. Several thousand individuals, primarily male, are employed in the approximately 450 restaurants in Chinatown (Kwong, 1987: 26). Chinese expansion in New York's garment industry since the mid-1960s has been remarkable. The 30 Chinese-owned firms in 1965 grew to about 500 firms within a little more than two decades and the current 20,000 Chinese workers compose more than one-sixth of the city's apparel labor force.

Sociologist Roger Waldinger (1986) emphasized the importance of the departure from the industry by earlier immigrants and their offspring, chiefly Jews and Italians. Waldinger's survey of Jewish and Italian factory owners provides clues to their reasons for leaving the business as well as the disinclination of the children to take over from their parents. Central to this change is the perception of occupational alternatives. What has occurred is a process of ethnic succession in which the Chinese had an opportunity as competition with more established groups in the industry declined.

To explain why the Chinese have been particularly successful in getting into the industry, Waldinger (1986) suggested that various cultural and psychological forces have an impact, and he provided an interesting perspective on the particular motives of the Chinese by a comparison with another group that has made inroads into the industry: Dominicans. For the Chinese, entrepreneurship is perceived as the most realistic way to achieve social mobility, while for the Dominicans it is a means to escape the oppressive work routines of the manual laborer. This suggests that the Chinese have goals similar to the Jews and Italians that preceded them in the industry and are thus likely to exit it if other occupational possibilities emerge. The influx of new immigrants has caused intense competition for jobs in these immigrant industries. Many workers are forced to rely on more than one job to survive economically. Working hours are generally long and the pay is low (Kinkead, 1992: 66; Zhou and Logan, 1989).

Chinatown continues to thrive on tourist dollars because a highly romanticized and exotic image has been maintained. This gilded ghetto is still beset by many serious problems, among which are health problems. Kinkead (1992: 84) reported that Chinatown suffers from a lower life expectancy and a high infant mortality rate because of such health problems as parasites, intestinal ailments, hepatitis, malnutrition, and anemia. The community also continues to suffer from high rates of mental illness and suicide.

This enclave economy, unlike the Cuban, exploits workers. Thus, the male-dominated restaurant industry and the female-dominated garment industry demand long work hours for very low pay (at or below minimum wage) and without the provision of fringe benefits. Employees, for example, are generally without health insurance, thereby compounding the health problems noted earlier. Housing also continues to be substandard, unsafe, unhealthy, overcrowded, and overpriced. Chinatown lacks adequate recreational facilities.

Crime has become a more serious problem and is intimately linked to the role of tongs, or youth gangs. Countless gangs currently operate in Chinatown, usually with a membership of between 30 and 50 members. Gangs pit different elements of the Chinese community against one another: Cantonese versus Mandarin, Hong Kong Chinese versus Taiwan Chinese, new arrivals versus youth who have been in America for some time, and so forth. They are involved in turf wars and a variety of criminal activities. Gangs routinely extort "protection" money from Chinatown businesses. Kinkead (1992: 66) wrote that more than 80 percent of Chinese restaurants and about two-thirds of all businesses indicate that regular protection payments are made to various gangs. Recently gangs have become involved in drug trafficking. The FBI estimates that as much as half of the heroin smuggled into the United States does so under the control of criminal syndicates in Chinatown.

Traditionally, the ruling elite of Chinatown controlled the secret societies or tongs. Whether they are able to do so effectively today is not clear. Nonetheless, the Chinese Consolidated Benevolent Association (CCBA) remains a powerful force in Chinatown, functioning as the unofficial governing body of the community as in the past. Housed in a building on Mott Street, the CCBA's headquarters operates something like a city hall, with the president's role being seen—as in the nineteenth century—as akin to that of a mayor.

Within the CCBA umbrella are two subdivisions that reflect the internal divisions in Chinatown: fongs, or village associations, and about 40 family associations, composed of people sharing the last surnames. Both serve important functions, including organizing recreational activities and celebrations on Chinese holidays; running schools designed to provide cultural and language instruction to youth; promoting traditional religious practices associated with ancestor worship; and providing various services, including loans and jobs for new arrivals, credit clubs, translation services, and lodging for the elderly and unemployed. In addition, district associations settle disputes, thereby permitting Chinatown residents to avoid the American judicial system except as a last resort (Wong, 1987: 247-248; Wong, 1982; Kuo, 1977).

The present role of the CCBA reflects the vitality of the traditional ethnic community. According to Bernard Wong (1987: 247), however, "the community is no longer controlled by the monolithic power structure of the CCBA and its affiliates." New organizations have been created, many by new immigrants and many with the support of federal and state funding. These include modern social service agencies such as the Chinatown Planning Council, the Chinatown Advisory Council, and the Chinese Health Clinic. More than 200 organizations have been created on the basis of educational backgrounds (such as alumni groups) and professional or business interests. The Organization of Chinese-Americans for example, is a civil rights organization concerned with combating prejudice and discrimination (Wong, 1987: 248–249).

What is significant about these new organizations is that they reflect a different orientation toward American society. Rather than seeking to keep Chinese isolated in ethnic communities, their purpose is to prepare Chinese for entry into the larger society. According to Wong (1987: 249), there are two distinct orientations toward the larger society in contemporary Chinatown:

> Having lived in an era of intense racism against Chinese, old settlers came to feel that any intimate contacts with the larger society would invite trouble and they isolated, and still isolate, themselves from the mainstream of American society. Most of the new immigrants do not want to isolate themselves and the community from the larger society. On the contrary, they would like to see their community as an integral part of the city as well as of the wider U.S. society. Thus, Chinatown is not an

"unmeltable" ethnic community. Rather, it is an assimilable community with an interest in changing its boundaries.

At present, it is unclear how likely assimilation is. This depends on economic opportunities and options, as well as political and cultural factors. Thus, we can only speculate about if and how those boundaries might change.

Korean Americans

The 1990 census reports that 837,000 Koreans live in the United States, so Koreans continue to rank fourth in size among Asian groups (U.S. Bureau of the Census, 1992). The vast majority of Korean Americans are here as a result of post-1965 immigration. Indeed, the small size of the Korean American community that had been created by the first two waves of immigration — after the turn of the century and in the wake of the Korean War — meant that they had only a minimal impact on America's ethnic mix (Melendy, 1977). Between 1950 and 1965, only 18,797 Koreans were admitted into the country as permanent residents. In the two decades between 1970 and 1990, however, the Korean population increased almost twelvefold. Koreans have settled in large numbers in a few major cities where their presence is especially felt: Los Angeles, New York, and Chicago.

During the period of mass migration, South Korea became an important economic force in Asia, with an expanding industrial base. In this context of economic expansion, what were the migratory push forces that contributed to the contemporary Korean diaspora? Korean immigration has been largely a middle-class phenomenon. In this regard, they are most like Cubans and Filipinos. Koreans are one of the most highly educated groups among the new immigrants. Many Koreans came to the United States not only with college degrees, but also with various kinds of post-graduate professional credentials. One might assume that it is precisely this class that had the most to gain by South Korean industrialization, and indeed the professional middle-class has grown. As In-Jin Yoon (1992: 3) showed, however, the rapid expansion of a new urban middle class resulted in a situation where many in this class experienced "a widening gap between their expectations of upward mobility and the limited opportunities available in South Korea."

The provisions of the 1965 Immigration Act facilitated Korean immigration to America, for it was precisely middle-class professionals who were accorded preferential treatment. The choice of the United States was also influenced by political and cultural ties that existed between the nations. Many institutions of higher education in Korea had been established by Christian missionaries from the United States, beginning in the latter part of the nineteenth century, and many prominent Koreans have been educated in these institutions.

Many educated in these schools converted to Christianity—largely Protestant Christianity. This provided an important cultural link to the United States (Kim, 1977; Kitano and Daniels, 1988; 106–110). The political dimension became important in the years after the Korean War, when U.S. military and economic aid was a major factor in making the transition from an agrarian to a market-based industrial economy (Yoon, 1992; Cha, 1977). These factors merged with purely economic considerations to motivate members of Korea's educated middle class to emigrate.

In recent years, the class composition of Korean immigration has changed as middle-class immigration has tapered off, while the percentage of non-white collar workers has increased (Yoon, 1992). As we have seen with Cubans recently and Germans a century ago, this is not an atypical pattern. Many recent arrivals do not possess the education or specific job skills that permit easy entry into the mainstream American economy. In addition, many from this cadre have more limited English-language proficiencies. As a result, they are far more dependent on the Korean ethnic economy for jobs than were the earlier migrants. They can also begin the adjustment process by relying on social networks and organizations established by the middle class.

Immigrant Entrepreneurs

Many Koreans experienced an initial period of downward mobility (Daniels and Kitano, 1988: 112). For some professionals, this was the inevitable consequence of the need to acquire additional educational training or recredentialing to enter American white-collar occupations. Koreans can be found in a range of professions, but are especially concentrated in health care and education. The number of Koreans teaching in higher education is attested to by the existence of an academic organization called the Association of Korean Christian Scholars in North America (Kivisto, 1993: 96). Although this move into the mainstream economy has been the route to upward mobility pursued by some, Koreans are disproportionately involved in small businesses.

In a study conducted by the U.S. Bureau of the Census (1984: 8), Koreans ranked first among 17 recent immigrant groups in their rate of self-employment. The proportion of Koreans who were self-employed in 1980 was almost twice that of the U.S. average. Pyong Gap Min (1991: 231) determined that the Census report undercounts the number of self-employed Koreans, and he contended that the rate of self-employment has actually increased since 1980. Won Moo Hurh and Kwang Chang Kim (1984) estimated that one-third of all Korean adults in Los Angeles are either owners or managers of small businesses, and other researchers have arrived at comparable percentages in other cites, such as New York and Atlanta (Kim, 1981; Min 1988).

Self-employment means that immigrants own their own businesses. These businesses tend to be small enterprises that frequently involve families. Korean women have a very high labor-force participation rate, and this is chiefly because they work in family-owned businesses. Koreans own a wide range of small businesses, including grocery stores, fruit stands, flower shops, liquor stores, apparel shops, wig shops, repair shops, and restaurants. Although their businesses are visible in a number of cities where Koreans constitute a small group, they are particularly important in Los Angeles, New York, and Chicago. In these cities Koreans are involved in a wide range of business activities, but are highly concentrated in a few businesses—including produce, liquor, and wigs. Los Angeles has the most highly developed enclave economy (Light and Bonacich, 1988; Kim, 1981; Kim and Hurh, 1985; Yoon, 1991).

Korean entrepreneurs frequently use ethnic resources when getting started in business. As with Chinese, Japanese, and West Indians, Koreans operate rotating credit associations, known in the Korean community as *Kye*, which provide start-up capital. Other ethnic resources that assist with entrepreneurial activities include loans from kin, friends, and Korean banks. In addition, informal ethnic networks provide information and advice. Although the role of ethnic resources is a crucial factor in explaining the high level of Korean business activity, not all Korean merchants rely on the ethnic community to get started. Many enter into business by investing their own personal savings, and others make use of loans from American banks. Yoon (1991) discovered that although ethnic resources do play an important role for many at the beginning of business formation, they become less important over time.

Conflict Between Koreans and African Americans

In contrast with Cubans, Koreans have established many businesses outside of the residential ethnic enclaves. The large Koreatown in Los Angeles and the smaller residential enclave in Chicago have many Korean businesses, but even more businesses are located outside of the ethnic neighborhood. In New York, Koreans live in various suburban areas, but operate most of their businesses in the city.

Particularly significant to new forms of interracial conflict is the presence of Korean-owned businesses in black neighborhoods. By the early 1970s, Koreans had begun to operate businesses in black inner-city ghettos. In part this can be seen as an example of ethnic succession, for until that point various European-origin groups, especially Jews, had been a prominent presence in ghettos. Jews and other white merchants, however, did not aspire to hand their businesses over to their children, who often went to college in preparation for entering the professional middle class. The urban upheavals of the late 1960s destroyed many of these businesses and prompted many merchants to leave the ghetto for good. Black entrepreneurs did not fill the economic void left by this mass departure, so there were opportunities for the newly arriving Korean immigrants. And they took advantage of the opportunities. There is evidence that Koreans have displaced black stores as well as white stores (Neufeld, 1990: 5).

In Spike Lee's 1989 film *Do the Right Thing*, a trio of older black men bemoan the fact that the corner market is owned by Koreans and not by African Americans. As the racial tensions escalate, the Koreans become targets of black animosity. At the climax of the movie, the Italian-owned Sal's pizzeria is set ablaze, and as the crowd begins to move on the Korean market, the owner protests, proclaiming that he, too, is black. The message implies that America is ultimately divided between whites on the one hand and all people of color on the other. Whether the crowd agreed is never made clear. The store is spared from attack, however.

Considerable tension exists between blacks and Koreans. In a study of ethnic conflict in Chicago, Steven Neufeld (1990) found that black complaints about Korean (and other "outsiders," such as Arabs) merchants were widespread. At the most general level, the Koreans were considered to be exploiters. More specifically, people complained about the quality of merchandise, the high prices, refund and exchange policies, and disrespectful treatment of customers. Koreans were faulted for not hiring enough blacks and for not investing in the black community by failing to use black suppliers, banks, and so forth. Black community organizers had, at various times, attempted to press for changes by calling for boycotts of Korean-owned businesses. These efforts have proved to be futile.

In contrast to the fictional riot of Lee's film, the 1992 Los Angeles riot resulted in large-scale destruction of Korean businesses. More than 1,000 Korean businesses were destroyed, with an estimated price tag of $300 million (Burton, 1992). Koreans were viewed sympathetically as innocent victims by the public at large. In the aftermath of the riot, many of those who remained readily express bitter resentment at those who took part in the riot. Gun merchants report a brisk trade in automatic weapons by those intent on being prepared for any future racial confrontations. Whether those whose businesses were destroyed will rebuild in the same area is uncertain. Perhaps like Jews a quarter of a century ago, they, too, will exit. Whether Koreans will continue doing business in black neighborhoods remains to be seen.

Korean Ethnic Churches

Koreans have created ethnic communities replete with charitable and mutual aid societies; senior citizen, handicapped, and youth centers; business and professional associations; musical societies; sports associations, which include judo and tae kwon do clubs, and other distinctly ethnic organizations (Lee, 1992).

One institution in particular is central to the Korean American community: the ethnic church. Although Christianity is a minority religion in Korea—approximately 16 percent of Koreans are affiliated with Protestant churches and 5 percent with Roman Catholic churches—about 70 percent of Korean Americans report their religion as Christian. In other words, Korean immigrants have come disproportionately from the Korean Christian community. This implies a class connection because Christianity is more prevalent among the Korean middle class than among other classes. In addition, many Christian Koreans fled from North Korea during and before the Korean War, and thus do not have especially strong ties to the South. This has probably made them more willing to emigrate than those from the South (Warner, 1992; Min, 1991; Hurh and Kim, 1990; Shin and Park, 1988; Kim, 1977).

Koreans have not generally joined existing Protestant or Catholic parishes. Instead, they have created over 2,000 ethnic congregations. Many of the congregations are quite small. For example, in New York City, the median number of members is 82 (Min, 1991: 229). Some congregations meet in the parish halls of established American churches, at least during the congregation's formative period.

By remaining distinctive, religious affiliation served practical functions in helping Korean immigrants adjust to their new homeland. Min (1991: 228–230) contended that one of the most important functions is to provide fellowship with other Koreans. Many churches provide the benefits of a primary group, and people derive their most intimate friendships from among the congregation's members. Larger parishes often create district meetings (*Kuyok Yebae*) in which church members in the same residential areas meet in members' homes for religious services and dinner parties.

By facilitating and encouraging such social relationships, churches reinforce the bonds of ethnic attachment. Korean churches also reinforce Korean culture. Church services, even children's services, are usually conducted in Korean, not English. The church is the key institution in programs designed to promote the retention of the Korean language among young people. In addition, the church is the place where many traditional cultural practices are enacted, and where the preservation of traditional values is observed.

Adhesive Adaptation

One important value that Korean churches attempt to instill in young people is filial piety. This value is rooted in Confucianism, but it is reinforced by Korean Christianity. Filial piety grants parents a high degree of authority over their children, who are expected to defer to, respect, and show devotion to their parents. As Korean children encounter and interact with American youth, especially in school, many of them increasingly question the tradition of filial piety. Min and Min (1992) identified two major sources of intergenerational strain and conflict. The first is differences regarding traditional values. Children frequently complain that their parents are too traditional and are too strict, not permitting them the kind of freedom most American school children take for granted. Korean parents often believe that their children do not work enough and do not expend sufficient effort to learn the Korean language and culture. The second source of tension is produced by the parental demand that children perform well in school. Some students think their parents' expectations are unrealistic and they resent the pressure to succeed.

However real the conflict between parents and school-aged youth is, it should not be overestimated. One reason is that Korean parents have also been Americanized, so they are not as traditional as their children might sometimes claim. They are engaged in what Hurh and Kim (1984) called a process of "adhesive adaptation," meaning that Koreans are engaged in grafting onto the traditional culture certain aspects of American culture and social relations. In other words, rather than abandoning the ethnic past, they connect it to the present.

This is seen in the high labor force participation rate of Korean women, despite their traditional role in the household. Many Koreans explain this shift as the result of economic necessity: as with most struggling members of the middle class, two incomes are needed to support their lifestyle. Although adaptation has occurred, the essentially patriarchal structure of the family remains intact. Hurh and Kim (1984: 122–128) noted that despite working outside of the home, women still are expected to perform most household work. Family decisions are still primarily made by men rather than shared (Um, 1992).

In another example of adhesive adaptation, changes in definitions of filial piety were detected in a study of elderly Koreans and their adult children (Kim and Hurh, 1992). The researchers noted that although both groups are committed to the ideal of filial piety, they have modified their understanding of what such piety means. Adult children tend to live separately from their aging parents, rather than taking them into their homes as would have been expected in the past. Many of the elderly continue to reside in the urban enclaves of initial settlement, while the children, having better economic situations than their parents, have moved to the suburbs. The adult children still visit and in other ways express their concern for their parents, but their expressions of piety have been modified.

Scenarios for the Future

Most Koreans are first or second generation ethnics, so they have not been in the United States for a long time. This means that the ethnic community, including churches and the family, continues to play a vital role in the adjustment process. Certain trends suggest that the future of Koreans might most resemble that of the Japanese. This is to say, Koreans may be assimilating to a greater degree than other Asian groups such as the Chinese and the Vietnamese.

First, by placing a premium on education, Koreans do not seem intent on handing ethnic enterprises on to their offspring. Rather, Koreans appear to want their children to become white-collar professionals. Although many college-educated Koreans have not obtained such jobs themselves, or have found themselves marginalized in various professions, they probably attribute this lack of success to language and cultural difficulties that the American born will not confront (Shin and Chang, 1988). White-collar jobs would promote entry into the mainstream and erode the institutional structure of the ethnic community.

Second, although most Korean marriages are endogamous, the rate of intermarriage for Koreans is higher than for some other Asian groups, and it is increasing. In a study of intermarriage patterns in the San Francisco–Oakland metropolitan area, Kumiko Shibuya (1992) found that for six Asian groups, the Japanese outmarriage rate was the highest at 47 percent, while the Chinese was the lowest at 17.2 percent. Slightly above the Chinese rate were the Vietnamese and Asian Indian. The Korean rate was 30.2 percent, close to the 33.6 percent reported for Filipinos. This suggests that Koreans are increasingly willing to look beyond the confines of the ethnic community for marital partners. Two points should be noted about this trend. First, most outmarriages take place between Koreans and members of other Asian groups. Second, women are four times more likely than men to marry a non-Korean. Korean women may be searching for more egalitarian marriages than they think is likely if they marry a Korean.

Filipino Americans

The Filipino immigration wave that began after 1965 resulted in an eightfold increase in population during the three decades beginning in 1960, when the figure was 181,614. In 1990 the 1,450,512 Filipinos in the United States represented the second largest Asian group (U.S. Bureau of the Census, 1992). These new arrivals differed considerably from those who came during the earliest immigration period, both in educational achievement and occupational backgrounds. To appreciate how different they were, a brief overview of pre-World War II immigration is necessary.

The earliest mass immigration began around 1910 and lasted for more than two decades, though the relatively small numbers meant that Filipinos did not have the impact that Chinese and Japanese immigrants did. Like their Chinese counterparts, this immigrant group was overwhelmingly composed of single males with few occupational skills and little education. Most were peasants, with no experience in an industrial setting. They were heavily concentrated in Hawaii and California, where many had been recruited by agricultural concerns such as the Hawaiian Sugar Planters Association (Bulosan, 1973; Melendy, 1977: 31–41; Kitano and Daniels, 1988: 79). They worked under the padrone system and suffered from the economic exploitation inherent in that system. Although there were several instances when Filipino workers attempted to organize unions to improve their economic conditions, they nonetheless were frequently criticized by white workers for undercutting wage levels (Jiobu, 1988: 50).

Economically based ethnic animosity was exacerbated because Filipino men, unlike other Asians, sought out the company of white women. One way this occurred was by an institution known as the taxi-dance hall, a place where Filipino men would pay to dance with white women. These halls, which were immensely popular with this bachelor society, were often fronts for prostitution. Interracial sexual relations — both commercial sexual relations and intimate ones — intensified anti-Filipino sentiment.

Thus, when Filipino men began to marry white women in California, an effort was made to prevent such unions by invoking the state's antimiscegenation statute. When the state's Supreme Court determined that the law did not apply to Filipinos, who were defined as members of the Malay race, the state quickly amended the law to prohibit Malay unions with Caucasians. Similar laws were passed in Oregon, Nevada, and Washington. In stark contrast with other Asian groups, interracial intermarriages before 1950 were not uncommon among Filipinos (Kitano and Daniels, 1988: 81). Although relatively little is known about these marriages, Barbara Posadas's (1981) study of Filipinos in Chicago found that most involved Filipino men and second generation women from various Eastern European ethnic groups.

Hostility toward interracial marriages was widespread. For some it conjured up the fear of racial degeneracy, as reflected in the words a prominent anti-Asian nativist: "The Filipino tends to interbreed with near-moron white girls" (quoted in Melendy, 1977: 61). Filipinos were characterized as being unassimilable. They were depicted as being "primitive"—unintelligent, disease-carrying, lazy, and morally suspect. Moreover, they were, like other Asian groups, the periodic victims of racist violence, including serious attacks during the 1920s and 1930s in the California communities of Exeter, Watsonville, and Modesto (Jiobu, 1988: 52; Pido, 1986).

The skewed sex ratio in the Filipino community and the termination of immigration caused the size of the community to decline over time. As Roger Daniels (1990: 358) wrote, "Between 1934 and the end of World War II, the Filipino population in the United States aged and dwindled, [while] the war years changed the image of the Filipinos to that of loyal allies against the Japanese." This was important in reducing levels of prejudice and discrimination. In this, the Filipino experience parallels that of the Chinese.

Immigration Since 1945

As with the Chinese and Koreans, the 1965 immigration act proved to be a watershed event in the Filipino community. A more limited wave of immigration took place between 1945 and 1965, however, during which the Filipino population in the United States almost doubled. The Philippines became independent in 1946, and during that year they became eligible for naturalization. The annual quota was raised to 100, and after 1954 to 1,300. More Filipinos were non-quota immigrants than were quota immigrants. Many arrived with tourist or student visas, and subsequently changed their immigrant status to remain in the country permanently. Many newcomers were women, which reduced the sex imbalance considerably. This resulted in the development of a sizeable second generation (Melendy, 1980: 361).

One unique group of immigrants constituted part of this immigration wave: the thousands of Filipinos, some in an organization known as the Philippine Scouts, who had served in the U.S. Navy. They were granted citizenship rights even before entering the United States, so many immigrated with their families (Daniels, 1990: 358–359).

The post-1965 immigrants were quite different from their predecessors, and thus much about the Filipino American ethnic group changed dramatically during the past quarter century. Perhaps as many as two-thirds of recent immigrants are educated, white-collar professionals. In contrast, the earlier arriving immigrants and their offspring were and are characterized by relatively low levels of educational achievement and by their concentration in unskilled jobs in industry and agriculture. The newcomers were also better educated and trained than those who remained in the Philippines (Pido, 1986; Melendy, 1980).

Like the earlier immigrants, the post-1965 immigrants were primarily motivated by economic considerations. They believed that they could earn more in a professional occupation if they emigrated, rather than remaining in their birthplace. In an interview with Alfredo Muñoz (1971: 29), one immigrant explained that a person could earn in a day in America what would be a month's salary in the Philippines. Thus, these immigrants are part of the "brain drain" from Third World countries (Rumbaut, 1991; Jasso and Rosenzweig, 1990).

Although a wide range of professions are represented among this group, including engineers, accountants, lawyers, and teachers, the most typical immigrant is a member of the health professions, including doctors, pharmacists, and nurses. About half of these immigrants are women, and nursing is by far the most common profession for them. During the 1970s, about 20 percent of nurses graduating from Philippine nursing schools emigrated to find work in the United States (Daniels, 1990: 359). Some immigrants report instances of discrimination in hiring, difficulties with adapting to the new culture, and language problems.

Many professionals have experienced a period of downward mobility, being forced to worked in unskilled or semiskilled jobs while obtaining the credentials needed to resume their profession. This was least problematic for nurses because of acute nursing shortages in many public hospitals, different levels of licensing, and the fact that the nursing curriculum used in the Philippines was similar to that used in the United States. Thus, perhaps as many as 33 percent of all licenses issued to foreign nurses went to Filipinas (Melendy, 1980: 362).

As with other Asian groups, Filipinos are highly concentrated in western states. The 1990 census revealed that 68.4 percent resided in this part of the country, most of them in two states — California and Hawaii (U.S. Bureau of the Census, 1992). In this regard they are most like the Japanese. Although many earlier immigrants lived in rural areas or smaller cities in agricultural areas, the new immigrants are highly concentrated in larger cities, especially Los Angeles, Honolulu, Chicago, and New York.

The Ethnic Community

Of the four major Asian groups, the Filipinos have created the least institutionally complete ethnic community. There are no "Little Manilas" in large cities. Though Filipinos in cities such as San Francisco and Los Angeles tend to cluster in neighborhoods with kin and friends, these neighborhoods have not developed into ethnic enclaves and have essentially disappeared. Rather than establishing mutual aid societies, fraternals, social halls, and the like, Filipinos tend to rely on more informal networks for assistance during difficult times (Yu, 1980). This reliance on informal relationships involving friends and relatives is reminiscent of the Mexican American community in an earlier stage of its development.

Unlike Koreans, Filipinos have not founded churches. Nominally Roman Catholic, Filipinos have been noted for their relative lack of involvement in American Catholicism. Those who are active join local parishes that are multi-ethnic, rather than chiefly Filipino (Pido, 1986; Cordova, 1983). Thus, for Filipinos there is no fusion of religious and ethnic identities that reinforces group distinctiveness and cohesiveness. This group differs from Koreans (and other Asian groups) in yet another way: very few Filipinos own small businesses (Min, 1987). The pre-1965 immigrants did not engage in entrepreneurship to a significant extent due to a lack of capital. The post-1965 immigrants have worked to get recredentialed as quickly as possible to obtain professional employment, rather than opting for business ownership.

One reason for the lack of cohesion among Filipino Americans is that regional and linguistic loyalties transplanted from the Philippines have divided rather than united Filipinos in America. In the Philippines there are eight major languages, with about 200 different dialects. Immigrants who speak, as their first language, three of these languages are well represented: Tagalog (the most widely spoken and common language), Ilocano, and Visayan (Mangiafico, 1988; Pido, 1986). According to H. Brett Melendy (1980: 362), most immigrants can speak both English and Tagalog. Thus, there is a linguistic basis for ethnic group unity. At present, however, regional differences remain sufficiently powerful to make such unity difficult.

Compounding these differences are political differences. During the regime of Ferdinand Marcos, expatriates in America remained acutely interested in homeland politics. Marcos had both supporters and detractors in America, and the level of animosity between the two sides made cooperative political undertakings infrequent. Partly for this reason, Filipinos have not been particularly successful in organizing politically in this country to advance their collective interests. Even after Marcos was driven from power in 1986 (as the evidence accumulated about the regime's high level of corruption) and the reformist Corazon Aquino became head of state, political differences persisted (Kitano and Daniels, 1988: 87). The ongoing instability of the Philippine political system is reflected in divisions within Filipino America: some continue to support Aquino, while others are more sympathetic to some of her powerful political challengers. Although communist guerrillas have operated in the Philippines for decades, and have had considerable success in controlling some areas of the country, few Filipino Americans are sympathetic to leftist revolutionary politics.

The second generation is now coming of age. These young adults have had little or no exposure to their homeland and are far more Americanized than their parents. It is not clear what the homeland means to them. Both at school and in the labor force, their worlds are shaped by their encounters with the larger society. The immigrant generation has made relatively minimal efforts to use language schools and cultural centers to preserve a distinctively Filipino American identity among the American-born.

This suggests that over time, Filipino Americans might be far less likely to maintain their ethnic identities than will many other recent immigrant groups. Though racial distinctiveness may prove to impede inclusion into the larger society, it appears that Filipinos differ somewhat from other Asians in this regard. Both physical features and names make the Filipinos in some ways similar to Hispanic rather than Asian groups. The implications of their somewhat ambiguous identities are unclear, so it is too early to predict whether assimilation or exclusion is a more likely future outcome. As long as immigration continues, the situation will remain fluid.

Summary

Although Asians remain a distinct numerical minority in the United States, their presence has become more visible and consequential since 1965. This is partially due to the heavy concentration of Asians on the West coast, especially in California and Hawaii. It is also due to the prominent roles Asians play compared with other groups in various arenas of social life. This is the case for Korean shopkeepers in black ghettos, for Chinese in the garment industry, and in institutions of higher education where whites increasingly feel the competition of highly prepared and hard working Asian students.

This chapter examined the four largest Asian groups of the dozens in the United States: Japanese, Chinese, Korean, and Filipino. Although these groups do have many things in common, especially because the images and stereotypes employed by many white Americans tend to lump all Asians together, this chapter reveals the significant differences that have created rather different experiences in America.

For example, Japanese Americans, unlike the other three groups, have not had large numbers of new immigrants arriving during the past quarter of a century, so there is comparatively less contact with and familiarity about the homeland. The life world of

Figure 12.3   *Thanksgiving Day for Japanese Americans, 1949.*

Source: Saburo and Michiyo Inouye Photographs courtesy of the Balch Institute Library.

Japanese Americans is shaped by one world—America—rather than two. Moreover, comparatively speaking, the Japanese American community is an older one. Its educational attainment level and occupational status, combined with the high rate of intermarriage to whites raises the possibility that assimilation might result in the end of the Japanese American ethnic community.

The other three groups have grown because of recent immigration. Mass immigration in recent years has revitalized the Chinese American community, considerably expanded the number of Filipinos without strengthening the institutional fabric of the ethnic community, and created a variety of new institutions by Korean Americans. Unlike the Chinese, among the Korean and Filipino immigrants are large numbers of middle class professionals, part of the third world "brain drain." The different class compositions of the respective groups accounts to a considerable degree for the different levels of economic success discussed in this chapter. It is too soon to tell what the ultimate futures of these groups will be, but it is conceivable that if immigration declines, some of these groups may have a future similar to that of Japanese Americans.

EPILOGUE

The detailed historical, social structural, and comparative analyses of race and ethnic relations in America contained in the preceding twelve chapters make it obvious that none of the images discussed in Chapter 1 adequately captures the nation's complexity: its diversity, the constant change, and the ever-present admixture of opportunity for some groups and the denial of opportunity to others. For some groups, especially those of European origin, the nation does in many respects resemble a melting pot. But even for these groups, the melting pot oversimplifies a far more complicated situation, one in which ethnic identities continue to affect the present. For other groups, who have either been excluded from full incorporation or have chosen to retain a distinct sense of peoplehood, their social world perhaps more closely resembles a salad bowl or mosaic. Even so, much of their sense of personal identity is shaped by a shared American experience. Using the orchestra image, both beautiful harmonic melodies and a cacophony of harsh and competing sounds have been and continue to be heard.

American history involves a ceaseless interplay between diversity and unity, between allegiance to discrete ethnic and racial identities and embracing a sense of being a part of "one people." The contemporary debates over multiculturalism illustrate this well. On the one hand, exponents of multiculturalism criticize the very notion of assimilation, decrying what they perceive to be the Eurocentrism of the concept. That is, they see the call for assimilation as entailing the loss of distinctive ethnic and racial identities by non-Europeans. They emphasize differences rather than those

"Valentine's Day."

Source: Art Spiegelman's "Valentine's Day" first appeared as the cover art for *The New Yorker*, February 15, 1993. ©1993 by Art Spiegelman. Reprinted with permission of Wylie, Aitken & Stone, Inc. and with special permission of *The New Yorker*.

things which Americans share in common. On the other hand, others express concern that an overemphasis on differences tends to undermine a necessary sense of commonality and with it a common civic culture (Takaki, 1993; West, 1993; Gitlin, 1993; Taylor, et al., 1992; Schlesinger, 1992; Fuchs, 1990).

The persistent dilemma confronting American society is revealed in microcosm in the controversial Valentine's Day cover of *The New Yorker* magazine painted by Art Spiegelman. The painting depicts an Hasidic Jew passionately kissing an African American woman. The artist describes his work as knowingly naive, calling it "a wish for the reconciliation of seemingly unbridgeable differences in the form of a symbolic kiss." As Kay S. Hymowitz (1993) pointed out, blacks were angered by the painting because it recalled the sexual exploitation of black women by white men. Orthodox Jews were equally upset because Hasidic men are not permitted to express such emotions in public.

Neither embracing differences nor seeking to deny them is adequate. Neither romanticizing differences as many multiculturalists tend to do, nor denigrating them as some hostile to multiculturalism do, will help to overcome past legacies of injustice and provide the basis for a more equitable and humane society.

What is needed is greater understanding. This includes understanding the internal dynamics of the ethnic and racial groups that make up the composite American population. It involves understanding the nature of intergroup relations over time. It requires locating these groups and patterns of relationships in terms of the economic, political, and cultural character of the larger American society. This book has been an attempt to assist in that task, seeking to show how, as we approach the end of the twentieth century, we have failed as a nation to adequately address what Du Bois, at the beginning of the century, (1961 [1903]: 23) so aptly termed "the problem of the color-line."

References

Abramson, Harold J. 1973. *Ethnic Diversity in Catholic America*. New York: John Wiley and Sons.

_____. 1975. "The Religioethnic Factor and the American Experience." *Ethnicity* 2 (July): 165–177.

_____. 1980. "Assimilation and Pluralism." 150–160 in *Harvard Encyclopedia of American Ethnic Groups*, edited by Stephan Thernstrom, Ann Orlov, and Oscar Handlin. Cambridge, MA: Harvard University Press.

Adamic, Louis. 1944. *A Nation of Nations*. New York: Harper.

Adorno, T.W., Else Frenkel-Brunswik, Daniel J. Levinson, and R. Nevitt Sanford. 1950. *The Authoritarian Personality*. New York: John Wiley and Sons.

"A Guide to Understanding Chippewa Treaty Rights" ndl. Odauah, WI: Great Lakes Indian Fish and Wildlife Commission.

Aho, James A. 1990. *The Politics of Righteousness: Idaho Christian Patnotism*. Seattle: University of Washington Press.

Alba, Richard D. 1981. "The Twilight of Ethnicity Among American Catholics of European Ancestry." *Annals* 454 (March): 86–97.

_____. 1985a. "Interracial and Interethnic Marriage in the 1980 Census." Paper presented at the 1985 meetings of the American Sociological Association.

_____. 1985b. *Italian Americans: Into the Twilight of Ethnicity*. Englewood Cliffs, NJ: Prentice-Hall.

_____. 1990. *Ethnic Identity: The Transformation of White America*. New Haven: Yale University Press.

Alexander, Adele Logan. 1991. *Ambiguous Lives: Free Women of Color in Rural Georgia, 1789–1879*. Fayetteville: The University of Arkansas Press.

Allen, Irving Lewis. 1990. *Unkind Words: Ethnic Labeling From Redskin to WASP.* New York: Bergin & Garvey.

Allen, James Paul and Eugene James Turner. 1988. *We the People: An Atlas of America's Ethnic Diversity*. New York: Macmillan.

Allport, Gordon. 1958. *The Nature of Prejudice*. Garden City, NY: Doubleday.

Ander, O.F. 1931. *T.N. Hasselquist*. Rock Island, IL: Augustana Historical Society.

Anderson, Charles H. 1970. *White Protestant Americans: From National Origins to Religious Group*. Englewood Cliffs, NJ: Prentice-Hall.

Anderson, Elijah. 1990. *Streetwise: Race Class, and Change in an Urban Community*. Chicago: The University of Chicago Press.

Angelou, Maya. 1969. *I Know Why the Caged Bird Sings*. New York: Random House.

Annual Report of the Commissioner General of Immigration for 1930. Washington, D.C.: Government Printing Office.

Anthias, Floya. 1990. "Race and Class Revisited—Conceptualizing Race and Racisms." *The Sociological Review* 38 (1): 19–42.

Aponte, Robert. 1991. "Urban Hispanic Poverty: Disaggregations and Explanations." *Social Problems*, 38 (4): 516–528.

Appel, John. 1961. "Hansen's Third Generation 'Law' and the Origins of the American Jewish Historical Society." *Jewish Social Studies* 23 (January): 3–20.

Aptheker, Herbert. 1943. *American Negro Slave Revolts.* New York: Columbia University Press.

Archdeacon, Thomas. 1983. *Becoming American: An Ethnic History.* New York: The Free Press.

_____. 1985. "Problems and Possibilities in the Study of American Immigration and Ethnic History." *International Migration Review* 19 (Spring): 112–134.

_____. 1990. "Hansen's Hypothesis as a Model of Immigrant Assimilation." 42–63 in *American Immigrants and Their Generations: Studies and Commentaries on the Hansen Thesis After Fifty Years,* edited by Peter Kivisto and Dag Blanck. Urbana: University of Illinois Press.

Arendt, Hannah. 1974. *Rahel Varnhagen: The Life of a Jewish Woman.* New York: Harcourt Brace Jovanovich.

The Arizona Republic. 1987. "Fraud in Indian Country." October 11: 34.

Auletta, Ken. 1982. *The Underclass.* New York: Random House.

Awanohara, Susumu. 1991. "Tyros, Triads, Tycoons: Chinatown Ghettos Versus Arriviste Suburbs." *Far Eastern Economic Review* 153 (July 18): 50–51.

Babchuk, Nicholas and Ralph V. Thompson. 1962. "The Voluntary Associations of Negroes." *American Sociological Review* 27 (5): 647–655.

Baer, Hans A. and Merrill Singer. 1992. *African-American Religion in the Twentieth Century: Varieties of Protest and Accommodation.* Knoxville: The University of Tennessee Press.

Baily, Samuel L. 1983. "The Adjustment of Italian Immigrants in Buenos Aires and New York, 1870–1914," *The American Historical Review* 88 (2): 281–305.

Bailyn, Bernard. 1967. *The Ideological Origins of the American Revolution.* Cambridge, MA: The Belknap Press of Harvard University Press.

_____. 1986a. *The Peopling of North America: An Introduction.* New York: Alfred A. Knopf.

_____. 1986b. *Voyagers to the West: A Passage in the Peopling of America on the Eve of the Revolution.* New York: Alfred A. Knopf.

Baker, Ray Stannard. 1964 [1908]. *Following the Color Line: American Negro Citizenship in the Progressive Era.* New York: Harper Torchbooks.

Balch, Emily. 1910. *Our Slavic Fellow Citizens.* New York: Charities Publication Committee.

Baltzell, E. Digby. 1979. *Puritan Boston and Quaker Philadelphia: Two Protestant Ethics and the Spirit of Class Authority and Leadership.* New York: The Free Press.

Banner-Haley, Charles T. 1994. *The Fruits of Integration: Black Middle-Class Ideology and Culture, 1960–1990.* Jackson: University Press of Mississippi.

Banton, Michael. 1983. *Racial and Ethnic Competition.* Cambridge: Cambridge University Press.

_____. 1987. *Racial Theories.* Cambridge: Cambridge University Press.

Banton, Michael and Jonathan Harwood. 1975. *The Race Concept.* New York: Praeger.

Barkan, Elazar. 1992. *The Retreat of Scientific Racism: Changing Concepts of Race in Britain and the United States Between the World Wars.* Cambridge: Cambridge University Press.

Barrera, Mario. 1979. *Race and Class in the Southwest.* Notre Dame, IN: University of Notre Dame Press.

_____. 1985. "The Historical Evolution of Chicano Ethnic Goals: A Bibliographic Essay." *Sage Race Relations Abstracts* 10 (1): 1–48.

Barringer, Herbert, Robert W. Gardner, and Michael J. Levin. 1993. *Asians and Pacific Islanders in the United States.* New York: Russell Sage Foundation.

Barth, Fredrik, ed. 1969. *Ethnic Groups and Boundaries.* Boston: Little, Brown.

Barth, Gunther. 1964. *Bitter Strength: A History of the Chinese in the United States, 1850–1870.* Cambridge, MA: Harvard University Press.

Barton, Josef J. 1975. *Peasants and Strangers: Italians, Rumanians, and Slovaks in an American City, 1890–1950.* Cambridge, MA: Harvard University Press.

Bataille, Gretchen and Charles L.P. Silet. 1980. "The Entertaining Anachronism: Indians in American Film." 36–53 in *The Kaleidoscopic Lens: How Hollywood Views Ethnic Groups.* Englewood, NJ: Jerome S. Ozer.

Baudrillard, Jean. 1988. *America.* London: Verso.

Baum, Dan. 1990. "Blackfeet Flight Oil Exploration on Sacred Land" *Denver Post,* December 16: 1–3.

Bayor, Ronald H. 1978. *Neighbors in Conflict: The Irish, Germans, Jews, and Italians of New York City, 1929–1941.* Baltimore: The Johns Hopkins University Press.

Bean, Frank D. and Marta Tienda. 1987. *The Hispanic Population of the United States.* New York: Russell Sage Foundation.

Becerra, Rosina M. 1988. "The Mexican American Family." 141–172 in *Ethnic Families in America: Patterns and Variations,* ed. Charles H. Mindel, et al. New York: Elsevier.

Beer, William R. 1987. "Resolute Ignorance: Social Science and Affirmative Action." *Society* 24: 63–69.

Bell, Daniel. 1965. *The End of Ideology: On the Exhaustion of Political Ideas in the Fifties.* New York: Free Press.

———. 1973. *The Coming of Post-Industrial Society: A Venture in Social Forecasting.* New York: Basic Books.

Bellah, Robert, Richard Madsen, William M. Sullivan, Ann Swidler, and Stephen M. Tipton. 1985. *Habits of the Heart: Individualism and Commitment in American Life.* Berkeley: University of California Press.

Benedict, Roth. 1959. *Race: Science and Politics.* New York: The Viking Press.

Benjamin, Lois. 1992. *The Black Elite: Facing the Color Line in the Twilight of the Twentieth Century.* Chicago: Nelson-Hall.

Bensman, Joseph and Arthur J. Vidich. 1971. *The New American Society: The Revolution of the Middle Class.* Chicago: Quadrangle Books.

Berger, Bennett. 1960. *Working-Class Suburb: A Study of Auto Workers in Suburbia.* Berkeley: University of California Press.

Bergquist, James M. 1984. "German Communities in American Cities: An Interpretation of the Nineteenth-Century Experience," *Journal of American Ethnic History* 4 (Fall): 9–30.

Berle, Beatrice. 1959. *Eighty Puerto Rican Families in New York City.* New York: Columbia University Press.

Berlin, Ira. 1974. *Slaves Without Masters: The Free Negro in the Antebellum South.* New York: Pantheon Books.

Bernal, Martin. 1987. *Black Athena: The Afroasiatic Roots of Classical Civilization,* vol. I. New Brunswick, NJ: Rutgers University Press.

Berry, Brewton. 1963. *Almost White.* New York: Macmillan.

Berthoff, Rowland. 1971. *An Unsettled People: Social Order and Disorder in American History.* New York: Harper and Row.

Billigmeier, Robert Henry. 1974. *Americans from Germany: A Study in Cultural Diversity.* Belmont, CA: Wadsworth.

Billington, Roy. 1938. *The Protestant Crusade 1800–1860: A Study of the Origins of American Nativism.* New York: Macmillan.

Blackwell, James E. 1985. *The Black Community: Diversity and Unity.* New York: Harper and Row.

Blake, Casey Nelson. 1990. *Beloved Community: The Cultural Criticism of Randolph Bourne, Van Wyck Brooks, Waldo Frank and Lewis Mumford.* Chapel Hill: The University of North Carolina Press.

Blalock, Hubert M. 1967. *Toward a Theory of Minority-Group Relations.* New York: John Wiley and Sons.

Blassingame, John W. 1972. *The Slave Community: Plantation Life in the Antebellum South.* New York: Oxford University Press.

Blauner, Robert. 1969. "Internal Colonialism and Ghetto Revolt." *Social Problems* 16 (Spring): 393–408.

Blessing, Patrick J. 1980. "Irish." 524–545 in the *Harvard Encyclopedia of American Ethnic Groups,* edited by Stephan Thernstrom, Ann Orlov, and Oscar Handlin. Cambridge, MA: Harvard University Press.

Bloom, Jack M. 1987. *Class, Race, and the Civil Rights Movement.* Bloomington: Indiana University Press.

Blumberg, Rhoda Lois. 1984. *Civil Rights: The 1960s Freedom Struggle.* Boston: Twayne.

Blumer, Herbert. 1954. "What is Wrong with Social Theory?" *American Sociological Review* 19: 3–10.

———. 1958. "Race Prejudice as a Sense of Group Position." *Pacific Sociological Review* 1: 3–7.

———. 1965. "The Future of the Color Line." 322–336 in *The South in Continuity and Change,* edited by John McKinney and E.T. Thompson. Durham, NC: Duke University Press.

Bobo, Lawrence. 1983. "Whites' Opposition to Busing: Symbolic Racism or Realistic Group Conflict." *Journal of Personality and Social Psychology* 45 (6): 1196–1210.

Bodnar, John. 1976. "Materialism and Morality: Slavic-American Immigrants and Education, 1890–1940." *The Journal of Ethnic Studies* 3 (4): 1–19.

———. 1982. *Workers' World: Kinship, Community, and Protest in an Industrial Society, 1900–1940.* Baltimore: The John Hopkins University Press.

———. 1985. *The Transplanted: A History of Immigrants in Urban America.* Bloomington: Indiana University Press.

Bodnar, John, Roger Simon, and Michael P. Weber. 1982. *Lives of Their Own: Blacks, Italians, and Poles in Pittsburgh, 1900–1960.* Urbana: University of Illinois Press.

Bogardus, Emory. 1933. "A Social Distance Scale." *Sociology and Social Research* 17 (January-February): 265–271.

———. 1934. *The Mexican in the United States.* Los Angeles: University of Southern California Press.

———. 1959. *Social Distance.* Yellow Springs, OH: Antioch Press.

Bolt, Christine. 1971. *Victorian Attitudes to Race.* London: Routledge and Kegan Paul.

———. 1987. *American Indian Policy and American Reform.* London: Unwin Hyman.

Bonacich, Edna. 1972. "A Theory of Ethnic Antagonism: The Split Labor Market." *American Sociological Review* 37: 547–559.

_____. 1973. "A Theory of Middlemen Minorities." *American Sociological Review* 38 (4): 583–594.

_____. 1980. "Class Approaches to Ethnicity and Race." *Insurgent Sociologist* 10 (2): 9–23.

_____. 1992. "Alienation Among Asian and Latino Immigrants in the Los Angeles Garment Industry: The Need for New Forms of Class Struggle in the Late Twentieth Century." 165–180 in *Alienation, Society and the Individual*, ed. Feliz Geyer and Walter R. Heinz. New Brunswick, NJ: Transaction Publishers.

Bonilla, Frank and Ricardo Campos. 1981. "A Wealth of Poor: Puerto Ricans in the New Economic Order." *Daedalus* (110): 133–176.

Borjas, George J. 1990. *Friends or Strangers: The Impact of Immigrants on the U.S. Economy.* New York: Basic Books.

Boswell, Thomas D. and James R. Curtis. 1983. *The Cuban-American Experience: Culture, Images, and Perspectives.* Totowa, NJ: Rowman and Allanheld.

Bourne, Randolph. 1977. *The Radical Will: Selected Writings 1911–1918.* New York: Urizen Books.

Bouvier, Leon F. 1992. *Peaceful Invasions: Immigration and Changing America.* Lanham, MD: University Press of America.

Brace, Charles Loring. 1872. *The Dangerous Classes of New York and Twenty Years' Work Among Them.* New York: Wynkoop and Hallenbeck.

Bredemeier, Harry. 1955. *The Federal Public Housing Movement: A Case Study of Social Change.* Ph.D. dissertation, Columbia University.

Breton, Raymond. 1964. "Institutional Completeness of Ethnic Communities and the Personal Relations of Immigrants." *American Journal of Sociology* 70 (2): 193–205.

Briquets, Sergio Diaz and Lizandro Perez. 1981. *Cuba: The Demography of Revolution.* Washington, D.C.: Population Reference Bureau, vol. 36, no. 1.

Broderick, Francis L. 1959. *W.E.B. Du Bois: Negro Leader in a Time of Crisis.* Stanford, CA: Stanford University Press.

Brown, Dee. 1970. *Bury My Heart at Wounded Knee.* New York: Holt, Rinehart, and Winston.

Brown, Francis J. and Joseph S. Roucek, eds. 1937. *Our Racial and National Minorities.* New York: Prentice-Hall.

Brown, Thomas N. 1966. *Irish-American Nationalism.* Philadelphia: J.B. Lippincott.

Brownlaw, Kevin. 1990. *Behind the Mask of Innocence.* New York: Alfred A. Knopf.

Bugelski, B.R. 1961. "Assimilation Through Intermarriage." *Social Forces* 40 (December): 148–153.

Bukowczyk, John J. 1987. *And My Children Did Not Know Me: A History of the Polish-Americans.* Bloomington: Indiana University Press.

Bulosan, Carlos. 1973 [1946]. *America Is in the Heart.* Seattle: University of Washington Press.

Burma, John. 1954. *Spanish-Speaking Groups in the United States.* Durham, NC: Duke University Press.

Burt, Larry W. 1982. *Tribalism in Crisis: Federal Indian Policy, 1953–1961.* Albuquerque: University of New Mexico Press.

Burton, Jonathan. 1992. "Razed Hopes: Korean Americans Struggle to Rebuild After Riots." *Far Eastern Economic Review* 55 (October): 26–27.

Butler, Jon. 1983. *The Huguenots in America: A Refugee People in New World Society.* Cambridge, MA: Harvard University Press.

_____. 1990. *Awash in a Sea of Faith: Christianizing the American Republic.* Cambridge: Cambridge University Press.

Camarillo, Albert. 1979. *Chicanos in a Changing Society: From Mexican Pueblos to American Barrios in Santa Barbara and Southern California, 1848–1930.* Cambridge, MA: Harvard University Press.

Carling, Alan. 1991. *Social Division.* London: Verso.

Carmichael, Stokely and Charles V. Hamilton. 1967. *Black Power: The Politics of Liberation in America.* New York: Random House.

Caroli, Betty Boyd. 1973. *Italian Repatriation from the United States, 1900–1914.* New York: Center for Migration Studies.

Caroli, Betty Boyd and Thomas Kessner. 1978. "New Immigrant Women at Work: Italians and Jews in New York City, 1880–1905. *The Journal of Ethnic Studies* 28 (Winter): 5:21.

Carter, Stephen L. 1991. *Reflections of an Affirmative Action Baby.* New York: Basic Books.

Cha, Marn J. 1977. "An Ethnic Political Orientations as a Function of Assimilation: With Reference to Koreans in Los Angeles." 191–203 in *The Korean Diaspora,* edited by Hyung-chan Kim. Santa Barbara, CA: ABC-Clio.

Champagne, Duane. 1992. *Social Order and Political Change: Constitutional Government Among the Cherokee, the Choctaw, the Chickasaw, and the Creek.* Stanford, CA: Stanford University Press.

Chan, Sucheng. 1991. *Asian Americans: An Interpretive History.* Boston: Twayne.

Chavez, John R. 1984. *The Lost Land: The Chicano Image of the Southwest.* Albuquerque: University of New Mexico Press.

Chavez, Linda. 1991. *Out of the Barrio: Toward a New Politics of Hispanic Assimilation.* New York: Basic Books.

Chen, Hsiang-Shiu. 1992. *Chinatown No More: Taiwan Immigrants in Contemporary New York.* Ithaca, NY: Cornell University Press.

Chen, Jack. 1980. *The Chinese of America.* San Francisco: Harper and Row.

Cinel, Dino. 1981. "Between Change and Continuity: Regionalism Among Immigrants from the Italian Northwest." *Journal of Ethnic Studies* 9: 19–36.

———. 1982a. *From Italy to San Francisco: The Immigrant Experience.* Stanford, CA: Stanford University Press.

———. 1982b. "The Seasonal Emigrations of Italians in the Nineteenth Century: From Internal to International Destinations." *Journal of Ethnic Studies* 10: 43–68.

Clark, Dennis J. 1977. "The Irish Catholics: A Postponed Perspective." 48–68 in *Immigrants and Religion in Urban America,* ed., Randall M. Miller and Thomas D. Marzik. Philadelphia: Temple University Press.

Clark, Terry. 1975. "The Irish Ethnic and the Spirit of Patronage." *Ethnicity* 2: 305–359.

Cohen, Lizabeth. 1990. *Making a New Deal: Industrial Workers in Chicago, 1919–1939.* New York: Cambridge University Press.

Cohen, Steven M. 1988. *American Assimilation or Jewish Revival?* Bloomington: Indiana University Press.

Cohen, Steven M. and Leonard J. Fein. 1985. "From Integration to Survival: American Jewish Anxieties in Transition." *The Annals of the American Academy of Political and Social Sciences* 480 (July): 75–88.

Coleman, James S., Thomas Hoffer, and Sally Kilgore. 1981. *Public Private Schools.* Chicago: National Opinion Research Center.

Coleman, James S., Sara D. Kelly, and John A. Moore. 1975. *Trends in School Segregation 1968–1973.* Washington, D.C.: Urban Institute.

Coleman, James, Ernest Q. Campbell, Carol J. Hobson, James McPartlarl, Alexander Mood, Frederick D. Weinfield, and Robert L. York. 1966. *Equality of Educational Opportunity.* Washington, D.C.: Government Printing Office.

Collier, John. 1945. "United States Indian Administration as a Laboratory of Ethnic Relations." *Social Research* 12 (2): 265–303.

Commager, Henry Steele. 1977. *The Empire of Reason: How Europe Imagined and America Realized the Enlightenment.* Garden City, New York: Anchor Press.

Connell, K.H. 1950. *The Population of Ireland, 1750–1845.* London: Oxford University Press.

Connor, Walker. 1978. "A Nation is a Nation, is a State, is an Ethnic Group, is a . . ." *Ethnic and Racial Studies,* 1 (4): 377–400.

Conzen, Kathleen Neils. 1976. *Immigrant Milwaukee, 1836–1860: Accommodation and Community in a Frontier City.* Cambridge, MA: Harvard University Press.

———. 1980. "Germans." 405–425 in *Harvard Encyclopedia of American Ethnic Groups,* edited by Stephan Thernstrom, Ann Orlov, and Oscar Handlin. Cambridge, MA: Harvard University Press.

———. 1985. "Peasant Pioneers: Generational Succession Among German Farmers in Frontier Minnesota." 259–292, in *The Countryside in the Age of Capitalist Transformation,* edited by Steven Hahn. Chapel Hill: University of North Carolina Press.

———. 1991. "Ethnic Patterns in America Cities: Historiographical Trends." Paper presented in Vaxjo, Sweden, May 31.

Conzen, Kathleen Neils, David A. Gerber, Ewa Morawska, George E. Pozzetta, and Rudolph J. Vecoli. 1990. "The Invention of Ethnicity: A Perspective from the USA." *Altreitalie* 3: 37–62.

Coon, Carleton S. 1965. *The Living Races of Man.* New York: Alfred A. Knopf.

Cordova, Fred. 1983. *Filipinos.* Dubuque, IA: Kendall-Hunt.

Cornell, Stephan. 1988. *The Return of the Native: American Indian Political Resurgence.* New York: Oxford University Press.

Cortés, Carlos. 1980. "Mexicans." 697–719 in *Harvard Encyclopedia of American Ethnic Groups,* edited by Stephan Thernstrom, Ann Orlov, and Oscar Handlin. Cambridge, MA: Harvard University Press.

Cottle, Thomas J. 1976. *Busing.* Boston: Beacon Press.

Covello, Leonard. 1972. *The Social Background of the Italo-American School Child.* Totowa, NJ: Rowan and Littlefield.

Cowell, D.D. 1985. "Funerals, Family, and Forefathers: A View of Italian-American Funeral Practices." *Omega* 16: 69–85.

Cox, Oliver C. 1948. *Caste, Class, and Race.* New York: Monthly Review Press.

CQ Researcher. 1992. *Illegal Immigration.* Washington, D.C.: Congressional Quarterly, April 24.

Craven, Wesley Frank. 1971. "Twenty Negroes to Jamestown in 1619?" *Virginia Quarterly Review* 47: 416–420.

Cravens, Hamilton. 1978. *The Triumph of Evolution: American Scientists and the Hereditary-Environment Controversy, 1900–1941.* Philadelphia: University of Pennsylvania Press.

Creel, Margaret Washington. 1988. *"A Peculiar People": Slave Religion and Community-Culture Among the Gullahs.* New York: New York University Press.

Creelan, Paul and Robert Granfield. 1986. "The Polish Peasant and the Pilgrim's Progress: Morality and Myth in W. I. Thomas' Social Theory." *Journal for the Scientific Study of Religion* 25 (2): 162–179.

Crispino, James A. 1980. *The Assimilation of Ethnic Groups: The Italian Case.* Staten Island, NY: Center for Migration Studies.

Cronon, E. David. 1955. *Black Moses: The Story of Marcus Garvey and the Universal Negro Improvement Association*. Madison: University of Wisconsin Press.

Cross, William E., Jr. 1991. *Shades of Black: Diversity in African-American Identity*. Philadelphia: Temple University Press.

Curti, Merle, with the assistance of Robert Daniel, Shaw Livermore, Jr., Joseph Van Hise, and Margaret W. Curti. 1959. *The Making of an American Community: A Case Study of Democracy in a Frontier County*. Stanford, CA: Stanford University Press.

Curtin, Philip. 1969. *The Atlantic Slave Trade*. Madison: University of Wisconsin Press.

Dadrian, Vahakn N. 1989. "Genocide as a Problem of National and International Law: The World War I Armenian Case and its Contemporary Legal Ramifications." *Yale Journal of International Law* 14 (2): 221–334.

Daniel, Pete. 1985. *Breaking the Land: The Transformation of Cotton, Tobacco, and Rice Cultures Since 1880*. Urbana: University of Illinois Press.

Daniels, Roger. 1972. *Concentration Camps, U.S.A., Japanese Americans and World War II*. New York: Holt, Rinehart, and Winston.

_____. 1988. *Asian America: Chinese and Japanese in the United States Since 1850*. Seattle: University of Washington Press.

_____. 1990. *Coming to America: A History of Immigration and Ethnicity in American Life*. New York: Harper Collins.

Danzger, Herbert M. 1989. *Returning to Tradition: The Contemporary Revival of Orthodox Judaism*. New Haven: Yale University Press.

Dashefsky, Arnold, ed. 1976. *Ethnic Identity in Society*. Chicago: Rand McNally.

Davis, Allison, Burleigh B. Gardner, and Mary R. Gardner. 1941. *Deep South: A Social Anthropological Study of Caste and Class*. Chicago: The University of Chicago Press.

Davis, David Brion. 1966. *The Problem of Slavery in Western Culture*. Ithaca, New York: Cornell University Press.

Davis, F. James. 1991. *Who is Black? One Nation's Definition*. University Park, PA: Pennsylvania State University Press.

Debo, Angie. 1970. *A History of the Indians of the United States*. Norman: University of Oklahoma Press.

DeConde, Alexander. 1992. *Ethnicity, Race and American Foreign Policy*. Boston: Northeastern University Press.

de Crèvecoeur, J. Hector St. John. 1904 [1782]. *Letters from an American Farmer*. New York: Fox, Duffield.

Degler, Carl. 1991. *In Search of Human Nature: The Decline and Revival of Darwinism in American Social Thought*. New York: Oxford University Press.

Delgado, Héctor L. 1993. *New Immigrants, Old Unions: Organizing Undocumented Workers in Los Angeles*. Philadelphia: Temple University Press.

Deloria, Vine, Jr., ed. 1985. *American Indian Policy in the Twentieth Century*. Norman: University of Oklahoma Press.

Denevan, William M., ed. 1976. *The Native Population of the Americas in 1492*. Madison: University of Wisconsin Press.

Denton, Nancy A. and Douglas S. Massey. 1989. "Racial Identity Among Caribbean Hispanics: The Effect of Double Minority Status on Residential Segregation." *American Sociological Review* 54 (5): 790–808.

Department of Housing and Urban Development. 1980. *Condominium Conversions*. Washington, D.C.: Government Printing Office.

de Toqueville, Alexis. 1981 [1835]. *Democracy in America.* New York: The Modern Library.

Deutsch, Sarah. 1987. *No Separate Refuge: Culture, Class, and Gender on an Anglo-Hispanic Frontier in the American Southwest, 1880–1940.* New York: Oxford University Press.

di Leonardo, Micaela. 1984. *The Varieties of Ethnic Experience: Kinship, Class, and Gender Among California Italian-Americans.* Ithaca, N.Y.: Cornell University Press.

Diner, Hasia R. 1983. *Erin's Daughters in America: Irish Immigrant Women in the Nineteenth Century.* Baltimore: The Johns Hopkins University Press.

Dinnerstein, Leonard and David M. Reimers. 1988. *Ethnic Americans: A History of Immigration.* New York: Harper and Row.

Dinnerstein, Leonard, Roger L. Nichols, and David M. Reimers. 1990. *Natives and Strangers: Blacks, Indians, and Immigrants in America.* New York: Oxford University Press.

Dolan, Jay. 1975. *The Immigrant Church: New York's Irish and German Catholics, 1815–1865.* Baltimore: The Johns Hopkins University Press.

Dollard, John. 1937. *Caste and Class in a Southern Town.* New Haven: Yale University Press.

Donaldson, Gordon. 1980. "Scots." 908–916 in *Harvard Encyclopedia of American Ethnic Groups,* edited by Stephan Thernstrom, Ann Orlov, and Oscar Handlin. Cambridge, MA: Harvard University Press.

Dore, R.F. 1959. *Land Reform in Japan.* New York: Oxford University Press.

Dorris, Michael A. 1981. "The Grass Still Grows, The Rivers Still Flow: Contemporary Native Americans." *Daedalus* 110 (Spring): 43–69.

Douglass, William A. and John Bilbao. 1975. *Amerikanauk: The Basques in the New World.* Reno: University of Nevada Press.

Douglass, William A. and Stanford Lyman. 1976. "L'ethnie: Structure, processus, et saillance." *Cahiers Internationale de Sociologie* 61: 342–358.

Dowd, Gregory Evans. 1991. *A Spirited Resistance: The North American Indian Struggle for Unity, 1745–1815.* Baltimore: The John Hopkins University Press.

Doyle, Bertram W. 1936. "The Etiquette of Race Relations—Past, Present, and Future." *Journal of Negro Education* 5: 191–208.

Drake, St. Clair and Horace R. Cayton. 1962 [1945]. *Black Metropolis: A Study of Negro Life in a Northern City.* New York: Harper and Row.

Driver, Harold E. 1969. *Indians of North America.* Chicago: The University of Chicago Press.

Dubinin, N.P. 1956. "Race and Contemporary Genetics." 68–94 in *Race, Science and Society,* Leo Kuper, ed. Paris: The Unesco Press.

Dublin, Thomas. 1993. *Immigrant Voice New Lives in America, 1773–1986.* Urbana: University of Illinois Press.

Dubofsky, Melvyn. 1969. *We Shall Be All: A History of the Industrial Workers of The World.* Chicago: Quadrangle.

Du Bois, W.E.B. 1961 [1903]. *The Souls of Black Folk.* New York: Fawcett World Library.

————. 1969 [1896]. *The Suppression of the African Slave-Trade to the United States of America, 1638–1870.* New York: Schocken Books.

————. 1970 [1909]. *The Negro American Family.* Cambridge, MA: MIT Press.

————. 1973 [1935]. *Black Reconstruction in America: An Essay Toward a History of the Part Which Black Folk Played in the Attempt to Reconstruct Democracy in America, 1860–1880.* New York: Atheneum.

Dunn, L. C. and Th. Dobzhansky. 1952. *Heredity, Race, and Society.* New York: The New American Library.

Duster, Troy. 1990. *Backdoor to Eugenics.* New York: Routledge.

Early, Gerald, ed. 1993. *Lure and Loathing: Essays on Race, Identity, and the Ambivalence of Assimilation*. New York: The Penguin Press.

Easterlin, Richard A., David Ward, William S. Bernard, and Reed Ueda. 1980. *Immigration*. Cambridge, MA: The Belknap Press of Harvard University Press.

The Economist. 1990. "American Survey," September 29: 41–42.

Edsall, Thomas Byrne and Mary D. Edsall. 1991. "Race." *The Atlantic Monthly* 267 (5): 53–86.

Elkins, Stanley M. 1959. *Slavery: A Problem in American Institutional and Intellectual Life*. Chicago: The University of Chicago Press.

Erickson, Charlotte. 1972. *Invisible Immigrants: The Adaptation of English and Scottish Immigrants in Nineteenth-Century America*. Coral Gables, FL: University of Miami Press.

————. 1980. "English." 319–336 in *Harvard Encyclopedia of American Ethnic Groups*, edited by Stephan Thernstrom, Ann Orlov, and Oscar Handlin. Cambridge, MA: Harvard University Press.

Erie, Steven P. 1988. *Rainbow's End: Irish-Americans and the Dilemmas of Urban Machine Politics, 1840–1985*. Berkeley: University of California Press.

Ewen, Elizabeth. 1980. "City Lights: Immigrant Women and the Rise of the Movies." *Signs* 5 (3): 45–65.

Ezorsky, Gertrude. 1991. *Racism and Justice: The Case for Affirmative Action*. Ithaca, NY: Cornell University Press.

Fairchild, Henry Pratt. 1926. *The Melting Pot Mistake*. Boston: Little, Brown.

Falcon, Luis M., Douglas T. Gurak, and Mary G. Powers. 1990. "Labor Force Participation of Puerto Rican Women in Greater New York City." *Sociology and Social Research*. 74 (2): 110–117.

Fallows, Marjorie R. 1979. *Irish Americans: Identity and Assimilation*. Englewood Cliffs, NJ: Prentice-Hall.

Farber, Bernard, Charles H. Mindel, and Bernard Lazerwitz. 1988. "The Jewish American Family." 400–437 in *Ethnic Families in America: Patterns and Variations*, edited by Charles H. Mindel, Robert W. Habenstein, and Roosevelt Wright, Jr. New York: Elsevier.

Farley, John E. 1982. *Majority-Minority Relations*. Englewood Cliffs, NJ: Prentice-Hall.

Farley, Reynolds. 1984. *Blacks and Whites: Narrowing the Gap?* Cambridge, MA: Harvard University Press.

————. 1990. "Blacks, Hispanics, and White Ethnic Groups: Are Blacks Uniquely Disadvantaged?" *The American Economic Review* 80 (2): 237–241.

Farley, Reynolds and Walter R. Allen. 1989. *The Color Line and the Quality of Life in America*. New York: Oxford University Press.

Farley, Reynolds and William H. Frey. 1994. "Changes in the Segregation of Whites From Blacks During the 1980s: Small Steps Toward a More Integrated Society." *American Sociological Review* 59 (1): 23–45.

Farley, Reynolds, Howard Schumun, Suzanne Biachi, Diane Colasyto, and Shirley Hatchett. 1978. "Chocolate City, Vanilla Suburbs: Will the Trend Toward Racially Separate Communities Continue?" *Social Science Research* 7 (December): 319–344.

Farley, Reynolds, Toni Richards, and Clarence Wurdock. 1980. "School Desegregation and White Flight: An Investigation of Competing Models and Their Discrepant Findings." *Sociology of Education* 53: 123–139.

Fass, Paula S. 1989. *Outside In: Minorities and the Transformation of American Education*. New York: Oxford University Press.

Faust, Albert B. 1909. *The German Element in the United States, With Special Reference to its Political, Moral, Social, and Educational Influence*. Vols. 1 and 2. Boston, MA: Houghton Mifflin.

Feagin, Joe R. 1984. *Racial and Ethnic Relations*. Englewood Cliffs, NJ: Prentice-Hall, Inc.

————. 1991. "The Continuing Significance of Race: Antiblack Discrimination in Public Places." *American Sociological Review* 56 (1): 101–116.

Feinberg, William E. 1985. "Are Affirmative Action and Economic Growth Alternative Paths to Racial Equality?" *American Sociological Review* 50 (4): 561–571.

Femminella, Francis X., ed. 1985. *Irish and Italian Interaction*. New York: Italian-American Historical Association.

Ferraro, Thomas. 1993. *Ethnic Passages: Literary Immigrants in Twentieth-Century America*. Chicago: The University of Chicago Press.

Fischer, David Hackett. 1989. *Albion's Seed: Four British Folkways in America*. New York: Oxford University Press.

Fishel, Leslie H., Jr. and Benjamin Quarles. 1970. *The Black American: A Brief Documentary History*. Glenview, IL: Scott, Foresman.

Fisher, Alan M. 1979. "Realignment of the Jewish Vote?" *Political Science Quarterly* 94: 97–116.

Fisher, Robert. 1959. *Twenty Years of Public Housing*. New York: Harper and Brothers.

Fishman, Joshua, ed. 1966. *Language Loyalty in the United States*. The Hague: Mouton.

Fishman, Joshua, Michael H. Gertner, Esther G. Lowy, and William G. Milán. 1985. *The Rise and Fall of the Ethnic Revival*. Berlin: Mouton.

Fishman, Sylvia Barack. 1987. *Learning About Learning: Insights on Contemporary Jewish Education from Jewish Population Studies*. Research Report 2, Center for Modern Jewish Studies, Brandeis University.

Fitzhugh, George. 1854. "Sociology for the South: Or the Failure of Free Society." Salem, NH: Ayer Company.

Fitzpatrick, Joseph P. 1980. "Puerto Ricans." 858–867 in *Harvard Encyclopedia of American Ethnic Groups*, edited by Stephan Thernstrom, Ann Orlov, and Oscar Handlin. Cambridge, MA: Harvard University Press.

————. 1987. *Puerto Rican Americans: The Meaning of Migration to the Mainland*. Englewood Cliffs, NJ: Prentice-Hall.

Fixico, Donald L. 1986. *Termination and Relocation: Federal Indian Policy, 1945–1960*. Albuquerque: University of New Mexico Press.

————. 1985. "Tribal Leaders and The Demand for Natural Energy Resources on Tribal Lands." 42–78 in *The Plains Indians of the Twentieth Century* ed. Peter Iverson. Norman: University of Oklahoma Press.

Fligstein, Neil. 1981. *Going North: Migration of Blacks and Whites from the South, 1900–1950*. New York: Academic Press.

Flores, Juan. 1985. "Que Assimilated Brother, Yo Soy Asimilao": The Structuring of Puerto Rican Identity in the U.S." *The Journal of Ethnic Studies* 13 (3): 1–16.

Foerster, Robert S. 1919. *The Italian Emigration of Our Times*. Cambridge, MA: Harvard University Press.

Fogel, Robert William. 1989. *Without Consent or Contract: The Rise and Fall of American Slavery*. New York: W.W. Norton.

Fogel, Robert William and Stanley L. Engerman. 1974. *Time on the Cross: The Economics of American Negro Slavery*. Boston: Little, Brown.

Foner, Eric. 1988. *Reconstruction: America's Unfinished Revolution, 1863–1877*. New York: Harper and Row.

———. 1990. "Blacks and the U.S. Constitution, 1789–1989." *New Left Review*, no. 183 (September/October): 63–74.

Fong, Timothy P. 1994. *The First Suburban Chinatown: The Remaking of Monterey Park, California*. Philadelphia: Temple University Press.

Formisano, Ronald P. 1991. *Boston Against Busing: Race, Class, and Ethnicity in the 1960s and 1970s*. Chapel Hill: University of North Carolina Press.

Foster, Morris W. 1991. *Being Comanche: A Social History of an American Indian Community*. Tucson: University of Arizona Press.

Foucault, Michel. 1979. *Discipline and Punish: The Birth of the Prison*. New York: Vintage Books.

Fox-Genovese, Elizabeth and Eugene D. Genovese. 1983. *Fruits of Merchant Capital: Slavery and Bourgeois Property in the Rise and Expansion of Capitalism*. New York: Oxford University Press.

Francis, E.K. 1947. "The Nature of the Ethnic Group." *American Journal of Sociology* 52 (5): 393–400.

———. 1951. "Minority Groups—A Revision of Concepts." *British Journal of Sociology* 2: 219–229.

———. 1976. *Interethnic Relations: An Essay in Sociological Theory*. New York: Elsevier.

Franklin, John Hope. 1967. *From Slavery to Freedom: A History of Negro Americans*. New York: Alfred A. Knopf.

Franklin, Raymond S. 1991. *Shadows of Race and Class*. Minneapolis: University of Minnesota Press.

Frazier, E. Franklin. 1939. *The Negro Family in the United States*. Chicago: The University of Chicago Press.

———. 1949. *The Negro in the United States*. New York: Macmillany.

———. 1957. *Black Bourgeoisie: The Rise of a New Middle Class in the United States*. New York: The Free Press.

———. 1963. *The Negro Church in America*. New York: Schocken Books.

Fredrickson, George M. 1981. *White Supremacy: A Comparative Study in American and South African History*. New York: Oxford University Press.

Freehling, William W. 1986. "Denmark Vesey's Peculiar Reality." 25–47 in *Race and Slavery in America: Essays in Honor of Kenneth M. Stampp*, edited by Robert H. Abzug and Stephen E. Maizlish. Lexington: The University Press of Kentucky.

Freeman, Leonard. 1969. *Public Housing: The Politics of Poverty*. New York: Holt, Rinehart, and Winston.

Friedman, Lawrence. 1978. *Government and Slum Housing*. New York: Arno Press.

Fuchs, Lawrence H. 1990. *The American Kaleidoscope: Race, Ethnicity, and the Civic Culture*. Hanover, NH: Wesleyan University Press.

Fugita, Stephen S. and David J. O'Brien. 1991. *Japanese American Ethnicity: The Persistence of Community*. Seattle: University of Washington Press.

Fukuda, Yoshiaki. 1990. *My Six Years of Internment: An Issei's Struggle for Justice*. San Francisco: The Konko Church.

Fullinwider, Robert K. 1980. *The Reverse Discrimination Controversy*. Totowa, NJ: Rowan and Littlefield.

Furer, Howard B. 1972. *The British in America 1578–1970: A Chronology and Fact Book*. Dobbs Ferry, NY: Oceana Publications.

Gabaccia, Donna. 1988. *Militants and Migrants: Rural Sicilians Become American Workers.* New Brunswick, NJ: Rutgers University Press.

Gambino, Richard. 1974. *Blood of My Blood.* New York: Anchor Books.

Gans, Herbert. 1956. "American Jewry Present and Future." *Commentary* 21 (5): 422–430.

———. 1962. *The Urban Villagers: Group and Class in the Life of Italian-Americans.* Glencoe, IL: The Free Press.

———. 1967. *The Levittouners: Ways of Life and Politics in a New Suburban Community.* New York: Pantheon Books.

———. 1979. "Symbolic Ethnicity: The Future of Ethnic Groups and Cultures in America." 193–220 in *On the Making of Americans: Essays in Honor of David Riesman*, edited by Herbert J. Gans, Nathan Glazer, Joseph R. Gusfield, and Christopher Jencks. Philadelphia: University of Pennsylvania Press.

———. 1985. "Ethnicity, Ideology, and the Insider Problem." *Contemporary Sociology* 14 (3): 303–304.

———. 1992. "Comment: Ethnic Invention and Acculturation, A Bumpy-Line Approach." *Journal of American Ethnic History* 12 (1): 42–52.

Garcia, Mario T. 1981. *Desert Immigrants: The Mexicans of El Paso, 1880–1920.* New Haven: Yale University Press.

———. 1989. *Mexican Americans: Leadership, Ideology, and Identity, 1930–1960.* New Haven: Yale University Press.

Garcia, Richard A. 1991. *Rise of the Mexican Middle Class: San Antonio, 1929–1941.* College Station: Texas A&M University Press.

Garrow, David J. 1978. *Protest at Selma: Martin Luther King, Jr., and the Voting Rights Act of 1965.* New Haven: Yale University Press.

Geertz, Clifford. 1973. *The Interpretation of Culture.* New York: Basic Books.

Gellner, Ernest. 1983. *Nations and Nationalism.* Ithaca, New York: Cornell University Press.

Genovese, Eugene D. 1969. *The World the Slaveholders Made: Two Essays in Interpretation.* New York: Pantheon Books.

———. 1972. *Roll, Jordan, Roll: The World the Slaves Made.* New York: Pantheon Books.

———. 1979. *From Rebellion to Revolution: Afro-American Slave Revolts in the Making of the Modern World.* Baton Rouge: Louisiana State University Press.

Geschwender, James. 1978. *Racial Stratification in America.* Dubuque, IA: William C. Brown.

Giddens, Anthony. 1973. *The Class Structure of the Advanced Societies.* New York: Harper and Row.

———. 1984. *The Constitution of Society: Outline of a Theory of Structuration.* Berkeley: University of California Press.

Giddings, Franklin Henry. 1893. *Philanthropy and Social Progress.* New York: Thomas Y. Crowell.

Gitlin, Todd. 1993. "The Rise of 'Identity Politics'." *Dissent* (Spring): 172–177.

Glazer, Nathan. 1957. *American Judaism.* Chicago: The University of Chicago Press.

———. 1975. *Affirmative Discrimination: Ethnic Inequality and Public Policy.* New York: Basic Books.

———. 1985. "On Jewish Forbodings." *Commentary* 80 (2): 32–36.

Glazer, Nathan and Daniel P. Moynihan. 1963. *Beyond the Melting Pot.* Cambridge, MA: MIT Press and Harvard University Press.

———. 1975. "Introduction." 1–26 in *Ethnicity: Theory and Experience*, edited by Nathan Glazer and Daniel P. Moynihan. Cambridge, MA: Harvard University Press.

Gleason, Philip. 1964. "The Melting Pot: Symbol of Fusion or Confusion?" *American Quarterly* 16 (1): 20–46.

_____. 1983. "Identifying Identity: A Semantic History." *Journal of American History* 69 (4): 428–453.

_____. 1991. "Minorities (Almost) All: The Minority Concept in American Social Thought." *American Quarterly* 43 (3): 392–424.

_____. 1992. *Speaking of Diversity: Language and Ethnicity in Twentieth-Century America.* Baltimore: The John Hopkins University Press.

Glenn, Evelyn Nakano. 1986. *Issei, Nisei, War Bride: Three Generations of Japanese American Women in Domestic Service.* Philadelphia: Temple University Press.

Glenn, Norvall D. 1982. "Interreligious Marriage in the United States." *Journal of Marriage and the Family* 44: 555–565.

Glenn, Susan A. 1990. *Daughters of the Shtetl: Life and Labor in the Immigrant Generation.* Ithaca, New York: Cornell University Press.

Gobineau, Arthur de. 1915 [1853–55]. *The Inequality of Human Races.* London: Heinemann.

Goering, John M. 1971. "The Emergence of Ethnic Interests: A Case of Serendipity." *Social Forces* 48 (March): 379–384.

_____. 1986. "Minority Housing Needs and Civil Rights Enforcement." 195–215 in *Race, Ethnicity, and Minority Housing in the United States*, edited by Jamshid A. Momeni. Westport, CT: Greenwood Press.

Goffman, Erving. 1961. *Asylums: Essays on the Social Situation of Mental Patients and Other Inmates.* Garden City, New York: Doubleday.

Golab, Caroline. 1977. *Immigrant Destinations.* Philadelphia: Temple University Press.

Gold, Steven J. 1992. "Chinese-Vietnamese Entrepreneurs in California." Paper presented at the annual meeting of the American Sociological Association, Pittsburgh, PA.

Goldscheider, Calvin. 1986. *Jewish Continuity and Change.* Bloomington: Indiana University Press.

Goldscheider, Calvin and Alan S. Zuckerman. 1984. *The Transformation of the Jews.* Chicago: The University of Chicago Press.

Gomez-Quiñones, Juan. 1990. *Chicano Politics: Reality and Promise, 1940–1990.* Albuquerque: University of New Mexico Press.

Gonzalez, David. 1992a. "What's the Problem with 'Hispanic'? Just Ask a 'Latino'." *New York Times*, November 15: E6.

_____. 1992b. "Dominican Immigration Alters Hispanic New York." *New York Times*, September 1, A1 and A11.

Goodwyn, Lawrence. 1978. *The Populist Movement.* New York: Oxford University Press.

Gordon, Milton M. 1964. *Assimilation in American Life: The Role of Race, Religion, and National Origins.* New York: Oxford University Press.

Goren, Arthur A. 1980. "Jews." 571–598 in *Harvard Encyclopedia of American Ethnic Groups*, edited by Stephan Thernstrom, Ann Orlov, and Oscar Handlin. Cambridge, MA: Harvard University Press.

Gossett, Thomas. 1965. *Race: The History of an Idea in America.* Dallas: Southern Methodist University Press.

Graham, Ian Charles. 1956. *Colonists from Scotland: Emigration to North America, 1707–1783.* Ithaca, NY: Cornell University Press.

Grant, Madison. 1916. *The Passing of the Great Race.* New York: C. Scribner's Sons.

Greeley, Andrew M. 1971. *Why Can't They Be Like Us? America's White Ethnic Groups.* New York: E.P. Dutton.

———. 1974. *Ethnicity in the United States: A Preliminary Reconnaissance.* New York: John Wiley and Sons.

———. 1975. "A Model for Ethnic Political Socialization." *American Journal of Political Science* 19: 187–206.

———. 1988. "The Success and Assimilation of Irish Protestants and Irish Catholics in the United States." *Sociology and Social Research* 72: 229–236.

Greeley, Andrew and William C. McCready. 1975. "The Transmission of Cultural Heritages: The Case of the Italians and the Irish." 209–235 in *Ethnicity: Theory and Experience*, edited by Nathan Glazer and Daniel P. Moynihan. Cambridge, MA: Harvard University Press.

Greeley, Andrew, William C. McCready and Gary Theisen. 1980. *Ethnic Drinking Subcultures.* New York: Praeger.

Green, George N. 1992. "The Felix Longoria Affair." *The Journal of Ethnic Studies* 19 (3): 23–49.

Greenbaum, Susan D. 1991. "A Comparison of African American and Euro-American Mutual Aid Societies in 19th Century America." *The Journal of Ethnic Studies* 19 (3): 95–119.

Greene, Victor R. 1968. *The Slavic Community on Strike.* Notre Dame, IN: University of Notre Dame Press.

———. 1975. *For God and Country.* Madison: Wisconsin State Historical Society.

———. 1980. "Poles." 787–803 in *Harvard Encyclopedia of American Ethnic Groups*, edited by Stephan Thernstrom, Ann Orlov, and Oscar Handlin. Cambridge, MA: Harvard University Press.

———. 1987. *American Immigrant Leaders 1800–1910: Marginality and Identity.* Baltimore: The Johns Hopkins University Press.

———. 1990. "Old-time Folk Dancing and Music Among the Second Generation, 1920–50." 142–163 in *American Immigrants and Their Generations*, edited by Peter Kivisto and Dag Blanck. Urbana: University of Illinois Press.

Griswold del Castillo, Richard. 1979. *The Los Angeles Barrio, 1850–1890: A Social History.* Berkeley: University of California Press.

Grossman, James. 1989. *Land of Hope: Chicago, Black Southerners, and the Great Migration.* Chicago: The University of Chicago Press.

Gutierrez, Armando and Herbert Hirsch. 1970. "The Militant Challenge to the American Ethos: 'Chicanos' and 'Mexican Americans'." *Social Science Quarterly* 53 (March): 830–845.

Gutierrez, David G. 1991. "Sin *Fronteras*?: Chicanos, Mexican Americans, and the Emergence of the Contemporary Mexican Immigration Debate, 1968–1978." *Journal of American Ethnic History,* 10 (4): 5–37.

Gutman, Herbert. 1976. *The Black Family in Slavery and Freedom, 1750–1925.* New York: Pantheon Books.

Hacker, Andrew. 1992. *Two Nations: Black and White, Separate, Hostile, Unequal.* New York: Charles Scribner's Sons.

Haines, Herbert H. 1988. *Black Radicals and the Civil Rights Mainstream, 1954–1970.* Knoxville: The University of Tennessee Press.

Handlin, Oscar. 1948. *Race and Nationality in American Life.* Boston: Little, Brown.

———. 1959. *Immigration as a Factor in American History.* Englewood Cliffs, NJ: Prentice-Hall.

———. 1970. *Boston's Immigrants.* New York: Atheneum.

———. 1973. *The Uprooted.* Boston: Little, Brown.

Handlin, Oscar and Lilian Handlin. 1982. *A Restless People: Americans in Rebellion, 1770–1787.* Garden City, NJ: Anchor Press.

Hanke, Lewis. 1970. *Aristotle and the American Indians.* Bloomington: Indiana University Press

Hannerz, Ulf. 1969. *Soulside: Inquires into Ghetto Culture and Community.* New York: Columbia University Press.

Hansen, Marcus Lee. 1938. "The Problem of the Third Generation Immigrant." Rock Island, IL: Augustana Historical Society.

_____. 1940a. *The Atlantic Migration, 1607–1860: A History of the Continuing Settlement of the United States.* Cambridge, MA: Harvard University Press.

_____. 1940b. *The Immigrant in American History.* Cambridge, MA: Harvard University Press.

Hansen, Marcus Lee and John Bartlett Brebner. 1940. *The Mingling of the Canadian and American Peoples*, Vol. I. Historical. New Haven: Yale University Press.

Harding, Sandra, ed. 1987. *Feminism and Methodology.* Bloomington: Indiana University Press.

Harlan, Louis. 1983. *Booker T. Washington: The Wizard of Tuskegee, 1901–1915.* New York: Oxford University Press.

Harney, Robert F. 1976. "The Italian Experience in the United States." 1–18 in *A Handbook for Teachers of Italian*, edited by Anthony Mollica. New York: American Association of Teachers of Italian.

Harney, Robert F. and J. Vincenza Scarpaci, eds. 1981. *Little Italies in North America.* Toronto: The Multicultural History Society of Ontario.

Harrington, Michael. 1962. *The Other America: Poverty in the United States.* Baltimore: Penguin Books.

Hauptman, Laurence M. and James D. Wherry. 1990. *The Pequots in Southern New England: The Fall and Rise of an American Indian Nation.* Norman: University of Oklahoma Press.

Hawgood, John A. 1940. *The Tragedy of German America: The Germans in the United States of America During the Nineteenth Century—and After.* New York: G.P. Putnam's Sons.

Hechter, Michael. 1986. "Rational Choice and the Study of Race and Ethnic Relations." 264–279 in *Theories of Race and Ethnic Relations*, edited by John Rex and David Mason. Cambridge: Cambridge University Press.

Hechter, Michael, Debra Friedman and M. Appelbaum. 1982. "A Theory of Ethnic Collective Action." *International Migration Review* 16: 412–434.

Heer, David M. 1990. *Undocumented Mexicans in the United States.* Cambridge: Cambridge University Press.

Heilman, Samuel C. and Steven M. Cohen. 1989. *Cosmopolitans and Parochials: Modern Orthodox Jewish America.* Chicago: The University of Chicago Press.

Heller, Scott. 1991. "Anthropologists Examine Commemorations of Columbus's Fateful Voyage." *The Chronicle of Higher Education* 38 (17): A9–A10. (December 18).

Herberg, Will. 1955. *Protestant-Catholic-Jew: An Essay in American Religious Sociology.* Garden City, NY: Doubleday.

Hero, Rodney E. 1992. *Latinos and the U.S. Political System: Two-Tiered Pluralism.* Philadelphia: Temple University Press.

Herskovits, M.J. 1941. *The Myth of the Negro Past.* New York: Harper and Brothers.

Hertzberg, Arthur. 1989. *The Jews in America. Four Centuries of an Uneasy Encounter: A History.* New York: Simon and Schuster.

_____. 1989. "The End of American Jewish History." *The New York Review of Books* 36: 26–30.

Heyman, Josiah McC. 1991. *Life and Labor on the Border: Working People of Northeastern Sonora, Mexico, 1886–1986*. Tucson: University of Arizona Press.

Higgs, Robert. 1978. "Landless by Law: Japanese Immigrants in California Agriculture to 1941." *Journal of Economic History* (38) (1): 205–225.

Higham, John. 1970. *Strangers in the Land*. New York: Atheneum.

———, ed. 1978. *Ethnic Leadership in America*. Baltimore: The Johns Hopkins University Press.

———. 1982. "Current Trends in the Study of Ethnicity in the United States." *Journal of American Ethnic History* 2 (1): 5–15.

Hill, Herbert. 1966. *Anger, and Beyond: The Negro Writer in the United States*. New York: Harper and Row.

———. 1973. "Anti-Oriental Agitation and the Rise of Working-Class Racism." *Transaction* 10 (2): 43–54.

Hirata, Lucie Cheny. 1975. "Free, Indentured, Enslaved: Chinese Prostitutes in Nineteenth Century America." *Signs* 5 (Autumn): 3–29.

Hirschman, Charles. 1983. "America's Melting Pot Reconsidered." *Annual Review of Sociology* 9: 397–423.

"The Hispanic Population in the United States: March 1991." *Current Population Reports*, Series p. 20, no. 455. Washington: Government Printing Office.

Hobsbawm, E. J. 1959. *Primitive Rebels: Studies in Archaic Forms of Social Movement in the 19th and 20th Centuries*. New York: W.W. Norton.

———. 1969. *Industry and Empire*. New York: Penguin Books.

———. 1983. "Introduction: Inventing Traditions." 1–14 in *The Invention of Tradition*, edited by Eric Hobsbawm and Terence Ranger. Cambridge: Cambridge University Press.

———. 1991. "The Perils of the New Nationalism." *The Nation*, November 4: 537–556.

Hochschild, Jennifer. 1985. *Thirty Years After Brown*. Washington, D.C.: Joint Center for Political Studies.

Hoffman, Abraham. 1974. *Unwanted Mexican Americans in the Great Depression: Repatriation Pressures, 1929–1938*. Tucson: University of Arizona Press.

Holli, Melvin G. 1981. "The Great War Sinks Chicago's German *Kultur*" 460–512 in *Ethnic Chicago*, edited by Peter d'A Jones and Melvin G. Holli. Grand Rapids, MI: Eerdmans.

Holloway, Joseph E., ed. 1990. *Africanisms in American Culture*. Bloomington: Indiana University Press.

Holt, Hamilton, ed. 1991 [1906]. *Life Stories of Undistinguished Americans, as Told by Themselves* (introduction by Werner Sollors). New York: Routledge.

Horgan, Ellen Somers. 1988. "The American Catholic Irish Family." 45–75 in *Ethnic Families in American: Patterns and Variations*, edited by Charles H. Mindel, Robert W. Habenstein, and Roosevelt Wright, Jr. New York: Elsevier.

Horowitz, Donald L. 1985. *Ethnic Groups in Conflict*. Berkeley: University of California Press.

Horowitz, Ruth. 1983. *Honor and the American Dream: Culture and Identity in a Chicano Community*. New Brunswick, NJ: Rutgers University Press.

Hosokawa, Bill. 1982. *JACL in Quest in Justice*. New York: William Morrow.

Hout, Michael and Joshua R. Goldstein. 1994. "How 4.5 Million Irish Immigrants Became 40 Million Irish Americans: Demographic and Subjective Aspects of the Ethnic Composition of White Americans. *American Sociological Review* 59 (1): 64–82.

Howe, Irving. 1976. *World of Our Fathers*. New York: Harcourt Brace Jovanovich.

Hraba, Joseph. 1979. *American Ethnicity*. Itasca, IL: F.E. Peacock Publishers.

Huggins, Nathan Irvin. 1971. *Harlem Renaissance*. New York: Oxford University Press.

————. 1980. *Slave and Citizen: The Life of Frederick Douglass*. Boston: Little, Brown.

Hughes, Everett C. 1943. *French Canada in Transition*. Chicago: The University of Chicago Press.

Hughes, Everett Cherrington and Helen MacGill Hughes. 1952. *Where Peoples Meet: Racial and Ethnic Frontiers*. Glencoe, IL: The Free Press.

Hughes, Henry. 1854. *A Treatise on Sociology, Theoretical and Practical*. Philadelphia: Lippincott and Grambo.

Hurh, Won Moo and Kwang Chang Kim. 1984. *Korean Immigrants in America: A Structural Analysis of Ethnic Confinement and Adhesive Adaptation*. Cranbury, NJ: Fairleigh Dickinson University Press.

————. 1990. "Religious Participation of Korean Immigrants in the United States." *Journal for the Scientific Study of Religion* 29 (March): 19–34.

Hurston, Zora Neale. 1978 [1937]. *Their Eyes Were Watching God*. Urbana: University of Illinois Press.

Hutchinson, Edward P. 1956. *Immigrants and Their Children, 1850–1950*. New York: John Wiley and Sons.

————. 1981. *Legislative History of America Immigration Policy, 1789–1965*. Philadelphia: University of Pennsylvania Press.

Hutchison, Ray. 1992. "Immigration and Family Networks in Chicago's Hispanic Community." Paper presented at the annual meeting of the American Sociological Association, Pittsburgh, PA.

Hwang, Sean-Shongend and Steve H. Murdock. 1988. "Residential Segregation and Ethnic Identification Among Hispanics in Texas." *Urban Affairs Quarterly* 23 (3): 329–345.

Hymowitz, Kay S. 1993. "Multiculturalism is Anti-Culture." *The New York Times*, March 25: A15.

Iamurri, Gabriel A. 1951. *The True Story of an Immigrant*. Boston: Christopher Publishing House.

Indian Health Service. 1987. *Chart Book Series*. Washington, D.C.: Department of Health and Human Services.

Isaacs, Harold R. 1975. *Idols of the Tribe: Group Identity and Political Change*. New York: Harper and Row.

Isajiw, Wsevolod W. 1979. *Definitions of Ethnicity*. Occasional Papers in Ethnic and Immigration Studies. Toronto: The Multicultural History Society of Ontario.

Ivey, Mike. 1990. "Report Targets Racism as Basis for Indian Treaty Rights Tension." *Capital Times* (Madison, Wisconsin), January 17: E14.

Jackson, Helen Hunt. 1881. *A Century of Dishonor*. Boston: Roberts Brothers.

Jaret, Charles. 1979. "The Greek, Italian, and Jewish American Press: A Comparative Analysis." *Journal of Ethnic Studies* 7: 47–70.

Jarvenpa, Robert. 1985. "The Political Economy and Political Ethnicity of American Indian Adaptations and Identities." *Ethnic and Racial Studies* 8 (1): 29–48.

Jasso, G. and M.R. Rosenzweig. 1990. *The New Chosen People*. New York: Russell Sage Foundation.

Jaynes, Gerald David and Robin M. Williams, Jr., editors. 1989. *A Common Destiny: Blacks and American Society*. Washington, D.C.: National Academy Press.

Jen, Gish. 1991. *Typical American*. Boston: Houghton Mifflin.

Jenkins, J. Craig and Craig M. Eckert. 1986. "Channeling Black Insurgency: Elite Patronage and Professional Social Movement Organizations in the Development of the Black Movement." *American Sociological Review* 51 (December): 812–829.

Jennings, Francis. 1976. *The Invasion of America: Indians, Colonialism, and the Cant of Conquest*. New York: W.W. Norton.

Jiobu, Robert M. 1988. *Ethnicity and Assimilation: Blacks, Chinese, Filipinos, Japanese, Koreans, Mexicans, Vietnames, and Whites*. Albany: State University of New York Press.

Jo, Moon H. and Daniel D. Mast. 1993. "Changing Images of Asian Americans." *International Journal of Politics, Culture and Society*, 6 (3): 417–441.

John, Robert. 1988. "The Native American Family." 325–363 in *Ethnic Families in America*, edited by Charles H. Mindel, Robert W. Habenstein, and Roosevelt Wright, Jr. New York: Elsevier.

Johnson, Guy B. 1934. "Some Factors in the Development of Negro Institutions in the United States." *American Journal of Sociology* 40 (3): 329–337.

Jones, LeRoi. 1963. *Blues People: The Negro Experience in White America and the Music that Developed from It*. New York: William Morrow.

Jones, Maldwyn Allen. 1960. *American Immigration*. Chicago: The University of Chicago Press.

―――――. 1980. "Scotch-Irish" 895–908 in *Harvard Encyclopedia of American Ethnic Groups*, edited by Stephan Thernstrom, Ann Orlov, and Oscar Handlin. Cambridge, MA: Harvard University Press.

Jordon, Winthrop D. 1968. *White Over Black: American Attitudes Toward the Negro, 1550–1812*. Chapel Hill: University of North Carolina Press.

Jorgensen, Joseph G. 1984. "Native American and Rural Anglos: Conflicts and Cultural Responses to Energy Developments." *Human Organization* 43 (Summer): 178–185.

Josephy, Alvin M., Jr. 1969. *The Indian Heritage of America*. New York: Alfred A. Knopf.

―――――. 1971. *The Nez Perce Indians and the Opening of the Northwest*. New Haven: Yale University Press.

Kahn, Arcadus. 1978. "Economic Choices and Opportunities: The Jewish Immigrants, 1880–1914." *Journal of Economic History* 38 (March): 235–251.

Kallen, Horace M. 1924. *Culture and Democracy in the United States. Studies in the Group Psychology of the American People*. Salem, NH: Ayer Company.

Kamphoefner, Walter D. 1987. *The Westfalians: From Germany to Missouri*. Princeton: Princeton University Press.

Kantowicz, Edward R. 1975. *Polish-American Politics in Chicago, 1888–1940*. Chicago: The University of Chicago Press.

Kaplan, Charles and Thomas L. VanValey. 1980. *Census '80: Continuing the Fact Finder Tradition*. Washington, D.C.: Government Printing Office.

Kashima, Tetsuden. 1980. "Japanese-American Internees Return, 1945 to 1955: Readjustment and Social Amnesia." *Phylon*, XLI (Summer): 107–115.

Katz, Daniel and Kenneth Braly. 1933. "Racial Stereotypes of One Hundred College Students." *Journal of Abnormal and Social Psychology* 28: 280–290.

Katz, Michael B. 1989. *The Underserving Poor: From the War on Poverty to the War on Welfare*. New York: Pantheon Books.

Katzman, David M. 1973. *Before the Ghetto: Black Detroit in the Nineteenth Century*. Urbana: University of Illinois Press.

Katznelson, Ira. 1981. *City Trenches: Urban Politics and the Patterning of Class in the United States*. New York: Pantheon Books.

Kaufman, Debra Renee. 1991. *Rachel's Daughter: Newly Orthodox Jewish Women.* New Brunswick, N.J.: Rutgers University Press.

Kaups, Matti. 1986. "A Commentary Concerning the Legend of St. Uhro." *Finnish Americana* 7: 13–17.

Kedourie, Eli. 1985. *Nationalism.* London: Hutchinson.

Keil, Charles. 1979. "Class and Ethnicity in Polish America." *Journal of Ethnic Studies* (Summer): 37–45.

Keil, Harmut and John B. Jentz, eds. 1983. *German Workers in Industrial Chicago, 1850–1910: A Comparative Perspective.* DeKalb: Northern Illinois University Press.

Kennedy, Ruby Jo Reeves. 1944. "Single or Triple Melting-Pot? Intermarriage Trends in New Haven, 1870–1940." *American Journal of Sociology* 49 (4): 331–339.

Kerr, Louise Ano Nuevo. 1984. "Mexican Chicago: Chicano Assimilation Aborted, 1939–1954." 269–298 in *Ethnic Chicago,* ed. Melvin G. Hollis and Peter d'A. James. Grand Rapids, MI: William B. Eerdmans.

Kessner, Thomas. 1977. *The Golden Door: Italian and Jewish Mobility in New York City, 1880–1915.* New York: Oxford University Press.

Killian, Lewis M. 1970. "Herbert Blumer's Contributions to Race Relations." 179–190 in *Human Nature and Collective Behavior: Papers in Honor of Herbert Blumer,* edited by Tamotsu Shibutani. New Brunswick, NJ: Transaction Books.

_____. 1975. *The Impossible Revolution, Phase II: Black Power and the American Dream.* New York: Random House.

_____. 1984. "Organization, Rationality, and Spontaneity in the Civil Rights Movement." *American Sociological Review* 49 (December): 770–783.

_____. 1991. "Gandhi, Frederick Douglass and Affirmative Action." *International Journal of Politics, Culture, and Society* 5 (2): 167–182.

Kilson, Martin. 1983. "The Black Bourgeoisie Revisited: From E. Franklin Frazier to the Present." *Dissent* 30 (Winter): 85–96.

Kim, Hyung-chan. 1977. "The History and Role of the Church in the Korean American Community." 47–63 in *The Korean Diaspora,* edited by Hyung-chan Kim. Santa Barbara, CA: ABC-Clio.

Kim, Illsoo. 1981. *New Urban Immigrants: The Korean Community in New York.* Princeton: Princeton University Press.

Kim, Kwang Chung and Won Moo Hurh. 1992. "Generation Differences in Korean Immigrants' Life Experiences in the United States." Paper presented at the American Sociological Association annual meeting, Pittsburgh, PA.

_____. 1985. "Ethnic Resources Utilization of Korean Immigrant Entrepreneurs in the Chicago Minority Area." *International Migration Review* 19 (1): 82–111.

Kinkead, Gwen. 1992. *Chinatown: A Portrait of a Closed Society.* New York: Harper Collins.

Kinlock, Graham C. 1974. *The Dynamics of Race Relations: A Sociological Analysis.* New York: McGraw-Hill.

Kitano, Harry H.L. 1969. *Japanese Americans: The Evolution of a Subculture.* Englewood Cliffs, NJ: Prentice-Hal.

_____. 1988. "The Japanese American Family." 258–275 in *Ethnic Families in America: Patterns and Variations,* eds. Charles H. Mindell, Robert W. Habenstein and Roosevelt Wright, Jr. New York: Elsevier.

_____. 1991. *Race Relations.* Englewood Cliffs, NJ: Prentice-Hall.

Kitano, Harry H.L. and Roger Daniels. 1988. *Asian Americans: Emerging Minorities.* Englewood Cliffs, NJ: Prentice-Hall.

Kitano, Harry H., Wai-tsang Yeung, Lynn Chai, and Herb Hatanaka. 1984. "Asian American Interracial Marriage." *Journal of Marriage and the Family* 46 (February): 179–190.

Kivisto, Peter. 1978. "Sumner on Race Relations: An Example of a Theoretical Short-Circuit in the Quest for Certitude." *Free Inquiry* 6 (2): 48–59.

————. 1984. *Immigrant Socialists in the United States: The Case of Finns and the Left.* Rutherford, NJ: Fairleigh Dickinson University Press.

————. 1986. "An Historical Review of Public Housing Policies and Their Impact on Minorities." 1–18 in *Race, Ethnicity, and Housing in the United States,* edited by Jamshid Momeni. Westport, CT: Greenwood Press.

————. 1989. "Overview: Thinking About Ethnicity." 11–23 in *The Ethnic Enigma,* edited by Peter Kivisto. Philadelphia: The Balch Institute Press.

————. 1990. "The Transplanted Then and Now: The Reorientation of Immigration Studies from the Chicago School to the New Social History." *Ethnic and Racial Studies* 13 (4): 455–481.

————. 1991. "What Did Americanization Mean for the Finns?" Paper presented at the Making of Finnish America Conference, University of Minnesota.

————. 1993. "Religions and the New Immigrants." 92–108 in *A Future for Religion? New Paradigms for Social Analysis,* edited by William H. Swatos, Jr. Newbury Park, CA: Sage Publications.

Kivisto, Peter and Dag Blanck, eds. 1990. *American Immigrants and Their Generations.* Urbana: University of Illinois Press.

Koivukangas, Olavi. 1988. *Delaware 350.* Turku, Finland: Institute of Migration.

Korman, Gerd. 1967. *Industrialization, Immigrants, and Americanizers: The View from Milwaukee, 1866–1921.* Madison: The State Historical Society of Wisconsin.

Kosmin, Barry, Sidney Goldstein, Joseph Waksberg, Nava Lerer, Ariella Keysar, and Jeffrey Scheckner. 1991. *Highlights of the CJF 1990 National Jewish Population Survey.* New York: Council of Jewish Federations.

Kovel, Joel. 1970. *White Racism: A Psychohistory.* New York: Vintage Books.

Kristeva, Julia. 1993. *Nations Without Nationalism.* New York: Columbia University Press.

Kuo, Chia-Ling. 1977. *Social and Political Change in New York's Chinatown: The Role of Voluntary Associations.* New York: Praeger.

Kuper, Leo. 1975. *Race, Class, and Power: Ideology and Revolutionary Change in Plural Societies.* Chicago: Aldine Publishing.

Kwoh, Beulah Ong. 1947. "The Occupational Status of American-born Chinese Male Graduates." *American Journal of Sociology* 53 (3): 192–200.

Kwong, Peter. 1987. *The New Chinatown.* New York: Hill and Wang.

LaBarre, Weston. 1975. *The Peyote Cult.* New York: Schocken.

Lal, Barbara Ballis. 1983. "Perspectives on Ethnicity: Old Wine in New Bottles." *Ethnic and Racial Studies* 6 (2): 154–173.

————. 1986. "The 'Chicago School' of American Sociology, Symbolic Interactionism, and Race Relations Theory." 280–298 in *Theories of Race and Ethnic Relations,* edited by John Rex and David Mason. Cambridge: Cambridge University Press.

————. 1990. *The Romance of Culture in an Urban Civilization.* London: Routledge.

Lamphere, Louise, ed. 1992. *Structuring Diversity: Ethnographic Perspectives on the New Immigration.* Chicago: The University of Chicago Press.

Landry, Bart. 1987. *The New Black Middle Class.* Berkeley: University of California Press.

Langer, Elinor. 1990. "The American Neo-Nazi Movement Today." *The Nation* (July 16/23): 82–107.

LaSorte, Michael. 1985. *LaMerica: Images of Italian Greenhorn Experience*. Philadelphia: Temple University Press.

Lavander, Abraham. 1977. *A Coat of Many Colors: Jewish Subcommunities in the Unites States*. Westport, CT: Greenwood Press.

Lavender, Abraham D. and John M. Forsyth. 1976. "The Sociological Study of Minority Groups as Reflected by Leading Sociological Journals: Who Gets Studied and Who Gets Neglected?" *Ethnicity* 3: 338–398.

Lazerwitz, Bernard and Louis Rowitz. 1964. "The Three-Generations Hypothesis." *American Journal of Sociology* 69 (March): 529–538.

Leacock, Eleanor Burke and Nancy Oestreich Lurie, eds. 1988. *North American Indians in Historical Perspective*. Prospect Heights, IL: Waveland Press.

Lee, Dong Ok. 1992. "Commodification of Ethnicity: The Sociospatial Reproduction of Immigrant Entrepreneurs." *Urban Affairs Quarterly* 28 (December): 258–275.

Lee, Rose Hum. 1949. "The Decline of Chinatown in the U.S." *American Journal of Sociology* 54 (5): 425–433.

Legters, Lyman H. and Fremont J. Lyden, eds. 1994. *American Indian Policy: Self-Governance and Economic Development*. Westport, CT: Greenwood Press.

Lemann, Nicholas. 1991. *The Promised Land: The Great Black Migration and How It Changed America*. New York: Alfred A. Knopf.

Levine, Edward M. 1966. *The Irish and Irish Politicians: A Study of Cultural and Social Alienation*. Notre Dame, IN: University of Notre Dame Press.

Levine, Gene N. and Darrel M. Montero. 1973. "Socioeconomic Mobility Among Three Generations of Japanese Americans." *Journal of Social Issues* 29 (2): 33–48.

Levine, Gene N. and Colbert Rhodes. 1981. *The Japanese American Community: A Three-Generation Study*. New York: Praeger.

Levine, Lawrence W. 1977. *Black Culture and Black Consciousness*. New York: Oxford University Press.

LeVine, Robert A and Donald T. Campbell. 1972. *Ethnocentrism: Theories of Conflict, Ethnic Attitudes and Group Behavior*. New York: John Wiley and Sons.

Levitan, Sar. and Robert Taggart. 1976. *The Promise of Greatness*. Cambridge, MA: Harvard University Press.

Lewis, David Levering. 1981. *When Harlem Was in Vogue*. New York: Alfred A. Knopf.

Lieberson, Stanley, 1985. "Unhyphenated Whites in the United States." 159–180 in *Ethnicity and Race in the U.S.A.: Toward the Twenty-First Century*. London: Routledge and Kegan Paul.

Lieberson, Stanley and Mary C. Waters. 1985. "Ethnic Mixtures in The United States." *Sociology and Social Research* 70: 43–52.

———. 1986. "Ethnic Groups in Flux: The Changing Ethnic Responses of American Whites." *The Annals of the American Academy of Political and Social Science* 487 (September): 79–91.

———. 1988. *From Many Strands: Ethnic and Racial Groups in Contemporary America*. New York: Russell Sage Foundation.

Liebman, Arthur. 1979. *Jews and the Left*. New York: John Wiley and Sons.

Liebman, Charles S. 1973. *The Ambivalent American Jew: Politics, Religion, and Family in American Jewish Life*. Philadelphia: The Jewish Publication Society of America.

Liebow, Elliot. 1967. *Tally's Corner: A Study of Negro Streetcorner Men*. Boston: Little, Brown.

Light, Ivan. 1972. *Ethnic Enterprise in America: Business and Welfare Among Chinese, Japanese, and Blacks*. Berkeley: University of California Press.

Light, Ivan and Edna Bonacich. 1988. *Immigrant Entrepreneurs: Koreans in Los Angeles, 1965–1982*. Berkeley: University of California Press.

Lincoln, C. Eric and Lawrence H. Mamiya. 1990. *The Black Church in the African American Experience*. Durham, NC: Duke University Press.

Lindemann, Albert S. 1991. *The Jew Accused: Three Anti-Semitic Affairs (Dreyfus, Beilis, Frank) 1894–1915*. Cambridge: Cambridge University Press.

Lipset, Seymour Martin. 1963. *The First New Nation: The United States in Historical and Comparative Perspective*. New York: Basic Books.

Lipset, Seymour Martin and William Schneider. 1978. "The Bakke Case: How Would It Be Decided at the Court of Public Opinion?" *Public Opinion* (March/April): 38–44.

Litwack, Leon F. 1979. *Been in the Storm So Long: The Aftermath of Slavery*. New York: Alfred A. Knopf.

Livingstone, Frank B. 1962. "On the Non-Existence of Human Races." *Current Anthropology* 3 (3): 279–281.

Lockhart, Audrey. 1976. *Some Aspects of Emigration from Ireland to the North American Colonies Between 1600 and 1775*. New York: Arno Press.

Lockwood, William W. 1954. *The Economic Development of Japan: Growth and Structural Change, 1868–1938*. Princeton, NJ: Princeton University Press.

Loewen, James W. 1988. *The Mississippi Chinese: Between Black and White*. Prospect Heights, IL: Waveland Press.

Long, Larry and Diane DiAve. 1981. "Suburbanization of Blacks." *American Demographics* 3: 16–44.

Lopata, Helena Znaniecki. 1994. *Polish Americans*, Second, Revised Edition. New Brunswick, NJ: Transaction Publishers.

Lopreato, Joseph. 1970. *Italian Americans*. New York: Random House.

_____. 1990. "From Social Evolution to Biocultural Evolutionism." *Sociological Forum* 5 (2): 187–212.

Low, W. Augustus and Virgil A. Cliff. 1981. *Encyclopedia of Black America*. New York: McGraw-Hill.

Luebke, Frederick L. 1990. *Germans in the New World: Essays in the History of Immigration*. Urbana: University of Illinois Press.

Lurie, Nancy O. 1968. "Historical Background." 49–81 in *The American Indian Today*. Baltimore: Penguin Books

Lyman, Stanford M. 1972. *The Black American in Sociological Thought*. New York: Capricorn Books.

_____. 1974. *Chinese Americans*. New York: Random House.

_____. 1977. *The Asian in North America*. Santa Barbara, CA: ABC-Clio.

_____. 1984. "Interactionism and the Study of Race Relations at the Macro-Sociological Level: The Contribution of Herbert Blumer." *Symbolic Interaction* 7 (1): 107–120.

_____. 1986. *Chinatown and Little Tokyo: Power, Conflict, and Community Among Chinese and Japanese Immigrants in America*. Millwood, NY: Associated Faculty Press.

_____. 1990a. "The Drama in the Routine: A Prolegomenon to a Praxiological Sociology." *Sociological Theory* 8 (2): 216–223.

_____. 1990b. "Race, Sex and Servitude: Images of Blacks in American Cinema." *International Journal of Politics, Culture, and Society* 4 (1): 49–77.

————. 1991. "The Race Question and Liberalism: Casuistries in American Constitutional Law." *International Journal of Politics, Culture, and Society,* 5 (2): 183–247.

————. 1992. *Militarism, Imperialism, and Racial Accommodation.* Fayetteville: The University of Arkansas Press.

————. 1994. *Color, Culture, Civilization: Race and Minority Issues in American Society.* Urbana: University of Illinois Press.

Lynd, Robert S. and Helen Merrell Lynd. 1929. *Middletown: A Study in American Culture.* New York: Harcourt, Brace.

————. 1937. *Middletown in Transition: A Study in Cultural Conflict.* New York: Harcourt, Brace.

Majka, Linda C. and Theo J. Majka. 1982. *Farm Workers, Agribusiness, and the State.* Philadelphia: Temple University Press.

Mangiafico, Luciano. 1988. *Contemporary American Immigrants: Patterns of Filipino, Korean, and Chinese Settlement in the United States.* New York: Praeger.

Mangione, Jerre. 1978. *An Ethnic at Large: A Memoir of America in the Thirties and Forties.* New York: G.P. Putnam's Sons.

Mann, Arthur. 1979. *The One and the Many: Reflections on the American Identity.* Chicago: The University of Chicago Press.

Marable, Manning. 1983. *How Capitalism Underdeveloped Black America: Problems in Race, Political Economy and Society.* Boston: South End Press.

Marcus, Jacob R. 1970. *The Colonial American Jew, 1492–1776,* 3 vols. Detroit: Wayne State University Press.

Marger, Martin, and Phillip Obermiller. 1983. "Urban Appalachians and Canadian Maritime Migrants: A Comparative Study of Emergent Ethnicity." *International Journal of Comparative Sociology* 24 (September/December): 229–243.

Marks, Carole. 1989. *Farewell—We're Good and Gone: The Great Black Migration.* Bloomington: Indiana University Press.

Marriott, Michael. 1992. "Indians Turing to Tribal Colleges for Opportunity and Cultural Values." *New York Times,* February 26: A13.

Martin, Joel W. 1991. *Sacred Revolt: The Muskogees' Struggle for a New World.* Boston: Beacon Press.

Mass, Amy Iwasaki. 1992. "Interracial Japanese Americans: The Best of Both Worlds or the End of the Japanese American Community?" 265–279 in *Racially Mixed People in America,* edited by Maria P.P. Root. Newbury Park, CA: Sage Publications.

Massey, Douglas S. and Nancy A. Denton. 1988. "Suburbanization and Segregation in U.S. Metropolitan Areas." *American Journal of Sociology* 94 (3): 592–626.

Massey, Douglas S. and Eric Fong. 1990. "Segregation and Neighborhood Quality: Blacks, Hispanics, and Asians in the San Francisco Metropolitan Area." *Social Forces* 69 (1): 15–32.

Matthews, Fred H. 1978. *The Quest for Community: Robert Park and the Chicago School of American Sociology.* Montreal: McGill-Queen's University Press.

————. 1987. "Louis Wirth and American Ethnic Studies: The World of Enlightened Assimilationism, 1925–1950." 123–143 in *The Jews of North America,* edited by Moses Rischin. Detroit: Wayne State University Press.

Mayer, Egon. 1979. *From Suburb to Stetl: The Jews of Boro Park.* Philadelphia: Temple University Press.

————. 1980. "Processes and Outcomes in Marriages Between Jews and Non-Jews." *American Behavioral Scientist* 23: 487–518.

Mazón, Mauricio. 1984. *The Zoot-Suit Riots: The Psychology of Symbolic Annihilation.* Austin: University of Texas Press.

McAdam, Doug. 1982. *Political Process and the Development of Black Insurgency, 1930–1970.* Chicago: The University of Chicago Press.

_____. 1988. *Freedom Summer.* New York: Oxford University Press.

McCaffrey, Lawrence J. 1976. *The Irish Diaspora in America.* Bloomington: Indiana University Press.

McCarthy, John D. and Mayer N. Zald. 1977. "Resource Mobilization and Social Movements: A Partial Theory." *American Journal of Sociology* 82 (6): 1212–1241.

McKay, James. 1982. "An Exploratory Synthesis of Primordial and Mobilizationist Approaches to Ethnic Phenomena." *Ethnic and Racial Studies* 5 (4): 395–420.

McNickle, D'Arcy. 1962. *The Indian Tribes of the United States: Ethnic and Cultural Survival.* New York: Oxford University Press.

McPhail, Clark. 1971. "Civil Disorder Participation: A Critical Examination of Recent Research." *American Sociological Review* 36: 1058–1073.

McPherson, James M. 1982. *Ordeal by Fire: The Civil War and Reconstruction.* New York: Alfred A. Knopf.

McWilliam, Carey. 1948. *North from Mexico: The Spanish Speaking People.* Philadelphia: J.B. Lippincott.

Meier, August and Elliot Rudwick. 1973. *CORE, A Study of the Civil Rights Movement, 1942–1968.* New York: Oxford University Press.

Melendy, H. Brett. 1977. *Asians in America: Filipinos, Koreans, and East Indians.* Boston: Twayne Publishers.

_____. 1980. "Filipinos." 354–362 in *Harvard Encyclopedia of American Ethnic Groups,* edited by Stephan Thernstrom, Ann Orlov, and Oscar Handlin. Cambridge, MA: Harvard University Press.

Melville, Herman. 1964 [1857]. *The Confidence-Man: His Masquerade.* New York: New American Library.

Melville, Margarita. 1983. "Ethnicity: An Analysis of Its Dynamism and Variability Focusing on Mexican/Anglo/Mexican American Interface." *American Ethnologist* 10 (2): 272–289.

Merton, Robert K. 1972. "Insiders and Outsiders: A Chapter in the Sociology Knowledge." *American Journal of Sociology* 24 (1): 9–47.

_____. 1976. *Sociological Ambivalence and Other Essays.* New York: Free Press.

Metzger, Isaac, ed. 1971. *A Bintel Brief: "A Bundle of Letters" to the Jewish Daily Forward.* New York: Doubleday.

Meyer, Michael. 1992. "Los Angeles 2010: A Latino Subcontinent." *Newsweek,* November 9: 32–33.

Miller, Kerby A. 1985. *Emigrants and Exiles: Ireland and the Irish Exodus to North America.* New York: Oxford University Press.

Miller, Randall M. 1978. *Ethnic Images in American Film and Television.* Philadelphia: Balch Institute Press.

Mills, C. Wright. 1951. *White Collar: The American Middle Class.* New York: Oxford University Press.

Mills, C. Wright, Clarence Senior, and Rose Kohn Goldsen. 1950. *The Puerto Rican Journey: New York's Newest Immigrants.* New York: Harper and Row.

Min, Pyong Gap. 1987. "Filipino and Korean Immigrants in Small Business: A Comparative Analysis." *Amerasia* 13 (Spring): 53–71.

_____. 1988. *Ethnic Business Enterprise: Korean Small Business in Atlanta*. New York: Center for Migration Studies.

_____. 1991. "Cultural and Economic Boundaries of Korean Ethnicity: A Comparative Analysis." *Ethnic and Racial Studies* 14 (2): 225–241.

Mintz, Sidney W. 1960. *Worker in the Cane: A Puerto Rican Life History*. New Haven: Yale University Press.

Model, Suzanne. 1992. "The Ethnic Economy: Cubans and Chinese Reconsidered." *The Sociological Quarterly* 33 (1): 63–82.

Mohl, Raymond A. 1985. "An Ethnic 'Boiling Pot': Cubans and Haitians in Miami." *The Journal of Ethnic Studies* 13 (Summer): 51–74.

Momaday, N. Scott. 1976. *The Names: A Memoir*. New York: Harper and Row.

Moore, Joan. 1970. *Mexican Americans*. Englewood Cliffs, NJ: Prentice-Hall.

_____. 1978. *Homeboys*. Philadelphia: Temple University Press.

Moore, Joan and Harry Pachon. 1985. *Hispanics in the United States*. Englewood Cliffs, NJ: Prentice-Hall.

Moore, Joan W. and James Diego Vigil. 1987. "Chicano Gangs: Group Norms and Individual Factors Related to Adult Criminality." *Aztlan* 18 (2): 27–44.

Moore, Michael. 1988. "Scapegoats Again: 'Hate Crimes' Against Asian American the Rise." *The Progressive*, February 25: 9.

Moore, William. 1969. *The Vertical Ghetto*. New York: Random House.

Morawska, Ewa. 1985. *For Bread With Butter: The Life-Worlds of East Central Europeans in Johnstown, Pennsylvania, 1890–1940*. Cambridge: Cambridge University Press.

_____. 1989. "Labor Migrations of Poles in the Atlantic World Economy, 1880–1914." *Comparative Studies in Society and History* 31 (2): 237–272.

_____. 1990. "The Sociology and Historiography of Immigration." 187–238 in *Immigration Reconsidered: History, Sociology, and Politics*, edited by Virginia Yans-McLaughlin. New York: Oxford University Press.

_____. 1994. "In Defense of the Assimilation Model." *Journal of American Ethnic History* 13 (2): 76–87.

Morris, Aldon D. 1984. *The Origins of the Civil Rights Movement: Black Communities Organizing for Change*. New York: The Free Press.

Moynihan, Daniel Patrick. 1965. *The Negro Family: The Case for National Action*. Washington, D.C.: Office of Policy Planning and Research, United States Department of Labor.

Mucha, Janusz. 1984. "American Indian Success in the Urban Setting." *Urban Anthropology* 13 (4): 329–354.

Muñoz, Alfredo. 1971. *The Filipinos in the United States*. Los Angeles: Mountain View Publishers.

Murray, Charles. 1984. *Losing Ground: American Social Policy, 1950–1980*. New York: Basic Books.

Myrdal, Gunnar. 1944. *An American Dilemma: The Negro Problem and Modern Democracy*. New York: Harper and Brothers.

Nabokov, Peter, ed. 1991. *Native American Testimony: A Chronicle of Indian-White Relations from Prophecy to the Present, 1492–1992*. New York: Viking.

Naff, Alixa. 1985. *Becoming American: The Early Arab Immigrant Experience*. Carbondale: Southern Illinois University Press.

Nagel, Joane. 1994. *American Indian Ethnic Revival: Red Power and the Resurgence of Identity and Culture*. New York: Oxford University Press.

Nagel, Joane and Susan Olzak. 1982. "Ethnic Mobilization in New and Old States: An Extension of the Competition Model." *Social Problems* 30 (1): 127–143.

Nahiray, Vladimir and Joshua Fishman. 1965. "American Immigrant Groups: Ethnic Identification and the Problem of Generations." *Sociological Review* 13 (November): 311–326.

Naison, Mark. 1983. *Communists in Harlem During the Depression*. Urbana: University of Illinois Press.

Nakamaru, Robert Tsuneo. 1993. "Assimilation and the Japanese American Experience" Paper presented at the annual Illinois Sociological Association meeting, October 21, Rockford, IL.

Nash, Gary B. 1990. *Race and Revolution*. Madison, WI: Madison House.

Nash, Manning. 1989. *The Cauldron of Ethnicity in the Modern World*. Chicago: The University of Chicago Press.

National Opinion Research Center. 1991. *General Social Survey*. Chicago: National Opinion Research Center.

Nee, Victor and Brett Nee. 1973. *Longtime Californ': A Study of an American Chinatown*. New York: Pantheon Books.

Nee, Victor and Herbert Y. Wong. 1985. "Asian American Socioeconomic Achievement: The Strength of the Family Bond." *Sociological Perspectives* 28 (3): 281–306.

Nefzger, Ben and Peter Kivisto. 1990. "Studying the Changing Conditions of Jewish Life in a Middle-Sized American City." *Sociological Focus* 23 (3): 177–201.

Nelli, Humbert S. 1970. *The Italians in Chicago*. New York: Oxford University Press.

_____. 1980. "Italians," 545–560 in *Harvard Encyclopedia of American Ethnic Groups*, edited by Stephan Thernstrom, Ann Orlov, and Oscar Handlin. Cambridge, MA: Harvard University Press.

_____. 1983. *From Immigrants to Ethnics: The Italian Americans*. New York: Oxford University Press.

Nelson, Lowry. 1943. "Intermarriage Among Nationality Groups in a Rural Area of Minnesota." *American Journal of Sociology* 48 (5): 585–592.

Neufeld, Steven. 1990. "Ethnic Conflict and Community Mobilization: Arab-Owned and Korean-Owned Businesses in Predominantly Black Neighborhoods." Paper presented at the Midwest Sociogical Society annual meeting, Chicago, IL.

Newman, William M. 1973. *American Pluralism: A Study of Minority Groups and Social Theory*. New York: Harper and Row.

The New Yorker, February 15, 1993: 6.

New York Times. 1984. "Sioux Indians in South Dakota Awaiting $606 million in Compensation," July 16: 17.

_____. 1984. "Moapa Band of Paiute Indians Proposes Setting Up a Brothel on Reservation." November 4: A31.

_____. 1989. "Southern Pacific Transportation Company to Pay Walker River Paiutes $1.2 million," August 13: 26.

_____. 1990. "The Mosaic Thing." January 3, 1990: 20.

_____. 1990. "Puyallup Tribe Signs Away Claim to Much of its Land," March 25: 33.

_____. 1992. "Gambling is a Billion Dollar a Year Business," January 6: A17.

_____. 1992. "New York Irish March as Gay Group Protest," and "Proud to Be Gay and Irish, But Sad as Marchers Go By," March 18: A16.

Niehardt, John G. 1961. *Black Elk Speaks: Being a Life Story of a Holy Man of the Oglala Sioux*. Lincoln: University of Nebraska Press.

Nielsen, Francois. 1985. "Toward a Theory of Ethnic Solidarity in Modern Society." *American Sociological Review* 50 (2): 133–149.

Noriega, Chon. 1991. "Citizen Chicano: The Trials and Titillations of Ethnicity in the American Cinema, 1935–1962." *Social Research* 58 (2): 413–438.

Norman, Hans and Harald Runblom. 1988. *Transatlantic Connections: Nordic Migration to the New World After 1800*. Oslo: Norwegian University Press.

Novak, Michael. 1971. *The Rise of the Unmeltable Ethnics*. New York: Macmillan.

_____. 1972. *The Rise of the Unmeltable Ethnics: Politics and Culture in the Seventies*. New York: Macmillan.

O'Brien, Conor Cruise. 1991. "Nationalists and Democrats." *New York Review of Books*, August 15: 29–31.

O'Brien, David J. and Stephen S. Fugita. 1991. *The Japanese American Experience*. Bloomington: Indiana University Press.

O'Grady, Joseph P. 1973. *How the Irish Became Americans*. New York: Twayne Publishers.

Oliver, Lawrence J. 1987. "'Great Equalizer' or 'Cruel Stepmother?' Image of the School in Italian American Literature." *Journal of Ethnic Studies* 15: 113–130.

Olzak, Susan. 1992. *The Dynamics of Ethnic Competition and Conflict*. Stanford, CA: Stanford University Press.

Omi, Michael and Howard Winant. 1986. *Racial Formation in the United States: From the 1960s to the 1980s*. New York: Routledge and Kegan Paul.

Orfield, Gary. 1983. *Public School Desegregation in the United States, 1968–1980*. Washington, D.C.: Joint Center for Political Studies.

Orfield, Gary and Franklin Monfort. 1988. *Change in the Racial Composition and Segregation of Large School Districts, 1967–1986*. Alexandria, VA: National School Boards Association.

Ortiz, Vilma. 1986. "Changes in the Characteristics of Puerto Rican Migrants from 1955 to 1980." *International Migration Review* 20 (3): 612–628.

Orzell, Lawrence J. 1982. "The 'National Catholic' Response: Franciszek Hodur and his Followers, 1897–1907." 117–182 in *The Polish Presence in Canada and America*, edited by Frank Renkiewicz. Toronto: The Multicultural History Society of Ontario.

Osako, Masako M. 1984. "Japanese-Americans: Melting into the All-American Pot?" 513–544 in *Ethnic Chicago*, edited by Melvin G. Holli and Peter d'A. Jones. Grand Rapids, MI: William B. Eerdmans.

Padilla, Felix. 1987. *Puerto Rican Chicago*. Notre Dame, IN: University of Notre Dame Press.

Parenti, Michael. 1967. "Ethnic Politics and the Persistence of Ethnic Identification." *American Political Science Review* 61: 717–726.

Park, Robert Ezra. 1950. *Race and Culture: The Collected Papers of R.E. Park*. Glencoe, IL: The Free Press.

Parkin, Frank. 1979. *Marxism and Class Theory: A Bourgeois Critique*. London: Tavistock.

Parot, Joseph. 1981. *Polish Catholics in Chicago, 1850–1920*. DeKalb: Northern Illinois University Press.

Patterson, James. 1981. *Americans' Struggle Against Poverty*. Cambridge, MA: Harvard University Press.

Patterson, Orlando. 1982. *Slavery and Social Death: A Comparative Study*. Cambridge, MA: Harvard University Press.

————. 1991. *Freedom. Volume I: Freedom in the Making of Western Culture*. New York: Basic Books.

Peach, Cheri. 1980. "Which Triple Melting Pot? A Re-examination of Ethnic Intermarriage in New Haven, 1900–1950." *Ethnic and Racial Studies* 3: 1–16.

Pearce, Roy Harvey. 1967. *Savagism and Civilization: A Study of the Indian and the American Mind*. Baltimore: The Johns Hopkins University Press.

Pedraza-Bailey, Silvia. 1990. "Immigration Research: A Conceptual Map." *Social Science History* 14 (1): 43–67.

Pérez, Lisandro. 1980. "Cubans." 256–261 in *Harvard Encyclopedia of American Ethnic Groups* edited by Stephan Thernstrom, Ann Orlov, and Oscar Handlin. Cambridge, MA: Harvard University Press.

————. 1986. "Immigrant Economic Adjustment and Family Organization: The Cuban Success Story Reexamined." *International Migration Review* 20 (1): 4–20

Perlman, Robert. 1991. *Bridging Three Worlds: Hungarian-Jewish Americans, 1848–1914*. Amherst: The University of Massachusetts Press.

Pernicone, Nicholas. 1979. "Carlo Tresca and the Sacco-Vanzetti Case." *Journal of American History* 66: 535–547.

Persons, Stow. 1987. *Ethnic Studies at Chicago 1905–45*. Urbana: University of Illinois Press.

Petersen, William. 1971. *Japanese Americans*. New York: Random House.

————. 1982. "Concepts of Ethnicity." 1–26 in *Concepts of Ethnicity*, William Peterson, Michael Novak and Philip Gleason. Cambridge, MA: The Belknap Press of Harvard University Press.

Pettigrew, Thomas F. 1958. "Personality and Sociocultural Factors in Intergroup Attitudes." *Journal of Conflict Resolution* 2: 29–42.

————. 1979. "The Changing—Not Declining—Significance of Race." 111–116 in *The Caste and Class Controversy*, edited by Charles Vert Willie. Bayside, NY: General Hall.

Pettigrew, Thomas F., and Robert F. Green. 1976. "School Desegregation in Large Cities: A Critique of the Coleman White Flight Thesis." *Harvard Educational Review* 46 (February): 1–53.

Phillips, Ulrich B. 1918. *American Negro Slavery*. New York: D. Appleton.

Piatt, Bill. 1990. *Only English? Law and Language Policy in the United States*. Albuquerque: University of New Mexico Press.

Pido, Antonio J.A. 1986. *The Filipinos in America*. New York: Center for Migration Studies.

Pieterse, Jan Nederveen. 1992. *White on Black: Images of Africa and Blacks in Western Popular Culture*. New Haven: Yale University Press.

Pinderhughes, Dianne. 1987. *Race and Ethnicity in Chicago Politics: A Reexamination of Pluralist Theory*. Urbana: University of Illinois Press.

Pinkney, Alphonso. 1984. *The Myth of Black Progress*. Cambridge: Cambridge University Press.

————. 1987. *Black Americans*. Englewood Cliffs, NJ: Prentice-Hall.

Piore, Michael. 1979. *Birds of Passage: Migrant Labor and Industrial Societies*. Cambridge: Cambridge University Press.

Piven, Frances Fox and Richard Cloward. 1971. *Regulating the Poor: The Functions of Public Welfare*. New York: Vintage Press.

Polenberg, Richard. 1980. *One Nation Divisible: Class, Race, and Ethnicity in the United States Since 1938*. New York: Viking Press.

Portes, Alejandro and Alex Stepick. 1985. "Unwelcome Immigrants: The Labor Market Experiences of 1980 (Mariel) Cuban and Haitian Refugees in South Florida." *American Sociological Review* 50 (4): 493–514.

Portes, Alejandro and Rafael Mozo. 1985. "The Political Adaptation Process of Cubans and Other Ethnic Minorities in the United States: A Preliminary Analysis." *International Migration Review.* 19 (1): 35–63.

Portes, Alejandro and Leif Jensen. 1989. "The Enclave and the Entrants: Patterns of Ethnic Enterprise Before and After Mariel." *American Sociological Review* 54 (6): 929–949.

Portes, Alejandro and Ruben G. Rumbaut. 1990. *Immigrant America: A Portrait.* Berkeley: University of California Press.

Posadas, Barbara M. 1981. "Crossed Boundaries in Interracial Chicago: Philpino American Families Since 1925." *Amerasia Journal* 8 (1): 31—52.

Powledge, Fred. 1991. *Free At Last? The Civil Rights Movement and the People Who Made It.* Boston: Little, Brown.

Pozzetta, George and Gary Mormino. 1986. *The Immigrant World of Ybor City.* Urbana: University of Illinois Press.

Prucha, Francis Paul. 1985. *The Indians in American Society: From the Revolutionary War to the Present.* Berkeley: University of California Press.

Pula, James S. and Eugene E. Dziedzic. 1990. *United We Stand: The Role of Polish Workers in the New York Mills Textile Strikes, 1912 and 1916.* New York: Eastern European Monographs.

Quan, Robert Seto. 1982. *Lotus Among the Magnolias: The Mississippi Chinese.* Jackson: University Press of Mississippi.

Rachleff, Peter. 1984. *Black Labor in the South: Richmond, Virginia, 1865–1890.* Philadelphia: Temple University Press.

Radzialowski, Thaddeus. 1976. "The Competition for Jobs and Racial Stereotypes: Poles and Blacks in Chicago." *Polish American Studies* 33 (2): 5–18.

_____. 1982. "Ethnic Conflict and the Polish Americans of Detroit, 1921–42." 195–207 in *The Polish Presence in Canada and America,* edited by Frank Renkiewicz. Toronto: The Multicultural History Society of Ontario.

Rainwater, Lee. 1970. *Behind Ghetto Walls: Black Family Life in a Federal Slum.* Chicago: Aldine Publishing.

Rainwater, Lee and William L. Yancey, eds. 1967. *The Moynihan Report and the Politics of Controversy.* Cambridge, MA: The MIT Press.

Ramella, Franco. 1991. "Emigration from an Area of Intense Industrial Development: The Case of Northwestern Italy." 261–274 in *A Century of European Migrations, 1830–1930,* edited by Rudolph J. Vecoli and Suzanne M. Sinke. Urbana: University of Illinois Press.

Raper, Arthur F. 1933. *The Tragedy of Southern Lynching.* Chapel Hill: University of North Carolina Press.

Redkey, Edwin S. 1969. *Black Exodus: Black Nationalist and Back-to-Africa Movements, 1890–1910.* New Haven: Yale University Press.

Reed, Adolph L., Jr. 1986. *The Jesse Jackson Phenomenon: The Crisis of Purpose in Afro-American Politics.* New Haven: Yale University Press.

The Report of the President's Commission on Housing. 1982. Washington, D.C.: Government Printing Office.

Rex, John. 1983. *Race Relations in Sociology Theory.* London: Routledge and Kegan Paul.

Ribuffo, Leo P. 1986. "Henry Ford and *The International Jew.*" 175–190 in *The American Jewish Experience*, edited by Jonathan D. Sarna. New York: Holmes and Meier.

Rieder, Jonathan. 1985. *Canarsie: The Jews and Italians of Brooklyn Against Liberalism.* Cambridge, MA: Harvard University Press.

Riesman, David, with Nathan Glazer and Revel Denney. 1950. *The Lonely Crowd: A Study of the Changing American Character.* New Haven: Yale University Press.

Riis, Jacob. 1971 [1890]. *How the Other Half Lives: Studies Among the Tenements of New York.* New York: Dover.

Rippley, LaVern J. 1984. *The German-Americans.* Lanham, MD: University Press of America.

Rischin, Moses. 1962. *The Promised City: New York's Jews, 1870–1914.* Cambridge, MA: Harvard University Press.

———. 1990. "Just Call Me John: Ethnicity as *Mentalite.*" 64–82 in *American Immigrants and Their Generations: Studies and Commentaries on the Hansen Thesis after Fifty Years,* edited by Peter Kivisto and Dag Blanck. Urbana: University of Illinois Press.

Rodriguez, Clara. 1989. *Puerto Ricans: Born in the U.S.A.* Boston: Unwin Hyman.

Rodriguez, Richard. 1981. *Hunger of Memory: The Education of Richard Rodriguez.* Boston: David R. Godine.

Roediger, David R. 1991. *The Wages of Whiteness: Race and the Making of the American Working Class.* London: Verso.

Rokeach, Milton. 1960. *The Open and Closed Mind.* New York: Basic Books.

Rollins, Judith. 1986. "Part of a Whole: The Interdependence of the Civil Rights Movement and Other Social Movements." *Phylon* 47 (1): 61–70.

Romo, Ricardo. 1983. *East Los Angeles: History of a Barrio.* Austin: University of Texas Press.

Roosens, Eugene E. 1989. *Creating Ethnicity: The Process of Ethnogenesis.* Newbury Park, CA: Sage Publications.

Rose, Arnold. 1951. *The Roots of Prejudice.* Paris: UNESCO.

Rose, Arnold and Caroline Rose. 1948. *America Divided: Minority Group Relations in the United States.* New York: Alfred A. Knopf.

Rose, Peter I. 1968. *The Subject is Race: Traditional Ideologies and the Teaching of Race Relations.* New York: Oxford University Press.

———. 1978. *"Nobody Knows the Trouble I've Seen": Some Reflections on the Insider-Outsider Debate.* Northhampton, MA: Smith College.

Ross, Edward A. 1914. *The Old World in the New.* New York: Century.

Rossell, Christine H. 1976. "School Desegregation and White Flight." *Political Science Quarterly* 90 (Winter): 675–695.

———. 1988. "Is It the Busing or the Blacks?" *Urban Affairs Quarterly* 24 (1): 138–148.

Rothschild, Joseph. 1981. *Ethnopolitics: A Conceptual Framework.* New York: Columbia University Press.

Royce, Anya Peterson. 1982. *Ethnic Identity: Strategies of Diversity.* Bloomington: Indiana University Press.

Rumbaut, Ruben G. 1991. "Passages to America." 208–243 in *America at Century's End*, edited by Alan Wolfe. Berkeley: University of California Press.

Ryan, William. 1971. *Blaming the Victim.* New York: Random House.

Sahlins, Marshall. 1972. *Stone Age Economics.* Chicago: Aldine-Atherton.

———. 1976. *The Uses and Abuses of Biology.* Ann Arbor: University of Michigan Press.

Sale, Kirkpatrick. 1990. *The Conquest of Paradise: Christopher Columbus and the Columbian Legacy.* New York: Alfred A. Knopf.

Saloutos, Theodore. 1964. *The Greeks in the United States.* Cambridge, MA: Harvard University Press.

Salvemini, Gaetano. 1977. *Italian Fascist Activities in the United States.* New York: Center for Migration Studies.

Sánchez-Ayéndez, Melba. 1988. "The Puerto Rican American Family." 173–195 in *Ethnic Families in America,* edited by Charles H. Mindel, Robert W. Hubenstein, and Roosevelt Wright, Jr. New York: Elsevier.

Sandberg, Neil C. 1974. *Ethnic Identity and Assimilation: The Polish-American.* New York: Praeger.

———. 1986. *Jewish Life in Los Angeles.* Lanham, MD: University Press of America.

Sandefur, Gary D. and Trudy McKinnel. 1986. "American Indian Intermarriage." *Social Science Research* 15 (December): 347–371.

Sanders, Jimy M. and Victor Nee. 1987. "Limits of Ethnic Solidarity in the Enclave Economy." *American Sociological Review* 52 (6): 745–767.

San Miguel, Guadalupe. 1987. *Let All of Them Take Heed: Mexican-Americans and the Campaign for Educational Equality in Texas, 1910–1981.* Austin: University of Texas Press.

Sarna, Jonathan. 1978. "From Immigrants to Ethnics: Toward a New Theory of 'Ethnicization'." *Ethnicity* 5: 370–378.

Savas, Emmanual. 1979. *Federal Housing Policy: An Agenda.* Unpublished manuscript.

Saxton, Alexander. 1971. *The Indispensable Enemy: Labor and the Anti-Chinese Movement in California.* Berkeley: University of California Press.

———. 1990. *The Rise and Fall of the White Republic: Class Politics and Mass Culture in Nineteenth-Century America.* London: Verso.

Schaefer, Richard T. 1988. *Racial and Ethnic Groups.* Glenview, IL: Scott, Foresman.

Schermerhorn, R.A. 1978. *Comparative Ethnic Relations: A Framework for Theory and Research.* New York: Random House.

Schlesinger, Arthur M., Jr. 1992. *The Disuniting of America: Reflections on a Multicultural Society.* New York: W.W. Norton.

Schneider, Jo Anne. 1990. "Defining Boundaries, Creating Contacts: Puerto Rican and Polish Presentation of Group Identity Through Ethnic Parades." *The Journal of Ethnic Studies* 18 (1): 33–57.

Schneider, Keith. 1992. "Grants Stir Interest in Nuclear Waste Site," *New York Times,* January 9: A10.

Schuman, Howard, Charlotte Steeh, and Lawrence Bobo. 1985. *Racial Attitudes in America: Trends and Interpretations.* Cambridge, MA: Harvard University Press.

Schwartz, Michael. 1988. *Radical Protest and Social Structure: The Southern Farmers' Alliance and Cotton Tenancy, 1880–1890.* Chicago: The University of Chicago Press.

Schweninger, Loren. 1990. *Black Property Owners in the South, 1790–1915.* Urbana: University of Illinois Press.

Scott, Anne Firor. 1984. "On Seeing and Not Seeing: A Case of Historical Invisibility." *The Journal of American History* 71 (1): 7–21.

Scott, Franklin D. 1963. *The Peopling of America: Perspectives on Immigration.* Washington, D.C.: American Historical Association.

Scott, George M., Jr. 1990. "A Resynthesis of the Primordial and Circumstantial Approaches to Ethnic Group Solidarity: Towards an Explanatory Model." *Ethnic and Racial Studies* 13 (2): 147–171.

Scott, Rebecca J. 1994. "Defining the Boundaries of Freedom in the World of Cane: Cuba, Brazil, and Louisiana after Emancipation." *American Historical Review* 99 (1): 70–102.

Sears, David O., and Donald R. Kinder. 1985. "Whites' Opposition to Busing: On Conceptualizing and Operationalizing Group Conflict." *Journal of Personality and Social Psychology* 48 (5): 1141–1147.

See, Katherine O'Sullivan and William J. Wilson. 1988. "Race and Ethnicity." 223–242 in *Handbook of Sociology*, edited by Neil Smelser. Newbury Park, CA: Sage Publications.

Senior, Clarence. 1965. *The Puerto Ricans*. Chicago: Quadrangle Books.

Sexton, Patricia Cayo. 1966. *Spanish Harlem: Anatomy of Poverty*. New York: Harper and Row.

Shannon, William V. 1963. *The American Irish*. New York: Macmillan.

Shapiro, Herbert. 1988. *White Violence and Black Response: From Reconstruction to Montgomery*. Amherst: University of Massachusetts Press.

Sharfman, Harold. 1977. *Jews on the Frontier*. Chicago: Regnery.

Shepperson, Wilbur S. 1965. *Emigration and Disenchantment: Portraits of Englishmen Repatriated from the United States*. Norman: University of Oklahoma Press.

Sherif, Muzafer and Carolyn W. Sherif. 1953. *Groups in Harmony and Tension: An Integration of Studies in Intergroup Relations*. New York: Harper and Brothers.

Shibutani, Tamotso and Kian M. Kwan. 1965. *Ethnic Stratification: A Comparative Approach*. New York: Macmillan.

Shibuya, Kumiko. 1992. "Patterns and Determinants of Minority Intermarriage in the San Franciso-Oakland Metropolitan Area, 1980." Paper presented at the American Sociological Association annual meeting, Pittsburgh, PA.

Shils, Edward. 1975. *Center and Periphery: Essays in Macrosociology*. Chicago: The University of Chicago Press.

Shin, Eui Hang and Hyung Park. 1988. "Peripheralization of Immigrant Professionals: Korean Physicians in the United States." *International Migration Review* (22): 609–626.

Shin, Eui Hang and Kyung-Sun Chang. 1988. "Peripheralization of Immigrant Professionals: Korean Physicians in the United States." *International Migration Review* 22 (4): 609–626.

_____. 1988. "An Analysis of Causes of Schisms in Ethnic Churches: The Case of Korean-American Churches." *Sociological Analysis* 49 (3): 234–248.

Shklar, Judith N. 1991. *American Citizenship: The Quest for Inclusion*. Cambridge, MA: Harvard University Press.

Shokeid, Moshe. 1988. *Children of Circumstances: Israeli Emigrants in New York*. Ithaca, NY: Cornell University Press.

Sigelman, Lee, and Susan Welch. 1991. *Black Americans' Views of Racial Inequality: The Dream Deferred*. Cambridge: Cambridge University Press.

Silberman, Charles E. 1985. *A Certain People: American Jews and Their Lives Today*. New York: Summit Books

Simmel, Georg. 1955. *Conflict and the Web of Group Affiliations*. New York: The Free Press.

Sinclair, Upton. 1906. *The Jungle*. New York: New American Library.

Sindler, Allen P. 1978. *Bakke, DeFunis, and Minority Admissions: The Quest for Equal Opportunity*. New York: Longman.

Singer, David, ed. 1988. *American Jewish Yearbook, 1989*. New York: American Jewish Committee.

Siu, Paul. 1952. "The Sojourner." *American Journal of Sociology,* 58: 34–44.

Skardal, Dorothy Burton. 1974. *The Divided Heart: Scandinavian Immigrant Experience through Literary Sources*. Lincoln: University of Nebraska Press.

Sklare, Marshall. 1971. *America's Jews*. New York: Random House.

————. 1972 [1955]. *Conservative Judaism: An American Religious Movement*. New York: Schocken.

Sklare, Marshall and Joseph Greenblum. 1967. *Jewish Identity on the Suburban Frontier*. New York: Basic Books.

Slayton, Robert A. 1986. *Back of the Yards: The Making of a Local Democracy*. Chicago: The University of Chicago Press.

Sleeper, Jim. 1990. *The Closet of Strangers: Liberalism and the Politics of Race in New York*. New York: W.W. Norton.

Smith, Anthony. 1981. *The Ethnic Revival*. Cambridge: Cambridge University Press.

————. 1986. *The Ethnic Origins of Nations*. Oxford: Blackwell.

Smith, Charles V. and Lewis M. Killian. 1990. "Sociological Foundations of the Civil Rights Movement." 105–116 in *Sociology in America*, edited by Herbert Gans. Newbury Park, CA: Sage Publications.

Smith, Dorothy. 1990. *Texts, Facts, and Femininity*. London: Routledge and Kegan Paul.

Smith, J. Owens. 1987. *The Politics of Racial Inequality: A Systematic Comparative Macro-Analysis from the Colonial Period to 1970*. New York: Greenwood Press.

Smith, M. Estell. 1982. "Tourism and Native Americans." *Cultural Survival Quarterly* 6 (Summer): 10–12.

Smith, M.G. 1982. "Ethnicity and Ethnic Groups in America: The View from Harvard." *Ethnic and Racial Studies* 5 (1): 1–22.

Smith, Timothy L. 1969. "Immigrant Social Aspirations and American Education, 1880–1930." *American Quarterly* 21 (3): 523–543.

Snipp, C. Matthew. 1989. *American Indians: The First of This Land*. New York: Russell Sage Foundation.

Sollors, Werner. 1981. "Theory of American Ethnicity, or: "?S Ethnic?/Ti and American/Ti, De or United (w) States S Sl and Theor?" *American Quarterly* 33 (3): 257–283.

————. ed. 1989. *The Invention of Ethnicity*. New York: Oxford University Press.

Solomon, Barbara Miller. 1956. *Ancestors and Immigrants: A Changing New England Tradition*. Cambridge, MA: Harvard University Press.

Sorin, Gerald. 1985. *The Prophetic Minority: American Jewish Immigrant Radicals, 1880–1920*. Bloomington: Indiana University Press.

Southern, David W. 1987. *Gunnar Myrdal and Black-White Relations: The Use and Abuse of An American Dilemma, 1944–1969*. Baton Rouge: Louisiana State University Press.

Sowell, Thomas. 1981. *Ethnic America: A History*. New York: Basic Books.

————. 1981. *Pink and Brown People and Other Controversial Essays*. Stanford, CA: Hoover Institution Press.

————. 1989. "Affirmative Action: A Worldwide Disaster." *Commentary* 88: 21–41.

Spicer, Edward H. 1962. *Cycles of Conquest: The Impact of Spain, Mexico, and the United States on the Indians of the Southwest*. Tucson: University of Arizona Press.

————. 1980. "American Indians." 58–122.

Spickard, Paul R. 1989. *Mixed Blood: Intermarriage and Ethnic Identity in Twentieth Century America*. Madison: University of Wisconsin Press.

Spindler, George and Louise Spindler. 1984. *Dreamers Without Power: The Menominee*. Prospect Heights, IL: Waveland Press.

Spitzberg, Irving J., Jr. 1987. *Racial Politics in Little Rock, 1954–1964.* New York: Garland.

Stack, Carol. 1974. *All Our Kin: Strategies for Survival in a Black Community.* New York: Harper and Row.

Stampp, Kenneth M. 1956. *The Peculiar Institution: Slavery in the Ante-Bellum South.* New York: Alfred A. Knopf.

Stanton, William. 1960. *The Leopard's Spots: Scientific Attitudes Towards Race in America, 1815–1859.* Chicago: The University of Chicago Press.

Staples, Robert. 1988. "The Black American Family." 303–324 in *Ethnic Families in America: Patterns and Variations,* edited by Charles H. Mindel, Robert W. Habenstein, and Roosevelt Wright, Jr. New York: Elsevier.

Starr, Paul. 1992. "Social Categories and Claims in the Liberal State." *Social Research* 59 (2): 263–295.

Steele, Shelby. 1990. *The Content of Our Character: A New Vision of Race in America.* New York: St. Martin's Press.

Stein, Howard F. and Robert F. Hill. 1977. *The Ethnic Imperative: Examining the New White Ethnic Movement.*

Steinberg, Stephen. 1981. *The Ethnic Myth: Race, Ethnicity, and Class in America.* New York: Atheneum.

Steiner, Stan. 1968. *The New Indians.* New York: Dell.

————. 1970. *La Raza: The Mexican Americans.* New York: Harper and Row.

Stoddard, Ellwyn R. 1973. *Mexican Americans.* New York: Random House.

————. 1987. *Maquilla: Assembly Plants in Northern Mexico.* El Paso: Texas Western Press.

Stoddard, Lothrop. 1920. *The Rising Tide of Color Against White World-Supremacy.* New York: Charles Scribner's Sons.

Stone, John. 1985. *Racial Conflict in Contemporary Society.* Cambridge, MA: Harvard University Press.

Storti, Craig. 1991. *Incident at Bitter Creek: The Story of the Rock Springs Chinese Massacre.* Ames: Iowa State University Press.

Strauss, Anselm. 1991. *Creating Sociological Awareness: Collective Images and Symbolic Representation.* New Brunswick, NJ: Transaction Publishers.

Stuckey, Sterling. 1987. *Slave Culture: Nationalist Theory and the Foundation of Black America.* New York: Oxford University Press.

Struyck, Raymond, Neil Mayer, and John A. Tuccillo. 1983. *Federal Housing Policy at President Reagan's Midterm.* Washington, D.C.: The Urban Institute Press.

Sullivan, Teresa A. 1984. "The Occupational Prestige of Women Immigrants: A Comparison of Cubans and Mexicans." *International Migration Review.* 18 (4): 1045–1062.

Sumka, Howard. 1978. "Displacement in Revitalizing Neighborhoods: A Review and Research Strategy. *Occasion Papers in Housing and Community Affairs,* Vol 2. Washington, D.C.: Department of Housing and Urban Development: 134–167.

Sumner, William Graham. 1940 [1906]. *Folkways: A Study of the Sociological Importance of Usages, Manners, Customs, Mores, and Morals.* Boston: Ginn.

Sung, Betty Lee. 1967. *Mountain of Gold.* New York: Macmillan.

Swatez, Marc Jon. 1990. "United We Stand: The Merging of the German and Eastern European Jews in Chicago." Paper presented at the annual meeting of the Midwest Sociological Society, Chicago.

Swierenga, Robert P., ed. 1985. *The Dutch in America: Immigration, Settlement, and Cultural Change.* New Brunswick, NJ: Rutgers University Press.

Taeuber, Karl B. 1983. *Racial Residential Segregation, 28 Cities, 1970–1980.* Working paper 83-12. Madison: Center for Demography and Ecology, University of Wisconsin.

Tajfel, Henri. 1969. "Cognitive Aspects of Prejudice." *Journal of Biosocial Science*, Supplement no. 1.

_____. 1978. *The Social Psychology of Minorities.* London: Minority Rights Groups.

_____. 1981. *Human Groups and Social Categories.* Cambridge: Cambridge University Press.

Takaki, Ronald. 1979. *Iron Cages: Race and Culture in 19th- Century America.* New York: Alfred A. Knopf.

_____. 1989. *Strangers From a Different Shore: A History of Asian Americans.* Boston: Little, Brown.

_____. 1993. *A Different Mirror: A History of Multicultural America.* Boston: Little, Brown.

Tannenbaum, Frank. 1946. *Slave and Citizen.* New York: Random House.

Taylor, Charles, with commentary by Amy Gutmann, Steven C. Rockefeller, Michael Walzer, and Susan Wolf. 1992. *Multiculturalism and "The Politics of Recognition.* Princeton: Princeton University Press.

Taylor, D. Garth, Paul B. Sheatsley, and Andrew M. Greeley. 1978. "Attitudes Toward Racial Integration." *Scientific American* 238 (June): 42–51.

Taylor, Lawrence J. 1983. *Dutchmen on the Bay: The Ethnohistory of a Contractual Community.* Philadelphia: University of Pennsylvania Press.

Taylor, Philip. 1971. *The Distant Magnet: European Emigration to the U.S.A.* New York: Harper and Row.

TeSelle, Sallie, ed. 1973. *The Rediscovery of Ethnicity.* New York: Harper and Row.

Terry, Don. 1991. "Indian Treaty Accord in Wisconsin." *New York Times*, May 21: A8.

Thernstrom, Stephan. 1973. *The Other Bostonians.* Cambridge, MA: Harvard University Press.

Thernstrom, Stephan, Ann Orlov, and Oscar Handlin, eds. 1980. *Harvard Encyclopedia of American Ethnic Groups.* Cambridge, MA: Belknap Press of the Harvard University Press.

Thistlethwaite, Frank. 1960. "Migrations from Europe Overseas in the Nineteenth and Twentieth Centuries." XIe Congres International des Sciences Historiques, *Rapports* (Uppsala, Sweden) 5: 32–60.

Thomas, Melvin E. 1993. "Race, Class, and Personal Income: An Empirical Test of the Declining Significance of Race Thesis, 1968–1988." *Social Problems* 40 (3): 328–342.

Thomas, Piri. 1967. *Down These Mean Streets.* New York: Alfred A. Knopf.

Thomas, Robert K. 1968. "Pan-Indianism." 128–140 in *The American Indian Today*, eds. Stuart Levine and Nancy Oestreich Luine. Baltimore: Penquin Books.

Thomas, William Isaac. 1909. *Source Book for Social Origins: Ethnological Materials, Psychological Standpoint, Classified and Annotated Bibliographics for the Interpretation of Savage Societies.* Boston: Badger.

Thomas, W. I. and Florian Znaniecki. 1918. *The Polish Peasant in Europe and America.* New York: Alfred A. Knopf.

Thomsen, Craig. 1993. "After Making a Run for the Border: A Historical and Economic Analysis of Illegal Mexican Immigrants in the United States." Unpublished paper.

Thornton, Russell. 1987. *American Indian Holocaust and Survival: A Population History Since 1492.* Norman: University of Oklahoma Press.

_____. 1990. *The Cherokees: A Population History.* Lincoln: University of Nebraska Press.

Tienda, Marta. 1989. "Puerto Ricans and The Underclass Debate." *Annals* vol. 501 (January): 105–119.

Tienda, Marta and Ding-Tzann Lii. 1987. "Minority Concentration and Earnings Inequality: Blacks, Hispanics, and Asians Compared." *American Journal of Sociology* 93 (1): 141–165.

Tilly, Charles. 1990. "The Weight of the Past on American Immigration." Unpublished paper.

Tippeconnic, John W., III. 1990. "American Indians: Education, Demographics, and the 1990s." 249–257 in *U.S. Race Relations in the 1980s and 1990s*, ed. Gail E. Thomas. New York: Hemisphere.

Tolnay, Stewart E. and E. M. Beck. 1992. "Racial Violence and Black Migration in the American South, 1910 to 1930." *American Sociological Review* 57 (1): 103–116.

Tomasi, Lydio F. 1978. *The Italian in America: The Progressive View, 1892–1914*. New York: Center for Migration Studies.

Tomasi, Silvano M. 1975. *Piety and Power: The Role of the Italian Parishes in the New York Metropolitan Area, 1880–1930*. New York: Center for Migration Studies.

Tricarico, Donald. 1984. *The Italians of Greenwich Village*. New York: Center for Migration Studies.

_____. 1989. "In a New Light: Italian-American Ethnicity in the Mainstream." 24–46 in *The Ethnic Enigma*, edited by Peter Kivisto. Philadelphia: Balch Institute Press.

Tsukashima, Ronald Tadao. 1991. "Cultural Endowment, Disadvantaged Status, and Economic Niche: The Development of an Ethnic Trade." *International Migration Review* 25 (2): 333–354.

Ueda, Reed. 1992. "American National Identity and Race in Immigrant Generations: Reconsidering Hansen's 'Law'." *Journal of Interdisciplinary History* 22 (3): 483–491.

Um, Shin Ja. 1992. "Korean Married Immigrant Woman Working in the Dallas Garment Industry: Looking for Feminist Threads in Patriarchial Cloth." Paper presented at the Midwest Sociological Society annual meeting, Kansas City, MO.

Ungehever, Frederick. 1987. "A New Band of Tribal Tycoons." *Time* 129 (March 16): 56–59.

U.S. Bureau of the Census. 1909. *A Century of Population Growth*. Washington, D.C: Government Printing Office.

_____. 1971. "The Social and Economic Status of the Black Population in the United States, 1971." *Current Population Reports*, Series p. 23, no. 42. Washington, D.C.: Government Printing Office.

_____. 1975. *Historical Statistics of the United States: Colonial Times to 1970*. Part 1. Washington D.C.: Government Printing Office.

_____. 1980. *General Social and Economic Characteristics, 1980, United States Summary*. Washington, D.C.: Government Printing Office.

_____. 1983. *Ancestry of the Population by State: 1980*. Washington, D.C.: Government Printing Office.

_____. 1984. *1980 Census of the Population*, PC80-1-D1-A. Washington, D.C.: Government Printing Office.

_____. 1986. *Projections of the Hispanic Population of the United States: 1983–2080*. Washington D.C.: Government Printing Office.

_____. 1987. *Statistical Abstract of the United States*. Washington, D.C.: Government Printing Office.

_____. 1989. *The Hispanic Population in the United States*, Current Population Reports, Series P-20, No. 438. Washington, D.C.: Government Printing Office.

_____. 1991a. *The Hispanic Population in the United States*, Current Population Reports, Series P-20, No. 455. Washington, D.C.: Government Printing Office.

_____. 1991b. *Statistical Abstract of the United States*. Washington, D.C.: Government Printing Office.

_____. 1991c. "The Economic Status of Hispanics in the United States." *Current Population Reports*. Washington, D.C.: Government Printing Office.

_____. 1992. *The Black Population in the United States*, Current Population Reports, Series P-20, No. 462. Washington, D.C.: Government Printing Office.

U.S. Immigration and Naturalization Service. 1985. Statistical Yearbook. Washington D.C.: Government Printing Office.

Valdes, Dennis Nodin. 1991. *Al Norte: Agricultural Workers in the Great Lakes Region, 1917–1970*. Austin: University of Texas Press.

Valentine, Charles A. 1968. *Culture and Poverty: Critique and Counter Proposals*. Chicago: The University of Chicago Press.

Van den Berghe, Pierre L. 1965. *South Africa: A Study in Conflict*. Middletown, CT: Wesleyan University Press.

_____. 1967. *Race and Racism: A Comparative Perspective*. New York: John Wiley and Sons.

_____. 1970. *Race and Ethnicity: Essays in Comparative Sociology*. New York: Basic Books.

_____. 1978. "Race and Ethnicity: A Sociobiological Perspective." *Ethnic and Racial Studies* 1 (4): 401–411.

_____. 1981. *The Ethnic Phenomenon*. New York: Elsevier.

_____. 1986. "Ethnicity and the Sociobiology Debate." 246–263 in *Theories of Race and Ethnic Relations*, edited by John Rex and David Mason. Cambridge: Cambridge University Press.

_____. 1990. "Why Most Sociologists Don't (and Won't) Think Evolutionarily." *Sociological Forum* 5 (2): 173–185.

Vander Zanden, James W. 1973. *American Minority Relations*. New York: Plenum.

Vecoli, Rudolph J. 1964. "Contadini in Chicago: A Critique of *The Uprooted.*" *Journal of American History* 51: 404–417.

_____. 1970. "Ethnicity: A Neglected Dimension of American History." 70–88 in *The State of American History*, edited by Herbert J. Bass. Chicago: Quadrangle Books.

_____. 1979. "The Resurgence of American Immigration History." *American Studies International*.

_____. 1987. *Italian Immigration in Rural and Small Town America*. New York: Italian America Historical Association.

_____. 1991. "Inter-Ethnic Perspectives on American Immigration History." Paper presented in Vaxjo, Sweden, May 31.

Vidich, Arthur J. 1992. "Boston's North End: An American Epic." *Journal of Contemporary Ethnography* 21 (April): 80–102.

Vidich, Arthur J. and Joseph Bensman. 1958. *Small Town in Mass Society: Class Power, and Religion in a Rural Community*. Princeton, NJ: Princeton University Press.

Vinje, David. 1985. "Cultural Values and Economic Development on Reservations." 155–175 in *American Indian Policy in the Twentieth Century*, edited by Vine Delona, Jr. Norman: University of Oklahoma Press.

Vogel, Virgil J. 1972. *This Country Was Ours*. New York: Harper and Row.

Vogt, Evan Z. 1957. "The Acculturation of American Indians." *Annals of the American Academy of Political and Social Science* 311: 137–146.

Wacker, R. Fred. 1983. *Ethnicity Pluralism, and Race: Race Relations Theory in America Before Myrdal*. Westport, CT: Greenwood Press.

Waddell, Jack O. and O. Michael Watson, eds. 1971. *The American Indian in Urban Society.* Boston: Little, Brown.

Wakatsuki, Yasuo. 1979. "Japanese Emigration to the United States." *Perspectives in American History* 12: 395–465.

Waldinger, Roger. 1986. *Through the Eye of the Needle: Immigrants and Enterprise in New York's Garment Trades.* New York: New York University Press.

_____. 1994. "The Making of an Immigrant Niche." *International Migration Review* 28 (1): 3–30.

Wallerstein, Immanuel. 1974. *The Modern World-System: Capitalist Agriculture and the Origins of the European World-Economy in the Sixteenth Century.* New York: John Wiley and Sons.

Ward, David. 1980. "Settlement Patterns and Spatial Distribution." 35–74 in *Immigration*, Richard A. Easterlin, David Ward, William S. Bernard, and Reed Ueda. Cambridge: The Belknap Press of Harvard University Press.

Ware, Caroline F. 1935. *Greenwich Village, 1920–1930.* Boston: Houghton Mifflin.

_____. 1940. "Cultural Groups in the United States." 62–73 in *The Cultural Approach to History*, edited by Caroline F. Ware. New York: Gordon Press.

Warner, R. Stephen. 1992. "Religious Institutions Emerging Among New (Post-1965) Immigrant Groups in the U.S." Paper presented at the Midwest Sociological Society annual meeting, Kansas City, MO.

Washington, Booker T. 1963 [1901]. *Up From Slavery.* New York: Bantam Books.

Waters, Mary C. 1990. *Ethnic Options Choosing Identities in America.* Berkeley: University of California Press.

Wattenberg, Ben. 1991. *The First Universal Nation: Leading Indicators and Ideas About the Surge of America in the 1990s.* New York: The Free Press.

Wax, Murray L. 1971. *Indian Americans: Unity and Diversity.* Englewood Cliffs, NJ: Prentice-Hall, Inc.

Waxman, Chaim I. 1983. *America's Jews in Transition.* Philadelphia: Temple University Press.

Weber, David J. 1973. *Foreigners in Their Native Land.* Albuquerque: University of New Mexico Press.

_____. 1982. *The Mexican Frontier, 1821–1846.* Albuquerque: University of New Mexico Press.

Weed, Perry. 1971. *The White Ethnic Movement and Ethnic Politics.* New York: Macmillan.

Weibel-Orlando, Joan. 1991. *Indian Country, L.A.: Maintaining Ethnic Community in a Complex Society.* Urbana: University of Illinois Press

Weinberg, Sydney Stahl. 1988. *The World of Our Mothers.* Chapel Hill: University of North Carolina Press.

Weiss, Bernard, ed. 1982. *American Education and the European Immigrant.* Urbana: University of Illinois Press.

Wells, Robert V. 1975. *The Population of the British Colonies in America Before 1776: A Survey of Census Data.* Princeton, NJ: Princeton University Press.

Weslager, C.A. 1988. *New Sweden on the Delaware: 1638–1655.* Wilmington, DE: The Middle Atlantic Press.

West, Cornel. 1993. *Race Matters.* Boston: Beacon Press.

White, Ronald C., Jr. 1990. *Liberty and Justice for All: Racial Reform and the Social Gospel.* New York: Harper and Row.

Whyte, William Foote. 1943. *Street Corner Society: The Social Structure of an Italian Slum.* Chicago: The University of Chicago Press.

Wiley, Norbert. 1986. "Early American Sociology and the *Polish Peasant.*" *Sociological Theory* 4 (Spring): 20–40.

Wilhelm, Sidney M. 1970. *Who Needs the Negro?* Garden City, NY: Doubleday.

Williams, Norma. 1980. *The Mexican American Family: Tradition and Change.* Dix Hills, NY: General Hall.

Williams, Richard. 1990. *Hierarchial Structures and Social Value: The Creation of Black and Irish Identities in the United States.* Cambridge: Cambridge University Press.

Williams, Robin M., Jr. 1977. *Mutual Accommodation: Ethnic Conflict and Cooperation.* Minneapolis: University of Minnesota Press.

Williamson, Joel. 1980. *New People: Miscegenation and Mulattoes in the United States.* New York: The Free Press.

_____. 1986. *A Rage for Order: Black-White Relations in the American South Since Emancipation.* New York: Oxford University Press.

Willie, Charles Vert. 1979. "The Inclining Significance of Race." 145–158 in *The Caste and Class Controversy,* edited by Charles Vert Willie. Bayside, NY: General Hall.

Wilson, Kenneth L. and Alejandro Portes. 1980. "Immigrant Enclaves: An Analysis of the Labor Market Experiences of Cubans in Miami." *American Journal of Sociology* 86 (2): 295–319.

Wilson, Kenneth L. and W. Allen Martin. 1982. "Ethnic Enclaves: A Comparison of the Cuban and Black Economies in Miami." *American Journal of Sociology* 88 (1): 135–160.

Wilson, William Julius. 1978. *The Declining Significance of Race: Blacks and Changing American Institution.* Chicago: The University of Chicago Press.

_____. 1987. *The Truly Disadvantaged: The Inner City, The Underclass, and Public Policy.* Chicago: The University of Chicago Press.

_____. 1991. "Studying Inner-City Social Dislocations: The Challenge of Public Agenda Research." *American Sociological Review* 56 (1): 1–14.

Wirth, Louis. 1956 [1928]. *The Ghetto.* Chicago: The University of Chicago Press.

_____. 1945. "The Problem of Minority Groups." 347–372 in *The Science of Man in the World Crisis,* edited by Ralph Linton. New York: Columbia University Press.

_____. 1956 [1928]. *The Ghetto.* Chicago: The University of Chicago Press.

Wittke, Carl. 1939. *We Who Built America: The Saga of the Immigrant.* New York: Prentice-Hall.

_____. 1952. *Refugees of Revolution: The German Forty-Eighters in America.* Philadelphia: University of Pennsylvania Press.

_____. 1956. *The Irish in America.* Baton Rouge: Louisiana State University Press.

Woll, Allen L. and Randall M. Miller. 1987. *Ethnic and Racial Images in American Film and Television: Historical Essays and Bibliography.* New York: Garland.

Wong, Bernard. 1982. *Chinatown: Economic Adaptation and Ethnic Identity of the Chinese.* New York: CBS College.

_____. 1987. "The Chinese: New Immigrants in New York's Chinatown." 243–271 in *New Immigrants in New York,* edited by Nancy Foner. New York: Columbia University Press.

Wong, Jade Snow. 1945. *Fifth Chinese Daughter.* New York: Harper and Brothers.

Wong, Morrison G. 1988. "The Chinese American Family." 230–257 in *Ethnic Families in America: Patterns and Variations*, edited by Charles H. Mindel, Robert W. Habenstein, and Roosevelt Wright, Jr. New York: Elsevier.

Woocher, Jonathan. 1986. *Sacred Survival: The Civil Religion of American Jews*. Bloomington: Indiana University Press.

Wood, Forrest G. 1990. *The Arrogance of Faith: Christianity and Race in America from the Colonial Era to the Twentieth Century*. New York: Alfred A. Knopf.

Woods, Robert A. 1903. *Americans in Process: A Settlement Study*. Boston: Houghton, Mifflin and Company.

Woodson, Carter. 1968. *The Education of the Negro Prior to 1861*. New York: Arno Press.

Woodward, C. Vann. 1971. *American Counterpoint: Slavery and Racism in the North-South Dialogue*. Boston: Little, Brown.

_____. 1974. *The Strange Career of Jim Crow*. New York: Oxford University Press.

Wright, Richard. 1937. *Black Boy: A Record of Childhood and Youth*. New York: Harper and Brothers.

Wrobel, Paul. 1979. *Our Way: Family Parish, and Neighborhood in a Polish-American Community*. Notre Dame, IN: University of Notre Dame Press.

Wyman, David S. 1984. *The Abandonment of the Jews: America and the Holocaust*. New York: Pantheon Books.

Yanagisako, Sylvia J. 1985. *Transforming the Past*. Stanford, CA: Stanford University Press.

Yancey, William L., Eugene P. Ericksen, and Richard N. Juliani. 1976. "Emergent Ethnicity: A Review and Reformulation." *American Sociological Review* 41 (3): 391–403.

Yancey, William L., Eugene P. Ericksen, and George Leon. 1985. "The Structure of Pluralism: 'We're All Italian Around Here, Aren't We, Mrs. O'Brien?'" 94–116 in *Ethnicity and Race in the U.S.A.: Toward the Twenty-First Century*. London: Routledge and Kegan Paul.

Yans-McLaughlin, Virginia. 1977. *Family and Community: Italian Immigrants in Buffalo, 1880–1930*. Ithaca, NY: Cornell University Press.

Yinger, J. Milton. 1985. "Ethnicity." *Annual Review of Sociology* 11: 151–180.

_____. 1986. "Intersecting Strands in the Theorization of Race and Ethnic Relations." 20–41 in *Theories of Race and Ethnic Relations*, edited by John Rex and David Mason. Cambridge: Cambridge University Press.

Yoon, In-Jin. 1991. "The Changing Significance of Ethnic and Class Resources in Immigrant Business: The Case of Korean Immigrant Business in Chicago." *International Migration Review* 25 (2): 303–332.

_____. 1992. "The Social Origins of Korean Immigration to the United States, 1965-Present." Paper presented at the American Sociological Association annual meeting, Pittsburgh, PA.

Young, Donald. 1932. *American Minority Peoples: A Study in Racial and Cultural Conflicts in the United States*. New York: Harper and Brothers.

Yu, Elena S.H. 1980. "Filipino Migration and Community Organizations in the United States." *California Sociologist* 3 (Summer): 76–102

Zangwill, Israel. 1909. *The Melting-Pot: A Drama in Four Acts*. New York: Macmillan.

Zeul, Carolyn R. and Craig R. Humphrey. 1971. "The Integratives of Black Residents in Suburban Neighborhoods: A Reexamination of the Contact Hypothesis." *Social Problems* 18 (4): 462–474.

Zhou, Min and John R. Logan. 1989. "Returns on Human Capital in Ethnic Enclaves: New York City's Chinatown." *American Sociological Review* 54 (5): 809–820.

_____. 1991. "In and Out of Chinatown: Residential Mobility and Segregation of New York City's Chinese. *Social Forces* 70 (2): 387–407.

Zorbaugh, Harvey. 1929. *The Gold Coast and the Slum*. Chicago: The University of Chicago Press.

Zunz, Olivier. 1982. *The Changing Face of Inequality: Urbanization, Industrial Development, and Immigrants in Detroit, 1880–1920*. Chicago: The University of Chicago Press.

_____. 1985. "American History and the Changing Meaning of Assimilation." *Journal of American Ethnic History* 4 (2): 53–72.

Zweigenhaft, Richard L. and G. William Domhoff. 1991. *Blacks in the White Establishment? A Study of Race and Class in America*. New Haven: Yale University Press.

Index

A

Abolitionist Movement, 168–169
Adamic, Louis, 34
Addams, Jane, 23, 184
Adhesive adaptation, 450–451
Adorno, T. W., 63
Affirmative action, 326–336
  consequences of, 332–334
  public opinion and, 331–332
  quotas in, 332
  reverse discrimination and, 328–331
African Americans, 13, 223–238, 308–354
  affirmative action and, 326–336
  caste pluralism and, 146, 155–169, 232–234
  in cities, 96, 97, 235–236, 351–352
  citizenship rights of, 3
  civil rights movement and, 311–336
  community of, 236–237
  defining, 17–18
  demographics of, 73, 89–98, 341–342, 385
  depression and, 334
  education of, 225, 227, 229, 317, 321–326, 335–336
  employment of, 224, 225, 231–232
  enslavement of. See Slavery
  ethnic experiences of, 8–9
  European American attitudes toward, 301–306
  families of, 163–165, 229, 350–351
  in films, 225, 226, 238, 346, 351, 354, 447–448
  "free persons of color," 167–168
  Great Migration of, 92–98, 234–236, 310
  heterogeneity of, 91
  ideology of racism and, 157–159
  immigration of, 89–98, 155–169
  labor unions and, 237
  leadership of, 228–231
  militancy of, 318–321
  as minority group, 36–37
  music of, 237
  naming, 18
  nationalism among, 34
  origins of culture of, 161–163, 237–238
  politics and, 225, 227, 315–316, 353
  population growth among, 89–92
  poverty among, 349–352
  race theories and, 39, 40, 157–159
  in Reconstruction era, 223–226
  relations with other ethnic groups, 37, 201–202, 231–234, 398, 410, 447–448
  school desegregation and, 317, 321–326
  segregated housing of, 336–342
  social class of, 231–234, 345–349
  social standing of, 275
  Southern race relations and, 231–234
  stereotypes of, 65, 162
  violence against, 8–9, 165, 166, 232, 311, 317
  voting rights of, 3, 224, 315, 318
  women, 164–165, 224, 350–351
African Union Society, 168
Afro American, 18. See also African Americans
Aid to Families with Dependent Children (AFDC), 338, 350
Alba, Richard D., 187, 278, 287–288, 289–290, 292
Alcoholism, among American Indians, 378–379
Alexander, Adele Logan, 167
Alexander v. Holmes (1969), 322
Alianza Federal de Mercedes, 416–417
Alianza Hispano-Americano, 413
Alien Labor Contract Law of 1885, 83
Alien Land Act of 1913, 259
Allen, Walter R., 92
Allport, Gordon, 63
America (film), 269
American Civil Liberties Union, 262
American Dilemma, An (Myrdal), 308–310
American Federation of Labor, 214, 249
American Indian Defense Association, 270
American Indian Movement (AIM), 365–367, 375
American Indians, 263–271, 355–384
  alcoholism among, 378–379
  assimilation of, 356–357, 358, 367–368, 382–383

in cities, 80, 81, 271,
    359–364
citizenship rights of, 3
coercive pluralism and,
    145–146, 147–154
as colonized peoples, 69
community of, 363–364
conflict over land of,
    151–154, 267, 368–374
culture of, 361
demographics of, 74–80,
    81, 360, 385
diseases among, 75
economics and, 149–151,
    361, 374–376
education of, 382–383
ethnic experiences of,
    10–11
families of, 266
in films, 269, 380–381
future of, 382–383
genocide and, 47
Ghost Dance movement of,
    267–268
government policies on,
    356–359
health of, 75, 378–379
housing of, 377
intermarriage among,
    362–363
naming, 18, 364
nationalism among, 34
natural resources of,
    369–375
New Deal program for,
    269–271, 355–356
ongoing conflict with
    white America,
    368–374
political activism of,
    364–368
political goals of, 367–368
population decline and
    recovery of, 74–76
populations of various
    tribes, 77
poverty among, 375–376
prejudice and
    discrimination
    against, 271
religion and, 268, 360
relocation of, 153–154
on reservations, 77–80,
    263–265, 374–379,
    382–383

social standing of, 275
stereotypes of, 269
trade with European
    settlers, 149–151
tribal organization of,
    147–148
white attitudes toward,
    379–382
Americanization, 49
American Minority Peoples
    (Young), 35
American Protestant
    Association, 123
Amish, 45, 61
Analysis, levels of, 5–6, 16
Anderson, Charles, 124
Anderson, Elijah, 351
Anderson v. S.F. Unified School
    District (1971), 328–329
And My Children Did Not
    Know Me (Bukowczyk),
    203
Angelou, Maya, 8–9, 12
Anglicanism, 122
Anglo-conformity, 49
Anglo Saxon Clubs, 231
Anglo Saxon Protestants, 37,
    83, 117, 124
Anti-Semitism, 37, 87, 206,
    211–212, 277, 294, 295,
    300
Appalachian identity, 291
Aptheker, Herbert, 165
Aquino, Corazon, 456
Archdeacon, Thomas, 124,
    290
Aristotle, 170
Ashkenazic Jews, 204
Asian Americans, 249–263,
    424–459
    assimilation of, 433,
        456–457, 458
    in cities, 252–253,
        255–256, 258,
        437–438, 439–444
    coercive pluralism and,
        173–176
    community of, 252–253,
        255–256, 260–262,
        432–435, 455–457
    demographics of, 102–109,
        249, 250, 258, 385,
        395, 435–436
    discrimination against,
        253–255, 256,
        259–260, 425,
        430–431, 452–453, 455

economics and, 441–442,
    445–447
education of, 255–256,
    425, 437
employment of, 252,
    255–256, 258, 259,
    260–261, 429–431,
    437, 441–442,
    445–447, 454–455, 456
ethnic experiences of,
    9–10
families of, 251–252, 259,
    432, 435, 449–451
in films, 428, 434
future of, 451–452
gangs and, 438, 442
generational change
    among, 261–262,
    429–432, 449–451,
    456–457
immigration of, 19,
    102–109, 173–176,
    249–251, 257–259,
    436, 444–446, 452,
    453–455, 458
intermarriage among,
    434–435, 452–453
internment of, 262–263,
    429
as model minority,
    425–427
perceptions of American
    culture, 21
politics and, 433–434,
    438–439, 456
poverty among, 437–438,
    440
prejudice and, 175–176,
    253–255, 256,
    259–260, 425,
    427–429, 430–431,
    452–453, 455
relations with other ethnic
    groups, 447–448
religion and, 251–252,
    261, 432–433, 445,
    448–449, 455
restrictions on
    immigration of, 19,
    105, 249–251, 436
settlement patterns of,
    254, 258
social class of, 436–438,
    439–440, 444–445,
    458–459
social standing of, 275

stereotypes of, 65
violence against, 254
women, 251, 253, 259, 436, 451–452
See also specific ethnic groups
Assimilation, 22–26
of American Indians, 356–357, 358, 367–368, 382–383
of Asian Americans, 433, 456–457, 458
of Cuban Americans, 398–399
defined, 48
ethnicity vs., 19–20, 48–52, 70, 278–283, 287–288, 460–462
of Jewish Americans, 295–300, 306
modified, 50–52
pluralism vs., 19–20
types of, 49
Asylums (Goffman), 160
"Atlanta Compromise" speech (B. T. Washington), 229
Awful Disclosures of the Hotel Dieu Nunnery of Montreal (Monk), 135
Aztec empire, 170

B

Bailyn, Bernard, 115
Baker, Ella, 312
Bakke v. Regents of the University of California (1978), 329–330
Baldwin, Roger, 262
Bank of Italy, 188
Barrera, Mario, 417
Barth, Fredrik, 61
Basic Naturalization Act of 1906, 85
Bataille, Gretchen, 381
Batista, Fulgencio, 248, 391
Baudrillard, Jean, 22
Bay of Pigs invasion, 392
Beban, George, 192
Beecher, Lyman, 135
Bell, Daniel, 189
Bellah, Robert, 116
Benedict, Ruth, 31
Benjamin, Lois, 334
Berger, Victor L., 215

Berthoff, Rowland, 112, 119–120
Beyond the Melting Pot (Glazer and Moynihan), 27, 50, 284–285
Bilingual Education Act of 1968, 388–389
Bilingualism, 19, 387–390
Birth of a Nation, The (film), 225, 226, 238
Black Bourgeoisie (Frazier), 345–346
Black Boy (Wright), 9
Black codes, 223–224
Blackfeet oil exploration dispute, 371–372
Black Hand, The (film), 192
Black Metropolis (Drake and Cayton), 32, 236–237
Black Muslims, 319
Black nationalism, 318–321
Black Panthers, 319–320
Black Power, 319
Blacks, 17–18. *See also* African Americans
Blassingame, John, 91, 164
Blauner, Robert, 240
Blessing, Patrick J., 130, 214
Blumer, Herbert, 46, 60, 64
B'nai B'rith, 205–206
Boas, Franz, 31
Bobo, Lawrence, 325
Bodnar, John, 180, 200, 201
Bogardus, Emory, 188, 246
Bolt, Christine, 270
Bonacich, Edna, 69, 396
Border Industrialization Program, 386
Border Patrol, 243
Bordertown (film), 246
Borjas, George, 413
Boston, Italian Americans in, 277–278
Boundaries, ethnic, 16–18, 61
Bourne, Randolph, 26, 117
Boycotts, in civil rights movement, 315
Boyz N the Hood (film), 351
Brace, Charles Loring, 184–185
Bracero program, 246, 410
Braly, Kenneth, 188
Breton, Raymond, 61–62, 141, 211

British immigrants, 82, 113–125
culture of, 117, 119–120, 121, 124–125
number of, 114, 120
religion and, 113, 118, 122–123
Broken Arrow (film), 380–381
Brown, Francis J., 34, 35
Brown, Jerry, 415
Brown, John, 166
Brown v. Board of Education of Topeka, Kansas (1954), 318, 331
Buddhism, 432, 433
Buffalo Bill and the Indians (film), 381
Bugelski, B.R., 283
Bukowczyk, John, 197, 199–200, 202–203
Bureau of Indian Affairs (BIA), 265–266, 270, 356, 357, 358, 366–367, 377
Buses
desegregation of, 314–315
school desegregation and, 317, 321–326, 335–336
Bush, George, 305, 330, 332, 359
Butler, Jon, 143

C

Canada, Québecois separatists in, 34, 48
Carmichael, Stokely, 319
Carnegie Corporation, 308
Carroll, John, 132
Cass, Lewis, 152
Caste pluralism, 146, 155–169, 232–234
Castro, Fidel, 101, 392, 394
Catholicism
German Americans and, 141, 217
Hispanic Americans and, 240, 247, 408, 413–414
Irish Americans and, 123, 124, 125, 126, 127, 131, 132–133, 217
Italian Americans and, 186
Polish Americans and, 196–197
prejudice and, 135
Caughnawagas, 271
Cavaliers, 118

Cayton, Horace R., 32, 236–237

Census, 72–74, 287–288

Chan, Sucheng, 175

Chaney, James, 317

Charitable Irish Society of Boston, 131

Chavez, Cesar, 415

Chavez, John, 171, 173

Chavez, Linda, 390, 418

Cherokee Nation v. Georgia (1831), 154

Chiang Kai-shek, 436, 438

Chicago School of Sociology, 31–32, 46, 193

Chicanismo, 416–417. *See also* Mexican Americans

Chinatowns, 252–253, 255–256, 437–438, 439–444

Chinese Americans, 249–256, 435–444
  coercive pluralism and, 173–176
  community of, 252–253, 255–256
  demographics of, 103–104, 109, 250, 435–436
  economics and, 441–442
  education of, 255–256, 437
  employment of, 252, 255–256, 437, 441–442
  ethnic experiences of, 9–10
  families of, 251–252
  gangs and, 438, 442
  health of, 442
  middle class, 436–438, 439–440
  politics and, 438–439
  poverty among, 437–438, 440
  prejudice and, 175–176, 253–255, 256
  religion and, 251–252
  restrictions on immigration of, 19, 249–251, 436
  settlement patterns of, 254
  social standing of, 275
  violence against, 254
  women, 251, 253, 436
  See also Asian Americans

Chinese Consolidated Benevolent Association (CCBA), 252, 442–443

Chinese Exclusion Act of 1882, 19, 105, 436

Chippewa spearfishing dispute, 369–371

Cimino, Michael, 428

Cinel, Dino, 183

Circumstantialism, 52

Cisneros, Henry, 417

Cities
  African Americans in, 96, 97, 235–236, 351–352
  American Indians in, 80, 81, 271, 359–364
  Asian Americans in, 252–253, 255–256, 258, 437–438, 439–444
  German Americans in, 139–140
  Hispanic Americans in, 96, 97, 385–386, 394–396, 399, 402, 404, 405–406, 407–409, 410
  Italian Americans in, 184, 277–278
  segregation in, 97
  white flight from, 324–326

Citizenship, meaning for ethnic groups, 3

Civil Liberties Act of 1988, 434

Civil Rights Act of 1866, 224, 341

Civil Rights Act of 1964, 318, 322, 327–328, 332, 341, 389

Civil Rights Act of 1968, 318, 341

Civil rights movement, 311–336
  affirmative action and, 326–336
  busing and school desegregation and, 317, 321–326, 335–336
  judicial decisions concerning, 317–318, 322–323, 328–331
  legislation concerning, 224, 312–318, 322, 327–328, 332, 341, 389
  militancy and black nationalism and, 318–321
  nonviolent confrontation and legislative lobbying and, 312–318

reverse discrimination and, 328–331
  white responses to, 316–317

Clansman, The (Dixon), 226

Clark, Mark, 320

Class. *See* Social class

Cleaver, Eldridge, 319

Coercive pluralism, 145–176
  African Americans and, 146, 155–169
  American Indians and, 145–146, 147–154
  Asian Americans and, 173–176
  Hispanic Americans and, 170–173

Cohen, Lizabeth, 200

Cohen, Steven M., 296–298

Coleman, James, 324, 335

Collier, John, 270, 355–356

Colonized peoples, 69

Colored Alliance, 232

Come See the Paradise (film), 434

Community. *See* Ethnic communities

Comte, Auguste, 158

Confidence Man, The (Melville), 152

Conflict period of European settlement, 151–154

Confucianism, 449

Congress of Industrial Organizations (CIO), 199–200, 217, 237, 248

Congress of Racial Equality (CORE), 312, 315

Congress of Spanish-Speaking People, 248, 413

Conzen, Kathleen Neils, 59, 60, 138

Cornell, Stephen, 148, 149–150, 154, 263, 265, 367

Cortés, Hernando, 170

Cottle, Thomas, 323

Coughlin, Charles, 217

Council of Energy Resource Tribes (CERT), 374–375

Cox, Oliver, 343

Creek War of 1813–1814, 152

Crèvecoeur, J. Hector St. John de, 22–23, 138

Crime
  among Chinese
    Americans, 438, 442
  among Hispanic
    Americans, 422
  among Italian Americans,
    188–189, 192
Crispino, James A., 281–283
Croatian Americans, 4
Cromwell, Oliver, 125
Cronkite, Walter, 390
Cuban Americans, 386, 387,
    390–399
  assimilation of, 398–399
  demographics of, 100–101
  economics and, 396–397
  employment of, 397
  immigration of, 68, 248,
    391–394
  Marielitos, 101, 393–394
  politics and, 397–398
  religion and, 396
  settlement patterns of,
    394–396
  women, 397
  See also Hispanic
    Americans
Cuban missile crisis, 392–393
Cullen, Countee, 237
Cultural assimilation, 49, 70
Cultural pluralism, 26–27, 70
Culture
  African American,
    161–163, 237–238
  American Indian, 361
  assimilation vs. ethnicity,
    19–20, 48–52, 70,
    278–283, 287–288,
    460–462
  British, 116–117, 119–120,
    121, 124–125
  ethnic groups and, 42–43,
    70
  European American,
    116–117, 119–120,
    121, 124–125
  Polish American, 200–201
  transmission of, 278–283
Curtain, Philip, 91

D

Daley, Richard, 198, 216
Daniels, Roger, 175, 261, 453
Darwinism, 39–40
Davis, Allison, 232–233

Davis, David Brion, 155
Dawes Act of 1887, 265–267,
    270
*Declining Significance of Race,
    The* (Wilson), 343–345
DeConde, Alexander, 439
Deer Hunter, The (film), 428
DeFunis v. Odegaard, 329
Degler, Carl, 31
Democracy in America
    (Tocqueville), 22, 116
Demographics, 72–110
  of African Americans, 73,
    89–98, 341–342, 385
  of American Indians,
    74–80, 81, 360, 385
  of Asian Americans,
    102–109, 249, 250,
    258, 295, 385, 435–436
  on ethnicity vs.
    assimilation, 287–288
  of European Americans,
    80–89, 90, 385
  of Hispanic Americans,
    98–102, 385, 405–406
  of Jewish Americans, 204,
    295, 296, 297
Denevan, William, 74–75
Depression
  African Americans and,
    334
  Hispanic Americans and,
    243–244
Desegregation
  of municipal buses,
    314–315
  of schools, 317, 321–326,
    335–336
De Soto, Hernando, 148
Deutsch, Sarah, 239
Diaz, Porfirio, 241
di Leonardo, Micaela, 293
Diner, Hasia, 129, 130
Dinkins, David, 27
Discrimination
  against American Indians,
    271
  against Asian Americans,
    253–255, 256,
    259–260, 425,
    430–431, 452–453, 455
  employment, 70
  gender, 9, 10
  against Hispanic
    Americans, 244–246

institutional, 66
  reverse, 328–331
  social structure and, 3–4
  sociology of, 64–66
Displaced Persons Act, 436
Diversity, 2–3. *See also*
    Ethnicity
Dixon, Thomas, 226
Doak, William, 243
Dollard, John, 232–234
Do the Right Thing (film), 354,
    447–448
Douglass, Frederick, 169, 230
Douglass, William A., 58
Dowd, Gregory Evans, 153
Down These Mean Streets
    (Thomas), 404
Doyle, Bertram, 232
Drake, St. Clair, 32, 236–237
Dreamer Movement, 268
Drug abuse, 351–352
Drum Cult, 268
Drums Along the Mohawk
    (film), 269
Dual allegiances, 3
Dubinin, N.P., 41
Du Bois, W.E.B., 164, 222,
    228, 230, 309, 462
Duke, David, 304–305
Dukmejian, George, 420
Dunkers, 137
Duster, Troy, 40
Dutch immigrants, 113, 114
Dziedzic, Eugene, 198

E

Eckert, Craig, 313
Economics
  American Indians and,
    149–151, 361, 374–376
  Asian Americans and,
    441–442, 445–447
  ethnic groups and, 19,
    69–70
  European Americans and,
    112–115, 127–128,
    139–140
  Hispanic Americans and,
    396–397, 400,
    401–402, 403–407,
    418–420
  immigration and, 82–83,
    112–115, 121,
    127–128, 139–140
  language and, 390

slavery and, 159–161, 169
social class and, 69–70
Education
    of African Americans, 225,
        227, 229, 317,
        321–326, 335–336
    of American Indians,
        382–383
    of Asian Americans,
        255–256, 425, 437
    bilingual, 19, 388–390
    of Hispanic Americans,
        419
    of Italian Americans, 67,
        186–188
    of Jewish Americans, 212
    of Polish Americans, 200
    school desegregation and,
        317, 321–326, 335–336
Elk, John, 269
Elk v. Wilkins, 269
Elkins, Stanley M., 165
Emancipation, 223–226
Emergent ethnicity, 58
Emerson, Ralph Waldo, 23
Employment
    of African Americans, 224,
        225, 231–232
    of Asian Americans, 252,
        255–256, 258, 259,
        260–261, 429–431,
        437, 441–442,
        445–447, 454–455, 456
    discrimination in, 70
    of German Americans,
        213–215
    of Hispanic Americans,
        242–243, 246, 397,
        401–402, 403–406,
        410–411, 419, 420
    of Irish Americans,
        128–130, 132, 213–215
    of Italian Americans,
        182–183, 187–188
    of Jewish Americans, 60,
        70, 86–87, 207
    labor unions and, 185–186
    of Polish Americans,
        195–196
    self-employment, 446–447
    of women, 129–130, 208,
        397, 403
Engerman, Stanley L., 169
English immigrants. *See*
    British immigrants

Equal Employment
    Opportunity Commission
    (EEOC), 327–328
Equal opportunity housing,
    340–342
Ericksen, Eugene, 58
Erickson, Charlotte, 120, 121
Erie, Steven, 131
Ethical Culture Society, 210
Ethnic America
    alternative images of,
        27–28
    melting pot image of,
        22–26
Ethnic boundaries, 16–18, 61
Ethnic communities
    African American,
        236–237
    American Indian, 363–364
    Asian American, 252–253,
        255–256, 260–262,
        432–435, 455–457
    Chinese American,
        252–253, 255–256
    Filipino American,
        455–457
    German American, 138,
        217–218
    Hispanic American,
        246–248, 386–387,
        407–409
    Irish American, 217–218
    Italian American, 183–188
    Japanese American,
        260–262, 432–435
    Jewish American,
        205–211, 294–295, 296
    Mexican American,
        246–248
    Polish American, 196–197
    Puerto Rican, 407–409
    slave, 163–165
Ethnic experiences, 6–16
    African American, 8–9
    American Indian, 10–11
    Chinese American, 9–10
    Italian American, 6–7
    Mexican American, 7–8
Ethnic groups, 16–21, 42–46
    assimilation of. *See*
        Assimilation
    culture and, 42–43, 70
    definitions and
        boundaries of, 16–18,
        44, 61

differences in positions of,
    66–70
economics and, 19, 69–70
mode of incorporation into
    U.S., 67–69
names of, 18
pluralism and, 19–20,
    26–27, 50–52
political power of, 19, 70
position of, 62–70
racial, 45–46
religious, 44–45
stereotypes of. *See*
    Stereotypes
terminology for, 33–38
variables affecting
    importance of, 55
*See also specific ethnic
    groups*
Ethnic identity, 274–307
    attachment to, 288–289
    collective, 62
    cultural transmission and,
        278–283
    developing model of,
        52–56
    erosion of, 278–290
    of European Americans,
        281–283, 292–294
    of Jewish Americans,
        294–300
    pluralism and, 51
    regional, 291–292
    revival of, 283–286
    suburbanization and,
        276–278
Ethnicity
    assimilation vs., 19–20,
        48–52, 70, 278–283,
        287–288, 460–462
    defining, 43–44
    emergent, 58
    erosion of, 278–290
    invention of, 58–62,
        290–294
    political, 284–286
    privatization of, 289–290
    revival of, 283–286
    social class and, 54
    social construction of,
        56–62
    symbolic, 286–290
Ethnicization, 57

Ethnic relations, 46–52
    of African Americans, 37,
        201–202, 231–234,
        398, 410, 447–448
    genocide and, 46–47
    of German Americans, 202
    of Hispanic Americans, 37,
        398, 410
    interethnic, 18–21, 30
    intraethnic, 30
    of Jewish Americans, 37,
        202, 447
    of Korean Americans,
        447–448
    of Polish Americans,
        201–202
    treatment of immigrants
        and, 19, 47–48
Ethnic studies
    emergence of, 30–32
    pitfalls in, 14–16
Ethnocentrism, 14–15, 42
Ethnogenesis, 57
Eugenics, 39–40
European Americans,
    274–307
    American Indians and,
        148–154
    cultural forces and,
        116–117, 119–120,
        121, 124–125
    demographics of, 80–89,
        90, 385
    economics and, 112–115,
        127–128, 139–140
    ethnic erosion among,
        278–290
    ethnic identity of,
        281–283, 292–294
    in films, 189, 191–192, 218
    immigration of, 81–87,
        112–144, 179
    intermarriage among,
        88–89, 218–219
    politics and, 115, 130–131,
        134–135, 142,
        189–190, 198–200,
        215–217, 284–286
    racial attitudes of,
        300–306, 379–382
    regional identities of,
        291–292
    social standing of, 275
    suburbanization of,
        276–278

    symbolic ethnicity among,
        286–290
    *See also specific ethnic
        groups*
Ewen, Elizabeth, 191–192
Experimental Housing
    Allowance Program
    (EHAP), 339

F

Fair Employment Practices
    Commission, 310
Fair Housing Law, 318
Families
    African American,
        163–165, 229, 350–351
    American Indian, 266
    Asian American, 251–252,
        259, 432, 435, 449–451
    Hispanic American, 36,
        397, 399, 407
    Italian American, 185, 191
    Jewish American, 207–208
    slave, 163–165
Farley, Reynolds, 92, 95
Farnham, Thomas, 75
Fascism, 189–190, 304–305
Faubus, Orval, 317, 321
Feagin, Joe R., 349
Feinberg, William E., 333
Fictive kin, 407
Fifteenth Amendment, 224,
    227
Filial piety, 449–451
Filipino Americans, 452–457
    assimilation of, 456–457
    community of, 455–457
    demographics of, 103,
        106–107, 109
    employment of, 454–455,
        456
    immigration of, 452,
        453–455
    intermarriage among,
        452–453
    language and, 456
    politics and, 456
    prejudice and, 452–453,
        455
    religion and, 455
    See also Asian Americans
Films
    African Americans in, 225,
        226, 238, 346, 351,
        354, 447–448

    American Indians in, 269,
        380–381
    Asian Americans in, 428,
        434
    European Americans in,
        189, 191–192, 218
    German Americans in, 218
    Hispanic Americans in,
        244–246
    Irish Americans in, 218
    Italian Americans in, 189,
        191–192
Finnish Americans, 280–281,
    290
*Firefighters Local Union No.
    1784 v. Stotts* (1984), 331
Fischer, David Hackett, 117
Fishman, Joshua, 280
Fitzhugh, George, 158
Five Civilized Tribes, 153–154
Flint Knife (Blackfeet Indian),
    267
Fogel, Robert W., 169
Folkways (Sumner), 43
Foner, Eric, 145, 225
For Bread with Butter
    (Morawska), 195
Ford, Henry, 26
Ford, John, 269
*Foreign Conspiracy Against the
    Liberties of the United
    States, A* (Morse), 135
Formisano, Ronald P., 323
Forty-eighters, 140, 142
Fourier, Charles, 158
Fourteenth Amendment, 224
Francis, E. K., 43
Frank, Leo, 211
Franklin, Benjamin, 19, 138
Fraternal and mutual aid
    societies, 205–206,
    208–210
Frazier, E. Franklin, 32, 161,
    164, 345–346
Fredrickson, George, 157
Free African Society, 167
Freedmen's Bureau, 223, 225
Freedom Riders, 317
Freehling, William, 161
French Canada in Transition
    (Hughes), 32
French immigrants, 114, 120
Fuchs, Lawrence, 145
Fugita, Stephen S., 433
Fugitive Slave Law, 168–169

G

Gadsden Purchase, 172
Gaelic language, 123, 124
Galton, Francis, 39
Gambino, Richard, 187
Gambling, economic development through, 376
Gangs
    Asian American, 438, 442
    Hispanic American, 422
Gans, Herbert, 58, 277–278, 279, 286–287, 296
Gantt, Harvey, 332
Garcia, Mario T., 248
Gardner, Burleigh, 232–233
Gardner, Mary, 233
Garrison, William Lloyd, 169
Garrity, W. Arthur, 323
Garvey, Marcus, 228, 230–231, 319
Geary Act, 251
Geertz, Clifford, 51, 52
Gemeinschaft groups, 43
Gender discrimination, 9, 10
Gender roles, 208
Generational change
    among Asian Americans, 261–262, 429–432, 449–451, 456–457
    among Italian Americans, 190–192, 281–283
    among Japanese Americans, 261–262, 429–432
    among Polish Americans, 202–203, 281
Genetics, and race, 39–41
Genocide, 46–47
Genovese, Eugene, 164, 166, 169
"Gentleman's Agreement," 105, 259
German Americans, 213–219
    in cities, 139–140
    community of, 138, 217–218
    economics and, 139–140
    employment of, 213–215
    immigration of, 114, 136–143
    intermarriage among, 218–219
    intraethnic conflict among, 140–143

labor unions and, 214–215
politics and, 142, 216–217
relations with Polish Americans, 202
religion and, 136–137, 139, 140, 141–143, 216, 217
settlement patterns of, 136–138, 139–140
social status of, 143
stereotypes of, 65
upward mobility of, 214
Germantowns, 141
Ghetto, The (Wirth), 32
Ghost Dance movement, 267–268
Giddings, Franklin Henry, 39–40
Glazer, Nathan, 27, 50, 284–285
Gleason, Philip, 22, 24, 35
Glenn, Evelyn Nakano, 259
Gobineau, Arthur de, 38–39
Goering, John, 285
Goffman, Erving, 160
Goldscheider, Calvin, 203, 296
Gomez-Quiñones, Juan, 415
Gompers, Samuel, 249
Gone with the Wind (Mitchell), 159, 238
Gonzales, Rodolfo ("Corky"), 416
Gonzalez, David, 387, 406
Goodman, Andrew, 317
Gordon, Milton, 48–49, 343
Gorras Blancas, 239
Grant, Madison, 25, 39
Greaser's Revenge, The (film), 244
Great Famine (Ireland), 127–128
Great Migration, 92–98, 234–236, 310
Great Society program, 339
Greek Americans, 20, 178
Greeley, Andrew, 14, 278–280
Green v. New Kent Co. (1968), 322
Greene, Victor, 198
Griffith, D.W., 225, 226, 269
Group analysis, 5, 16
Groups
    Gemeinschaft, 43
    minority, 35–38

nationality, 33–35
racial, 45–46
religio-ethnic, 44–45
See also Ethnic groups
Guadalupe Hidalgo, Treaty of, 98, 172
Gumplowicz, Ludwig, 53
Gutman, Herbert, 164

H

Hacker, Andrew, 329–330, 333
Hampton, Fred, 320
Handlin, Oscar, 34, 81, 179–180, 181, 193, 206
Hannerz, Ulf, 349–350
Hansen, Marcus Lee, 190, 283–284
Hansen thesis, 283–284
Harlem Renaissance, 237–238
Harney, Robert, 184
Harrington, Michael, 312
Harvard Encyclopedia of American Ethnic Groups (HEAEG) (Thernstrom et al.), 17, 43–44
Hasidic Jews, 61, 294
Hawaii, Japanese immigrants in, 258
Hayakawa, S.I., 389
Hayes, Ira, 270
Hayes, Rutherford, 249–250
Haywood, "Big Bill," 215
Head Start program, 335
Health
    of American Indians, 75, 378–379
    of Chinese Americans, 442
Hearst, William Randolph, 262
Heer, David, 411–412
Helms, Jesse, 332
Herberg, Will, 218
Herrnstein, Richard, 40
Herskovits, Melville J., 161–162
Hertzberg, Arthur, 208
Hidalgo y Costilla, Miguel, 171
Higham, John, 211
Hispanic Americans, 238–249, 385–423
    assimilation of, 398–399
    bilingualism of, 387–390, 399

bracero program for, 246, 410
in cities, 96, 97, 385–386, 394–396, 399, 402, 404, 405–406, 407–409, 410
coercive pluralism and, 170–173
community of, 246–248, 386–387, 407–409
conquest of Mexico and, 170–173
defining, 16
demographics of, 98–102, 385, 405–406
depression and, 243–244
discrimination against, 244–246
economics and, 396–397, 400, 401–402, 403–407, 418–420
education of, 419
employment of, 242–243, 246, 397, 401–402, 403–406, 410–411, 419, 420
ethnic experiences of, 7–8
families of, 36, 397, 399, 407
in films, 244–246
future of, 423
gangs and, 422
immigration of, 68, 98–102, 170–173, 238–243, 248–249, 386, 391–394, 398–399, 410–413
labor unions and, 242–243, 248, 415–416
naming, 18, 387
politics and, 247–248, 397–398, 400–401, 409, 413–418
poverty among, 420
prejudice and, 244–246
relations with other ethnic groups, 37, 398, 410
religion and, 240, 247, 396, 408, 413–414
settlement patterns of, 239–240, 242, 394–396, 402–403
social standing of, 275
states with largest populations of, 99
voting rights of, 401, 414

women, 397, 403, 406–407
See also specific ethnic groups
Hitler, Adolf, 216–217
Hobsbawm, E.J., 58, 175
Hodur, Francis, 197
Hoffer, Thomas, 335
Hoffman, Abraham, 244
Holt, Hamilton, 12–13, 184
Horowitz, Ruth, 422
Horseshoe Bend, Battle of (1814), 153
Housing
equal opportunity, 340–342
public, 336–339
on reservations, 377
segregation in, 336–342
Housing Act of 1937, 337
Housing Act of 1949, 336
Howe, Irving, 209–210
Hughes, Everett, 32
Hughes, Henry, 158–159, 226
Hughes, Langston, 237
Huguenots, 120
Hunger of Memory (Rodriguez), 7–8
Hurh, Won Moo, 450
Hurston, Zora Neale, 228, 237
Hutchison, Ray, 422
Hutterites, 45
Hymowitz, Kay S., 462

1

Iamurri, Gabriel, 182
Identity. *See* Ethnic identity
Illegal aliens, 411–413
Images
of ethnic America, 22–28
of ethnic groups, 64–65
Immigration Restriction League, 40 FIX IN TEXT; MOVE
Immigrants, 179–180
African, 89–98, 155–169
alienation of, 179–180
Asian, 19, 102–109, 173–176, 249–251, 257–259, 436, 444–446, 452, 453–455, 458
Chinese, 19, 105, 249–251, 436, 439
Cuban, 68, 248, 391–394

cultural forces and, 116–117, 119–120, 121, 124–125
economics and, 82–83, 112–115, 121, 127–128, 139–140
European, 81–87, 112–144, 179
Filipino, 452, 453–455
Hispanic, 68, 98–102, 170–173, 238–243, 248–249, 386, 391–394, 398–399, 410–413
history of, 19, 47–48
illegal, 411–413
Irish, 114, 124–136, 217
Italian, 85–86, 180–182
Japanese, 105, 257–259
Jewish, 68, 73, 84, 86–87, 88–89, 114, 203–205
Korean, 444–446
laws concerning, 19, 83, 85, 104, 105–108, 249–251, 258–259, 412, 436, 445
Mexican, 170–173, 238–243, 386, 410–413
numbers of, 114, 179, 181, 213
Polish, 192–196
Puerto Rican, 248–249, 399–400, 406–407
restrictions on number of, 19, 40, 105, 249–251, 436
Scotch-Irish, 119, 122–124
voluntary vs. involuntary, 67–69
voting rights of, 145
Immigration Act of 1875, 83
Immigration Act of 1907, 105
Immigration and Naturalization Act of 1965, 104, 107, 445
Immigration Reform and Control Act of 1986, 412
Imperial Edict of 1712 (China), 173
Indentured servants, 121
Indian. *See* American Indians
Indian Allotment (Dawes) Act of 1887, 265–267, 270
Indian Educational Assistance and Self-Determination Act of 1975, 358, 368

Indian Reorganization Act of 1934, 270, 355–356, 358
Individual analysis, 5
Individualism, 116
Industrialization
    class structure and, 69–70
    immigration and, 82–83, 121
Inequality of Human Races, The (Gobineau), 38–39
Insider-outsider debate, 15–16
Institutional completeness, 61–62
Institutional discrimination, 66
Intermarriage
    among American Indians, 362–363
    among Asian Americans, 434–435, 452–453
    among European Americans, 88–89, 218–219
    among Jewish Americans, 296–297, 298–300
    laws on, 453
    racial, 301–302
Internment, of Japanese Americans, 262–263, 429
Ireland, 125–128
Irish Americans, 213–219
    communal activities and organizations of, 130–132
    community of, 217–218
    culture of, 124–125
    employment of, 128–130, 132, 213–215
    ethnic boundaries and, 61
    ethnicity of, 290–291
    immigration of, 114, 124–136, 217
    intermarriage among, 218–219
    labor unions and, 214–215
    nativism and, 133–136
    politics and, 130–131, 134–135, 215–216, 217, 285
    prejudice and, 133–136
    religion and, 123, 124, 125–127, 131, 132–133, 135, 217
    settlement patterns of, 128
    upward mobility of, 214

Irish Free State, 216
Irish Republican Army, 216
Irredentist movements, 48
Isaacs, Harold, 51
Isajiw, Wsevold, 43, 44
Italian, The (film), 192
Italian Americans, 180–192
    in cities, 184, 277–278
    community of, 183–188
    defining, 16–17
    education of, 67, 186–188
    employment of, 182–183, 187–188
    ethnic experiences of, 6–7
    ethnic identity of, 281–283
    families of, 185, 191
    in films, 189, 191–192
    generational change among, 190–192, 281–283
    immigration of, 85–86, 180–182
    labor unions and, 185–186
    politics and, 189–190, 285–286
    religion and, 186
    similarities to Polish Americans, 193–194
    stereotypes of, 65, 188–189
    upward mobility of, 67, 186–188
Italian Blood (film), 192

J

Jackson, Andrew, 152, 154
Jackson, Helen Hunt, 154
Jackson, Jesse, 353
Japanese American Citizens League (JACL), 433–434
Japanese Americans, 65, 256–263, 429–435
    assimilation of, 433, 458
    community of, 260–262, 432–435
    demographics of, 103, 104–106, 109, 250, 258, 295
    discrimination against, 259–260, 430–431
    employment of, 258, 259, 260–261, 429–431
    families of, 259, 432, 435

generational change among, 261–262, 429–432
    immigration of, 105, 257–259
    intermarriage among, 434–435
    internment of, 262–263, 429
    politics and, 433–434
    prejudice and, 259–260, 427–429, 430–431
    religion and, 261, 432–433
    settlement patterns of, 258
    social class of, 431–432
    social standing of, 275
    women, 259
    See also Asian Americans
Jaynes, Gerald David, 326
Jefferson, Thomas, 155
Jen, Gish, 21
Jenkins, J. Craig, 313
Jensen, Arthur, 40
Jewish Americans, 203–213
    anti-Semitism and, 37, 87, 206, 211–212, 277, 294, 295, 300
    assimilation of, 295–300, 306
    community of, 205–211, 294–295, 296
    Conservative, 210–211
    demographics of, 204, 295, 296, 297
    education of, 212
    employment of, 60, 70, 86–87, 207
    ethnic boundaries and, 61
    ethnic identity of, 294–300
    families of, 207–208
    fraternal and mutual aid societies of, 205–206, 208–210
    Hasidic, 61, 294
    immigration of, 68, 73, 84, 86–87, 88–89, 114, 203–205
    intermarriage and, 296–297, 298–300
    labor unions and, 211
    language and, 209–210
    as minority group, 36–37
    politics and, 211, 285–286
    Reform, 210

relations with other ethnic groups, 37, 202, 447
religion and, 44–45, 210–211
settlement patterns of, 204–205
social standing of, 275
stereotypes of, 65, 212
suburbanization and, 277
support of civil rights movement by, 313
upward mobility of, 66–67, 187, 212–213
Jewish Theological Seminary, 210–211
Jim Crow laws, 227–228, 314–316, 318
Jo, Moon H., 425
Johnson, Andrew, 223–224
Johnson, Lyndon, 326, 328, 330, 339
Jones v. Mayer, 341
Joseph, chief of Nez Perce tribe, 263–264
Judd, Walter H., 438
Judicial decisions, concerning civil rights, 317–318
Juliani, Richard, 58
Jungle, The (Sinclair), 196
Jungle Fever (film), 351

𝒦

Kallen, Horace, 26–27
Kashima, Tetsuden, 263
Katz, Daniel, 188
Katznelson, Ira, 201
Kearney, Denis, 214
Kelly, Sara, 324
Kennedy, John F., 313, 327, 341, 358, 392, 414
Kennedy, Robert F., 415
Kennedy, Ruby Jo Reeves, 218, 219
Kessner, Thomas, 184, 187
Keyes v. Denver School District No. 1 (1973), 323
Kilgore, Sally, 335
Kilson, Martin, 347
Kim, Kwang Chang, 450
Kinder, Donald, 325
King, Martin Luther, Jr., 311, 312, 315, 319, 320, 354
Kinkead, Gwen, 442
Kitano, Harry H.L., 261, 429
Knights of Labor, 215

Knights of the White Camellia, 232
Knowland, William F., 438
Know-Nothing party, 133–134
Korean Americans, 444–452
adhesive adaptation among, 450–451
demographics of, 103, 107–108, 109
entrepreneurship among, 445–447
families of, 449–451
future of, 451–452
immigration of, 444–446
relations with other ethnic groups, 447–448
religion and, 445, 448–449
social class of, 444–445
See also Asian Americans
Kosciuszko, Thaddeus, 193
Kroeber, Alfred L., 31
Ku Klux Klan, 211, 217, 231, 232, 236, 300, 304, 317, 347, 365
Kwong, Peter, 440–441

𝓛

Labor unions
African Americans and, 237
German Americans and, 214–215
Hispanic Americans and, 242–243, 248, 415–416
Irish Americans and, 214–215
Italian Americans and, 185–186
Jewish Americans and, 211
Polish Americans and, 198–200
Land
conflict with American Indians over, 151–154, 267, 368–374
conflict with Mexico over, 170–173
laws on ownership of, 259–260
Landry, Bart, 347
Landsmannschaften, 205–206, 209

Language
American Indians and, 360–361
bilingualism, 19, 387–390, 399
economics and, 390
European immigrants and, 121, 123, 138, 141, 209–210
Filipino Americans and, 456
German Americans and, 138, 141
Jewish Americans and, 209–210
loyalty to, 280
La Raza Unida, 417
Las Casas, Bartolomé de, 170
Latino, 18, 386–387. *See also* Hispanic Americans
Lau v. Nichols (1974), 389
Laws
on bilingual education, 388–389
on civil rights, 224, 312–318, 322, 327–328, 332, 341, 389
on housing, 336, 337
on immigration, 19, 83, 85, 104, 105–108, 249–251, 258–259, 412, 436, 445
on intermarriage, 453
Jim Crow, 227–228, 314–316, 318
lobbying for, 312–318
on ownership of land, 259–260
Reconstruction, 223–224
termination, 357
on treatment of American Indians, 265–267, 270, 355–356, 357, 358, 368
See also specific laws
League of United Latin American Citizens (LULAC), 247–248, 412, 413
Leased Housing Program, 339
Lee, Spike, 346, 351, 354, 447–448
Letters from an American Farmer (Crèvecoeur), 22–23
Levine, Edward, 215
Levine, Lawrence W., 162

Levittown, 277
Liberty City race riot, 386, 398
Lieberson, Stanley, 287–288
Liebow, Elliot, 11, 349, 350
Life Stories of Undistinguished Americans, As Told by Themselves (Holt), 13
Light, Ivan, 259
Lincoln, Abraham, 223
Lincoln, C. Eric, 163
Lincoln County War, 239–240
Linnaeus, Carolus, 38
Lippmann, Walter, 262
Lipset, Seymour Martin, 115, 116
Little Big Man (film), 381
Little Italies, 184
Little Tokyos, 258
Livingstone, Frank, 40
Lobbying, in civil rights movement, 312–318
Locke, Alain, 237, 238
Loewen, James, 255
Lonely Crowd, The (Riesman), 276
Longoria, Felix, 413
Lopata, Helena, 201
Los Angeles riots, 320, 386, 448
Lowie, Robert, 31
Luce, Henry, 438
Lutheranism, 137, 139, 141–142, 216, 280
Lyman, Stanford, 58, 64, 252, 270, 327
Lynd, Helen, 236
Lynd, Robert, 236

M

MacMurrough, Dermot, 125
Macro level of analysis, 5–6
Madero, Francisco I., 241
Mafia, 188–189, 192
Malcolm X, 319, 354
Mamiya, Lawrence H., 163
Man Called Horse, A (film), 381
Manchurian Candidate (film), 428
Mangione, Jerre, 6–7, 12
Manifest Destiny, 151
Mano Negro, 239
Mao Tse-tung, 436, 438, 439

Maquiladora industries, 386, 423
Marcos, Ferdinand, 456
Marger, Martin, 291
Marielitos, 101, 393–394
Marin, Luis Muñoz, 400, 401
Mariott, Michael, 383
Marital assimilation, 49
Market period of European settlement, 149–151
Marriage. *See* Families; Intermarriage
Marshall, Thurgood, 330–331
Martin, Joel, 153
Marx, Karl, 205
Marxism, 53–54
Mass, Amy Iwaskai, 435
Mast, Daniel D., 425
Mayer, Egon, 300
Mazzoli, Romano, 412
McAdam, Doug, 310–311, 320
McCarran-Walter Act of 1952, 436
McCarthy, Joseph, 438–439
McGovern, George, 415
McKay, Claude, 237
McWilliams, Carey, 262
Mead, Margaret, 31
"Melting Pot, The" (Zangwill), 23–25
"Melting pot" metaphor, 22–26, 460. *See also* Assimilation
Melville, Herman, 152
Mennonites, 136
Merton, Robert, 15, 66
Metzger, Tom, 304
Mexican American Legal Defense Educational Fund (MALDEF), 412
Mexican Americans, 98–100, 410–422
   bracero program for, 246, 410
   community of, 246–248
   conquest of Mexico and, 170–173
   depression and, 243–244
   discrimination against, 244–246
   education of, 419
   employment of, 242–243, 410–411
   ethnic experiences of, 7–8
   families of, 36

   forced repatriation of, 243–244
   gangs and, 422
   immigration of, 170–173, 238–243, 386, 410–413
   labor unions and, 242–243, 248, 415–416
   politics and, 413–418
   poverty among, 420
   religion and, 413–414
   settlement patterns of, 239–240, 242
   social standing of, 275
   socioeconomic status of, 418–420
   See also Hispanic Americans
Mexican Revolution, 99, 241
Mexican War, 172
Mexico, land disputes with, 170–173
Miami
   Cuban Americans in, 394–396, 399
   race riots in, 386, 398
Micro level of analysis, 5
Militancy, of African Americans, 318–321
Miller, Randall, 244–245
Mills, C. Wright, 274, 276
Minority groups, 35–38
Missouri Synod, 216, 217
Mitchell, Margaret, 159
Mixed race, 17, 45
Mohl, Raymond, 395
Moieties, 147
Molly Maguires, 215
Momaday, N. Scott, 10–11, 12, 267, 381
Monk, Maria, 135
Moore, John, 324
Morawska, Ewa, 53, 195
Mormons, 44–45
Morris, Aldon, 312
Morse, Samuel, 135
Movies. *See* Films
Moynihan, Daniel P., 27, 50, 284–285, 350–351
Moynihan Report, 350–351
Mucha, Janusz, 361
Muhammad, Elijah, 319
Mühlenberg, Heinrich Melchior, 137
Mulatto, 17, 45, 404
Muñoz, Alfredo, 454

Mussolini, Benito, 189–190, 217

Myer, Dillon S., 357

Myrdal, Gunnar, 300, 308–310

Myth of the Negro Past, The (Herskovits), 161–162

N

Names, The (Momaday), 10–11

Nantes, Edict of, 120

Nash, Gary, 168

Nast, Thomas, 225

National Association for the Advancement of Colored People (NAACP), 230, 309, 310, 312, 314

National Committee Against Discrimination in Housing, 342

National Congress of American Indians (NCAI), 357, 364–365

National German–American Alliance, 215

National Indian Youth Council (NIYC), 365

Nationalism, 33–35

Nationality groups, 33–35

National Origins Act of 1924, 85

National Urban League, 310, 312

Nation of Nations, A (Adamic), 34

Native Americans, 18, 364. *See also* American Indians

Nativism, 133–136

Natural resources, of American Indians, 369–375

Nature of Prejudice, The (Allport), 63

Negro, 18. *See also* African Americans

Negro Family in the United States, The (Frazier), 32

Negro in the United States, The (Frazier), 32

Nelli, Humbert, 185

Nelson, Lowrey, 219

Neo-Nazi groups, 304–305

Neufeld, Steven, 448

Newman, William, 49, 50

Newton, Huey, 319

New York City
Chinese Americans in, 440–444
Puerto Ricans in, 402, 404, 405–406, 407–409, 410

Nixon, Richard, 303, 328, 339, 358

Noriega, Chon, 246

Novak, Michael, 27, 283

O

Obermiller, Phillip, 291

O'Brien, David J., 433

Odum, Howard, 31

Office of Economic Opportunity, 358

Oil exploration dispute with Blackfeet, 371–372

"Old City" (Davis, Gardner, and Gardner), 232–233

Old World in the New, The (Ross), 39

Omi, Michael, 303–304

One More American (film), 192

Optionalists, 52

Organization of Chinese-Americans, 443

Osako, Masako M., 435

Our Racial and National Minorities (Brown and Roucek), 34, 35

Ozawa v. United States, 260

P

Padrone (labor boss), 182–183

"Paper son" migration, 251

Paris, Treaty of, 151

Park, Robert E., 31, 32, 45, 53, 104, 161, 193, 235, 436

Parks, Rosa, 315

Passing of the Great Race, The (Grant), 25, 39

Patterson, Orlando, 155

Peach, Cheri, 219

Pearce, Roy Harvey, 151

Penal Laws (Britain), 126

Penn, Arthur, 381

Penn, William, 136

Pequot War of 1637, 150

Perry, Matthew, 104, 256

Petersen, William, 429

Pettigrew, Thomas, 345

Peyote cult, 268

Phagan, Mary, 211

Phillips, Ulrich B., 166

Picture brides, 107, 259

Pinderhughes, Dianne, 198

Plea for the West, A (Beecher), 135

Plessy v. Ferguson (1896), 227, 318

Pluralism, 50–52
assimilation vs., 19–20
caste, 146, 155–169, 232–234
circumstantialism and, 52
coercive. *See* Coercive pluralism
cultural, 26–27, 70
primordialism and, 51–52, 56
voluntary, 147

Polish Americans, 192–203
community of, 196–197
cultural values of, 200–201
education of, 200
employment of, 195–196
ethnic identity of, 281
generational change among, 202–203, 281
immigration of, 192–196
labor unions and, 198–200
nationalism of, 194–195
politics and, 198–200
relations with other ethnic groups, 201–202
religion and, 196–197
settlement patterns of, 196
similarities to Italian Americans, 193–194
stereotypes of, 65, 202
upward mobility of, 200–201

Polish National Alliance, 197

Polish National Church, 197

Polish Peasant in Europe and America, The (Thomas and Znaniecki), 31, 192–193

Polish Roman Catholic Union, 197

Political ethnicity, 284–286

Politics
African Americans and, 225, 227, 315–316, 353
American Indians and, 364–368
Asian Americans and, 433–434, 438–439, 456

Cuban Americans and, 397–398
European Americans and, 115, 130–131, 134–135, 142, 189–190, 198–200, 215–217, 284–286
German Americans and, 142, 216–217
Hispanic Americans and, 247–248, 397–398, 400–401, 409, 413–418
immigration and, 115
Irish Americans and, 130–131, 134–135, 215–216, 217, 285
Italian Americans and, 189–190, 285–286
Jewish Americans and, 211, 285–286
land disputes with Mexico and, 170–173
Polish Americans and, 198–200
power of ethnic groups in, 19, 70
race and, 304–306
Population statistics. *See* Demographics
Portes, Alejandro, 72, 396
Posada, Barbara, 453
Poverty
among African Americans, 349–352
among American Indians, 375–376
among Asian Americans, 437–438, 440
among Hispanic Americans, 420
War on, 339, 352
Powderly, Terence V., 215
Prejudice
American Indians and, 271
Asian Americans and, 175–176, 253–255, 256, 259–260, 425, 427–429, 430–431, 452–453, 455
Catholicism and, 135
Hispanic Americans and, 244–246
Irish Americans and, 133–136
Mexican Americans and, 244–246

nativism and, 133–136
psychology of, 63–64
sociology of, 64–66
Presbyterianism, 122
Primordialism, 51–52, 56
Prince Hall Masonic Lodge, 168
"Problem of the Third Generation Immigrant, The" (Hansen), 190
Prosser, Gabriel, 166
Protestant Ascendancy, 126
Protestant-Catholic-Jew (Herberg), 218
Protestant ethic, 124
Protestantism, 178. *See also specific denominations*
Prucha, Francis Paul, 356, 366
Public housing, 336–339
Puerto Ricans, 390, 399–410
community of, 407–409
demographics of, 100
economics and, 400, 401–402, 403–407
employment of, 401–402, 403–406
families of, 407
immigrants' return, 406–407
immigration of, 248–249, 399–400
legal status of, 248, 399
politics and, 401, 409
racial classification of, 403–404
relations with other ethnic groups, 410
religion and, 408
self-help organizations of, 407–408
settlement patterns of, 402–403
voting rights of, 401
women, 403, 406–407
See also Hispanic Americans
Pula, James, 198
Pulaski, Casimir, 193
Puritans, 118, 125

Q

Quakers, 118, 167, 360
Quan, Robert Seto, 255
Québecois separatists, 34, 48

Quotas, in affirmative action, 332

R

Race, 38–42
Darwinism and, 39–40
declining significance of, 343–345
divisions caused by, 222
European Americans on, 300–306, 379–382
intermarriage and, 301–302
mixed, 17, 45
nineteenth century thought on, 38–39
1920s thought on, 40–41
politics and, 304–306
sociobiology and, 41–42
Race and Nationality in American Life (Handlin), 34
Race relations, 30
government and, 302–304
Myrdal's projections about, 308–310
See also Ethnic relations
Race riots, 235–236, 320, 386, 398, 448
Rachleff, Peter, 232
Racial classification, of Puerto Ricans, 403–404
Racial groups, 45–46
Racism
ideology of, 157–159
symbolic, 325
See also Prejudice
Radzialowski, Thaddeus, 201
Rainbow Coalition, 353
Randolph, A. Philip, 310, 311, 315
Rational choice theory, 54–56
Ratzenhofer, Gustav, 53
Reagan, Ronald, 270, 303, 305, 330, 332, 340, 358–359, 375, 398, 412, 434
Reconstruction era, 223–226
Red Power movement, 365–367
Regional identities, 291–292
Religio-ethnic groups, 44–45
Religion
American Indians and, 268, 360

Asian Americans and, 251–252, 261, 432–433, 445, 448–449, 455
British immigrants and, 113, 118, 122–123
German Americans and, 136–137, 139, 140, 141–143, 216, 217
Hispanic Americans and, 240, 247, 396, 408, 413–414
Irish Americans and, 123, 124, 125–127, 131, 132–133, 135, 217
Italian Americans and, 186
Jewish Americans and, 44–45, 210–211
Polish Americans and, 196–197
slavery and, 162–163
Relocation policy, and American Indians, 153–154
Report of the President's Commission on Housing (1982), 340
Reservations, 77–80, 263–265, 374–379, 382–383
health on, 378–379
housing on, 377
quality of life on, 376–379
Reuter, Edward B., 31
Reverse discrimination, 328–331
Rieder, Jonathan, 285
Riesman, David, 276
Riis, Jacob, 184
Riots, race, 235–236, 320, 386, 398, 448
Rise of the Unmeltable Ethnics, The (Novak), 27
Rodriguez, Richard, 7–8, 12, 390
Roosens, Eugene, 57
Roosevelt, Franklin Delano, 262, 270, 310, 327, 400
Roosevelt, Theodore, 23, 229, 259
Rose, Arnold, 63
Rose, Peter, 15, 16
Ross, Edward Alsworth, 39
Rossell, Christine, 325, 326
Roucek, Joseph S., 34, 35
Royce, Anya Peterson, 54
Rumbaut, Ruben G., 72

Rush, Benjamin, 138
Rustin, Bayard, 312
Rydings-McDuffie Act of 1934, 106

S

Sacco, Nicola, 189
Sahlins, Marshall, 42
Sánchez-Ayéndez, Melba, 407
Sandberg, Neil, 281
Santeria, 396
Sarna, Jonathan, 57
Savagism and Civilization (Pearce), 151
Scandinavian Americans, 280–281, 290
Schermerhorn, R. A., 46
Schlesinger, Arthur, Sr., 60
Schneider, Jo Anne, 409
Schneider, Keith, 375
School Daze (film), 346
School desegregation, 317, 321–326, 335–336
Schwarzenau Brethren, 137
Schwerner, Mickey, 317
Scotch immigrants, 114, 119, 122–124
Scotch-Irish immigrants, 119, 122–124
Scott, Anne Firor, 14
Scott, Franklin, 114
Seale, Bobby, 319
Sears, David, 325
See, Katherine O'Sullivan, 63
Segregation, 227
in cities, 97
de facto, 323
in housing, 336–342
on municipal buses, 314–315
in schools, 317, 321–326, 335–336
"Separate but equal" doctrine, 227
Sephardic Jews, 203–204
Sepúlveda, Juan Ginés de, 170
Serna v. Portales Municipal Schools (1974), 389
Servants, indentured, 121
Settlement patterns
Chinese American, 254
Cuban American, 394–396
German American, 136–138, 139–140
Irish American, 128

Japanese American, 258
Jewish American, 204–205
Mexican American, 239–240, 242
Polish American, 196
Puerto Rican, 402–403
Sex discrimination, 9, 10
Sex roles, 208
Shelley v. Kramer, 340
Shepperson, Wilbur, 121
Shibuya, Kumiko, 451
Shils, Edward, 51, 52
Shintoism, 432, 433
Shtetl, 207–208
Shufeldt Treaty of 1882, 107
Sigelman, Lee, 331
Silet, Charles L.P., 381
Simmel, Georg, 54, 206
Simpson, Alan, 412
Sinclair, Upton, 196
Sit-ins, 315
Six Companies, 252
Sklare, Marshall, 298–299
Slavery, 155–169
Abolitionist Movement and, 168–169
African American culture and, 161–163
caste pluralism and, 146, 155–157
community and, 163–165
demographics of, 73, 89–92
economics and, 159–161, 169
end of, 223, 327
external challenges to, 168–169
family and, 163–165
ideology of racism and, 157–159
as institutional discrimination, 66
plantations and, 159–161
race theory and, 39
religion and, 162–163
slave revolts and, 165–167
slave trade and, 2, 69, 89–92, 155–157
women and, 163–164
Slayton, Robert, 247
"Slot racket" migration, 251
Smith, Anthony, 284
Smith, M.G., 46

Snipp, C. Matthew, 74, 75, 382
Social class
    of African Americans,
        231–234, 345–349
    Asian American, 436–438,
        439–440, 444–445,
        458–459
    black vs. white, 348
    economics and, 69–70
    Japanese American,
        431–432
    Marxism and, 53–54
    Mexican American,
        418–420
    middle class, 345–349,
        436–438, 439–440,
        444–445, 458–459
Social Gospel movement, 227,
    229
Social standings, ranking by
    ethnic groups, 275
Social structure, 3–5
Society of Friends (Quakers),
    118, 167, 360
Sociobiology, 41–42
"Sociology for the South"
    (Fitzhugh), 158
Soldier Blue (film), 381
Sollors, Werner, 43, 58–59
Sorin, Gerald, 211
Soulside (Hannerz), 349–350
South
    race relations in, 231–234
    Reconstruction era in,
        223–226
Southern Christian
    Leadership Conference
    (SCLC), 312
Southern Farmers' Alliance,
    232
"Southerntown" (Dollard),
    232–234
Sowell, Thomas, 66, 67
Spanish-American War, 101,
    177
Spanish Society of Castes, 172
Spearfishing dispute
    (Chippewas), 369–371
Spicer, Edward, 359
Spiegelman, Art, 462
Spitzberg, Irving, Jr., 322
Stagecoach (film), 269
Stampp, Kenneth, 159, 160
Standard Metropolitan
    Statistical Areas (SMSAs),
    95, 96, 341

Stanton, William, 39
Staples, Robert, 163–164
Steinberg, Stephen, 67
Stereotypes, 64–65, 162
    African American, 65, 162
    American Indian, 269
    Asian American, 65
    Italian American, 65,
        188–189
    Jewish American, 65, 212
    Polish American, 65, 202
Straight out of Brooklyn (film),
    351
Strauss, Anselm, 22
Street Corner Society (Whyte),
    11, 192
Structural assimilation, 49
Student Nonviolent
    Coordinating Committee
    (SNCC), 312–313
Suburbanization, 276–278,
    324–326
Sumner, William Graham, 14,
    42, 43, 309
Sung, Betty Lee, 251
*Swann v. Charlotte-
    Mecklenberg* (1971), 322
Swedish immigrants, 113, 136
Symbolic ethnicity, 286–290
Symbolic interactionism, 46
Symbolic racism, 325

T

Taft, William Howard, 229
Taiping Rebellion (China),
    103, 173
Takaki, Ronald, 105, 152, 252,
    253
Tally's Corner (Liebow), 11,
    349, 350
Tammany Hall, 215
Tanton, John, 389, 390
Taylor, Philip, 134
Tell Them Willie Boy Is Here
    (film), 381
Termination laws, 357
Texas Rangers, 243
Their Eyes Were Watching God
    (Hurston), 228
Theories
    circumstantialism, 52
    Darwinism, 39–40
    eugenics, 39–40
    Marxism, 53–54
    primordialism, 51–52

    of race, 38–42, 157–159
    rational choice, 54–56
Thirteenth Amendment, 223,
    327
Thomas, Clarence, 330, 331
Thomas, Piri, 404
Thomas, Robert, 364
Thomas, William I., 31–32,
    192–193
Thornton, Russell, 47
Tienda, Marta, 405
Till, Emmett, 311
Time, cultural concepts of,
    361
Tocqueville, Alexis de, 21–22,
    116
Tongs, 442
Tony the Greaser (film), 244
Toomer, Jean, 237
Tourism
    in American Indian
        community, 375
    in Chinese American
        community, 441–442
Trade
    with American Indians,
        149–151
    in slaves, 2, 69, 89–92,
        155–157
Trail of Broken Treaties
    march, 366
Trail of Tears, 154
*Transformation of the Jews,
    The* (Goldscheider and
    Zuckerman), 203
Transplanted, The (Bodnar),
    180
Treatise on Sociology (Hughes),
    158–159
Tresca, Carlo, 189
Tribes, 77, 147–148, 153–154
Trigueños, 404
Truman, Harry S, 311, 327,
    401
Tugwell, Rexford, 400, 401
Turner, Frederick Jackson, 23
Turner, Nat, 166
Tuskegee Institute, 229, 230

U

Underground Railroad,
    168–169
Unions. *See* Labor unions
United Farm Workers (UFW),
    415, 420

U.S. Bureau of the Census, 72–73
U.S. Constitution
  Fifteenth Amendment to, 224, 227
  Fourteenth Amendment to, 224
  Thirteenth Amendment to, 223, 327
U.S. Immigration and Naturalization Service, 243
U.S. Supreme Court
  on American Indians, 154
  on civil rights, 318, 322–323, 328–331
  on housing, 340
  on school desegregation, 322–323
United States v. Paradise, 331
Universal Negro Improvement Association (U.N.I.A.), 231
Uprooted, The (Handlin), 179–180, 206
Upward mobility
  German American, 214
  Irish American, 214
  Italian American, 67, 186–188
  Jewish American, 66–67, 187, 212–213
  Polish American, 200–201

V

van den Berghe, Pierre, 41–42, 51–52
Vanishing American, The (film), 269
Vanzetti, Bartolomeo, 189
Varnhagen, Rahel, 205
Vecoli, Rudolph, 21, 185
Vesey, Denmark, 166, 167
Voting rights
  of African Americans, 3, 224, 315, 318
  of Hispanic Americans, 401, 414
  of immigrants, 145
  of women, 145
Voting Rights Act of 1965, 318

W

Waldinger, Roger, 441
Walker, David, 169
Wallace, George, 317

Walther, C.F.W., 142
Ware, Caroline, 190
Warner, W. Lloyd, 43
Warranteeism, 158
Warren, Earl, 262
Washington, Booker T., 228–230, 309
Washington, George, 152
Waters, Mary C., 287–289, 293–294
Watt, James, 270
Watts riots, 320
Wax, Murray, 154, 271
Weber v. Kaiser Aluminum and Chemical Corporation (1979), 330
Weibel-Orlando, Joan, 364
Welch, Susan, 331
West, Cornel, 354
Wetback, 411
White Anglo Saxon Protestants (WASPS), 37, 83, 117, 124. *See also* British immigrants; European Americans
White Armed Resistance, 304
White flight, 324–326
Who Needs the Negro? (Wilhelm), 94
Whyte, William Foote, 11, 192
Wilhelm, Sidney, 94
Wilkins, Roy, 309
Williams, Robin M., Jr., 326
Williamson, Joel, 228, 230
Willie, Charles Vert, 345
Wilson, Kenneth, 396
Wilson, William Julius, 63, 332–333, 343–345, 347, 349, 352
Wilson, Woodrow, 216
Winant, Howard, 303–304
Wirth, Louis, 32, 36
Woll, Allen, 244–245
Women
  African American, 164–165, 224, 350–351
  Asian American, 251, 253, 259, 436, 451–452
  employment of, 129–130, 208, 397, 403
  gender discrimination and, 9, 10
  gender roles of, 208
  Hispanic American, 397, 403, 406–407

slavery and, 163–164
  voting rights of, 145
Wong, Bernard, 443–444
Wong, Jade Snow, 9–10, 12, 256
Woodward, C. Vann, 227
Worcester v. Georgia (1832), 154
Wounded Knee, 366–367
Wovoka (Paiute Indian), 268
Wright, Richard, 9

Y

Yancey, William, 58
"Yankee City" study, 43
Yiddish language, 209–210
Yinger, J. Milton, 52–53
Yoon, In-Jin, 447
Young, Donald, 35

Z

Zangwill, Israel, 23–25
Zinzendorf, Nikolaus Ludwig von, 137
Znaniecki, Florian, 31, 192–193
Zorbaugh, Harvey, 184
Zuckerman, Alan S., 203